Ireland in the Virginian Sea

The freres

KRAGFARGVS·
TOWNE·

KRAGFARGVS
CASTELL·

Ireland

IN THE

Virginian Sea

Colonialism in the British Atlantic

 AUDREY HORNING

Published for the
Omohundro Institute of Early American
History and Culture, Williamsburg, Virginia,
by the University of North Carolina Press,
Chapel Hill

The Omohundro Institute of Early American History and Culture is sponsored jointly by the College of William and Mary and the Colonial Williamsburg Foundation. On November 15, 1996, the Institute adopted the present name in honor of a bequest from Malvern H. Omohundro, Jr.

Library of Congress Cataloging-in-Publication Data
Horning, Audrey J.
Ireland in the Virginian sea: colonialism in the British Atlantic /
Audrey Horning.
pages cm
Includes bibliographical references and index.
ISBN 978-1-4696-1072-6 (hardback)
1. Great Britain—Colonies—History—16th century. 2. Colonization—
History—16th century. 3. Ireland—Colonization—History—16th
century. 4. Virginia—Colonization—History—16th century. 5. North
Atlantic Region—History—16th century. I. Title.
DA16.H655 2013
941.605—dc23
2013022515

17 16 15 14 13   5 4 3 2 1

For my mother, and in memory of my father

Preface

Histories exist in and shape the present. This study comparing and contrasting English expansion into Ireland and the New World has been written over many years and over a period of considerable transition in Northern Ireland—the place I now call home. Throughout the writing process, I have been acutely aware of the contemporary ramifications of my historical and archaeological forays into the character of late medieval Gaelic life, the experiences of incoming settlers and their impact on the Irish, and especially of the conflict that marked that process and resonates into the present. At the same time, material and documentary evidence for the emergence of syncretic practices undermine the stark narratives of planter-versus-Gael, just as they complicate understandings of the relationship between English settlers and New World Natives.

Challenging historical memories of the nature of plantation in contemporary Northern Ireland is not merely an academic endeavor. Society remains divided between two communities with plantation-era roots: broadly drawn, one is Catholic, nationalist, and self-identifies as heirs of the Gaels; the other is Protestant, unionist, and self-identifies as heirs of the planters. More than 90 percent of schoolchildren in Northern Ireland are educated in either maintained majority-Catholic or controlled majority-Protestant schools. In Belfast, physical boundaries—so-called peace walls—still divide neighborhoods. Settlement across the province is sharply defined by community identity. Memories of plantation are routinely invoked by partisans from both traditions to illustrate and explain the violence characterizing the most recent conflict, "the Troubles," which began in 1968 and claimed more than 3,700 lives. Debates over whether the Troubles are best understood as the result of economic, social, or religious tensions are not easily resolved. Regardless, the practice and presentation of historical scholarship are inevitably implicated. In short, sectarian historical narratives remain deeply rooted and resistant to change.[1]

1. Marie Smyth and Jennifer Hamilton, "The Human Costs of the Troubles," in Owen Hargie and David Dickson, eds., *Researching the Troubles: Social Science Perspectives on the Northern Ireland Conflict* (Edinburgh, 2003), 15–36; Brendan O'Leary and John McGarry, *The Politics of Antagonism: Understanding Northern Ireland* (London, 1993); Frances McLernon et al., "Memories of Recent Conflict and Forgiveness in Northern Ireland," in Ed Cairns and Mícheál D. Roe, eds.,

As an archaeologist, I engage in work that is, by its very nature, public-facing. The plantation-era sites I research exist and are understood (or misunderstood) in the present. They have much to tell us about the actualities of past encounters between individuals, communities, and cultures, but the stories that are revealed are seldom the same as those that are remembered. As such, drawing immediate and overt links between the past and the present risks losing the attention of a public hypersensitized to the slightest hint of partisanship, in a land where even the name you use for one of Northern Ireland's largest settlements—Derry/Londonderry—is construed as a statement of political allegiance rooted in the history of plantation.

Place-names are not the only troublesome terms in Northern Ireland. The word "colony" is also challenging when significant numbers of the unionist community would not self-identify as colonists. Many of Scots descent, in fact, claim the north of Ireland as their ancestral homeland. By contrast, the nationalist community has long answered the question of whether Ireland was a colony in the affirmative. On both sides of the Atlantic, historical tropes that liken the Gaelic Irish to New World Native peoples still inform beliefs in the equivalency of colonial experiences. But the history of British expansion into Ireland cannot be simply understood as a colonial episode akin to the colonization of North America. There are significant divergences between the processes and experience of British expansion in both lands that undermine assumptions of equivalency. Decoupling the two fields of colonial endeavor allows for a deeper consideration of the ambiguities of early modern colonialism. Recognition of those ambiguities carries implications for the present-day negotiation of identity.

Outside of Ireland, many people find it impossible to understand how memories of the events of the seventeenth century can still structure daily life, yet public interpretations of the significance of British colonization of North America are also constructed in the present and reify contemporary notions of national identity. Memories of colonialism are ever present, albeit neutralized, in the ubiquitous appearance of the word "colonial" in branding for pancake houses, motels, car dealerships, and housing subdivisions. Such uses are clearly not intended to evoke the violence, uncertainties, and unresolved conflicts of colonial entanglements seemingly so much more evident

---

The Role of Memory in Ethnic Conflict (New York, 2003), 125–143; Keith C. Barton and Alan McCully, "History Teaching and the Perpetuation of Memories: The Northern Ireland Experience," ibid., 107–124; Mairáed Nic Craith, Culture and Identity Politics in Northern Ireland (London, 2003). As of 2013, there are sixty-two integrated schools in Northern Ireland, building upon the 1981 establishment of the first integrated school, Lagan College.

in Ireland. A significant challenge is posed by the need to acknowledge the unresolved violence of colonial encounters in North America while decentering bloodshed in understandings of colonialism and Irish history. The first step in confronting the power of such dichotomous historical narratives and their influence on contemporary society is to reexamine the history and archaeology of English, and later British, expansion into Ireland and into eastern North America—which is the aim of this volume. On that basis, we can begin to engage with the present implications of such a reenvisioning of the past.[2]

2. The most obvious example is the celebratory rhetoric associated with the 2007 commemoration of the settlement of Jamestown as the "birthplace of America." For critical discussion of the Jamestown anniversary, see Christopher Grasso and Karin Wulf, "Nothing Says 'Democracy' Like a Visit from the Queen: Reflections on Empire and Nation in Early American Histories," *Journal of American History*, XCV (2008), 764–781; Audrey Horning, "Archaeology and the Construction of America's Jamestown," *Post-Medieval Archaeology*, XL, part 1 (2006), 1–27. One could also view the public presentation and celebration of the 2010 four hundredth anniversary of the settlement of Cupid's Cove, Newfoundland, dubbed "the birthplace of English Canada," as inevitably referencing identity and language politics in twenty-first-century Canada.

Acknowledgments

I would like to express my gratitude to Fredrika Teute, Nadine Zimmerli, and the Omohundro Institute of Early American History and Culture for taking a chance on publishing a work by a historical archaeologist, and especially for their continual encouragement and sensible suggestions. I am most grateful to Kathryn Burdette for her excellent copy-editing and consistent good humor. Peter Pope dedicated much time and effort in suggesting ways to expand and improve the study, for which I extend my considerable thanks. I would also like to thank Warren Hofstra for his thoughtful and helpful suggestions on my initial manuscript, and especially for recognizing the value of understanding the past in the context of present-day Northern Ireland. For helping me to refine my thoughts and my prose, I thank the following individuals for reading and offering comments on earlier drafts: Nick Brannon, Marley Brown, Andrew Edwards, Elizabeth FitzPatrick, Robert Heslip, Chris King, Deirdre O'Sullivan, and Beverly Straube. Shannon Mahoney, Debbie Miles-Williams, and Elizabeth Mulqueeny kindly produced maps and drawings included in this book. The support and counsel of Matthew Johnson, Martin Hall, Colin Haselgrove, Marilyn Palmer, and Sarah Tarlow has been invaluable.

My research has been supported by a range of funding bodies and institutions. They include the British Academy, the British Council, the Academy of Irish Cultural Heritages at the University of Ulster, the Colonial Williamsburg Foundation, the Department of Anthropology and the Reves Center for International Studies at the College of William and Mary, the Leverhulme Trust, the Northern Ireland Environment Agency and its predecessor, the Environment and Heritage Service, the School of Archaeology and Ancient History at the University of Leicester, the School of Geography, Archaeology and Palaeoecology and the Institute of Irish Studies at Queen's University Belfast, the United States National Park Service, and the University of Pennsylvania. I am also grateful to the staff of a range of institutions for assistance over the years, including the British Library, the British Museum, the Guildhall Library and London Metropolitan Archives, the Jamestown-Yorktown Foundation, the Lambeth Palace Library, the Linen Hall Library, the Monuments and Buildings Record of Northern Ireland, the National Library of Ireland, the National Maritime Museum, the Public Record Office of Northern Ireland, the John D. Rockefeller Jr. Library at the Colonial Williamsburg Foundation, the Earl Gregg Swem Library at the College of William and Mary, Trinity College Library, Dublin, the Ulster Museum, and the Worshipful Company of Mercers.

A number of scholars have generously shared their research and unpublished data, including Dennis Blanton, Nick Brannon, Colin Breen, Joanne Bowen, David Caldwell, Colm Donnelly, Andrew Edwards, Martin Gallivan, Mark Gardiner, Valerie Hall, Charley Hodges, Connie Kelleher, Julie King, Bruce Larson, Paul Logue, Nick Luccketti, Hank Lutton, James Lyttleton, Martha McCartney, Henry Miller, Danielle Moretti-Langholtz, Eiméar Nelis, Ruairí Ó Baoill, John O'Keeffe, James O'Neill, Luke Pecoraro, the late David Phelps, Meredith Poole, William Roulston, Colin Rynne, Kim Sloan, Beverly Straube, Clay Swindell, Karen Bellinger Wehner, and Buck Woodard. Tom Davidson, Raymond Gillespie, Gillian Hutchinson, Kelly Ladd-Kostro, Kathryn Sikes, Eric Speth, and Grace Turner each cheerfully answered seemingly random queries that were, in fact, essential to my interpretations.

Early in my career, I was entrusted with the responsibility of running the first large-scale archaeological fieldwork in the Jamestown townsite since the 1950s, alongside longtime friend and valued colleague Andrew Edwards. Marley Brown III and Cary Carson generously allowed me my head in pursuing Jamestown-related researches, even when some of my critical readings of this iconic site were a bit too passionately stated. Robert Schuyler at the University of Pennsylvania supported me when I drastically changed directions in my research from Appalachia to comparative colonialism in the Atlantic, while David Orr made certain I could pursue both interests. Jamestown research was facilitated by David Orr, Curt Gaul, James Haskett, Kirk Kehrberg, David Riggs, Chuck Rafkind, Karen Rehm, and Diane Stalling. Fieldwork was carried out by the most professional crew ever assembled, including Anna Agbe-Davies, Alison Bell, Amber Bennett, Shannon Dawdy, Eric Deetz, Maria Franklin, Grant Gilmore, Michael Jarvis, Elizabeth Grzymala Jordan, Seth Mallios, Elise Manning-Sterling, Fred Smith, and Karen Bellinger Wehner, with support from Greg Brown, Pegeen McLaughlin, and William Pitman. Colleagues working on the Jamestown Rediscovery excavations have been consistently generous with their time and information, and I owe them a considerable debt for allowing me to discuss some of the findings from their ongoing research. I am particularly grateful to Beverly Straube, William Kelso, Jamie May, and David Given. Virginia's Indian communities remain a significant source of inspiration. Working alongside Shirley "Little Dove" Custalow McGowan in the Jamestown

Settlement Museum while I was still a student gave me the opportunity to meet many Virginia Indians who collectively helped to shape my perspective on Chesapeake history.

My research on the island of Ireland has been equally dependent upon a range of supportive colleagues. First and foremost is Nick Brannon, former Director of Built Heritage for the Northern Ireland Environment and Heritage Service, for his wealth of knowledge about the archaeology of the Ulster Plantation, for graciously allowing me to subject it to new readings, and for always insisting on the "why." Friends and colleagues in the Irish Post-Medieval Archaeology Group have been a source of inspiration for many years. My excavations on the Northern Ireland sites discussed in this volume would not have happened without the support of landowners Derek Crockett, Jackie Crockett, Bobby McLister, and Cherry McLister; the fieldwork contributions of Colm Donnelly, Shannon Dunn, Sarah Gormley, Helen Legge, Ruth Logue, Ronan McHugh, Cormac McSparron, Emily Murray, Sapphire Mussen, and Ruairí Ó Baoill; the facilitation from Nick Brannon, Tony Corey, Claire Foley, Paul Logue, Gail Pollock, Rhonda Robinson, John O'Keeffe, and Brian Williams; and the support of Tracy Collins, Frank Coyne, Robert Heslip, Kevin MacDonald, Theresa MacDonald, Nick Maxwell, and Helen Perry.

In addition to those already acknowledged above, I would also like to thank the following individuals for helping me to formulate my ideas (while not being responsible for them!): Michael Blakey, Kathleen Bragdon, Alasdair Brooks, Minette Church, David Edwards, Grey Gundaker, Sinéad McCartan, Stephen Mrozowski, Franc Myles, Tadhg O'Keeffe, Charles Orser, Mary Voigt, and Ruth Young. Andrew Edwards and Robert Lyon have provided strength and friendship throughout. I thank Eve Brannon and Fay Decodts for their generosity. My mother, Joy Ramsey Horning, my sister, Wendy Tobin, and my late father, John Horning, deserve my thanks for good-naturedly tolerating my transatlantic existence. This book would never have been completed without the support, knowledge, and red pen of my husband, Nick. Thank you.

Students at Queen's University Belfast, the University of Leicester, the University of Ulster, and the College of William and Mary all helped me to refine my ideas. Members of a wide range of local history societies, schools, and community groups in Northern Ireland have generously shared their own perspectives regarding the ongoing legacies of early modern British expansion. Their experiences and hopes for the future are a constant reminder of why it all matters.

Contents

List of Illustrations

Ireland in the Virginian Sea

Ireland and the Virginian Sea

"I had rather labour with my hands in the plantation of Ulster," declared Sir Arthur Chichester, accomplished military man and Lord Deputy of Ireland, "than dance or play in that of Virginia." Chichester's 1610 statement references the contemporary entanglement of two of England's colonial ventures: one just about to begin in the north of nearby Ireland, and the other barely clinging to life across the Atlantic, in the land known to its Powhatan inhabitants as Tsenacommacah. Within a decade, association of the two was routine, reflected in the chronicler Fynes Moryson's casual 1617 description of Ireland as "this famous Island in the Virginian Sea."[1]

Observers have long noted connections between Ireland and England's New World expansion, and indeed, mention of Ireland has become de rigueur for Atlantic histories. What has been missing is a detailed comparative consideration of early modern colonialism in both lands that gives equal weight to each region. What were the actual similarities? Was Moryson correct in viewing Ireland as immersed in a Virginian, rather than Atlantic, sea? Do his comments imply that Ireland is better understood as situated on the far side of the Atlantic rather than just upon England's doorstep? Should we take more seriously the oft-quoted contemporary chroniclers who elided the perceived barbarity of the Irish with that of New World Natives? Did Ireland in any way serve as a model for the New World? Or is such an assumption rendered moot by the reality that most plantation efforts in Ireland postdated both the Roanoke and Jamestown settlements? Is it even appropriate to consider Ireland as a colony akin to Virginia, given that Ireland remained a separate kingdom until the nineteenth century? This study offers a fresh look at the convergence and divergence of British expansion into both lands, with emphasis upon applying anthropological insights to

1. Sir Arthur Chichester to the king, Oct. 31, 1610, in C. W. Russell and John P. Prendergast, eds., *Calendar of the State Papers, Relating to Ireland, of the Reign of James I*, 5 vols. (London, 1872–1880), III, *1608–1610*, 520; Fynes Moryson, *An Itinerary: Containing His Ten Yeeres Travell . . .* , 4 vols. ([1617]; Glasgow, 1907–1908), IV, 185.

understanding the relations between natives and newcomers that shape all colonial encounters.[2]

Ireland and eastern North America were very different places and very different kinds of colonial enterprises. Yet analysis of cultural relations between

2. Following first the lead of David Beers Quinn (*Ireland and America: Their Early Association* [Liverpool, 1991]) and then Nicholas Canny (*Kingdom and Colony: Ireland in the Atlantic World, 1560–1800* [Baltimore, 1987]), scholars have granted Ireland a regular place at the Atlantic table. Consider the comments of Alison Games: "Colonial historians often think of Ireland as a formative place in shaping English plantations in America" (Games, "Beyond the Atlantic: English Globetrotters and Transoceanic Connections," *William and Mary Quarterly*, 3d Ser., LXIII [2006]), 675–692. See also Eliga Gould's assertion that "colonists in North America and the West Indies" viewed "Ireland's coordinate relationship with England as an appropriate model for 'ancient' colonies like Virginia, Massachusetts, and Barbados" (Gould, "Revolution and Counter-Revolution," in David Armitage and Michael J. Braddick, eds., *The British Atlantic World, 1500–1800* [Basingstoke, 2002], 197). Similarly, Andrew Hadfield suggests, "When the Jamestown colony was established in 1607, colonial experience in Ireland formed the only serious precedent and means of making sense of the New World" (Hadfield, "Irish Colonies and America," in Robert Appelbaum and John Wood Sweet, eds., *Envisioning an English Empire: Jamestown and the Making of the North Atlantic World* [Philadelphia, 2005], 174). Other scholars extend Ireland's influence on North American colonization even farther back in time. James Muldoon asserts, "By the end of the sixteenth century, as the English were beginning to attempt the colonization of North America, they could call upon four centuries of experience in overseas colonization and a significant body of literature analyzing the failure of English policy in Ireland" (Muldoon, *Identity on the Medieval Irish Frontier: Degenerate Englishmen, Wild Irishmen, Middle Nations* [Gainesville, Fla., 2003], 91). Acceptance of the connections between British expansion in North America and Ireland is not limited to American historiography. Ulster historian Jonathan Bardon compares the two ventures: "Elizabethan conquest was therefore followed by Jacobean plantation, a colonising enterprise matching in scale and character the contemporary English migrations to the New World" (Bardon, *A History of Ulster* [Belfast, 1992], 115). In summarizing what is known of the archaeology of the province of Munster between 1570 and 1670, Colin Breen refers more directly to the presumed role of Ireland in American colonization: "Ireland then became a trial ground for future colonial activity and form[ed] future projects in the Americas and elsewhere" (Breen, *An Archaeology of Southwest Ireland, 1570–1670* [Dublin, 2007], 190). Comparative discussions of Ireland and America are generally framed from the perspective of one or the other region, oversimplifying or at times misrepresenting the history of the comparator. In an exhaustive consideration of the cultural geography of Ireland in the period 1530–1750, William Smyth evokes the New World comparison to explain why the plantation process was uneven. He asserts that, because New World Natives readily capitulated to disease and warfare, North America presented a terra nullius or tabula rasa for colonial society (Smyth, *Map-Making, Landscapes, and Memory: A Geography of Colonial and Early Modern Ireland, c. 1530–1750* [Cork, 2006], 437). Nothing could be further from the truth in terms of Native persistence. Looking the other direction, Warren Billings states that the Virginia Company "modeled the first settlement [of Jamestown] in the manner of fortified garrison towns in Ulster that had proven effective in the conquest of Northern Ireland," a comment that ignores the reality that the Jamestown colony preceded the Ulster Plantation as well as the fact that there was no political entity known as Northern Ireland until the twentieth century (Billings, *Sir William Berkeley and the Forging of Colonial Virginia* [Baton Rouge, La., 2004], 45).

indigenous and incoming peoples in both lands takes us closer to understanding the delicate balance between structure and agency in guiding human behavior. The contradictions inherent to colonial entanglements—where individuals of differing backgrounds can, on one day, find themselves sharing their labor, languages, material culture, food, drink, and cultural practices more generally and, on the next day, find themselves locked in mortal combat—are exposed in both lands. Dissecting the process of English (and, after 1603, British) expansion into both lands also brings into sharp relief the often chaotic and haphazard character of early modern colonialism. There were no accepted models, and disaster was a frequent outcome. In the New World, lack of knowledge, inadequate planning, and overambitious expectations put paid to the dreams of many adventurers. In Ireland, given the intimate connections between the two lands that stretched back millennia, the problem was never lack of knowledge; it was familiarity. The Irish who resisted English incursions were aided by their considerable knowledge of English culture and military tactics. At the same time, promoters of plantation schemes, which were efforts to plant loyal settlers on confiscated Irish lands, struggled to convince Englishmen of means to relocate to a land well known for its challenging terrain, lack of mineral wealth, and recalcitrant population.

This examination of Ireland and Atlantic world colonialism encompasses the tumultuous century between 1550 and 1650. In that period, Ireland witnessed the forces of Reformation, warfare and conquest, and plantation settlement. The second decade of the seventeenth century brought a period of relative peace that lasted until the outbreak of violence associated with the 1641 Rising / Rebellion and Ireland's subsequent immersion in the War of the Three Kingdoms. The aftermath of this last conflict saw enactment of the 1652 Act of Settlement, which reordered Irish lands and government in a fashion that diverged significantly from that of early-seventeenth-century plantations. The story of post-1650 Ireland and its connections to the New World is a subject for a different study. Events in Ireland during the period 1550–1650 must be understood in the context of England's sixteenth-century turn toward the New World, marked by the increasing exploitation of North Atlantic fisheries, the search for the Northwest Passage, the disastrous efforts to plant a colony at Roanoke, and eventually the settlement of overseas colonies in Virginia, Bermuda, New England, Newfoundland, and Maryland.[3]

3. Throughout this work, I refer to the events of 1641 as a "Rising / Rebellion" in recognition of the lasting power of perceptions of this event. From a British perspective, the conflict was a

Within this New World comparative context, the focus is on the Chesapeake and Albemarle regions, with a particular consideration of the relationship between the diverse indigenous inhabitants of the wider region and the incoming Europeans. The experiences of the Roanoke adventurers informed the later Jamestown venture. Knowledge about the Algonquian peoples of the Roanoke region, gathered by the polymath Thomas Hariot and the artist John White, was selectively applied to inform the Jamestown settlers' expectations of the Powhatan peoples of Tsenacommacah. Although the Carolina Algonquians and the Powhatans of tidewater Virginia represented a range of independent polities with disparate languages and cultural practices, the societies shared enough characteristics to render the Powhatan people seemingly familiar to those cognizant of the work of Hariot and White. Conversely, knowledge of the failings of the all-male colonial model employed by the first Roanoke colony, and the financial risks associated with reliance upon private investment, did not prevent the Virginia Company from adopting the same structure for the Jamestown colony.

The establishment of the Virginia colony (1607) and the implementation of the Ulster Plantation (launched 1609–1610) in the north of Ireland occurred essentially at the same time, involved many of the same personalities, and, crucially, were financially intertwined. Funding for the official Ulster Plantation, designed to supplant native Irish with loyal English and Scottish settlers, came from the same sources as for the Jamestown colony—the coffers of the London Companies and individual investors. As such, each project affected and, to varying extents, influenced the other—but in no way can it be said that early Virginia followed an established Irish model, nor plantation-era Ulster a New World model. Settlers in both lands struggled to execute idealized plans and replicate familiar forms to meet their own needs and ensure profitable commodities for the crown and for private investors. They acted not dissimilarly to those within England and Scotland also seeking to reformulate society and, in particular, to recast the role of urban places. At the same time, local populations in each land devised their own strategies and responses to British expansion—strategies very much consistent with their own social and political structures and knowledge of the incomers.

---

rebellion; from an Irish perspective, it was a rising. I am following the lead of Smyth in his *Map-Making, Landscapes and Memory*, 105. I also prefer the term "War of the Three Kingdoms" over "English Civil War" or "Revolution" to describe the conflicts of midcentury, as it gives equal weight to the conflicts taking place in Ireland and Scotland.

The Ulster Plantation commends itself for comparative study of colonialism because, of all the Tudor and Stuart efforts to subdue Ireland through the importation of settlers, it was the most carefully planned, most closely regulated, and most likely to succeed. Its closest comparator, the Munster Plantation (1587–1598, reestablished 1601), was also overtly designed upon colonial principles but structurally was an unlikely colony from the start. Its lands were noncontiguous, and it enjoyed an established urban network. Plantation-era Munster thus looked much like late medieval Munster, without the extensive reordering or development of new forms of settlement implied by application of a colonial model. Old English (descendants of the twelfth-century Anglo-Norman invaders) and Gaelic lords retained influence within the new political structure, as would also be the case in the early-seventeenth-century efforts to plant the Irish Midlands. Ulster was very different.

The most northerly of all four Irish provinces, late medieval Ulster lacked an extensive urban network. The centrality of towns to the formal Ulster Plantation scheme, applied to Counties Armagh, Cavan, Donegal, Fermanagh, Tyrone, and the newly created County Londonderry, wrought significant physical and social changes on the Ulster landscape, even if the number of towns established fell far short of expectations. The power of the Gaelic lordships in Ulster was also far more severely eroded than elsewhere in Ireland. Although some Gaelic and Old English elites retained landholdings and accepted positions of responsibility within the new plantation order, their holdings were scattered among the much larger land areas made available for plantation settlement. The displacement of Irish tenants in favor of British settlers was also an overt element of the Ulster Plantation design. This doctrine was most explicitly stated in the plans for the Londonderry Plantation. An area encompassing more than two thousand square kilometers was carved out of the former O'Cahan lordship, renamed County Londonderry, and assigned to the twelve premier London Companies in a bid to ensure financial investment in the reordering of Ulster. Under the 1610 Articles of Plantation, the companies were directed to remove all Irish from their lands. Although efforts to carry out this requirement were haphazard and incomplete, overall the official Ulster Plantation and the unofficial plantation of counties Antrim and Down did manage to attract sufficient numbers of undertakers (one who undertakes to plant settlers) and tenants to effect a physical change that is still evident in the landscape. Sixteen new towns were established, fortified manor houses built, fields enclosed or reordered, communication networks enhanced, and Ulster's chief resources, timber and fish, extensively exploited. In intent and implementation, the Ulster Plantation was the most colonial of all plantation efforts in Ireland.[4]

On the other side of the Atlantic, Roanoke and particularly the Jamestown colony readily commend themselves for comparison with Ireland. Most significant is the involvement of many of the same individuals in both the New World and Irish ventures. The Roanoke experience of these Atlantic adventurers was more influential on later colonial practice in Ireland than their previous experiences in Ireland were upon the Roanoke venture. Furthermore, the nearly contemporary establishment of the Jamestown colony with that of the Ulster Plantation affords a valuable opportunity to assess the degree to which the two ventures were intertwined and, from a material perspective, to evaluate the levels of investment in both colonial projects. Other commonalities include the relative role of religion and economics. Both the Ulster Plantation and the Virginia colony were intended to be peopled by Protestants loyal to the established church, but in practice, both prioritized economic development and political control over religion. Although reality seldom reflected intention in terms of the religious identities of planters and settlers, these two colonial societies stand in contrast to the Puritan settlement of 1620s New England and the Roman Catholic settlement of Maryland in the 1630s. There, the threat of religious prosecution was paramount in both colonial ideology and the execution of colonization plans.

ANY COMPARATIVE STUDY of colonialism must define problematic terms such as "colonial," "colonialism," and "colonization." Inevitably, there is a disjuncture between the ways in which historians, archaeologists, anthropologists, geographers, and literary / cultural scholars employ the terms. At the most basic level, colonization is a process of territorial acquisition, a colony is a sociopolitical organization, and colonialism is a system of domi-

---

4. For general discussions of the Ulster Plantation, see Bardon, *History of Ulster;* Bardon, *The Plantation of Ulster: The British Colonisation of the North of Ireland in the Seventeenth Century* (Dublin, 2011); Nicholas P. Canny, *Making Ireland British: 1580–1650* (Oxford, 2001); James Stevens Curl, *The Londonderry Plantation* (Southampton, 1986); Curl, *The Honourable the Irish Society and the Plantation of Ulster, 1608–2000: A History and Critique* (Chichester, 2000); Rolf Loeber, *The Geography and Practice of English Colonisation in Ireland from 1534–1609,* Irish Settlement Studies, no. 3 (n.p., 1991); Philip Robinson, *The Plantation of Ulster* (1984; rpt. Belfast, 2000); George Hill, *An Historical Account of the Plantation in Ulster at the Commencement of the Seventeenth Century, 1608–1620* (1877; rpt. Shannon, 1970); T. W. Moody, *The Londonderry Plantation* (Belfast, 1939).

nation. Each term can be interlinked as part of the expansion of a society beyond its recognized boundaries and can be applied to episodes across space
and time. Colonialism in the post-1500 world is generally distinguished
from earlier forms both by an emphasis upon cultural difference and by the
centrality of dispossession and acquisition of lands, employing *terra nullius*
(derived from *res nullius*). This principle justified the acquisition of any land
or territory that was deemed to be inappropriately used, generally meaning "not cultivated." With the exception of the uninhabited Bermuda, no
British colonial terrain was truly terra nullius; as such, the British expended
considerable effort upon justifying the acquisition of lands clearly in use and
clearly inhabited by other peoples.

In Ireland, the mechanisms for land acquisition primarily relied upon
the participation, be it partial and coerced, of native elites. Legal policies of
surrender and regrant transferred landownership from the administration
of traditional Brehon law—drawing upon practices established in the early
medieval period—to English law. Under newly issued grants, landholders
would receive back much, but not all, of their land, now held under English
title. Once they were subject to English law, such lands could be (and often
were) deemed to be escheated if the owners opposed English activities.[5]

No such legal niceties structured land acquisition in early colonial British
North America. Concepts familiar to settlers regarding the alienability of
land were incompatible with Native understandings of place and its linkage
to community identities, even within the hierarchical Powhatan world. As
recorded by John Smith, werowances (political leaders of individual tribes
or sub-chiefdoms) controlled "their severall lands, and habitations, and
limits, to fish, fowle, or hunt in, but they hold all of their great Werowance
Powhatan." From an English perspective, this practice was understood as

5. For discussion of terminology in relation to colonialism, see the very useful overview provided by Jürgen Osterhammel, *Colonialism: A Theoretical Overview* (Princeton, N.J., 1995). Chris
Gosden explicitly considers colonialism and archaeology from the ancient to modern worlds in
Gosden, *Archaeology and Colonialism: Cultural Contact from 5000 BC to the Present* (Cambridge,
2004), 116. The Gaelic legal system was administered by the legal class known as Brehons, the
anglicized form of the Irish word for "judge," *breitheamh*. Brehons served, in effect, as arbitra-
tors, particularly in cases of succession as well as a range of personal claims. Rulings took into
account personal status, as determined by rank and by property, and maintained Gaelic social
hierarchies. Like any legal system, Brehon law evolved over time. For the changes associated
with the arrival of the Anglo-Normans in the twelfth century up through the sixteenth century,
see Katharine Simms, *From Kings to Warlords: The Changing Political Structure of Gaelic Ireland
in the Later Middle Ages* (Woodbridge, Suffolk, 2000); for a general overview of Brehon law
in medieval Ireland, see Kenneth W. Nicholls, *Gaelic and Gaelicised Ireland in the Middle Ages*
(Dublin, 2003), 50–76.

Wahunsenacawh's holding title to land. In reality, he acted as a steward who allocated the use of lands according to political favor.[6]

In reconstructing the cultural contexts of Ulster and the Chesapeake / Albemarle regions in the sixteenth and seventeenth centuries, this study is interdisciplinary in its use of sources and theoretical perspectives. It highlights the centrality, rather than peripherality, of material evidence in eliciting understandings of the complexity of colonial relations in the early modern Atlantic world. Archaeological evidence can do far more than just illuminate the documentary record. Often, it complicates and even contradicts documentary reportage. For example, enthusiastic reports of plantation progress often allude to the construction of new buildings and alteration of landscapes—information that is contradicted by the physical evidence of reuse of existing structures and adaptation to existing patterns of land exploitation. Such a contradiction illuminates the actualities of the plantation process and the lengths to which commentators were invested in promoting their own particular views. Archaeological evidence can also yield insight into the experiences of those whose lives seldom feature directly in the written record. In episodes of plantation and colonization, it is at the level of the ordinary individual that we can begin to see the microscale impacts of these macroscale processes in daily, materially brokered contestations. The mix of Native and English goods found in the early deposits of James Fort divulge the intimacy of encounter often omitted from the documentary record. Objects changed hands, unfamiliar foods were shared, all leaving behind traces that demand explanation.

Objects, buildings, and landscapes, like documents, are also susceptible to ambiguity and to multiple readings. It is the critical analysis of all available sources, however fragmentary or awkward they might be, that provides the best opportunity to recast understandings of colonial imbroglios in the early modern Atlantic world, even if it is at the price of further complication rather than simple explication.[7]

6. John Smith, *A Map of Virginia, with a Description of the Countrey, the Commodities, People, Government and Religion* (1612), in Philip L. Barbour, ed., *The Complete Works of Captain John Smith (1580–1631),* 3 vols. (Chapel Hill, N.C., 1986), I, 174.

7. For a consideration of the potential value of archaeology for historians, see Alan Mayne, "On the Edges of History: Reflections on Historical Archaeology," *American Historical Review,* CXIII (2008), 93–118. Material similarities between British colonial efforts in Ireland and North America have long been noted. Anthony N. B. Garvan was the first to explicitly consider the similarities between Ulster Plantation villages and those of New England in his 1951 *Architecture and Town Planning in Colonial Connecticut* (New Haven, Conn., 1951). John L. Cotter referenced the Ulster settlements in interpreting his pioneering excavations at James-

Comparing archaeological and historical studies of Ireland and North America also requires acknowledgment of the very different approaches employed by scholars in both regions. Most American historical archaeologists are trained in anthropology and tend to view their archaeological sites and sources through a lens that prioritizes an understanding of cultural behavior, be it patterned or intuited. Some will have had additional training in history but are equally likely to have had training in the sciences. By contrast, Irish medieval and postmedieval archaeologists are trained in archaeology as a stand-alone field and have greater affinities with the study of prehistory, history, and historical geography. By and large, documentary evidence takes greater precedence for the study of this period in Ireland.

The study of Irish sixteenth- and seventeenth-century plantation sites is dominated by the study of architecture, with a focus upon the upstanding remains of masonry bawns (enclosures) and fortified English and Scottish planter dwellings. Accompanying these studies are intensive examinations of map data, given the English emphasis upon conquest through cartography, discussed in greater depth in Chapter 1. Archaeologists in eastern North America, on the other hand, have little upstanding early-seventeenth-century architecture to study, owing to the widespread use of timber rather than stone. Excavated evidence, architectural and otherwise, assumes a greater significance. Part and parcel of the Chesapeake archaeological approach is the inclusion of landscape and environmental evidence. Although

---

town; see Cotter, *Archaeological Excavations at Jamestown, Virginia* (Washington, D.C., 1958). Ivor Noël Hume fueled interest in the comparative analysis of Ireland and the Chesapeake in his popular archaeological account of the short life (1618–1622) of the enclosed settlement of Wolstenholmetowne at Martin's Hundred on Virginia's James River. See Noël Hume, *Martin's Hundred* (New York, 1982); Noël Hume, *The Virginia Adventure: Roanoke to James Towne; An Archaeological and Historical Odyssey* (Charlottesville, Va., 1997); Ivor Noël Hume and Audrey Noël Hume, *The Archaeology of Martin's Hundred* (Philadelphia, 2001). Charles T. Hodges, "Private Fortifications in 17th Century Virginia: Six Representative Works," in Theodore R. Reinhart and Dennis J. Pogue, eds., *The Archaeology of Seventeenth Century Virginia,* Archaeological Society of Virginia Special Publication no. 30 (Richmond, Va., 1993), 183–222; and James Deetz, *Flowerdew Hundred: The Archaeology of a Virginia Plantation, 1619–1864* (Charlottesville, Va., 1993), also interpreted seventeenth-century fortified settlements along the James River as echoing the bawns (fortified enclosures) of Ireland. The English inspiration for the layout of these bawns has been considered by Robert Blair St. George, "Bawns and Beliefs: Architecture, Commerce, and Conversion in Early New England," *Winterthur Portfolio,* XXV (1990), 241–287. More recently, scholars affiliated with the Jamestown Rediscovery program, which has unearthed traces of James Fort on Jamestown Island, have linked the fortification and the armaments found within its deposits to the Irish experiences of the Jamestown soldiers. See Beverly A. Straube, "'Unfitt for Any Moderne Service'? Arms and Armour from James Fort," *Post-Medieval Archaeology,* XL (2006), 33–61.

landscape plays a part in analyses of late medieval Gaelic Ireland, it is chiefly approached through map data. Comparable cartographic data does not exist for early colonial British America; hence the greater reliance upon climatic, geological, and biological sources. Environmental analysis is extensively used in the study of Irish prehistory, but it seldom figures in the examination and interpretation of postmedieval sites.[8]

Another significant difference in practice lies in the tendency of American archaeology to divide sharply between prehistorians with interests in pre-European expansion Native life and historical archaeologists who focus upon European settlement. Until very recently, the latter group seldom took into account the archaeology of Native peoples, particularly in early colonial contexts. Similarly, the former group tended to lose interest in Native sites once traces of European material culture appeared in the record. These variations in method and research questions render comparisons problematic while nonetheless highlighting alternative interpretations. Regardless of sources employed and approaches adopted by scholars in both lands, a shared concern is the cultural impact of the meetings of disparate groups of people and the role of material culture in fostering changes. This shift in emphasis reflects the developments in postcolonial thought on contemporary practice and the recognition that the disciplines of anthropology and archaeology are themselves embedded in the structures of colonialism.[9]

There are three differing ways of viewing the historical changes inherent to colonial entanglements: acculturation, maintenance of tradition, and hybridity / creolization. In the first, the culture of an indigenous group or groups becomes submerged and dominated by that of the colonizer, often a presumed inevitability. Acculturation models have their origins in nineteenth-century ideas of cultural evolution, where efforts to "acculturate" were seen as the positive development of backward or primitive non-Western societies. From an archaeological perspective, acculturation studies presume a one-to-one correlation between acquisition and use of material culture with degrees of acculturation. In other words, the recovery of significant quantities of European goods from a site associated with Native

8. Michael Avery, "Review of *Pieces of the Past* (Archaeological Excavations of the Department of the Environment for Northern Ireland [1970–1986], edited by Ann Hamlin and Chris Lynn, Belfast HMSO 1988)," *Ulster Journal of Archaeology*, 3d Ser., LI (1988), 141–142.

9. For discussion and critique of the divide between prehistorians and historical archaeologists in relation to Native experiences in colonial contexts, see Stephen W. Silliman, "Culture Contact or Colonialism? Challenges in the Archaeology of Native North America," *American Antiquity*, LXX (2005), 55–74; Kent G. Lightfoot, "Culture Contact Studies: Redefining the Relationship between Prehistoric and Historical Archaeology," ibid., LX (1995), 199–217.

peoples could indicate the corresponding loss of Native identities. What this perspective misses is that the presence of European-made objects on a site does not necessarily tell us how they were used or perceived. In addition to overlooking the multiple uses and meanings of material culture, acculturation models presume that the dominant culture is never significantly influenced by the colonized other.[10]

The second approach, focusing upon the ways in which colonized peoples resisted change and maintained traditional cultures, is again linked to anthropological models of culture change and is associated with the development of ethnography in the twentieth century. In studying groups situated in isolated locales, anthropologists presumed that these societies had not been influenced by colonialism and that their traditional practices were authentically rooted in the past. In this formulation, indigenous cultures are either static, capable only of providing a window into the past, or are viewed as having successfully resisted outside forces. Either way, they can only be understood in reference to the forces of western colonialism and imperialism. The only action is reaction. As with acculturation, there is little room to consider influences upon the colonizer or to ponder the emergence of new identities.

The third approach allows for a greater degree of complexity as well as ambiguity in understanding colonial impacts, as it recognizes that change (precolonial, colonial, and postcolonial) is a constant for all human cultures. Methodologies emphasizing hybridity or syncretism seek to understand the new cultural forms that emerge from the meeting of peoples and practices, with all parties acting upon one another, whereas creolization studies emphasize dynamism. Material culture becomes less a reflection of iden-

10. For a classic statement of acculturation and material culture studies, see George I. Quimby and Alexander Spoehr, "Acculturation and Material Culture," *Fieldiana: Anthropology* XXXVI (1951), 107–147; and also George Irving Quimby, *Indian Culture and European Trade Goods* (Madison, Wis., 1966). Historical archaeologists who have effectively critiqued the acculturation model include Patricia Rubertone, "Archaeology, Colonialism, and 17th-Century Native America: Towards an Alternative Interpretation," in Robert Layton, ed., *Conflict in the Archaeology of Living Traditions* (London, 1989); Rubertone, "The Historical Archaeology of Native Americans," *Annual Review of Anthropology*, XXIX (2000), 425–446; James G. Cusick, "Historiography of Acculturation: An Evaluation of Concepts and Their Application in Archaeology," in Cusick, ed., *Studies in Culture Contact Interaction, Cultural Change and Archaeology* (Carbondale, Ill., 1998), 126–145. Bruce G. Trigger, "Archaeology and the Ethnographic Present," *Anthropologica*, XXIII (1981), 3–17, was among the first archaeologists to take aim at the assumptions underlying the Quimby-Spoehr acculturation model. See also his *Natives and Newcomers: Canada's Heroic Age Reconsidered* (Toronto, 1985) for a critique of simplistic views of Native-European relations within colonial contexts.

tity than an active constituent in dynamic processes of identity formation. Whereas some approaches stressing hybridity or syncretism have been critiqued for overlooking inequality and power relations in their emphasis on cultural exchange, others foreground the ambivalence and ambiguity attendant upon encounter and exchange. The acceptance of complexity and, by extension, the multiple meanings of artifacts in contact situations illustrates a turn from more general models of colonialism to ones that emphasize the local and particular. Such approaches challenge and complicate the way in which we interpret assemblages in light of such local contexts but have, in turn, been critiqued for downplaying the effects of the broader structures of European expansion. There is a risk in these models of avoiding discussions of violence, trauma, and strategies of resistance, themes that are considered in greater depth in later chapters.[11]

This study does not sidestep violence and resistance. It does acknowledge dynamism and complexity in terms of relations between the Gaelic Irish, Old English, New English, and Scots, as considered in Chapters 1 and 3, and between the diverse Algonquian polities of eastern North America and European explorers and settlers, as discussed in Chapters 2 and 4. However, making use of insights drawn from postcolonial cultural criticism should not be construed as an acknowledgment that processes of colonialism, defined as systems of domination, were wholly similar in implementation in Ireland and the New World. There were important structural differences between plantation in Ireland and colonization in the New World. On paper, the Ulster Plantation was an Irish solution to an Irish problem, approved and implemented by the Irish Parliament, not by the English Parliament as an invading colonial power. Although the old ruling orders in Ireland suffered defeat, Ireland remained legally a separate kingdom, sharing its monarch with the kingdom of England and, after 1603, with the kingdom of Scotland.

A distinction also has to be drawn between the more abstract discourses of colonialism and the actual processes of plantation. Outside of Ulster, plantation efforts routinely relied upon the integral participation of Gaelic and Old English elites, a far cry from the practices employed in colonizing eastern North America. There, extremes of cultural distance prohibited par-

11. For a consideration of the importance of ambiguity, see Homi K. Bhabha, *The Location of Culture* (London, 1994). A focused discussion of violence as evidence of the closeness of intercultural relations can be found in Audrey Horning, "'Such Was the End of Their Feast': Violence, Intimacy and Mimetic Practice in Early Modern Ireland," in Timothy Clack, ed., *Archaeology, Syncretism, and Creolisation* (forthcoming).

ticipation. Indigenous Americans were no more likely to see advantage in taking on the mantle of English governance than the English were likely to allow themselves to become situated as a subordinate Powhatan chiefdom, despite efforts by the Powhatan paramount chief Wahunsenacawh to do just that. Cultural relations in Ireland were politically and economically unequal, but they were not always framed as colonial, even if, in hindsight, we can intuit the operation of ideologies and practices associated more closely with colonialism in other lands.[12]

This study tacks back and forth across the Atlantic to compare the Irish and Chesapeake / Albemarle colonial engagements. The individual experiences and perceptions of prominent men in both lands, such as Ralph Lane, Christopher Carleill, Francis Drake, Arthur Chichester, and Daniel Gooch Jr., personalize the narrative. All colonial enterprises depended upon the participation of individuals, whose actions were often dictated by personal motivations and loyalties. It is also at the level of the personal that we can best see how the contradictions of colonialism play out.

To set the stage for comparative analysis, Chapter 1 reconsiders whether the English experience in sixteenth-century Ireland truly provides an appropriate model for interpreting New World colonialism. Arguably, similarities lie in process and persona, whereas differences are rooted in historical, political, and cultural contexts as well as geography. Documentary, cartographic, literary, and archaeological sources relating to sixteenth-century Gaelic culture and rural settlement counter and contextualize contemporary portrayals of the Irish as wild and uncivilized. Sixteenth-century efforts to plant Ireland, and the reasons behind their uniform failure, are then considered. The chapter also reflects upon the post-Roanoke career of the failed colony's governor, Ralph Lane, as an Irish servitor. Lane's New World experience was disastrous, and he made no effort to return. Instead, he focused his energies upon designing schemes to defend and subdue Ulster and enhancing his own social and economic status. In the Irish career of Ralph Lane, we can see the influence of the New World.

Chapter 2 challenges the usual comparisons between Irish and New World cultures by focusing upon the complexity of sixteenth-century Native American societies in the eastern North Carolina and Chesapeake regions. This chapter also traces the story of early English expansion in the

12. Nicholas Canny, ed., *The Origins of Empire: British Overseas Enterprise to the Close of the Seventeenth Century*, Oxford History of the British Empire, I (Oxford, 1998); Canny, *Making Ireland British*. See also discussion in Stephen Howe, *Ireland and Empire: Colonial Legacies in Irish History and Culture* (Oxford, 2000), 25.

New World with a focus, first upon Roanoke, and then upon relations between English settlers and the Powhatan peoples as well as the ways in which material evidence sheds light on those relations. Of particular importance is the distinction between the extensively documented and studied Powhatan paramount chiefdom of tidewater Virginia and the less-studied, smaller Algonquian polities encountered by the Roanoke colonists in eastern North Carolina. Archaeological data drawn from a range of unpublished or underpublished studies from the region highlight the diversity of Native life and the ways in which different Native polities engaged with Europeans.

Chapter 3 examines the history and archaeology of the Ulster Plantation in particular and evaluates its colonial character and impact. Here, consideration of the experiences of two men, English servitor Sir Thomas Phillips and Gaelic lord Donal Ballagh O'Cahan, humanize the process of plantation and underscore its many contradictions. O'Cahan was one of many Irish lords who saw personal advantage in surrendering his lands in exchange for English title and a knighthood. But in 1608, he found himself under arrest for treason (a groundless accusation) and his lands confiscated. O'Cahan's Country, as it was then known, became County Londonderry and was granted to the London Companies in a scheme partially drafted by Sir Thomas Phillips, who also acquired O'Cahan's chief castle at Limavady for himself. Plantation ruined both men. O'Cahan died in the Tower of London, having never been granted a trial. Phillips died bankrupt, financially drained by his efforts to punish the London Companies for not ridding the Londonderry Plantation of Irish natives. In addition to telling the stories of these men, Chapter 3 places the Ulster Plantation into its Irish context, considering efforts to plant the Midlands and revive the failed Munster Plantation. The central role of urbanization in plantation strategy is also examined in the context of British colonial efforts more generally. The chapter ends with a consideration of what plantation did and did not achieve in the years up to the outbreak of violence in 1641 and the realignment of Protestant control in the 1650s, with attention to the emergence of syncretic practices.

The following chapter turns to Jamestown, the principal English settlement in the seventeenth-century Chesapeake. The commonalities and divergences between the history and archaeology of the Ulster Plantation and that of the Virginia colony are addressed in this chapter. Here, again, the stories of individuals flesh out the inner workings of colonialism and highlight the connections between the North American colonies and the plantations of Ireland. Sir Arthur Chichester, who had so vociferously insisted that he would rather labor in Ulster than dance or play in Virginia, nonetheless was drawn into the Virginia adventure. In the wake of the Powhatan Uprising of 1622 and the subsequent revocation of the Virginia Company's charter, Chichester helped to draft the recommendations that led to the establishment of Virginia as a royal colony. Another key figure is Governor Sir John Harvey. Much like Sir Thomas Phillips, Harvey was a strong advocate of crown policy and power, and he sought to impose English civil society upon Virginia through ideology associated with economic diversification. A proper colonial society, as in Ulster, needed to be served by and administered through the mechanism of a proper incorporated town.

Just as Chapter 3 considers the interplay between Irish and English within the new plantations of the seventeenth century, Chapter 4 also addresses the mutual effects of the entanglement of English settlers and Algonquian Natives. Here, the archaeological record is particularly illuminating. The overwhelming dominance of Native ceramics in the archaeological assemblages of early James Fort breaks the intentional silence of the documentary record. The assemblages demonstrate the degree to which the early colony survived because of the Powhatans' decision to permit, and initially facilitate, its existence. In the first years of the Jamestown colony, settlers were in no position to exercise colonial hegemony. As would be the case in the much-later encounters between British mariners and Pacific Islanders, the balance of power was originally held by the indigenous people. Elsewhere in the British colonial world, Native peoples would react differently to European incursions. Whatever the initial responses, all were changed through prolonged encounter. That the distribution of English settlements maps closely onto the Native settlements recorded by John Smith in his *Map of Virginia* is only one example of the manner in which the Powhatan world shaped the colonial Virginia world.[13]

13. See the influential work of Marshall Sahlins on Captain Cook and the Hawaiian encounter for a consideration of power dynamics in encounter situations (Sahlins, *Islands of History* [Chicago, 1985]) and also Nicholas Thomas's studies of colonial relations on Melanesia (Thomas, *Entangled Objects: Exchange, Material Culture, and Colonialism in the Pacific* [Cambridge, Mass., 1991]). For consideration of colonialism and the intentional silences in colonial records, see M. Trouillot, *Silencing the Past: Power and the Production of History* (Boston, 1996). For information on the relative percentages of Native ceramics in the Jamestown archaeological record, see William Kelso and Beverly Straube, eds., "2000–2006 Interim Report on the APVA Excavations at Jamestown, Virginia," unpublished report by the Association for the Preservation of Virginia Antiquities, Williamsburg, Va., 2008; Kelso, *Jamestown: The Buried Truth* (Charlottesville, Va., 2006). April Hatfield has specifically considered the influence of Powhatan

By 1650, the colonial Chesapeake had achieved a measure of stability, in contrast to war-torn Ireland. Tobacco had become the Chesapeake's principal export commodity, ensuring continued dependency upon the colonial core for finished products but providing a focus for and structure to the colonial economy. Although the Chesapeake lacked a functioning urban network and its main colonies, Virginia and Maryland, were divided by politics and religion, the balance of power was now firmly in favor of the colonizers even as they remained outnumbered by indigenous populations. In Virginia, the last concerted effort at armed resistance by the Powhatans, led by Opechancanough in 1644, had ended in defeat. Although the Powhatan chiefdom had fragmented, Virginia Indian communities nonetheless persevered, refashioning their Native identities through the regulation of their cultural engagements with the wider colonial world. Native societies elsewhere in British colonial America employed similar strategies. Just south of the Virginia colony, Albemarle Native communities had yet to experience any serious European challenge to their sovereignty and settlements since their ancestors had first interfaced with Hariot, White, Lane, and the other Roanoke adventurers. Settlers would not begin to encroach upon Albemarle territories until the latter half of the 1650s. The structuring of British-Native colonial relations in North America was far from complete by 1650. British-Irish relations were similarly unresolved. The cracks in the plantation system led to armed conflict throughout Ireland, giving way to the post-1650 introduction of a more rigid colonial power structure.[14]

Early modern British expansion into the Atlantic world was neither a monolithic nor an inevitable process. Outcomes of colonial encounter and entanglement were variable, unpredictable, and ongoing. Ireland, with its long-standing continental cultural and religious connections, was an unlikely practice ground for the colonization of the Americas, yet its history became intertwined with that of colonial America. Ireland sat both within a Virginian Sea and, at the same time, firmly within Europe.

---

geographies on English settlement; see Hatfield, *Atlantic Virginia: Intercolonial Relations in the Seventeenth Century* (Philadelphia, 2004); Hatfield, "Spanish Colonization Literature, Powhatan Geographies, and English Perceptions of Tsenacommacah/Virginia," *Journal of Southern History,* LXIX (2003), 249.

14. The issue of stability in the Virginia colony has long been the subject of debate. See, for example, Jon Kukla, "Order and Chaos in Early America: Political and Social Stability in Pre-Restoration Virginia," *AHR,* XC (1985), 275–298. For the purposes of this discussion, it is the contrast with Ireland that is most salient. Virginia was no paradise, but by the 1650s, a reasonably stable sociopolitical and economic framework had been established.

CHAPTER ONE

Toward a Colonial Ireland?
The Sixteenth Century

Introduction

The idea of Ireland as a testing ground for Elizabeth's New World colonial adventures hinges upon the sixteenth-century actions of the English in Ireland and their changing attitudes toward their western neighbor. In the wake of the Reformation, recalcitrant Catholic Ireland served as an ever-present cause of anxiety and an object of fear, soon translated into a subject for conquest. Ireland was recast as a savage land occupied by people in need of control and improvement. Unlike the New World and its indigenous inhabitants, sixteenth-century Ireland was long known to the English, and the English were long known to the Irish. Yet by the end of the sixteenth century, Ireland became unknown through the construction of difference, or otherness, a process integral to early modern colonialism. In the words of English soldier and commentator Barnaby Riche, the Irish were "more uncivill, more uncleanly, more barbarous, and more brutish in their customs and demeanures, than any other part of the world that is known." This discourse of inferiority underpinned English activities in Ireland, which included protocolonial efforts to plant settlements as well as outright warfare.[1]

---

1. See, for example, discussion in Chris Gosden, *Archaeology and Colonialism: Cultural Contact from 5000 BC to the Present* (Cambridge, 2004), 135–136, which emphasizes the unequal, pejorative character of early modern "othering." For Barnaby Riche, see Barnabe Rych, *A Short Survey of Ireland, Truly Discovering Who It Is That Hath So Armed the Hearts of That People, with Disobediences to Their Princes* (London, [1609]), 2; C. Litton Falkiner, "Barnaby Rich's 'Remembrances of the State of Ireland, 1612,' with Notices of Other Manuscript Reports, by the Same Writer, on Ireland under James the First," in *Proceedings of the Royal Irish Academy, Section C: Archaeology, Celtic Studies, History, Linguistics, Literature*, XXVI (1906), 125–142; John Leon Lievsay, "A Word about Barnaby Rich," *Journal of English and Germanic Philology*, LV (1956), 381–392; Brendan Bradshaw, "Sword, Word and Strategy in the Reformation in Ireland," *Historical Journal*, XXI (1978), 475–502. There is a considerable literature about the evolution of

Examination of Irish life and culture in the sixteenth century belies the stark characterizations of Barnaby Riche and his contemporaries and permits a critical evaluation of English colonial strategy from the vantage point of Ireland and its inhabitants. Drawing from documentary as well as material sources, this discussion considers the complex identities of late medieval Ireland, particularly the Gaels, the Old English (descendants of the twelfth-century Anglo-Norman invaders), and the Highland Scots whose territories straddled the north coast of Ulster and the Isles. However, much of the evidence pertains to the elite of these three groups and to the structure of the *oireacht,* or lordship, that was central to political and social life. The challenge of eliciting information about the lower orders of society in Ireland is addressed through consideration of case studies drawn principally from the north of Ireland.

Sixteenth-century English efforts to subdue Ireland have also traditionally been viewed as critical for understanding English activities in the New World, just as descriptions of the Irish penned by hostile commentators such as Riche have provided fertile ground for comparing the perceived savagery of the Irish with that assigned to New World Natives. Yet the two lands share few commonalities. Instead, what links Ireland with the New World is the haphazard character of English attempts to wield control in both lands. There was no accepted model, and failure was commonplace. English colonial efforts in Ireland and the New World were marked by uncertainty and political intrigue, marred by brutality, and dependent upon greed. Reexamination of the material legacy of relations between England and Ireland and consideration of the role of Elizabeth's adventurers in both lands also suggests that the Roanoke colonists' experiences in the 1580s wielded a far more lasting influence over subsequent plantation settlements in Ireland than the sixteenth-century Irish plantations ever did upon New World ventures. The

---

English attitudes toward the Irish as well as the comparators with Native Americans. See, for example, Nicholas P. Canny, "The Ideology of English Colonization: From Ireland to America," *William and Mary Quarterly,* 3d Ser., XXX (1973), 575–598; Joep Leerssen, *Mere Irish and Fíor-Ghael: Studies in the Idea of Irish Nationality, Its Development and Literary Expression prior to the Nineteenth Century* (Amsterdam, 1986); Leerssen, "Wildness, Wilderness, and Ireland: Medieval and Early-Modern Patterns in the Demarcation of Civility," *Journal of the History of Ideas,* LVI (1995), 25–39; James E. Doan, "'An Island in the Virginia Sea': Native Americans and the Irish in English Discourse, 1585–1640," *New Hibernia Review,* I, no. 1 (Spring 1997), 79–99; David Harding, "Objects of English Colonial Discourse: The Irish and Native Americans," *Nordic Irish Studies,* IV (2005), 37–60; Keith Pluymers, "Taming the Wilderness in Sixteenth- and Seventeenth-Century Ireland and Virginia," *Environmental History,* XVI (2011), 610–632.

seventeenth century, explored in later chapters, witnessed far greater overlap between colonial efforts in both lands.

Medieval Background

English sway over Irish affairs was no new phenomenon in the sixteenth century. From the late twelfth century, Anglo-Norman involvement in Ireland precipitated English rule, introduced new people and manorial-style settlements, and accelerated urbanism. The greatest impact occurred east of a line stretching southwest from Strangford Lough in the north to Bantry Bay in the southwest. Throughout Ireland, the engagement of Gaelic lordships with Anglo-Norman peoples and practices was highly variable. In a general sense, Gaelic clan hierarchies, customs, and social structures continued to dominate west of that arbitrary line through the sixteenth century. Certainly for some visitors, these lands "beyond the Pale" embodied the very unknown, as epitomized by the comments of Francesco Chiericati, papal nuncio to England, who visited Dublin and Armagh in 1517: "I have heard that in places farther north people are more uncivilised, going about nude, living in mountain caves and eating raw meat."[2]

Despite such perceptions, medieval towns played a significant role in guiding the economic fortunes of the country. Extensive shipping routes connected Ireland with the southwest coast of England, linking the Continent with port towns such as Galway, Cork, and Waterford. These were run by small numbers of established merchants and politicos who were predominantly the descendants of the Anglo-Norman invaders, henceforth referred to as the Old English. They profited from the trade in raw materials to England, with Gaelic lordships often controlling the acquisition of such items. The sixteenth-century development of Ireland was predicated upon this mercantile system: port towns collecting commodities from the hinterlands through time-honored trading relationships between the Old English and Gaelic lordships, exporting items such as fish, hides, wool, linen, and timber in exchange for goods such as wine, iron, and salt. The growth and

2. For discussion of the nature and effect of Anglo-Norman settlement in Ireland, see the essays in Art Cosgrove, ed., *A New History of Ireland II: Medieval Ireland, 1169–1534* (Oxford, 1987); see also the essays in David Edwards, *Regions and Rulers in Ireland, 1100–1650* (Dublin, 2004); and, for a consideration of the later medieval Gaelic political structure and its relationship to Anglo-Norman practices, see chap. 2 in Katharine Simms, *From Kings to Warlords: The Changing Political Structure of Gaelic Ireland in the Later Middle Ages* (Woodbridge, Suffolk, 1987); Mary Purcell, "St. Patrick's Purgatory: Francesco Chiericati's Letter to Isabella d'Este," *Seanchas Ardmhacha*, XII (1986–1987), 1–10.

independent functioning of Ireland's late medieval towns is comparable with the development of city-states in terms of their individual hegemony and interplay with the English ports of Chester, Liverpool, and Bristol. Thus the historic development of Ireland, to the sixteenth-century mind, was predicated upon the control of a merchant class over the development of urban areas and over trade in primary materials. When advantageous for the crown, the import and even existence of Irish towns could be readily denied—particularly if there was a need to justify the invasion of an apparently uncivilized land.[3]

From an archaeological perspective, it is not difficult to pin down the material influence of England and the Continent in medieval Ireland. Excavations in Galway have highlighted the well-established trade networks of the west coast port, especially by revealing extensive ceramic assemblages of Iberian and French wares. Dominated by the so-called "tribes," or the families of leading merchants, Galway functioned as a semiautonomous city only nominally under the influence of the Dublin administration. Throughout the late medieval period, Galway was engaged in a vibrant transit trade with France and Spain. Galway's merchant elite relied upon the Gaelic Uí Fhlaith-bheartaigh (O'Flaherty) lordship, which extended across much of Connemara, to provide many of the goods traded to the continental merchants, principally hides, wool, and cloth, and to serve as a market for imported commodities such as salt and French wine and brandy. Although the significance of relations between Galway and Spain may be overstated through historical memory, Spanish connections are clearly reflected in the material record. For example, 714 sherds of postmedieval Iberian wares were identified from a series of (often small) urban excavations between 1987 and 1998, representing at least 87 individual vessels. These imports included olive jars that served as the containers for other commodities, as well as tablewares (bowls, plates, candlesticks, and vases) destined for domestic use. Such objects, although not overwhelming in number, arguably underscore the significant connections between Galway and Spain, not least of which was a common religious identity. Inevitably, their Catholicism and strong links

---

3. For consideration of the character of Irish towns and the role of the Old English elite, see Anthony Sheehan, "Irish Towns in a Period of Change, 1558–1625," in Ciaran Brady and Raymond Gillespie, eds., *Natives and Newcomers: Essays on the Making of Irish Colonial Society, 1534–1641* (Suffolk, 1986), 93–119, esp. 104. The classification of Irish towns as city-states comes from R. A. Butlin, "Irish Towns in the Sixteenth and Seventeenth Centuries," in Butlin, ed., *The Development of the Irish Town* (London, 1977), 65. See also F. H. A. Aalen, *Man and the Landscape in Ireland* (London, 1978), 137.

with Spain brought the Galway elite into conflict with the English crown. The establishment of an English garrison in the town in 1579 reflects not only the English desire to protect commerce and shipping interests in the west but the perceived need to exercise closer supervision over the Old English tribes. It is no coincidence that the earliest English maps of the town date to this period.[4]

The Galway Old English merchants maintained alliances by balancing their religious and mercantile interests with those of physical and economic security. Architectural styles reflect their awareness of both English and continental fashions. In particular, the tower houses of the mercantile elite incorporate a range of late Gothic and Renaissance features, including decorative roundels and heraldic sculpture bearing coats of arms and merchants' marks. A 1613 account, attributed to the servitor and future Lord Deputy of Ireland Sir Oliver St. John, provides some insight on the town's composition: "Their commonalty is composed of the descendants of the ancient English founders of the town, and rarely admit any new English to have freedom or education among them, and never any of the Irish." St. John emphasizes the Old English mercantile class's strict control but evades the reality of interdependence upon the Gaelic hinterland.[5]

Whereas Galway's merchants were comprised of the Old English, albeit reliant on the Gaelic Uí Fhlaithbheartaigh, there were Gaelic elites directly involved in trade and town development elsewhere in Ireland. Both Cavan and Longford could be described as Gaelic market towns, with Cavan developed and controlled by the O'Reilly and MacBrady families of Breifne,

4. Excavations in Galway are covered by Elizabeth FitzPatrick, Madeline O'Brien, and Paul Walsh, eds., *Archaeological Investigations in Galway City, 1987–1998* (Bray, 2004); for Iberian sherd count, see 364. Paul Naessens discusses the role of the Uí Fhlaithbheartaigh lords in Galway in "Gaelic Lords of the Sea: The Coastal Tower Houses of South Connemara," in Linda Dornan and James Lyttleton, eds., *Lordship in Medieval Ireland: Image and Reality* (Dublin, 2007), 217–253, esp. 223. Alexandra Hartnett cautions against overemphasizing the Spanish connections with Galway in "The Port of Galway: Infrastructure, Trade, and Commodities," in FitzPatrick, O'Brien, and Walsh, eds., *Archaeological Investigations in Galway City,* 292–308. The presence of Iberian pottery is commented upon in FitzPatrick, "The Finds," ibid., 364, whereas the full analysis of ceramic data from the Galway excavations can be found in Rosanne Meenan, "Pottery of the Late Medieval and Post-Medieval Periods," 376–404. Paul Walsh discusses the contemporary map evidence from Galway in "The Post-Medieval Archaeology of Galway, 1550–1850: A Historical Outline," in Audrey Horning et al., eds., *The Post-Medieval Archaeology of Ireland, 1550–1850* (Dublin, 2007), 155.

5. Walsh, "Post-Medieval Archaeology of Galway," in Horning et al., eds., *Post-Medieval Archaeology of Ireland,* 155–157; Oliver St. John, "A Description of Connaght," in J. S. Brewer and William Bullen, eds., *Calendar of the Carew Manuscripts, Preserved in the Archiepiscopal Library at Lambeth,* VI, *1603–1624* (London, 1873), 292–299, esp. 295.

a Gaelic territory adjacent to the English Pale. In Connacht, the Gaelic O'Connors capitalized upon the thirteenth-century Anglo-Norman establishment of the town of Sligo, enhancing the growth of the settlement as a significant port as well as an ecclesiastical and military center. Control over the export of salmon and herring from Sligo was firmly held by the Gaelic O'Crean family. Other Gaelic lords also extensively exploited maritime resources. At Dunboy, Berehaven, in Bantry Bay, West Cork, the O'Sullivan Beares maintained a tower house that oversaw fishing activity, particularly through the collection of fees and tribute from foreign fishing fleets. A report from 1600 notes that communities on the Blasket Islands and around the County Cork port of Baltimore had become fluent in Spanish, testimony to the extensive and well-established presence of Spanish fishing fleets off the south and west coast. Materials unearthed from excavations at the Dunboy tower house include a wide range of sixteenth-century French and Spanish wares, suggesting direct trade with vessels from those countries, whereas four sherds from a single Chinese Ming porcelain bowl attest to the reach of expanding European contacts with the Far East. Spanish activities on the Irish coast were a source of particular irritation to the English.[6]

Similarly, the O'Driscolls tightly controlled fishing activities in the barony of West Carbery, centered on Baltimore harbor. There they maintained strategically placed coastal castles: "Every ship or boat that fishes there is to pay the lord in money sixteen shillings and two-pence, a barrel of flour,

6. Jonathan Cherry considers the role of Gaelic elites in Cavan in "Colonial Appropriation of Gaelic Urban Space: Creating the First Ulster Plantation Town," *Irish Geography,* XL (2007), 114–116. For Sligo, see Butlin, "Irish Towns," in Butlin, ed., *Development of the Irish Town,* 74. For the Creans, see S. J. Connolly, *Contested Island: Ireland, 1460–1630* (Oxford, 2007), 24, which describes the Creans as a "native merchant dynasty"; see also Mary O'Dowd, *Power, Politics, and Land: Early Modern Sligo, 1568–1688* (Belfast, 1991). For the involvement of the Spanish in southwest fishing activity, see Diarmaid Ó Catháin, "Some Reflexes of Latin Learning and of the Renaissance in Ireland, c.1450–c.1600," in Jason Harris and Keith Sidwell, eds., *Making Ireland Roman: Irish Neo-Latin Writers and the Republic of Letters* (Cork, 2009), 16–17; Ciaran O'Scea, "The Significance and Legacy of Spanish Intervention in West Munster during the Battle of Kinsale," in Thomas O'Conor and Mary Ann Lyons, eds., *Irish Migrants in Europe after Kinsale, 1602–1820* (Dublin, 2003), 32–63; and Colin Breen, "The Maritime Cultural Landscape in Medieval Gaelic Ireland," in Patrick J. Duffy, David Edwards, and Elizabeth FitzPatrick, eds., *Gaelic Ireland, c. 1250–1650: Land, Lordship, and Settlement* (Dublin, 2001), 426–429. Breen also presents the archaeological evidence underscoring the continental connections of the O'Sullivan Beares. Spanish fishing in Irish waters was particularly unwelcome for the English. In the 1560s, England competed against Dutch and Scandinavian fishing fleets in Icelandic waters, against the French in the Newfoundland fisheries, and against the Spanish on the Irish seacoast. See R. C. L. Sgroi, "Piscatorial Politics Revisited: The Language of Economic Debate and the Evolution of Fishing Policy in Elizabethan England," *Albion,* XXXV (2003), 5.

a barrel of salt, a hogshead of beer, a dish of fish three times a week from every boat, and if they dry their fish in any part of the said country to pay thirteen shillings for the rocks." The lucrative fishery attracted considerable English attention, with Baltimore featuring in a number of proposed plantation schemes that aimed to capitalize upon the fishing and limit the power of the O'Driscolls. A series of extant stone-built fish palaces attests to both the intensity and longevity of the O'Driscolls' maritime industry.[7]

Extant customs accounts from the port of Bristol illuminate the nature of the trade between southwestern Ireland and Britain, highlighting an increasing demand for an ever-widening array of goods. Early in the sixteenth century, Irish imports from Bristol consisted predominantly of spices and foodstuffs, including dried peas and beans. By the end of the century, Irish merchants were purchasing a range of fashionable goods, including silk, taffeta, and velvet cloth and clothing; combs, mirrors, and spectacles; New World products such as tobacco and Atlantic fish; tablewares such as French drinking glasses; books; and looking glasses. Although the evidence from Bristol provides only a hint of the material goods circulating in sixteenth-century Ireland, given direct trade to the Continent, widespread smuggling, and the lack of documentation for other English ports, the Bristol port books make it very clear that there was a market in Ireland for the most up-to-date fashions and global commodities. Who was purchasing these items, once they traveled from the Old English–controlled port towns such as Waterford and Cork, is less certain. The Old and New English elite are an obvious audience for these items, but the Gaelic elite also desired and acquired them.[8]

7. Connie Kelleher discusses the activities of the O'Driscoll lords in "The Gaelic O'Driscoll Lords of Baltimore, Co. Cork: Settlement, Economy, and Conflict in a Maritime Cultural Landscape," in Dornan and Lyttleton, eds., *Lordship in Medieval Ireland*, 140. The payments extracted by the O'Driscolls are noted in Hans Claude Hamilton, Ernest G. Atkinson, and Robert Pentland Mahaffy, eds., *Calendar of the State Papers, Relating to Ireland, of the Reigns of Henry VIII., Edward VI., Mary, and Elizabeth . . .* , 11 vols. (London, 1860–1912), I, *1509–1573*, 197. The O'Driscolls kept a weather eye on their political vulnerability, professing loyalty to the crown while simultaneously providing support to the Spanish on the eve of the Battle of Kinsale in 1601, which saw the English defeat Irish and Spanish forces. See Kelleher,"Gaelic O'Driscoll Lords," in Dornan and Lyttleton, eds., *Lordship in Medieval Ireland*, 138, for efforts to control the power of the O'Driscolls, and 141 for consideration of the archaeological evidence for fish palaces.

8. Susan Flavin, "Consumption and Material Culture in Sixteenth-Century Ireland," *Economic History Review*, LXIV (2011), 1144–1174; Flavin and Evan T. Jones, eds., *Bristol's Trade with Ireland and the Continent, 1503–1601: The Evidence of the Exchequer Customs Accounts* (Dublin, 2009). Joan Thirsk, *Economic Policy and Projects: The Development of a Consumer Society in Early Modern England* (Oxford, 1978), 125 n. 47, attributes the demand to the presence of soldiers in

The extensive trade connections between Ireland, Britain, and the Continent fostered a shared desire for luxury goods that contrasts sharply with the way in which New World peoples would relate to the introduction of European material culture. European goods were more selectively incorporated into Native repertoires and often used in ways unintended by their manufacturers. Glass bottles were knapped into knives, copper kettles transformed into symbolic objects, and iron broadaxes employed as intertribal communication devices. Although the Irish and the English likely diverged in their use and understandings of luxury goods, such differences were subtle rather than obvious, reflecting variations rather than absences in shared understandings. A hat was still a hat, even if its social meaning was recast.[9]

The trade and contacts between the Gaelic elite and the foreign merchants and politicos was facilitated by the widespread use of Latin, also the language of choice for the educated Gaelic Irish in communications with the English. That Latin was understood by the learned classes even in the most rural parts of Ireland is clear from the testimony of the Spanish sailor Francisco de Cuellar, who was shipwrecked off the Sligo coast in the aftermath of the 1588 Spanish Armada. De Cuellar recounted in a letter how he had sought and received shelter in an Irish home,

> where they did not do me harm, because there was in them one who knew Latin; and in the necessity of the circumstances, our Lord was pleased that we should understand one another, talking Latin. I narrated to them my hardships. The Latin-speaking man sheltered me in his hut that night he dressed my wound, gave me supper, and a place where I might sleep

Ireland, whereas Flavin herself identifies the consumers as "Anglo-Irish" in "Consumption and Material Culture," 1170.

9. The transformation of meaning of European goods in Native contexts is evidenced by the presence of knapped glass found at Jamestown; see Kelso and Straube, eds., "2000–2006 Interim Report"; and Audrey J. Horning and Andrew C. Edwards, *Archaeology in New Towne, 1993–1995* (Williamsburg, Va., 2000). For repurposing of copper objects, see D. B. Blanton and C. C. Hudgins, "Archaeological Evidence for Native Prestige Commodity Devaluation: Analysis of Copper Artifacts from 44YO687 and 44YO693," in Blanton, ed., "Archaeological Evaluation of Eight Prehistoric–Native American Sites at Naval Weapons Station Yorktown, Virginia," report submitted to the Atlantic Division, Naval Facilities Engineering Command, Norfolk, Va., I1–I14; and Martin Gallivan, "The Archaeology of Native Societies in the Chesapeake: New Investigations and Interpretations," *Journal of Archaeological Research,* XIX (2011), 281–325. In 1681, the Maryland Piscataways sent a sharpened broadaxe to the Senecas, an invitation to war against the English. See Julia A. King and Dennis C. Curry, "'Forced to Fall to Making of Bows and Arrows': The Material Conditions of Indian Life in the Chesapeake, 1660–1710," paper presented at the Society for Historical Archaeology Annual Conference, January 2010, and *Archives of Maryland,* XXVII, 5–7.

upon some straw. In the middle of the night his father arrived and his brothers, loaded with plunder and our things, and it did not displease the old man that I had been sheltered in his house and well treated.

Although this narrative can only confirm the presence of a single Latin-educated Irishman in Sligo, the fact that the Latin speaker was residing in the family home suggests that he was educated locally and might have been part of a local community of learned scholars.[10]

In 1541, Henry VIII declared himself king (not just lord) of Ireland. Control was to be achieved through a range of government-sponsored and individual strategies, each inextricably associated with the forces of Reformation. New fortifications were constructed, lands were granted to loyal followers, and monastic property was confiscated and redistributed. In addition, loyal adventurers were encouraged and expected to take responsibility for subduing any dissent on their new lands. Disloyalty was countered by transportation and confiscation of properties. A policy of surrender and regrant promised security of land tenure through the granting of charters and the conferring of an English title upon native elites who swore allegiance to the crown.

Initially, English efforts at shoring up the hold on Ireland were concentrated upon protecting Dublin and the Pale. To that end, the first official plantation efforts were implemented in Counties Laois and Offaly in 1551. Two forts were established: Fort Protector (later Maryborough, now Portlaoise) and Fort Governor (later Phillipstown and now Daingean). Plans for the settlement of what became, in 1557, Queen's County (now Laois) and King's County (Offaly) relied upon grants made to a total of forty planters, drawn from the Old English, New English, and Gaelic populations. Unlike later efforts, the criterion for acquiring a grant was, not ethnic or religious identity, but professed loyalty to the crown; the "Instructions of Philip and Mary" divided the lands up between "our loving subjects, English and Irish," with two-thirds designated for "Englishmen born in England or Ireland, and the third part to Irishmen of birth and blood." Although the two forts evolved into towns, the plantation effort itself was doomed from the start. No adequate surveys had been drawn up, nor were the leaseholds perma-

---

10. Ó Catháin, "Latin Learning," in Harris and Sidwell, eds., *Making Ireland Roman*, 18; J. P. O'Reilly, trans., "Remarks on Certain Passages in Captain Cuellar's Narrative of His Adventures in Ireland after the Wreck of the Spanish Armada in 1588–89, Followed by a Literal Translation of That Narrative," *Proceedings of the Royal Irish Academy (1889–1901)*, III (1893–1896), 202. Patricia Palmer lists a number of occasions where the sixteenth-century Gaelic elite employ Latin in *Language and Conquest in Early Modern Ireland: English Renaissance Literature and Elizabethan Imperial Expansion* (Cambridge, 2001), 185–188.

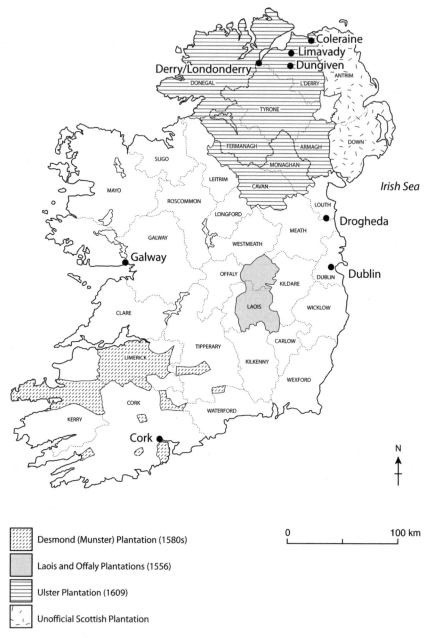

Figure 1. Map of Plantation-era Ireland. Produced for the author
by Elizabeth Mulqueeny, Queen's University, Belfast

nent. Eighteen revolts between 1551 and 1608 rendered this quasi-colonial scheme untenable.[11]

From Diplomacy to Conquest

The progress of Reformation in Ireland, begun under Henry VIII, is best described as variable and incomplete. The Irish Parliament in Dublin passed the Act of Supremacy in 1536, declaring Henry VIII to be the head of the Church of Ireland and beginning the long process of dissolution; but efforts to reform the church doctrine itself were not seriously imposed until the reign of Edward VI (1547–1553). Any gains were soon countered by the accession of Mary I in 1553, when the Catholic Church was reestablished. Under Elizabeth I, efforts to impose the Reformation were redoubled, with every citizen required to attend the Protestant church on a weekly basis or face a stiff fine. Enforcement of this decree, part of the 1560 Act of Uniformity, was infeasible.

Initial English efforts to extend their control over Ireland relied upon negotiation both with the Old English descendants of the Normans and with the Gaelic lords. Under Elizabeth I, the conquest of Catholic Ireland was increasingly seen as critical in the competition against Catholic Spain, tying into the same rationale for Elizabethan interest in the New World. In recognition that control would come only through conquest, English forces in Ireland increased from a few hundred in the 1530s to twenty-one thousand by 1596. Military efforts were accompanied by renewed efforts to destabilize Gaelic culture and undercut the standing of the resolutely Catholic Old English leadership. To English eyes, these descendants of the Anglo-Normans were indistinguishable from the Gaelic Irish in terms of language, custom, and actions, as in the judgment of Lord Mountjoy's secretary Fynes Moryson: "Yet the English-Irish, forgetting their own country, are somewhat infected with the Irish rudeness." Increased use of Gaelic literature and a more sophisticated understanding of the structure of the Gaelic oireacht have illuminated the roles of elites and the organization of Irish political life. Combined with archaeological analyses, the resulting image undermines the

---

11. Rolf Loeber, "The Geography and Practice of English Colonisation in Ireland from 1534–1609," *Irish Settlement Studies,* no. 3 (1991). Quotation from "Instructions of Philip and Mary to Thomas Radcliffe, Lord Fitzwalter, Their Deputy in Ireland, Touching the Countries of Leix and Offaly," Apr. 28, 1556, Cotton MSS, Titus B.xi, no. 241, British Library, London, in Constantia Maxwell, *Irish History from Contemporary Sources, 1509–1610* (London, 1923), 229–232, esp. 232.

common belief in the stark contrast between the Gaelic Irish and the Old English by the late medieval period.[12]

Considerations of architecture, settlement, and material culture are central to the debate over the dichotomous nature of society in Ireland following the arrival of the Anglo-Normans. The nucleated Anglo-Norman manorial-style settlements, introduced in the thirteenth century, have been contrasted with more dispersed rural Gaelic settlements, characterized by the use of the *ráth,* or ringfort, a circular enclosed farmstead with early medieval origins. At the same time, the widespread distribution of tower houses in fifteenth-century Ireland suggests a shared Gaelic and Old English culture, though only at the level of elite architecture. Even earlier than the fifteenth century, some northern Irish elites incorporated the idea of the castle into their own lexicon. The Ulster elite learned quickly from the Anglo-Norman invaders, judging by the thirteenth-century earthen fortifications at Doonbought, Co. Antrim, and Coney Island, in Lough Neagh, as well as fourteenth-century stone castles such as Harry Avery's Castle, Co. Tyrone, built by the O'Neills.[13]

The Gaelic elite left behind a range of material responses to the introduction of castle building. Some lords chose to build in stone, but others sought continuity in maintaining their lordly residences on crannogs, or artificial islands, more commonly associated with the early medieval period. Similarly, the use of earthen (ráth) and stone cashel *(caisel)* ringforts into the late medieval period suggest continuity, although that does not imply cultural stasis. Despite the fact that more than forty-five thousand of these sites

12. It is worth reexamining the scholarly insistence upon discussing the Gaelic Irish and the Old English as separate identities, a practice rooted in Elizabethan policies and perspectives. Continued emphasis upon the divide between the two peoples—bearing in mind that by the time Elizabeth attained the throne the Old English had been in Ireland for four hundred years—arguably provides legitimacy to continued constructions of the descendants of the sixteenth- and seventeenth-century planters as colonists without a legitimate claim to any part of Ireland. See Fynes Moryson, *An Itinerary: Containing His Ten Yeeres Travell . . . ,* 4 vols. (1617; rpt. Glasgow, 1907–1908), III, 180; Nicholas P. Canny, *Making Ireland British: 1580–1650* (Oxford, 2001); Patrick J. Duffy, David Edwards, and Elizabeth FitzPatrick, "Recovering Gaelic Ireland, c. 1250–c. 1650," in Duffy, Edwards, and FitzPatrick, eds., *Gaelic Ireland,* 21–76.

13. Terry Barry, "Rural Settlement in Medieval Ireland," in Barry, ed., *A History of Settlement in Ireland* (London, 2000), 110–123; Kieran Denis O'Conor, *The Archaeology of Medieval Rural Settlement in Ireland,* Discovery Program Monographs, no. 3 (Dublin, 1998), 104; J. P. Mallory and T. E. McNeill, *The Archaeology of Ulster from Colonization to Plantation* (Belfast, 1991), 269–273. The exact construction history of Harry Avery's castle is unclear. The name relates to the O'Neill chief Henry Ambreidh O'Neill, who died around 1392 and who is traditionally associated with the building.

have been identified in the Irish landscape, their chronology remains poorly understood. Evidence from cashels, locally known as *cathracha* (plural), or *cathair* (singular), in the Burren, Co. Clare, suggests that, although such enclosures might have first been built in the early medieval period, they were adapted for domestic use by minor Gaelic elites. In the seventeenth century, English planters would also use these enclosed Irish settlements, in contravention of plantation regulations, because of their defensive qualities and their common presence on the landscape.[14]

Reconstructing Late Medieval Gaelic Life

The political structure of late medieval Ireland was characterized, not by unity, but by factionalism and regionalism that complicated both English efforts at conquering Ireland and the centralization of any Irish efforts at resisting England. Outside of the English administration in Dublin, hereditary chieftains or lords maintained political power through inherited territories and a complicated system of mutual obligation. Kin relationships, both familial and fictive, structured society, but their individual nature could vary between lordships. Customs of fosterage and gossiprid (a form of clientage) could provide a means of ensuring loyalty and affinity between nonrelated families, usually at the elite level. In fosterage, a child was sent, often for a fee, to be raised by another family, intended to ensure lifelong obligation. The system was founded upon the personal ties maintained by an individual lord, spurring competition and sporadic conflict between lordships. Regional differences were also significant. Gaelic elites in Leinster, situated close to the center of English administration in Dublin, felt the impact of English conquest more immediately than Gaelic elites in the north or far west. It is no surprise that the members of Leinster Gaelic lordships, such as those of the O'Byrnes and O'Tooles, might have viewed Gaelic elites from Ulster or Connacht with suspicion rather than comradeship.[15]

14. For a reevaluation of the chronology of enclosed settlement, see Elizabeth FitzPatrick, "Native Enclosed Settlement and the Problem of the Irish 'Ring-Fort,'" *Medieval Archaeology*, LIII (2009), 271–307. Evidence for the reuse of ráths by planters is considered in more detail in Chapter 2.

15. Gossiprid, as defined by Fiona Fitzsimons, "was essentially a pledge of fraternal association between a lord who thereby gained service, and his client who received protection, patronage and . . . preferential treatment of his suits in court" (Fitzsimons, "Fosterage and Gossiprid in Late Medieval Ireland: Some New Evidence," in Duffy, Edwards, and FitzPatrick, eds., *Gaelic Ireland*, 143). Christopher Maginn explores the O'Byrne and O'Toole lordships and their reaction to Tudor encroachment in *"Civilizing" Gaelic Leinster: The Extension of Tudor Rule in the O'Byrne and O'Toole Lordships* (Dublin, 2005). In additional to interregional distrust, Maginn

Oral tradition was central to historical understandings, although documentary insight into Gaelic and Old English elite life can be derived from the annals and from bardic poetry. Since these sources were compiled by scribes and poets enhancing the localized political and cultural position of their lordly patrons, the nuanced interpretation of these texts is a challenging exercise. Although the annals—more accurately, chronicles—contain occasional references to events that took place outside of Ireland, the reports are episodic and dependent upon the reliability of the source, likely a merchant or traveling cleric. The annalists primarily concentrated upon the listing of individual events related to particular places and lordships, often derived from earlier sources or oral traditions and presented according to a formalized prose style. Bardic poetry, by contrast, consists of lyrical paeans to lordly patrons, designed to commemorate their bravery, generosity, and power. Neither source can be read literally, but both the chronicles and poems offer an invaluable emic window into Gaelic values and understandings. In other words, rather than etic reports constructed by outsiders attempting to record Gaelic lifeways, these sources are themselves products of a Gaelic world. No such textual sources exist for the Algonquian peoples encountered by the English in the Roanoke and Chesapeake regions. Instead, historians have long prioritized English descriptions of Algonquian life, even when archaeological evidence contradicts or complicates those accounts. In the case of sixteenth-century Gaelic Ireland, the broader range of sources available and the closer relationships between archaeologists, historians, and geographers hold greater promise for balancing emic and etic perspectives than is currently the case for sixteenth-century Algonquian life. At the same time, the archaeological record pertaining to the habitations of the lower orders of Irish society has barely been examined, and many basic questions about daily life still remain.[16]

As difficult as it has been to reconstruct the mindsets and experience of the late medieval Gaelic elite, even with emic textual sources, a far more difficult task is reconstructing the everyday lives of the majority of the Irish

---

(186) speculates about animosity between upland and lowland branches of both septs. Although the comparison he uses for discussing this relationship—that of Native relations in piedmont versus mountain North Carolina—is not appropriate, given the cultural distance between Iroquoian- and Siouan-speaking Native societies versus the shared clan identity and Gaelic tongue of the O'Byrnes and O'Tooles, the example illustrates the lack of unity in Ireland even within kinship groups.

16. Bernadette Cunningham and Raymond Gillespie, *Stories from Gaelic Ireland* (Dublin, 2003), 23; Cunningham, "Native Culture and Political Change in Ireland, 1580–1640," in Brady and Gillespie, eds., *Natives and Newcomers*, 148–170.

population. Comparatively little is known about the nonelite Gaelic Irish in the later medieval period, even by contrast to knowledge of contact-period Native societies of eastern North America, however biased that knowledge may be. For sixteenth-century Ireland, we are dealing with regional identities linked to clans, yet the low population seemed to encourage some degree of mobility on the part of tenants, as lamented by the English governor of Connacht, Sir Richard Bingham, in 1592: "Every May the tenants are at liberty to remove from one landlord to another, to what place they will." Such mobility challenged the elite's ability to cultivate loyalties and concretize regional allegiances. A better understanding of the survival strategies employed by nonelite Gaels, including mobility and flexibility, is essential for considering native responses to the extensive plantation schemes of the seventeenth century.[17]

Mobility was associated with cattle pastoralism and seasonal transhumance, or moving with cattle between winter and summer pasturage. To what extent the practice of transhumance was exaggerated by chroniclers, or exacerbated by conflict, remains unclear. The accounts of the shipwrecked Spanish sailor Francisco de Cuellar convey hyperbole as well as a sense of palpable social disarray in 1588 Ulster:

> The custom of these savages is to live as the brute beasts among the mountains, which are very rugged in that part of Ireland where we lost ourselves. They live in huts made of straw. . . . They cover themselves with "mantas" and wear their hair down to their eyes. . . . The chief inclination of these people, is to be robbers, and to plunder each other. . . . They have therefore, no other remedy but to withdraw themselves to the mountains, with their women and cattle; for they possess no other property, nor more moveables nor clothing. They sleep upon the ground, on rushes, newly cut and full of water and ice. . . . The most of the women are very beautiful, but badly dressed. . . . In short, in this Kingdom there is neither justice nor right, and everybody does what he pleases.[18]

17. Sir Richard Bingham quoted in Cunningham and Gillespie, *Stories,* 31. For consideration of the movement of the tenantry, see Kenneth Nicholls, *Gaelic and Gaelicised Ireland in the Middle Ages* (Dublin, 1972).

18. Unpublished place-name research by Thomas McErlean for Ulster and Theresa McDonald for Achill Island, Co. Mayo, addresses the long-established patterns of movement within a clearly defined territory, in contradiction to the English emphasis on nomadism. For example, the Ordnance Survey Memoirs for Achill Island state, "It is a great habit among the people of the island to have two townlands and houses built on each where they remove occasionally with their cattle." For discussion of field systems, see Tadhg O'Keeffe, *Medieval Ireland: An Archae-*

Servitor and mapmaker Francis Jobson similarly attributed the rebellious-ness of the Irish to the practice of transhumance: "The greatest strength, riches, and relief of these rebellious people, in this Province and other parts of Ireland, consist chiefly upon great herds of cows, goats, and horse, which so long as they may have scope to range up and down in to pasture and feed, they both can and will ever at their pleasures (without regard of God, Prince, or humanity), rebel and make havoc." In imposing the rigors of plantation, Lord Deputy Arthur Chichester decreed in 1608 that the Ulster Irish were to be "drawn from their course of running up and down the country with their cattle . . . and are to settle themselves in towns and villages." Consider-ing that transhumance was also common in upland areas of England, Wales, and Scotland, and that lands in England were just undergoing the transition from an infield-outfield system to organized enclosure, English commen-tators on Irish land usage had some familiarity with pastoralism and sea-sonal movements linked to grazing lands. That they emphasized a presumed nomadism rather than transhumance suggests a desire to justify land acqui-sition on the basis that it was not owned or sufficiently used by the native population, a rationale repeated in the New World. A similar discomfort with regulated seasonal migration informed later British colonial efforts to en-force sedentism on North American Native people.[19]

Men like Chichester who drew up plans for the Ulster Plantation con-demned Irish impermanent architecture and associated seasonal movement as the antithesis of the "civilized" English timber-frame dwelling in a spa-tially constrained and ordered village, even when English settlers themselves often adopted Irish forms of dwellings. The emphasis upon converting the Irish from pastoralism and mobility to agriculture was inextricably linked with the colonizing and civilizing imperative. Taming the land equated tam-ing the people. If pastures were plowed and fields divided and ordered, it fol-lowed that the population would become more ordered. In reality, planters in both the sixteenth and seventeenth centuries adopted elements of the

---

ology (Stroud, 2000), 80. Quotation of de Cuellar can be found in Francisco de Cuellar, "Account of Captain Cuellar," in Maxwell, *Irish History from Contemporary Sources,* 318–319.

19. Jobson quotation from Francis Jobson, "Ulster's Unity" (1598), in Hamilton, Atkinson, and Mahaffy, eds., *CSPI of the Reigns of Henry VIII., Edward VI., Mary, and Elizabeth,* VII, *1598, January–1599, March,* 445; Chichester quotation from Arthur Chichester, "Certain Notes of Re-membrances Touching the Plantation and Settlement of the Escheated Lands in Ulster, Septem-ber 1608," in C. W. Russell and John P. Prendergast, eds., *Calendar of the State Papers, Relating to Ireland, of the Reign of James I,* 5 vols. (London, 1872–1880), III, *1608–1610,* 54–65, esp. 65.

Irish cattle economy, with trade in hides providing an important means of guaranteeing income.[20]

The unrelenting emphasis upon pastoralism found in sixteenth-century writings must be read in the context of the intensification of English agriculture and tillage in particular. As argued by Moryson, "The Irish thus given to idelness, naturally abhor from manual arts and civil trades to gain their own bread. . . . [They] gladly employed themselves in feeding of cows, that course of life was embraced by them as suitable to their innate sloth," whereas the poet Edmund Spenser more succinctly insisted, "This keeping of cows is of itself a very idle life." Yet cartographic evidence suggests not-infrequent representations of crops, even on the Richard Bartlett maps that chronicle the Ulster campaign of Charles Blount, Lord Mountjoy, during the Nine Years' War (1594–1603). The depiction of crops on English military maps reflects the practical need to feed troops, but the historic significance of cereal crop production can be traced back through pollen analysis and in texts to the period well before the twelfth-century Anglo-Norman invasions. In short, Ireland was not devoid of improved fields and cultivated crops. The emphasis on wilderness and on the supposed uncivilized character of a cattle-based economy reflected English anxiety over the close association between agricultural improvement and civility and justified English efforts to impose control over Ireland.[21]

20. See John Patrick Montaño, *The Roots of English Colonialism in Ireland* (Cambridge, 2011), for an argument emphasizing the connection between agricultural improvement and colonialism in Ireland; also considered by Pluymers, "Taming the Wilderness," *Environmental History,* XVI (2011), 610–632. Despite the difficulty of comprehending the lifeways of nonelite Gaelic Irish in the sixteenth century, the influence of the imposition of nomadism on the Irish continues to shape scholarship. See James A. Delle, "'A Good and Easy Speculation': Spatial Conflict, Collusion, and Resistance in Late Sixteenth-Century Munster, Ireland," *International Journal of Historical Archaeology,* III (1999), 32, where he explains his focus on elite architecture in an exploration of Gaelic resistance by dismissing the rest of Irish architecture as impermanent, because "the ordinary Irish people of the sixteenth century were largely transhumant pastoralists." For consideration of the imposition of reserves to curb Native seasonal mobility in North America, see Neal Ferris, *The Archaeology of Native-Lived Colonialism: Challenging History in the Great Lakes* (Tucson, Ariz., 2009), 59–62.

21. Fynes Moryson, "The Commonwealth of Ireland," in C. Litton Falkiner, ed., *Illustrations of Irish History and Topography, Mainly of the Seventeenth Century* (London, 1904), 249–250; Edmund Spenser, *A View of the Present State of Ireland: From the First Printed Edition,* ed. Andrew Hadfield and Willy Maley (Oxford, 1997), 149; Fergus Kelly, *Early Irish Farming: A Study Based Mainly on the Law-Texts of the 7th and 8th Centuries AD* (Dublin, 1997); Valerie A. Hall and Lynda Bunting, "Tephra-Dated Pollen Studies of Medieval Landscapes in the North of Ireland," in Duffy, Edwards, and FitzPatrick, eds., *Gaelic Ireland,* 220.

Accounts focusing upon population mobility and the insecurity of tenure also overlook the considerable evidence for established, nucleated settlements throughout late medieval Ireland. As discussed above, urban centers were present in areas most significantly affected by Anglo-Norman influence as well as in zones where Gaelic hierarchies predominated. Outside of urban zones, manorial-style settlements generally incorporated a church, mill, bakery, and agricultural units such as granaries, barns, dovecotes, fishponds, and rabbit warrens. Beyond the manors could be found moated sites, or defended farmsteads, of which more than one thousand have been identified, concentrated in the southeast and south of the country but also identified in areas outside of Anglo-Norman control. Additionally, a network of parish churches throughout all four provinces of Ireland ministered to the population and encouraged nucleation in their immediate vicinity. Traces of those settlements exist in the form of house platforms, enclosures, and, in some cases, adjacent tower houses. Many of these locales held markets, which drew the population together with traders. The countryside itself was no wilderness but instead was understood and administered through a system of political boundaries. In late medieval Ulster, land divisions ranged from the largest, the *ballybetagh,* to the quarter, the *ballyboe* (sometimes also referred to as *tate,* or *poll),* to the smallest, alternatively recorded as *sessagh, gort, gallon,* or *pottle.* The modern townland, averaging between two hundred and four hundred acres in size, corresponds with the ballyboe. Ballybetaghs and ballyboes correspond with clan or sept territories, where land was subject to periodic redistribution. Within the ballybetagh could be found the full range of land types necessary to support cattle-raising and grain (most often oat) cultivation. The system of land assessment and division facilitated the exaction of taxes and tributes by the Gaelic lords, as implied by the nomenclature *(ballyboe* likely derives from *baile bó,* or *cowland).* [22]

22. The different forms of settlement are discussed in O'Conor, *Archaeology of Medieval Rural Settlement,* 41–71; Terry Barry, "Rural Settlement in Ireland in the Middle Ages: An Overview," *Ruralia,* I (1995), 134–141; Barry, "'The People of the Country . . . Dwell Scattered': The Pattern of Rural Settlement in Ireland in the Later Middle Ages," in J. Bradley, ed., *Settlement and Society in Medieval Ireland* (Kilkenny, 1988), 345–360; O'Keeffe, *Medieval Ireland;* and Audrey Horning, "Ireland: Medieval Identities, Settlement and Land Use," in Neil Christie and Paul Stamper, eds., *Medieval Rural Settlement: Britain and Ireland, A.D. 800–1600* (Oxford 2011), 172–185. For consideration of manorial settlement forms, see Oliver Creighton and Terry Barry, "Seigneurial and Elite Sites in the Medieval Landscape," ibid., 63–80; G. DeHaene, "Medieval Rural Settlement beside Duncormick Motte, Co. Wexford," in Margaret Murphy and Michael Potterton, eds., *The Dublin Region in the Middle Ages: Settlement, Land-Use, and Economy* (Dublin, 2010), 59–66, 171. For moated sites, see Kieran D. O'Conor, "The Ethnicity of Irish Moated Sites,"

Elsewhere in Ireland, similar systems were in operation. In Connacht, lands were divided into the baile, then quarter, then (at the townland level) the *cartron,* or *gniv;* in Leinster and Munster, lands were assessed in units of quarters and a townland-level unit variously termed a *plowland, cowland, cartron, martland, carrowmeer,* or *colp.* These terms indicate Anglo-Norman influence. Ireland, then, was not devoid of organized settlement, despite population levels decimated by the plagues of the fifteenth century, conflicts endemic to Gaelic society, and worsening fights with the English. New diseases arrived with English servitors, who themselves fell prey to what has been described as Ireland's unique disease environment.[23]

English descriptions of Ireland overemphasized chaos and instability; Moryson observed, "Ireland after much bloud spilt in the Civill warres, became less populous." In his estimation, the decline in population was exacerbated by the "slothfulnesse" and "barbarousnesse" of the population, who "build no houses, but, like nomads living in cabins, remove from one place to another with their cows, and commonly retire them within thick woods not to be entered without a guide, delighting in this roguish life, as more free from the hand of justice and more fit to commit rapines." Similarly, Spenser believed that, in order to convert the Irish "from their delight of licensious barbarisme unto the love of goodnesse and civillity," they must be compelled to adopt husbandry instead of, or at least alongside, pastoralism. Furthermore, towns should be established near mountain grazing lands so that the Irish "may dwell together with neighbors, and be conversante in the vewe of the world." Plantation was cast as an improvement to a neglected land. As noted above, however, archaeological investigations, coupled with broader use of Gaelic literary sources, underscore the diversity of settlement

---

Ruralia, III (2000), 92–102; O'Conor, *Archaeology of Medieval Rural Settlement;* Terrence B. Barry, *The Medieval Moated Sites of South-Eastern Ireland: Counties Carlow, Kilkenny, Tipperary, and Wexford,* British Archaeological Reports, British Ser., no. 35 (Oxford, 1977); Barry, *The Archaeology of Medieval Ireland* (London, 1988). For consideration of parish settlement nucleation, see Elizabeth FitzPatrick, "The Material World of the Parish," in FitzPatrick and Raymond Gillespie, eds., *The Parish in Medieval and Early Modern Ireland: Community, Territory, and Building* (Dublin, 2006), 62–79; Patrick Nugent, "The Dynamics of Parish Formation in High Medieval and Late Medieval Clare," ibid., 186–210. See also Horning, "Ireland," in Christie and Stamper, eds., *Medieval Rural Settlement,* 172–185.

23. For discussion of townlands and land divisions, see Thomas McErlean, "The Irish Townland System of Landscape Organisation," in T. Reeves-Smyth and F. Hamond, eds., *Landscape Archaeology in Ireland,* British Archaeological Report, British Ser., no. 116 (Oxford, 1983), 315–339. For Ireland's disease environment, see Colm Lennon, *Sixteenth-Century Ireland: The Incomplete Conquest* (New York, 1995), 9.

forms present throughout late medieval Ireland alongside a range of pastoral and agricultural subsistence practices.[24]

Although Moryson and Spenser overstated the nomadic nature of Irish pastoralism, transhumance did feature in the seasonal round of rural Gaelic Ireland, and it can be elucidated in the archaeological record. Sites traditionally associated with seasonal grazing activities, or *booleying*, generally encompass a cluster of single-room structures with occasional annexes, built of stone or sod, possessing no chimneys or windows, and situated on high ground near fresh water. Documentary and oral historical sources confirm the seasonal use of some of these structures in the eighteenth and nineteenth centuries, although whether these structures and locales also reflect medieval practice remains an open question. Very few have been archaeologically examined, and those that have yield chronologically ambiguous results.

The challenge of understanding the relationship between sites associated with transhumance and the nature of late medieval rural life is illustrated through a reanalysis of thirty-eight County Antrim sites, listed as booleying locales on the Northern Ireland Sites and Monuments Record. These structures survive in upland locations in the form of low earthworks. All are situated in places that have never undergone plow-based cultivation, which would have removed all traces of their mainly earthen walls. This means that sites tend to survive in marginal upland environments, significantly skewing

24. Moryson, *Itinerary*, IV, 192, 195; Moryson, "Commonwealth of Ireland," in Falkiner, ed., *Illustrations of Irish History and Topography*, 246; Spenser, *View of the Present State*, ed. Hadfield and Maley, 149–150, 201–221. Understandings of rural and urban life during the late sixteenth and early seventeenth centuries have long concentrated upon documentary and cartographic sources on English and Scottish settlement and on the experiences of the Gaelic and Old English elite, lamenting the dearth of information on rural Gaelic land use. The presumed minimal visibility of the lower orders of Gaelic society has discouraged many scholars from even looking. Such assumptions are underscored by the comments of medievalist Tadhg O'Keeffe: "All strata of secular society beneath the castle-owning élite . . . are very difficult to isolate in the archaeological record. In consequence, archaeologists cannot draw from their own reservoir of data to speak independently and authoritatively about any subtle distinctions of social class and economic dependence around which mediaeval Gaelic society was organised." See O'Keeffe, *The Gaelic Peoples and Their Archaeological Identities, A.D. 1000–1650*, Quiggin Pamphlets on the Sources of Mediaeval Gaelic History, no. 7 (Cambridge, 2004), 20. A parallel can be drawn with the lack of attention paid to North American Native sites of the nineteenth and twentieth centuries, where presumptions of total material acculturation led to expectations that there would be no distinctive material signature. See Neal Ferris, *The Archaeology of Native-Lived Colonialism: Challenging History in the Great Lakes* (Tucson, Ariz., 2009); and Patricia E. Rubertone, "The Historical Archaeology of Native Americans," *Annual Review of Anthropology*, XXIX (2000), 425–446. For a call to pay greater attention to Gaelic sources, see Cunningham, "Native Culture and Political Change in Ireland," in Brady and Gillespie, eds., *Natives and Newcomers*, 148–170.

our image of late medieval rural life. Seven of these thirty-eight sites were at least partially excavated, but given the paucity of finds and lack of clear dating evidence, they could date anywhere from the thirteenth century to the eighteenth. Moreover, little evidence indicates whether particular sites were occupied only in the summer, as befitting their designation as booleying locales. Such dwellings are equally likely to have been the year-round homes of the lower orders of late medieval Gaelic society. Whether used for transhumance or not, the structures encountered in the Antrim study provide valuable, if frustratingly incomplete, insight into the material life of the nonelite.[25]

Based on the Antrim evidence, the ordinary homes of the rural population were modest in size and subrectangular in shape, with inside activities focused around a central hearth from which smoke escaped through a hole in the roof. Appending additional units onto the ends of the structures gave extra space. Such additions probably housed cattle, although opposing doorways on many of the principal dwellings suggest that some families also shared their homes with livestock (opposing doorways are needed to facilitate the movement of a cow, unable to turn around in the confined space of a dwelling). These structures tend to be clustered together in small numbers from two or three to no more than a dozen, indicating the residences of extended family groups.

The traces of three such subrectangular houses were investigated in 1982, in an upland location adjacent to the Glenmakeeran River in Glenmakee-

25. Considerations of booleying draws from the work of Jean Margaret Graham, "Transhumance in Ireland, with Special Reference to Its Bearing on the Evolution of Rural Communities in the West" (Ph.D. diss., Queen's University, Belfast, 1954); and E. Estyn Evans, "Field Archaeology in the Ballycastle District," *Ulster Journal of Archaeology,* 3d Ser., VIII (1945), 14–32. A key source for understanding the role of late medieval transhumance is Katharine Simms, "Nomadry in Medieval Ireland: The Origins of the Creaght, or Caoraigheacht," *Peritia,* V (1986), 379–391. See further discussions in Kieran D. O'Conor, "Housing in Later Medieval Gaelic Ireland," *Ruralia,* IV (2001), 201–210; and Stuart Rathbone, "Booley Houses, Hafods, and Shielings: A Comparative Study of Transhumant Settlements from around the Northern Basin of the Irish Sea," in Audrey Horning and Nick Brannon, eds., *Ireland and Britain in the Atlantic World* (Dublin, 2009), 111–130. Reconsideration of the function of these sites is addressed in Horning, "A Re-evaluation of the Archaeology of Transhumance in the North of Ireland," paper presented at the Second Annual Conference of the Irish Post-Medieval Archaeology Group, Trinity College, Dublin, February 2002; Horning, "Archaeological Explorations of Cultural Identity and Rural Economy in the North of Ireland: Goodland, County Antrim," *International Journal of Historical Archaeology,* VIII (2004), 28–31; Horning, "Materiality and Mutable Landscapes: Rethinking Seasonality and Marginality in Rural Ireland," ibid., XI (2007), 358–378. The Tildarg site is reported upon in N. F. Brannon, "A Small Excavation in Tildarg Townland, Near Ballyclare, County Antrim," *Ulster Journal of Archaeology,* 3d Ser., XLVII (1984), 163–170.

ran Townland, 6.4 kilometers southeast of the coastal settlement of Bally-castle. One of these dwellings—which was built of sods, measured 10.2 by 5.2 meters, and featured a central hearth—was excavated. Investigators en-countered no evidence for earthfast posts, so the building either had a roof supported on the sod walls or, more likely, employed a form of cruck tim-bering. A cruck roof system had advantages for a transhumant lifestyle, given the ease with which the roof timbers could be dismantled and trans-ferred to another site. The use of crucks, however, is certainly not predi-cated upon transhumance. Few finds were recovered from the building that speak directly to the date of the structure. Ceramics consisted of six sherds of Ulster coarse pottery. This hand-built regional Irish ware, also known as everted-rim ware, can be only generally dated to the late medieval period. The recovery of sherds of the same type of native pottery from an early-seventeenth-century context at Movanagher, Co. Londonderry, as well as in a third quarter of the seventeenth-century context at Salterstown, Co. Londonderry, expands the potential time frame of occupation well up to the eighteenth century. The lack of associated cultivation ridges suggests that the building was only seasonally occupied, supported by references indicat-ing that land in Glenmakeeran Townland still served as mountain grazing in the early nineteenth century. But even if the occupants did not practice any significant cultivation, that does not prove or disprove seasonal use of the dwelling. Small-scale domestic sites of this period in lowland as well as upland areas seldom exhibit much surviving material culture, reflecting the reliance upon perishable materials such as baskets and wooden and leather vessels. All that can be said for certain about Glenmakeeran is that the small cluster of dwellings dates to a roughly five hundred–year period and was occupied by people who were far from the top of society.[26]

A similar subrectangular stone and sod building was excavated adjacent

26. For Glenmakeeran, see B. B. Williams and P. S. Robinson, "The Excavation of Bronze Age Cists and a Medieval Booley House at Glenmakeeran, County Antrim, and a Discussion of Booleying in North Antrim," *Ulster Journal of Archaeology*, 3d Ser., XLVI (1983), 29–40; for a reconsideration of Ulster coarse pottery, see Cormac McSparron, "The Medieval Coarse Pot-tery of Ulster" (M.Phil. diss., Queen's University, Belfast, 2007); and McSparron, "The Medi-eval Coarse Pottery of Ulster," *Journal of Irish Archaeology*, XX (2011), 101–121. The Movanagher evidence is discussed in Audrey J. Horning, "'Dwelling Houses in the Old Irish Barbarous Man-ner': Archaeological Evidence for Gaelic Architecture in an Ulster Plantation Village," in Duffy, Edwards, and FitzPatrick, eds., *Gaelic Ireland*, 375–396; Horning, "On the Banks of the Bann: The Riverine Economy of an Ulster Plantation Village," *Historical Archaeology*, XLI (2007), 94–114. For Salterstown, see Orloff Garrik Miller, "Archaeological Investigations at Salters-town, County Londonderry, Northern Ireland" (Ph.D. diss., University of Pennsylvania, 1991).

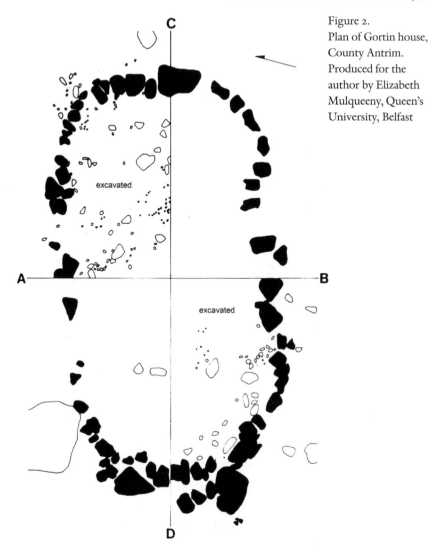

Figure 2.
Plan of Gortin house,
County Antrim.
Produced for the
author by Elizabeth
Mulqueeny, Queen's
University, Belfast

to the Carnlough River in Gortin Townland, Co. Antrim. Slightly smaller than the Glenmakeeran house, this structure measured 7.4 by 3.6 meters. Unfortunately, not a single artifact was recovered to provide any chronological framework for its interpretation. The lack of finds may relate to a very short-term use, to the material impoverishment of its occupants, or to their reliance on objects derived from perishable materials. Although absence of evidence is never evidence of absence, the lack of the more ubiquitous postmedieval artifacts such as clay tobacco pipestems and bottle glass implies a date earlier than the seventeenth or eighteenth centuries. Similarly, two small (2 m²) subrectangular structures were recorded and excavated in Ballyutoag Townland, Co. Antrim, but again, no finds were recovered. The most extensive settlement evidence has been recorded at Craigs, Co. Antrim, including cultivation ridges. Finds from a subrectangular structure there consisted entirely of Ulster coarse pottery, again pointing only generally to late medieval and early postmedieval occupation. In this case, however, the sod walls and charcoal from the central hearth yielded radiocarbon dates that support a sixteenth- to seventeenth-century date range. Given that the structural evidence from Craigs closely reflects that found at the above sites, the radiocarbon dates strengthen the case that these dwellings served as the homes of the so-called "mere Irish" in the late medieval and early modern periods.[27]

Another cluster of more than a dozen houses can be found in Coolnagoppoge Townland, along the banks of Turrybrennan Burn. The structures, which have not been excavated, survive as earthworks that are mainly subrectangular to rectangular in shape, measuring on average five by three meters. A desolate upland location today, this is a believable booleying locale, supported by its association with the placename of Crocknaboley. Yet the location also sustained permanent habitation in the eighteenth and nineteenth centuries, given the presence of a substantial ruined dwelling incorporating stone walls and a chimney, a flax retting dam adjacent to the burn, and the remains of a clustered nineteenth-century farming settlement less than a mile away. In the adjoining townland of Ballyvennacht lies another cluster of hut remains in association with Turrybrennan Burn. Situated in a small valley sheltered by hills on three sides, this is an ideal locale for seasonal pasturage, with cattle protected from the weather and from raids by the sides of the valley. Finds of bog butter reported in the *Ordnance Survey Memoirs* provide further support for pastoralism. But like Coolnagoppoge, the traces of subrectangular sod and stone-built houses are accompanied by at least one that incorporates a stone-built chimney, indicating a postmedieval date and also suggesting continuity of occupation at this site. The evidence of later permanent habitation challenges assumptions about the marginality

---

27. The Gortin site is reported by Mark Gardiner, *Excavations of a Late Medieval or Early Modern House at Gortin, Ardclinis, Co. Antrim,* Data Structure Report (Belfast, 2010); and the Ballyutoag site by Cormac McSparron, "A Note on the Discovery of Two Probable Booley Houses at Ballyutoag, County Antrim," *Ulster Journal of Archaeology,* 3d Ser., LXI (2002), 154–155; and B. B. Williams, "Excavations at Ballyutoag, County Antrim," ibid., XLVII (1984), 37–49. Excavations at Craigs are reported in Williams, A. Goddard, and M. McCorry, "A Late Medieval Rural Settlement at Craigs, County Antrim," ibid., LI (1988), 91–102.

of these upland environments and raises questions about the character and role of seasonality in the late medieval period.[28]

All this ambiguous and fragmentary evidence gives us extremely limited archaeological understandings of those members of the lower orders of Gaelic society referred to by the English as the "wild" or "mere" Irish. More extensive surveying and excavation of these subrectangular dwellings—incorporating sampling for floral and faunal remains to shed light upon seasonality—is needed to provide even a baseline understanding of late medieval Gaelic habitation. Such a program of excavation would have to rely upon an extensive radiocarbon dating exercise, given the paucity of dateable material culture associated with those few sites that have been studied. Such investigation should take place throughout Ireland, as similar booley sites can be found throughout the island, often exhibiting distinct regional differences in shape, size, and material that have yet to be understood. The upland *bothóg,* or booley hut, of County Donegal was typically cut into an earthen bank, with walls built up with sods and stone. Variation can be found even in the same locale: so-called booley villages on Achill Island, Co. Mayo, vary

28. The early-nineteenth-century Ordnance Survey Memoirs for the parish of Culfreightrin noted, "There is no town in the parish and no village deserving of the name. Coolnagoppag is the largest group of cabins." Whether this relates to the clustered farmsteads or to the structures along the burn is uncertain. Quotation from Angelique Day, Patrick McWilliams, and Nóirín Dobson, eds., *Ordnance Survey Memoirs of Ireland,* XXIV, *Parishes of County Antrim IX, 1830–32, 1835, 1838–9, North Antrim Coast and Rathlin* (Belfast, 1994), 39. Further complicating the association of these Antrim sites with transhumance is the likelihood that another designated booley site, in Tildarg Townland on the slopes of Big Colin Mountain near Ballyclare, may instead be the remains of a permanent moated settlement. Traces of a subrectangular structure included substantial remains of low sod and clay walls surviving as a raised platform, as well as a series of stakeholes and an ashy layer within the structure. Measuring approximately 6 by 16 meters, this sizeable structure was located within an unusual earthwork that might have served as a cattle enclosure. The use of clay and sod walling, in a locale with abundant stone, suggests that the walls themselves were not designed to bear the weight of the roof structure. Instead, the structure might have relied upon wooden crucks. Ambiguous archaeological evidence supporting this theory included a void in the wall and a shallow depression into which cruck timber supports might have been placed. The indicative thirteenth-century radiocarbon date (755 +– 50 B.P. [UB 2581], which calibrates within a 2 s.d. range of AD 1185–1375) corresponds to a documented period of climatic warming and suggests that occupation on this site was not necessarily constrained by seasonal marginality. On the north side of Big Colin Mountain, in the same townland, two more locales are identified as booleying sites, possibly also associated with the medieval usage of the land. No excavation has taken place at these sites to refine their usage. As illustrated by the Glenmakeeran, Gortin, and Ballyutoag investigations, excavation of the Big Colin sites still might not yield enough evidence to assign either chronology or function in terms of seasonality. See Brannon, "Small Excavation in Tildarg Townland," *Ulster Journal of Archaeology,* 3d Ser., XLVII (1984), 163–170. O'Conor has suggested that this may be a moated site; see *Archaeology of Medieval Rural Settlement,* 88–89.

from clusters of small, circular stone dwellings to groupings of multiroomed earthen and stone structures with distinct architectural features, including in-built niches and cupboards. Returning to Coolnagoppoge, structures there also include round as well as subrectangular forms. Whether these differences relate to date or function remains unknown. The relative physical invisibility of the ordinary Gael, particularly by comparison to the rich archaeological and architectural record associated with the elite, discourages sustained archaeological investigation. However, there is evidence still surviving and well worth exploring to shed light on late medieval Gaelic life.[29]

Constructing the Irish as "Other"

Regardless of the ability of physical evidence to inform understandings of late medieval Gaelic life, it is the English sources that have long framed both considerations of Gaelic society on the eve of plantation and comparisons with the Natives of the New World. These sources explicitly treated an undifferentiated Irish population as the other; a process with distinctly material associations. In imposing the Reformation, the English betrayed material anxieties as they legislated against Irishness. Owing to fear of familiarity and perhaps the loss of a newly constructed English identity, English servitors and soldiers were forbidden from wearing any Irish garb—as were the Irish themselves. Identity was proclaimed through and thus defined by appearance. The mark of loyalty to the crown could be read and proclaimed materially, according to the 1537 Act for the English Order, Habit, and Language:

> Werefore it be enacted . . . that no person or persons . . . shall use or wear any mantles, coat or hood made after the Irish fashion . . . every the said person or persons having or keeping any house or household, shall, to their power, knowledge, and ability, use and keep their houses and households, as near as ever they can, according to the English order, condition and manner.[30]

The Irish readily understood that display and the construction of difference was a weapon. According to one English chronicler, "It is to be observed in the proud condition of the Irish, that they disdain to sort

---

29. Robbie Hannan and Jonathan Bell, "The *Bothóg:* A Seasonal Dwelling from County Donegal," in Trefor M. Owen, ed., *From Corrib to Cultra: Folklife Essays in Honour of Alan Gailey* (Belfast, 2000), 71–81.

30. "An Act for the English Order, Habit, and Language," 28 Hen. VIII. c. 15, *Irish Statutes* (1786), I, 199–122, in Maxwell, *Irish History from Contemporary Sources,* 112.

themselves in fashion unto us, which in their opinion would more plainly manifest our conquest over them." Barnaby Riche was rather less measured in expressing his frustration: "The Irish had rather still retain themselves in their sluttishness, in their uncleanliness, in their rudeness, and in their inhuman loathsomeness, than they would take any example from the English, either of civility, humanity, or any manner of decency."[31]

By way of counterpart, an Irish perspective is provided in a sixteenth-century poem composed by the bard Laoiseach Mac an Bhaird, deriding an Irish man for sporting English fashion:

> O man who follow English ways, who cut your thick-clustering hair, graceful hand of my choice, you are not Donnchadh's good son! . . . A man who has never loved English ways is Eóghan Bán, beloved of noble ladies. To English ways he never gave his heart: a savage life he chose. . . . Little he cares for a mantle gold-embroidered, or a high ornamental collar, or a gold ring that would only be irksome, or a satin scarf down to the heels. . . . How unlike you are to Eoghan Ban—they laugh at your foot on the stepping-stone. Pity that you have not seen your fault, O man who follows English ways.[32]

Mac an Bhaird's poem indicates that he was well versed in the broader Renaissance language of costume. In recognizing the transformative, trans-naturing power of clothing, he demonstrates a shared cultural understanding with the English and with European Renaissance society more generally. Mac an Bhaird's complaints about elite Irishmen's adopting foreign frippery, and by extension endangering their identity, appears to have been justified. Bristol port books divulge the increasing importation of cloth and clothing to Ireland throughout the sixteenth century. Although rare, archaeological finds of luxury textiles such as continental silks and velvets also suggest that not all Irish were immune to the attractions of English fashions. Excavation of a ditch in-filled in late sixteenth-century Dublin uncovered a deposit of textile scraps interpreted as castoffs from a late-sixteenth-century tailor's shop. In the assemblage were ten fragments of velvet cloth, likely of

31. *A New Description of Ireland, together with the Manners, Customs, and Dispositions of the People* (1610), rpt. in James P. Myers Jr., ed., *Elizabethan Ireland: A Selection of Writings by Elizabethan Writers on Ireland* (Hamden, Conn., 1983), 126–145, esp. 131; E. C. S. [Sir Edward Cecil], *The Government of Ireland under . . . Sir John Perrot . . .* (London, 1626), in Maxwell, *Irish History from Contemporary Sources,* 350; Rych, *Short Survey of Ireland.*

32. "Poem by Laoiseach Mac an Bhaird," trans. Osborn Bergin, *Journal of the Ivernian Society,* V (1913), 212–213.

Italian manufacture, alongside twenty-four pieces of silk, a range of woolen cloths, and lengths of silken thread. Many of these items had apparently been recycled and reworked, highlighting their contemporary value. Clientele for this Dublin tailor probably included New English, Old English, and members of the Gaelic elite. Given the shared understanding of the language of costume, it is no surprise that the Irish elite (Old English and Gaelic) employed clothing as part of a strategy of code-switching. The rebellious earl of Desmond, Gerald FitzGerald, and his wife, Eleanor, were recorded as dressing in English clothes while the earl was under house arrest in London from 1567 to 1573, but both donned traditional garb when they returned to their lands and tenants in the province of Munster.[33]

English anxiety over Irish materiality conforms to the practice of othering inherent to early modern colonialism. Reference to the derided Irish mantle forms a part of later English descriptions of Native Americans. Jamestown colonist William Strachey compared the clothing of the Powhatan tribes with that of the Irish, noting, "The better sort use large mantells of deeres' skynnes, not much differing from the Irish falings." Similarly, Captain John Smith reported that the clothing of the paramount Powhatan chief, Wahunsenacawh, was a "faire Robe of skins as large as an Irish mantle." This robe may be the one acquired by John Tredescant the Younger in the 1620s. Now a centerpiece in the colonial collections of the Ashmolean Museum, Powhatan's Mantle, as it is still known, is constructed of four deerskins decorated with shells that depict a human, two animals, and more than thirty circles (generally interpreted as the political units within the paramount chiefdom).[34]

No matter how the mantle was construed as the material manifestation

33. For in-depth consideration of the meaning of clothing in the sixteenth century, see Ann Rosalind Jones and Peter Stallybrass, *Renaissance Clothing and the Materials of Memory* (Cambridge, 2000). For the Bristol evidence, see Flavin and Jones, eds., *Bristol's Trade with Ireland and the Continent*. Discussion of the Dublin finds is in Elizabeth Wincott Heckett, "Town and Country: An Overview of Irish Archaeological Cloth and Clothing, 1550–1850," in Horning et al., eds., *Post-Medieval Archaeology of Ireland*, 453–466. For Irish clothing more generally, see Mairéad Dunlevy, *Dress in Ireland* (London, 1989).

34. William Strachey, *The Historie of Travaile into Virginia Brittanie: Expressing the Cosmographie and Commodities of the Country, Together with the Manners and Customes of the People*, ed. R[ichard] H[enry] Major (London, 1849), 65. John Smith also uses the same comparison in his "Description of Virginia," in Smith, *The Generall Historie of Virginia, New England, and the Summer Isles* . . . (Glasgow, 1907), I, 62, when he states that the Powhatans wore "large mantels of Deare skins, not much differing in fashion from the Irish mantels"; and see Edward Arber, ed., *Capt. John Smith of Willoughby by Alford, Lincolnshire: President of Virginia, and Admiral of New England, Works, 1608–1631*, 3 vols. (Birmingham, 1884), I, 102.

Plate 1. "An Irish Banquet." From John Derricke, *Image of Irelande,*
with a Discoverie of Woodkarne . . . (London, 1581)

of the other, use of the mantle itself soon traversed supposedly impermeable
colonial boundaries. The Irish mantle was simultaneously legislated against
and appropriated by the English elite as an article of fashion. Even Elizabeth
I was portrayed resplendent in a brightly colored cloak trimmed like an Irish
mantle, illustrative, perhaps, of her desire for sovereignty over the Irish. The
selective adoption of the Irish mantle by the English is a clear instance of mimetic practice, which involves the interpretation and imitation of behavior.
It is a strategy employed not only by the colonized other but also by those
in authority, like Queen Elizabeth, who were engaging with and endeavoring to understand the behavior of those over whom they wielded power.[35]

35. Whether Powhatan's Mantle was actually a garment or, alternatively, a temple hanging is debatable. What is germane to this discussion is the use of the term "mantle." See David
Beers Quinn, *The Elizabethans and the Irish* (Ithaca, N.Y., 1966), 24; Ann Rosalind Jones and
Peter Stallybrass, "'Rugges of London and the Divell's Band': Irish Mantles and Yellow Starch
as Hybrid London Fashion," in Lena Cowen Orlin, ed., *Material London, ca. 1600* (Philadelphia,
2000), 128–149; Jones and Stallybrass, "Dismantling Irena: The Sexualizing of Ireland in Early
Modern England," in Andrew Parker et al., eds., *Nationalisms and Sexualities* (London, 1992),
157–171; Michael Neill, "Broken English and Broken Irish: Nation, Language, and the Optic

The emphasis upon replacing "Irish" habits with "English" habits implies the existence of an essential and recognizable "English manner"—but this must be viewed as aspirational rather than representational. Sixteenth-century England was hardly a unified country with a fossilized identity; it was a land undergoing uneven but discomforting transformation, marked by the Reformation-triggered privatization of church lands, by sporadic enclosure, by increasing urbanism, and by developing industries. The enclosure of the medieval open fields of England has been described as a "rational" process, improving the economic efficiency of the land while altering traditional social and legal relationships. Although the pattern of enclosure was not consistent between and even within regions, the cumulative effect was a rising number of impoverished, landless individuals and families in the sixteenth and seventeenth centuries. Quantifying how many English men, women, and children were landless and unemployed is difficult, but the perception at the time was that vagrancy was rampant. As such, efforts were made by government officials to calculate the actual numbers of vagrants, although estimates ranged from fifteen thousand to as many as eighty thousand. These numbers are hardly exact, but they suggest that vagrancy was, in fact, not a major problem, as even by the highest of those figures it affected less than 2 percent of the population in 1603. More significant was the perception of a problem, perhaps worsened by the fact that the majority of vagrants were young males.[36]

Whatever the true extent of vagrancy, there is no denying the impact of nascent enclosures. The enclosure of nearly seventy thousand acres in the

---

of Power in Shakespeare's Histories," *Shakespeare Quarterly,* XLV (1994), 24–25; and Barbara Fuchs, "Conquering Islands: Contextualizing *The Tempest,*" ibid., XLVIII (1997), 45–62. For mimesis, see Michael Taussig, *Mimesis and Alterity: A Particular History of the Senses* (New York, 1993); and for a consideration of the use of mimesis by the colonizing force, see Neil Mclean, "Mimesis and Pacification: The Colonial Legacy in Papua, New Guinea," *History and Anthropology,* XI (1998), 75–118.

36. For the rationality of enclosure, see Matthew H. Johnson, "Enclosure and Capitalism: The History of a Process," in Robert W. Preucel, ed., *Processual and Post-Processual Archaeologies: Multiple Ways of Knowing the Past,* Center for Archaeological Investigations, Southern Illinois University at Carbondale, Occasional Paper no. 10 (Carbondale, Ill., 1991), 162. Leonard Cantor summarizes the subsequent population disruption thus: "The more substantial and energetic peasants consolidated their holdings as the weaker went to the wall and were forced to give up their land so that a class of yeomen and minor gentry emerged, at the expense of an increase in the number of landless who were forced to become wage-labourers or, in some cases, were reduced to poverty and destitution" (Cantor, *The Changing English Countryside, 1400–1700* [London, 1987], 36). The problem of vagrancy is discussed by A. L. Beier, "Vagrants and the Social Order in Elizabethan England," *Past and Present,* no. 64 (August 1974), 5.

Midlands between 1578 and 1607 resulted in the mass protest known as the Midlands Revolt. Over a six-week period, an estimated five thousand protesters dug up hedges, filled in ditches, and ultimately engaged in hand-to-hand combat against the forces of the local gentry. Although the suppression of this rural English rising has been touted as a class victory for the wealthy landowners, it also shows that enclosure was neither a complete nor an accepted practice. Archaeological investigations throughout England have revealed that the enclosure of fields occurred gradually, particularly outside of the Midlands region. Nevertheless, enclosure allowed for the consolidation of landholdings and experimentation in specialized, profit-oriented agricultural enterprises and encouraged—and sometimes forced—laborers and small farmers to migrate in search of better economic prospects. Lesser numbers of rural dwellers were displaced via the creation of parklands surrounding country manor houses, which also accounted, in part, for the phenomenon of deserted villages.[37]

Unlike the enclosure of fields of the English countryside, many lands on the edges of towns and cities were opened to settlement through the sixteenth-century dissolution of the monasteries. The phenomenal geographic expansion of London was only possible because former monastic property beyond its walls became available for development. London grew from approximately 120,000 residents in 1550 to 490,000 residents by 1700 and alone accounted for half of the growth of the English urban population between 1500 and 1700. Population growth was a key factor in the rise of towns, although debate continues over the rate and extent of demographic change. The most extreme estimates suggest that the population of England doubled between the mid-fifteenth and mid-seventeenth centuries, in contrast to continental growth rates of around one-quarter of 1 percent per

---

37. For the Midlands Revolt and reconsideration of the impacts of enclosure and its uneven application, see Beier, "Vagrants," *Past and Present*, no. 64 (August 1974), 46; Tom Williamson and Liz Bellamy, *Property and Landscape: A Social History of Land Ownership and the English Countryside* (London, 1987); and Steve Hindle, "Imagining Insurrection in Seventeenth-Century England: Representations of the Midland Rising of 1607," *History Workshop Journal*, LXVI (2008), 24. Archival sources, as noted by archaeologist David Crossley, tend to emphasize "particular events and problems, which overshadow gradual change. In the case of enclosure, sixteenth-century litigation and commissions of enquiry concentrated on hard cases. . . . Just as these records understate the long-term changes such as piecemeal enclosure by agreement, so other aspects of improvement are distorted." See Crossley, *Post-Medieval Archaeology in Britain* (Leicester, 1990), 7. The classic source for abandoned medieval villages is Maurice Beresford and John G. Hurst, *Medieval Deserted Villages* (London, 1971). See also Cantor, *Changing English Countryside*; Neil Christie and Paul Stamper, eds., *Medieval Rural Settlement*.

year. A more realistic population estimate, derived through the analysis of taxation records and parish registers, suggests that the English of the 1520s numbered around 2.4 million. By 1580, the population increased to 3.6 million, exhibiting an annual growth rate of 1.1 percent in the 1570s and 1580s. This expansion may be linked more to an overall decline in mortality caused by a reduction in epidemic disease outbreaks than to an increase in fertility.[38]

Despite the fears of many who promoted New World colonization as a means of relieving overpopulation, the sixteenth and seventeenth centuries were not a time of uncontrolled population increase. Rather, the two centuries witnessed a slow and steady increase in population, which did strain available resources but at the same time provided a labor force and a consumer force to encourage the development of urban and rural manufactures.

Changes in the English landscape were integral to improvement, itself a hallmark of modernity. Although improvement is generally considered a phenomenon of the eighteenth and nineteenth centuries—as expressed through agricultural innovation and an emphasis upon morality, health, and education—the term does appear in sixteenth- and seventeenth-century writings in relation to both agriculture and morality. Ultimately, improvement would come to signal "both profit and moral benefit." The importance of this nascent process to a new English identity (constructed in opposition to an Irish identity) can be read in the comments of Irish attorney general Sir John Davies:

> For, though the Irishry be a Nation of great Antiquity, and wanted neither wit nor valour; and though they had received the Christian Faith, above 1,200 yeares since; and were Lovers of Musicke, Poetry, and all kinde of learning . . . yet (which is strange to bee related) they did never builde any houses of Brick or stone . . . plant any Gardens or Orchards, Inclose or improve their lands, live together in setled Villages or Townes, nor made any provision for posterity; which being against all common sense and reason, must needs be imputed to those unreasonable Customes, which made their estates so uncertaine and transitory in their possessions.

38. For the growth of London, see A. L. Beier and Roger Finlay, *London, 1500–1700: The Making of the Metropolis* (London, 1985), 2. According to Alan Dyer, between the mid-fifteenth and mid-seventeenth centuries, England's population doubled, which occasioned crowding in the countryside and an excess of labor. See Dyer, *Decline and Growth in English Towns, 1400–1640* (London, 1991); see also John Patten, *English Towns, 1500–1700* (Chatham, Kent, 1978), 95. The reduction in mortality due to epidemic disease is considered by Keith Wrightson, *Earthly Necessities: Economic Lives in Early Modern Britain* (New Haven, Conn., 2000), 120–128.

Davies would seem to be speaking as much to an English audience in need of being convinced of the necessity of enclosure and improvement as to an Irish audience in need of civilizing. In fact, some Irish lands, as was the case in the Ards Peninsula of County Down, were already partially enclosed during the medieval period, long before the English enclosure movement was felt in Ireland. Similarly, enclosure was the norm in the Burren region of County Clare. In constructing their images of Ireland and of Irish identity, early commentators like Davies were perforce constructing an identity for the English. Ethnic groups are defined as much by their perceived difference from other identities as they are by their own shared characteristics.[39]

Early modern Irish scholars also sought to codify their identity by contradicting negative English portrayals. In the early seventeenth century, Don Philip O'Sullivan Beare took, as his theme in his *Natural History of Ireland,* the refutation of Giraldus Cambrensis's (Gerald of Wales) unflattering twelfth-century description of Ireland. Cambrensis's writings were given a significant boost by the Old English writer Richard Stanihurst, who incorporated and further popularized them in his 1584 *De Rebus in Hibernia Gestis.* Although Stanihurst was an ardent Catholic, he also sought to distinguish the character of the Old English from that of the Gaelic Irish, a purpose for which the work of Cambrensis provided ample support. Cambrensis thus was widely used by English writers including William Camden and was also referenced by servitors such as Ralph Lane. Their reliance on Cambrensis incensed O'Sullivan Beare, who opened his book with the heading *"Quae Geraldi dicta sunt hic refellenda* [What are the things that were said by Gyraldus that need to be refuted here]?" O'Sullivan Beare concluded his work, "What I have taken up I seem to have accomplished: that Ireland is not deserted, without roads, and boggy, as Gyraldus would have it, but that it is heaped with glory under many headings." Notably, the works of O'Sullivan Beare were not widely published or distributed at the time, and, in fact, his *Natural History* was translated into English from the original Latin only

---

39. See John O'Keeffe, "The Archaeology of the Later Historical Cultural Landscape in Northern Ireland: Developing Historic Landscape Investigation for the Management of the Archaeological Resource: A Case Study of the Ards, County Down" (Ph.D. diss., University of Ulster, 2008). On improvement and moral benefit, see Sarah Tarlow, *The Archaeology of Improvement in Britain* (Cambridge, 2007), 12. Davies quotation from Sir John Davies, *Discovery of the True Causes Why Ireland Was Never Entirely Subdued* (1612; rpt. Shannon, 1969), 169–170. For the Burren, see FitzPatrick, "Native Enclosed Settlement." The relational nature of identity was argued by social anthropologist Fredrik Barth in his *Ethnic Groups and Boundaries: The Social Organization of Culture Difference* (London, 1969).

in the early twenty-first century. Remarkably, the writings of Cambrensis continue to influence scholarship on medieval Gaelic society extrapolated to understandings of Irish life in the sixteenth and early seventeenth centuries. O'Sullivan Beare failed in his mission to refute the twelfth-century polemicist and, by extension, the similar writings of his sixteenth-century advocates such as Stanihurst, Camden, and Lane.[40]

Cartography

Cartographic knowledge was another weapon in the English arsenal, as efforts to gain more credible knowledge of Gaelic territories intensified. Sixteenth-century maps first and foremost defined known political boundaries, outlined landscape characteristics, and pinpointed troublesome inhabitants and potentially defensible structures. When employed for colonial as well as military purposes, maps highlighted exploitable commodities and delineated territories presented as being available, and were central to early modern European colonizing ventures around the world.[41]

40. Giraldus Cambrensis, *Topography of Ireland*, trans. Thomas Forester (Ontario, 2000). Camden's use of Cambrensis and its promotion by Richard Stanihurst is explored in John Barry, "Derricke and Stanihurst: A Dialogue," in Harris and Sidwell, eds., *Making Ireland Roman*, 36–47; and David Finnegan, "Old English Views of Irish History," in Brain Mac Cuarta, ed., *Reshaping Ireland, 1550–1700: Colonization and Its Consequences; Essays Presented to Nicholas Canny* (Dublin, 2011), 192–193. For O'Sullivan Beare's perspective, see Philip O'Sullivan Beare, *The Natural History of Ireland: Included in Book One of the Zoilomastix of Don Philip O'Sullivan Beare*, ed. and trans. Denis C. O'Sullivan (Cork, 2009), 30–31, 267. The lingering influence of Cambrensis's description of the Irish is exemplified by the work of James Muldoon, who draws comparisons between Cambrensis's medieval descriptions of the Irish and John Smith's descriptions of the Powhatans (Muldoon, *Identity on the Medieval Irish Frontier: Degenerate Englishmen, Wild Irishmen, Middle Nations* [Gainesville, Fla., 2003], 92).

41. John H. Andrews, "The Mapping of Ireland's Cultural Landscape, 1550–1630," in Duffy, Edwards, and FitzPatrick, *Gaelic Ireland*, 179; Bernard Klein, *Maps and the Writing of Space in Early Modern England and Ireland* (Hampshire, 2001). For broader colonial and postcolonial perspectives on cartography, see, for example, Jeremy Black, *Maps and History: Constructing Images of the Past* (New Haven, Conn., 1997); Jeffrey C. Stone, "Imperialism, Colonialism, and Cartography," *Transactions of the Institute of British Geographers*, XIII (1988), 57–64; Simon Ryan, *The Cartographic Eye: How Explorers Saw Australia* (Cambridge, 1996). Annaleigh Margey has also summarized the practice of early modern cartography in the Ulster Plantation; see "Representing Plantation Landscapes: The Mapping of Ulster, c. 1560–1640," in James Lyttleton and Colin Rynne, eds., *Plantation Ireland: Settlement and Material Culture, c. 1550–1700* (Dublin, 2009), 140–164; and Margey, "After the Flight: The Impact of Plantation on the Ulster Landscape," in David Finnegan, Éamonn Ó Ciardha, and Marie-Claire Harrigan, eds., *The Flight of the Earls: Imeacht na nIarlaí* (Derry, 2010). Margey's "Representing Colonial Landscapes: Early English Maps of Ulster and Virginia, 1580–1612," in Mac Cuarta, ed., *Reshaping Ireland*, 61–81, compares the mapping of Ulster with the creation of John Smith's *Map of Virginia* but betrays a lacks of awareness of the Virginia landscape and an understanding of the specific cultural contexts of the Powhatan world.

A considerable number of sixteenth- and early-seventeenth-century cartographers captured Ireland on parchment, including Baptiste Boazio, Francis Jobson, Richard Bartlett, two mapmakers by the name of John Browne, Captain James Carlyle, John Norden, Thomas Fleming, Captain Nicholas Dawtrey, Brian Fitzpatrick, Thomas Raven, William Jones, Captain John Baxter, John Thomas, James Grafton, and Robert Lythe. Former Roanoke governor Ralph Lane also engaged in a cartographic exercise in order to produce a map of East Ulster that underscored his own claim to territory around Strangford Lough. Mapmakers might have created as many as four hundred maps of Irish territory, of which more than two hundred survive. These have been invaluable to scholars not just for the territories, structures, and events they depict but also for what they reveal about English preoccupations. To create a map of Ireland was to claim control, as symbolized by the Tudor arms and/or the cross of Saint George that frequently appear in cartographic cartouches.[42]

Cartographic knowledge of Ireland was still in short supply when the Ulster Plantation was launched in 1609–1610. Attorney General Sir John Davies made a somewhat hyperbolic complaint that the territory of Tyrone was "as unknown to the English here as the most inland part of Virginia is yet unknown to our English colony there." Later plantation maps, such as the 1625 survey of north County Down by Thomas Raven, purport to depict the extensive commodities available to planters while symbolically subduing the land (and its people) through surveillance. As on the maps of the Chesapeake drawn by Roanoke governor John White, the land represents future possibilities while downplaying past human activity. Abundant fish leap from the waters in the White maps; deer and rabbits cavort through newly delineated fertile fields on the Raven maps. Yet on a closer look, the native Irish can be found lingering on the edges of the map, evident in the often schematic representation of their dwellings, rendered no more substantial than a haystack or animal burrow.[43]

Whatever the intention of the cartographer, and whatever the perception of those who employed the maps to stake a claim, they are uneasy docu-

42. J. H. Andrews, *The Queen's Last Map-Maker: Richard Bartlett in Ireland, 1600–3* (Dublin, 2008), 1; Bernhard Klein, "English Cartographers and the Mapping of Ireland in the Early Modern Period," *Journal for the Study of British Cultures,* II (1995), 115–139.

43. For quotation, see G. D. Owen, ed., *Calendar of the Manuscripts of the Most Hon. the Marquess of Salisbury . . . ,* XXI (London, 1883), 121. For a consideration of Raven, see Raymond Gillespie, "Thomas Raven and the Mapping of the Claneboy Estates," *Bangor Historical Society Journal,* I (1981), 6–7, 9; and Klein, "English Cartographers," *Journal for the Study of British Cultures,* II (1995), 116.

ments, as problematic in their production as in their interpretation. Indeed, the plane table as an instrument of war was well understood by those who found themselves captured in a map, as Sir John Davies reported on the fate of cartographer Richard Bartlett: "Their geographers do not forget what entertainment the Irish of Tyrconnell gave to a map-maker . . . being appointed . . . to draw a true and perfect map of the north parts of Ulster . . . when he came into Tyrconnell, the inhabitants took off his head, because they would not have the country discovered." Bartlett produced a vivid visual record of the triumphs of Lord Mountjoy during his Ulster campaigns of 1600–1603. It is likely that Bartlett lost his head in late summer of 1603, following the submission of Hugh O'Neill and the granting of an earldom to Rory O'Donnell, hereditary chief of Tyrconnell (Donegal).[44]

Sixteenth-Century Ulster

The territories of Ulster that Bartlett endeavored to capture on parchment represented the most Gaelic and, from an English perspective, most wild part of Ireland. With the exception of the English garrison towns of Carrickfergus and Newry, much of the rest of the province remained under Irish or Scottish power in the sixteenth century. Irish control was divided between several Gaelic lordships, of which the most powerful was that of the O'Neills, concentrated in mid-Ulster. Each of these lords enjoyed the fealty of lesser lords, or sept leaders representing kin groups, who paid tribute in exchange for maintaining their local authority. The relationship of the Gaelic lords with the English crown was variable and principally dependent upon localized political struggles. Conn Bacach O'Neill had acquired the title of earl of Tyrone through the surrender and regrant of O'Neill lands under Henry VIII, but his son Shane O'Neill angered the English through his efforts to wrest the earldom from his father's heir, Shane's illegitimate brother Matthew. The O'Neill clan and sept leaders recognized Shane as the O'Neill, whereas the English recognized Matthew as the earl of Tyrone. Shane O'Neill murdered Matthew in 1558 and in 1563 submitted to Elizabeth I. In a subsequent power struggle exacerbated by the hostility of Irish Lord Deputy Henry Sidney, O'Neill attempted to engage the support of the Scottish MacDonnells against the crown. Murdered by the MacDonnells as

44. Quotation from Sir John Davies to earl of Salisbury, Aug. 28, 1609, in Russell and Prendergast, eds., *CSPI of the Reign of James I*, III, 280. For further discussion of Bartlett's fate, see Andrews, *Queen's Last Map-Maker*, 35–36.

part of their own efforts to manipulate Sidney, Shane O'Neill epitomizes the convoluted power relations of sixteenth-century Ulster.

Further complicating English efforts at gaining control over Ulster were the increasing numbers of Scots migrating to Ulster in the sixteenth century; this combined with Randal MacDonnell's efforts to rejuvenate the medieval Lordship of the Isles, when the MacDonnells held sway over western Scotland, the Isles, and the north of Ireland. The activities of MacDonnell and the Scots in north Antrim presented Queen Elizabeth with an even greater headache than had political intrigue in the rest of Ireland. On the one hand, the linked resources of Gaelic Ulster and Gaelic Scotland promised a very real threat to English plans to subdue Ireland, whereas inter- and intra-clan politics jeopardized English efforts to cultivate and retain uneasy allegiances with the Gaelic leadership. Connections between the north of Ireland and Scotland stretch well back into prehistory and are reliably documented throughout the medieval period. In the early twelfth century, King John granted the coastline and glens of north Antrim to Norman Scots, and throughout the medieval period, Highland clans and native Irish vied for control over the territory. The sea, far from being a barrier between Scotland and Ireland, held the two lands together.[45]

By the late sixteenth century, there were significant numbers of Scots in the Glens. Many appear to have practiced a pastoral lifestyle akin to that of the rural Irish. The settlers of the Glens were described in a 1584 report to Elizabeth's secretary of state, Francis Walsingham, by Martin Couche: "The woodes which we call the Glyne being the place of strengthe where the usurpinge Skotts contynewe themselves with theere cattell, which wee properlie term create." "Creating" was another term applied to the practice of transhumance in Ireland. An English soldier's description of a skirmish that occurred in the same year suggests that, despite a similarity in cultural practices, competition characterized the relationship between the Scots and the Irish:

45. For the strength of connections between Antrim and the Isles, see Jane H. Ohlmeyer, *Civil War and Restoration in the Three Stuart Kingdoms: The Career of Randal McDonnell, Marquis of Antrim, 1609–1683* (Cambridge, 1993), 7; and also Simon Kingston, *Ulster and the Isles in the Fifteenth Century: The Lordship of the Clann Domhnaill of Antrim* (Dublin, 2004). Challenging the perspective that the two regions shared a unified culture is the research of Wilson McLeod in bardic poetry, which suggests that Irish Gaelic culture was far more influential upon Scottish Gaelic society than the reverse. See McLeod, *Divided Gaels: Gaelic Cultural Identities in Scotland and Ireland, c. 1200–1650* (Oxford, 2004).

We [the English] were drawn uppon all the creates that the Scottes had, wheare we had the spoyle of the value of five or six thousand pound . . . we brought awaye three thousand cowes and garrans, . . . we have taken a Scottishe-woman that telleth us manie strange tales of their determyna-con . . . the contrye people hearing that the Scottes forsooke their goodes and repayred again to the Glynnes followed the spoyle and did them as much hurt as was possible to be done.

The tactical potential for worsening conflict between the Antrim Scots and Irish was not lost on the English. The English military leader and later Irish Lord Deputy Arthur Chichester described the Highlanders as

a very savage and heathenish people, speaking Irish, wavering and un-certain, better affected to this nation than to us, liking their manners and dissolute living better than our justice and living under law; which makes me doubtful of them being in great numbers, and a few can do us no good. But were there an army in the field or strong garrisons in Tyrone, good use might be made of them for a time.

Chichester's comments underscore the similarity between the lifeways of the north Antrim Irish and the Scots of the Isles as well as the pragmatism that lay at the heart of English military strategy.[46]

English servitor Henry Bagenal (whose father, Nicholas, was marshal of the army and later chief commissioner of Ulster) provided a further report on the influence of the Scots in the Glens of Antrim in 1586.

The Glynnes so called because it is full of rocky and wooded dalles, it stretcheth in length 24 miles (on the one side being backed with a very steepe and bogie mounteyne and on th' other parte with the sea), on whiche side there are many small creekes between rockes and thickets, where the Scottishe galleys do commonlie land; at either end are very nar-rowe entries and passages into this countery, which lieth directlie oppo-site to Cantire in Scotland, from which it is 18 miles distant. . . . The

46. Martin Couche, "Relation of the Journey to the Woods called the Glynns against the Usurping Scots" (1584), in George Hill, ed., *An Historical Account of the MacDonnells of An-trim: Including Notices of Some Other Septs, Irish and Scottish* (Belfast, 1873), 175; report of soldier E. Barkley, February 1584, ibid., 176; Chichester to Secretary Cecil, Dec. 29, 1601, in Hamilton, Atkinson, and Mahaffy, eds., *CSPI of the Reigns of Henry VIII., Edward VI., Mary, and Eliza-beth*, XI, 1601–3 (with Addenda, 1565–1654), and of the Hanmer Papers, 245. See also Gerard Anthony Hayes-McCoy, *Scots Mercenary Forces in Ireland (1565–1603): An Account of Their Service during that Period, of the Reaction of Their Activities on Scottish Affairs, and of the Effect of Their Presence in Ire-land, Together with an Examination of the Gallóglaigh, or Galloglas* (Dublin, 1964), 333.

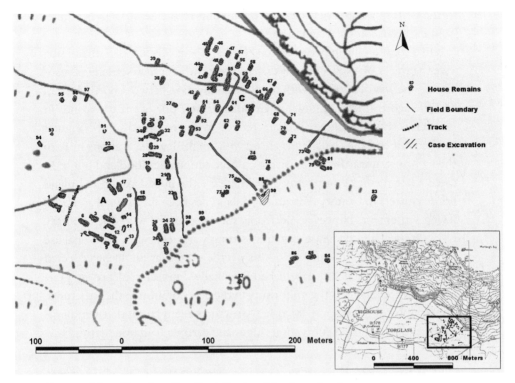

Figure 3. Map of hut sites, Goodland. Produced for the author by
Shannon Mahoney, College of William and Mary

force of this countrey is uncertaine, for that they are supplied as neede re-
quireth from Scotland, with what numbers they list to call, by making of
fiers upon certain steepe rockes hanginge over the sea. The auncient followers of the country . . . are most desirous to lyve under the Scottes, because they do better defende and lesse spende them then the Irishe Lorde
dothe . . . the confininge so neare to the Iles of Scotland, and the con-
tynuall comerce which the Irishry have with the people of those partes,
occassionethe the often cominge in of them, to the greate hurt of this
Province and the subjects which dwell there.

Bagenal's commentary highlights the often conflicting loyalties of the region inextricably linked to the shared culture of the Isles and the northern
reaches of Ulster that remained significant well into the seventeenth century. He also spells out the ease of movement between the two regions and
adds another layer of difficulty to the effort to tease out the material traces
of nonelite rural life in Ireland. The reported similarity between the lifestyles

of the Ulster Irish and of the Gaelic inhabitants of the Scottish Isles implies a similar archaeological signature.[47]

On a coastal hilltop between Tor Head and Fair Head, Co. Antrim, survive the traces of a sixteenth- or early-seventeenth-century settlement associated, one way or another, with the close connection between north Antrim and the Scottish Isles. Known as Goodland, after one of the townlands in which it is situated, the site is characterized by 129 recorded subrectangular earthen huts on the chalk lands above Murlough Bay. Excavations in 1949 through 1950 unearthed extensive Neolithic activity at Goodland but indicated a late medieval or postmedieval date for the huts. Like other upland house clusters in County Antrim, Goodland has been interpreted as a booleying settlement. However, electronic survey, coupled with documentary research and a limited new excavation, strongly argues against a seasonal use for the Goodland structures. No huts overlie others, as might be expected for a site reoccupied and refurbished seasonally. Further evidence suggesting contemporaneity is the uniformity in the deterioration of the structures. Topography and a respect for other structures seem to guide their alignment, as do associated cultivation ridges and earthen field boundaries.[48]

47. Marshal Bagenal, Herbert F. Hore, and Lord Burghley, "Marshal Bagenal's Description of Ulster, Anno 1586," *Ulster Journal of Archaeology*, 1st Ser., II (1854), 137–160.

48. Jean M. Sidebotham, "A Settlement in Goodland Townland, Co. Antrim," *Ulster Journal of Archaeology*, 3d Ser., XIII (1950), 44–53, esp. 48. In addition to more than one hundred sherds of Neolithic pottery, "two small pieces of red pottery, with a yellow glaze on the inside surface . . . and a fragment of the stem of a clay pipe" were recovered from one of the huts. Neither further description nor trace of these finds survives with the site archive. Further excavations in 1952 and 1953 sought to demonstrate that the huts were actually Neolithic, but again postmedieval materials were recovered, including glazed pottery, pipestems, late medieval Ulster coarse pottery, and even a silver brooch. With the exception of a single sherd of Ulster coarse pottery, the postmedieval materials were never turned over to the Ulster Museum, which houses the Neolithic artifacts. The likeliest scenario is that the late materials were perceived as insignificant, and thus they were not curated. An overview of the site and the previous excavations can be found in Horning, "Archaeological Explorations of Cultural Identity," *International Journal of Historical Archaeology*, VIII (2004), 28–31; Horning and Nick Brannon, "Rediscovering Goodland: Neolithic Ritual Site, Seasonal Booley Settlement, or Lost Scottish Village?" *Archaeology Ireland*, XVIII, no. 3 (Autumn 2004), 28–31. The 1940s and 1950s research is presented in Humphrey Case, "Settlement Patterns in the North Irish Neolithic," *Ulster Journal of Archaeology*, 3d Ser., XXXII (1969), 3–27; Case, "A Ritual Site in North-East Ireland," in Glyn Daniel and Poul Kjærum, eds., *Megalithic Graves and Ritual: Papers Presented at the III Atlantic Colloquium, Moesgård 1969* (Copenhagen, 1973); Case et al., "Land Use in Goodland Townland, Co. Antrim, from Neolithic Times until Today," *Journal of the Royal Society of Antiquaries of Ireland*, XCIX (1969), 39–53; and Graham, "Transhumance in Ireland." The prehistoric artifacts from the site have been reinterpreted by Eiméar L. Nelis, "Lithics of the Northern Irish Neolithic" (Ph.D. diss., Queen's University, Belfast, 2003). Long before twentieth-century archaeologists looked

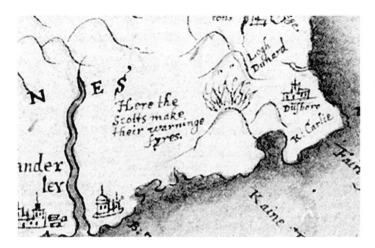

Plate 2.
Scots' warning fire.
Detail, 1601 Map of
East Ulster, National
Maritime Museum
P49(25). ©National
Maritime Museum,
Greenwich, London

The locale of the site, the character of its architecture, and documentary sources all suggest a Scottish connection. Cartographic sources show beacon fires lit on the clifftop to draw MacDonnell forces from Kintyre. A 1601 map of East Ulster includes the phrase, "Here the Scotts make their warninge fyres," and depicts a bonfire above Murlough Bay. John Norden's 1610 map of Ireland follows suit with an inscription in the same location, stating, "At this marke the Scottes used to make their warning-fires." Those responding to the call to arms would have landed and moored their craft in Murlough Bay, which contains deep waters and a moderately sheltered cove. Nevertheless, one can ascend from the bay to the top of the cliff in about fifteen minutes. The now-ruined medieval church of Drumnakill added to the appeal of the site while being chiefly accessible via the sea.[49]

---

for Neolithic farmers in the earthen huts, local people had their own explanations for the complex of buildings. In the 1830s, local traditions were recorded by Ordnance Survey mapmakers, including these contrasting views of the Goodland huts: "Local conjecture as regards those ancient dwellings is quite opposite and unsettled. Many call them booley ⟨bolia⟩ houses, as being erected for summer dwellings by the local inhabitants, who, in the latter seasons of the year, repaired with their cattle to mountain grazing. . . . Others ascribe their erection and occupation to the Danes and other strangers who in ancient times so frequently infested different parts of the kingdom. Others ascribe their foundation . . . to the ancient Irish at periods when the lowlands were in general under woods and likewise the seats of wolves ⟨wolfs⟩ and other ferocious animals." Folklife scholar Emyr Estyn Evans described Goodland as "the most interesting and extensive collection of booleys." See Day, McWilliams, and Dobson, *Ordnance Survey Memoirs,* 78; Evans, "Field Archaeology," *Ulster Journal of Archaeology,* 3d Ser., VIII (1945), 30.

49. John Norden, *The Plot of Ireland with the Confines,* Public Record Office, Kew, U.K. The map was likely commissioned by Ralph Lane and is discussed in detail later in this chapter. It is housed in the National Maritime Museum, Greenwich, P49(25). As interpreted by the

Limited excavation of one of the houses elucidated construction details while leaving the question of cultural affiliation still unanswered. Like the Glenmakeeran, Gortin, and Craigs examples, the Goodland house was built of sods with the occasional layer of loose gravel and an entrance lined with large stones. In the center of the house, the wall collapse sealed an occupation layer and a well-defined area of ash correlating to an open hearth. A number of Neolithic artifacts, including three sherds of pottery and secondary thinning flakes of local flint, were recovered, having been unintentionally incorporated by the house builders into the sods that served as the primary walling material. Only one artifact relating to the occupation of the house was found: a minuscule sherd of Ulster coarse pottery. The lack of any vessel glass, pipe fragments, or refined ceramics in the assemblage provides some support for a late-sixteenth- or early-seventeenth-century date, given that wine bottle glass and tablewares become ubiquitous on both urban and rural sites from the mid-seventeenth century onward. Like the other Antrim sod-built dwellings, this house incorporated a central hearth around which occupants would have slept and upon which their meals were cooked in hand-built ceramic pots. Perishable materials such as wood, leather, textiles, and basketry presumably provided other necessary items but have left no physical trace.[50]

Goodland may reflect a MacDonnell military encampment of the sixteenth century or possibly an early-seventeenth-century Scottish plantation settlement associated with the earl of Antrim, Randall MacDonnell. Despite remaining Roman Catholic, MacDonnell managed to curry and maintain favor with James VI of Scotland, even after James acceded to the English throne as James I. MacDonnell controlled more than 300,000 acres of land in north Antrim, and in 1620, he granted Alexander Magee (Mackay), from the Rinns in Islay, "the lands of Ballygicon, containing 80 acres;

---

nineteenth-century antiquarian George Hill, "the precise spot was probably on the high land of Ballyuchan [an earlier name for Goodland], adjoining Murloch Bay," whereas, in 1822, the Reverend W. Hamilton noted that the Tor Head vicinity was known as "'The Scots Warning Fyre,' from the Scots who had settled in those parts making fires on it, to bring over their friends to their assistance, when about to be assailed by the English or Irish." See Hill, *MacDonnells of Antrim,* 132–133; W. Hamilton, *Letters concerning the Northern Coast of the County of Antrim; Containing Observations on the Antiquities, Manners, and Customs of That Country with the Natural History of the Basaltes, Illustrated by an Accurate Map of the Country of Antrim and Views of the Most Interesting Objects on the Coast* (Belfast, 1822), 241.

50. Audrey Horning and Nick Brannon, "Summary Report on Excavations at Goodland, Co. Antrim, April 2007," unpublished report submitted to Northern Ireland Environment Agency, Belfast.

half of Turnaroan, 60 acres; Ballycregah, 120 acres, and the quarter of Dow-
corry, 20 acres"—land that encompasses the Goodland hut sites. In July
1630, Magee and his brother Donal were again granted leaseholds that are
today the townlands of Bighouse, Goodland, Knockbrack, Torglass, and
Tornaroon, neatly corresponding to the boundaries of the archaeological
site as delineated by its Scheduled Historic Monument status. The regrant-
ing of the lease suggests that the Magees had earned retention of the land by
planting settlers. In 1659, one Daniel (most likely Donal) Magee held land
at Ballygicon (Ballyuchan) upon which resided fourteen taxable persons described as Irish. These figures are based upon poll tax data and recorded identity only as either British or Irish. A Highland Catholic Scot could easily
have been recorded as Irish, especially since many of the "Irish" names in
the 1659 survey are clearly of Scottish origin, including both the Magee and
MacDonnell surnames.[51]

In addition to the documentary evidence linking Goodland with Islay,
there are intriguing similarities between the Goodland huts and several
structures unearthed at Finlaggan on Islay. Finlaggan was the traditional
center of the Lordship of the Isles and consisted of a densely built-up island
within an interior lake. Although most of the buildings at Finlaggan relate
to the fourteenth-century heyday of the Lordship of the Isles, five house
types dating from the sixteenth through nineteenth centuries were also
identified. One of these, typical of the seventeenth century, is a subrectangular dwelling employing opposing doorways, which reflects those structures
found at Goodland and elsewhere in north Antrim. As in Gaelic Ulster, Islay
was supported by a pastoral economy, underscored by the yearly export of
upward of one thousand cattle.[52]

Materially, life in both north Antrim and the Isles would have looked

51. The leases are recorded in the *Inquisitionum in officio rotulorum cancellariae Hiberniae asser-
vatorum reportorium,* II, *Ultonia* (Dublin, 1829), and noted in Hill, *MacDonnells of Antrim,* 117.
The 1659 figures are based upon poll tax data and can be found in Séamus Pender, *A Census of
Ireland, circa 1659, with Supplementary Material from the Poll Money Ordinances (1660–1661)* (Dublin, 1939), 17. It is worth noting that the Antrim returns for 1659 do not allow for "Scottish" as a
category—individuals were categorized as either "English" or "Irish," leaving open the question
of the cultural affiliation of the Ballyuchan inhabitants. Of the "principall Irish names" noted
in the survey, many appear to be of Scottish origin, including Magee, MacDonnell, Stuart,
McAlester, and McCampbell.

52. David H. Caldwell, Roger McWhee, and Nigel A. Ruckley, "Post-Medieval Settlement
in Islay: Some Recent Research," in John A. Atkinson, Iain Banks, and Gavin MacGregor,
eds., *Townships to Farmsteads: Rural Settlement Studies in Scotland, England, and Wales,* British
Archaeological Reports, no. 293 (Oxford, 2000).

very much the same, complicating our ability to identify and distinguish between archaeological traces pertaining to Irish and Scots rural inhabitants. The same challenge was faced by English military leaders, unable to always identify their foes' allegiances. The English were on somewhat firmer ground when it came to operating within Ulster's more formal settlements.

Sixteenth-Century Plantations in Ulster

By contrast to our current, limited understanding of nonelite rural life in sixteenth-century Ulster, somewhat more information is available on towns and on English efforts at controlling and planting settlements. Unlike Leinster and Munster and portions of Connacht, the province of Ulster did not experience much urbanization following the Anglo-Norman invasions. Carrickfergus and Newry alone provided England with the sixteenth-century urban toeholds in the north. The County Down port town of Newry was established as an Anglo-Norman stronghold in the late twelfth century. By the sixteenth century, it was of increasing strategic importance to the English forces. In 1552, Nicholas Bagenal, the marshal of the English army in Ireland and member of the Irish Privy Council, was granted the lands and buildings of the recently dissolved Newry Abbey. Bagenal established a garrison and constructed a new castle within the town. Once believed to have been demolished, substantial standing remains of the 8.53 by 14.63–meter tower house were rediscovered in 1996 encased within the fabric of a nineteenth-century bakery. Architectural traces and a surviving sixteenth-century elevation drawing of the structure indicate that Bagenal augmented the defensive characteristics of the tower house (gun loops and a machicolation over the doorway) with more fashionable features, including four soaring chimney stacks and transomed windows with decorative hood moldings. The multiple architectural grammars he employed—combining medieval defensive qualities with more elite and up-to-date flourishes—is consistent with his strategy in developing Newry: he balanced his allegiances to the English, Old English, Gaelic Irish, and Scots. Late medieval Newry was home to a mixture of Irish, Old English, and New English and could never be read as a colonial settlement in the sense of a replacement of natives by transplanted settlers.[53]

53. The most recent coverage of the 1996 discovery and attribution of Bagenal's Castle can be found in Claire Foley, "Bagenal's Castle, Newry, County Down: Discovery and Re-use," *Ulster Journal of Archaeology,* 3d Ser., LXVIII (2009), 141–151. See also John J. Ó Néill, "Nicholas Bagnall's Castle at Newry, County Down," ibid., LXI (2002), 117–124; Liam McQuillan, "Bagenal's Castle, Newry," in Isabel Bennett, ed., *Excavations 1999: Summary Accounts of Archaeological Ex-*

Ulster's other late medieval garrison town, Carrickfergus, was strength-ened under Captain William Piers, who held command of the Anglo-Norman castle from the 1550s to 1580. Situated on the western banks of Belfast Lough in County Antrim, Carrickfergus traces its origins back to the Anglo-Norman lord John de Courcy, who led a successful invasion of Ulster in 1177. De Courcy began construction of a fortification at Carrick-fergus sometime between 1177 and 1181, soon followed by the building of a church and, later, a walled town. Medieval features within the town high-light extensive trade links with England and the Continent in the form of pottery imports, as well as a thirteenth-century kiln operated by potters brought in from Chester. Although established as an Anglo-Norman center, medieval Carrickfergus was not exclusively Old English. The Gaelic Clande-boye O'Neill lords of East Ulster were primary patrons of the Franciscan friary at Carrickfergus until its disestablishment early in the reign of Eliza-beth I. The sixteenth-century presence of native Irish in Carrickfergus is evident in two maps. The first, dated to 1560 and produced by an unidenti-fied cartographer, depicts circular wattlework Irish houses adjacent to the twelve masonry tower houses that formed the core of the settlement. Simi-larly, a 1567 map by Robert Lythe depicts the same types of small dwellings throughout the town. Although no archaeological trace of these dwellings has been found, their depiction on two separate period maps supports their existence. Excavations at Carrickfergus unearthed late medieval rubbish pits containing a mixture of locally made Ulster coarse pottery as well as conti-nental and English imports, further attesting to the proximity of relations between the English and Irish. On his 1567 map, Lythe also indicated the poor state of the town defenses; these would become the focus for extensive reedification work within a decade, given Carrickfergus's strategic location on Belfast Lough and bordering on lands held both by the Gaelic Clande-boye O'Neills and the Scots of north Antrim.[54]

cavations in Ireland, XLVIII (Dublin, 1999); D. Moore, "Bagenal's Castle (McCann's Bakery), Newry," ibid., 48.

54. The Lythe map is in Trinity College Library, Dublin (MS 1209[26]). For Carrickfergus history and archaeology, see T. E. McNeill, *Carrickfergus Castle, County Antrim* (Belfast, 1981); Ruairí Ó Baoill, "Archaeology of Post-Medieval Carrickfergus and Belfast, 1550–1750," in Horn-ing et al., eds., *Post-Medieval Archaeology of Ireland,* 91–116; Ó Baoill, *Carrickfergus: The Story of the Castle and Walled Town* (Belfast, 2008); M. L. Simpson and N. F. Brannon, "Uncovering the Past in a Busy Town: Carrickfergus, Co. Antrim," in Ann Hamlin and Chris Lynn, eds., *Pieces of the Past: Archaeological Excavations by the Department of the Environment for Northern Ireland, 1970–1986* (Belfast, 1986), 64–66; Simpson et al., eds., "An Early Thirteenth-Century Double-Flued Pottery Kiln at Carrickfergus, Co. Antrim: An Interim Report," *Medieval Ceramics,* III (1979), 41–52.

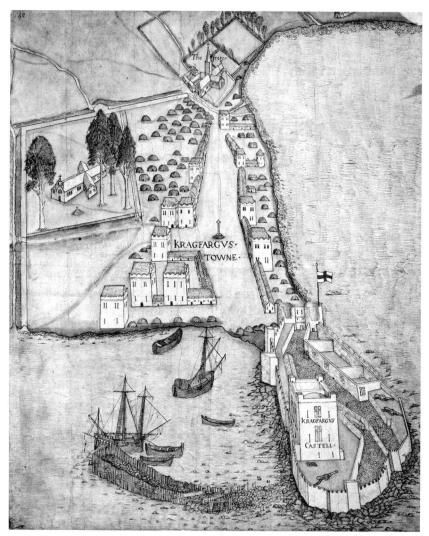

Plate 3. Carrickfergus, 1560. ©The British Library Board, Cotton Augustus I,ii, f.42

Like Bagenal at Newry, Captain William Piers maintained control at Carrickfergus through diplomacy, cultivating the loyalty of the Gaelic O'Neills
and the Scottish MacDonnells while simultaneously denouncing them both
in official communiqués to the English government. The extent of Piers's
connections and duplicity is evidenced in his role in the 1567 assassination
of Shane O'Neill at the hands of the Scottish MacDonnell clan but with
the support of Sir Brian MacPhelim O'Neill, lord of Clandeboye. Piers allegedly promised the MacDonnells, on behalf of Lord Deputy Sidney, that

they would be permitted to remain on their Ulster lands. Piers's diplomatic strategies occasionally backfired, as witness his imprisonment in 1573, following allegations by Walter Devereaux, the earl of Essex, that he served as a spy for the O'Neills. Essex, frustrated in a plan to colonize County Antrim, was forced to retreat to the relative safety of Carrickfergus in 1575, and it is perhaps not surprising that he and the pragmatic Piers did not see eye to eye.[55]

Whereas Piers was focused on his efforts to maintain Carrickfergus as an English base and the center of his own power, others viewed their service in Ireland as just one of many potential postings. The career of sea captain Christopher Carleill, who served as constable of Carrickfergus and governor of Ulster in the late 1580s, illustrates the perspective of those adventurers whose service to Elizabeth encompassed activity in both Ireland and the Americas. A stepson of Sir Francis Walsingham, Carleill first came to Ireland in 1584 following a career as a soldier in the Low Countries and France and in the wake of a failed bid to lead a New World colonization effort. Carleill, who enjoyed a close relationship with the mapmaker Abraham Ortelius, had already made his name as an adventurer with a 1583 discourse on New World colonization, which emphasized the economic and cultural potential of English clothing.[56]

To secure the financial backing of the Muscovy Company, Carleill set out his plans for a voyage and subsequent commercial settlement, highlighting the potential riches to be had:

> In the Northerlie may be expected not onely an especiall good fishing for Salmon, Codde, and Whales, but also any other such commodities, as the Easterne Countreys doe yield us now: as Pitch, Tarre, Hempe, and thereof cordage, Masts, Losshe hides, rich Furres, and other such like without being in any sort beholding to a king of Denmarke, or other prince or state. . . . As for those partes which lie West and to the Southwardes, it may well bee hoped they will yield Wines with a small helpe,

55. Ciaran Brady, *The Chief Governors: The Rise and Fall of Reform Government in Tudor Ireland, 1536–1588* (Cambridge, 1994), 258–259; Brady, "The Killing of Shane O'Neill: Some New Evidence," *Irish Sword,* XV (1982–1983), 116–123; Canny, *Making Ireland British,* 85–90; Canny, *Elizabethan Conquest of Ireland: A Pattern Established, 1565–76* (New York, 1976), 70–71. Henry Sidney provides a contemporary account of Piers's activities in "Sir Henry Sidney's Memoir of His Government of Ireland, 1583," *Ulster Journal of Archaeology,* 1st Ser., III (1855), 91, 93.

56. D. J. B. Trim, "Carleill, Christopher (1551?–1593)," *Oxford Dictionary of National Biography* (Oxford, 2004–2011); Rachel Lloyd, *Elizabethan Adventurer: A Life of Captain Christopher Carleill* (London, 1974).

since the grapes doe growe there of themselves alreadie very faire and in great abundance. Olives being once planted, will yeelde the like Oyle as Spaine, Province and Italie.[57]

Carleill was similarly optimistic over the readiness of the indigenous people of the New World to "forsake their barbarous and savage living" and "have wonderfull great use of our sayde English Clothes, after they shall come once to knowe the commodite thereof." Carleill's focus upon the need to clothe the Natives of the New World reveals multiple concerns of the English, as earlier reflected in the concern over the use of the Irish mantle. On a basic economic level, cloth and clothing comprised one of the major products of later medieval England, and the discovery or creation of a new market was bound to appeal to the expanding English mercantile elite. Fashion also served as a marker of social status in English society. By adopting the grammar of English fashion, native people would become readable and knowable rather than savage and inscrutable.[58]

Failing to attain financial backing for his New World adventuring, Carleill instead sailed to Ireland to offer his service in capturing pirates. He soon found himself engaged for a different purpose when he was given the charge of a poorly provisioned garrison at Coleraine, situated on the north coast of Ulster at the mouth of the River Bann. The posting was not a success, as Carleill became embroiled in arguments over pay with Lord Deputy John Perrot. A year later, Carleill finally found himself sailing across the Atlantic, under the command of Sir Francis Drake. Drake's fleet pillaged the Spanish settlements at San Domingo, Cartageña, and Saint Augustine and completed their time in the New World with the rescue of the surviving Roanoke colonists under the leadership of Ralph Lane. Both Carleill and Lane returned to service in Ulster, Carleill holding the castle at Carrickfergus and Lane receiving various postings, including the title of mustermaster general of the forces and control of the castle at Belfast. Both would spend the remainder of their careers petitioning the queen for offices and favors.[59]

---

57. Christopher Carlile, "A Briefe and Summarie Discourse upon the Intended Voyage to the Hithermost Parts of America, Written by Captaine Carlile in April 1583," in Richard Hakluyt, *The Principall Navigations, Voyages, Traffiques, and Discoveries of the English Nation Made by Sea or Overland to the Remote and Farthest Distant Quarters of the Earth at any Time within the Compass of These 1600 Years* (London, 1926), VI, 84–85.

58. Carlile, "Briefe and Summarie Discourse," in Hakluyt, *Principall Navigations*, VI, 85. On the significance of nakedness in the English colonial mindset, see discussion in Karen Ordahl Kupperman, *Indians and English: Facing off in Early America* (Ithaca, N.Y., 2000), 41–76.

59. Trim, "Carliell, Christopher"; Lloyd, *Elizabethan Adventurer*; Sir Rafe Lane to the queen,

In the 1570s — before Carleill began pondering the sartorial markets of the New World but while William Piers conspired with the Scots — portions of East Ulster were allocated for plantation through private investment. The attainder of the recently beheaded Shane O'Neill in 1569 ostensibly opened up lands in the territory of Counties Down and Antrim (officially created in 1570 and 1571) to English influence, provided that one overlooked the competing claims of Sir Brian MacPhelim O'Neill as well as the MacDonnells. Whereas Essex attempted to master control over portions of County Antrim, a more carefully conceived plantation effort was that of Sir Thomas Smith in the Ards Peninsula, Co. Down, between 1572 and 1575.

Smith was a classical scholar and committed Protestant who had served as secretary of state under Edward Seymour, duke of Somerset, during the regency of Edward IV. Although he suffered from Somerset's downfall in 1548, Smith regained favor and served Elizabeth first as ambassador to France and then again as secretary of state. Smith designed his Ards venture along Roman colonial principles: the colony was to be organized around nucleated villages linked to towns, based upon cultivation rather than Irish pastoralism, and was to yield profit for private investors. Smith employed biblical metaphors to justify his mission, describing Ireland as a "lande that floweth with milke and hony," and flattered the queen by intimating that, like ancient Macedonia at the time of Alexander, England was a strong nation well situated to take forward colonizing enterprises. Smith also appears to have been informed by Spanish colonial practice, suggesting he was well aware of the nascent racialization of indigenous populations.[60]

Certainly, Sir Thomas Smith placed confidence in the strategy of legis-

---

Lane to Lord Burghley, Feb. 14, Feb. 16, 1595, both in Hamilton, Atkinson, and Mahaffy, eds., *CSPI of the Reigns of Henry VIII., Edward VI., Mary, and Elizabeth*, V, *1592, October–1596, June*, 297.

60. See "A Letter Sent by T. B. Gentleman unto His Very Frende Mayster R. C. Esquire, Wherin is Conteined a Large Discourse of the Peopling and Inhabiting the Cuntrie Called the Ardes . . . ," in Hill, *MacDonnells of Antrim*, 405–415, esp. 409, for a statement of Smith's colonizing philosophy. Canny has argued for the Spanish influence on Smith in *Elizabethan Conquest of Ireland*, 133, in reference to Smith's familiarity with Peter Martyr's *De Orbe Novo*. See also Hiram Morgan, "The Colonial Venture of Sir Thomas Smith in Ulster, 1571–1575," *Historical Journal*, XXVIII (1985), 261–278; and David Beers Quinn, "Sir Thomas Smith (1513–1577) and the Beginnings of English Colonial Theory," *Proceedings of the American Philosophical Society*, LXXXIX (1945), 543–560. For a broader consideration of the role of Roman history in shaping English understandings of their relationship with Ireland, see John E. Curran, *Roman Invasions: The British History, Protestant Anti-Romanism, and the Historical Imagination in England, 1530–1660* (Cranbury, N.J., 2002); and Paulina Kewes, "Henry Savile's Tacitus and the Politics of Roman History in Late Elizabethan England," *Huntingdon Library Quarterly*, LXXIV (2011), 515–551.

lating materiality, but in an inversion of previous legislation, Smith sought to permanently mark the Irish as inferior and materially different: "Everie Irishman shalbe forbidden to weare Englishe apparell or weapon upon payne of deathe . . . no Irishman borne of Irish race and brought up Irishe shall purchace land, beare office, be chosen of any jurie." In late August of 1572, Smith's son (also Thomas) left Liverpool to take up his father's grant in Ulster, supported only by a force of one hundred men and fed on the dreams of his father: "Irelande once inhabited with Englishe men, and polliced with Englishe lawes, would be as great commoditie to the Prince as the realme of England . . . there cannot be (sayeth he) a more fertile soil thorowe out the worlde for that climate than it is, a more pleasant, healthful, full of springs, rivers, great fresh lakes, fishe, and foule, and of moste commodious herbers. . . . There is Timber, stone, plaister, and slate commodious for building everywhere aboundant." This optimistic description, written by the elder Smith but caged as a dialogue between one T. B., Gent., and one R. C., Esq., underestimated the political realities of the Ards. Smith's colony was to be established in the Clandeboye territories of north Down traditionally held by Sir Brian MacPhelim O'Neill. Before Smith the younger had even set out for Ireland, O'Neill had already lodged an official complaint with the Dublin administration as well as with the crown over his belief in the illegality of the grants to Smith.[61]

When his complaint was not upheld, the Clandeboye leader turned to physical force. As soon as Smith arrived, his small band immediately encountered strong resistance. To prevent Smith from employing the long-established English practice of commandeering Irish ecclesiastical structures for use as English garrisons, O'Neill burned church buildings on Smith's grant—including the dissolved Cistercian house at Greyabbey and monastic holdings in Bangor, Movilla, Newtownards, and Holywood.[62]

O'Neill's preemptive strike not only robbed Smith and his men of a con-

---

61. Quinn, *Elizabethans and the Irish,* 108; Mary Dewar, *Sir Thomas Smith: A Tudor Intellectual in Office* (London, 1964), 159. For quotations, see C. L. Kingsford, ed., *Report on the Manuscripts of Lord del'Isle and Dudley Preserved at Penhurst Palace* (London, 1934), II, 14; "A Letter Sent by T. B. Gentleman," in Hill, *MacDonnells of Antrim,* 406–409.

62. For example, an English garrison was first stationed at the twelfth-century Cistercian Abbey of Boyle, Co. Roscommon, in 1566. Boyle continued to serve as an English military stronghold throughout much of the seventeenth century. See Kieran O'Conor, "English Settlement and Change in Roscommon during the Late Sixteenth and Seventeenth Centuries," in Horning et al., eds., *Post-Medieval Archaeology of Ireland,* 189–204; Thomas McErlean, Rosemary McConkey, and Wes Forsythe, *Strangford Lough: An Archaeological Survey of the Maritime Cultural Landscape* (Belfast, 2002), 106.

venient defensible base but denied them the opportunity to demonstrate Protestant hegemony over the old faith. They were forced to take refuge to the south, temporarily occupying Ringhaddy Castle, a fifteenth-century tower house situated on a tidal island on the western side of Strangford Lough. Sometime during the winter of 1572, Smith and his men managed to hastily construct a fortification near Comber, Co. Down. No trace of this defensive structure survives, suggesting that it was built of timber and earth, not unlike the early forts of English America. The only possible depiction of this fort can be found on Richard Bartlett's 1602 "Map of Military Installations," which shows a diamond-shaped fortification with two angle bastions, situated between Comber and Newtownards.[63]

The Ards Plantation effort received a fatal blow in 1573, when Thomas Smith the Younger was murdered by his Irish servants (possibly in the pay of Neal Mac Brian Fertagh O'Neill) in Comber. As reported by the earl of Essex to the Privy Council, Thomas fell prey to "the revolting of certain Irishmen of his own household to whom he overmuch trusted, whereof one . . . killed him with a shot." Notwithstanding the loss of his son, the elder Smith threw himself into rescuing his colonial venture, outlining the importance of townbuilding as a defensive strategy: "The chief strength to fortify a colony is to have a principal city or town of strength well walled and defended." Smith sent another expedition out in 1573, but the sailors and their captain instead engaged in piracy, never making it to the Ards. Smith's brother George led a third and final expedition partnered with Jerome Brett, who himself had schemed with Humphrey Gilbert and Sir Warham Saint Leger in 1569 to colonize south Munster. Smith's final effort at developing his colony in Ireland received financial support from the Berkeleys of Gloucestershire, a family that, along with its Somerset branch, would become intimately involved in the seventeenth-century Virginia colony. Smith's venture enjoyed no success, and he reluctantly turned his grant over to Essex. Any gains that might have been achieved were destroyed by O'Neill's combined forces of Irish and Scots. This English colonial foray into Ireland was successfully repelled.[64]

63. See McErlean, McConkey, and Forsythe, *Strangford Lough,* 289, drawing after NLI 16 L 32(5).

64. For Essex quotation, see State Paper Office, State Papers Ireland, Elizabeth I to George III, SP 63/42/55, f.118, National Archives, Kew; and Dewar, *Sir Thomas Smith,* 163, 165. Gilbert styled himself "Humfrey"; however, the spelling "Humphrey" is used throughout this manuscript for consistency with other historical scholarship. See usage in Peter E. Pope, *Fish into Wine: The Newfoundland Plantation in the Seventeenth Century* (Chapel Hill, N.C., 2004). For the involvement of the Smith and Berkeley families, see Dewar, *Sir Thomas Smith,* 168. For the

With the exception of medieval buildings employed by the colonizers, such as Ringhaddy Castle, there are no extant buildings or sites today that can be confidently attributed to the Smith Plantation. The only comparable contemporary sites in the Strangford Lough vicinity are Mahee Castle and Castle Ward. Mahee Castle, a tower house built by Thomas Browne in 1570, was intended to be the center of an English settlement. Browne was no more successful than Smith, losing his castle and his lands by 1574 to the O'Neill forces. From an architectural perspective, Browne's choice of a shore-side tower house was hardly symbolic of a new order as dreamed by Sir Thomas Smith. Neither was Castle Ward, on the west shore of Strangford Lough, believed to have been built by Nicholas Ward in the 1570s. Instead, both dwellings reflected continuity with medieval fortified dwellings and were clearly influenced, and most likely built, by local Irish masons.[65]

The failed Smith Plantation could not inform New World colonial ventures. Rather, the Ards colony and Roanoke shared elements that contributed to their respective downfalls: reliance on private capital, insufficient supplies, and recourse to violence rather than diplomacy. The Smith project, like early New World ventures, reflects the influence of Roman colonial history on Renaissance intellectuals. A range of Roman colonial histories were becoming widely available to English scholars and colonial theorists in the latter half of the sixteenth century, in both Latin and in English translation, and individuals including Smith, Humphrey Gilbert, and Edmund Spenser deliberated the value of the Roman experience as a template for subduing Ireland.[66]

Munster effort, see Michael MacCarthy-Morrogh, *The Munster Plantation: English Migration to Southern Ireland, 1583–1641* (Oxford, 1986), 20–21. The second and third Smith expeditions are briefly described in Morgan, "Colonial Venture of Sir Thomas Smith," *Historical Journal,* XXVIII (1985), 261–278.

65. O'Keeffe, "Later Historical Cultural Landscape," 238, suggests that the extant structure known as the White House, in Ballyspurge Townland, may relate to the Smith venture. The building has been traditionally attributed to the mid-seventeenth century, albeit not on the basis of any clear documentary or archaeological grounds. Further excavation is required to elucidate the building's history. For descriptions of Mahee Castle and Castle Ward, see Archaeological Survey of Northern Ireland, *An Archaeological Survey of County Down* (Belfast, 1966), 231–233, 244–245; and McErlean, McConkey, and Forsythe, *Strangford Lough,* 112–114, 202. No date for the construction of Castle Ward is known, but it was likely built by the 1580s.

66. Notwithstanding the complete failure of the Ards Colony, some historians have wanted to see it as formative for the New World. For example, Steven G. Ellis, *Tudor Ireland: Crown, Community and the Conflict of Cultures, 1470–1603* (London, 1985), 268, argues that the significance of the Smith plantation was to "point the way to the Hakluyts, Gilbert, Grenville, and Raleigh in colonizing America." The influence of Roman colonial history on Tudor intellectuals gazing towards Ireland is discussed by Lisa Jardine, "Mastering the Uncouth: Gabriel Harvey,

Despite augmenting his own lands with Smith's, the earl of Essex also failed to plant his grant. Like Smith, Essex had gambled his own money and that of others, mortgaging his lands in England in exchange for a royal loan of £10,000 and military support from the queen. Essex had envisioned taking control of much of County Antrim simply by expelling the Scots. Instead, he found his efforts staunchly opposed not only by the MacDonnells and their followers but also by the Clandeboye O'Neills. Infuriated by his inability to control, let alone plant, his lands, Essex began plotting his revenge.[67]

Essex retaliated against Sir Brian MacPhelim O'Neill in a remarkable fashion in 1574, as recorded in the *Annals of the Four Masters*:

> Peace, sociality, and friendship, were established between Brian, the son of Felim Bacagh O'Neill, and the Earl of Essex; and a feast was afterwards prepared by Brian, to which the Lord Justice and the chiefs of his people were invited; and they passed three nights and days together pleasantly and cheerfully. At the expiration of this time, however, as they were agreeably drinking and making merry, Brian, his brother, and his wife, were seized upon by the Earl, and all his people put unsparingly to the sword, men, women, youths, and maidens, in Brian's own presence. Brian was afterwards sent to Dublin, together with his wife and brother, where they were cut in quarters. Such was the end of their feast. This unexpected massacre, this wicked and treacherous murder of the lord of the race of Hugh Boy O'Neill, the head and the senior of the race of Eoghan, son of Niall of the Nine Hostages, and of all the Gaels, a few only excepted, was a sufficient cause of hatred and disgust *of the English* to the Irish.[68]

Essex's version of his actions was less colorful. "With the advice and consents of all the captains in the camp, I gave order to lay hold of Brian in the

---

Edmund Spenser, and the English Experience in Ireland," in John Harvey and Sarah Hutton, eds., *New Perspectives on Renaissance Thought: Essays in the History of Science, Education, and Philosophy* (London, 1991), 68–81; and by David J. Baker, "'Wildehirissheman:' Colonialist Representation in Shakespeare's Henry V," *English Literary Renaissance*, XXII (1992), 37–61; and in Rolf Loeber, "Certeyn Notes: Biblical and Foreign Signposts to the Ulster Plantation," in Lyttleton and Rynne, eds., *Plantation Ireland*, 24–25; as well as by Montaño, *Roots of English Colonialism in Ireland*, 256, 258–259; and Canny, *Making Ireland British*, 121–122, with particular reference to the Smith venture.

67. Canny, *Elizabethan Conquest*, 88–89, 130; Lennon, *Sixteenth-Century Ireland*, 282–284.

68. John O'Donovan, *Annals of the Kingdom of Ireland by the Four Masters, from the Earliest Period to the Year 1616* (Dublin, 1854), VM1574.4, 1677.

castle of Belfast where he lay. Resistance was offered by his men lodged in the town and 125 of them were slain. Sir Brian and his wife, Rory Óg and Brian Mac Revelin were taken." If the account from the *Annals* is correct, Essex's plan succeeded because he understood that Gaelic hospitality would compel O'Neill to entertain his English guests. Lavish displays involving feasting and toasting were a means of demonstrating the power and status of the chiefly elite, as chronicled in bardic poetry. In violating the rules of hospitality, Essex not only inflicted maximum humiliation on O'Neill through his disdain of Irish custom; he also sent an aggressive message to the Gaelic leadership. Most important, he revealed the depth of his understanding of Gaelic culture—an understanding that proved its tactical worth.[69]

Six months later, Essex was apparently still smarting from the loss of his colonial enterprise. Determined to exact his revenge on the Scots of the north, and eager as ever to impress Queen Elizabeth, Essex ordered John Norris and Francis Drake to attack the Scottish base on Rathlin Island, off the north coast of County Antrim. On July 31, Essex reported to the queen that Norris and his men had "slain that came out of the castle all sorts 200 . . . and have slain that they have found in caves and in the cliffs of the sea to the number of 300 or 400 more." Essex was blunter in writing to Walsingham on the same day, reporting that 600 people had been killed, including the families of Sorley Boy MacDonnell and his followers. Essex closed his letter to Walsingham by relating information from a spy: "Sorley then also stood upon the main land of the Glens and saw the taking of the island and was like to run mad for sorrow (as the spy says) tearing and tormenting himself and saying that he then lost all that ever he had." Essex's actions violated contemporary military discipline, yet he still managed to retain support from the queen, who declared him Earl Marshal of Ireland in 1576. He died of dysentery in the same year, before having the opportunity to fully exploit his new role.[70]

69. Quotation is from earl of Essex to Lord Deputy Fitzwilliam, Nov. 14, 1574, in Mary O'Dowd, ed., *Calendar of State Papers, Ireland, Tudor Period, 1571–1575* (Kew, 2000), entry 1162.3, 688. For a discussion of hospitality, see Katharine Simms, "Guesting and Feasting in Gaelic Ireland," *Journal of the Royal Society of Antiquaries of Ireland*, CVIII (1978), 67–100; for a consideration of the tactical use of understandings of hospitality, see Audrey Horning, "'The Root of All Vice and Bestiality': Exploring the Cultural Role of the Alehouse in the Ulster Plantation," in Lyttleton and Rynne, eds., *Plantation Ireland*, 117–118.

70. Essex to the queen, Jul. 31, 1575, in O'Dowd, ed., *CSPI Tudor Period*, 880–882, entry 1495 (SP 63/52, no. 77); Essex to Sir Francis Walsingham, Jul. 31, 1575, ibid., 882–883, entry 1497 (SP 63/52, no 79). Allegations of poisoning were raised at the time, but never proved. It is now presumed that Essex died from dysentery. See Paul E. J. Hammer, *The Polarisation of Eliza-*

Essex was hardly the only English soldier to resort to extremes of violence in the Irish campaigns. Another oft-cited episode occurred in November 1580. Spanish and Italian troops that had come to the aid of Irish forces surrendered to the English army of Arthur Grey, fourteenth baron of Wilton, at Smerwick Harbor in County Kerry, expecting clemency. But in his own words, Grey "put . . . in certain bands, who straight fell to execution. There were 600 slain." Those certain bands were led by Walter Raleigh, as observed by John Hooker: "Capteine Raleigh together with capteine macworth, who had the ward of that daie, enterede into the castell and made a great slaughter, manie or the most part of them being put to the sword." In William Camden's version, the decision to massacre the prisoners of war was motivated by pragmatism: "The English were so destitute of food and clothing that they would have mutinied if they had not been relieved out of the spoil taken from the enemy's fort, and there were no ships to carry the enemy away."[71]

Raleigh and servitor MacWorth were accompanied by the commander of the queen's ship *Foresight,* Martin Frobisher, best known for his abortive efforts to find the Northwest Passage from 1576 to 1578. Smerwick Harbor held unhappy memories for Frobisher. Two years earlier, on its return journey from his settlement on Baffin Island, Frobisher's ship, the *Emmanuel of Bridgwater,* foundered and sank off the Irish coast near Smerwick Harbor. The ship was laden with Frobisher's "gold," rocks that soldiers and sailors had laboriously mined from the frozen ground of Baffin Island and that excited the imaginations of Frobisher's investors. Philip Sidney, poet son of Sir Henry Sidney, enthused, "This ore shows sure signs that the island is so metal-rich as far to surpass the regions of Peru." Excavated by the Smithsonian Institution, the remains of Frobisher's Baffin Island camps lie surrounded by abandoned mines and workplaces where the adventurers quarried Frobisher's "gold." Misled by an assayer who declared that some of the

bethan Politics: The Political Career of Robert Devereux, 2nd Earl of Essex, 1585–1597 (Cambridge, 1999), 17–18, 31.

71. Lord Grey to the queen, Nov. 12, 1580, in Hamilton, Atkinson, and Mahaffy, eds., *CSPI of the Reigns of Henry VIII., Edward VI., Mary, and Elizabeth,* II, *1574–1585,* lxix–lxxvi, esp. lxxiii; John Hooker, "The Supplie of This Irish Chronicle, Continued from the Death of King Henrie the Eight, 1546 untill This Present Yeare 1586 . . . ," in Raphael Holinshed, *The Third Volume of the Chronicles . . .* (London, 1587), 107–183, esp. 165; see discussion in Vincent Carey, "Atrocity and History: Grey, Spenser, and the Slaughter of Smerwick (1580)," in David Edwards, Pádraig Lenihan, and Clodagh Tait, eds., *Age of Atrocity: Violence and Political Conflict in Early Modern Ireland* (Dublin, 2007), 79–94, esp. 84–85; William Camden, *Annales rerum Anglicarum et Hibernicarum, regnante Elizabetha, ad Annum Salutis 1589* (1615), 293–296, in Maxwell, *Irish History from Contemporary Sources,* 170–171.

specimens actually contained gold, Frobisher convinced investors, like the courtier Sidney and his mother, to back his scheme to search out, mine, and process what turned out to be worthless Arctic hornblende. When the *Emmanuel of Bridgwater* sank off the Kerry coast, the seas claimed more than the ship's cargo. Frobisher's dreams plummeted to the seabed along with his "golden" ballast. Thus Frobisher spent 1580 fighting for Elizabeth in Ireland and dining on rations of dried Newfoundland cod rather than eating fresh fish while presiding over his own venture to exploit the riches of the New World.[72]

Captain Christopher Carleill, who would sail with Frobisher on Drake's pillaging voyage to the New World in 1585, obliquely referred to Frobisher's experience as a cautionary tale in his 1583 discourse aiming to convince the Muscovy Company to support his own New World aspirations:

> What Minerall matter may fall out to bee found, is a thing left in suspence, until some better knowledge, because there be many men, who having long since expected some profits herein, upon the great promises that have bene made them, and being as yet in no point satisfied, doe thereupon conceive that they be but wordes purposely cast out for the inducing of men to bee the more ready and willing to furnish their money towards the charge of the first discoverie.

Carleill, however pointed or accurate his observation, was no more successful in his aspirations for the New World than Martin Frobisher was in his.[73]

The willingness of adventurers such as Frobisher and Raleigh to brutalize their foes in Ireland was shared by another celebrated soldier and explorer, Raleigh's half-brother Sir Humphrey Gilbert. Gilbert was notable for the extreme nature of his tactics in Ireland, which included advocating the killing

---

72. Albert Feuillerat, ed., *The Complete Works of Sir Philip Sidney,* III (Cambridge, 1923), letter 31, 116–118. Sidney and his mother had each pledged £25 to support Frobisher's first voyage in 1576. See Roger Kuin, "Querre-Muhaui: Sir Philip Sidney and the New World," *Renaissance Quarterly,* LI (1998), 562. Convinced by the veracity of the assayer's claims, Sidney invested a further £50 in Frobisher's second voyage and £67 10s. in Frobisher's third voyage; see H. R. Woudhuysen, "Sidney, Sir Philip (1554–1586)," *Oxford Dictionary of National Biography* online, Oxford University Press, 2004–, http://www.oxforddnb.com/view/article/25522; William W. Fitzhugh and Jacqueline S. Olin, eds., *Archeology of the Frobisher Voyages* (Washington, D.C., 1993); see also James McDermott, *Martin Frobisher: Elizabethan Privateer* (New Haven, Conn., 2001); Burghley to William Glaseour, "For Taking up Certain Newfoundland Cod-Fish for Ireland," Oct. 14, 1580, in Hamilton, Atkinson, and Mahaffy, eds., *CSPI of the Reigns of Henry VIII., Edward VI., Mary, and Elizabeth,* II, 260.

73. Carlile, "A Briefe and Summarie Discourse," in Hakluyt, *Principall Navigations,* VI, 86.

of noncombatants. According to Raleigh, there was no "man more feared than he is among the Irish nation. The most unbridled traitors would come in were it but known that he were come among them." As described by the English poet Thomas Churchyard, Gilbert insisted that "the heads of all those . . . which were killed in the day should be cut off from their bodies and brought to the place where he encamped at night, and should there be laid on the ground by each side of the way leading into his own tent. . . . And yet did it bring great terrour to the people when they sawe the heddes of their dedde fathers, brothers, children, kinsfolk and friends, lye on the grounde before their faces." Gilbert's tactic was potent and no doubt effective.[74]

Defiling the bodies of the enemy Irish served as an emblem for conquest. Not only was Elizabeth I often the recipient of severed heads—including the pickled head of Shane O'Neill—but she permitted the desecration of Irish graves, as during the Desmond Rebellions (1569–1573 and 1579–1583). The Irish understood the significance of English attitudes toward enemy bodies as clearly as they did the language of clothing. In 1583, the dying rebel James Fitzmaurice FitzGerald entreated his own men to behead him and conceal his remains. But English soldiers hunted down and retrieved his corpse, then used it for target practice in Dublin.[75]

Although Humphrey Gilbert received a knighthood for his success in Ireland, such harsh practices did not go entirely unremarked. In 1583, Sir James Croft lamented "these unexpert captains and soldiers that hath slain and destroyed as well the unarmed as armed, even to the plowman that never bare weapon, extending cruelty upon both sexes and upon all ages, from the babe in the cradle to the decrepit age, in sort not to be named and by Christian people not to be looked upon." Notwithstanding Croft's concerns, brutality remained a hallmark of the English campaigns in Ireland well after the death of Gilbert in 1583, when he was lost at sea on the return from his own voyage to the New World.[76]

74. Walter Raleigh to Walsingham, Feb. 25, 1581, in Hamilton, Atkinson, and Mahaffy, eds., *CSPI of the Reigns of Henry VIII., Edward VI., Mary, and Elizabeth*, II, 289; Canny, *Elizabethan Conquest of Ireland*, 122; Quinn, *Elizabethans and the Irish*, 127–128. The intended symbolism of these displays is further discussed in William Palmer, "That 'Insolent Liberty': Honor, Rites of Power, and Persuasion in Sixteenth-Century Ireland," *Renaissance Quarterly*, XLVI (1993), 314.

75. Palmer, "That 'Insolent Liberty,'" *Renaissance Quarterly*, XLVI (1993), 315. As discussed in James P. Myers Jr., "'Murdering Heart . . . Murdering Hand': Captain Thomas Lee of Ireland, Elizabethan Assassin," *Sixteenth Century Journal*, XXII (1991), 47–60, Elizabeth tacitly approved of the actions of Captain Thomas Lee, described as an assassin, who sent her the head of the murdered rebel Feagh MacHugh O'Byrne in 1597.

76. Quinn, *Elizabethans and the Irish*, 133.

Evidence for English forces' ruthlessness in Ireland can be found as early as the 1520s and 1530s, suggesting that, in their use of terror, preemptive attacks, and indiscriminate killing, the English viewed the Irish as objects of conquest rather than as subjects to be governed. Gaelic society itself was also martial, with lordly power in part maintained (and challenged) through raids and ambushes. Illustrating wider European awareness of Irish culture, the sixteenth-century Italian historian Paolo Giovio highlighted both the centrality of conflict in Gaelic society as well as the controlled mortality of Gaelic tactics. In considering the warlike pursuits of Conn O'Neill, Giovio notes that the Gaelic lords "set a higher value on military pursuits than on profits from trade. The custom is not to sustain disputes for long, since there is no place for advocates." [77]

English documentary sources from the period often emphasize a perceived contrast in martial strategy between the Irish and the English. An example can be found in the 1618 work by soldier T. E. Gainsford, *The Glory of England*. Gainsford served in Ireland during the Nine Years' War and described the land and its defenders thus:

> The country and kingdome of Ireland is generally for naturall aire, and commoditie of blessings, sufficient to satisfie a covetous or curious appetite: but withal divided into such fastness of mountaine, bogg, and wood, that it hath emboldned the inhabitants to presume on hereditary securitie, as if disobedience had a protection. For the mountaines denie any cariages, but by great industry and strength of men (so have we drawne the Cannon over the deepest bogs, and stoniest hils), and the passages are every way dangerous, both for unfirmenes of ground, and the lurking rebell, who will plash downe whole trees over the pa[ss]es, and so intricately winde them, or lay them, that they shall be a strong barracado, and then lurke in ambush amongst the standing wood, playing upon all commers as they intend to goe along.

77. David Edwards, "The Escalation of Violence in Sixteenth-Century Ireland," in Edwards, Lenihan, and Tait, eds., *Age of Atrocity*, 59, 61. Edwards draws a direct link between Irish and Native North American forms of warfare: "As historians of native society in sixteenth- and seventeenth-century North America have shown, endemic violence among tribal or lineage groups was actually not greatly destructive of life. Because warfare was a matter of raids and counter-raids, ambushes and skirmishes, combat mortality was usually low" (43). In actuality, the nature and deadliness of intertribal conflicts in the Chesapeake region is not as well understood as Edwards implies. Evidence for fortifications underscores the role of violence in the emergence of the expansive Powhatan paramount chiefdom during the sixteenth century, as discussed in Chapter 2. For Giovio, see Jason Harris, "Ireland in Europe: Paolo Giovio's *Descriptio*," *Irish Historical Studies*, XXXV (2006–2007), 265–288, esp. 287.

The Irish forces clearly made strategic and effective use of their superior knowledge of their local landscape.[78]

Parallels between Irish and Native North American warfare have been drawn at least since the late seventeenth century, when the Puritan leader Samuel Gorton stated in a letter to Connecticut governor John Winthrop Jr., "I remember the time of the warres in Ireland; (when I was young, in Queene Elizabeths dayes of famous memory,) where much English blood was spilt by a people much like unto these [Natives] . . . where many valiant souldiers lost their lives, both horse and foot, by meanes of woods, bushes, boggs, and quagmires." Gorton references the Irish use of landscape features as a means of slowing down or trapping the English. Such a tactic proved highly successful in the 1598 Battle of the Yellow Ford, when O'Neill's forces mired the English artillery, under the command of Sir Henry Bagenal, in a bog. Efforts to reclaim a valuable saker from the bog split the troops, who were first picked off by O'Neill's men using woodland for cover and then surprised by a combined Irish attack from the rear.[79]

78. See, for example, Lennon's description of Lord Grey's troops in 1580: "The brightly clad soldiers with their scarlet and blue doublets and white hose were easy targets for the allied fighters, waiting behind their natural shelter of trees and boulders with their guns, bows, and axes" (*Sixteenth-Century Ireland*, 178). For Gainsford, see T[homas] G[ainsford], *The Glory of England; or, A True Description of Many Excellent Prerogatives and Remarkable Blessings* . . . (London, 1618), 144; Maxwell, *Irish History from Contemporary Sources*, 218.

79. Lane to [Burghley], Dec. 15, 1595, in Hamilton, Atkinson, and Mahaffy, eds., *CSPI of the Reigns of Henry VIII., Edward VI., Mary, and Elizabeth*, V, 439; Samuel Gorton to John Winthrop Jr., in Adam Winthrop et al., *The Winthrop Papers*, Massachusetts Historical Society, *Collections*, 4th Ser., VII (Boston, 1865), 629–630; James E. Doan, "'An Island in the Virginian Sea': Native Americans and the Irish in English Discourse, 1585–1640," *New Hibernia Review*, I (1997), 99. For an analysis of the Battle of the Yellow Ford, see Paul Logue and James O'Neill, "The Battlefield Archaeology of the Yellow Ford," in Horning and Brannon, eds., *Ireland and Britain in the Atlantic World*, 7–30. North American historical archaeologists have accepted these accounts in support of comparisons between the Irish and Native American use of guerrilla-style military tactics. Virginia fortifications at the Nansemond Fort site and at Wolstenholmetowne at Martin's Hundred have been described as resembling "the fortified compounds of English settlement in Ireland," suggesting that they represent "an adaptation, or vernacular development, perhaps based on Irish precedents, in military architecture primarily meant to deter Native American bowmen and not European military bombardment"; see Nicholas M. Luccketti, "The Road to James Fort," in William M. Kelso, Luccketti, and Beverly A. Straube, *Jamestown Rediscovery V* (Richmond, Va., 1999), 32. In analyzing the types of weaponry recovered from early-seventeenth-century deposits from James Fort on Jamestown Island, the presence of bucklers and body armor has been interpreted as a response to guerrilla-style warfare, referencing the English experience in Ireland: "The English had already colonized successfully in Ireland, where they also faced a resistant native population that engaged in guerrilla warfare" (Beverly A. Straube, "'Unfitt for Any Moderne Service'? Arms and Armour from James Fort," *Post-Medieval Archaeology*, XL [2006], 34). In reality, the English had not yet "colonized successfully" in Ire-

Irish battles were not conducted in ways directly analogous to Native American conflicts, given the Irish reliance on cavalry and the use of continental weaponry. As again outlined by Giovio, "A horseman is protected by armour and a helmet; he carries a Spanish lance and the reins together in his left hand, and with his right he hurls with great strength a javelin fitted with a leather strap." An Irish foot soldier was similarly clad in armor and "uses a German axe after he has thrown his javelin at the beginning of battle." Furthermore, there is growing evidence that the Irish forces fighting under Hugh O'Neill during the Nine Years' War employed English and continental European military techniques, whereas English forces, according to Ralph Lane, suffered "extreme peril . . . in the late encounter in Ulster for lack of military knowledge." By the end of the sixteenth century, Gaelic leaders were employing up-to-date tactics, learned not only through conflict with the English but by serving alongside them on the Continent.[80]

Firsthand knowledge of English strategies against the Irish, although occasionally overstated, also inevitably affected New World methods. Queen Elizabeth withdrew Ralph Lane, an expert in fortifications, from his newly attained post in Ireland and selected him to serve as the governor for Raleigh's Roanoke colony in 1585. Such a choice presaged the conflict between the English and the local Algonquian tribes that led to the abandonment of Lane's colony. In a glowing letter written to Richard Hakluyt shortly after arrival in North America, Lane reported upon both the commodities and the people of the New World. According to Lane, the Roanoke region was "the goodliest and most pleasing territory of the world," and he boasted, "What commodities soever Spain, France, Italy, or the East parts do yield unto us in wines of all sorts, in oils, in flax, in rosins, pitch, frankincense, currants, sugars, and such-like, these parts do abound with the growth of them all, but, being savages that possess the land, they know no use of the same." Lane then echoes Carleill's obsession with cloth: "The people naturally are most courteous and very desirous to have clothes, but especially of coarse cloth rather than silk."[81]

---

land by the time of Jamestown's establishment in 1607. The Laois and Offaly Plantations were long forgotten, the Munster Plantation in ruins, and plans for the Ulster Plantation not yet on the drawing board. For the Yellow Ford, see Logue and O'Neill, "Battlefield Archaeology of the Yellow Ford," in Horning and Brannon, eds., *Ireland and Britain in the Atlantic World*, 7–30.

80. Harris, "Ireland in Europe," *Irish Historical Studies*, XXXV (2006–2007), 287; Lane to [Burghley], Dec. 15, 1595, in Hamilton, Atkinson, and Mahaffy, eds., *CSPI of the Reigns of Henry VIII., Edward VI., Mary, and Elizabeth*, V, 439.

81. Rafe Lane, "Glowing Prospects for Raleigh's Colony" (1585), in Louis B. Wright, ed., *The Elizabethans' America: A Collection of Early Reports by Englishmen on the New World* (Cambridge,

Propaganda by Roanoke chroniclers suggested that conquering the native inhabitants of North America would prove far easier than conquering the Irish. On the face of reports from Virginia, Richard Hakluyt claimed, "One hundred men will doe more nowe among the naked and unarmed people in Virginiea, then one thousande were able then to doe in Irelande against that armed and warlike nation." The initial willingness of the early-seventeenth-century Jamestown colonists to develop trade relations reflects not only awareness of their dependency on the Powhatan tribes but possibly an instilled, if naive, belief in the quiescence of the Natives and their susceptibility to English commodities.[82]

Violence as a strategy would prove inevitable, as Lane's martial training overwhelmed his enthusiasm. Although Lane's decision to abandon the Roanoke settlement might have been partly influenced by his disgust at not discovering any precious metals ready for extraction, the failure of the 1585–1586 Roanoke colony is more clearly attributable to Lane's aggressive treatment of the Roanoke Indians. Following a series of confrontations between the English and the Roanokes, Lane led an attack on their chief, Pemisipan (Wingina), and his men. Edward Nugent, who had served with Lane in Ireland, killed the native leader: "In the end," Lane reported, "an Irish man serving me, one Nugent. . . . undertooke him, and following him in the woods, overtooke him . . . we met him returning out of the woods with Pemisapan's head in his hand." The Irish presence among English forces was common enough that Nugent's ethnicity was no impediment to his service. Nor did his Irish identity hinder him from applying the same tactic of beheading that Gilbert had employed so effectively in his Irish campaigns. But the attack on Wingina was ill conceived. Faced with starvation—given that his settlers had not planted crops and no longer could count upon the assistance of the local inhabitants—Ralph Lane evacuated his colony when Francis Drake and his captains, including Christopher Carleill, arrived at Roanoke in June 1586.[83]

Mass., 1965), 113–114. In January 1583, reference is made to "the Queen's promise for Mr. Ralph Lane to go into Ireland with some reasonable pension to make fortifications" (earl of Ormond to Walsingham, Jan. 8, 1583, in Hamilton, Atkinson, and Mahaffy, eds., *CSPI of the Reigns of Henry VIII., Edward VI., Mary, and Elizabeth,* II, 423). See also Feb. 8, 1585, "Warrant by the Queen to the Lord Deputy Perrot and to Wallop: For the Government of Kerry and Clanmorris, with 20 Horse and 40 Foot, to Have Been Delivered to Rafe Lane . . ." (ibid., 551).

82. Richard Hakluyt, "Epistle Dedicatory to Sir Walter Ralegh," in E. G. R. Taylor, ed., *The Original Writings and Correspondence of the Two Richard Hakluyts* (London, 1935), II, 377; Shannon Miller, *Invested with Meaning: The Raleigh Circle in the New World* (Philadelphia, 1998), 55.

83. Carole Shammas argues for the lack of marketable commodities as a key factor in the

Six years after his return from Roanoke, Lane was appointed as muster-master general for the English forces in Ireland. Although this was a position of importance that contributed to his being knighted in 1593, Lane often complained about "the barrenness of his entertainment and allowance as Muster Master." In early 1595, Lane had reached the end of his tether, petitioning "Queen Elizabeth for her warrant to the Lord Deputy for the Surveyorship of the Parish Clerks of Ireland, a base place with something, which is better than greater employment with nothing." Two days later, he was in deeper despair, petitioning Lord Burghley for "a grant of the office of Chief Bellringer of Ireland." In 1598, Lane was finally rewarded:

> Grant to sir Raphe Lane, knt.; of the custody of the castle of Belfaste; and for the better maintenance of it, certain lands adjoining, called the Falle and Moyellon, with the toaughe of land called the Synnamente which stretches along by the water side between Belfaste and Carickfergus, and the wardenship of the woods, mines, and minerals of both Clandeboyes, Kilulto, Kilwarlen, and Killeleyrto, and of the loughs and islands in the same. He is to have all the profits of the premises and the fishing of the river Laggan. He is also empowered to take from the woodmen of those parts, such bonnaghts as they have answered to the earl of Tyrone or the Scots, if he can win the good will of the captains of those countries.[84]

Rather than occupy Belfast Castle—most likely the tower house built by the O'Neills, in which Essex had betrayed Brian MacPhelim O'Neill—Lane chose to reedify Ringhaddy Castle, where the ill-fated Thomas Smith the Younger had sought refuge in 1572. Although Lane's choice to eschew Belfast may seem odd given the settlement's later predominance, the Strangford region was arguably of greater economic and political significance in the late

---

abandonment of the colony in "English Commercial Development and American Colonization, 1560–1620," in Kenneth R. Andrews, Nicholas P. Canny, and P. E. H. Hair, eds., *The Westward Enterprise: English Activities in Ireland, the Atlantic, and America, 1480–1650* (Liverpool, 1978), 161. See also "17 August 1585–18 June 1586: Ralph Lane's Discourse on the First Colony," in David Beers Quinn, ed., *The Roanoke Voyages, 1584–1590: Documents to Illustrate the English Voyages to North America under the Patent Granted to Walter Raleigh in 1584* (London, 1955), I, 287–288; Quinn, *England and the Discovery of America, 1481–1606: From the Bristol Voyages of the Fifteenth Century to the Pilgrim Settlement at Plymouth* . . . (New York, 1974); Quinn, *Set Fair for Roanoke: Voyages and Colonies, 1584–1606* (Chapel Hill, N.C., 1985).

84. Lane to Burghley, Sept. 24, 1594, in Hamilton, Atkinson, and Mahaffy, eds., *CSPI of the Reigns of Henry VIII., Edward VI., Mary, and Elizabeth,* V, 274; Lane to Elizabeth I, Feb. 14, 1594/5, ibid., 297; Lane to Burghley, Feb. 16, 1594/5, ibid., 297; "Entry 6235," in *The Irish Fiants of the Tudor Sovereigns during the Reigns of Henry VIII, Edward VI, Philip and Mary, and Elizabeth I,* III, *1586–1603* (1875; rpt. Dublin, 1994), 326.

sixteenth century. By contrast, Belfast consisted primarily of a ford defended by a decayed castle. An unsigned map of the East Ulster region, most likely commissioned by Ralph Lane and considered in detail below, depicts only a handful of cabins at the ford. Effectively a failed medieval settlement, Belfast would continue to be overshadowed by its northern neighbor Carrickfergus throughout the first few decades of the seventeenth century.[85]

Lane's assumptions of security at Ringhaddy are reflected in his alteration of the extant medieval tower house from a readily defensible, albeit "medieval," edifice into a fashionable, Jacobean gabled dwelling with characteristically large windows. Lane was convinced of the potential of his lands and the efficacy of colonization and laid plans to import settlers, including "men of trade of Manchester, Liverpool, and of Lancashire." In a 1602 missive to Robert Cecil, secretary of state, Lane enthused about the potential of the Strangford Lough region, describing it as

> the only safe and stately harbour to make a perpetual standing arsenal and, as it were, a mother-garrison for galleys and ships of any burthen, full of fish within itself and upon that shore to victual an army perpetual, full of islands shore-deep to make magazines and storehouses, accoasted upon the edge of it with the greatest woods and fairest timber trees of Ireland . . . the best corn ground in Ireland . . . as with 200 men to be guarded against all the forces of Spain.

Considering Lane's disenchantment with settlement in North America, it is not hard to imagine his being far more optimistic about attracting English artisans and settlers to people his County Down lands, in a familiar climate and requiring a rather shorter journey. That said, his optimistic missives regarding the commodities and advantages of Roanoke give us pause in discerning the "truth" of his County Down claims.[86]

In his letter to Cecil, Lane refers to a "map describing only that part of Ulster called the Clandebois and the sea-coasts of Kentere in Scotland affronting the coast of Ulster." Although this map is recorded as "Missing" in the edited state papers, it is most likely the detailed map of East Ulster

85. Archaeological Survey of Northern Ireland, *Archaeological Survey of County Down*, 24; Raymond Gillespie and Stephen A. Royle, *Irish Historic Towns Atlas No. 12: Belfast Part 1, to 1840* (Dublin, 2003), 1; Ó Baoill, "Carrickfergus and Belfast," in Horning et al., eds., *Post-Medieval Archaeology of Ireland*, 91–116; Ó Baoill, *Hidden History below Our Feet: The Archaeological Story of Belfast* (Belfast, 2011).

86. Quinn, *Elizabethans and the Irish*, 118; Lane to Robert Cecil, Mar. 5, 1602, in Hamilton, Atkinson, and Mahaffy, eds., *CSPI of the Reigns of Henry VIII., Edward VI., Mary, and Elizabeth*, XI, 315–319, esp. 315, 318.

Plate 4. Ringhaddy Castle, County Down, reedified by Ralph Lane.
Photograph by the author

housed in the National Maritime Museum. The map provides an unusual
insight into Lane's attitude toward Ireland and his role in its conquest.
Apposite to the military man that he was, and reflecting his knowledge
of Cambrensis, Lane stressed the achievements of John de Courcy on this
map and in his letter to Cecil. Lane noted that de Courcy landed in Strangford Lough and "entered with 100 ships and an army and shortly subdued
the Clandeboyes, and all Ulster east of the Bann, having first descended on
the Duffraine from that lough." Lane's map is augmented with cartouches
outlining the history of de Courcy's conquest, including a portrayal of de
Courcy himself resplendent in armor and elaborate helmet, standing tall
ahead of three kneeling native Irish leaders wearing only the vilified mantle
and raising their hands in supplication to the Anglo-Norman conqueror.
Clearly Lane saw himself in de Courcy and used this rendering as a none-
too-subtle piece of propaganda to underscore the tactical advantages of his
lands along Strangford Lough.[87]

87. Historical geographer John Andrews suggests that the map is likely not by Lane himself but by one of his staff members, Captain James Carlyle, albeit with significant input from
Lane. See Andrews, *Queen's Last Map-Maker,* 39–40; Lane to Cecil, Mar. 5, 1602, in Hamilton,
Atkinson, and Mahaffy, eds., *CSPI of the Reigns of Henry VIII., Edward VI., Mary, and Elizabeth,* XI, 315–319, esp. 316.

Plate 5. Strangford Lough region. Detail, 1601 map of East Ulster, National Maritime Museum P49(25). ©National Maritime Museum, Greenwich, London

Lane further argued that the Spanish could readily acquire "a supply of galleys from the Redshanks who, within 20 days' warning, could at all times transport 4,000 of them and their ordnance. . . . Strangford river is most favourably placed of any in Ireland for a landing, both because its natural strength renders it easily fortifiable and because it passes through the country of the rebels." To illustrate this point, a total of fourteen galleys appear on the map, the majority sailing from Scotland toward Strangford Lough. An unfortified Strangford Lough could serve as a "nursery" for the Spanish, where they could construct ships, feed their soldiers, and prepare for an attack on the English coast. Even if they could not enter the Lough itself, Spanish and Irish forces would have been able to reach the lough from the lands of the Dufferin, as "the rebels" had done "all these wars till I entered and built the castle of Ranahaddy on it." Despite Lane's emphasis on the military importance of his plantation scheme, the physical evidence at Ringhaddy itself suggests, as noted above, that Lane was equally concerned with constructing a fashionable abode befitting an English gentleman.[88]

88. Lane to Cecil, Mar. 5, 1602, in Hamilton, Atkinson, and Mahaffy, eds., *CSPI of the Reigns of Henry VIII., Edward VI., Mary, and Elizabeth*, XI, 317.

However well respected Lane might have been by the queen and Privy Council, he was still awaiting an answer to his suit in October 1602. In pleading his case this time, he included a letter of support from Sir Arthur Chichester, then governor of Carrickfergus, who described Lane's plantation scheme as deserving "all favour." Chichester noted that, until Lane had taken over the castle at Ringhaddy, Strangford Lough had been used to supply rebel forces "by a frequent trade into it of Scottish barques with munition, cloth, wine and *aqua vitae*." Lane's presence, the letter implied, was sufficient to dissuade these Scottish traders from entering the lough.[89]

Chichester, who would later become Irish Lord Deputy and preside over the implementation of the Ulster Plantation scheme, was himself no stranger to the New World. In 1595, he accompanied Francis Drake and the English slave trader John Hawkins on a crown-sanctioned voyage to plunder the Spanish settlements of Panama and the Caribbean. The voyage was far from a success. As Drake's forces (including five hundred men under Chichester's command) amassed off the coast of Puerto Rico in October 1595, illness claimed Hawkins's life. Spanish forces repelled efforts to attack San Juan, and the English fleet, less one-fifth of its original complement, was forced to retreat. On the voyage back to England, Drake himself died. Chichester's one foray into the New World had been a resounding failure, and he dismissed the New World as playing any viable role in his own future. The golden age of Elizabethan privateering was on the wane, Raleigh's dreams for the Roanoke colony were long dashed, and plans for other colonial settlements on the eastern seaboard and for the permanent settlement of the fishing stations of Newfoundland would not advance until the reign of James I / VI. Perhaps Chichester and Lane traded notes about their less-than-positive experiences in the New World, within the relative comfort of Ringhaddy or from Chichester's base in the imposing Anglo-Norman castle at Carrickfergus. Certainly both men ultimately opted to seek their fortune in Ireland rather than across the Atlantic.[90]

In addition to Chichester's letter, Lane received support for his plan via a testimony from Constable William Debdall. Debdall related how Lane's

89. Chichester to Cecil, May 12, 1602, ibid., 505.

90. K. R. Andrews, ed., *The Last Voyage of Drake and Hawkins* (Cambridge, 1972); John McCavitt, *Sir Arthur Chichester: Lord Deputy of Ireland, 1605–16* (Belfast, 1998), 6–7; Basil Morgan, "Hawkins, Sir John (1532–1595)," *Oxford Dictionary of National Biography*, http://www.oxforddnb.com/view/article/12672?docPos=1; Kenneth R. Andrews, *Trade, Plunder and Settlement: Maritime Enterprise and the Genesis of the British Empire, 1480–1630* (Cambridge, 1984); Gillian T. Cell, "The Newfoundland Company: A Study of Subscribers to a Colonizing Venture," *WMQ*, XXII (1965), 611–625.

men had captured several Irish "knaves" who "lay in the woods of Ranna-haddy and spoilt the poor tenants who went for wood. They brought in one head and four prisoners . . . I set up the head on the top of the castle to stand as a sentinel for the terrifying of other knaves." Debdall indicates not only the nature of English military tactics in Ireland but also Lane's possible exaggeration of the extent to which he had pacified the Strangford region. The leader of Lane's men was himself ambushed by Irishmen under Brian McArt O'Neill "as he was going from Rannahaddy Castle to a castle which he had built on a neck of land leased to him [by Lane], called Randuffren." Lane promised that, if he received funding to strengthen his forces, "there would be an interchange of heads as current in that part as in any part of Ulster." From Roanoke to Ireland, Lane relied consistently upon violence and, in particular, upon the symbolic value of decapitation. Removing the head of an enemy was the ultimate assertion of power, as the head was believed to be the locus of power, consciousness, and the soul.[91]

Lane did not comment upon the ideological underpinnings for the conquest of Ireland or, for that matter, the New World. His writings focus instead on military matters and his own personal well-being and profit rather than upon matters of religion or culture. By contrast, one of his subordinates seems to have been inflamed with hatred for Irish Catholics. In the aftermath of the 1601 Battle of Kinsale, Ralph Birkensha, Lane's comptroller of the Muster, penned a vitriolic pamphlet and poem. Birkensha railed against "blind Papists, Priests and filthie Friars" and presented the Irish as "champions of hell," "idolators," and "bastards." One wonders how much Lane the adventurer sympathized with his underling's sentiments. Whatever Lane's personal convictions, this quintessential military man died of natural causes before he could prove himself to be the reincarnation of Ulster's Anglo-Norman conqueror de Courcy.[92]

91. William Debdall to Sir Geoffrey Fenton, May 31, 1602, in Hamilton, Atkinson, and Mahaffy, eds., *CSPI of the Reigns of Henry VIII., Edward VI., Mary, and Elizabeth*, XI, 505–506. The ambushed individual was named John White but is not likely to have been the artist and Roanoke governor. See petition of Ralph Lane, ibid., 502–503. The symbolic power of beheading is discussed by Sarah Tarlow, *Ritual, Belief and the Dead in Early Modern Britain and Ireland* (Cambridge, 2011), 148–149; Palmer, "That 'Insolent Liberty,'" *Renaissance Quarterly*, XLVI (1993), 308–327; and for Ireland specifically in Edwards, "Escalation of Violence," in Edwards, Lenihan, and Tait, eds., *Age of Atrocity*, 56–58. See also Jacques Le Goff, "Head or Heart? The Political Use of Body Metaphors in the Middle Ages," in M. Feher, ed., *Fragments for a History of the Human Body* (New York, 1989), 13–26.

92. Hiram Morgan, "Birkensha's Discourse," in Morgan, ed., *The Battle of Kinsale* (Bray, 2004), 391–407.

Akin to Lane, Gilbert, Chichester, and Carleill, a number of notable early Jamestown colonists—such as Thomas Gates, Thomas West, the Lord De la Warr, and Thomas Dale, who together imposed martial law on the Jamestown colonists in 1611—also honed their skills and attitudes as soldiers for Elizabeth in Ireland and in the Netherlands. The draconian punishments meted out to those who violated Dale's martial code (hanging, burning, staking, shooting, and being broken upon a wheel) make it clear that violence as a control tactic was not reserved solely for use against cultural "others." The oft-cited similarities between the fortified bawns of Ireland and the wooden forts of the Chesapeake, such as James Fort, Wolstenholmetowne, Flowerdew Hundred, and Harbor View, may owe much to the expertise and the expectations of Elizabeth's soldiers. Yet it is important to note that, in the case of Ralph Lane, he had only been in Ireland fewer than two years before being called upon to serve the queen on the Roanoke project. His knowledge of fortifications drew upon his broader military experience on the Continent rather than his time in Ireland specifically. Lane's experience in the New World had more of an impact upon his subsequent attitude toward Ireland and the Irish than the reverse. Lane was initially unimpressed with Ireland, noting only a few months after his first posting there that he had "chosen in the end of his 20 years service about Her Majesty's person to employ himself in Her desolate kingdom of Ireland." It would appear, however, that following his time in the New World, Ireland appeared a better prospect for his future. Lane spent the last ten years of his life, 1593 to 1603, fighting against the Irish while developing his own ideal plantation settlement. Although American history remembers him for his brief time on Roanoke Island (less than one year), his endeavors in Ireland were of greater personal significance.[93]

93. Gates, West, and Dale were serving in Ireland in 1599 but were in the Netherlands immediately before their time in Virginia. See Ancient Planters of Virginia, "A Brief Declaration," in Edward Wright Haile, ed., *Jamestown Narratives: Eyewitness Accounts of the Virginia Colony; The First Decade, 1607–1617* (Champlain, Va., 1998), 900. Similarities between fortifications in both lands is touched upon in Eric C. Klingelhöfer, *Castles and Colonists: An Archaeology of Elizabethan Ireland* (Manchester, 2010), 55–58. See also (and especially) Charles T. Hodges, "Private Fortifications in 17th-Century Virginia: A Study of Six Representative Works," in Theodore R. Reinhart and Dennis J. Pogue, eds., *The Archaeology of Seventeenth-Century Virginia*, Archaeological Society of Virginia Special Publication no. 30 (Richmond, Va., 1993); and Hodges, "Forts of the Chieftains: A Study of Vernacular, Classical, and Renaissance Influence on Defensible Town and Villa Plans in 17th-Century Virginia" (M.A. thesis, College of William and Mary, 2003), for a full discussion. Note Hodges's caution that "in the Chesapeake the word 'bawn' has been more often used to mystify rather than clarify cultural meanings" (ibid., 525). For quotation, see Lane to Burghley, Apr. 4, 1583, in Hamilton, Atkinson, and Mahaffy, eds., *CSPI of the Reigns of Henry VIII., Edward VI., Mary, and Elizabeth*, II, 505.

The Munster Plantation

Just as Ralph Lane is ahistorically assumed to have imposed his Irish experience on Roanoke, the Munster Plantation of the 1580s is often viewed as a blueprint for New World colonial settlement. But the Roanoke venture was already faltering by the time Raleigh received his grant in Munster. More accurately described as the Desmond Plantation, the Munster Plantation was an attempt to reallocate the forfeited lands of Gerald Fitz-Gerald, the earl of Desmond, following his failed rebellions (1569–1573 and 1579–1583). The lands to be planted were noncontiguous and included property in counties Cork, Kerry, Limerick, Waterford, and Tipperary. In contrast to the Roanoke effort and the abortive Ulster plantations of the 1570s, and perhaps in recognition of the reasons behind their failure, the Munster Plantation was to be directed by the government rather than established and administered via private speculation. Plans for the confiscated lands were bandied about for years before an official plantation scheme was announced in the summer of 1586, with lands in the possession of most of the plantation undertakers by 1588. Old English and Gaelic lords who were not deeply implicated in the rebellion retained their lands adjacent to the confiscated territories, whereas the larger towns were not included in the scheme.[94]

The underlying philosophy for the Munster Plantation scheme was the notion of res nullius, that one could start anew—unrealistic, given that Munster was dotted with tower houses and medieval settlements and given the noncontiguous nature of the lands to be planted. Recognizing the lessons learned from the failed Laois and Offaly Plantations and reflecting the hardening of English attitudes toward the Irish, the Gaelic Irish and the Old English were officially forbidden from participating. Between 4,500 and 5,000 English settlers were persuaded to people the forfeited lands of Desmond, although, as would be the case for the Ulster Plantation, ridding the lands of its native inhabitants proved unrealistic as well as imprudent.[95]

The Munster Plantation was developed by individuals familiar with

94. For example, Delle, "'A Good and Easy Speculation,'" *International Journal of Historical Archaeology,* III (1999), 12, argues, "In many ways, the Munster Plantation set the precedents for these later and more popularly understood colonial enterprises, and, in fact, involved several historical characters, like Walter Raleigh, who would contribute greatly to the shaping of the early English colonies in North America." The possibility that Roanoke was more influential in Ireland has also been raised by cultural theorist Shannon Miller, who suggested that Ireland became "a space for colonizing in large part because of the colonization project undertaken overseas" *(Invested with Meaning,* 53).

95. Canny, *Making Ireland British,* esp. 121–164; Loeber, "Geography and Practice," *Irish Settlement Studies,* no. 3 (1991), 48–53; MacCarthy-Morrogh, *Munster Plantation.*

efforts to explore and exploit the New World. A total of seven of the Munster Plantation undertakers had already personally supported New World colonial ventures. The Southampton merchant Henry Oughtred had invested in Frobisher's efforts to find the Northwest Passage, funded attacks on Portuguese ships involved in the Newfoundland fishery in 1582, and supported Humphrey Gilbert's Norumbega enterprise of 1583. Others set their sights on the New World from the vantage point of Munster. One of the designers of the Munster Plantation was Attorney General John Popham, whose nephew George (with Raleigh Gilbert, half-nephew of Walter Raleigh) would later lead the Plymouth Company's failed settlement in Maine in 1607. Res nullius informed these English New World ventures and, on paper, was intended to direct the Munster settlement. In reality, most Munster planters opted to develop existing settlements. Certainly taking over dwellings and cultivated fields required far less of an investment than establishing completely new English-style settlements. The fragmented nature of the Munster Plantation also made a mockery of the idea that planters were starting with an empty landscape ready to be molded into some sort of a reflection of England, a belief as ill-founded as Sir Thomas Smith's expectation that the lands of the Ards were only marginally inhabited and represented "waste" to be cultivated. The haphazard implementation of the paper plan also undermines interpretations of the Munster Plantation as exemplifying the successful application of early capitalist ideology. Had the plan been executed as constructed, one could assign a degree of rationalism. But that was not the case.[96]

There were to be nine seigniories of twelve thousand acres, each accommodating 91 English planters and each divided into a manor with adjacent freeholds. The regulated land divisions were designed to maintain a balance of power through the settlement. Such an approach would later be employed with far greater success in seventeenth-century Bermuda and the colonies of Nevis, Saint Christopher, and Providence. By contrast, the Munster Plantation scheme was immediately undermined by Walter Raleigh. Cashing in on his popularity with the queen, Raleigh acquired a massive grant of forty

---

96. MacCarthy-Morrogh, *Munster Plantation*, 50; Gillian T. Cell, *English Enterprise in Newfoundland, 1577–1660* (Toronto, 1969), 24; Jeffrey P. Brain, *Fort St. George: Archaeological Investigation of the 1607–1608 Popham Colony on the Kennebec River in Maine* (Salem, Mass., 1995); Nicholas P. Canny, "Select Documents XXXIV: Rowland White's 'Discors Touching Ireland,'" c. 1569," *Irish Historical Studies*, XX (1976–1977), 439–463; Hiram Morgan, "The Colonial Venture of Sir Thomas Smith in Ulster, 1571–1575," *Historical Journal*, XXVIII (1985), 261–278. The Munster Plantation as an example of capitalism is argued by Delle, "'A Good and Easy Speculation,'" *International Journal of Historical Archaeology*, III (1999), 12.

thousand acres in the Munster Plantation, despite the intended seigniorial divisions. Though seldom resident in Ireland, Raleigh directed the exploitation of his lands, encouraging timber harvesting, establishing Ireland's first blast furnaces, and exemplifying the commodification of nature central to early modern European expansion. Within a period of three years, Raleigh exported approximately 340,000 barrel staves produced from his Munster forests by 200 imported English laborers.[97]

Raleigh was not the only entrepreneur to recognize the commercial value of Munster's forest resources. Sir Francis Willoughby—notable for his development of the Nottinghamshire coal fields and for his experiments with glassmaking and woad cultivation on his grounds at Wollaton near Nottingham—similarly saw potential in Ireland. Willoughby evidently acquired woodlands in Munster in the hopes of developing an iron manufactory at Kinalmeaky in association with the Munster undertaker and London haberdasher Phane Becher. Another partner in this venture was Robert Payne, a previous business associate of Willoughby's. In 1589, Payne wrote enthusiastically to his backers about the abundance of iron ore in Munster and of the "great store of Lead ore, and Wood sufficient to mayntane divers Iron and lead works (with good husbandrie) forever." Payne further extolled Becher's "honest and plaine dealing" and claimed, "Many are desirous to inhabitte with him." Payne's enthusiasm, Becher's honesty, and Willoughby's capital would not prove sufficient to overcome local political realities. Becher's grant, including the Castle O'Mahoney, had long been contested by the O'Mahoney chief, Donal Graney. Graney's frustrations culminated in violence, as he captured and burned the castle in 1589, ransacking all of the undertaker's property. For Willoughby, this would be just another drain on the family coffers; responsibility for his extensive debts would pass to his son-in-law Percival Willoughby. Taking a leaf from the older man's book, Percival attempted to recoup the family fortune by promoting the mining and processing of iron ore in the Newfoundland colony of the early seventeenth century. His efforts would also prove unsuccessful.[98]

97. Virginia Bernhard, "Bermuda and Virginia in the Seventeenth Century: A Comparative View," *Journal of Social History,* XIX (1985), 59–61. Raleigh's iron industry is discussed in Colin Rynne, "The Origins and Technical Development of the Blast Furnace in Ireland, c. 1596–c. 1740," in Conleth Manning, ed., *From Ringforts to Fortified Houses: Studies on Castles and Other Monuments in Honour of David Sweetman* (Bray, 2007), 389; and Rynne, "The Social Archaeology of Plantation-Period Ironworks in Ireland: Immigrant Industrial Communities and Technology Transfer, c. 1560–1640," in Lyttleton and Rynne, eds., *Plantation Ireland,* 248–264; David Beers Quinn, *Raleigh and the British Empire* (London, 1947), 153.

98. Robert Payne, *A Briefe Description of Ireland: Made in This Yeare, 1589, by Robert Payne unto*

Like Willoughby, Raleigh explicitly viewed his Munster holdings in terms of their potential for economic gain. In addition to his exploitation of the forest and the establishment of an ironworking industry, Raleigh also obtained financial support from London backers by interesting them in land speculation. Archaeological investigation of two settlements on Raleigh's lands at Mogeely, captured on a detailed estate map of 1598, reveals the traces of possible late-sixteenth-century habitations associated with Raleigh's tenants. Remains of what might have been a sizable timber-frame manor house were unearthed, alongside ephemeral evidence for two other domestic buildings of vernacular Irish form. The structures were not in association with any sixteenth-century materials, so attribution to Raleigh's plantation is not certain. Even if the structures date to the 1590s, there is nothing to suggest that Raleigh had a direct influence on the approach of the settlers. Rather, he was content to reap the profits denied him in the New World. In short, the nameless tenants whose abodes are depicted on the Mogeely estate map paid rents to an absentee landlord in England, whose principal concern was recouping investment rather than reproducing some version of England in Ireland. By 1598, Raleigh had evidently lost interest in his Irish venture and tried to sell off his interests entirely. In 1603, Raleigh, then imprisoned in the Tower, penned a letter to Cecil lamenting that his remaining Munster "tenants refuse to pay my wife her rent. . . . Alas! all goes to ruin of that littell which remayneth. My woods ar cutt down; my grounds wast; my stock—which made up my rent—sold. And except sume end be had, by your good favor to the Kinge, I perish every waye." Viewed from the Tower, Ireland must have seemed an expensive mistake.[99]

Raleigh was not alone in his hope that investing in the Munster Plantation would prove easier than the effort to plant a colony at Roanoke. Following his return from Roanoke in 1586, scientist and chronicler Thomas

---

XXV of His Partners for Whom He Is Undertaker There (London, 1590), 6; "Answer of Richard Harison, Attorney, unto Phane Becher, Esq., to the Articles Set down by the Commissioners," Sept. 17, 1589, in Hamilton, Atkinson, and Mahaffy, eds., CSPI of the Reigns of Henry VIII., Edward VI., Mary, and Elizabeth, IV, 238; S. [T.] M[cCarthy], "The Mahonys of Kerry," Kerry Archaeological Magazine, IV (1917–1918), 171–190, 223–255; Cell, "The Newfoundland Company," WMQ, 3d Ser., XXII (1965), 611–625.

99. MacCarthy-Morrogh, Munster Plantation, 124. Despite the equivocal evidence from Mogeely, the excavator Eric Klingelhöfer argued that the combination of cartographic and material data "suggest that they [Raleigh's settlers] were trying to create stable, permanent communities on the English model." See Klingelhöfer, "Elizabethan Settlements: Mogeely Castle, Curraglass, and Carrigeen, Co. Cork (Part II)," Journal of the Cork Historical and Archaeological Society, CV (2000), 174; Sir John Pope Hennessy, Sir Walter Ralegh in Ireland (London, 1883), 58.

Hariot ensconced himself in the dissolved Molana Abbey while former Roanoke governor and artist John White lived out his days in County Cork after
failing to rescue the 1587 Lost Colony. Sir Richard Grenville, Lane's partner and nemesis in the 1585 Roanoke colony effort, endeavored to acquire a
seignory in the Munster Plantation to realize an earlier, failed venture he had
shared with his uncle Sir Warham Saint Leger in the late 1560s. Failing to do
so, Grenville found himself again in the service of Elizabeth, facing down
the Spanish in English waters in 1588. Grenville died in the aftermath of the
Armada, never achieving any of his colonial dreams.[100]

The most celebrated Munster planter was the poet Edmund Spenser,
credited for advocating the use of violence to conquer Ireland in the pages of
his literary masterpiece, *The Faerie Queene*. Drawing in part on his firsthand
experience of the slaughter at Smerwick and containing a spirited defense of
Smerwick commander Lord Grey (then Spenser's chief patron), *The Faerie
Queene* is also replete with references to Roanoke. Spenser's knowledge of
the failed colony can be attributed to Raleigh, whom Spenser notably entertained in Kilcolman Castle, Co. Cork. Spenser acquired the castle and an
adjacent 3,028 acres, and, like most English planters, chose to occupy the
existing tower house rather than build entirely anew. Excavations at Kilcolman revealed that Spenser had appended a parlor to the castle and established pleasure gardens to mark his status as an English gentleman. Archaeological evidence suggests that Spenser's new construction work was of a
poor quality and neglected defensive needs.[101]

The Munster planters saw their efforts, confident or otherwise, almost entirely reversed in October 1598 as the Nine Years' War between the English
and the Irish forces led by Hugh O'Neill intensified throughout Ireland.
Spenser's poorly defended, if fashionably augmented, castle was burned at
the culmination of Desmond heir James Fitzmaurice FitzGerald's rebellious actions. Owny O'Moore, an agent of Hugh O'Neill, led coordinated
attacks upon plantation settlements, structures, and planters. As the new
planters fled, the former occupants swiftly reclaimed their confiscated lands,

---

100. Canny, *Making Ireland British;* Paul Hulton, *America 1585: The Complete Drawings of John
White* (Chapel Hill, N.C., 1985); Quinn, *Elizabethans and the Irish.*

101. Vincent P. Carey, "Atrocity and History: Grey, Spenser, and the Slaughter at Smerwick," in Edwards, Lenihan, and Tait, eds., *Age of Atrocity,* 81–82; Kim Sloan, *A New World:
England's First View of America* (Chapel Hill, N.C., 2007), 49; Eric Klingelhöfer, "The Architecture of Empire: Elizabethan Country Houses in Ireland," in Susan Lawrence, ed., *Archaeologies
of the British: Explorations of Identity in Great Britain and Its Colonies, 1600–1945* (London, 2003),
111; Klingelhöfer, *Castles and Colonists,* 154.

occasioning much soul-searching by the planters and the plantation ideo-logues. Spenser wrote, seemingly without irony, "Before new buildings were erected, the old should have been plucked down." Although Spenser's words were intended as a metaphor for relations between the English and Irish, the fate of Kilcolman and his own slapdash refurbishment must have been on his mind.[102]

Not all Munster planters abandoned their investments when the vio-lence broke out. Francis Berkeley, great-uncle to one of seventeenth-century Virginia's most notable governors, William Berkeley, reclaimed his seat at Askeaton Castle and was knighted by Essex in 1599. Considered an energetic planter, Berkeley had managed to obtain the chief seat of the Desmonds, which he used as a base for his seigneury. The castle itself, of fourteenth-century origin, was situated on an island and boasted an impressive ban-queting hall and residential tower. Its natural defenses aided its service as a refuge in November 1598, despite the fact that Berkeley did not maintain a force, as he reported to the queen: "The revolt of the country was sudden and unexpected, my provision only fitting a private gentleman's house. The English that neighboured me . . . came, of gentlemen and others that had lived in good sort, and few that maintained not a household, into the castle, not so few as five hundred men, women and children, who brought nothing with them, for the most part, but such things as the extremity of their fear would give them leave to lay their hands on." Askeaton Castle was a tem-porary refuge for the displaced English settlers, with its fourteenth-century defenses serving Berkeley better than any expedient new construction.[103]

Whereas Berkeley was honored for maintaining his foothold in Munster, Fynes Moryson blamed the undertakers in general for the destruction of the Munster Plantation. In his estimation, the planters were "in great part the cause . . . of their owne fatall miseries. For whereas they should have built Castles, and brought over Colonies of English, and have admitted no Irish Tenant, but onely English, these and like covenants were in no part per-formed by them. Of whom the men of best quality never came over, but made profit of the land . . . and all entertained Irish servants and tenants." Moryson's complaints would be routinely echoed by critics of the Ulster

102. Edmund Spenser, "Lament of Edward Spenser: A Brief Note of Ireland" (1598), in Maxwell, *Irish History from Contemporary Sources*, 250–252.

103. MacCarthy-Morrogh, *Munster Plantation*, 138; T. E. McNeill, *Castles in Ireland: Feu-dal Power in a Gaelic World* (London, 1997), 178; Captain Francis Barkley to the Lords Justices Loftus and Gardener, Nov. 3, 1598, in Hamilton, Atkinson, and Mahaffy, eds., *CSPI of the Reigns of Henry VIII., Edward VI., Mary, and Elizabeth*, VII, 347–348.

Plantation. The fundamental challenge for all plantation efforts was secur-
ing sufficient numbers of loyal tenants willing to relocate to Ireland and
risk a very uncertain future. It was inevitable that planters would be compelled to rely upon Irish laborers and tenants. It must be remembered that
the Munster Plantation, in particular, was also designed to play a key role in
England's defense against Spain. Relying on Irish tenantry to prop up the
plantation settlement was better than having no foothold in Ireland at all.
Indeed, only a year after the first official grants for Munster plantation land
were issued, English fears of a Spanish invasion were realized as a fleet of 130
Spanish ships appeared in the English Channel on July 29, 1588.[104]

Ireland and the Spanish Armada

Under the leadership of Alonso Perez de Guzman el Bueno, duke
of Medina Sidonia, the ships sighted in the Channel were en route to the
Netherlands, to pick up Spanish troops before attacking England. The English forces that responded included individuals experienced in both the
Irish wars and the race for the New World. Francis Drake captained a ship,
as did would-be Munster planter Richard Grenville. Martin Frobisher captained the *Triumph,* leading the first day's attack on the Spanish alongside
Drake's ship the *Revenge* and the *Victory,* captained by the slave trader and
privateer Sir John Hawkins. Outmaneuvered by the English, the Spanish
fleet never made it to the Netherlands. Instead, they were compelled to cir-
cumnavigate Scotland and Ireland as they endeavored to return to Spain. The
retreat of the Armada left a tangible legacy in Ireland. The ships encountered
not only rough weather but the maritime charts that were, at best, schematic
when it came to representing nothern and western Ireland's treacherous
coastline. At least twenty-three ships were lost, with shipwrecked survivors
experiencing welcomes from the Irish that ranged from generous hospitality to indifference to outright violence. When Juan de Saavedra's ship,
the *Zuñiga,* managed to navigate into the port of Tralee, the locals refused
"to allow us to obtain water; nor would they sell us food." These were "rus-
tic savages, devoted to England." Saavedra was far more fortunate than the
Spanish mariners who sought refuge on Clare Island, where they were killed
by Dubhdarach Roe O'Malley and his men for their gold. By contrast, many
of those whose ships grounded or sank off the coast of Donegal received
assistance and hospitality from local clans under the leadership of the Mac-
Sweenys. The experiences of the aforementioned Francisco de Cuellar, who

104. Moryson, *Itinerary,* II, 219.

received assistance from a Latin-speaking Irishman, provide insight into the lack of political unity in the north of Ireland: he was welcomed by the O'Rourkes, rejected by the O'Cahans, and alternatively housed and robbed by Irish peasants.[105]

Although the Lord Deputy Sir William Fitzwilliam ordered the capture and execution of any stranded mariners—a pragmatic response to the English soldiers under his command—apparently not all English soldiers complied. The fate of a handful of the mariners on board the *Girona*, a Neapolitan galleass that wrecked near Lacada Point off the Antrim coast on October 28, 1588, is hinted at by the Italian historian Petruccio Ubaldino: "Fourteen Spaniards who had saved themselves from their wrecked ship" encountered the would-be American adventurer Christopher Carleill, then governor of Carrickfergus. According to Carleill's biographer, the men begged "that as a soldier he [Carleill] should spare their lives. It seemed to him that he should use military pity, and therefore he received them chivalrously without cruelty or grudging." Tradition suggests that, following a dispute with the Lord Deputy Fitzwilliam, who insisted that Carleill execute the refugees, Carleill paid some Scottish sailors to take the men to Scotland.[106]

A supply ship designed to carry only 500 men, the *Girona* was laden with some 1,300 survivors of other Armada shipwrecks en route from their refuge in Killybegs Harbor, Co. Donegal—where they had been supported by the local population—to relative safety in Scotland. Nearly all aboard the *Girona* perished, with the exception of those reportedly rescued by Carleill. The cargo included an array of gems and coinage. A total of 1,276 coins from six countries and representing sixty denominations were recovered from the wreck site in 1968, as were twelve gold chains, one dozen gold rings, a set of portrait cameos carved of lapis lazuli and set in gold, and lavish tablewares including silver serving dishes, candlesticks, and silver forks. These articles

105. Colin Martin and Geoffrey Parker, *The Spanish Armada* (New York, 1988); Niall Fallon, *The Armada in Ireland* (Middletown, Conn., 1978); Stephen Usherwood, ed., *The Great Enterprise: The History of the Spanish Armada as Revealed in Contemporary Documents* (London, 1978); Karl Brady and Connie Kelleher, *National Inventory of Wrecks and Wrecking* (Dublin, 2003); Edward J. Bourke, *Shipwrecks of the Irish Coast*, I, *1105–1993* (Dublin, 1994); Bourke, *Shipwrecks of the Irish Coast*, II, *932–1997* (Dublin, 1998); Juan De Saavedra to the king, Oct. 4, 1588, in Martin A. S. Hume, ed., *Calendar of Letters and State Papers Relating to English Affairs . . .* , IV, *Elizabeth, 1587–1603* (London, 1899), 456–457; O'Reilly, trans., "Remarks on Certain Passages in Captain Cuellar's Narrative," in *Proceedings of the Royal Irish Academy (1889–1901)*, III (1893–1896), 175–217. Richard Grenville was commander of the fleet that took Lane and his men to Roanoke; he returned with supplies barely a month after Lane abandoned the colony.

106. Lloyd, *Elizabethan Adventurer*, 151.

are a reminder of the riches extracted by the Spanish in the New World and of the avariciousness of colonial enterprise that inspired jealousy among Elizabeth's grasping adventurers.[107]

The fourth largest vessel in the Spanish fleet, *La Trinidad Valencera*, wrecked in Kinnagoe Bay, Co. Donegal, on September 12, 1588. All but forty of those aboard were reportedly rescued. Excavation has revealed that its cargo included Remigy siege guns intended for an attack on London, along with fragments of clothing (wool and velvet), a campaign tent, wine-skin stoppers, and barrels, staves, and bungs, providing insights into both the practicalities of shipboard life and the kinds of articles the Irish might have salvaged. Although Irish forces might have hoped for a Spanish victory over the English, it was their own rugged landscape that devastated the Spanish fleet.[108]

Nine Years' War

The English victory over the Spanish Armada and the subsequent loss of so many ships off the Irish coast was a serious blow for Spain, but the conflict with England would not conclude until the early seventeenth century. The defeat of Irish and Spanish forces at Kinsale, Co. Cork, in 1601 signaled the ending of the Anglo-Spanish War and was a turning point in the Nine Years' War. As discussed earlier, Irish fighters used their superior geographic knowledge and stealth honed by centuries of raiding. However, examination of Hugh O'Neill's activities suggests a more savvy amalgamation of techniques. Landscape analysis of the Yellow Ford, where the English suffered their most humiliating defeat in 1598, demonstrates O'Neill's

107. The *Girona* was investigated under the direction of Belgian underwater archaeologist Robert Sténuit in 1968. See Laurence Flanagan, *Girona* (Belfast, 1974); and Brian Williams, "Maritime Archaeology in Northern Ireland: A Holistic Approach," in Carol Ruppé and Jon Barstan, eds., *International Handbook of Underwater Archaeology* (New York, 2002), 424. Also held by the Ulster Museum are materials associated with another Armada wreck, that of the *Santa Maria de la Rosa*, which sank off the Blasket Islands in County Kerry.

108. *La Trinidad Valencera* was located by the City of Derry Sub-Aqua Club in 1971 and excavated by Colin Martin in the 1970s and 1980s, with ongoing work by the Underwater Archaeology Unit of the Republic of Ireland Department of the Environment, Heritage, and Local Government. See Connie Kelleher, "Connections and Conflict by Sea: The Maritime Interrelationship between Ireland, Britain, and the Wider Atlantic," in Horning and Brannon, eds., *Ireland and Britain in the Atlantic World*, 53–82; Williams, "Maritime Archaeology in Northern Ireland," in Ruppé and Barstan, eds., *International Handbook of Underwater Archaeology*, 425; and Colin Breen and Aidan O'Sullivan, "Maritime Archaeology in the Republic of Ireland," ibid., 411. Possible traces of another Armada wreck, the *Juliana*, were located at Streedagh Strand, Co. Sligo, in 1985. The remains included a rudder and gun carriage.

canny use of the local environment and topography to trap the numerically superior English forces. At the same time, archaeological evidence indicates that O'Neill incorporated up-to-date continental weapons, tactics, and fortifications to beat the English at their own game. Even Walter Raleigh, in his *Discourse Touching a War with Spain,* acknowledged that the Irish employed contemporary weaponry:

> I remember also, when myself was a captain in Ireland, that a hundred foot and a hundred horse would have beaten all the forces of the strongest provinces: but of late, I have known an Easterling fight hand to hand with one of her majesty's ships; and the Irish have, in this last war, been overthrown with an even, or a far less number. The Netherlands, in those days, had wooden guns, and the Irish had darts, but the one is now furnished with as great a number of English ordnance as ourselves, and the other with as good pikes and muskets as England hath.

Some of these Irish armaments were purchased from the Spanish along with other commodities, whereas guns captured from the English were no doubt put to good use. Similarly, Irish, English, and Scottish forces recovered sunken weaponry from the wrecked Armada ships. The Highlander Sorley Boy MacDonnell salvaged cannon from the wreck of the *Girona* and mounted them at Dunluce Castle on the north coast of County Antrim.[109]

O'Neill's fortifications at Dungannon and along the shores of Lough Neagh reveal patterns that differ little from contemporary English defenses. This is to be expected, considering that O'Neill had spent part of his child-

109. Walter Raleigh, "A Discourse Touching a War with Spain and of the Protecting of the Netherlands," in Raleigh, *The Works of Sir Walter Raleigh . . .* , VIII (Oxford, 1829), 304–305. Thomas Maria Wingfield, brother of Virginia governor Edward Maria Wingfield, led the English in their tactical retreat from the Yellow Ford. See Colm J. Donnelly and Kathy Cluny, "'Here Tirone Fortifieth': Gaelic Military Fortifications and the Defence of the O'Neill Household Lands in Ulster during the Nine Years War, 1594–1603," paper presented at the Society for Historical Archaeology's 40th Annual Conference on Historical and Underwater Archaeology, Williamsburg, Va., Jan. 10–14, 2007; James O'Neill, "An Introduction to Firearms in Post-Medieval Ireland, 1500–1700," in Horning et al., eds., *Post-Medieval Archaeology of Ireland,* 467–484; Logue and O'Neill, "Battlefield Archaeology of the Yellow Ford," in Horning and Brannon, eds., *Ireland and Britain in the Atlantic World,* 7–30. The antiquarian Henry Lawlor noted in 1928, "A letter written in 1548 on behalf of Rowland White, afterwards of the Dufferin, to the Lord Deputy Bellingham, pressing for supplies of war matériel, asks for 'one falcon of brass, two dozen of moryce pikes and 40 sheaffes of arrows,'" suggesting that firearms remained uncommon at that time. However, by the 1570s, the Irish were employing firearms, as witness the fate of Thomas Smythe's son, who was shot dead by an Irish servant in his household. See Lawlor, *Ulster: Its Archaeology and Antiquities* (Belfast, 1928).

hood in the Pale, in the household of a New English settler, Giles Hoven-
den, and had fought with the earl of Essex against the Scots. O'Neill readily
traversed cultural boundaries, as witness Elizabeth's regretful description
of him as "a creature of our own." Furthermore, Elizabeth's troops were
comprised not only of English men but also Irish soldiers for hire. Some
of these individuals offered O'Neill their services and, by extension, their
understanding of English military tactics, strengths, and weaknesses.[110]

Notwithstanding his English education, O'Neill, like other Gaelic military leaders, also made apt use of crannogs, or defensible artificial islands,
as munitions stores, refuges, and hospitals. Crannogs, fortified by wooden
pilings and protected by water, were an unfamiliar feature to the English sol-
diery and occasioned much comment. In reporting to the crown in 1567 on
Shane O'Neill's defenses, English soldier Thomas Phettiplace noted:

> That fortification that he only dependeth upon *is in sartin freshwater loghes*
> in his country, which from the sea there come neither ship nor boat to
> approach them; it is thought that there in the said *fortified* islands lyeth
> all his plate, wch is much, and money, prisoners, and gages, wch islands
> hath in wars before been attempted, and now of late again by the Lord
> Deputy Sr Harry Sydney, wch for want of means for safe conduct upon
> the water, it hath not prevailed.[111]

Although standard treatments of Irish archaeology attribute crannogs to
the early medieval period, paralleling the construction of ráths, a number
of crannogs throughout the island have yielded predominantly fifteenth-,
sixteenth-, and even seventeenth-century artifacts. A hoard of sixteenth-
century coins and goldwork recovered from the Cherry Island crannog on
Lough Ennell, Co. Westmeath, is attributed to Gaelic lords' practice of stor-
ing their treasurers as well as ammunition on crannogs. Island McHugh, a
crannog in Lough Catherine, Co. Tyrone, served as a notable lordly center
and residence for the O'Neills well into the sixteenth century. Its tower house
attests to a continuity of purpose regarding the site's defensive strengths.

---

110. Donnelly and Cluny, "'Here Tirone Fortifieth'"; Donnelly, personal communication,
October 2008; John J. Marshall, "The Hovendens: Foster Brothers of Aodh O'Neill, Prince of
Ulster (Earl of Tireoghan)," *Ulster Journal of Archaeology*, 2d Ser., XIII (1907), 5; Hiram Morgan, *Tyrone's Rebellion: The Outbreak of the Nine Years War in Tudor Ireland* (Woodbridge, Suffolk, 1993), 85, 214.

111. Aidan O'Sullivan, *The Archaeology of Lake Settlement in Ireland* (Dublin, 1998), 170; W. G.
Wood-Martin, *The Lake-Dwellings of Ireland or Ancient Lacustrine Habitations of Erin Commonly
Called Crannogs* (Dublin, 1886), 146–147.

At Lough Island Reavy crannog, Co. Down, sixteenth-century German stoneware, querns, whetstones, Tudor coinage, as well as cannonballs and musketballs suggest domestic use punctuated by military activity; the presence of German stoneware also underscores the participation of the Gaelic elite in continental trade. Dendrochronological analysis of structural timbers from Carrick Lough and Lough Eyes crannogs in County Fermanagh likewise yielded sixteenth-century dates.[112]

Antiquarian excavation of a crannog in Lough Henry, Co. Down, reportedly unearthed a late medieval helmet and fragments of chainmail, possibly associated with the early-seventeenth-century occupation of Tool McPhelim McIvor. Crannogs continued to be used militarily by the Irish throughout the seventeenth century, with documented skirmishes during the 1641 Rising / Rebellion as well as the Williamite Wars. This sustained use flouted English legislation, as expressed in this 1604 decree "that none of the Irish do build any house on loughs, but be enjoined to build castles or houses upon the firm land, and those houses that now are built upon loughs to be defaced." The English, it seems, were well aware of both the crannog's defensive and cultural roles in Gaelic society.[113]

The most detailed pictorial evidence for the continued use of crannogs in the postmedieval period can be found in the maps rendered by the ill-fated Richard Bartlett, which chronicle the advances of Lord Mountjoy against Tyrone's rebelling forces. One illustration depicts an attack on a crannog believed to be the one still present within Lough Roughan, Co. Tyrone, a locale captured by Mountjoy on July 1, 1602. Bartlett shows several buildings on the crannog, including three small, thatched structures and a timber frame for another, surrounded by a wickerwork fence, through which Irish forces are returning the fire of the English.[114]

Mountjoy's scorched-earth campaigns echoed the ferocity of Gilbert

112. O'Sullivan, *Archaeology of Lake Settlement in Ireland,* 170; Wood-Martin, *Lake-Dwellings of Ireland,* 147; Niall Brady and Kieran O'Conor, "The Later Medieval Usage of Crannogs in Ireland," *Ruralia,* V (2003), 129–130. Excavations were carried out by C. W. Dickinson but never brought to final report stage. Finds reported in David M. Wilson and D. Gillian Hurst, "Medieval Britain in 1962 and 1963," *Medieval Archaeology,* VIII (1964), 276. See Mallory and McNeill, *Archaeology of Ulster,* 292. The Lough Island Reavy sixteenth-century finds are also mentioned by A. E. P. Collins, "Excavations at Dressogagh Rath, Co. Armagh," *Ulster Journal of Archaeology,* 3d Ser., XXIX (1966), 117–129. For the dendrochronological analysis, see M. G. L. Baillie, "An Interim Statement on Dendrochronology at Belfast," ibid., XLII (1979), 79.

113. For Lough Henry, see *Archaeological Survey of County Down,* 18. Quotation from "Memorials for the Better Reformation of the Kingdom of Ireland," in Russell and Prendergast, eds., *CSPI of the Reign of James I,* I, *1603–1606,* 135.

114. G. A. Hayes-McCoy, ed., *Ulster and Other Irish Maps, c. 1600* (Dublin, 1964), 9–10.

Plate 6. Richard Bartlett, "Attack on a Crannog." This image is reproduced courtesy of the National Library of Ireland, NLI MS 2656/5

and Grey's activities in Munster. Fynes Moryson, Mountjoy's secretary, chronicled the suffering in the aftermath: "And no spectacle was more frequent in the Ditches of Townes, and especiallie in wasted Countries, then to see multitudes of these poor people dead with their mouthes all coloured greene by eating nettles, docks, and all things they could rend up above ground." Bartlett's maps, most accurately described as a narrative of conquest, record this destruction. In his map of Armagh, he juxtaposes the roofless, ruined monastic and domestic dwellings against the tidy, thatched-roof dwellings of the English garrison sheltering within the triangular-bastioned Mullin Fort.[115]

Armagh, once the ecclesiastical capital of Ireland, was repeatedly laid waste during the latter half of the sixteenth century. As described by Henry Bagenal in 1586, Armagh was "a small villadge, having the church and other the Frieries there for the most part broken and defaced." The symbolic impact of this destruction of sacred space was no doubt eclipsed by the policy of terror and starvation imposed by Mountjoy's forces and expressed by

115. Moryson, *Itinerary,* III, 283.

Chichester: "A million swords will not do them so much harm as one winter's famine." Mountjoy himself acknowledged the harshness of their campaign: "We do now continually hunt all their woods, spoil their corn, burn their houses, and kill so many churls, as it grieveth me to think that it is necessary to do it." Mountjoy nonetheless relied upon this tactic in his Ulster campaign.[116]

The destruction wrought by Mountjoy's forces and the defeat of O'Neill at Kinsale in 1601 laid the groundwork for the plantation of Ulster, established after the departure of O'Neill in 1607, in the event known as the Flight of the Earls. The "flight" occurred on September 14, just after the Jamestown colonists had endured their first sweltering Virginia summer. Hugh O'Neill set sail for Spain accompanied by Rory O'Donnell, the earl of Tyrconnell, and Cúchonnacht Maguire, lord of Fermanagh, and their followers. Presumably en route to reengage Spanish military support, their vessel wound up in Normandy, from where they were ultimately expelled to Rome. The void in Ulster Gaelic leadership left in the wake of the earls ensured little immediate resistance to the confiscation of their lands.[117]

---

116. Although the destruction of Armagh depicted by Bartlett is supported by a range of documentary references, it should be noted that his depiction of Mullin Fort may be more aspirational than accurate. The location of the fort is atop what is today a featureless hill. Although clearly a tactical location in terms of visibility over the landscape, there is little surface evidence for the type of textbook defenses Bartlett rendered; see Marshal Bagenal, Herbert F. Hore, and Lord Burghley, "Marshal Bagenal's Description of Ulster, Anno 1586," *Ulster Journal of Archaeology*, 1st Ser., II (1854), 137–160, esp. 151. Armagh is situated in a broader ritual landscape associated with the Iron Age center of Emaínn Macha, or Navan Fort. Recognition of the continuity in the sacred nature of this locale is implied by Bartlett's depiction of the mound of Emaínn Macha on his map of Armagh; see McCavitt, *Chichester*, 10; State Paper Office, State Papers Ireland, Elizabeth I to George III, SP 63/207 iii/53, National Archives, Kew; Mountjoy to Sir George Carew, Jul. 2, 1602, in J. S. Brewer and William Bullen, eds., *Calendar of the Carew Manuscripts, Preserved in the Archiepiscopal Library at Lambeth*, IV, *1601–1603* (London, 1870), 263–264. Analysis of the Armagh picture map by Paul Logue suggests an alternative thesis to the juxtaposition of a ruined Armagh and a tidy Mullan Fort: that the ruined monastic buildings had been refurbished by English troops, as evidenced by the depiction of gunloops and a soldier's platform (Paul Logue, personal communication, May 2013).

117. John McCavitt, *The Flight of the Earls* (Dublin, 2002); John McGurk, "The Flight of the Earls: Escape or Strategic Regrouping?" *History Ireland*, XV, no. 4 (July/August 2007), 16–21. Plans for a reinvigoration of the Hiberno-Spanish alliance came to naught. Whether the Spanish would have even entertained such a notion is also questionable, given that one of the rationales for joining the engagement at Kinsale was, in fact, to alleviate the pressures of Irish immigration to Spain, which had particularly manifested in fractious relations between the Old English and Gaels who had taken up residence in Madrid. See discussion in Enrique García Hernán, "Irish Clerics in Madrid, 1598–1665," in Thomas O'Connor and Mary Ann Lyons, eds., *Irish Communities in Early-Modern Europe* (Dublin, 2006), 270–272.

Despite the ambiguity of Hugh O'Neill's own identity, he has come to symbolize the destruction of a supposedly pristine and traditional Gaelic society by an English colonial power, analogous to the conquest of native New World societies. Such simplistic interpretation denies the sly civility or duplomacy practiced by individuals like the O'Neill. Hugh O'Neill was far from the only Gaelic lord knowledgeable of English culture who sought to subvert and capitalize upon the increased English attention to Ireland. Lesser Ulster lords like Donal Ballagh O'Cahan (whose story is considered in greater detail in Chapter 3, below) furthered political aims through selective use of the English legal system. In O'Cahan's case, he envisioned freedom from his O'Neill overlord by applying English concepts of property ownership. Similarly, the MacGiollapadraigs of Upper Ossory cultivated knowledge of the English language and customs to inform their own strategies for retaining control of their lands, whereas the O'Dwyers of Kilmanagh conformed to English law in a bid to maintain traditional holdings. By presenting a veneer of English acculturation, these Gaelic elites endeavored to deflect the English gaze. Elsewhere, the O'Sullivan Beare of the Beara Peninsula exploited fishing grounds with all the enthusiasm of a New World adventurer, landing himself occasionally in difficulties through his harsh treatment of English captains who did not play by his rules. Like the O'Neills of Ulster, the O'Sullivan Beare sept would find their power and long hegemony eroded through the implementation of plantation in the seventeenth century. Once again, the fragmented character of Irish lordship ensured a range of responses to the threat of English incursion—responses that were entirely consistent with the existing Gaelic and Old English political frameworks.[118]

Conclusion

Late medieval Irish society was far from uniform in its cultural practices, economic activities, and political allegiances. Gaelic and Old English elite engaged with the New English and the forces of Elizabethan expansion in divergent fashion, from full collaboration to outright violent resistance. The Highland Scots of the north of Ireland employed their multiple

---

118. See Chapter 3 for the O'Cahan case. For the MacGiollapadraigs, see David Edwards, "Collaboration without Anglicization: The MacGiollapadraig Lordship and Tudor Reform," in Duffy, Edwards, and FitzPatrick, eds., *Gaelic Ireland*, 77–97. For the O'Dwyers, see John Morrissey, "Contours of Colonialism: Gaelic Ireland and the Early Colonial Subject," *Irish Geography*, XXXVII (2004), 88–102. For the O'Sullivan Beare, see Colin Breen, *The Gaelic Lordship of the O'Sullivan Beare: A Landscape Cultural History* (Dublin, 2005), 117.

identities as a tool, contingent upon which allegiance was the more advantageous. Elizabethan adventurers like Essex and Lane approached Ireland armored with their prejudices and selfish motivations but seldom with any clear, proven plan for success. Violence was ever present and often the fallback position, more often than not visited upon the lower orders of Gaelic society: the churls (peasants) and the mobile woodkerne. Their stories are challenging to elicit from the documentary record, as they appear only as an undifferentiated mass under the appellation of "wild Irish." Understanding of their material lives is only beginning to emerge from the increasing recognition of late medieval domestic habitations and a more critical consideration of the nature and role of transhumance.

In considering the sixteenth-century English efforts to control Ireland through plantation, a distinction must also be made between the "top down" creation of a society as designed by plantation theorists like Thomas Smith and what actually happened. And what actually happened takes us closer to a critical understanding of relations between natives and newcomers beyond what the plantation theorists intended them to be. In spite of all the rhetoric and the construction of the Irish as other, Ireland was not a res nullius. Any practical plan for settlement would have to rely on the participation of the native population, a reality that intellectuals like Smith and military men like Essex and Lane refused to contemplate. Expediency and pragmatism would take precedence over ideology and over the desire for military conquest as plantation played out in the seventeenth century. With the exception of a brief, and to some degree unsuccessful, period in the late sixteenth and early seventeenth centuries, the postmedieval development of Ireland does not truly adhere to a colonial model as it would be understood in North America, Africa, or India. This development was an uncertain process riven with violence, insecurity, and incompletion. Although the portrait of sixteenth-century Ireland and its English conquerors remains unfinished, this reanalysis suggests that the influence of the New World on English activities in sixteenth-century Ireland was far greater than the reverse. With that in mind, it is time to turn to the New World.

CHAPTER TWO

❦ Across the Virginian Sea
Contact and Encounter

Introduction

Following the cessation of the sixteen-year-long Anglo-Spanish War and the concomitant end of armed conflict in Ireland in the wake of Hugh O'Neill's 1603 submission, England once again began focusing upon the territories of the New World. Spurred by the 1598 publication of the second edition of Hakluyt's *Principall Navigations, Voyages, Traffiques, and Discoveries of the English Nation,* numerous adventurers pledged to throw themselves with renewed vigor into exploration and colonization in North America. With the lessons of Raleigh's underfunded and unsuccessful attempts to found a colony at Roanoke Island at least partially learned, the newest venture to colonize Virginia was to rely upon the collective wealth of a group of investors. Petitioning the newly ascended James I (VI) in 1605, the newly formed Virginia Company of London received a charter the following year for the planting of a settlement in Virginia. A second division of the joint-stock company, based in Plymouth, was poised to colonize the northerly reaches of Virginia above the forty-first parallel. Backed by London capital, members of the company, predominantly merchants and gentlemen, set about planning their ventures. Little did they know that the king would soon demand their participation in his Ulster Plantation scheme, which would severely tax their finances and cripple their ability to support the Virginia colony.

Three ships set out from London in December 1606, arriving at the mouth of the Chesapeake Bay in April. A two-week expedition resulted in the choice of what became known as Jamestown Island—in reality, a peninsula at the time—as the location for the principal settlement. Although hindsight suggests that the low-lying, marshy island with its brackish water was not the best selection for a colonial outpost, at the time the island's appeal rested in the fact that it was seemingly uninhabited and possessed a deep harbor close to shore, to anchor and protect the English vessels from Spanish predation. The colonists' early hardships are well known and discussed in detail in Chapter 4, below. The most significant factor in Jamestown's perseverance was the character of relations between the settlers and the Native peoples, predominantly Algonquian-speaking members of the paramount Powhatan chiefdom. Significant quantities of Native-made materials have been unearthed from deposits associated with James Fort, underscoring the frequency and intensity of daily contacts. Considering that the struggling English outpost was literally surrounded by Native villages, as indicated by the density of settlements recorded on John Smith's map of Virginia, the conclusion to be drawn is that the Powhatan people permitted the English colony to survive for reasons related both to their own political entanglements and to their expectations of Europeans, founded upon nearly a century of encounter. Only once the complexity of the encounters between North American Natives and the English are appreciated can we begin to evaluate the subsequent impact upon English attitudes toward the Irish.

In the previous chapter, England's relationship with sixteenth-century Ireland served as the focus for a consideration of the character of Irish culture and the extent to which Gaelic Ireland did not conform to the portrayals penned by commentators such as Spenser, Moryson, and Rich. Archaeological evidence for the extent of Ireland's continental trade, for example, belies characterization of the land as wild and unfamiliar. Turning to the New World, we can put the descriptions penned by individuals like Thomas Hariot, John Smith, William Strachey, and George Percy about eastern North American Native societies to a similar test. English descriptions of Native New World peoples tell us as much about English notions of the "other" as they do about the lifeways of those they encountered.

Archaeological evidence pertaining to Algonquian lifeways provides not only a yardstick against which to measure the veracity of English descriptions but, crucially, also reveals the diversity of regional societies and the longevity of Native identities in the face of disruption, disease, and displacement. Traditional assumptions about Native capitulation in the form of a simplistic "fatal impact" narrative are simply not supported by evidence from the Americas. Native societies persevered through a diverse array of strategies to manage their intercultural dealings in the early years of colonial exploration and settlement, which informed a range of coping mechanisms during the centuries of Euro-American domination. Furthermore, as was the case in Ireland, the interplay between incoming settlers and Native peoples shaped the colonial societies that emerged in the seventeenth century. No one was unchanged by the experience.[1]

It would be wholly inaccurate and inappropriate to downplay the myriad negative impacts of the colonial encounter on Native societies, from the violence of initial encounter to the centuries of sociopolitical domination and persecution. To do so would be to undermine the significance of the persistence of Native identities in the present. However, considering the agency of indigenous peoples is the first step toward acknowledging not only the complexity of responses to so-called contact encounters but also, more critically, recognizing that the unequal power relations that defined later Euro American–indigenous relations were by no means guaranteed in the early years of exploration and settlement.

Even where Native societies did succumb to the negative impacts of European expansion and settlement, as with the nineteenth-century loss of the Newfoundland Beothuks, it is clear that Native peoples engaged in a range of intentional and self-aware strategies to preserve and protect their integrity. The Beothuks themselves coped with the increasing presence of European fishing fleets in the sixteenth century and the establishment of colonial settlements in the seventeenth century through avoidance coupled with lim-

---

1. When scholars of early modern Ireland make reference to New World parallels for British expansion into the island, their arguments generally do not take into account the complexity and diversity of Native New World experiences. Instead, the varied responses of the Irish population to the imposition of English authority is situated as nuanced and not straightforward by comparison with what is presumed to be the ready capitulation of the North American Native, overwhelmed by the traditional forces of military might, technology, and, of course, devastating epidemic diseases. William J. Smyth explores the connections between the settlement of Ireland and North America in his 2006 examination of the role of cartography in early modern Ireland. He argues for numerous parallels in strategy and ideology but contrasts the process and outcomes, concluding, "The American experience was, in short, a more straightforward dialogue between a new society and a strange environment; there were fewer existing local and regional institutions to filter and reshape the process of adjustment" (Smyth, *Map-Making, Landscapes, and Memory: A Geography of Colonial and Early Modern Ireland, c. 1530–1750* [Notre Dame, Ind., 2006], 437). Although Smyth rightly highlights the complexity of the Irish landscape with its urban settlements as well as "wild" regions, his description of North America is predicated upon the assumption that "the overall impact of the Indian cultures on the emerging American societies and landscapes was rather slight, since their populations were decimated by epidemic diseases, demoralization, and war. In the rediscovery and resettlement on the eastern seaboard, the English colonist, inadvertently in part, had created a depopulated wasteland, ready for a new forging, a new imprint" (ibid.). His belief that Native American societies were readily conquered and destroyed echoes Jonathan Bardon: "Unlike native Americans, who were all but wiped out by disease and slaughter, the Ulster Irish survived" (Bardon, *A History of Ulster* [Belfast, 1992], 115–116). The use of the phrase "depopulated wasteland" is no more appropriate for North America than it was for the Ards Peninsula in the early seventeenth century.

ited and regulated engagement. Some Beothuks shifted their settlements from the outer coast to the sheltered bays and coves, as well as further inland, to reduce contact and thus conflict. This strategy of avoidance was qualified. The Beothuks selectively incorporated European goods, particularly metal-work, into their material repertoire. In 1612, Englishmen Henry Crout, who was serving as agent on behalf of the governor of the London and Bristol Company for the plantation of Newfoundland, noted the presence of cop-per kettles and a variety of European fishing implements. Whereas some items were acquired via direct trade, many were taken from the summer fishing stations when their occupants departed for the winter. This Native exploitation of European goods had a negative impact on the sustainability of the fishing stations, contributing to the establishment of more perma-nent fishing settlements and illustrating the significant influence of Native decision-making on European activities even when avoiding direct contact. That the Beothuks and many other Native groups elected to incorporate new materials into their own worlds should similarly not be understood as the first domino falling in an inexorable tumble to acculturation. Cultural meanings may be encoded in objects, but those meanings change according to context. Ownership of a previously unfamiliar object does not change one's identity. To assume that European contact and the introduction of the unfamiliar somehow made Native people less themselves is to assume that Native cultures were entirely static before their encounters with "dynamic" European societies. Recognizing that all cultures are dynamic highlights the intricacies of colonial entanglements and contradicts the idea that "contact" was a momentous watershed with only one possible outcome.[2]

English colonists and the indigenous inhabitants of eastern North America clearly engaged in complicated negotiations and accommodations structured by culturally rooted practices, understandings, and experiences and ranging from avoidance to targeted engagement. In the Chesapeake region, for much of the seventeenth century, English territory and under-standings of the landscape were shaped by the extent of the contact-period

2. William Gilbert, "'. . . Great Good Done': Beothuk-European Relations in Trinity Bay, 1612 to 1622," *Newfoundland Quarterly,* LXXXVI, no. 3 (Summer–Fall 1992), 8; Donald H. Holly Jr., "Social Aspects and Implications of 'Running to the Hills': The Case of the Beo-thuk Indians of Newfoundland," *Journal of Island and Coastal Archaeology,* III (2008), 170–190; Holly Jr., "The Beothuk on the Eve of Their Extinction," *Arctic Anthropology,* XXXVII, no. 1 (2000), 79–95; Laurie McLean, "Beothuk Iron — Evidence for European trade?" *Newfoundland Studies,* VI (1990), 168–176; Peter Pope, "Scavengers and Caretakers: Beothuk / European Settle-ment Dynamics in Seventeenth-Century Newfoundland," ibid., IX (1993), 279–293; Pope, *Fish into Wine: The Newfoundland Plantation in the Seventeenth Century* (Chapel Hill, N.C., 2004), 73.

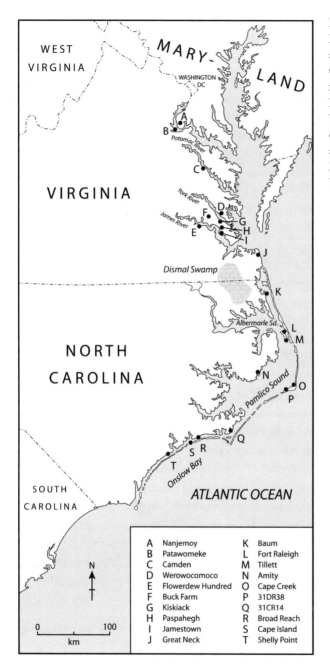

Figure 4. Location of sites discussed in Chapter 2. Produced for the author by Debbie Miles-Williams, University of Leicester, and Elizabeth Mulqueeny, Queen's University, Belfast

WEST VIRGINIA

MARY-LAND

WASHINGTON DC

VIRGINIA

Potomac River

York River

James River

Dismal Swamp

Albermarle Sd.

NORTH CAROLINA

Pamlico Sound

Onslow Bay

SOUTH CAROLINA

ATLANTIC OCEAN

N

0   100
km

A	Nanjemoy	K	Baum
B	Patawomeke	L	Fort Raleigh
C	Camden	M	Tillett
D	Werowocomoco	N	Amity
E	Flowerdew Hundred	O	Cape Creek
F	Buck Farm	P	31DR38
G	Kiskiack	Q	31CR14
H	Paspahegh	R	Broad Reach
I	Jamestown	S	Cape Island
J	Great Neck	T	Shelly Point

Powhatan sphere of influence. The view of colonial North America as a de-populated tabula rasa, a land far more malleable than fractious Ireland, is rooted in sixteenth-century colonial rhetoric but does not reflect reality.

An important difference between the ways in which the English viewed the New World and Ireland can be seen in the types of documents that con-temporary observers generated. Ralph Hamor, George Percy, John Smith, Henry Spelman, and others extensively chronicled their encounters with Native peoples. These individuals were aware, as they described the cus-toms and habits of the Indians, that their observations were of considerable interest to English scholars. By contrast, the planters who accepted land grants in Ireland did not feel the need to describe the familiar characteris-tics and lifeways of the Irish in any comparable fashion. Instead, the docu-mentary record of the Irish plantations concentrates on the progress (or lack thereof) of the projects themselves. Another difficulty in pursuing in-depth comparisons between Ireland and the Chesapeake lies in the differen-tial nature of archaeological research in both locales. More than forty years of continuous archaeological and historical investigation of colonial sites in the Chesapeake region have provided a wealth of information about daily life for settlers at nearly all levels of society, even as the interpretations of this material have considerably downplayed Native contributions. This vast corpus of scholarship stands in sharp contrast to the dearth of concentrated examinations of non-urban plantation-period sites in Ireland. One of the particular challenges for addressing the character of Native life in the Chesa-peake as well as Albemarle regions rests in the dominance of scholarship on the Powhatan Indians of the Virginia Coastal Plain. Considerations of other Algonquian-speaking peoples in the region, and particularly in eastern North Carolina, are often elided with understandings of the Powhatans in ways that obscure rather than illuminate. Yet it was knowledge of the Roa-noke encounters that spread through the coastal Native worlds, informed later expectations on the part of Jamestown's colonists, and arguably also informed English attitudes to plantation in Ireland following the failure of the Roanoke venture.[3]

3. The historiography of the Powhatan chiefdom itself is as rich, varied, and often contra-dictory as are the early reports of Virginia Native society, and debate about the exact nature of Powhatan sociopolitical structure promises to be healthy and unresolved for a long time to come. Such is not the case for the societies first encountered by Raleigh's adventurers in the 1580s. Archaeological evidence from the region seldom figures in historical examinations of the relations between Natives and the Roanoke adventurers, because much of the data from exca-vations on protohistoric Native sites remains unpublished. See, for example, Lewis Binford, "Archaeological and Ethnohistorical Investigation of Cultural Diversity and Progressive Devel-

European and Native Contacts before Roanoke and Jamestown

Direct contact between Europeans and the Indians in the Chesapeake region is usually traced to the mid-sixteenth century, when a Spanish Jesuit mission was established on the York River between 1570 and 1572. However, Spanish, English, French, and Portuguese vessels began extensively plying the waters of the Atlantic and the eastern coast of North America from the late fifteenth century, precipitating the first contacts between Europeans and Natives in the Chesapeake and wider region.[4] Although the Bristol-based Zuan Caboto, or John Cabot, originally set his sights on the legendary island of Hy-Brasil, it was likely Newfoundland that he encountered on a 1497 voyage, precipitating the development of its lucrative fishery.[5] His son Sebastian came much closer to the Chesapeake, as he

---

opment among Aboriginal Cultures of Coastal Virginia and North Carolina" (Ph.D. diss., University of Michigan, Ann Arbor, 1964); Helen C. Rountree, *The Powhatan Indians of Virginia: Their Traditional Culture* (Norman, Okla., 1989); Rountree, *Pocahontas's People: The Powhatan Indians of Virginia through Four Centuries* (Norman Okla., 1990); Karen Ordahl Kupperman, *Indians and English: Facing off in Early America* (Ithaca, N.Y., 2000); Martin D. Gallivan, *James River Chiefdoms: The Rise of Social Inequality in the Chesapeake* (Lincoln, Neb., 2003); Margaret Holmes Williamson, *Powhatan Lords of Life and Death: Command and Consent in Seventeenth-Century Virginia* (Lincoln, Neb., 2003); Linwood "Little Bear" Custalow and Angela L. Daniel "Silver Star," *The True Story of Pocahontas: The Other Side of History* (Golden, Colo., 2007). Even the study by Michael Leroy Oberg, who overtly set out to "tell the story of the Roanoke ventures from the perspective of the Indians who confronted and attempted to make sense of Sir Walter's colonists," relies overwhelmingly upon historical literature and frankly acknowledged speculation. See Oberg, *The Head in Edward Nugent's Hand: Roanoke's Forgotten Indians* (Philadelphia, 2008), xiii. Historians Kupperman *(Indians and English)* and Oberg have focused their attention upon the nature of Algonquian society in the Roanoke region, as has the ethnohistorian Christian F. Feest. See Feest, "John White's New World," in Kim Sloan, ed., *A New World: England's First View of America* (London, 2007), 65–78. However, these scholars have not incorporated archaeological data into their discussions, primarily because much of the work that has been carried out in the region is not widely published. See extended discussion in Audrey Horning, "Past, Present, and Future: Exploring and Restoring Native perspectives on Roanoke and the Chesapeake," in Kim Sloan, ed., *European Visions, American Voices,* British Museum Research Publication no. 172 (London, 2009), 131–142.

4. David Beers Quinn, *England and the Discovery of America, 1481–1620: From the Bristol Voyages of the Fifteenth Century to the Pilgrim Settlement at Plymouth* . . . (New York, 1974); Frederic W. Gleach, *Powhatan's World and Colonial Virginia: A Conflict of Cultures* (Lincoln, Neb., 1997). Note that the French and the Portuguese had engaged in cod fishing off Newfoundland since at least the first decade of the sixteenth century. See Laurier Turgeon, "Codfish, Consumption, and Colonization: The Creation of the French Atlantic World during the Sixteenth Century," in Caroline A. Williams, ed., *Bridging the Early Modern Atlantic World: People, Products, and Practices on the Move* (Farnham, Surrey, 2009), 35–36.

5. Hy-Brasil is enshrined in Irish medieval folklore; see discussion of it and Cabot's voyages in John L. Allen, "From Cabot to Cartier: The Early Exploration of Eastern North America, 1497–1543," *Annals of the Association of American Geographers,* LXXXII, no. 3 (September 1992),

reportedly traversed the Atlantic coast from Newfoundland to Florida in 1508–1509. Despite the younger Cabot's journey, English mariners would remain more focused on the northerly waters of the Atlantic, whereas the Spanish remained focused upon their gold- and silver-bearing territories from the Caribbean southward.

In the 1520s, the voyages of the Florentine Giovanni da Verrazzano on behalf of the French crown brought sailors to the Carolina coast, even if Verrazzano made no report of the existence of the Chesapeake Bay. Verrazzano and his crew did encounter Native people, whom Verrazzano generally described in a favorable light when writing to Francis I. Despite Verrazzano's positive impression of the southeastern coast of North America, subsequent French voyages of discovery, such as under Jacques Cartier in the 1530s and 1540s, would focus upon penetrating the interior of the continent in what is now Canada, New England, and the Great Lakes region. There, contacts between Europeans and Natives centered on a nascent trade in furs, principally mediated by the Saint Lawrence Iroquois until the end of the sixteenth century. Relations were conditional, with the impact of the early fur trade uneven and, for some Native groups, inconsequential. Not all indigenous societies within the French and later British colonial sphere of interest participated in the fur trade. Even well into the nineteenth century, long after the emergence of the Hudson's Bay Company and the intensification of fur production and marketing, the Ojibwa of southern Ontario continued to hunt fur-bearing animals such as beaver, muskrat, and raccoon only in the quantities required to satisfy tribal needs. Archaeological evidence from that region does not support the wholesale transformation of Native hunting practices to service the European desire for pelts. Instead, Native groups chose their own degree of participation.[6]

For nearly the first three-quarters of the sixteenth century, Chesapeake

---

502–503. For the development of the fishery, see again Turgeon, "Codfish," in Williams, ed., *Bridging the Early Modern Atlantic World*, esp. 35–38.

6. David B. Quinn, *New American World: A Documentary History of North America to 1612*, I, *America from Concept to Discovery: Early Exploration of North America* (New York, 1979), 282; Allen, "From Cabot to Cartier," *Annals of the Association of American Geographers*, LXXXII, no. 3 (September 1992), 514. For discussion of the sixteenth-century fur trade, see Laurier Turgeon, "French Fishers, Fur Traders, and Amerindians during the Sixteenth Century: History and Archaeology," *William and Mary Quarterly*, 3d Ser., LV (1998), 585–610; and Turgeon, "The Tale of the Kettle: Odyssey of an Intercultural Object," *Ethnohistory*, XLIV (1997), 1–29. For the Ojibwas, see Neal Ferris, *The Archaeology of Native-Lived Colonialism: Challenging History in the Great Lakes* (Tucson, Ariz., 2009), 44–45.

and coastal Carolina Native peoples remained on the peripheries of intensive European activity to the north and to the south, generally ignored by the fur traders, fishers, privateers, and explorers. That their territories remained relatively unthreatened does not mean that they were unaware of European activities. In 1546, a French ship sailed into the Chesapeake Bay and reported being met by more than thirty canoes. During this encounter, the Chesapeake Natives apparently traded more than one thousand hides to the French in exchange for goods such as metal tools and cloth. Knowledge of the far-flung French fur trade had evidently already reached the Chesapeake. Although it is unlikely that hunting practices were altered to accommodate this uncertain trade mechanism, occasional fur exchange with Europeans widened the range of trade opportunities to be accommodated within traditional hunting and exchange practices and might have facilitated a desire for selected European goods that were absorbed into the Natives' material repertoire. By the time the first Roanoke colonists stepped ashore in the Outer Banks, and certainly by the time the *Godspeed, Discovery,* and *Susan Constant* discharged their passengers and crew on Jamestown Island in May 1607, Native peoples up and down the east coast of North America had amassed a considerable amount of knowledge about Europeans, certainly in comparison to what the English colonists knew about them. The importance of England's lack of familiarity with North American societies—particularly in contrast with its millennia of connections with Ireland and its people—cannot be overstated.[7]

Half a century before the English attempted to settle the Outer Banks, coastal Algonquian people felt the effects of Spanish colonization precipitated by the 1513 landing of Juan Ponce de León on the coast of Florida. De León's venture was followed by a series of violent incursions and settlement efforts, including that of Lucas Vásquez de Ayllón in 1526 at Sapelo Sound (present-day Georgia), where he and 350 of 600 settlers died within a two-month period. Linguistic analysis of the testimony of Francisco de Chicora relating to the Ayllón colonization venture strongly suggests that the Spanish explored as far north as Pamlico Sound (present-day North Carolina), encountering the Algonquian-speaking groups who would later engage with the Roanoke adventurers. The presence of Algonquian-derived

7. Quinn, *England and the Discovery of America,* 190; Clifford M. Lewis and Albert J. Loomie, *The Spanish Jesuit Mission in Virginia, 1570–1572* (Chapel Hill, N.C., 1953), 13; Stephen R. Potter, *Commoners, Tributes, and Chiefs: The Development of Algonquian Culture in the Potomac Valley* (Charlottesville, Va., 1993), 161.

words such as *Quexaga* (from *kewasówak,* meaning "gods," as later recorded by Thomas Hariot) in the de Chicora testimony suggests intensive interaction between the Spanish and the Algonquian Natives.[8]

Whatever the extent of the relations between the Carolina Algonquians and the Spanish in the early 1520s, territory as far north as the Chesapeake Bay was known to the Spanish, underscored by its appearance (as Bahia de Santa Maria) on contemporary Spanish maps. The strategic importance of the Chesapeake Bay was certainly recognized by the time Pedro Menéndez de Avilés served as governor of Florida in the 1560s. The bay was then viewed as the northern boundary of Spanish La Florida and the presumed extent of its habitable territory; it was also thought to be situated not far from the Strait of Anián, the sea route to the Far East analogous to the Northwest Passage. Like the English, the Spanish were keen to locate and control access to this passage to the Pacific, which would require the cooperation of Native populations—willing or unwilling. To that end, Menéndez planned to establish forts along the Atlantic coast and into the Chesapeake Bay that would provide protection for the Caribbean treasure fleet and ward off any further French intrusions.[9]

Well before Menéndez arrived, the effects of Hernando de Soto's wellmanned expedition westward from 1539 to 1543 also extended as far north as the Chesapeake. Soto's explorations have been linked to major alterations in the social structure of a number of southeastern Indian polities, particularly through its biological impact on Native populations. This venture has even been referred to as a "biological wrecking ball," although this is not supported by known mortuary evidence in the form of the mass graves that might be expected from epidemics. In reality, the predominance of young men in the Spanish exploratory parties meant that they were less likely to be carriers of smallpox—generally associated with children—or other acute, infectious diseases. Furthermore, the Atlantic passage was sufficiently long enough for many contagious diseases to burn out. Disease-linked demographic collapse among Native groups in the Spanish colonial southeast was more a feature of the extended contact and local conditions of later mission

8. Blair A. Rudes, "The First Description of an Iroquoian People: Spaniards among the Tuscaroras before 1522," paper presented at the Testimony of Chicora Conference on Iroquois Research, Rensselaerville, New York, October 2002.

9. Gallivan, *James River Chiefdoms,* 161; Lewis and Loomie, *Spanish Jesuit Mission,* 7; Charlotte M. Gradie, "The Powhatans in the Context of the Spanish Empire," in Helen C. Rountree, ed., *Powhatan Foreign Relations, 1500–1722* (Charlottesville, Va., 1993), 155–157.

settlements rather than a pan-southeastern phenomenon attributable to the early years of European exploration.[10]

English accounts suggest that the Roanoke colonists spread influenza to the coastal Algonquians, resulting in depopulation and the disappearance of the Delmarva village of Mashawatoc. These European reports of Native mortality are not entirely convincing. Thomas Hariot's chronicles of Algonquian deaths in the Roanoke area served the purposes of the English, who were keen to downplay Native strength in order to attract financial support and settlers. Hariot's statement that the Indians "could not tel whether to thinke us gods or men" because of disease is more than a little self-serving, particularly considering the likelihood of prior contacts between the peoples of the Albemarle Sound and European explorers. Discussions of the impact of European diseases on the Native peoples of the Roanoke region need to take into account not only documentary sources but also data from archaeological sites, which are more likely to yield concrete evidence regarding demographic collapse (as reflected in bioarchaeological data) and widespread settlement abandonment or disruption.[11]

In neither the Albemarle nor the Chesapeake region is there compelling evidence for immediate or widespread deaths from communicable diseases. Mortuary studies of human remains from late Woodland and protohistoric

10. Rebecca Saunders, "Seasonality, Sedentism, Subsistence, and Disease in the Protohistoric: Archaeological versus Ethnohistoric Data along the Lower Atlantic Coast," in Cameron B. Wesson and Mark A. Rees, eds., *Between Contacts and Colonies: Archaeological Perspectives on the Protohistoric Southeast* (Tuscaloosa, Ala., 2002). See the work of historian Paul Kelton, who notes, "Early European encounters have been overrated in their ability to facilitate the spread of new germs" (Kelton, *Epidemics and Enslavement: Biological Catastrophe in the Native Southeast, 1492–1715* [Lincoln, Neb., 2007], 98). For an archaeological perspective that corroborates the lack of evidence for epidemics before intense colonization, see Celeste Marie Gagnon, "Stability in a Time of Change: Contact Period Health in the Lower Susquehanna Valley," *Archaeology of Eastern North America*, XXXII (2004), 101–121. For a perspective on the impact of European epidemic diseases in the Northeast, see Dean R. Snow and Kim M. Lanphear, "European Contact and Indian Depopulation in the Northeast: The Timing of the First Epidemics," *Ethnohistory*, XXXV (1988), 15–33. A continued willingness to uncritically accept the notion that European diseases rapidly decimated Native societies constitutes an a priori denial of Native contributions to postcontact American society as well as continuity in Native identities in eastern North America.

11. The depopulation and disappearance of Mashawatocs was recorded by the Roanoke adventurers, but not by John Smith, twenty-two years later. See Peter B. Mires, "Contact and Contagion: The Roanoke Colony and Influenza," *Historical Archaeology*, XXVIII, no. 3 (1994), 30–38; "February 1588: Thomas Hariot, *A Briefe and True Report*," in David Beers Quinn, ed., *The Roanoke Voyages, 1584–1590: Documents to Illustrate the English Voyages to North America under the Patent Granted to Walter Raleigh in 1584* (London, 1955), I, 379.

Native burials in Maryland and also North Carolina speak to Native health. Fractured bones were a frequent occurrence, and syphilis (the nonvenereal, childhood strain known as *endemic syphilis,* or *bejel*) was common. For the Chesapeake area specifically, the first documented case of smallpox dates to 1667, well after the first encounters between European and Native peoples in the region and thirty-four years after a smallpox epidemic in the Northeast. Furthermore, the most devastating illness found in the colonial Chesapeake was, not smallpox, but a strain of malaria introduced from Africa. No archaeological evidence for sixteenth-century mass mortality has been identified anywhere within the Roanoke and Chesapeake regions. Archaeological and documentary evidence of the seventeenth century supports the shifting of Native settlements in the Powhatan heartland, clearly attributable to disruption caused by English encroachment. In the Roanoke region, continuity in Native settlement patterns remained the norm well into the eighteenth century. The Chesapeake and Albemarle regions were not rapidly depopulated and were no more readily transformable into an English colonial society than was Ireland, with its settled population and existent sociopolitical structures.[12]

Before the colonization efforts of the English at Roanoke, the French had also explored and attempted to settle along the east coast, establishing a brief foothold on Parris Island, South Carolina, under Jean Ribault in 1562. News of this endeavor is likely to have been disseminated through coastal Native communication channels. Ribault's colony was abandoned within a year, although it was to have been resupplied in a joint venture between the French and the English. Queen Elizabeth charged the adventurer Sir Thomas Stukeley with leading a fleet to rescue the French Protestant colonists as a means of establishing an English foothold in the Florida territory, but instead, Stukeley took the ships (which had been prepared for

12. Elizabeth I. Monahan, "Bioarchaeological Analysis of the Mortuary Practices at the Broad Reach Site (31CR218), Coastal North Carolina," *Southern Indian Studies,* XLIV (1995), 37–69; Dennis C. Curry, *Feast of the Dead: Aboriginal Ossuaries in Maryland* (Crownsville, Md., 1999), 60. Some of these conclusions can only be regarded as tentative, however, as the majority of these human remains have not been subjected to rigorous forensic analysis, and many were poorly excavated in the first place; see Douglas H. Ubelaker and Philip D. Curtin, "Human Biology of Populations in the Chesapeake Watershed," in Curtin, Grace S. Brush, and George W. Fisher, eds., *Discovering the Chesapeake: The History of an Ecosystem* (Baltimore, 2001), 127–148. For discussion of smallpox in the Northeast, see Snow and Lanphear, "European Contact and Indian Depopulation," *Ethnohistory,* XXXV (1988), 15–33. The New World demographics contradict Smyth's arguments in *Map-Making, Landscapes, and Memory,* 437, regarding rapid demographic collapse and the presumed ease with which the English were able to take over Native lands.

their voyage in the Old English port of Waterford, on the southeastern coast of Ireland) on a privateering mission. Stukeley inadvertently did rescue the colonists: he seized a twenty-ton ship that had been cobbled together by Parris Island survivors, who had reportedly been forced into cannibalism before abandoning their fort. The sailors claimed to have rigged their makeshift ship with Indian-made rope. This seemingly insignificant detail actually raises core questions about relations between the French settlers and the local Native inhabitants. Between 1,000 and 2,800 meters of rope would have been needed to rig a twenty-ton, sixteenth-century sailing craft. Such lengths of rope are unlikely to have been readily available in Native storehouses; instead, the Natives would have fashioned cordage for house construction or for fishing gear. The production of the rigging rope implies sustained and reasonably stable relations between the French and the Native ropemakers, who would have had to source the raw materials, prepare them for use, and then fabricate the rope itself. Exactly what the French provided in return was not recorded. Perhaps their departure was reward enough.[13]

In the aftermath of his privateering venture, Stukeley failed to reingratiate himself with an annoyed Queen Elizabeth, duplicitously courting her enemy Shane O'Neill in Ireland and allegedly treating with the Spanish. Stukeley was soon imprisoned in Dublin under the charge of corresponding with Spain's Philip II. Following his release from prison, and perhaps out of spite at his treatment by Elizabeth, Stukeley headed to Spain, where he set about fomenting support for an invasion of Ireland in expectation of substantial personal reward. In the estimation of Lord Justice Fitzwilliam, Stukeley could also expect commendation from the pope, who "cannot for honour's sake but reward Stukeley." Fitzwilliam feared Stukeley's influence in Ireland, noting, "In Waterford they think him holy by reason of his so often going barefoot and barelegged up and down their streets and churches in the same Lent in which he built and furnished his bark and went away with it." Memories of Stukeley's deceit were fresh in the mind of Sir Thomas Smith when he set about establishing his colony on the Ards Peninsula of Ulster in 1572–1573. In considering his son's intended role in the Irish colony, the elder Smith wrote, "I had rather he should adventure his life than that we both should be accounted deceivers of men and enterprisers of

13. Karen Ordahl Kupperman, *The Jamestown Project* (Cambridge, Mass., 2007), 45–47. Rigging estimate based upon comparison with the pinnace *Discovery* and discussion with maritime archaeologists Kathryn Sikes and Grace Turner and curators Hazel Forsythe (Museum of the Docklands, London) and Thomas Davidson and Eric Speth (Jamestown Settlement Museum, Virginia).

Stewelie's voyage of Terra Florida, or a lottery, as some evil tongues did term it." Smith was well aware of the opprobrium directed toward Stukeley in presenting his own project as morally superior; he also tacitly acknowledged the role of New World colonial efforts in shaping his ideas for Ireland.[14]

Following Stukeley's rescue of the French colonists, the Spanish, led by Pedro Menéndez de Avilés, supplanted the French on Parris Island by establishing the somewhat more successful settlement of Santa Elena in 1566. Excavations at Santa Elena yielded material evidence for extensive contact between Native Carolinians and Spanish settlers. Ceramic assemblages contained equivalent amounts of locally produced Native wares and imported Spanish wares, possibly reflecting the Spanish tendency of taking Native wives, one of the significant differences between Spanish and British colonial practices. A similar pattern has been noted in the Spanish settlement of Saint Augustine, where household kitchen assemblages are dominated by Native cooking wares, indicative of the Native cultural impact on Spanish colonial society, transmitted by Native women through their influence within the home. Whereas this cross-cultural mixing strengthened the Saint Augustine community, it evidently had the opposite effect at Santa Elena. There, the Spanish abandoned their settlement at Parris Island in response to the strength and aggression of Native people. European diseases did not play a significant role in subduing Native societies in the Parris Island area, given the locals' success in evicting the Spanish.[15]

With the exception of the Guale and Mocama peoples of northern Florida,

14. John Izon, *Stucley c. 1525–1578: Traitor Extraordinary* (London, 1956); William Fitzwilliam to Lord Burghley, May 24, 1571, State Paper Office, State Papers Ireland, Elizabeth I to George III, SP 63/32, no. 44, National Archives, Kew; Sir Thomas Smith to Fitzwilliam, Apr. 27, 1573, Carte MSS 56, f. 57, Bodleian Library, University of Oxford; see also discussion in David Beers . Quinn, *The Elizabethans and the Irish* (Ithaca, N.Y., 1966), 109; Quinn, "Sir Thomas Smith (1513–1577) and the Beginnings of English Colonial Theory," *Proceedings of the American Philosophical Society,* LXXXIX (1945), 543–560.

15. According to the excavator Stanley South, "In the town of Santa Elena there was as much locally-made ware as Spanish pottery" (South, *Archaeology at Santa Elena: Doorway to the Past* [Columbia, S.C., 1991], 77); see also South, Russell K. Skowronek, and Richard E. Johnson, *Spanish Artifacts from Santa Elena,* Anthropological Studies, no. 7 (Columbia, S.C., 1988); and Michael Gannon, "The New Alliance of History and Archaeology in the Eastern Spanish Borderlands," *WMQ,* 3d Ser., XLIX (1992), 327. For Saint Augustine, see Kathleen Deagan, "Colonial Origins and Colonial Transformations in Spanish America," *Historical Archaeology,* XXXVII, no. 4 (2003), 3–13. Kelton, *Epidemics and Enslavement,* 77, notes that the Spanish on Parris Island "received little help from diseases in reaching their imperialistic goals. At most a combination of typhus, malaria, and common waterborne illnesses made indigenous people sick, but not to the extent that they became receptive to Catholicism and willing to submit to Spanish rule."

who were incorporated into Saint Augustine through Jesuit mission activities, most southeast coastal societies maintained their autonomy from European colonizers well into the seventeenth century, and some well beyond. At the same time, existing Native communication and trade routes ensured that information and material culture traveled readily between worlds, facilitated by the missionized groups as well as direct Native-Spanish contacts. One of the more compelling stories of direct Spanish–Virginia Indian contact is the extraordinary experience of Don Luís de Velasco, a young Native man, also known as Paqaquineo, who was captured by a Spanish ship in the Chesapeake Bay in 1561. Identified in Spanish sources as a *cacique,* or Native chief, Paqaquineo was taken first to Mexico, then educated at the court of Philip II in Spain, and then transferred to Havana. In 1566, Menéndez charged Paqaquineo with guiding an expedition of two Dominican friars and thirty-seven Spanish soldiers from Mexico City northward to the Chesapeake Bay. Part of Menéndez's scheme to control the coast and locate the Strait of Anián, this venture was intended to result in the establishment of a mission and the placing of a formal Spanish claim to the territory of the Chesapeake Bay. The expedition dependend upon Paqaquineo. When he claimed not to recognize any of the coastline encountered by the voyagers, and when fierce weather threatened, the expedition was abandoned.[16]

In 1570, Paqaquineo helped engineer an effort to establish a Jesuit mission on the York River. This time, he had no difficulty in leading the Spanish voyage back to his homeland—perhaps because no soldiers accompanied him. The adventurers were reportedly astonished at the conditions they found upon returning to Virginia:

> We find the land of Don Luís in quite another condition than expected, not because he was at fault in his description of it, but because Our Lord has chastised it with six years of famine and death, which has brought it about that there is much less population than usual. Since many have died and many also have moved to other regions to ease their hunger, there remain but few of the tribe and, whose leaders say that they wish to die where their fathers have died, although they have no maize, and have not

16. Victor D. Thompson and John E. Worth, "Dwellers by the Sea: Native American Adaptations along the Southern Coasts of Eastern North America," *Journal of Archaeological Research,* XIX (2011), 51–101, esp. 80–82; Lewis and Loomie, *Spanish Jesuit Mission;* and see Williamson, *Powhatan Lords of Life and Death,* 70, 83, 143–144, for discussion of Paqaquineo's status as a werowance. Note, however, that Gradie, "Powhatans in the Context of the Spanish Empire," in Rountree, ed., *Powhatan Foreign Relations,* describes him as the son of a chief rather than as a chief himself (65).

found wild fruit, which they are accustomed to eat. Neither roots nor anything else can be had, save for a small amount obtained with great labor from the soil, which is very parched.

The dismal condition of the Natives has been attributed to the presumed widespread (if unquantified) impact of European disease but was more likely the result of a protracted drought, revealed through dendrochronological analysis of bald cypress in the Chesapeake and Dismal Swamp regions. Rainfall during the growing seasons in the period of 1562 to 1571 was considerably below average. This period of drought would have had a significant impact upon yearly food production and would also have increased the salinity of the rivers, affecting the availability of riverine food resources.[17]

Shortly after his arrival in Virginia, Paqaquineo returned to his kinspeople, possibly the Paspaheghs or the Kiskiacks, and later led an attack upon the mission. Although the Spanish sent a force against the Indians, killing at least twenty individuals, the mission was abandoned. Only Paqaquineo and a Spanish boy named Alonso survived from the original group, with Alonso living among the Indians for another year and a half. Although Paqaquineo might have always intended to destroy the mission and return to his people, a more compelling explanation for the Indian attack points to European violations of Native gift exchange practices. The Spanish neglected to reciprocate the food supplies and assistance gifted by the Indians, then, adding insult to injury, traded desirable iron tools to a rival tribal group. Such actions conveyed a lack of respect for Paqaquineo's people; such humiliation was unlikely to have been tolerated. Coupled with this loss of cultural understanding between the two groups, Paqaquineo's reaction to returning home must be taken into account. No matter how transformative his experience with the Spanish must have been, confronting former friends, family, social structures, and a once–intimately known environment must have been destabilizing. Engaging anew with what had been the everyday would have struck to the core of the young man's identity. Paqaquineo was likely susceptible to the counsel of Native elders who had taught him in his youth. At the same time, his local standing was enhanced by his knowledge of people and worlds far beyond the Chesapeake.[18]

17. Luis de Quirós and Juan Baptista Segura to Juan de Hinistrosa, Sept. 12, 1570, in Lewis and Loomie, *Spanish Jesuit Mission,* 89; Gleach, *Powhatan's World,* 91; Dennis B. Blanton, "Drought as a Factor in the Jamestown Colony, 1607–1612," *Historical Archaeology,* XXXIV (2000), 74–81; David W. Stahle et al., "The Lost Colony and Jamestown Droughts," *Science,* CCLXXX, no. 5363 (Apr. 24, 1998), 564–567.

18. Helen C. Rountree and E. Randolph Turner III, *Before and after Jamestown: Virginia's*

The identity of Paqaquineo has long intrigued scholars, particularly the suggestion that he was Opechancanough, brother to the paramount chief Powhatan, or Wahunsenacawh. Opechancanough is remembered in English sources principally for his leadership during what has been labeled the third, and final, Anglo-Powhatan War of the 1640s. The suggestion that Opechancanough was Paqaquineo is based upon the writings of Robert Beverley in the early eighteenth century and not upon any clear contemporary sources. He would have to have been extremely long-lived: described as a teenager in 1561, Paqaquineo would have been in his twenties in 1570, when the mission was established on the York River. Assuming the Spanish descriptions to be accurate, Paqaquineo must have been born no later than 1548, and quite likely earlier, given that he was already recognized as a werowance in 1561. Opechancanough led a last uprising in 1644 against the English, who assassinated him in 1645. It is unlikely that he led his people into revolt while in his late nineties.[19]

Notwithstanding Paqaquineo's identity within the Powhatan hierarchy, he played a significant role in brokering relations between the Powhatans and Europeans. His personal observation of Spanish treatment of Caribbean and Mexican Native peoples, although not likely to have fostered any pan-Indian sense of unity, would nevertheless have ensured understanding of the capacity for violence inherent to Spanish colonial society. Similarly,

---

Powhatans and Their Predecessors (Gainesville, Fla., 2002); Gradie, "Powhatans in the Context of the Spanish Empire," in Rountree, ed., Powhatan Foreign Relations, 155–157; Seth W. Mallios, "Exchange and Violence at Ajacan, Roanoke, and Jamestown," in Dennis B. Blanton and Julia A. King, Indian and European Contact in Context (Gainesville, Fla., 2004), 126–148, esp. 138–140; Mallios, "Gift Exchange and the Ossomocomuck Balance of Power: Explaining Carolina Algonquian Socioeconomic Aberrations at Contact," in E. Thomson Shields Jr. and Charles R. Ewen, eds., Searching for the Roanoke Colonies: An Interdisciplinary Collection (Raleigh, N.C., 2003), 142–158; Mallios, The Deadly Politics of Giving: Exchange and Violence at Ajacan, Roanoke, and Jamestown (Tuscaloosa, Ala., 2006). Pierre Bourdieu's concept of habitus is useful for framing an understanding of the overwhelming impact that returning to the Chesapeake and to his family must have had upon Paqaquineo; see Outline of a Theory of Practice, trans. Richard Nice, Cambridge Studies in Social and Cultural Anthropology (Cambridge, 1977).

19. James Horn is among scholars who have revived the notion that the two were one and the same; see Horn, A Land as God Made It: Jamestown and the Birth of America (New York, 2005), 15. Helen C. Rountree argues that Paqaquineo was born between 1540 and 1550 and further asserts that he came from a different family than Opechancanough, as Paqaquineo was a Paspahegh, whereas Opechancanough was affiliated with one of six polities: Pamunkey, Youghtanund, Mattaponi, Powhatan, Arrohateck, and Appomatuck (Rountree, Pocahontas, Powhatan, Opechancanough: Three Indian Lives Changed by Jamestown [Charlottesville, Va., 2005], 27–28). Rountree defines the term werowance (or weroance) as that of a subchief in Powhatan Indians of Virginia, 16, noting as well that the Algonquian term translates as "commander."

his firsthand experience of Spanish military tactics, ceremony, and symbols of political and religious hierarchy, derived from his time in Madrid, would prove very useful for the Powhatans in their later relations with the English. The Powhatans were no strangers to hierarchy in their own complex chiefdom, so evidence for similar differentiation among Europeans was readily comprehensible. Such knowledge and its attendant insecurities undoubtedly penetrated well inland from the Chesapeake Bay.[20]

The 1570–1572 Jesuit mission that brought Paqaquineo back to eastern Virginia, although yet to be archaeologically pinpointed, lies within the territory that formed the settlement core of the Kiskiack people, members of the Powhatan chiefdom, at the time of the 1607 Jamestown settlement. The mission was short-lived, but it must have had far-reaching impact in terms of direct contact between Natives and the missionaries and the rapid spread of stories and material culture throughout the Chesapeake region. Nueva Cádiz drawn-glass beads recovered from seventeenth-century contexts in Virginia, including Jamestown and the village of Paspahegh at the confluence of the Chickahominy and James Rivers, may represent material originating from the mission or other Spanish ventures into the Chesapeake. Nueva Cádiz beads are traditionally associated with Spanish exploration and settlement in the sixteenth century, although that does not preclude the recognition by other European explorers of their potential value in constructing relations with Native peoples. A hint of the possible complexity of material exchanges between Spanish and Algonquian people is presented by the incorporation of peach pits in a late Woodland–period ossuary at Sinepuxent Bay, Maryland; peach trees are not native to North America.[21]

<hr />

20. For consideration of Paqaquineo as cultural mediator, see Gallivan, *James River Chiefdoms,* 162.

21. The location of the former mission is likely either in the vicinity of King and Queen's Creek, on lands that are part of the U. S. Naval Supply Center at Cheatham Annex (near Williamsburg) or in the adjacent area now encompassed by the federal installation of Camp Peary. See Lewis and Loomie, *Spanish Jesuit Mission,* 26–54; Charlotte M. Gradie, "Spanish Jesuits in Virginia: The Mission That Failed," *Virginia Magazine of History and Biography,* XCVI (1988), 131–156; Gradie, "Powhatans in the Context of the Spanish Empire," in Rountree, ed., *Powhatan Foreign Relations,* 165–172; Nicholas Luccketti and Beverly Straube, *1997 Interim Report on the APVA Excavations at Jamestown, Virginia* (Richmond, Va., 1998); Heather A. Lapham, "More Than 'A Few Blue Beads': The Glass and Stone Beads from Jamestown Rediscovery's 1994–1997 Excavations," *Journal of the Jamestown Rediscovery Center,* I (2001), http://www .preservationvirginia.org/rediscovery/page.php?page_id=235. Historical archaeologist Ivor Noël Hume cites other objects possibly relating to Spanish incursions into what is now Virginia, although all in the form of undocumented, unprovenanced European metal objects. These

Regardless of the physical exchanges between the Spanish and Chesapeake communities, personal and tribal memories of the mission and of Spanish aggression must still have been strong at the time the English landed at Jamestown. The Powhatans' willingness to engage with the English colonists suggests that they had no difficulty distinguishing between different European identities, given their previous experience with the Spanish and their likely knowledge of the English through either direct encounter or intertribal communications from Roanoke. The Virginia Company's three ships, the *Susan Constant, Godspeed,* and *Discovery,* were certainly not the first English vessels to catch the eyes of the local inhabitants of the Chesapeake Bay. The bay figured prominently in the explorations of the Roanoke adventurers in the 1580s, with direct contacts made between the English and local inhabitants. When the English arrived in Powhatan territory in 1607, they did not go unnoticed: Natives tracked their arrival from the three ships' first entry into the Chesapeake Bay that April. When the English sent out a landing party under the leadership of Captain Christopher Newport, they were attacked by a group of Native men. As described by John Smith, *"Maister Wingfield, Gosnoll,* and *Newport,* with 30 others, recreating themselves on shore, were assaulted by 5 Salvages; who hurt 2 of the English very dangerously."* This show of force was designed to demonstrate Native superiority, but not to annihilate the English.[22]

---

include a Dutch bronze mortar of late-sixteenth-century date "found in a field near Richmond" and a "Catholic bronze seal matrix found near Smithfield and . . . dateable to the first half of the sixteenth century." As interpreted by Noël Hume, "Whether this latest treasure is a relic of a Spanish presence in Virginia prior to 1607 or all these relics were subsequently traded as 'toys' to Indians remains anybody's guess." See *The Virginia Adventure: Roanoke to James Towne; An Archaeological and Historical Odyssey* (Charlottesville, Va., 1997), 190–191; Curry, *Feast of the Dead,* 60.

22. Despite the considerable interactions of Native people with Europeans before the establishment of the Jamestown colony, popular versions of the meeting of the English and the Indians presumes isolation and naiveté on the part of the Powhatans while concomitantly ignoring the previous Spanish settlement of the region. For example, the series of paintings by the artist Sydney King, commissioned for the 1957 Jamestown anniversary, portray the early colonial landscape of Jamestown Island as a wilderness. One image depicts several Native men peering from beyond trees at the recently constructed fort and the three ships. The visual implication is surprise and awe on the part of the Native peoples. Nothing could be further from the truth regarding the first encounters between the English of the Jamestown venture and the Powhatan people. See John Smith, "The Proceedings of the English Colony in Virginia . . . ," in Edward Arber, ed., *Travels and Works of Captain John Smith, President of Virginia, and Admiral of New England, 1580–1631,* I (Edinburgh, 1910), 91.

Roanoke and Ossomocomuck

Before considering the Roanoke colony's impact on Powhatan and Powhatan-affiliated tribal groups in the Virginia Coastal Plain, the experience of Native people in the Albemarle and Roanoke regions—known as Ossomocomuck to some of its sixteenth-century inhabitants—needs to be examined. The archaeological and historical record pinpoints significant differences between Native peoples in what are now eastern Virginia and eastern North Carolina. Although the Native people encountered by the Roanoke and Jamestown settlers shared a common linguistic heritage in Eastern Algonquian, it does not follow that their related dialects were entirely intelligible. The Virginia and Carolina Algonquian languages were related, but much of our knowledge rests only upon a handful of colonial-era word lists. The significant variability between the archaeological evidence for settlements in both regions suggests greater differences between the cultures that might also have been reflected linguistically.[23]

Although societies in both regions relied upon mixed horticulture and maintained semi-permanent settlement clusters, political organization was varied. The eastern Carolina Algonquian polities appear to have been less hierarchically structured than was the case in the Virginia Coastal Plain. In eastern North Carolina, individual Native groups engaged with the Roanoke explorers and colonists in disparate fashion, reflecting their individual identities as well as political exigencies, whereas a paramount chief centralized control over Native peoples in the Chesapeake. In addition to intertribal competition, North Carolina coastal groups also had to cope with the aggressiveness of this expanding Powhatan paramount chiefdom to the north as well as conflict with Siouan and Iroquoian societies immediately to the west. Protohistoric Siouan-speaking groups in the northeastern piedmont North Carolina region include the Saponis and Tutelos, whereas Iroquoian-speaking peoples include the Tuscaroras, Meherrins, and Nottoways. The English might not have been initially capable of distinguishing between Native groups, but Native interlocutors soon educated them in the separate tribal cultural identities.

23. See Ives Goddard, "Eastern Algonquian as Genetic Subgrouping," in William Cowan, ed., *Papers of the Eleventh Algonquian Conference* (Ottawa, 1980), 143–158; Blair A. Rudes, "Giving Voice to Powhatan's People: The Creation of the Virginia Algonquian Dialog for 'The New World,'" 2006, www.coastalcarolinaindians.com, accessed Feb. 14, 2013; Frank T. Seibert, "Resurrecting Virginia Algonquian from the Dead: The Reconstituted and Historical Phonology of Powhatan," in J. M. Crawford, *Studies in Southeastern Indian Languages* (Athens, Ga., 1975), 285–453.

On the first expedition in 1584, organized by Sir Walter Raleigh, explorers led by Philip Amadas and Arthur Barlowe enlisted two Algonquian-speaking Indians as translators: Manteo, a Croatoan Indian, and Wanchese, a Roanoke. During the month the explorers spent in North Carolina, they appear to have enjoyed cordial relations with the local Indians, principally the Roanoke polity led by Chief Wingina. In Barlowe's estimation, "A more kinde and loving people, there cannot be found in the world, as farre as have hitherto had triall." Although much of Barlowe's account concentrates upon extolling the commodities of the new land, he also provides some insight into Native life—which must nevertheless be filtered through his aim to assure his patron Walter Raleigh of the country's advantages. Of note is the way in which Barlowe learns to distinguish between different Native communities: he refers to the "very handsome, and goodly people" of Roanoke Island and their leader Wingina; the Chowanocs, whose leader, Pooneno, "is not subject to the King of Wingandacoa" (Wingina); "another king, whom they call Menatoan"; and the town of Sequotan, "neere unto which, six and twentie yeeres past, there was a shippe cast away, whereof some of the people where saved, and those were white people, whom the Countrey people preserved." Direct contact between peoples of the North Carolina coast and the Spanish had come in the form of a handful of survivors from a Spanish shipwreck off the Outer Banks in 1558, as noted by Barlowe. The Secotan Indians reportedly assisted the sailors, who endeavored to sail away in a ramshackle craft.[24]

Amadas and Barlowe took Manteo and Wanchese back to England at the end of their surveying venture. The Indians lodged at Walter Raleigh's London home, Durham House, and taught Thomas Hariot elements of Algonquian while they perfected their English. Some familiarity with Spanish might have aided Manteo and Wanchese in their English lessons. Within a year, the pair were competent enough in English to serve as translators for the 1585 colony, led by Ralph Lane. Hariot, for his part, had to engage with the complexities of a non-Indo-European language. His education in Algonquian grammar led him to construct a phonetic orthography, or a "universall Alphabet contenyning six and thirty letters, whereby may be

24. It is worth noting that not all participants in the Roanoke ventures were English. William S. Powell, "Who Came to Roanoke?" in Shields and Ewen, eds., *Searching for the Roanoke Colonies,* 51–52, notes that nine other nationalities were represented among the explorers and colonists, including Irish, German, Spanish, Portuguese, Danish, French, Scottish, and Welsh. On Barlowe, see "Arthur Barlowe's Discourse of the First Voyage," in Quinn, ed., *Roanoke Voyages,* I, 91–116, esp. 98, 110–112; Oberg, *Head in Edward Nugent's Hand,* 34–35.

expressed the lively image of mans voice in what language soever; first devised upon occasion to seeke for fit letters to expresse the Virginian speche." This orthography has been linked to the manner in which Hariot conceptualized algebra and geometry, raising the compelling prospect of a significant Algonquian contribution to Western mathematics. Unlike the ease with which men in Hariot's circle could communicate with learned Irish using Latin, linguistic communications between Hariot and the Algonquian men had to start from first principles. Hariot's desire to learn Algonquian should not be interpreted as indicative only of his considerable scientific curiosity but also as a pragmatic element of the extension of English power over the North Carolina Natives.[25]

An Irish parallel for Hariot's immersion in Algonquian can be seen in the decision of German-born Offaly planter Sir Matthew De Renzy—once a London-based textile merchant—to study Gaelic under the O'Brien historians, the MacBruadeadha, in the early seventeenth century. At one level, De Renzy employed the Irish language and engaged with Gaelic historiography to legitimize his role as a member of the Offaly elite. At another level, De Renzy's immersion in Gaelic literature was designed to afford him the knowledge required to understand, and thus predict, how the Irish viewed and responded to English incursions. At the same time that De Renzy strove to construct his own Irish pedigree, he was discomforted by what he perceived as the historical readiness of outsiders to assimilate into Irish culture. The ambiguity of De Renzy's enthusiastic immersion in Gaelic learning while he was simultaneously condemning Gaelic culture is another example of mimetic practice along the lines of the adoption of the Irish mantle by London's fashionable elite. For his part, Thomas Hariot was also engaging in mimetic practice as he struggled to understand and apply his newfound knowledge of Algonquian—knowledge that would be key to any successful effort to exploit and control Algonquian territories and peoples.[26]

After their stay in London, Manteo and Wanchese returned to their home-

25. Michael Booth, "Thomas Harriot's Translations," *Yale Journal of Criticism,* XVI (2003), 345–361; Vivian Salmon, "Thomas Harriot and the English Origins of Algonkian Linguistics," *The Durham Thomas Harriot Seminar,* Occasional Paper no. 8 (1993), 6, 33; Alden T. Vaughan, "Sir Walter Ralegh's Indian Interpreters," *WMQ,* 3d Ser., LIX (2002), 341–376.

26. In the estimation of S. J. Connolly, *Contested Island: Ireland, 1460–1630* (Oxford, 2007), 401, De Renzy "used his knowledge of Irish annals and mythology to legitimize plantation," a theme developed further by Brian Mac Cuarta, "'Sword' and 'Word' in the 1610s: Matthew De Renzy and Irish Reform," in Mac Cuarta, ed., *Reshaping Ireland, 1550–1700: Colonization and Its Consequences; Essays Presented to Nicholas Canny* (Dublin, 2011), 101–130. See Chapter 1 for discussion of the English attitude toward the Irish mantle as an exemplar of mimetic practice.

land as interpreters for Ralph Lane's 1585 venture. Aided by their presence, Lane initially continued the friendly relations with Wingina's people. He and his force of one hundred men also pushed northward and established relations with the Chesapeacks. With characteristic hyperbole, Lane described the land of the Chesapeacks as ideal for a future colony: "The Territorie and soyle of the Chesepians (being distant fifteene miles from the shoare) was for pleasantnes of seate, for temperature of Climate, for fertilitie of soyle, and for the commoditie of the Sea, besides multitude of beares (being an excellent good victual, with great woods of Sassafras, and Wall nut trees) is not to be excelled by any other whatsoever." Yet peace between Lane's men and the coastal Algonquians was not to last. Although Lane and his men still enjoyed Manteo's counsel and cooperation, Wanchese departed from the English and worked against them, capitalizing upon the knowledge he had gained while in Hariot's household. Wingina and his people were well aware that they could not wholly trust Lane and his men, not least because of Wanchese's firsthand experience with the English. That Wingina was wary of English intentions is underscored by the fact that he changed his name to Pemisapan, in effect becoming a different person poised to recast the nature of his foreign relations with the English. Lane, conditioned to negotiate through violence, launched an assault on Pemisapan and his people in July 1586. It was during this attack that Lane's Irish servant, Edward Nugent, beheaded the Algonquian leader. The killing of Pemisapan and the disintegration of all pretenses at diplomacy and accommodation precipitated the decision to abandon the colony. Ralph Lane's brief career as a New World adventurer was not an illustrious one. Ireland represented a far more knowable field of endeavor for Lane, and one that, as we have seen, he pursued for the remainder of his military service.[27]

Lane's difficulties at Roanoke led Raleigh to decide that the next expedition, to be governed by John White, should land instead in the territory of the Chesapeacks immediately south of the Chesapeake Bay. Despite these plans, the ships landed back at Roanoke following a rebellion reportedly led by the Portuguese ship's pilot, Simão Fernandes. Their conflict with Wingina's people resumed. The dispute over the landing at Roanoke and interpretations of the overall failure of Raleigh's colonial adventure have to be read and understood in terms of the centrality of privateering and profiteer-

27. "17 August 1585–18 June 1586: Ralph Lane's Discourse on the First Colony," in Quinn, ed., *Roanoke Voyages,* I, 257–258; Kupperman, *Indians and English,* 186; Quinn, *England and the Discovery of America;* David Stick, *Roanoke Island: The Beginnings of English America* (Chapel Hill, N.C., 1983).

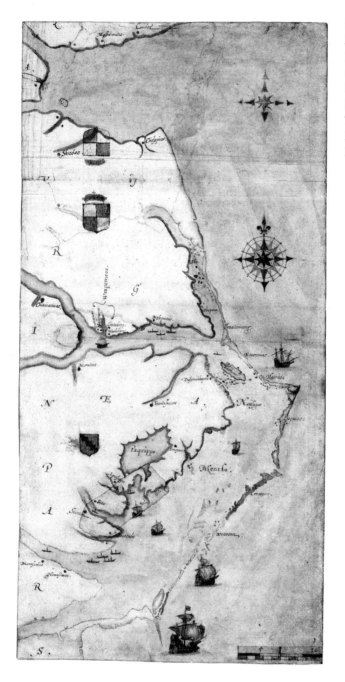

Plate 7.
La Virginea Pars.
John White's map
of the Chesapeake
Bay to Cape
Lookout. ©The
Trustees of the
British Museum,
BM 1906,0509.1.3

ing. As the treacherous Stukeley recognized more than twenty years earlier, the only sure way for an adventurer to recoup investment and to gain prestige was by capturing Spanish or other foreign ships and looting the cargo—far more expedient than awaiting the scant profits of a colonial enterprise.[28]

The goals of colonization and the necessity of swiftly repaying private investors, whether in Ireland or the New World, were antithetical. Establishing and supporting an overseas community of settlers required long-term support by way of supplies and defense and patience in awaiting a return on the investment; England was simply not in a position to provide such financial underwriting, let alone the required administrative support. Raleigh's private investors were hardly likely to countenance a wait of decades to recoup their initial investments. Fernandes was sensible in engineering the return to Roanoke, given that the Outer Banks provided a far more effective base for attacking Spanish ships than the more open Chesapeake Bay vicinity. Still pursuing his own goal of establishing and leading a self-sufficient agricultural community in the New World, White ordered the colonists to shift "50 miles further up into the maine" before he went back to England to fetch more supplies. Open conflict with the Spanish and the Portuguese prevented White from returning until 1590, by which time the colonists were not to be found.[29]

Scholars continue to debate the fate of the colonists. An early-twenty-first-century revisitation of the Lost Colony story suggests that small groups of the colonists not only joined the Croatans and Chowanocs, Algonquian-speaking coastal groups, but also were taken in by the Iroquoian-speaking Tuscaroras. Given the cultural distance between Algonquian and Iroquoian groups and the hostilities between the Tuscaroras and the Chowanocs, this is an unlikely explanation. If true, this dispersal would have required the divided colonists to effectively choose to become enemies. The answer to the riddle of the Lost Colony remains far more likely to be phrased in an Algonquian tongue. The discovery of a hitherto hidden symbol on John White's La Virginea Pars map could lend weight to the possibility that some of the colonists joined with the Algonquian Chowanocs. The symbol, covered by a patch, represents a fort in an inland location near the principal settlement of the Chowanocs. A more plausible explanation is that the notation was

28. Karen Ordahl Kupperman, *Roanoke: The Abandoned Colony,* 2d ed. (Lanham, Md., 2007), 45; Steven G. Ellis, *Tudor Ireland: Crown, Community, and the Conflict of Cultures, 1485–1603* (London, 1985), 268.

29. "1587: John White's Narrative of His Voyage," in Quinn, ed., *Roanoke Voyages,* II, 533.

covered because it depicts one of a series of forts that Ralph Lane was supposed to construct along the coastline and never did.[30]

30. David Beers Quinn's documentary researches suggested that the survivors moved closer
to the Chesapeake Bay in White's absence, affiliating themselves with the Chesapeack Indians,
who were subsequently wiped out in 1607 on the orders of the Powhatan paramount chief,
Wahunsenacawh. See Quinn, *The Lost Colonists and Their Probable Fate* (Raleigh, N.C., 1984).
Alden T. Vaughan further asserted that the lost colonists "melded during the next two decades
with neighboring natives to produce, to some extent, an ethnically and culturally mixed society" (Vaughan, "Sir Walter Raleigh's Indian Interpreters, 1584–1618," *WMQ*, 3d Ser., LXIX
[2002], 341–376). By contrast, Rountree and Turner reject the notion that some of the colonists
might have been among those killed by the forces of Wahunsenacawh: "For us it is questionable whether any of them would have survived that long, given Englishmen's documented arro-
gance and Europeans' lack of immunity to local 'bugs'" (*Before and after Jamestown*, 54). See also
James Horn, *A Kingdom Strange: The Brief and Tragic History of the Lost Colony of Roanoke* (New
York, 2010), 234; Paul Hulton, *America 1585: The Complete Drawings of John White* (Chapel Hill,
N.C., 1984); Stick, *Roanoke Island*; Quinn, *England and the Discovery of America*. For the discovery of the fort symbol, see Janet Ambers et al., "Examination of Patches on a Map of the East
Coast of North America by John White (La Virginea Pars, 1906, 0509.1.3)," report by the Department of Science and Conservation, British Museum, http://www.firstcolonyfoundation
.org/news/british_museum_findings.pdf. Scholarly and popular explanations for the disappearance of the colonists during Governor White's absence inevitably intersect with contemporary
cultural values and agendas. For members of North Carolina tribal groups, the question of the
fate of the lost colonists has never been in doubt. They *know* that the colonists were absorbed
into Native society. According to Christopher Arris Oakley, *Keeping the Circle: American Indian
Identity in Eastern North Carolina, 1885–2004* (Lincoln, Neb., 2005), 36, "every Indian community
in the state has, at one time or another, claimed a relationship to the ill-fated settlement." By
contrast, Euro-American oral traditions in eastern North Carolina also endeavor to account for
the fate of the colonists, relying, not on narratives of Native incorporation, but upon the highly
improbable survival of the settlers in cultural isolation. See Karen Baldwin, "Remembrance and
Renewal: Modern Belief and Legend in the Region of the 'Lost Colony,'" in Shields and Ewen,
eds., *Searching for the Roanoke Colonies*, 6–15. The existence of a successful, if undocumented,
settler community thus accounts for the oft-cited continuance of Lost Colony surnames in eastern North Carolina and the apparent survival of sixteenth-century folk practices. Such practices
include an Outer Banks festival that celebrates Christmas according to the Julian calendar rather
than the Gregorian calendar. This is hardly significant, given that the Gregorian calendar was not
widely adopted by the English until the mid-eighteenth century. Euro-American folk traditions
go to great lengths in order to provide an explanation for the fate of the Lost Colony that re-
jects the notion of incorporation into local Native society; this seems indicative of deeply rooted
intercultural anxieties. Such anxieties may stem from eighteenth- and nineteenth-century conceptions of whiteness, to judge from John Lawson's more matter-of-fact 1701 discussion of
the blending of English and Native culture in reference to the Hatteras Indians: "These tell us
that several of their ancestors were white people and could talk in a book as we do, the truth of
which is confirmed by gray eyes being found frequently amongst these Indians and no others.
They value themselves extremely for their affinity to the English, and are ready to do them all
friendly offices. It is probable that this settlement miscarried for want of timely supplies from
England or through the treachery of the natives, for we may reasonably suppose that the English
were forced to cohabit with them for relief and conversation and that in process of time they
conformed themselves to the manners of their Indian relatives." See Quinn, *Lost Colonists*, 50.

The Native site of Cape Creek in Buxton, on Hatteras Island, offers some insight into the Croatans and their relationship with the lost colonists. The locale appears to have supported occupation from approximately 500 CE into the eighteenth century and accommodated ten to fifteen dwellings. The continuous use of the site by the historic Croatans and their ancestors encompasses the period of European exploration, the Roanoke settlement and its abandonment, and the subsequent expansion of the colonial settlement from Virginia southward in the latter half of the seventeenth century. Significantly, there is little material evidence to suggest a major change in cultural practice resultant of colonial interactions. Deposits indicate only a selective incorporation of European material culture. Such goods include Spanish olive jar fragments and a sixteenth-century gold signet ring bearing the insignia of the Kendall family. Although a Kendall was part of the Lane colony, the ring itself was recovered from a seventeenth-century context and thus cannot be confidently associated with the Roanoke settlement. The fact that the ring appeared to be highly curated (worn and missing much of its shank) suggests that it might have been an heirloom dating back to the Roanoke colony but passed down through Croatan family lines.[31]

Reconstructing Carolina Algonquian Life

The writings of Thomas Hariot and the watercolors of John White constitute a critical record of Native society in the Coastal Plain area, albeit a record filtered through an English lens and colored by the financial imperatives underpinning the Roanoke project. The White watercolors stand as a unique visual account of Carolina Algonquian society on the eve of English

31. Site designation is 31DR1. See William G. Haag, "The Archaeology of Coastal North Carolina," Louisiana State University Studies, Coastal Study Ser., no. 2 (1956; rpt. Baton Rouge, La., 1958); Clay Swindell, personal communication, Sept. 24, 2007; accession record, sixteenth-century signet ring from Cape Creek site, Buxton, Special Collections Department, Joyner Library, East Carolina University, Greenville, N.C.; Nancy Gray, "Unearthing Clues to Lost Worlds: An Archaeological Dig on the Outer Banks of North Carolina Reveals Evidence of the Croatan Indians and Possible Links to the Lost Colony," *The ECU Report,* XXVIII, no. 2 (September 1997); Dane T. Magoon, "'Chesapeake' Pipes and Uncritical Assumptions: A View from Northeastern North Carolina," *North Carolina Archaeology,* XLVIII (1999), 107–126. The meaning attached to the ring by its Croatan owner or owners was surely divergent from whatever meaning it held for its original English owner, as well as being a far cry from the meaning attached to it in the present. The prioritization of this ring's European history in media reports of the Buxton excavation, rendering it a potent material connection to the Lost Colony, effectively alienated the object from its Indian cultural context. Consider the following newspaper headline written by Catherine Kozak: "Seeking the Lost Colony: Archaeologists Look for Signs of English among the Croatans," *Virginian Pilot,* Jul. 2, 2006.

The towne of Pomeiock and true forme of their howses, couered and enclosed some wth matts, and some wth barcks of trees. All compassed abowt wth smale poles stock thick together in stedd of a wall.

Plate 8. John White, watercolor of the palisaded village of Pomeiooc.
© The Trustees of the British Museum, BM 1906.0509.1

colonization, but the paintings are at best a stylized snapshot in time, un-likely to inform in any deeper diachronic sense. It is necessary to combine these sources with archaeological evidence from North Carolina and Vir-ginia to produce a more informed understanding of Native life, highlight-ing essential differences not just between the regions but between individual polities. Social stratification and political hierarchies defined the societies in the Roanoke vicinity, as evidenced by Hariot's description of Native titles and White's depiction of individuals sporting ornamentation from shells to pearl to copper. The character and material manifestation of status likely dif-fered between communities and regions. Although commonalities do exist between the eastern Algonquian societies in terms of subsistence strategies and some religious practices, these do not translate into a single Native identity, with ample archaeological and documentary evidence indicating considerable friction between Algonquian-speaking polities.[32]

The Native towns described by Hariot and painted by White incorporated twelve to eighteen houses, with estimated populations of 120 to 200 persons, subsisting on an abundant and varied range of cultivars. These included corn, sunflower, pumpkin, and wild plants; fish and shellfish caught with a selection of weirs, nets, hooks, and spears; and mammals such as deer and bear. Maize cultivation in the wider North Carolina and Virginia region seems to have begun and increased in the period after circa 1200 CE, to judge from environmental evidence. Ethnobotanical remains from the most recent excavations at the Patawomeke site on the Potomac River suggest the use of a diverse range of plants, including an equivalent reliance upon both wild and domesticated species. Osteoarchaeological examination of the human remains from North Carolina Algonquian burials highlights the commonality of dental caries related to a diet incorporating maize, although research into dental health accords with the paleobotanical evidence for diversity. The late Woodland populations of the eastern Carolina region did rely upon maize, but they still enjoyed a diverse diet drawing on wild plants and especially upon estuarine foods. Such appears to be a relatively common archaeological pattern for the mid-Atlantic region, in spite of early Jamestown sources that emphasized the vast quantities of maize being grown by the Powhatans. These claims are more illustrative of the desires of English colonists than the actual subsistence patterns of Native people, with the English overstating the amount of available corn as part of colonial propaganda.[33]

Hariot's writings, which include thirty-three Algonquian words learned from Manteo and Wanchese, provide extensive descriptions of the religion,

32. Hulton, *America 1585*; Horning, "Past, Present, and Future," in Kim Sloan, ed., *European Visions, American Voices*. Stephen Clucas, "Thomas Harriot's *A Briefe and True Report*: Knowledge-Making and the Roanoke Voyage," ibid., 17, suggests, "While their work may have generated knowledge which to 20th-century eyes at least has an objective value of its own, their work was fundamentally driven by the financial aims of the expedition."

33. Dennis B. Blanton et al., *The Potomac Creek Site (44ST2) Revisited*, Virginia Department of Historic Resources Research Report Ser., no. 10 (Williamsburg, Va., 1999), 83–84; Elizabeth Monahan Driscoll and David S. Weaver, "Dental Health and Late Woodland Subsistence in Coastal North Carolina," in Patricia M. Lambert, ed., *Bioarchaeological Studies of Life in the Age of Agriculture: A View from the Southeast* (Tuscaloosa, Ala., 2000), 148–167, esp. 165; E. Randolph Turner III, "The Virginia Coastal Plain during the Late Woodland Period," in Theodore R. Reinhart and Mary Ellen N. Hodges, eds., *Middle and Late Woodland Research in Virginia: A Synthesis* (Richmond, Va., 1992), 108; Martin Gallivan, "The Archaeology of Native Societies in the Chesapeake: New Investigations and Interpretations," *Journal of Archaeological Research*, XIX (2011), 281–325.

agriculture, clothing, and houses of the Algonquians, although Hariot can hardly be considered an unbiased ethnographer. One of Hariot's aims was to promote the New World settlement, and as such, he spent much time describing potentially lucrative commodities and emphasizing how the local population was likely to cooperate with the English. He interpreted the Native religion as somewhat analogous to Christianity, with the Indians worshiping "one onely chiefe and great God, which hath bene from all eternitie." Hariot saw this commonality as advantageous for the conversion of the Natives to Christianity, an optimistic notion considering the existence of many other deities beyond this principal god, recorded by Hariot as Kiwasa (from *kewasówak),* in the Carolina Algonquian pantheon. The Powhatans had a parallel religious structure; their practice focused upon the appeasement of the god Okeus but included room for a creator god, Ahone, as well as lesser deities.[34]

Similarly, in illustrating the Native towns of Secotan and Pomeiooc, John White stressed commonalities with English notions of architecture in depicting the houses with sharp, right-angled corners. The few late Woodland (c. 900–1500) and protohistoric (c. 1500–1607) village sites that have been excavated in Tidewater North Carolina and Virginia all share some general characteristics, both substantiating and contradicting the White imagery. Most important, the longhouses, or *yahecans,* painted by White as rectangles, are more usually subrectangular to oval in shape as delineated by patterns of post molds—surviving soil stains from where bent saplings were driven into the ground. Hariot recorded the dwellings as built of "small poles made fast at the tops in round forme after the maner as is used in many arbories in our gardens in England." Experimental archaeology makes it clear that the structures built in an oval or subrectangular shape are far more stable than those with squared ends as depicted by White. By giving the houses corners, White renders them familiar as dwellings. It is worth noting, as well, that Hariot does not comment upon the similarities in shape between the Algonquian dwellings and those of the rural Irish described in the previous chapter. Hariot's experience in Ireland postdates his time in the New World rather than the reverse. The only analogy he draws between the Carolina Algonquians and the Irish relates to the use of spears. In discussing the fishing techniques of the Native Carolinians, Hariot notes: "The inhabitants

34. Hariot, *Briefe and True Report,* in Quinn, ed., *Roanoke Voyages,* I, 372; Christian Feest, "North Carolina Algonquians," in Bruce G. Trigger, ed., *Handbook of North American Indians,* XV, *Northeast* (Washington, D.C., 1978), 271–281; Rountree, *Powhatan Indians of Virginia,* 136–139.

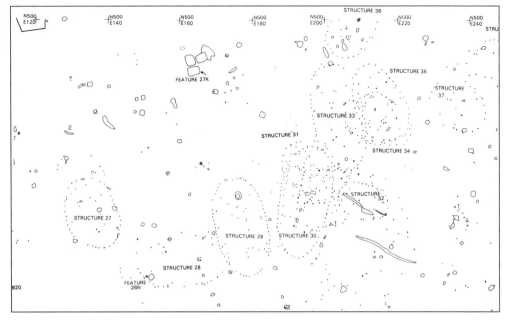

Figure 5. Plan of postmolds of a Paspahegh dwelling, 44JC308, James City County, Va. Courtesy, James River Institute for Archaeology

use to take them two maner of wayes, the one is by a kinde of wear made of reedes which in that countrey are very strong. The other way which is more strange, is with poles made sharpe at one ende, by shooting them into the fish after the maner as Irishmen cast dartes; either as they are rowing in their boates or els as they are wading in the shallowes for the purpose." Hariot presumably drew this analogy based either upon Ralph Lane's comments or direct discourse with the five Irishmen (Edward Nugent, Darby Gland, Edward Kelly, John Costigan, and James Lacie) who participated in the venture. Here, as in later centuries, Irishmen were full participants within an English-led colonial venture.[35]

Algonquian settlements were often surrounded by palisades. Some of these demarcated ritual space; others can be interpreted as defensive, reflecting intertribal conflict. In addition to White's depiction of a palisade at Pomeiooc, archaeological evidence sheds further light on Algonquian palisades. At the Amity site, located in Hyde County, North Carolina, not far

35. Hariot, *Briefe and True Report,* in Quinn, ed., *Roanoke Voyages,* I, 360, 370; list of Irishmen involved in the Roanoke venture as identified by Quinn, ibid., 195–197. Far more problematic than the number of sites excavated is the lack of publications about the sites, some of which have never been fully analyzed.

from the likely location of Pomeiooc, two subrectangular houses were excavated along with portions of a circular wooden stockade sixteen meters in diameter. Dating to the seventeenth century, this site highlights continuity in the use of palisades, as also observed by the early-eighteenth-century Virginia commentator Robert Beverley:

> Their Fortifications consist only of a Palisado, of about ten or twelve foot high; and when they would make themselves very safe, they treble the Pale. They often encompass their whole Town: But for the most part only their Kings Houses, and as many others as they judge sufficient to harbour all their People, when an Enemy comes against them. They never fail to secure within their Palisado, all their Religious Reliques, and the Remains of their Princes. Within this Inclosure, they likewise take care to have a supply of Water, and to make a place for a Fire, which they frequently dance round with great solemnity.

Beverley's description hints at both the defensive and the ritual nature of palisaded sites. The Amity stockade itself might have functioned as an occasional retreat and at other times as sacred space. The spatial separation provided by a palisade was clearly related to social status and spiritual beliefs. A small palisade at the Patawomeke site, a protohistoric village on the Potomac River in northern Virginia, enclosed two ossuaries and a small possible mortuary structure.[36]

Palisades therefore answered a range of needs, and defense was not the least of these, given the endemic conflict between Native polities. John Smith noted that the Powhatans "have many enimies, namely all their westernely Countries beyond the mountaines, and the heads of the rivers." In particular, Smith mentions the Siouan-speaking Monacans and Manahoacs to the west and the Patawomecks, Pautuxents, and the Iroquian Susquehannocks to the north. The increased use of palisades during the protohistoric period might also have been related to the uncertainties associated with increasing

36. Robert Beverley, *The History and Present State of Virginia: A New Edition with an Introduction by Susan Scott Parrish* (Chapel Hill, N.C., 2013), 139. It should be noted that Beverley was likely conflating his observations with much earlier descriptions. For the multi-purpose use of stockaded sites, see Paul S. Gardner, *Excavations at the Amity Site: Final Report of the Pomeiooc Project, 1984–1989*, Archaeological Research Report no. 7 (Greenville, N.C., 1990), a possibility also suggested by archaeologist Clay Swindell, personal communication, Sept. 24, 2007. See also consideration of palisades as multi-purpose constructions in Christopher Shephard, "A Late Woodland Protohistoric Compound on the Chickahominy River: Multiscalar Investigations of the Buck Farm Site," *Journal of Middle Atlantic Archaeology*, XXV (2009), 111–117; Blanton et al., *Potomac Creek Site Revisited*.

contact with Europeans. Certainly the Chesapeack Indians had good reason to palisade their principal town: their homeland was close to what are now the boundaries of Virginia and North Carolina. By 1607, when the English arrived at Jamestown, the Chesapeacks had had numerous engagements with the English in relation to the Roanoke venture and, more than likely, also with the Spanish. Unusually for the Virginia coastal region, the Chesapeacks resisted incorporation into the Powhatan paramount chiefdom and paid dearly. The Chesapeack people were reportedly wiped out by Powhatan forces in an uncharacteristically violent confrontation around the time of the Jamestown settlement. As reported by William Strachey, Wahunsenacawh "destroyed and put to the sword . . . all the inhabitants, the weroance, and his subjects of that province. And so remain all the Chessiopeians at this day and for this cause extinct." The veracity of Strachey's account is uncertain. His emphasis upon the violent nature of Wahunsenacawh's actions toward the Chesapeacks could easily be a rationalization of similar brutality on the part of the English toward Native people.[37]

Excavations in the 1980s on the west bank of Broad Bay (near Lynnhaven Inlet, within the confines of the city of Virginia Beach) unearthed the most likely candidate for the principal Chesapeack settlement. Known as the Great Neck site, it yielded a timber palisade, multiple longhouse dwellings, and burials presumed to be of high status because of the presence of grave goods. Like White's painting of Pomeiooc, the longhouses at Great Neck were situated parallel to the main palisade, but like those at the Amity site, they were subrectangular to oval in shape. Several other documented sites in the Lynnhaven River drainage have been dated to the protohistoric period and associated with the Chesapeacks, including one locale identified as the village of Apasus, which appears on the 1590 De Bry engraving of White's map. What emerges from these investigations is a clear sense of the diversity, rather than uniformity, of Algonquian settlement forms.[38]

37. John Smith, "Of the Naturall Inhabitants of Virginia," in Edward Arber, ed., *The Description of Virginia by Captaine Smith, in Travels and Works of Captain John Smith, President of Virginia, and Admiral of New England, 1580–1631* (Edinburgh, 1910), 71; Gallivan, *James River Chiefdoms*, 173. The violence of this encounter challenges the notion that Native conflicts were small-scale and nonlethal, as argued by David Edwards, "The Escalation of Violence in Sixteenth-Century Ireland," in Edwards, Pádraig Lenihan, and Clodagh Tait, eds., *Age of Atrocity: Violence and Political Conflict in Early Modern Ireland* (Dublin, 2007), 34–78. For Strachey's report, see William Strachey, "The History of Travel into Virginia Britannia: The First Book of the First Decade," in Edward Wright Haile, ed., *Jamestown Narratives: Eyewitness Accounts of the Virginia Colony; The First Decade, 1606–1617* (Champlain, Va., 1998), 662.

38. The state site number for Great Neck is 44VB7. See Keith Egloff and E. Randolph Turner

Multiple palisades were also unearthed at Patawomeke, located at the mouth of Potomac Creek in northern Virginia. These were constructed of saplings ranging from 5 to 7.5 centimeters in diameter, placed within a trench and driven directly into the ground, with spacing between the posts averaging around 20 centimeters. The largest palisade at the site measured at least 84 meters in diameter, enclosing the village itself. Across the river from Patawomeke, a total of seven palisade lines were uncovered at the Moyaone site on Accokeek Creek, Maryland, indicating the long-term maintenance of defenses. The Potomac River valley in Maryland and Virginia was frequently the locus for conflicts with the Susquehannocks from the north, who themselves were endeavoring to control the incursions of other northern Iroquoian groups. These sites were all located in zones of potential conflict, often near the boundaries of the Powhatan sphere of influence, or, like the Buck Farm site discussed below, associated with a group resistant to Powhatan power. Patawomeke, for example, was on the northerly edge of the Powhatan world and was most likely populated by relatively recent emigrants to the region, to judge from their distinctive ceramic tradition (more akin to materials found in the upper Susquehanna River region of Pennsylvania and New York). As noted previously, the Great Neck site was associated with the Chesapeack Indians, a society resisting incorporation by the Powhatan polity.[39]

III, "The Chesapeake Indians and Their Predecessors: Recent Excavations at Great Neck," *Notes on Virginia,* XXIV (1984), 36–39; Mary Ellen Norrisey Hodges, *Native American Settlement at Great Neck: Report on VDHR Archaeological Investigations of Woodland Components at Site 44VB7, Virginia Beach, Virginia, 1981–1987,* Virginia Department of Historic Resources Research Report Ser., no. 9 (Richmond, Va., 1998); E. Randolph Turner III and Anthony F. Opperman, "Archaeological Manifestations of the Virginia Company Period: A Summary of Surviving Powhatan and English Settlements in Tidewater Virginia, circa 1607–1624," in Theodore R. Reinhart and Dennis J. Pogue, eds., *The Archaeology of 17th Century Virginia,* Archaeological Society of Virginia, Special Publication no. 30 (Richmond, Va., 1993), 67–104.

39. The Patawomeke site state designations are 44ST1 and 44ST2; Accokeek Creek is 18PR8. See Blanton et al., *Potomac Creek Site Revisited;* Karl Schmitt Jr., "Patawomeke: An Historic Algonkian Site," *Quarterly Bulletin of the Archaeological Society of Virginia,* XX (1965), 1–36; Turner and Rountree, *Before and after Jamestown,* 47; Egloff and Turner, "Chesapeake Indians and Their Precursors," *Notes on Virginia,* XXIV (1984), 36–39; Robert L. Stephenson, Alice L. L. Ferguson, and Henry G. Ferguson, *The Accokeek Creek Site: A Middle Atlantic Seaboard Culture Sequence,* Anthropological Papers, Museum of Anthropology, University of Michigan, no. 20 (Ann Arbor, Mich., 1963); T. Dale Stewart, "Excavating the Indian Village of Patawomeke (Potomac)," *Explorations and Fieldwork of the Smithsonian Institution in 1938* (Washington, D.C., 1938), 87–90; Stewart, "Further Excavations at the Indian Village Site of of Patawomeke (Potomac)," *Explorations and Fieldwork of the Smithsonian Institution in 1939* (Washington, D.C., 1940), 79–82; Potter, *Commoners, Tributes, and Chiefs,* 149–152, 174–179.

The prevalence of palisaded settlements in the wider Algonquian settlement area of the Middle Atlantic relates to the longer pattern of population movements and cultural diversity in the region, where Algonquian communities interacted not only with others who shared the language group (if not political identity) but also Siouan- and Iroquoian-speaking communities. Archaeological sources are increasingly making it clear that late Woodland Native life was highly dynamic and punctuated by a wide variety of cultural interactions and the establishment and abandonment of settlements, independent from the as-yet-unquantified impacts of early European explorations. The established patterns of interaction and cultural knowledge of the Carolina and Virginia Algonquian people provided the basis for their dealings with first the Spanish and then the English and help to explain the range of strategies Native people employed in response to colonial expansion in the seventeenth century.

Both Carolina and Virginia Algonquian villages incorporated ritual buildings and spaces, many of which were also delineated by palisades. Compelling evidence for monumental architecture associated with ritual practices comes from the Buck Farm site in Charles County, Virginia. Sometime in the thirteenth century, a double-ditched palisade with wooden posts was constructed in a locale that had seen earlier Woodland-period settlement. The palisade enclosed an area of 24.3 by 18.3 meters and was destroyed by fire at the end of the sixteenth century. Inside were traces of three hearths, a series of pits, a single flexed human burial, and twelve animal burials. These features strongly suggest that defense was not its only function. Instead, the enclosed space may relate to the *quioccosan,* or priestly compound. A distinct lack of cultigens found in soil samples from the site further supports a sacred, rather than residential, use. The palisade might have protected the sacred space from incursion or, alternatively (if not concomitantly), protected the populace from the powerful spiritual forces bounded within the compound. The site can be attributed to the Chickahominies, who continue to live in the region. In the late sixteenth century, the Chickahominies were in the center of the Powhatan heartland but remained politically independent of the paramount chiefdom. Other palisaded villages in eastern Virginia that might have served ritual as well as defensive functions include a site on the Rappahannock River that appears to correspond to the village of Cuttawomen as depicted on John Smith's *Map of Virginia* and a settlement in Prince George's County on the James River, associated with an early-seventeenth-century Weyanoke village. Across the James, in Charles City County, traces of what may be another palisaded Weyanoke village site were unearthed in 1979. A dense array of small postholes indicate the long-term use of the site and the repair and rebuilding of a palisade line. Associated artifacts (albeit only from plowed contexts) pinpoint occupation during the late Woodland period, suggesting that the site was the principal settlement of the Weyanokes as depicted on the John Smith map.[40]

To return to the possible quioccosan at the Buck Farm site, in North Carolina Hariot was fascinated by the houses, or *machicomuck,* which lay within the priestly compounds he observed. There, the defleshed remains of priests, werowances, and other elite individuals were stored:

> The[y] builde a Scaffolde 9. or 10. foote hihe as is expressed in this figure under the tobs of thei[r] Weroans, or cheefe lordes which they cover with matts, and lai the dead corpses of their weroans theruppon in manner followinge. first the bowells are taken forthe. Then layinge downe the skinne, they cutt all the flesh cleane from the bones, which the drye in the sonne, and well dryed the inclose in Matts, and place at their feete. Then their bones (remaininge still fastened together with the ligaments whole and uncorrupted) are covered a gayne with leather, and their carcase fashioned as yf their flesh wear not taken away. They lapp eache corps in his owne skinne after the same i[s] thus handled, and lay yt in his order by the corpses of the other cheef lordes.

John Smith's 1612 description of Powhatan practice closely echoes Hariot's but notes that the insides of the dried corpses were stuffed "with copper beads and cover[ed] with a skin, hatchets, and such trash." These remains were stored for an indeterminate length of time and then were interred in ossuaries.[41]

Although Hariot concluded his description of the machicomuck by stating, "Thes[e] poore foules are thus instructed by nature to reverence their

40. M. D. Gallivan et al., *The Chickahominy River Survey: Native Communities in Tidewater Virginia, AD 200–1600* (Williamsburg, Va., 2009), 111–132; Christopher J. Shephard, "A Late Woodland Protohistoric Compound on the Chickahominy River: Multiscalar Investigations of the Buck Farm Site," *Journal of Middle Atlantic Archaeology,* XXV (2009), 111–117; Gallivan, "The Archaeology of Native Societies in the Chesapeake: New Investigations and Interpretations," *Journal of Archaeological Research,* XIX (2011), 298. The site designation for the possible Cutta-women site is 44ST3, and the probable Weyanock site is 44PG65. See Theodore R. Reinhart, ed., *The Archaeology of Shirley Plantation* (Charlottesville, Va., 1984), 198–202, for consideration of the possible Weyanock village in James City County.

41. Thomas Hariot, *A Briefe and True Report of the New Found Land of Virginia* (1590; rpt. New York, 1972), 72; Smith, "Description of Virginia," in Arber, ed., *Travels and Works of Captaine John Smith,* 75.

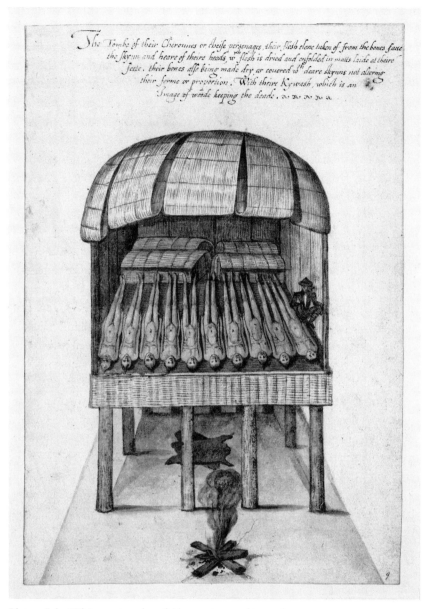

The Tombe of their Cheronnes or cheife personages, their flesh clene taken of from the bones saue
the skynn and heare of theire heads, wth flesh is dried and enfolded in mats laide at theire
feete. their bones also being made dry ar couered wth deare skynns not altering
their forme or proportion. With theire Kywash, which is an
Image of woode keeping the deade.

Plate 9. John White, watercolor of Algonquian *machicomuck*.
© The Trustees of the British Museum, BM 1906.0509.1.9

princes even after their death," he was hardly unfamiliar with practices such as the use of ossuaries and the veneration of the remains of the dead. The precise form of Algonquian mortuary houses might have been novel to White and Hariot, but both would have been accustomed to the notion that the bodies of the deceased could be spiritually powerful, even though the Catholic veneration of relics was forbidden in post-Reformation England. Certainly neither man was likely to be squeamish about mummified bodies, considering the widespread penchant for displaying the severed heads of executed criminals or captives of war as well as the common post-Dissolution practice of "translation," or movement of human remains from dissolved religious houses. Similarly, ritualized secondary burial was not common in England, but charnel burials are not unheard-of. The disarticulated remains of five individuals were discovered in a pit in the sixteenth-century nave of Saint Helen-on-the-Walls Church in York, where they had been carefully positioned in a square. Elsewhere, as in London's sixteenth-century New Churchyard, pits accommodated the mass burial of epidemic victims. Finally, secondary burials of disarticulated human remains routinely followed English gravediggers' disturbing earlier remains. Hariot's comments about the foolish Algonquians' venerating their dead priests perhaps lends weight to the accusations of atheism that cast a shadow over his post-Roanoke scientific career.[42]

Setting aside Hariot's judgments about preserving human remains, archaeological evidence supports his descriptions. Sites along the Eastern seaboard generally exhibit ossuaries filled with secondary deposits of disarticulated human remains that readily correspond to the descriptions of the temporary storage of human remains in above-ground mortuary houses and also to reinterment following exhumation and disarticulation. The early-sixteenth-century de Chicora testimony, which features words derived from Algonquian, also describes this process:

42. Hariot, *Briefe and True Report*, 72; Roberta Gilchrist, "'Dust to Dust': Revealing the Reformation Dead," in David Gaimster and Gilchrist, eds., *The Archaeology of Reformation, 1480–1580* (Leeds, 2003), 399–414; Sarah Tarlow, personal communication, Jul. 2, 2010. On Hariot's possible atheism, see Susanne S. Webb, "Raleigh, Hariot, and Atheism in Elizabethan and Early Stuart England," *Albion,* I (1969), 10–18; Jean Jacquot, "Thomas Harriot's Reputation for Impiety," *Notes and Records of the Royal Society of London,* IX (1952), 164–187. For a consideration of Hariot's attitude toward Native religious beliefs, see Stephen Greenblatt, "Invisible Bullets," in Greenblatt, *Shakespearean Negotiations: The Circulation of Social Energy in Renaissance England* (Berkeley, Calif., 1988), 21–65; and also William M. Hamlin, "Imagined Apotheoses: Drake, Harriot, and Ralegh in the Americas," *Journal of the History of Ideas,* LVII (1996), 405–428.

The natives celebrate a third festival, during which, after exhuming a long-buried skeleton, they erect a wooden cabin out in the country, leaving the top open so that the sky is visible; upon a plank placed in the center of the cabin they then spread out the bones. Only women surround the cabin, all of them weeping, and each of them offers such gifts as she can afford. The following day the bones are carried to the tomb and are henceforth considered sacred.

The accord between the ethnohistorical descriptions and the archaeological evidence supports the existence of a broadly shared Eastern Algonquian cosmology in relation to mortuary practices.[43]

Mortuary features and associated practice at Algonquian sites provide a valuable window into cultural beliefs and social organization. In eastern Maryland, some ossuaries incorporate the remains of up to six hundred individuals interred over several centuries, speaking to time depth and continuity for late Woodland complex society in this region. The earliest date for the use of ossuaries by Algonquian peoples in Maryland appears to be circa 1450 CE. Although far fewer ossuaries have been excavated in the wider Roanoke region, a calibrated radiocarbon date of 1168 CE (1-sigma 1032–1247) was reported at a small ossuary at the coastal Broad Reach site. This date hints at a longer continuity in burial practice and, by extension, cultural beliefs in the North Carolina area. The pit at Broad Reach included the remains of ten individuals in the form of bundle burials, consistent with the initial storage of bones in a mortuary house.[44]

Ossuaries have been recorded at several other coastal North Carolina sites

43. See "Testimony of Franciso de Chicora," in John R. Swanton, "The First Description of an Indian Tribe in the Territory of the Present United States," in Nathaniel M. Caffee and Thomas A. Kirby, *Studies for William A. Read: A Miscellany Presented by Some of His Colleagues and Friends* ([New Orleans], 1940), 326–328, esp. 330; and Blair Rudes, "The First Description of an Iroquoian People: Spaniards among the Tuscaroras before 1522," paper presented at the Testimony of Chicora Conference on Iroquois Research, Rensselaerville, N.Y., October 2002. See also Rudes, "Multilingualism in the South: A Carolinas Case Study," in Margaret Bender, ed., *Linguistic Diversity in the South: Changing Codes, Practices, and Ideology* (Athens, Ga., 2004), 37–49.

44. For a summary of Maryland Algonquian mortuary practices, see Curry, *Feast of the Dead;* Mark A. Mathis, "Mortuary Processes at the Broad Reach Site," paper presented at the 50th Annual Meeting of the Southeastern Archaeological Conference, Raleigh, N.C., November 1993 (available online at http://homepages.rootsweb.ancestry.com/~jmack/algonqin/mathis .htm). See further discussion in Elizabeth I. Monahan, "Bioarchaeological Analysis of the Mortuary Practices at the Broad Reach Site (31CR218), Coastal North Carolina," *Southern Indian Studies,* XLIV (1995), 37–69.

dating to the late Woodland Colington phase—a term that distinguishes coastal Algonquian late Woodland sites from interior sites inhabited by Iroquoian or Siouan-speaking peoples, such as the protohistoric Tusacaroras, Nottoways, and Meherrins, which are labeled "Cashie phase." Although projecting linguistic and cultural affiliations based upon protohistoric information into the centuries preceding the European arrival era is clearly problematic, there are distinctive material differences between Colington and Cashie phase artifacts, particularly ceramics. One common feature observed at Colington phase villages is the placement of ossuaries on the periphery or just outside of a village. The North Carolina coastal ossuaries, like Algonquian ossuaries elsewhere, include the remains of male and female individuals of all ages.[45]

Reanalysis of thirty-two excavated ossuaries in Maryland has yielded a better understanding of the presence and use of ossuaries by Algonquian groups in the wider Chesapeake region. Concurring with the observations of Hariot and White and the archaeological evidence from eastern North Carolina, the ossuaries tend be in association with village sites, albeit separate from habitation areas. The data suggest pre-interment treatment ranging from the scaffold burial and storage in a mortuary house to in-ground interment to cremation. One example, Nanjemoy Creek ossuary 3, was situated next to the traces of a six-meter-wide structure that has been interpreted as a mortuary house akin to that depicted by White. A radiocarbon date of 435+−155 B.P. was obtained from a charcoal sample within a postmold of this structure, which pinpoints its use to circa 1447 CE. Ethnographic sources do not mention cremation, yet 45 percent of the Maryland ossuaries contain evidence for the burial of cremated remains, most likely wrapped in bundles, akin to the burial of remains previously stored above ground. The archaeological record thus reveals variation in practice that ethnohistoric descriptions from one village and one point in time easily miss. Both need to be considered to understand the variety, complexity, and capacity for change over time that characterized Algonquian mortuary traditions and broader cultural practices.[46]

45. David Sutton Phelps, "Archaeology of the North Carolina Coast and Coastal Plain: Problems and Hypotheses," in Mark A. Mathis and Jeffrey J. Crow, eds., *The Prehistory of North Carolina: An Archaeological Symposium* (Raleigh, N.C., 1983), 41–43. These sites are critically important to understanding the character of local Native society on the eve of the Roanoke ventures, but at present they are unpublished and incompletely analyzed. Archaeologist Clay Swindell has begun the work of pulling together data on all of these sites.

46. The Maryland ossuaries tend to have been poorly excavated and poorly reported in the past, weakening any reinterpretation in the present. This caveat aside, there are a number of

The differential treatment of human remains before their interment in an ossuary could have related to the individual's status, further evidence of the stratified character of Algonquian society. Burials at an extensive late Woodland village in Virginia—believed to be related to the protohistoric Paspahegh settlement of Cinquoteck (destroyed by the English in 1611) and situated close to Jamestown—indicate three social ranks, distinguished by individual versus ossuary interment and the presence and nature of artifacts interred with the human remains. In addition to the remains of forty-five houses, twenty-one burials were excavated at the site. The mix of primary and secondary burials accords with the observations of Smith, who noted, "Their Kings they burie betwixt two mattes within their houses . . . the others in graves like ours." Three of these burials (one primary and two secondary) contained copper objects, including tubular beads and pendants. Compositional analysis of the thirty-one copper objects revealed that twenty-three were made from European copper. This was acquired either via trade with Native groups in the Southeast, who were directly engaging with the Spanish, or could have been obtained by the Paspaheghs from European explorers before the Jamestown settlement.[47]

What remains unanswered is the meaning of the differential burial practices. It should be remembered that funerary practices are more for the living than for the dead. Commingling secondary burials in ossuary pits suggests

---

features common to the sites that shed general light upon Algonquian practices. Most of the Maryland ossuaries were excavated under the auspices of the Smithsonian Institution in the nineteenth and early twentieth centuries, and as such the skeletal materials remain housed in Smithsonian collections. As non–federally recognized tribal entities, Native groups in Virginia and Maryland today cannot claim remains under the provisions of the Native American Graves Protection and Repatriation Act, nor do they have a legal right to advocate for or against future analysis of the skeletal remains. For Nanjemoy Creek specifics, see Curry, *Feast of the Dead*, 45; calibration following Minze Stuiver and Paula J. Reimer, "Extended 14C Data Base and Revised CALIB 3.0 14C Age Calibration Program," *Radiocarbon*, XXXV (1993), 215–230; Christine Jirokowic, "The Political Implications of a Cultural Practice: A New Perspective on Ossuary Burial in the Potomac Valley," *North American Archaeologist*, XI (1990), 361.

47. State site designation is 44JC308. See Mary Ellen N. Hodges and Charles T. Hodges, *Progress Report on Archaeological Investigations at 44JC308 at the Governor's Land at Two Rivers, James City County, Virginia* (Williamsburg, Va., 1991); Nicholas M. Luccketti, Mary Ellen N. Hodges, and Charles T. Hodges, eds., *Paspahegh Archaeology: Data Recovery Investigations of Site 44JC308 at the Governor's Land at Two Rivers, James City County, Virginia* (Williamsburg, Va., 1994); S. Fleming and C. Swann, "Final Report on the Technical Analysis of Copper-Based Artifacts from 44JC308 Governor's Land, Virginia" (Philadelphia, 1994); Beverly Straube and Nicholas Luccketti, *1995 Interim Report: Jamestown Rediscovery* ([Richmond, Va.], 1996); Smith, "A True Relation of Such Occurrences and Accidents of Note, as Hath Hapned at Virginia, since the First Planting of that Collony . . . ," in Arber, ed., *Travels and Works*, 22.

a value placed upon community over individuality and is not necessarily related to status. The use of communal mound burial in the Virginia piedmont
might have been a move to enhance solidarity among the Monacan people
in a period when relations with the Powhatans to the east were becoming
increasingly tense. This rationale could be extended to eastern Maryland,
when the earliest dates for ossuary burial coincide with the movement of
groups from the piedmont into the Coastal Plain.[48]

Ossuaries, then, not only emphasize communal identity and solidarity;
they also root a newly arrived group in space and place. Differences in burial
practice also likely relate to regional identities. The ossuaries of the Potomac
region are considerably larger than those found farther south in the James
and York River region and generally contain significantly higher quantities
of grave goods. Evidence for hierarchy is clear in both regions, but the ways
in which status was expressed through mortuary practice differed. In five
separate late Woodland sites at the Chickahominy heartland in Virginia,
few burials, ossuary or primary, contained any grave goods. The three primary burials related to individuals with skeletal markers suggesting that
the individuals had performed specialized, repetitive tasks that might have
contributed to their special treatment in death. One female burial exhibited
excessive wear to the teeth on the right side of her mouth, possibly indicating a repeated activity whereby the teeth were employed to hold on to or
strip something. The neck of a male burial displayed osteophytosis, an ar-
thritic condition related to the carrying of heavy weights. This individual
also exhibited traces of infection on his knees and hypertrophic muscular
attachments on the right clavicle and on both legs. His skeletal pathologies
suggested much time spent in a kneeling position and also carrying heavy
weights supported on his neck and shoulders. All of this evidence is a reminder of the diversity of Native identities in the region soon to be colonized by the English and helps to explain why individual Native polities did
not hold unified views toward the incomers.[49]

48. Debra L. Gold, "'Utmost Confusion' Reconsidered: Bioarchaeology and Secondary
Burial in Late Prehistoric Interior Virginia," in Patricia M. Lambert, ed., *Bioarchaeological Studies
of Life in the Age of Agriculture: A View from the Southeast* (Tuscaloosa, Ala., 2000), 195–218;
Julia A. King and Dennis C. Curry, "'Forced to Fall to Making of Bowes and Arrows': The Material Conditions of Indian Life in the Chesapeake, 1660–1710," paper presented at the Omohundro Institute of Early American History and Culture conference "The Early Chesapeake:
Reflections and Projections," November 2009.

49. Shannon S. Mahoney, "Mortuary Practices of the Chickahominy: Late Woodland Ceremonial Processes in Tidewater Virginia," *Journal of Middle Atlantic Archaeology*, XXV (2009),
133–140.

The artifacts found in association with burials further hint at the strati-fied nature of Native societies as well as the regional differences between groups. Although artifacts are generally scarce in late Woodland ossuaries—with the exception of quantities of shell beads often found with the bones of children—there is some evidence for differentiation in a small number of primary burials. The burial of an elderly man (aged between seventy and eighty years) at the Great Neck site in Virginia Beach contained more than thirty thousand shell beads that must have once decorated clothing.[50] This rare find may provide an archaeological corollary of sorts for Powhatan's Mantle. Similarly, the copper gorgets depicted by John White have clear ar-chaeological counterparts, particularly in postcontact burials. For example, an ossuary associated with an early- to mid-seventeenth-century Piscataway Indian settlement yielded a range of copper goods, including gorgets, disks, a copper spiral, tubular beads, and tinkling cones.[51]

The prevalence of copper objects in the Piscataway ossuary reflects the availability of European copper, which altered the spiritual and political power of the material within Native society. Native sources for copper in-clude sites in central and western Virginia and the Appalachian Mountains, as well as the Great Lakes. The closest sources of native copper to the Pow-hatan heartland can be found in the Virginia Blue Ridge Mountains, in present-day Madison, Greene, and Nelson Counties, although there is as yet no compelling archaeological evidence to support extensive Native exploi-tation of the Blue Ridge copper that would later attract nineteenth-century industrialists to the region.[52]

Whatever the source, the acquisition and display of copper before Euro-pean arrival were central to Algonquian society. The religious and social sig-nificance of copper seems to have, in part, dictated the relations between the eastern Algonquians and the Siouan peoples who controlled its flow. The

50. Floyd Painter, "The Great King of Great Neck: A Status Burial from Coastal Virginia," *The Chesopiean*, XVIII, nos. 3–6 (June–December 1980), 74–75.

51. Curry, *Feast of the Dead*, 28–34.

52. Lisa L. Heuvel, *Early Attempts of English Mineral Exploration in North America: The James-town Colony* (Charlottesville, Va., 2007), 18; Howard A. MacCord Sr., "Copper in Prehistoric Virginia," *Quart. Bull. Arch. Soc. Virg.*, LX (2005), 181–197. Traces of nineteenth-century copper mining can be identified within the boundaries of Shenandoah National Park, within Madison and Page Counties, Virginia. Opencast mining took place in both locales but failed to yield suf-ficient quantities of copper to sustain the activity. See A. Horning, "Overview and Assessment of Shenandoah National Park," report on file, Shenandoah National Park (Luray, Va., 2007), 69; B. Silliman Jr., *Reports on the Mineral Property of the Madison Mining Company* (Brooklyn, N.Y., 1955).

color of copper was key to its importance; Ralph Lane reported that the Algonquian Natives preferred English copper because "it is redder and harder." Red copper was linked to power of the spiritual realm and could only be handled by chiefs and priests. In the language of world systems theory, copper served as a preciosity, meaning a prestige item whose exchange value was rooted in its social role and its value specific to one exchange partner. Copper underscored Powhatan ritual and political power. Little wonder that Wahunsenacawh viewed the availability of European copper as a means for expanding his power base and gaining the upper hand in his foreign relations.[53]

Significant new thinking resultant from the ongoing excavations at the site of the James Fort further highlights the importance of the copper trade between the English and the Powhatans. The flooding of the market with English copper helped to ensure the survival of the English in the early years of the colony, but the influx destabilized the Native trade, which itself was founded upon a delicate balance of reciprocal relations between the Powhatan groups and the Siouan-speaking Monacans and Manahoacs to the west and northwest.[54] The Monacans and Manahoacs controlled access to whatever copper sources in the Blue Ridge Mountains were being exploited and appear also to have been the conduit for copper originating as far away as the Great Lakes. Although copper was an embodiment of political and sacred power for the Powhatans, to the English, it was a quantifiable commodity.

53. Gallivan, *James River Chiefdoms*, 164; Jeffrey L. Hantman, "Between Powhatan and Quirank: Reconstructing Monacan Culture and History in the Context of Jamestown," *American Anthropologist*, XCII (1990), 676–690. Ralph Lane quotation from "Ralph Lane's Discourse on the First Colony," in Quinn, *Roanoke Voyages*, I, 268. Frederic W. Gleach discusses the symbolic importance of the color red and of copper for a range of North American Native societies in Gleach, *Powhatan's World and Colonial Virginia: A Conflict of Cultures* (Lincoln, Neb., 1997), 56–57. For explication of the meaning of the term "preciosity" and the characteristics of preciosity exchange, see Immanuel Wallerstein, *The Capitalist World Economy* (Cambridge, 1979); and also Gil Stein, *Rethinking World Systems: Diasporas, Colonies, and Interactions in Uruk Mesopotamia* (Tucson, Ariz., 1999), esp. 12, 16, 30.

54. Seth Mallios and Shane Emmett, "Demand, Supply, and Elasticity in the Copper Trade at Early Jamestown," *Journal of the Jamestown Rediscovery Center*, II (2004); Mallios, "In the Hands of 'Indian Givers': Exchange and Violence at Ajacan, Roanoke, and Jamestown" (Ph.D. diss., University of Virginia, 1998); Carter C. Hudgins, Marcos Martinón-Torres, and Thilo Rehren, "From the Mines to the Colonies: Archaeological Evidence for the Exchange and Metallurgical Usage of English Copper in Early Seventeenth-Century Ireland and Virginia," in Audrey Horning and Nick Brannon, eds., *Ireland and Britain in the Atlantic World* (Dublin, 2009), 157–180; Hantman, "Between Powhatan and Quirank," *American Anthropologist*, XCII (1990). Hariot quotation from *Briefe and True Report*, 10; Lane's description of panning from "Ralph Lane's Discourse on the First Colony," in Quinn, *Roanoke Voyages*, I, 269.

Both Hariot and Lane extracted and recorded information about its location and acquisition from their Native informants. Hariot reported that copper as well as "whyte graynes of metall" could be found in mountainous rivers; he interpreted this white metal as silver (of greater value to the English than copper). Ralph Lane described in detail the practice of alluvial panning for copper deposits in mountain streams, as it was told to him.[55]

Archaeological information helps to balance out the overemphasis upon exploitable commodities in English descriptions of Native material culture. The surviving material culture associated with Algonquian late Woodland sites in North Carolina, Virginia, and Maryland includes stone, bone, and shell tools and a range of recognizable ceramics. Bone and antler were crafted into sewing items, ornaments, agricultural tools, and flintknapping implements. A remarkable set of five engraved busycon shell masks exhibiting a weeping eye motif were removed from an early-seventeenth-century burial site in Stafford County, Virginia, in 1869. The masks attest not only to the use of shell for display but also to wider contacts between the Powhatan people and other southeastern polities, where similar shell objects have been recorded.[56] Locally available quartz and quartzite were employed in knapping triangular projectile points for tipping arrows made of wood or reeds as well as for hafted triangular knives and specialized tools such as drills and scrapers. Given the far-flung extent of trade for copper, the Algonquian peoples did possess the networks to acquire lithic materials such as flint and chert, which are far more easily knapped than the locally available, coarse-grained quartz and quartzite, as we see by their occasional presence within assemblages. That copper nonetheless remained the principal preciosity acquired through long-distance trade underscores its cultural significance.

Undoubtedly, Native peoples enjoyed a rich material life involving a range of organic materials that seldom survive archaeologically. We can only imagine how many of the thousands of marginella shell beads exca-

55. Hariot, *Briefe and True Report*, 10; Dennis Blanton and Carter C. Hudgins, "Archaeological Evidence for Native Prestige Commodity Devaluation: An Example from the Chesapeake Associated with the Jamestown Colony," *Naval Weapons Station Yorktown*, www.nwsy.navy.mil/press/blanton.html, accessed Dec. 6, 2004; Hantman, "Between Powhatan and Quirank," *American Anthropologist*, XCII (1990), 676–690; Stephen R. Potter, "Early English Effects on Virginia Algonquian Exchange and Tribute in the Tidewater Potomac," in Peter H. Wood, Gregory A. Waselkov, and M. Thomas Hatley, eds., *Powhatan's Mantle: Indians in the Colonial Southeast* (Lincoln, Neb., 1989), 151–172.

56. Turner, "Virginia Coastal Plain," in Reinhart and Hodges, eds., *Middle and Late Woodland Research in Virginia,* 105; Marvin T. Smith and Julie Barnes Smith, "Engraved Shell Masks in North America," *Southeastern Archaeology,* VIII (1989), 9–18.

vated at Algonquian sites once decorated long-decayed leather garments or hangings such as Powhatan's Mantle. Pottery impressions give indirect evidence for basketry techniques, whereas scant traces of the waterproof mats woven by Native women (according to the ethnohistoric record) have been recovered—most recently within the confines of James Fort. A fragment of a marsh grass mat, bound with a bark fiber cord, was preserved through contact with copper fragments when deposited in an early-seventeenth-century pit. Ethnohistoric accounts also emphasize the use of organic materials for weapons. Arthur Barlowe noted of the Carolina Indians, "The weapons which themselves use, are bowes and arrowes: the arrowes are but of small canes, headed with a sharpe shell, or tooth of a fishe sufficient enough to kill a naked man. Their swordes are of wood hardened: likewise they use wooden breastplates for their defense." Any reimagining of the material lives of the eastern Algonquians must take into consideration the many purposes to which biodegradable natural resources were put—uses only hinted at by descriptions like Barlowe's and the fragmentary nature of the archaeological record, with its bias toward stone, shell, metals, and pottery.[57]

Canoes fashioned from tree trunks provided transport through the marshy Virginia Coastal Plain and Albemarle Sound region. Some of these vessels were, according to Hariot, so big that "being made in that sort of one tree that they have carried well xx [20] men at once, besides much baggage." William Strachey was similarly impressed: "They make them with one tree by burning and scraping away the coals with stones and shells till they have made them in form of a trough . . . some will transport 40 men; but the most ordinary are smaller, and will ferry 10 or 20, with some luggage, over their broadest rivers." In the 1960s, the waterlogged remains of one such canoe were located in Powhatan Creek, near Jamestown Island, and found to measure eight meters in length. Originally fashioned using the technique of burning described by Strachey, the canoe had been later altered employing metal implements. Interpreted at the time of its discovery as an Indian canoe acquired by early settlers in the 1630s, in reality the canoe cannot be tightly dated because of the nature of its recovery—nor can one assume that it was the English who wielded the iron tools that refashioned the vessel. Native people readily, if selectively, incorporated metal implements into their material repertoires, just as some English saw practical value in

57. William M. Kelso, *Jamestown: The Buried Truth* (Charlottesville, Va., 2006), 111–112, 115; "Arthur Barlowe's Discourse of the First Voyage," in Quinn, ed., *Roanoke Voyages,* I, 112.

the Indian canoe as a means of navigating the Chesapeake's riverine environment.[58]

Finds such as the Powhatan Creek canoe remain a rarity. As is inevitably the case in archaeology, it is the ceramics of the Algonquians that provide the bulk of material evidence. Extensive typologies aid in dating a range of Native-made ceramics and also in associating the pottery with the identity of its producers. The pointed cooking pots depicted by White were coil-built using local clays mixed with crushed and burned shell as a temper. Pots recovered from Colington phase sites in North Carolina are similar to ceramics found farther north into Virginia in terms of their production, size, shape, and decoration, including incised, fabric-impressed, and simple stamped treatment. The presence of these ceramic ware types—known as Roanoke Simple-Stamped and Gaston Ware—in both the Roanoke and James River vicinities is culturally meaningful. Their appearance in North Carolina during the late Woodland period has been interpreted as indicative of the late intrusion of Algonquian groups from the north, but this is at odds with the mortuary evidence for long-term cultural continuity. Rather than serving as a proxy for population migration and replacement, this pottery's appearance in North Carolina may instead reflect an acceleration of cultural interaction between the Algonquian-speaking peoples of the eastern coastal area. Such interaction was not always benign, as the presence of fortified settlements attests. A shared social practice such as pottery decoration or use of ossuaries can suggest an increase in interaction but does not equate to a single, shared identity.[59]

The recovery of a number of Native pots from sixteenth-century colonial contexts on Roanoke Island, including grit-tempered wares generally associated with Cashie phase interior sites, reference regional engagement. The presence of both locally produced and exotic pots in association with the Roanoke English settlement suggests that the colonists acquired them in trade rather than indicating a preexisting or abandoned Native site in the area selected by the colonists. Such a pattern was later repeated at Jamestown. The conical-shaped Native pots were designed to nestle down into

58. Hariot, *Briefe and True Report,* in Quinn, ed., *Roanoke Voyages,* I, 364; Strachey, "History of Travel," in Haile, ed., *Jamestown Narratives,* 638–639; Ben C. McCary, "An Indian Dugout Canoe, Reworked by Early Settlers, Found in Powhatan Creek, James City County, Virginia," *Quart. Bull. Arch. Soc. Virg.,* XIX (1964), 14–19.

59. H. Trawick Ward and R. P. Stephen Davis Jr., *Time before History: The Archaeology of North Carolina* (Chapel Hill, N.C., 1999), 194–228.

the coals for efficient and even cooking. It is unclear whether the English settlers at Roanoke adapted their own cooking techniques to make use of the Native pots or whether they were merely interested in the contents of the pots. Some early Jamestown settlers seem to have incorporated Powhatan cooking practices, to judge from the discovery of a conical pot lying broken, in situ, on a hearth within an early James Fort structure.[60]

Although simplistic comparisons between the culture of the Gaelic Irish and that of eastern Algonquians are unhelpful, it is notable that, from the perspective of material culture, dating a ceramic assemblage from an Algonquian site is easier than dating a rural Ulster assemblage if it contains only locally made Ulster coarse earthenware. The imbalance in understanding of ceramic traditions reflects the greater number of Algonquian sites investigated in comparison to rural Gaelic sites of the late medieval period; it does not necessarily imply continuity in Gaelic material traditions throughout the medieval period. Similarities in material culture of the rural Irish and of the Algonquians extend little further than the use of hand-built (as opposed to wheel-thrown) coarse-earthenware pottery, the superficially similar use of subrectangular house forms, and the wearing of mantles.[61]

Some Native pots saw use in mineralogical experimentation at Roanoke. As was the case for earlier English explorations to the New World—most notably, Frobisher's voyages in search of the Northwest Passage and Gilbert's Norumbega venture, which, according to Edward Hayes, included "Minerall men and Refiners"—the Roanoke expedition of 1585 included a number of individuals charged with investigating the mineralogical wealth of the new land. Chief among the scientists was the Prague mineralogist Joachim Gans, who might have been accompanied by the Saxon Daniel Höchstetter the Younger, later to become a director of the English Society of the Mines Royal. Excavations in 1991 and 1992 recovered tantalizing evidence of assaying activity on Roanoke Island. In association with what was described as Gans's laboratory floor, fragments of chemical glassware, crucibles, antimony, charcoal, French stoneware flasks, and copper residue were unearthed. Reanalysis of locally made bricks previously found in the same

60. Ibid., 272–275.

61. Jean Carl Harrington, *Search for the Cittie of Ralegh: Archaeological Excavations at Fort Raleigh National Historic Site, North Carolina,* Archaeological Research Ser., no. 6 (Washington, D.C., 1962); Harrington, "Plain Stamped, Shell Tempered Pottery from North Carolina," *American Antiquity,* XIII (1948), 251–252; William M. Kelso and Beverly Straube, eds., "2000–2006 Interim Report on the APVA Excavations at Jamestown, Virginia," unpublished report by the Association for the Preservation of Virginia Antiquities, Williamsburg, Va., 2008.

locale suggested they had once been employed as part of Gans's assaying furnace. Thomas Hariot reported that Gans's experiments with native copper rendered traces of silver. What the Native providers of Gans's copper thought about his experimentation can only be guessed at, although the apparent destruction of the copper in the assaying process could easily have been viewed as sacrilegious by Native observers, given the spiritual qualities with which they imbued copper.[62]

The English had a very different understanding of the power of copper. The discovery of significant silver deposits would have been welcome news for investors and speculators alike. At the time of the Roanoke venture, England remained dependent upon the Continent for refined copper and brass, despite the establishment of the Society of Mines Royal and the Society of Mineral and Battery Works in the 1560s to promote English copper mining and metallurgical prospecting. Ireland was also viewed as a potential source for copper and silver, as demonstrated by Francis Walsingham's search for copper and silver deposits near Youghal, Co. Cork, in the early years of the Munster Plantation.[63]

The speculative development of copper resources ensnared individuals as illustrious as Sir Humphrey Gilbert and Sir Thomas Smith. While Smith was designing his elaborate colony in the Ards Peninsula of County Down, he and Gilbert were duped into financing a scheme for copper processing spearheaded by William Medley and variously based in England, Cornwall, and Wales. On the basis of Medley's claims, Smith and Gilbert, along with the earl of Leicester and Lord Burghley, were together granted a patent by the queen giving them the "privilege for the making of copper and quicksilver by way of transmutation with other commodities growing of that mystery." The real mystery was how Medley managed to convince these men that he

62. [Edward Hayes], "A Report of the Voyage and Successe Thereof, Attempted in the Yeere of Our Lord 1583 by Sir Humfrey Gilbert, Knight," in Richard Hakluyt, *The Principal Navigations, Voyages, Traffiques, and Discoveries of the English Nation* . . . , 2d ed. (1598–1600; rpt. London, 1907), VI, 1–38, esp. 12; Kupperman, *Roanoke*, 172; Hariot, *Briefe and True Report*, in Quinn, ed., *Roanoke Voyages*, I, 333. The use of Native pots in mineralogical experimentation at Roanoke has been revealed by both renewed archaeological excavation and reconsideration of the mid-twentieth-century investigations. In a well-publicized, if not yet fully published, investigation in 1991 and 1992, archaeologists returned to an area on Roanoke Island previously investigated where they unearthed evidence of what was rather hyperbolically entitled "America's First Science Center." See discussion in Noël Hume, *Virginia Adventure*, 75–80; and Gary Carl Grassl, *The Search for the First English Settlement in America: America's First Science Center* (Bloomington, Ind., 2006).

63. Michael MacCarthy-Morrogh, *The Munster Plantation: English Migration to Southern Ireland, 1583–1641* (Oxford, 1986), 40.

could turn iron into copper; as Smith enthused to Burghley in 1574, "That it is true copper made of iron, I for my part do not doubt." Medley's schemes lost Smith more than one thousand pounds, just as he saw his plans for the perfect Irish colony washed away with the blood of his son. Successful copper and brass manufacturing continued to elude English entrepreneurs well into the seventeenth century, owing to the lack of available mineral ore or calamine stone. The identification of workable copper and calamine stone in the Roanoke and Jamestown vicinities would have certainly been perceived as significant for English efforts to develop self-sufficiency.[64]

The failure of the English to identify a ready source of marketable commodities or to develop any form of stable settlement at Roanoke meant that the people of Ossomocomuck enjoyed relative autonomy from Europeans for nearly a century after the abandonment of Raleigh's colony. Native polities controlled trade and cultural contacts with the seventeenth-century English colonial settlements to the north. The Croatan settlement at Cape Creek in Buxton might have been a center for the receipt of trade items flowing south from the Virginia colony and their subsequent redistribution to southeastern Native societies. Excavations at Cape Creek uncovered the remains of a mid- to late-seventeenth-century workshop that appears to have been used by the Croatan Indians for processing copper, shell, and bone into ornaments and for turning lead into shot. The transformation of bits of scrap copper into a range of objects, including one unusual animal figurine, indicates that copper might have retained some of its spiritual significance for Roanoke-area peoples regardless of its diminution in the eyes of the Powhatans. In Virginia, the surfeit of copper items brought by the English eroded its value as a preciosity, as it was no longer rare nor wholly in the control of the elite. Such evidence of continuity from Cape Creek, first occupied long before the arrival of Raleigh's adventurers, suggests that the Croatan culture of Manteo's time was still thriving a century after the cultural interlocutor taught Thomas Hariot his Algonquian tongue. By then, the Croatans were well accustomed to accommodating and rejecting material elements of English colonial society. The Native inhabitants of the Cape Creek vicinity maintained a separate and widely recognized Native identity through the

64. Mary Dewar, *Sir Thomas Smith: A Tudor Intellectual in Office* (London, 1964), 154; Smith to Burghley, Dec. 16, 1574, Lansdowne Manuscript Collection, 19/45, British Library, London; Carter C. Hudgins, "Elizabethan Industries in Jacobean Virginia? An Examination of the Industrial Origins and Metallurgic Functions of Scrap Copper at Jamestown, c. 1607–10" (Ph.D. diss., Royal Holloway College, 2006); Hudgins, Martinón-Torres, and Rehren, "From the Mines to the Colonies," in Horning and Brannon, eds., *Ireland and Britain*, 157–180.

eighteenth century, as attested to by a 1759 land grant of two hundred acres assigned to the Hatteras Indians.[65]

Jamestown and Tsenacommacah

By the time of the English arrival at Jamestown in 1607, Native society in the Virginia Coastal Plain was organized as a paramount chiefdom. Wahunsenacawh exerted control over thirty-two polities in a territory encompassing more than 6,500 square miles, from northern North Carolina to the Eastern Shore, as far north as the Potomac River and as far west as the geological fall line that marks the transition between the Coastal Plain and the piedmont region. This polity—or its geographical extent—was known as Tsenacommacah to its members, who numbered between 13,000 and 22,000 persons. Tsenacommacah can be characterized as an unequal, stratified society with meaningful social, political, economic, and ideological ties to groups as far away as the Potomac River, the Eastern Shore, and northern North Carolina. The combination of archaeological and ethnohistoric data from the Chesapeake paints an image of vibrant and dynamic societies long acquainted with European influences—for better or for worse. Documentary information regarding Native settlement in the early seventeenth century can be gleaned from the writings of John Smith and other early English explorers. Although working, to some extent, upon knowledge gained by the Roanoke adventurers, given that both Lane's *Discourse on the First Colony* and Hariot's *Briefe and True Report of the New Found Land of Virginia* were available, English understandings of Virginia Algonquian culture were nonetheless colored by misunderstandings, cultural bias, and faulty expectations.[66]

65. Cape Creek information from Clay Swindell, personal communication, Sept. 25, 2007; see also Jim Morrison, "In Search of the Lost Colony," *American Archaeology*, X (2006), 38–44; Magoon, "'Chesapeake' Pipes and Uncritical Assumptions," *North Carolina Archaeology*, XLVIII (1999), 115. Despite their continued presence as a recognized community through the eighteenth century, today direct links between groups like the Croatans and contemporary Native North Carolinians remain unclear. This stands in surprising contrast to the situation in Coastal Plain Virginia, where Powhatan descendants, whose lives were directly affected by the establishment of the Jamestown colony in 1607, have managed to maintain their Native identities through the centuries.

66. Rountree, *Powhatan Indians of Virginia*, 3–31, 140–152; Turner and Opperman, "Archaeological Manifestations," in Reinhart and Pogue, eds., *Archaeology of 17th Century Virginia*, 70; Binford, "Archaeological and Ethnohistorical Investigation of Cultural Diversity and Progressive Development"; Gallivan, *James River Chiefdoms*, 1–31; John F. Scarry and Mintcy D. Maxham, "Elite Actors in the Protohistoric: Elite Identities and Interaction with Europeans in the Apalachee and Powhatan Chiefdoms," in Cameron B. Wesson and Mark A. Rees, eds., *Be-*

The map of Virginia compiled by John Smith attests to the extent and density of Native settlement in the Chesapeake, its general accuracy confirmed through archaeological investigation. If we examine it, we may understand more readily the oft-derided decision of the English to make their permanent base on the swampy Jamestown Island—six miles downriver from a Paspahegh village situated at the confluence of the James and Chickahominy Rivers. However brackish the water, the island was defensible and contained a deep harbor close to shore. Perhaps more important, considering the density of Native settlement in the region, the island appeared to be uninhabited. Although it has been long assumed that Virginia's Powhatans eschewed the island because of its environmental drawbacks, archaeological evidence suggests instead that Native use of the landscape continued well into the late Woodland period. Archaeologists in the 1950s unearthed extensive deposits of Native material underlying plow zone and Civil War–period deposits in the vicinity of the James Fort; these included 303 sherds of pottery, most identified as late Woodland. In the early 2000s, Jamestown Rediscovery archaeologists, working in the same area, also unearthed an extensive late Woodland assemblage, including a nearly complete protohistoric Townsend pot, suggesting that the island had not been long abandoned before English arrival. These archaeologists also uncovered eleven post molds from a possible yahecan. Parallels between the shape and post-mold spacing of this structure with one from the Great Neck site at Lynnhaven may indicate that the structure is similarly late Woodland in date.[67]

Episodes of severe drought in the late sixteenth century, revealed through dendrochronological analysis, rendered Jamestown Island attractive only for seasonal use. Certainly when the three English ships sailed up the James from Cape Henry in May, those on board did not report any Native habi-

---

tween Contacts and Colonies: Archaeological Perspectives on the Protohistoric Southeast (Tuscaloosa, Ala., 2003), 142–169; E. Randolph Turner III, "A Re-examination of Powhatan Territorial Boundaries and Population, ca. A.D. 1607," *Quart. Bull. Arch. Soc. Virg.,* XXXVII (1982), 45–64.

67. The Jamestown settlers have been accused of "ignorance or carelessness" in disregarding the warning against "a low or moist place because it will prove unhealthful." See John W. Reps, *Tidewater Towns: City Planning in Colonial Virginia and Maryland* (Williamsburg, Va., 1972), 31. See also Joel L. Shiner, "A Jamestown Indian Site," *Quart. Bull. Arch. Soc. Virg.,* X (1955) (the finds led to Shiner's optimistic conclusion that it was "possible to date the site at not more than 10 or 20 years earlier than 1607" [ibid.]); Kelso and Straube, "2000–2006 Interim Report," 2. Evidence for Native use of this part of Jamestown Island over a period of thousands of years is also underscored by the recovery of Archaic-period lithic artifacts and Mockley and Prince George ceramics from an intact middle Woodland–period layer.

tation on Jamestown Island. Taking a broader perspective, 1990s analyses tracked environmental changes on the island over a period of twelve thousand years. Analysis of paleobotanical cores taken in several locations on the island reveals evidence for increasing human use of the island over the past one thousand years, exemplified by charcoal and pollen associated with plants that commonly grow in open spaces. Furthermore, over time, fire-intolerant plant species declined, indicating the use of fire to clear fields. That the fields were used for horticulture is supported by the presence of cultigens such as maize. It is possible that one of the reasons the English chose Jamestown Island for their outpost was because the locale presented a relatively open landscape, testament to centuries of human modification of the environment. Archaeological survey data supports the assertion that Native populations regularly visited and used the island. Evidence for Native activity on the island after 1200 CE is abundant, representing a 50 percent increase over identified sites from the middle Woodland period. These sites are all small in scale and density and accord with temporary camps rather than the sizable permanent bases, which were generally situated on higher ground with better freshwater resources than found on Jamestown in 1607. The selection of the island by the English, then, did not lead to instant conflict with local inhabitants, as the location was in relatively uncontested space.[68]

Shoreline and sea level analysis reveal significant erosion of the western side of the island, with the 1607 shoreline located more than 122 meters beyond the present western shore. Such intensive levels of erosion and submersion suggest the loss of indigenous cultural resources and were initially thought to indicate the loss of evidence associated with the early fort. In actuality, only a portion of the southwestern bulwark of the first fort was affected by erosion rates of up to fifty centimeters per year. When the colonists approached Jamestown Island, it was both larger than today and also connected to the mainland by an isthmus.[69]

68. Blanton, "Drought as a Factor in the Jamestown Colony," *Historical Archaeology*, XXXIV (2000), 74–81; Stahle et al., "The Lost Colony," *Science*, CCLXXX, no. 5363 (Apr. 24, 1998), 564–567; Gerald H. Johnson and Carl H. Hobbs III, "The Geology of Jamestown Island," in Johnson, Hobbs, et al., *Geological Development and Environmental Reconstruction of Jamestown Island* (Williamsburg, Va., 2001), 53; Dennis Blanton, Patricia Kandle, and Charles Downing, *Archaeological Survey of Jamestown Island*, Jamestown Archaeological Assessment Ser., no. 7 (Williamsburg, Va., 2000), 201.

69. Carried out as part of the 1990s National Park Service–sponsored Jamestown Archaeological Assessment; see Johnson and Hobbs, "Geology of Jamestown Island," in Johnson, Hobbs, et al., *Geological Development and Environmental Reconstruction of Jamestown Island*, 39.

One of the main paradoxes embedded in understandings of Powhatan society is an apparent disjuncture between documentary and archaeological evidence. Despite the richness of the ethnohistoric data in describing the social complexity of the Powhatan world, until recently little had been revealed archaeologically to support the long-term presence of a paramount chiefdom in the Coastal Plain region. The ethnohistorical record indicates that Wahunsenacawh inherited leadership over six sub-chiefdoms in the vicinity of the James River fall line and the upper reaches of the York River. From that base, he extended control over an additional twenty-six smaller-scale chiefdoms—control that might or might not have had deep roots. The documentary emphasis upon Wahunsenacawh as a uniquely powerful Native leader obscures the long-term presence of social complexity in the region and implicates European contact in the acceleration of such complexity. However, reconsiderations of the archaeological evidence for social hierarchy and inequality in the James River region pushes back the date for substantive change to the period between 1200 and 1500 CE.[70]

The dearth of physical evidence for long-term settlement hierarchy and status differentiation (often intuited from burial evidence) reflects the paucity of sites that have been investigated. Since the mid-1990s, considerable archaeological knowledge regarding the nature of Powhatan settlements has been unearthed in the Coastal Plain region and is beginning to address the seeming contradiction. Excavations at Werowocomoco—the seat of the Powhatan *mamanatowick* and the reported scene of the dramatic rescue of John Smith by Pocahontas—provides the most complete and convincing evidence for a complex, stratified society well before the arrival of Europeans. It also illustrates Wahunsenacawh's manipulation of early relations with the English. Located on Purtan Bay on the York River, the site

---

70. Gallivan, *James River Chiefdoms;* Hantman, "Between Powhatan and Quirank," *American Anthropologist*, XCII (1990), 676–690; Scarry and Maxham, "Elite Actors in the Protohistoric," in Wesson and Rees, eds., *Between Contacts and Colonies,* 142–169; Turner and Opperman, "Archaeological Manifestations," in Reinhart and Pogue, eds., *Archaeology of 17th Century Virginia,* 67–104. Many scholars have therefore argued for the relative newness of the paramount chiefdom as a political entity encouraged and established by Wahunsenacawh himself, implying that regional instabilities precipitated by those elusive European diseases allowed an individual like Wahunsenacawh to capitalize upon the disarray attendant upon European contacts. For example, Horn, *A Land as God Made It,* 11, views the emergence of the Powhatan paramount chiefdom as a "political development of the late sixteenth and early seventeenth centuries." By contrast, Gallivan argues, "The apparent disjuncture between ethnohistorically and archaeologically derived conceptions of Virginia's Indians largely disappears in the context of evidence recording a wholesale reorganization of Native social practices between AD 1200 and 1500" (*James River Chiefdoms,* 2).

was visited by the English six times between 1607 and 1609, when Wahun-senacawh left the village and headed inland to the town of Orapaks, near present-day Richmond. The chief's house was separated from the principal town, which housed a population of around 133–200 persons and has been identified along the river's edge. The symbolism of the placement of Wahunsenacawh's house would have been clear not only to members of Tsenacommacah but to the English, as well. Social and political hierarchy expressed through architecture and landscape was well established in the cultural grammar of late medieval England.[71]

As depicted on a map drawn by the Spanish spy Pedro Zuñiga, Werowocomoco has two odd "double-D" markings that would appear to correspond to two parallel ditches running for at least 210 meters and separating the riverside from an area of higher ground to the east. These curvilinear ditches may relate to above-ground earthworks that have since been plowed into oblivion. Reading this landscape against the ethnohistoric record suggests that Powhatan's house was situated on the rise east of the ditches, separate from the village site itself. The dates for the ditches, derived from radiocarbon as well as artifact types, indicate continued use from the thirteenth century into the seventeenth. The site as encountered by the English has great time depth—a product of long-term cultural dynamism.[72]

The use of earthworks in the York River vicinity is also supported by survey-level findings at the site of the Powhatan village of Kiskiack, on the south side of the river near Yorktown, Virginia. Kiskiack, depicted on Smith's map, is defined by a deep and extensive shell midden covering a series of landforms above Indian Creek. The dimensions of this midden reflect centuries of accumulation and indicate longevity of settlement. A concentration of Native activity along the south banks of the York River in the district of Kiskiack is underscored by the identification of twenty sites that date to the late Woodland and protohistoric periods. Early-twenty-first-century survey uncovered traces of a ditch (but no accompanying palisade), suggestive of a use of earthworks similar to that unearthed at Werowocomoco.[73]

71. The Werowocomoco project is also challenging the traditional practice of archaeological research in the Chesapeake, through the deliberate inclusion of Powhatan descendants in the research group. As advisors, researchers, and excavators, these individuals have influenced and guided the project from its inception.

72. Martin D. Gallivan, "Powhatan's Werowocomoco: Constructing Place, Polity, and Personhood in the Chespeake, C.E. 1200–C.E.1609," *American Anthropologist*, CIX (2007), 85–100.

73. The twenty sites are all located within the confines of the U.S. Naval Surface Weapons Station. See Dennis B. Blanton et al., *Archaeological Evaluation of Eight Prehistoric-Native American Sites at Naval Weapons Station, Yorktown, Virginia* (Williamsburg, Va., 2005); John R. Under-

In 2004, fragments of European copper were found in a midden deposit at Kiskiack dating to the early seventeenth century. The presence of the copper in the trash, as opposed to in a burial context, suggests its devaluation as a status item through the flooding of the market by the English. To quote John Smith, "But in short time, it followed, that could not be had for a pound of copper, which before was sold for an ounce." The instructions sent to incoming governor Sir Thomas Gates in 1609 state, "If you hope to winne them [the savages] and to provide for your selves by trade, you wilbe deceaved for already your Copper is embased by your abundance and neglect of prisinge it, and they will never feede you but for feare." In capitalist economies, of course, price is linked to the balance between supply and demand. The Native demand for copper that dropped so precipitously should have eventually recovered when the English supplies diminished. However, because the value of that copper lay in its spiritual significance, the prevalence of the metal in English supplies sapped its power. It was now demonstrably not rare and not controlled by those with spiritual knowledge. Subsequent efforts to regulate its availability were fruitless. The Powhatans no longer desired copper, whatever the price.[74]

Significant daily interactions between English and the Virginia Indians are attested to by the copper trade and reflected in the fact that approximately half of the recovered ceramics from 1607 to 1611 James Fort deposits are Native in manufacture. Yet this evidence should not be taken to mean that encounters were more cordial than the documents suggest. Although both the English and the Powhatans might have sought peaceable relations to serve their own interests, those interests were fundamentally incompatible inasmuch as each sought the political subordination of the other. Virginia Indians were not prepared to serve as docile laborers for the English; the English, assured of their own cultural superiority, professed bewilderment as to why the Indians did not wish to be "civilized" while at the same time expecting to subvert Indian political structures to their own ends, following the Spanish model. Just as Lane had employed violence as his prin-

wood et al., *Systematic Archaeological Survey of 6,000 Acres, Naval Weapons Station Yorktown, Virginia* (Williamsburg, Va., 2003).

74. Blanton and Hudgins, "Archaeological Evidence for Native Prestige Commodity Devaluation"; Hantman, "Between Powhatan and Quirank," *American Anthropologist*, XCII (1990), 676–690; instructions to Sir Thomas Gates, in Philip L. Barbour, *The Jamestown Voyages under the First Charter, 1606–1609: Documents relating to the Foundation of Jamestown and the History of the Jamestown Colony up to the Departure of Captain John Smith* . . . (Cambridge, 1969), II, 266; Mallios and Emmett, "Demand, Supply, and Elasticity," *Journal of the Jamestown Rediscovery Center*, II (2004).

cipal diplomatic tool at Roanoke, Jamestown's soldiers resorted to what they knew best.[75]

George Percy's "Trewe Relacyon" offers documentary evidence for violence directed against the Powhatan people. During the Starving Time of 1609–1610, then-governor George Percy sent Captain William Weste to obtain food supplies from the Patawomecks. Weste evidently succeeded in acquiring maize but then "used some harshe and Crewell dealinge by Cutteinge of towe of [the] Salvages heads and other extremetyes." As in Ireland, the English aimed to demonstrate their superiority by decapitating and defiling their enemies—even if, or perhaps because, they were reliant upon the Indians for food. In an earlier example, Percy had accompanied Captain John Martin in a raid on the Nansemonds in which they desecrated the remains of Nansemond elites: "[We] ransacked their Temples, Tooke downe the Corpes of their deade kings from of their Toambes, and Caryed away their pearles Copp[er] and braceletts wherew[i]th they doe decore their kings funeralles." Such actions were designed to incite anger and humiliation among the Natives. The destruction of Native items of worship also echoes the Protestant desecration of Catholic places of worship during the Reformation. That the English employed a similar approach to eradicating perceived idolatry among the Natives of Virginia does not come as a surprise; men like Percy were fully aware of the pain that the desecration of religious spaces and sacred objects could cause. It was a tried and true means of demonstrating power.[76]

Percy demonstrated his preferred tactic of violence on other occasions. In August 1610, despite the fact that the English had relied heavily on food supplies alternatively offered by and taken from the nearby Paspahegh village, Governor Sir Thomas Gates sent Percy to launch a vicious attack against the Paspaheghs. According to Percy's account, he and his men "fell in upon them, put some fifteen or sixteen to the sword," and captured the "queen and her children," most likely the wife and children of the Paspahegh wero-

75. As acknowledged by the historian Martin Quitt, "There is a hard lesson to be drawn from studying closely Anglo-Powhatan interaction during the period 1607–1609; mutual understanding does not necessarily engender mutual respect, tolerance, or civility" (Quitt, "Trade and Acculturation at Jamestown, 1607–1609: The Limits of Understanding," *WMQ*, 3d Ser., LII (1995), 227–258.

76. Mark Nicholls, "George Percy's 'Trewe Relacyon': A Primary Source for the Jamestown Settlement," *VMHB*, CXIII (2005), 212–275, esp. 214, 245, 248; George Percy, "A True Relation of the Proceedings and Occurrents of Moment Which Have Hap'ned in Virginia from the Time Sir Thomas Gates Was Shipwrack'd upon the Bermudes . . . ," in Haile, ed., *Jamestown Narratives*, 509–510.

wance Wowinchopunk. Although Percy professed a wish to spare them, he allowed his soldiers to throw the children into the river, whereupon his men commenced "shooting out their brains." The queen was then put to the sword. Whether Percy was influenced by his two trips to Ireland, where his brother Richard was serving as an army officer in Munster, is impossible to assess. He certainly was well aware of the central and often successful role violence played there. Regardless of the impetus, Percy's assault on the elite members of the Paspaheghs was a grave offense in Native terms: here was a direct attack on the Powhatan matrilineal social structure.[77]

Other Jamestown leaders similarly extended English settlement to the margins of the Powhatan world in an effort to implement and maintain surveillance over the Powhatan groups and their engagements with other Native peoples. Although the English might have hoped to supplant Native people by settling throughout the region, their own demographic inferiority and high mortality rates throughout the first fifteen years of the colony severely constrained these efforts. These outlying and complementary settlements were not the product of the same careful (if unrealized) planning that characterized the intended urban network of the Ulster Plantation towns, drafted well after the Jamestown settlement and considered in depth in Chapter 4. Instead, Virginia's early towns were defined by a mix of official and private efforts at speculative development and at territorial control. The placement of these settlements, however "unsuccessful" they might have been, provides an indirect means for extrapolating Native settle-

77. Nicholls, "George Percy's 'Trewe Relacyon,'" *VMHB,* CXIII (2005), 214; Percy, "True Relation," in Haile, ed., *Jamestown Narratives,* 509–510. Percy's vivid account is not only evocative for historians but remains a powerful source of memory and collective identity for today's Virginia Indians, as reflected in the comments of Chickahominy chief Stephen R. Adkins in 2006 Senate hearings over federal recognition: "I, and those Chiefs here with me, stand on the shoulders of the Paspahegh led by Chief Wowinchopunk, whose wife was captured and taken to Jamestown Fort and 'run through' with a sword, whose children were tossed overboard and then their brains were 'shot out' as they floundered in the water, and whose few remaining tribal members sought refuge with a nearby tribe, possibly the Chickahominy. With this horrific action in August 1610, a whole Nation was annihilated. A Nation who befriended strangers, and, ultimately died at the hands of those same strangers. As we commemorate Jamestown 2007 and the birth of our Nation today, those of Indian heritage in Virginia are reminded of this history" (*The Thomasina Jordan Indian Tribe of Virginia Federal Recognition Act and the Grand River Band of Ottawa Indians of Michigan Referral Act: Hearings on S. 480, Second Session, before the Committee on Indian Affairs,* 109th Cong. 86–89, June 21, 2006, Statement of Stephen R. Adkins, chief, Chickahominy Indian Tribe, Charles City, Va.). Regarding the Paspahegh reaction to the killings at the time, Rountree refers to the deaths as a "double atrocity" (Rountree, *Powhatan Foreign Relations,* 183).

ment, as places described as "Indian Fields" were routinely acquired and planted with English settlers. Virginia colonial settlement reflects Powhatan cultural geography, with the concept of Powhatan cultural boundaries influencing English ideas of the frontier. Although the English might have also been influenced by Spanish colonial models, wherein knowledge of Native political and economic structures offered a means of control, the spatiality of English settlement in Virginia is also evidence of agency on the part of Native people. Both the Powhatans and their Native neighbors determined the limits of colonial settlement for a century—something that no English commentator ever remarked upon, perhaps too accustomed to seeing only themselves as effective and central actors.[78]

One of the most important early Virginia English settlements was established atop the Native town of Kecoughtan in the vicinity of the present-day city of Hampton. In 1610, Governor Thomas Gates succeeded in removing the inhabitants of the Native town, spread across several thousand acres on the eastern side of the mouth of the Hampton River. By 1616, the settlement included twenty English residents, and in 1620, the Native name of Kecoughtan was changed to Elizabeth City. As was the case throughout early colonial Virginia, the acquisition of lands cleared and inhabited by Indians saved extensive effort on the part of English settlers. Rather than having to hew a settlement out of "virgin" forest, taking over an established settlement meant not only a cleared landscape but potentially also some extant buildings, fields, and landing sites. Furthermore, English settlers' readiness in adopting Indian crops such as maize as well as methods of hand cultivation accompanied their willingness to take over the same lands that supported Native horticulture.

As early as 1611, Sir Thomas Dale established Henrico, near present-day Richmond and on the edge of Tsenacommacah. In the following year, Dale established another settlement at Bermuda Hundred, situated on the north side of the Appomattox River, and proposed the establishment of Bermuda City, also known as Charles City, at the confluence of the James and Appo-

78. April Lee Hatfield, "Spanish Colonization Literature, Powhatan Geographies, and English Perceptions of Tsenacommacah/Virginia," *Journal of Southern History*, LXIX (2003), 245–282; Hatfield, *Atlantic Virginia: Intercolonial Relations in the Seventeenth Century* (Philadelphia, 2004). See also the discussion of demographic patterning in James D. Rice, *Nature and History in Potomac Country: From Hunter-Gatherers to the Age of Jefferson* (Baltimore, 2009), 255; and the reconsideration of urban planning in the Chesapeake in Paul Philip Musselwhite, "Towns in Mind: Urban Plans, Political Culture, and Empire in the Colonial Chesapeake, 1607–1722" (Ph.D., College of William and Mary, 2011).

mattox Rivers. Ralph Hamor optimistically described this enterprise as "a business of [the] greatest hope ever begun in our territories there." But Dale had another, political reason for establishing settlements in the territory of the Weanock and Appomattuck Indians: retribution. As related by George Percy, in 1610, the Appomattucks had lured a group of Englishmen into their homes with a promise of a feast but then turned on their guests, killing and wounding several. The Appomattuck territory served as a key interface between Coastal Plain polities and piedmont societies in the late Woodland period. To achieve his victory, Dale conceived of settlements he termed the New Bermudas, or Bermuda Incorporated, that would surround and ultimately displace the Appomattuck people. The aforementioned Bermuda City / Charles City and Bermuda Hundred, Digges Hundred, Upper Hundred / Curles Plantation, Rochdale Hundred, and West and Shirley Hundred were all established by 1613. The New Bermudas were designed to be as much a symbol of English authority over the Powhatans as they were to glorify the colonial enterprise. A closer examination of Bermuda City illustrates the premature character of such intent.[79]

As described by John Rolfe, the location of Bermuda / Charles City was advantageous for its strategic position: "a place so called there by reason of the strength of the situation, were it indifferently fortified." The c. 1617 Dutch chart of the James River, attributed to Johannes Vingboons, locates "Bermotho Citie" on a piece of land jutting out into the James River on the south side of the Appomattox River, correlating to the present-day location of City Point in the town of Hopewell, Virginia. On the Vingboons map, Bermuda City is symbolized by three buildings and is distinguished from Bermuda Hundred on the north side of the Appomattox. With its defensible promontory and fertile soils, the site Dale chose for Bermuda City had also long been attractive to generations of Native Americans, as indicated by scattered but significant evidence for late Woodland–period Native activity at City Point.[80]

The documentary record underscores the settlers' difficulties. In March 1617, following the agreed three-year period of servitude, laborers at

79. Ralph Hamor, *A True Discourse of the Present State of Virginia,* in Haile, ed., *Jamestown Narratives,* 815; Percy, "True Relation," ibid., 511.

80. Hamor, *True Discourse,* ibid., 826; John Rolfe, "A True Relation of the State of Virginia," ibid., 870; Michael Jarvis and Jeroen van Driel, "The Vingboons Chart of the James River, Virginia, circa 1617," *WMQ*, 3d Ser., LIV (1997), 377–394; David W. Lewes et al., *Windows into the Past: Archaeological Assessment of Three City Point Lots, City of Hopewell, Virginia* (Williamsburg, Va., 2003); Audrey Horning, *Cultural Overview of City Point, Petersburg National Battlefield, Hopewell, Virginia* (Williamsburg Va., 2004).

"Charles Hundred demanded our long-desired freedom from that common and general servitude," a request that was ultimately granted by Governor Yeardley. By the time of the 1619/1620 census, Bermuda City had been re-named Charles City and was inhabited by twenty-seven men, seven women, and three children. The census suggests that, despite their freedom from servitude to the company, the small group was living on the edge, with no horses and only one bull and three cows among them. According to *A Brief Declaration,* by the time of George Yeardley's arrival in 1619, Bermuda City consisted only of "six houses, much decayed," although it is likely that the Charles City settlement was at least partially fortified. Following the estab-lishment of Bermuda City, Dale noted his intention to "knock up pales," indicating the construction of palisades to enclose the new settlements and protect settlers and their livestock. Just across the Appomattox River from City Point lies the site of Dale's 1614 Bermuda Hundred settlement. Evidence for a ditch and berm, which served as part of the defensive pali-sade Dale erected across the peninsula between the James and Appomattox Rivers, still survives on the site today. Both settlements suffered in a coordi-nated attack by the Powhatans in March 1622, and despite instructions to reedify the locations, neither was rebuilt. When Captain Nathaniel Butler, governor of Bermuda, visited Virginia in the aftermath of the 1622 Uprising and penned his damning description of the state of the colony, he made spe-cific mention of the condition of Charles City:

> I found the Antient Plantaĉonss of Henrico and Charles Citty wholly quitted and lefte to the spoyle of the Indians who not onely burned the houses said to be once the best of all others, butt fell upon the Poultry, Hoggs, Cowes, Goats and Horses wherof they killed great nombers to the great griefe aswell as ruyne of the Olde Inhabitants, whoe stick not to affirme that these were not onely the best and healthiest parts of all others, butt might allso by their naturall strength of scituaĉion have been the most easefully preserved of all others.

Butler could see the advantages of the location chosen for the devastated settlement of Charles City, placing the blame for the failure to defend Charles City on the disorganization of the settlers. A year later, Ralph Hamor and other Ancient Planters (the term applied to those who arrived in Virginia before 1616 and were granted land patents under Dale) instead blamed the Virginia Company for the inhabitants' lack of preparedness. They com-plained in their *Brief Declaration,* part of a political protest directed against Virginia Company treasurer Thomas Smythe, that those who labored at

Charles City and Bermuda Hundred had received "very little allowance of clothing and victual" to support them in building the new settlements.[81]

The protohistoric Indian village at Jordan's Point, on the James River near modern-day Hopewell, provides insight into both a Powhatan settlement on the edges of Tsenacommacah and another early English fortified settlement. The Jordan's Point site encompassed an early-seventeenth-century English settlement, Jordan's Journey, atop the traces of what was probably a protohistoric Weyanoke/Weanock village, albeit one not named on early English maps. Extensive excavations on the point, which juts out into the bay created by the confluence of the James and Appomattox Rivers at City Point, unearthed elliptical post-in-ground houses, burials, and a series of pit features across a broad territory that has been divided into several different archaeological sites. The geographic extent of the associated features underscores the dispersed character of protohistoric Powhatan settlements. The presence of cleared, fertile agricultural land on the point no doubt also served as an enticement for English settlement. This settlement was materially attested to by the discovery of an extensive fortified compound believed to protect the home and dependencies of Samuel Jordan, who established Jordan's Journey sometime after 1619. Jordan represented Charles City in the first legislative assembly held at Jamestown in the summer of 1619. In 1620, he was granted a twelve-acre plot at Charles Hundred (Charles City), which already contained a house. The superposition of the Jordan occupation over the Weanock village illustrates the general process of English settlement in Virginia and its dependence upon and alternation of the existent cultural landscape of the Powhatan people.[82]

Farther downriver, evidence from Flowerdew Hundred also indicates

81. Martha W. McCartney, "An Early Census Reprised," *Quart. Bull. Arch. Soc. Virg.*, LIV (1999), 178–196, esp. 181–182; Ancient Planters of Virginia, "A Brief Declaration," in Haile, ed., *Jamestown Narratives*, 891–911, esp. 902, 904, 907; Dale, "Letter from Henrico, 10 June 1613," ibid., 778; Susan Myra Kingsbury, ed., *The Records of the Virginia Company of London: The Court Book, from the Manuscript in the Library of Congress* (Washington, D.C., 1906–1935), II, 374; Gleach, *Powhatan's World;* Turner and Opperman, "Archaeological Manifestations," in Reinhart and Pogue, eds., *Archaeology of 17th Century Virginia*, 67–104.

82. L. Daniel Mouer et al., "Jordan's Journey: A Preliminary Report on Archaeology at Site 44PG302, Prince George County, Virginia, 1990–1991," unpublished manuscript, Richmond, Va., 1992; Mouer, "Thomas Harris, Gent., as Related by His Second Sonne," *Historical Archaeology*, XXXII (1998), 4–14; Turner and Opperman, "Archaeological Manifestations," in Reinhart and Pogue, eds., *Archaeology of 17th Century Virginia*, 67–104; Martha W. McCartney, "The History of the Hopewell Airport Property, Jordan's Point, Prince George County, Virginia," unpublished report, Virginia Land Office Patent Book, VIII (Williamsburg, Va., 1987), 125.

continual Native American occupation from the Paleo-Indian period into the 1610s. Excavations in 1982 recovered brick fragments from a series of hearths associated with protohistoric Indian activity, suggesting that the lands were still used by the Weanocks in the years between 1607 and 1617, when Stanley Flowerdew first settled on the thousand-acre property. Sir George Yeardley, who was married to Flowerdew's sister Temperance, purchased the land in 1619 and set about defending the plantation through construction of a fortification: a ditch-set rectangular palisade measuring 72.5 by 24.4 meters, surrounding two dwellings and a structure interpreted as a combination warehouse, workhouse, and quarter, as well as an internal enclosure interpreted as a cattle pound. Immediately underlying the rectangular enclosure built by Yeardley (and subsequently by Abraham Peirsey, who acquired the land in 1624), small stakeholes indicate an Indian palisade in the same riverside locale. The difficulty of discerning Native from English features because of their close temporal and spatial associations was noted by the excavators, who nonetheless worked from the premise that the occupations had to be culturally and temporally separate. The site might well have appealed to the English because of its recent occupation, but equally the overlapping evidence may imply significant cultural interaction. The closeness of Native and English settlement at Flowerdew is clearly reflected in the artifactual record, given that fully 35 percent of the materials unearthed from the enclosed settlement were attributed to Native manufacture and include Native pottery and lithics. This same pattern of Native-English proximity echoes the deposits from the first years of the James Fort, showing the reliance of the English upon their Native neighbors.[83]

The presence of brick flecks in features at Flowerdew interpreted as Native hearths strongly suggests contemporaneity in terms of the presence of both Native and English occupants, as brick was produced by English settlers. Although the hearths were not constructed of brick, the flecks indicate some close interaction either with construction materials or with midden soils associated with English occupation. Despite the excavators'

83. James Deetz, *Flowerdew Hundred: The Archaeology of a Virginia Plantation, 1619–1864* (Charlottesville, Va., 1993), 31, 32, state site designation 44PG41/65; Charles T. Hodges, "Private Fortifications in 17th-Century Virginia: A Study of Six Representative Works," in Reinhart and Pogue, eds., *Archaeology of 17th Century Virginia*, 189–190; Norman F. Barka, "The Archaeology of Peirsey's Hundred, Virginia, within the Context of the Muster of 1624/5," in James B. Stoltman, ed., *Archaeology of Eastern North America: Papers in Honor of Stephen Williams,* Archaeological Reports 25, Mississippi Department of Archives and History (Jackson, Miss., 1993), 313–335, esp. 326, 330.

original confidence in separating the use of objects as exclusively Native or European, it is far more likely that a percentage of the European objects entered the material realm of the Weanock occupants, just as the English at Flowerdew were content to incorporate Native crops and methods of cultivation, and by extension some elements of Powhatan material culture, into their own repertoire. At the very least, Native ceramics in colonial assemblage are a direct reflection of the trade in the contents of those pots: food, so desperately sought by many early colonists.[84]

Other James River sites attest clearly to the overlap between Native and English settlement. Excavations at the extensive Hatch site in Prince George County recovered a mixture of Native features including structures, human interments, and more than one hundred dog burials, two in ritual association with human remains. In association with these recognizably Native features were the remains of three earthfast dwellings reflecting English building style. Accompanying assemblages from a range of pit features contained a mix of material culture derived from both Native and English traditions. Like Flowerdew and Jordan's Journey, the site is also believed to be affiliated with the Weyanoke / Weanock Indians documented by John Smith.[85]

Evidence from James Fort further confirms intercultural sharing of residences and settlements. The ubiquitous presence of Native objects in early deposits at James Fort represent more than mere markers of economic exchange. Rather, they reflect the complicated and variable relations between the English interlopers and the people of Tsenacommacah, who by turns tolerated and tormented the settlers. It is possible that Native women were resident in the fort before the arrival of English women in 1609, hinting at a practice of cohabitation, if not intermarriage, long denied in the documentary record but certainly common practice in Spanish colonial settings. If it was the case that Native women joined English men in the James Fort, then the decision to do so must have been tactical on the part of the women and

---

84. The tendency of archaeologists to presume a temporal separation between Native and English occupation has also been noted by Edward E. Chaney and Julia A. King: "Studies in Chesapeake historical archaeology have generally minimized the day-to-day role Native Americans played in English settlement" (King and Chaney, "Did the Chesapeake English Have a Contact Period?" in Blanton and King, eds., *Indian and European Contact in Context,* 193–221, esp. 196.

85. Leverette B. Gregory, "The Hatch Site: A Preliminary Report (Prince George County, Virginia)," *Quart. Bull. Arch. Soc. Virg.,* XXXIV (1979), 239–248; Paul M. Peebles, "Hatch Site Progress Report," *Newsletter of the Archaeological Society of Virginia,* LXXXIV (1983), 1–3; Turner, "The Virginia Coastal Plain," in Reinhart and Hodges, eds., *Middle and Late Woodland Research in Virginia,* 97–136.

the Powhatans more generally—perhaps part of Wahunsenacawh's ill-fated effort to incorporate the English as subjects.[86]

Another early James River colonial settlement, Wolstenholmetowne at Martin's Hundred, brings into sharp relief the challenge of reading English-Native relations through the material record. This "particular plantation" was chartered in 1618 by the Virginia Company of London on behalf of the Society for Martin's Hundred, a group of private investors hoping to capitalize upon New World settlement. The society was granted twenty thousand acres, and in 1619, they duly sent 220 individuals to Virginia to make good on the investment. On arrival, they constructed a fortified compound characterized by a rectangular timber palisade enclosing a number of dwellings and associated structures, which they named Wolstenholmetowne after one of their principal investors. The fortification as unearthed in the 1970s is reminiscent of the bawns erected by English settlers in Ireland, which were designed for periodic retreat, and reflects the colonial policy directing Virginia settlers to provide for their own defense. In contrast to early Jamestown and the assemblages from Flowerdew Hundred and Jordan's Journey, the published archaeological assemblages from Wolstenholmetowne list no Native ceramics or lithics, despite evidence from the surrounding property of intensive Native occupation in the middle and late Woodland periods. Outwardly, Martin's Hundred appears to have been constructed by a group of settlers concerned for their own defense and highly cautious in their dealings with Native people, if not averse to occupying a landscape bearing the traces of centuries of Native presence.[87]

Despite appearances, it is unlikely that the Martin's Hundred settlers eschewed engagement with Native people, given that the settlement suffered

86. The possibility of English men's cohabiting with Powhatan women was raised by William Kelso in "Digs and Discoveries," Jamestown Archaeological Forum, Omohundro Institute of Early American History and Culture / Society of Early Americanists joint conference, June 9, 2007, Jamestown, Va. For consideration of Spanish colonial practice and intermarriage with indigenous women, see Barbara L. Voss, "Domesticating Imperialism: Sexual Politics and the Archaeology of Empire," *American Anthropologist,* CX (2008), 191–203; Voss, "Gender, Race, and Labor in the Archaeology of the Spanish Colonial Americas," *Current Anthropology,* XLIX (2008), 861–893; Kathleen Deagan, "Colonial Transformation: Euro-American Cultural Genesis in the Early Spanish American Colonies," *Journal of Anthropological Research,* LII (1996), 135–160.

87. At the time of its discovery, this compound was explicitly compared to those of the Londonderry Plantation in Ulster, with particular reference to that built by the Merchant Taylors at Macosquin. See Ivor Noël Hume, *Martin's Hundred* (New York, 1982), 238. Assemblage data from Ivor Noël Hume and Audrey Noël Hume, *The Archaeology of Martin's Hundred: Part II, Artifact Catalog* (Philadelphia, 2001).

a very high casualty rate in the Powhatan attacks of 1622—which were facilitated by the ease of access to English settlements. The apparent dearth of Native goods in the archaeological record appears, instead, to be a factor of the post-excavation process, in which identification and analysis of the European and locally made English objects took precedence over items presumed to be residual prehistoric materials rather than Native-made items contemporary to the English occupation. The lesson of early Jamestown is that relations between Natives and English were not always predicated only upon avoidance or outright antagonism, notwithstanding the erection of defensive structures by the English. Sites like Martin's Hundred—excavated at a time when understandings of cultural relations in early colonial Virginia assumed a rigid separation—may yet reveal new stories.[88]

Like Wolstenholmetowne, the enclosed settlements at Jordan's Point and at Flowerdew Hundred share similarities with Ulster Plantation bawns but are best understood in light of more general Renaissance plans rather than any effort to replicate the Irish bawn in Virginia. George Yeardley had considerable military experience in the Low Countries and was well able to recognize the necessity and expediency of adapting designs to local contexts. Why would he copy another parochial application of Renaissance design when he could employ elements and influences that were more appropriate to the landscape and needs of Virginia? Regarding the similarity of fortifications and the use of continental models, many, if not most, of Ireland's servitors during the late sixteenth and into the seventeenth century had also served

88. Native materials were excavated at Wolstenholmetowne, even if they were not featured in the final publication (i.e., Noël Hume and Noël Hume, *Archaeology of Martin's Hundred*). In his earlier, popular book, *Martin's Hundred*, Noël Hume refers first to "traces of Indian occupation scattered both along the ridge and down toward the rear of the Company barn," noting that the excavators had "found a few quartzite points in the topsoil overlying the townsite, and these belonged to the Late Woodland period." Furthermore, they also excavated "a burned-out tree root system found southeast of the fort [that] had contained several fragments of Late Woodland pottery" (260). It should be noted that, in *Archaeology of Martin's Hundred*, the choice not to analyze Native artifacts is not explicitly explained, so that any scholar without access to the actual site archive and artifacts might believe that no Native materials were unearthed. There remain boxes of Native artifacts from the Wolstenholmetowne site that were not catalogued with the rest of the site material. Analysis by the author revealed the presence of pottery and lithics broadly dateable to the late Woodland / Protohistoric period in Virginia in Wolstenholmetowne deposits (including more than one hundred sherds of late Woodland pottery from Site C, the Company Compound), suggesting closer interactions between Natives and colonists than implied in the published studies of this site ("Native Materials from Martin's Hundred Sites, A, B, C, E, J, and H," unpublished report, October 2013; Kelly Ladd-Kostro, Curator of Archaeological Collections, Colonial Williamsburg Foundation, personal communication, Feb. 22, 2010).

in the Low Countries. The knowledge base was therefore shared. Commonalities between the material expressions of settlement layout in Virginia and in Ulster, considered further in the next two chapters, must be understood as the result of decisions made by individuals who shared similar backgrounds.[89]

The contemporaneity of efforts in Virginia and Ulster is exhibited in the specific example of Flowerdew Hundred. As noted above, Flowerdew Hundred takes its name from Stanley Flowerdew, who established himself on the thousand-acre property sometime between 1617 and 1619. By that time, his younger brother Thomas had settled in the barony of Clankelly, Co. Fermanagh, where it was reported that he had "built an Irish house with a chimney at the end, made of wattles, contrived in two rooms and a frame for a timber house of birch, most part of it to be set up with a Danes fort" (probably an early medieval ráth). A 1619 description states that, upon Thomas's Fermanagh proportion, "there is a large round Bawnne of Lyme and Stone," which suggests that he had taken advantage of a rarer stone cashel. Stanley's settlement in the Weanock village on the James and Thomas's reedified Gaelic enclosure and wattled Irish house show both brothers to have been comfortable with the idea of adapting non-English structures and landscapes. Although the younger Flowerdew later constructed a masonry tower house, he was initially content to live in the modest Irish timber and wattle house, which itself must have been constructed by an Irish builder. His decision to settle within a cashel reflects an understandable concern with defense and a prioritization of expediency over adhering to plantation regulations that required planters to build new defenses.[90]

89. The excavators of Jordan's Journey argue for direct parallels with the Vintner's Company bawn at Bellaghy; see Douglas C. McLearen and L. Daniel Mouer, "Jordan's Journey III: A Preliminary Report on the 1992–1993 Excavations at Archaeological Site 44PG307," unpublished manuscript, Virginia Department of Historic Resources, Richmond, Va., 1994, 6. McLearen and Mouer reference the Vintner's Company settlement at "Balleague," which should be "Bellaghy"; see Deetz, *Flowerdew Hundred*, 41. For extensive discussion of the continental and Renaissance origins of the bawn, see Charles Thomas Hodges, "Forts of the Chieftains: A Study of Vernacular, Classical, and Renaissance Influence on Defensible Town and Villa Plans in 17th-Century Virginia" (M.A. thesis, College of William and Mary, 2003), 528. Hodges argues, "When the functional use of buildings is considered between Ulster and Virginia plans overall, this information provides compelling evidence that the Virginia settlement models were not blindly copying the Ulster model at all—even from the beginning." Insofar as the Jamestown settlement predated activity in the Ulster Plantation, this is a given. Hodges also notes, "Had the English never settled in Ulster, not one single thing in Virginia would have changed. Both settlements were animated by larger classically and Renaissance-inspired models" (538).

90. J. S. Brewer and William Bullen, eds., *Calendar of the Carew Manuscripts, Preserved in the Archiepiscopal Library at Lambeth*, VI, *1603–1624* (London, 1873), 94.

The defensive advantages of ráths and cashels did not escape the notice of other planters besides Thomas Flowerdew. The O'Neill inauguration site of Tullahogue, held by the hereditary guardians the O'Hagans, was depicted by the cartographer Richard Bartlett in 1602 with two dwellings situated inside the circular earthwork. Although those dwellings likely relate to the O'Hagan use of the site—as Bartlett shows the undamaged inauguration chair just outside the ráth—the 1619 survey by Nicholas Pynnar indicates that the site was then used by the widow of the Scottish planter Robert Lindsay. "Mrs. Lindsey, late wife to *Robert Lindsey,* hath 1,000 acres, called *Tullaghoge.* Upon this there is a good strong Bawne of Earth, with a Quick-set Hedge upon it, and a Ditch about it. There is a Timber House within it, in which she and her Family dwell." A 1622 description of Mrs. Lindsay's holdings specifies "a Bawne of Sodds on the topp of the hill where the Great O'Neal was wont to be chosen." The earthen bawn with its ditch and hedge aptly describes a reused ráth.[91]

John Sedborough, who acquired land near Thomas Flowerdew in Fermanagh, also constructed his home within a ráth. By 1619, it was evident that Sedborough's plantation dream had failed, as Pynnar notes that Sedborough's land only boasted "a most poor Bawne of Sodds, being of a round forme, and most of it fallen down." Although Sedborough might have adapted an Irish ráth for reasons of economy, even some of the wealthier and better provisioned Scottish planters also opted to reuse existing ráths. For example, Sir George Carew noted in 1611 that the well-provisioned Scots planter Andrew Stewart, the third Lord Ochiltree, "hath built for his present use three houses of oak timber, one of 50 foot long and 22 wide, and two of 40 foot long, within an old fort, about which he is building a bawn." This "old fort" is likely an extant ráth located just outside of present-day Stewartstown, Co. Tyrone. Bawns described as constructed of earth or sods are not uncommon in records of plantation and may relate to the reuse of Irish-built ráths. The 1622 survey of Co. Armagh recorded four bawns constructed of earth or hedge and ditch, one enclosed by wooden pales, eleven built of stone, and one situated on an island, possibly a reused crannog.[92]

91. George Hill, *An Historical Account of the Plantation in Ulster at the Commencement of the Seventeenth Century, 1608–1620* ([1877]; Shannon, Ireland, 1970), 549; Victor Treadwell, "The Survey of Armagh and Tyrone, 1622," *Ulster Journal of Archaeology,* 3d Ser., XXIII (1960), 126–137; Treadwell, "The Survey of Armagh and Tyrone, 1622 (Continued)," ibid., XXVII (1964), 140–154, esp. 144.

92. Hill, *An Historical Account of the Plantation,* 482, 546; Treadwell, "Survey of Armagh and Tyrone," *Ulster Journal of Archaeology,* 3d Ser., XXIII (1960), 126–137; Treadwell, "Survey (Continued)," ibid., XXVII (1964), 140–154.

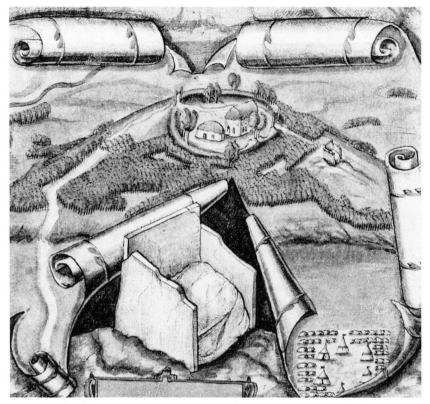

Plate 10. Richard Bartlett, Tullahogue, c. 1601, detail. This image is reproduced
courtesy of the National Library of Ireland, NLI MS2656/5

Along a similar line, Virginia leader Sir George Yeardley made use of
existing Native defenses at Flowerdew Hundred and at the confluence of
the James and Appomattox Rivers. Indicative of its long function as a buffer
or meeting zone between Native polities, the locale developed into a center for English-Indian trade, as reflected in finds of trade beads and copper
from Yeardley period deposits at Flowerdew. Despite the implied closeness
of relations between the Native population and the Flowerdew inhabitants,
Yeardley still maintained the defenses. He and other colonists had moved to
the margins of the Powhatan world in an effort to supplant them in their
own land. As the colonial population increased, so, naturally, did tensions
between the colonists and the Powhatan Indians, who increasingly found
themselves pushed off their ancestral lands. Under the leadership of the new
Powhatan paramount chief, Opechancanough, Powhatan warriors launched
a carefully planned and coordinated attack against the scattered colonial

plantation in March 1622. Like the Roanoke leader Wingina's transformation into Pemisapan when hostilities with the English reached their breaking point, Opechancanough changed his name to Mangopeesomon sometime in 1621—a clear warning sign to anyone who understood Algonquian customs. The 1622 attacks resulted in the deaths of nearly one-third of all the colonists. Many more would die of disease and starvation brought on by the decision to consolidate the settlers at selected population centers.[93]

Locations on the periphery of the chief settlement at Jamestown and in proximity to Native strongholds were ready targets for the Powhatans in their quest to reassert political and physical control over the lands rapidly being taken over by the ever-arriving English. Yeardley's caution and readiness in relation to the Flowerdew defenses was rewarded in 1622. Only six settlers at Flowerdew lost their lives in the Uprising, by comparison with a much higher death toll just across the river at Bermuda/Charles City. As recorded by Yeardley, "The settlers of the old Bermuda City and Hundred, the first free farmers, were nearly all killed." Although Charles City did not survive as a town, the locale of City Point continued to serve as an entrepôt for the English and for Native traders, marking a continuation of its traditional role as an interface zone for the Native peoples of the piedmont and tidewater.[94]

Surprisingly, the 1622 Uprising seemed to have caught settlers throughout the James River region unawares. It was the routine interactions between Indians and English that provided cover for the attackers, as recorded by Secretary Edward Waterhouse:

> As in other dayes before, they came unarmed into our houses, without Bowes or arrowes, or other weapons, with Deer, Turkies, Fish, Furres, and other provisions, to sell, and trucke with us, for glasse, beades, and other trifles: yea in some places, sate downe at Breakfast with our people at their tables, whom immediately with their owne tooles and weapons, eyther laid downe, or standing in their houses, they basely and barbarously murthered, not sparing eyther age or sexe, man, woman or childe: so sodaine in their cruell execution, that few or none discerned the weapon or blow that brought them to destruction. In which manner they

93. Hatfield, "Spanish Colonization Literature," *Journal of Southern History,* LXIX (2003), 245–282; Hatfield, *Atlantic Virginia,* 20–22; Gleach, *Powhatan's World,* 146.

94. Alexander Brown, *The First Republic in America: An Account of the Origin of This Nation, Written from the Records Then (1624) Concealed by the Council, Rather Than from the Histories Then Licensed by the Crown* (Boston, 1898), 467.

also slew many of our people then at their severall workes and husbandries in the fields . . . they well knowing in what places and what quarters each of our men were, in regard of their daily familiarity.

A total of 78 of 122 inhabitants of Martin's Hundred were killed in the Uprising. In fact, fully 22 percent of all English casualties were sustained at Martin's Hundred. The survivors fled to Jamestown, where they took up residence over the following year. As of 1625, only 27 settlers had returned to the 20,000-acre Martin's Hundred plantation.[95]

The 1622 Uprising claimed the lives of a reported 347 colonists. The same daily interactions between Natives and newcomers that facilitated the adoption of unfamiliar words, foods, and elements of material culture also facilitated the perpetration of violence, much as would be the case in Ireland at the time of the 1641 Rising / Rebellion. Numerous documents note the close relations between the Powhatans and the settlers. Upon arrival at Jamestown in 1617, the new governor, Samuel Argall, found that "the Salvages

95. Edward Waterhouse, "A Declaration of the State of the Colony and . . . a Relation of the Barbarous Massacre," in Kingsbury, ed., *Records of the Virginia Company of London*, III, 551–553; Noël Hume, *Martin's Hundred*, 64–65, 241–244. The violence of the attack on Martin's Hundred was magnified in the modern world through the sensationalized depictions of "massacre" victims in the pages of *National Geographic*, reporting upon the excavations of the 1970s. There, the archaeological discovery of a man's skull with a split through the forehead led to speculation about the manner of his death, presumed to be at the hands of Powhatan Indians. As imagined by Noël Hume, "First Look at a Lost Virginia Settlement," *National Geographic*, CLV (1979), 767: "Here lies testimony to a massacre. A bladed weapon, perhaps a spade or cleaver, split the man's forehead. . . . The back and sides of his skull were shattered, and a cut on the left brow suggests he was scalped." This speculation was transformed into tangible "reality" in the (now-closed) Winthrop Rockefeller Archaeology Museum, designed to house and display the finds from Martin's Hundred. There, visitors encountered a glass exhibit case in which a replica skull was featured with an iron spade embedded in its forehead, despite the fact that the no such spade was recovered anywhere near the interment, rendering the association spurious. For critique, see Marley R. Brown III and Edward A. Chappell, "Archaeological Authenticity and Reconstruction at Colonial Williamsburg," in John H. Jameson Jr., ed., *The Reconstructed Past: Reconstructions in the Public Interpretation of Archaeology and History* (Walnut Creek, Calif., 2003), 47–63. In a review of the exhibit, archaeologist Theresa Singleton described the concocted display and the use of the term "massacre" as "appalling," noting, "It is simply outrageous for a newly established museum to portray Native Americans in such a demeaning way" ("Carter's Grove: The Winthrop J. Rockefeller Archaeology Museum, Wolstenholme Towne, the Slave Quarter, and the Mansion; Long Term Exhibitions at Colonial Williamsburg," *American Anthropologist*, XCV [1993], 525–528, esp. 528). Elsewhere in the exhibit, the Wolstenholmetowne settlement was directly compared to English settlements in Ireland. The Martin's Hundred fortified compound was interpreted as fitting "a well-documented pattern of settlements in another English colony where fear of hostile natives made defense a key feature of the plan." The elision of perceived Irish and Indian savagery is clear in this association.

[were] as frequent in their houses as themselves, whereby they were become expert in our armes, and had a great many in their custodie and possession, the Colonie dispersed all about, planting Tobacco." In the aftermath of the violence, indentured servant Richard Frethorne expressed his fears in a letter home to England, noting that the local Native people possessed "peeces, Armour, sworde, all things fitt for Warre, so that they may now steale upon us and wee Cannot know them from English." Here, the subversion of identity can be seen as a clever and effective tactic of resistance. Following the Uprising, the crown revoked the Virginia Company charter, establishing Virginia as a Royal Colony. The events of 1622 also spurred an official inquiry by the English crown, with a series of recommendations proposed by Sir Arthur Chichester, formerly Lord Deputy of Ireland, chief architect of the Ulster Plantation, and a significant contributor to the drafting of Virginia's royal charter.[96]

From the Powhatan perspective, their victory should have at the very least chastened the English, stopping them from kidnapping Indian children for forced religious conversion and from expanding their settlements. The reverse turned out to be the case. The Uprising freed the English from any pretense of treating the Native people with kindness. Proving their own adaptability to guerilla-style tactics, the English began a series of raids on Powhatan villages, burning homes and storehouses and destroying crops and, in one incident, endeavoring to assassinate Opechancanough and other Native leaders by proffering poisoned sack. Such attacks remained unfettered until 1632, when they were limited by statute. At that time, hostile actions could only be engaged in if "provoked" by Native actions. By the 1630s, English settlement in Virginia had expanded to encompass the full length of the James River from the Chesapeake Bay to the fall line near present-day Richmond, and also the entirety of the lower Chickahominy River, the south side of the York River, and a significant proportion of the Eastern Shore. As explored in Chapter 4, the period after 1622 witnessed a sharp drop in the appearance of recognizably Native materials in assemblages excavated from sites associated with colonists. The intimacy of cultural relations before 1622, however uneasy, would not again be repeated in the Virginia colony.[97]

96. "The Government Devolved to Captaine Samuel Argall, 1617," in Smith, *Generall Historie*, I, 240; Richard Frethorne (1622), in Kingsbury, ed., *Records of the Virginia Company of London*, IV, 61.

97. Waterhouse, "Declaration," in Kingsbury, ed., *Records of the Virginia Company of London*,

The 1630s also saw the establishment of the Maryland colony along the Saint Mary's River, atop the village of Yaocomico. The inhabitants calculated that, by "freely" giving the lands to the English, they might reasonably expect the English to reciprocate favorably. Local Algonquian groups were under increasing pressure from the Iroquoian Susquehannocks, based on the northern fringes of the Chesapeake Bay, and saw the English as potential allies. Such would not be the case, with the southern Maryland Natives soon under such pressure from English expansion that in 1651 they would unsuccessfully petition the Maryland government for a dedicated reservation, competing with the English for possession of the rest of their lands. The new colony also impinged upon the lands of the Piscataways and threatened Piscataway-affiliated polities such as the Patuxents, Nanjemoys, Mattapanys, Portobagos, Mattawomans, and Chapticos, as well as Potomac River groups such as the Patawomekes. Back in Virginia, within two years of a final, unsuccessful attack on the English settlements in 1644, concerted violent resistance by the Powhatan groups of the Coastal Plain ended.[98]

Conclusion

The Native societies encountered by the English at Roanoke and at Jamestown and its hinterland were sophisticated in their sociopolitical organization, knowledgeable about Europeans from previous encounters and communications from afar, and savvy in their dealings with the encroaching English. Furthermore, Native peoples in the worlds of Ossomocomuck and Tsenacommacah did not view themselves as comprising a single entity in opposition to Europeans, just as the regional, clan, and cultural identities of the Gaels and Old English in Ireland ensured multiple and conflicting responses to English incursions in the sixteenth and early seventeenth centuries. Polities even within the Powhatan chiefdom itself conceived of themselves principally through the lens of tribal and kin affiliations. The idea that Native societies saw themselves as sharing a common foe in the ever-arriving Europeans is a product of historical hindsight. More often than not, explorers and settlers were perceived as potential allies in intertribal conflicts as well as suppliers of powerful spiritual and military objects and technologies. Native engagement with Europeans was shaped by locally contextualized expectations, needs, and traditions, not by the anticipation

III; Gleach, *Powhatan's World,* 170–171; Nell Marion Nugent, *Cavaliers and Pioneers: Abstracts of Virginia Land Patents and Grants, 1623–1800,* I (Richmond Va., 1934).

98. Rice, *Nature and History,* 98–100.

of an apocalyptic future. Long after Lane's settlers abandoned their colony and White's colonists disappeared, internal competition and carefully mediated relations with Siouan and Iroquoian peoples remained far more important to the Native people of the Carolinas than did their relations with Europeans. As is clear from the archaeological and documentary records, the descendants of Manteo's and Wanchese's people retained their independence and strength, selectively incorporating aspects of Euro-American material culture and serving as traders and brokers well into the eighteenth century. Despite the very different experience of Tsenacommacah's inhabitants—who fought two devastating wars against the English that culminated in their defeat in 1646—the descendants of the Powhatan polities of Pamunkey, Mattaponi, Nansemond, and Rappahannock and seven other Virginia Indian groups (including the independent Chickahominy) survive as state-recognized communities.[99]

The varied archaeological and historical records pertaining to Gaelic Ireland and to the Native worlds of the Chesapeake make it clear that commonalities between the peoples of both lands are illusory. One could point to competing polities in both lands, but the intertribal competitions of the Powhatans and their neighbors cannot be considered as more than superfi-

99. Just days before Elizabeth II and President George W. Bush ascended podiums at Jamestown to ponder the significance of the four hundredth anniversary of the settlement, the House of Representatives passed the Thomasina Jordan Indian Tribes of Virginia Federal Recognition Act H-1294, in what one local newspaper termed "a long-sought tribute to the American Indians whose early hospitality allowed that settlement [Jamestown] to survive" (Dale Eisman, "House OKs Recognition to 6 Virginia Indian Tribes," *Virginian Pilot* [May 9, 2007]). This tribute was not followed by similarly swift action in the Senate. Notwithstanding the fact that 2007 did not bring hoped-for federal recognition, Native Virginians did succeed in raising some degree of public awareness of their existence. As has been the case with other eastern Native groups—most notably the Mashantucket-Pequots, Eastern Pequots, and the Nipmucs of Massachusetts—some Virginia Indians have sought collaboration with anthropologists and archaeologists, as in the Werowocomoco project, as a means of connecting more closely with their ancestors while ensuring their contemporary voice is heard in constructions about their own past. See Stephen A. Mrozowski, "Pulling the Threads Together: Issues of Theory and Practice in an Archaeology of the Modern World," in Audrey Horning and Marilyn Palmer, eds., *Crossing Paths or Sharing Tracks? Future Directions in the Archaeological Study of Post-1500 Britain and Ireland,* Society for Post-Medieval Archaeology Monograph no. 5 (Woodbridge, Suffolk, 2009), 381–396; Mrozowski et al., "Magunkaquog: Native American Conversion and Cultural Persistence," in J. Campsi, *Eighteenth-Century Native Communities of Southern New England in the Colonial Context,* Mashantucket Museum and Research Center Occasional Paper no. 1 (2005), 57–71; Stephen W. Silliman, ed., *Collaborating at the Trowel's Edge: Teaching and Learning in Indigenous Archaeology* (Tucson, Ariz., 2008); Silliman, "Change and Continuity, Practice and Memory: Native American Persistence in Colonial New England," *American Antiquity,* LXXIV (2009), 211–230.

cially similar to the role of the clan in Ireland. Ireland could be described as a land divided into paramount chiefdoms somewhat akin to the Chesapeake region, but further comparisons become pointless when one considers the intensity and time depth of the Irish chiefs' relations with English and continental leaders and societies. The Powhatan people clearly had knowledge of Europeans before the establishment of Jamestown, but not centuries—certainly not millennia—of continual contact, as was the case for the Irish and English.

Language and religion constitute the significant differences between Indians and Irish in their relations with the English. Although the Native people of eastern Virginia and North Carolina might have shared a common language group in Algonquian, it is still far from clear how mutually intelligible their individual languages were, just as individual Indo-European tongues share commonalities but are not mutually intelligible. Certainly, religion has to be considered a central factor in English expansion into Ireland and to the New World, although whether being a non-Christian or being a Roman Catholic was more damning in English Protestant eyes remains a matter of some considerable debate. Regardless of the fervor with which the forces of Reformation turned their attention to correcting the deviant Irish church, there was still some notion of a common Christian heritage. The shared use of Latin in liturgy and scholarship is also significant. By contrast, the belief systems of the coastal Carolina Algonquians described by Hariot and those of the Powhatans as recorded by Englishmen were rather more alien to English eyes. More important, in terms of assessing relations between the Native peoples and the English, the Chesapeake Natives were working from a completely different spiritual framework within which to explain the actions of the English. The spiritual arguments employed by servitors in Ireland, on the other hand, were more readily understood, if nonetheless rejected, by the Catholic Irish. The impact of the sixteenth- and seventeenth-century meetings between English settlers and the diverse Native societies of the Chesapeake and Albemarle regions, once caged in a uniform narrative of exploitation followed by elimination, emerge as incomplete and unresolved. A similar story can be told of the Ulster Plantation.

CHAPTER THREE

Laboring in the Fields of Ulster

Introduction

The twenty-year period between the establishment of the last ill-fated colony at Roanoke in 1587 and the successful foothold gained by England at Jamestown in 1607 saw England's efforts to control Ireland devolve into outright warfare, ultimately delivering political control to the crown and paving the way for the most extensive plantation effort yet: the Ulster Plantation. As considered in Chapter 1, the scorched-earth policy of Lord Mountjoy during the Nine Years' War (1594–1603) devastated the countryside and, according to his secretary, Fynes Moryson, precipitated widespread starvation and disease. The intensification of this campaign in Ulster followed the English victory at Kinsale in 1601, which had routed Irish forces and destabilized their alliance with Spain; Hugh O'Neill capitulated in 1603, albeit under very favorable terms outlined in the Treaty of Mellifont. When James VI of Scotland ascended to the English throne as James I in that same year, England was finally in a position to profit from its hard-won authority over Ireland, although what form that "profit" would take was not immediately clear. Although O'Neill and his compatriots had surrendered, they emerged with English titles, retained control of their traditional lands, and were expected to behave as noble subjects. The latter was not to be the case. Frustrated at the loss of their influence even over their own traditional vassals, Rory O'Donnell (the earl of Tyrconnell) and Cúchonnacht Maguire (lord of Fermanagh) plotted to again enlist the Spanish to come to the aid of Ireland. O'Neill answered their summons when a ship set anchor at Rathmullan, Co. Donegal, bearing gifts from the king of Spain and poised to deliver the Gaelic leaders to the Continent. In September 1607, four and a half months after the establishment of Jamestown, this vessel set sail with O'Neill, Maguire, and O'Donnell aboard, alongside numerous family members and retainers. Any hopes of Spanish aid never came to fruition. Both Maguire and O'Donnell died not long after arriving on the Continent. O'Neill himself died in Rome in 1616 without ever returning to Ireland.

The Flight of the Earls, or Gaelic nobility, in 1607 resulted in the forfeiture of much of Counties Armagh, Cavan, Coleraine, Donegal, Fermanagh, and Tyrone to the crown; Old English lawyer Richard Hadsor opined, "The undutiful departure of the Earls of Tirone, Tirconell, and McGwyre offers good occasion for a plantation," echoing Irish Lord Deputy Sir Arthur Chichester's comment to James I: "There was never a fairer opportunity offered to any of His Highnesses predecessors to plant and reform that rude and irreligious corner of the North than by flight of the traitorous Earls Tyrone and Tyrconnell, with their co-partners and adherents; neither was there ever prince more wise and able to go through with so royal and memorable a work." This fortuitous event (from the plantation advocates' perspective) was followed in 1608 by the forfeiture of the Ulster lands belonging to Sir Cahir O'Doherty, Sir Donal Ballagh O'Cahan, and Niall Garbh O'Donnell after O'Doherty led a short-lived rebellion against English forces at Derry and Culmore. Although neither O'Cahan nor O'Donnell had participated—O'Cahan being in English custody at the time—the revolt convinced the English leadership that trusting any of the Gaelic clan leaders would be folly.[1]

On the advice of individuals including Sir Arthur Chichester and Sir John Davies, James I soon sought to plant the newly acquired lands in an effort to replace—or at least outnumber—the native population with loyal British subjects. Under what was labeled the Project of Plantation, the crown granted lands to "undertakers," often loyal soldiers or servitors who pledged or undertook to plant their lands with British settlers. To help fund his Ulster Plantation scheme, James coerced the Livery Companies of London into underwriting part of the effort. The companies were compensated with grants of land in the newly established County Londonderry, itself comprised of lands formerly known as O'Cahan's Country, after the Gaelic lordship of Donal Ballagh O'Cahan. The London Companies were forbidden to have Irish tenants and were ordered to construct villages on their individual lands (known as proportions), and to finance the establishment of two principal defended towns, Londonderry and Coleraine. The process was administered by a joint stock company, the Irish Society, consisting of representatives drawn from the fifty-five participating companies. By 1630, the

---

1. Richard Hadsor to earl of Salisbury, Sept. 23, 1607, in C. W. Russell and John P. Prendergast, eds., *Calendar of the State Papers, Relating to Ireland, of the Reign of James I,* 5 vols. (London, 1872–1880), II, *1606–1608,* 281; Sir Arthur Chichester to the king, ibid., III, *1608–1610,* 81.

companies had collectively, if begrudgingly, contributed between £60,000 and £70,000 to build and protect these settlements, located in what was considered to be the wildest and most vulnerable part of Ulster. By midcentury, much of the progress of plantation was damaged or destroyed by conflicts associated with the 1641 Irish Rising/Rebellion and by the Cromwellian campaigns of the 1640s and 1650s.[2]

Ulster's Irish hardly welcomed plantation, as expressed by an anonymous bard in reference to the loss of the Gaelic leaders and the changes to the country:

> In their place we have a conceited and impure swarm: of foreigners blood—of an excommunicated rabble—Saxons are there and Scotsmen. This the land of noble Niall's posterity they portion out among themselves without [leaving] a jot of Flann's milk-yielding plain [Ulster] but we find it [cut up] into acres. We have lived to see the tribal convention places emptied; the wealth perished away in the stream: dark thickets of the chase turned into streets. A borrish congregation is in the House of Saints . . . poets' and minstrels' bedclothes [thrown] to litter cattle; the mountain all in fenced fields. Fairs are held in places of the chase; the green is crossed by girdles of twisting fences.[3]

To some, the political and social changes wrought by the mechanism of plantation were catastrophic. Yet the Gaelic world was not wholly destroyed, nor did any of the seventeenth-century plantation schemes succeed as designed. For the Ulster Plantation in particular, the intended numbers and population influx were never achieved. Planters instead relied upon the existing Irish tenantry, which provided the space for significant, if long overlooked, Gaelic influence on the form and function of the Ulster Plantation settlements themselves.

This chapter focuses upon relations between planter and Gael through specific case studies, employing the combined analysis of documents and material sources. Particular attention is paid to evidence from the London

2. See Jonathan Bardon, *A History of Ulster* (Belfast, 1992); Nicholas Canny, *Making Ireland British: 1580–1650* (Oxford, 2001); James Stevens Curl, *The Londonderry Plantation, 1609–1914: The History, Architecture, and Planning of the Estates of the City of London and Its Livery Companies in Ulster* (Chichester, 1986); Curl, *The Honourable the Irish Society and the Plantation of Ulster, 1608–2000* (Chichester, 2000); Rolf Loeber, *The Geography and Practice of English Colonisation in Ireland from 1534–1609*, Irish Settlement Studies, no. 3 (n.p., 1991); T. W. Moody, *The Londonderry Plantation, 1609–41: The City of London and the Plantation in Ulster* (Belfast, 1939).

3. Poem by an anonymous bard, in Constantia Maxwell, *Irish History from Contemporary Sources, 1509–1610* (London, 1923), 290–291.

Company settlements as well as the processes of townbuilding in Coleraine, Londonderry, and Belfast. Consideration of two individuals central to the history of Ulster in the first decades of the seventeenth century—the clan chief Sir Donal Ballagh O'Cahan and the English servitor and architect of plantation Sir Thomas Phillips—both personalizes and complicates understandings of the seemingly dichotomous categories of planter and Gael.

The seventeenth-century Ulster Plantation settlements arguably left a far more visible and lasting mark on the built landscape than did contemporary efforts in the Chesapeake. Regardless of the variable success of plantation townbuilding and the reordering of the late medieval Gaelic world, monuments of plantation are common in contemporary Ulster. Aspiring planters' castles and manor houses still stand, albeit mostly in ruins. British settlers' masonry bawns survive intact in many locations, often encircling farmyards or incorporated into later estate divisions. Of the ninety-eight documented sites of late medieval and early-seventeenth-century castles and bawns, fifty-two still incorporate above-ground features. The city of Derry-Londonderry retains much of its seventeenth-century walls, completed by 1619, with the original diamond layout of the plantation street plan inside. Carrickfergus, similarly, is partially encircled by portions of both its medieval and seventeenth-century town walls. Even a lesser settlement such as Belfast retains traces of its plantation past in street names and in subsurface deposits.[4]

4. The archaeological study of the Ulster Plantation can be traced back to the nineteenth century, with the publication of a series of building studies in the *Ulster Journal of Archaeology*. In the twentieth century, scholars not only published drawn records of upstanding plantation castles and bawns but endeavored to produce synthetic discussions. For example, see E. M. Jope, "Moyry, Charlemont, Castleraw, and Richhill: Fortification to Architecture in the North of Ireland," *Ulster Journal of Archaeology*, 3d Ser., XXIII (1960), 97–123; Jope, "Castlecaulfield, Co. Tyrone," ibid., XXI (1958), 107; Jope, "Scottish Influences in the North of Ireland: Castles with Scottish Features, 1580–1640," ibid., XIV (1951), 31–47; D. M. Waterman, "Some Irish Seventeenth-Century Houses and Their Architectural Ancestry," in Jope, ed., *Studies in Building History: Essays in Recognition of the Work of B. H. St. J. O'Neil* (London, 1961), 251–274; Waterman, "Tully Castle, Co. Fermanagh," *Ulster Journal of Archaeology*, 3d Ser., XXII (1959), 123–126. For more recent discussions, see Colm J. Donnelly, "The Archaeology of the Ulster Plantation," in Audrey Horning et al., eds., *The Post-Medieval Archaeology of Ireland, c. 1550–1750* (Dublin, 2007), 37–50; Donnelly and Horning, "Post-Medieval and Industrial Archaeology in Ireland: An Overview," *Antiquity*, LXXVI (2002), 557–561; Nick Brannon, "Archives and Archaeology: The Ulster Plantations in the Landscape," in Geoff Egan and Ronald L. Michael, eds., *Old and New Worlds: Historical/Post Medieval Archaeology Papers from the Societies' Joint Conferences at Williamsburg and London, 1997* . . . (Oxford, 1999), 97–105. In the twentieth century, the work of geographers and folklife scholars also led to the wider recognition of postmedieval landscape features and the presence of late medieval and postmedieval booley huts, associated

Plate 11. Extant plantation bawn and fortified manor house,
Portora, County Fermanagh. Photograph by the author

The Ulster Plantation was unsuccessful in its aims and incomplete in its
execution. At the same time, the settlement of Virginia and the Ulster Plantation and the subsequent history of the north of Ireland are more closely
linked and reflective of one another than the sixteenth-century attempts at
plantation in Laois and Offaly and in Munster were in any way similar to
the unsuccessful English efforts in the New World. In fact, Sir Arthur Chi-

---

with seasonal transhumance. Subsurface examination of plantation-era sites, however, did not
begin until the mid- to late twentieth century. The urban excavation of plantation-period remains in Derry City, Belfast, Carrickfergus, and Coleraine owes an ironic debt to the bombs of
paramilitary forces that precipitated urban renewal; see Brannon, "Archives and Archaeology,"
99. The development of postmedieval archaeology in Northern Ireland also reflects broader political realities in that it occurred in tandem with the rise of postmedieval archaeology in Britain
beginning in the late 1960s, in contrast to the widespread lack of interest in the period within the
Republic of Ireland at that time. It is only since the early 2000s that the archaeological study of
postmedieval Ireland, north and south, has attained much professional recognition. See Audrey
Horning et al., "Foreword: Post-Medieval Archaeology in and of Ireland," in Horning et al.,
eds., *Post-Medieval Archaeology of Ireland*, xviii–xix; Colin Breen, "Twenty Years A'growing:
University-Based Teaching and Research of Historical Archaeology on the Island of Ireland,"
in Audrey Horning and Marilyn Palmer, eds., *Crossing Paths or Sharing Tracks? Future Directions
in the Archaeological Study of Post-1550 Britain and Ireland* (Woodbridge, Suffolk, 2009), 55–64.

chester referenced America when he penned "certain notes of remembrances touching the plantation and settlement of the escheated lands in Ulster" in 1608 as instructions to Sir James Ley and Sir John Davies:

> And as the churches in those later and the other countries, Cavan, Fermanagh, Donegall, and indeed of all Ulster, are so defaced, and the glebe and bishop's lands so obscured, that all is confused and out of order, as if it were in a wilderness, where neither Christianity nor religion was ever heard of. . . . He wishes . . . that the King may be pleased to make a new allotment to the bishops and church, as if His Majesty were to begin a new plantation in some part of America, from which it does not greatly differ. When this is done, he thinks they will have no great cause to take care for the inferior natives; for then all will settle themselves and their dependency upon the bishops, the undertakers, or the Irish landlords that shall be established by His Majesty's gracious favour; for most of them are by their nature inclined rather to be followers and tenants to others rather than lords or freeholders themselves.

Such a statement on Chichester's part seems both disingenuous and naive but reflects similar propaganda in relation to the presumed quiescence of New World Native people. Chichester's ready equation of Ireland and the New World signals his awareness of the Atlantic colonial projects, including the Jamestown colony, already under way.[5]

Chichester is perhaps better known for his comment about the Virginia and Ulster ventures, made to the king in a letter dated October 31, 1610: "If my poor endeavours may give any help and furtherance to so glorious and worthy a design, besides my obedience and duty to your Majesty, my heart is so well affected unto it, that I had rather labour with my hands in the plantation of Ulster, than dance or play in that of Virginia." Jamestown had been settled for three years when Chichester wrote this note, before the Ulster Plantation settlements had become a reality. Of course, very little dancing or playing was taking place in Virginia then. Only four months before, the few settlers who had survived the so-called Starving Time attempted to abandon the disease-ridden fort, only to be met by another fleet of settlers and supplies under Thomas West, Lord De la Warr. Had Chichester been more

---

5. Chichester's instructions to Sir James Ley and Sir John Davies, Oct. 14, 1608, in Russell and Prendergast, eds., *CSPI of the Reign of James I,* III, 64. Despite the clear failures of the Ulster Plantation, in popular memory, it is this period in Ulster's history that led inexorably to the conflicts and violence of the later twentieth century—conflicts and violence with a still-palpable legacy.

aware of the actual state of affairs in Virginia, he is unlikely to have viewed Virginia as the favored location for plantation. Chichester would come to know the Virginia colony very well in the 1620s, when he was called upon to assist in the drafting of Virginia's first royal charter.[6]

Creating the Ulster Plantation

As had been the case with the sixteenth-century plantation efforts, the Ulster Plantation as originally conceived allowed for the participation of loyal natives. In the estimation of Chichester, who spoke from long experience in Ireland, eviction or other harsh treatment of the native population would far more likely result in violence than would allowing "deserving" individuals to remain on their lands. His pragmatic approach to plantation is evident in his draft for the planting of Wexford: "By a reasonable mixture of English with Irish, the country may be better civilized, and that the present and apt means are not found to transplant the natives, nor is it seen whether they may be removed, it is allowed that every undertaker, according to his quantity, may make leases for years or lives to the present natives of all the rest of his proportion at reasonable rates." For the Ulster Plantation more specifically, Chichester argued, "The escheated lands should not be granted away in gross . . . but rather . . . the division should be amongst many and by reasonable portions, yet such as may encourage the particular undertakers to lay their fortunes upon the plantation and improvement thereof. Consideration must be had of the natives, who are many, that either the principal gentlemen, or else the honester sort and best deserving, may be so satisfied in this division as may quench envy." In both cases, Chichester recognized the need to make provisions for the existing Irish population as a means of ensuring peace.[7]

In 1609, Chichester spoke even more bluntly regarding the importance of paying heed to the native Irish, referencing the failure of the Munster Plantation:

Moreover, the daily conversation and dwelling of the Irish amongst the English gave free recourse to all their base followers and rogues to make

6. Chichester to the king, Oct. 31, 1610, in Russell and Prendergast, eds., *CSPI of the Reign of James I,* III, 520.

7. Chichester, "A Project for the Division and Plantation of the Several Small Territories in the County of Wexford," Feb. 28, 1616, in J. S. Brewer and William Bullen, eds., *Calendar of the Carew Manuscripts, Preserved in the Archiepiscopal Library at Lambeth,* VI, *1603–1624* (London, 1873), 323; Lord Deputy to the Privy Council, Oct. 14, 1608, in Russell and Prendergast, eds., *CSPI of the Reign of James I,* III, 68.

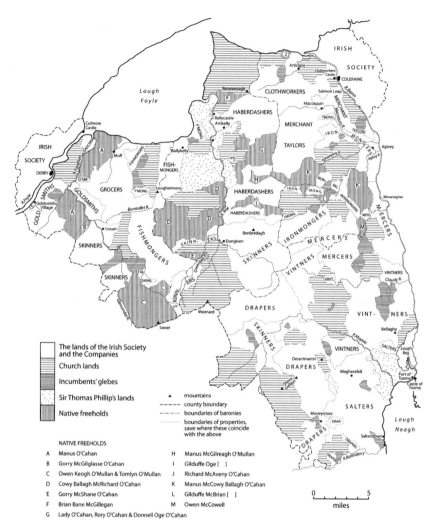

The lands of the Irish Society
and the Companies

Church lands

Incumbents' glebes

Sir Thomas Phillip's lands

Native freeholds

▲ mountains
----- county boundary
-·-·- boundaries of baronies
·········· boundaries of properties,
save where these coincide
with the above

NATIVE FREEHOLDS

A	Manus O'Cahan	H	Manus McGilreagh O'Mullan
B	Gorry McGilglasse O'Cahan	I	Gilduffe Oge [ ]
C	Owen Keogh O'Mullan & Tomlyn O'Mullan	J	Richard McAveny O'Cahan
D	Cowy Ballagh McRichard O'Cahan	K	Manus McCowy Ballagh O'Cahan
E	Gorry McShane O'Cahan	L	Gilduffe McBrian [ ]
F	Brian Bane McGillegan	M	Owen McCowell
G	Lady O'Cahan, Rory O'Cahan & Donnell Oge O'Cahan		

0   5

miles

Figure 6. Division of lands in the Ulster Plantation. Produced for the author
by Elizabeth Mulqueeny, Queen's University, Belfast, based upon the frontispiece
map in T. W. Moody, *The Londonderry Plantation* (Belfast, 1939)

espial and free passage amongst them, out of which late example he is
bold to say, that, as it is a matter of great consequence and necessity to
make meet provision for the natives, so it is very difficult and dangerous
to remove and transplant such a number of barbarous and warlike people
into any parts of the kingdom; besides that the other provinces are too
well acquainted with their lives and conditions, and will be as unapt to
receive them. . . . Wherever they are placed, they must be forced to leave

their creaghting and dwell together in town reeds as other the King's subjects.

Transplantation was not employed as a mechanism of the plantations of the early seventeenth century, although it would later serve as a key component of the postwar Cromwellian settlements. For Chichester, resettling native Irish within towns designed and administered according to English practice was a civilizing tool. Here Chichester was echoing the sentiments of the colonial theorist Francis Bacon, who in 1609 had argued strongly for the development of plantation towns to "secure the country against future perils" by facilitating the development of a stable society as well as a chain of defensible settlements.[8]

Sir John Davies addressed the position of Ulster's native Irish in his 1612 treatise *A Discoverie of the True Causes Why Ireland Was Never Entirely Subdued*. Davies encouraged the transportation of natives who were perceived to be resistant to English law, whereas others who were more amenable to becoming subjects could remain within the territory to be planted. As related by Davies, "the Irish were in some places transplanted from the Woods and Mountaines, into the Plaines and open Countries, that being removed (like wild fruit trees) they might better grow the milder, and beare the better and sweeter fruit." His use of agricultural metaphors reflects the prevailing emphasis upon the rhetoric of improvement and the belief in agriculture as emblematic of civility. In Davies's estimation, those Irish who remained and mixed with the incoming settlers would "grow up togither in one Nation" and effectively become English. Davies, like Bacon, viewed plantation as a means for social engineering and believed strongly that the native Irish could be convinced of the superiority of English civility. Chichester, on the other hand, recognized that peace could only be maintained through ensuring that the native leadership retained some vestige (preferably very limited) of power, regardless of how "English" they might act and appear.[9]

In the end, only one-quarter of lands in the Ulster Plantation were allocated to native landholders, possibly reflecting Davies's influence. Davies was fully prepared to permit the Irish to become subjects but less willing to extend any power to native leaders. He was unimpressed with the promises

8. Sir Arthur Chichester, "Certain Considerations Touching the Plantation of the Escheated Lands in Ulster," Jan. 27, 1609/10, in Russell and Prendergast, eds., *CSPI of the Reign of James I*, III, 357–359; Francis Bacon, "Certain Considerations Touching the Plantation in Ireland" (1608), in Maxwell, *Irish History from Contemporary Sources*, 269–273.

9. Sir John Davies, *Discoverie of the True Causes Why Ireland Was Never Entirely Subdued . . .* ([1612]; rpt. London, 1969), 281–282.

made by Sir Henry Docwra, commander of forces in the northwest, to native leaders that they be granted title to their traditional lands. O'Cahan and O'Doherty saw personal advantages in the English system of landholding, which would establish them as independent leaders rather than require them to pay O'Neill as an overlord in the traditional Gaelic fashion. O'Cahan even sought recourse in English law, bringing a suit against O'Neill in 1607, in which he stated to Chichester and the Council, "I am come hither to be protected by the King, and to the end that I and my kin may depend only on the King; if you send me down again to live under O'Neale and to hold my country at his pleasure, I must do as I have done, and be at his commandment in all actions he shall undertake." In his defense, O'Cahan noted that "he and his ancestors had for a thousand years been possessed of a country called O'Cahan's Country, lying betwixt the rivers of the Band [Bann] and Loughfoile" and that, at the end of the Nine Years' War, he had submitted "three-quarters of a year or more before the now Earl of Tyrone submitted himself" and "had letters patent granted him as custodia[n] by Sir H. Docwra and the then Lord Deputy, holding immediately from Her Majesty at the accustomed rent, with promise to have the absolute grant at convenient leisure." O'Cahan's abiding concern was maintaining his chiefly position, itself rooted in the control of the hereditary territory depicted on English maps simply as "O'Cahan's Country." Employing English law as a means of retaining these lands was a pragmatic and strategic decision.[10]

Sir Oliver St. John mooted sympathy for Sir Donal Ballagh O'Cahan in June 1607 when he described O'Cahan as "being weary of the tyranny of the O'Neales [and] . . . desirous to be made free by the benefit of the King's laws." St. John would later refer to O'Cahan and his attempts to engage with English law more disparagingly, considering O'Cahan, along with Niall Garbh O'Donnell and Cahir O'Doherty, as "men that have pride enough to think themselves worthy of much more than the King has reason to do for them." When O'Cahan's suit was heard in Dublin that same month, the outcome confirmed the status quo, with one-third of the lands claimed by O'Cahan assigned to O'Neill. Despite O'Neill's apparent victory, the ambiguities raised by the case might have precipitated his decision to leave Ulster, as O'Neill might have perceived the dispute as orches-

10. Sir John Davies to Salisbury, Jul. 1, 1607, in Russell and Prendergast, eds., *CSPI of the Reign of James I*, II, 212; "Petition of Donal Ballagh O'Cahan to the Lord Deputy and Council against the Earl of Tyrone," ibid., 143–144. Katharine Simms considers the relationship between O'Cahan and O'Neill in Simms, *From Kings to Warlords: The Changing Political Structure of Gaelic Ireland in the Later Middle Ages* (Woodbridge, Suffolk, 1987), 30–32, 142.

trated by the Lord Deputy to undermine him. Whatever disappointment O'Cahan himself felt at the outcome of his case against O'Neill—or elation following O'Neill's flight—paled when he found himself under suspicion of treason in the aftermath of the Flight of the Earls. O'Cahan was captured by Sir Thomas Phillips and sent to Dublin, where Lord Deputy Chichester ultimately charged him "with sundry misdemeanours and great presumption of treason" in February 1608. In Chichester's estimation, O'Cahan was a "barbarous unworthy man," a "man with a bold spirit, altogether unacquainted with the laws and civil conversation, and undoubtedly has much malice in him." This description is rather at odds with O'Cahan's attempted use of English law but is easily read as an effort to "other" the Irish leader. Considering Chichester's later involvement with the Virginia colony, it is noteworthy that, in October 1608, Chichester proposed to send O'Cahan and O'Donnell, who were reportedly endeavoring to escape from Dublin Castle, "to the new colony in Florida, from whence they may never return." Here Chichester betrays his disdain not only for the native leaders but for the New World colony of Virginia.[11]

Donal Ballagh O'Cahan's inconsistent treatment by the English reflects the chaos and cultural uncertainties of the period. When convenient, O'Cahan was treated as an ally and gentleman according to English custom, but he never enjoyed the trust of any of the English leaders, including Docwra. Although Docwra supported his case against Tyrone in 1607, in December 1601 Docwra had written triumphantly of laying waste to O'Cahan's lands and killing his brother: "I have burned all his corn and houses, whereof I found infinite store. . . . We slew many of his people . . . amongst

11. Sir Oliver St. John to Salisbury, June 1, 1607, in Russell and Prendergast, eds., *CSPI of the Reign of James I*, II, 157; St. John to Salisbury, Dec. 11, 1607, ibid., 357; John McGurk, *Sir Henry Docwra, 1564–1631: Derry's Second Founder* (Dublin, 2006), 215; see also Jerrold Casway, "The Decline and Fate of Dónal Ballagh O'Cahan and His Family," in Micheál Ó Siochrú, ed., *Kingdoms in Crisis: Ireland in the 1640s* (Dublin, 2001), 44–62; McGurk, "The Flight of the Earls: Escape or Strategic Regrouping?" *History Ireland*, XV, no. 4 (July/August 2007), 16–21; Chichester to the Privy Council, Nov. 28, 1607, in Russell and Prendergast, eds., *CSPI of the Reign of James I*, II, 337; Chichester to Salisbury, Feb. 17, 1608, ibid., 418; Sir Thomas Phillips to Salisbury, May 10, 1608, ibid., 519; Chichester to Salisbury, Oct. 18, 1608, ibid., III, 87. Chichester's use of "Florida" rather than "Virginia" as a shorthand for "North America" reflects not only the lack of news from the fledgling colony in 1608 and the previous common use of the term but arguably also reflects a memory within Ireland of Thomas Stukeley and his subversion of the English effort to rescue the French Protestant colony in Florida. Stukeley was infamous among the English forces in Ireland for his support for the cause of Shane O'Neill, as discussed in Chapter 2. By 1610, Chichester referred to the New World colony as being in Virginia. See David Beers Quinn, *The Elizabethans and the Irish* (Ithaca, N.Y., 1966), 121.

them Rory, his perfidious brother, who happily fell into my hands so as I sacrificed him quick. I burnt his camp." Certainly, Chichester never trusted O'Cahan. Writing in 1612, Chichester described the Irish prisoners in the Tower of London as "so subtill and full of practice, that I have kept continual Watch and espial upon the intelligence and advises they have had with their friends here, about two years since I lighted upon Letters written from Sir Donough O'Cahane to his Brother Manus, in which he declared his spleen to our Nation, and labored in them to make us more odious to this people and to incite them to withstand the plantation in those parts." O'Cahan never suspected, in venting his anger to his brother, that Manus would betray him to Chichester in his own attempt to retain some of the O'Cahan lordship. Although Chichester clearly overplayed Donal Ballagh O'Cahan's ability to foment rebellion from his prison, he recognized O'Cahan's fundamental motivation: control over his hereditary lands and opposition to its plantation.[12]

For O'Cahan's own part, his actions reflect a willingness to subvert Gaelic customs in order to supplant O'Neill, although his behavior is more indicative of traditional Gaelic rivalries and political machinations than any true desire to become an English subject. Ready parallels can be drawn with the ways in which the Natives of the Chesapeake endeavored to use the English settlers to their own benefit in their intertribal relations. Rather than view either the Irish or the Powhatan people on the eve of conquest as pawns in the face of colonization and plantation, one should acknowledge the self-aware actions of individuals on all sides—actions that seldom anticipated the future but very much reflected the worldviews of the time. To what extent was O'Cahan familiar with English culture? Unlike O'Neill, O'Cahan had not been educated in the English Pale but was certainly familiar with the character and behavior of Ulster's English military leaders. As O'Neill's son-in-law and *uirrithe* (hereditary subchief), O'Cahan also would have gained some understanding of English cultural practices as O'Neill implemented and understood them. A useful description of O'Neill's own household—and, by extension, O'Neill's use of mimetic practice—survives in a brief let-

12. Letter from Sir Henry Docwra, Dec. 6, 1601, in Hans Claude Hamilton, Ernest G. Atkinson, and Robert Pentland Mahaffy, eds., *Calendar of the State Papers, Relating to Ireland, of the Reigns of Henry VIII., Edward VI., Mary, and Elizabeth* . . . , 11 vols. (London, 1860–1912), XI, *1601–3 (with Addenda, 1565–1654), and of the Hanmer Papers,* 202; "The Lord Deputy to the Lord Privy Seal," Sept. 24, 1612, in R. Dudley Edwards, ed., "The Letter-Book of Sir Arthur Chichester, 1612–1614, in the Library of Trinity College, Dublin," *Analecta Hibernica*, no. 8 (1938), 45.

Plate 12. O'Neill inauguration. The O'Cahan casts a shoe over O'Neill's head as part of the ceremony. Detail, 1601 Map of East Ulster, National Maritime Museum, P49(25). ©National Maritime Museum, Greenwich, London

ter written by English military commander Sir John Harrington following a visit to O'Neill in 1599. Harrington found the chief's sons to be arrayed "in English clothes like a nobleman's sons; with velvet gerkins and gold lace . . . both of them [learning] the English tongue." Furthermore, Harrington reports that O'Neill was interested in his visitor's English translation of Lodovico Ariosto's 1591 *Orlando Furioso* and that he accordingly left a copy with the children's tutor, a Franciscan friar by the name of Nangle. Unlike his overlord O'Neill, O'Cahan does not appear to have been fluent in English. When petitioning his captors from Dublin Castle and later from the Tower of London, O'Cahan relied upon unidentified scribes, signing only his mark. The 1607 record of his petition to the Privy Council in his suit against O'Neill referred to him as "illiterate," likely owing to his inability to write in English. As a member of the Gaelic elite, however, O'Cahan was conversant in Latin, according to Fynes Moryson.[13]

13. "Report of a Journey into the North of Ireland Written to Justice Carey by Sir John Harington, 1599," in Sir John Harington, *Nugae Antiquae: Being a Miscellaneous Collection of Original Papers, in Prose and Verse . . .* (London, 1804), I, 247–252. By his own account, Harington was censured for this visit and personally chastised by the queen upon his return to England. See "Sir John Harington to Anthony Standen Knight," ibid., 309–311; petition of Donald O'Chane to the Privy Council, June 26, 1607, in Russell and Prendergast, eds., *CSPI of the Reign*

It is tempting to contemplate the interactions that might have taken place among the prisoners of the Tower of London during O'Cahan's 1609– c. 1616 confinement. The Gaelic chieftain was in the company not only of fellow Irish prisoners but also of Sir Walter Raleigh, who maintained reasonably well-appointed lodgings in the Bloody Tower from 1603 to 1616. There, Raleigh wrote his *History of the World* and entertained visitors, including the scientist and onetime Munster planter Thomas Hariot as well as several Guianan Natives Raleigh had brought back to England following his 1595 South American expedition. Raleigh's experiences as both a soldier and a planter in Ireland provided some basis for a relationship with the Irish prisoners, be it cordial or antagonistic.[14]

O'Cahan and O'Donnell would have also encountered the accused Catholic apologist Henry Percy, earl of Northumberland, imprisoned from 1605 to 1621 for his role in the 1605 Gunpowder Plot. An old friend of Raleigh's, Percy (dubbed the Wizard Earl) was celebrated for his extensive library and his role as a patron for scientists including Thomas Hariot. From the relative comfort of the Martin Tower, Percy financially supported the colonial activities of his younger brother George, who would be one of the few adventurers to survive the first years of the Jamestown colony. Before setting sail for Virginia, George Percy visited the Tower and presented his traveling clothes to Henry for inspection and approval. Upon George's return from Virginia in 1612, he remained dependent upon Henry, taking up residence in his brother's household; hence the younger Percy was likely a frequent visitor to the Tower. In respect of his visits to Ireland before the Jamestown adventure, George Percy possessed a baseline for understanding, positively or negatively, the situation of the Irish lords imprisoned in the Tower.[15]

Although the Irish state prisoners did not have the political or economic clout to support the freedoms granted to individuals like Northumberland

---

of James I, II, 200. Fynes Moryson describes O'Cahan as conversing with his guests "in the Latin tongue" (Moryson, *An Itinerary: Containing His Ten Yeeres Travell* . . . [1617; rpt. Glasgow, 1907–1908], IV, 237–238).

14. Alden T. Vaughan discusses the possible visits from Guianan Natives to the Tower in "Sir Walter Ralegh's Indian Interpreters, 1584–1618," *William and Mary Quarterly,* 3d Ser., LIX (2002), 341–376. See also Martin A. S. Hume, *Sir Walter Raleigh: The British Dominion of the West* (London, 1897), 288; Robert Lacey, *Sir Walter Raleigh* (New York, 1973), 325. At the start of Raleigh's incarceration, he might have encountered the Munster lord Florence MacCarthy, the MacCarthy Mór, who had been imprisoned in the Tower since 1601. He was transferred to another prison in 1604. See John Dorney, "Florence MacCarthy and the Conquest of Gaelic Munster, 1540–1640" (MA thesis, University College, Dublin, 2003).

15. Mark Nicholls, "George Percy's 'Trewe Relacyon': A Primary Source for the Jamestown Settlement," *Virginia Magazine of History and Biography,* CXIII (2005), 212–216.

and Raleigh, they were permitted visitors. In 1613, a warrant was granted to O'Cahan's wife, Honora, and Niall Garbh O'Donnell's sister Joan to visit the prisoners, chaperoned by an Irish interpreter. Honora would later be granted more general, albeit still chaperoned, access "at convenient tymes." Not all access to the prisoners seems to have been so highly regulated. Testimony given in 1617 against Edmund Oge O'Donnelly, an alleged Irish spy for the Spanish, noted that the accused "very often repairs into the Tower to confer with the Irish knights that are imprisoned there." If the testimony was accurate, then entertaining outside visitors was a routine activity.[16]

Discerning O'Cahan's character from written records is not a straightforward exercise. Beyond his own letters, sources range from bardic poetry extolling the O'Cahan's virtues to the more derisory commentaries by the English, which generally imply O'Cahan lost his lands because of his own personality flaws and inability to act rationally rather than through calculated English political maneuvering. Perhaps the most remarkable, if not necessarily reliable, English description of O'Cahan comes from the prolific pen of Fynes Moryson, who recounted the experience of the Czech noble and envoy of the Holy Roman Emperor Rudolph II, Jaroslav z Donína, baron of Dohna, who visited the O'Cahan at his Limavady stronghold in 1601:

> Comming to the house of Ocane a great Lord among them, was met at the doore with sixteene women, all naked, excepting their loose mantles;

16. "A Warrant to the Lieutennant of the Tower to Suffer Honora Ny Cahan, Wif unto Sir Donell O'Cahan, and Joane Ny Donell, Sister to Sir Neale O'Donell, Knighte, Prisoners in the Tower, to Have Accesse unto Them," Jul. 21, 1613, *Acts of the Privy Council of England*, N.S., XXXIII, *1613–1614* (London, 1921), 144; "A Letter to the Lieutennant of the Tower," Feb. 15, 1614, ibid., 345; "Neale Kinge's Information against Edmund Oge O'Donnelly," 1617, in Russell and Prendergast, eds., *CSPI of the Reign of James I*, V, *1615–1625*, 179. Visitors to the Tower of London today learn much about the imprisonment of Raleigh, the torture of recusants such as the Jesuit priest John Gerard, and the experiences of conspirators such as the earl of Northumberland. Despite the implicit recognition of religious conflict in the displays about torture in the museum, nowhere is there any mention of seventeenth-century Irish political prisoners. Despite the historical prominence of individuals like O'Cahan and O'Donnell, their presence and experiences in the Tower remain invisible in the public displays, reflecting the continuing ambiguity in the relationship between Britain and Ireland. The Troubles-era Republican bombing campaigns within Britain and the symbolism of the label "political prisoner" in precipitating the 1981 Hunger Strike at Long Kesh / Maze Prison might have influenced the decision over which stories to tell (or not tell) in the Tower. That O'Cahan's fate remains important today is clear in the contemporary O'Cahan / O'Kane clan's intention to petition for a retrospective pardon or declaration of innocence for Donal Ballagh O'Cahan, who was never formally convicted of any crime but nevertheless died while incarcerated. Information on the pardon effort from Danny O'Kane, personal communication, Limavady, Sept. 8, 2009.

whereof eight or ten were very faire, and two seemed very Nimphs: with which strange sight his eyes being dazelled, they led him into the house, and there sitting downe by the fier, with crossed legges like Taylors, and so low as could not but offend chast eyes, desired him to set downe with them. Soone after Ocane the Lord of the Countrie came in all naked excepting a loose mantle, and shooes, which he put off assoone as he came in, and entertaining the Barron after his best manner in the Latin tongue, desired him to put off his apparel, which he thought to be a burthen to him, and to sit naked by the fier with his naked company. But the Barron when he came to himselfe after some astonishment at this strange sight, professed that he was so inflamed therewith, as for shame he durst not put off his apparrell.

This description could be read as merely reflecting the sexualization of the "other," both as a tantalizing promise by Moryson to future servitors as well as a clear indication of the perceived immorality, incivility, and inferiority of the Irish. Read from another perspective, however, the tale may possibly contain some truth. It rings true in terms of the generosity of Gaelic hospitality and women's role in facilitating that hospitality. The wearing of scant apparel within the chief's dwelling likewise might conceivably have reflected generosity, given the many references to the fire that warmed the dwelling and rendered heavy clothing unnecessary. Finally, it is the baron, not O'Cahan, who suffers embarrassment at his inability to control his arousal. This account contains a hidden transcript. In describing the baron's humiliation, the virulently anti-Irish Moryson unintentionally reveals O'Cahan to be a powerful and self-controlled figure, despite his apparent violation of the rules of English apparel.[17]

17. Perhaps reflecting their reliance upon these English documentary sources, historians of the Londonderry Plantation have not been kind to Donal Ballagh O'Cahan. The nineteenth-century antiquarian the Reverend George Hill belittled O'Cahan as a "sulky" and "ill-starred simpleton"; the eminent mid-twentieth-century historian T. W. Moody dismissed him as "hot-tempered and reckless"; and, in seeming contrast, the London Company chronicler James Stevens Curl labeled him as "fearful and hostile." Meanwhile, Philip S. Robinson accords O'Cahan one mention in his 254-page history of the Ulster Plantation, suggesting that O'Cahan was implicated in the O'Doherty revolt (despite already being imprisoned in Dublin Castle), which justified the English development of his lands. See Hill, *An Historical Account of the Plantation in Ulster at the Commencement of the Seventeenth Century, 1608–1620* ([1877]; rpt. Shannon, 1970), 61, 234; Moody, *Londonderry Plantation, 1609–41*, 255; Curl, *The Honourable the Irish Society*, 29; Robinson, *The Plantation of Ulster: British Settlement in an Irish Landscape, 1600–1670* (1984; rpt. Belfast, 2000), 67; Moryson, *Itinerary*, IV, 237–238; Quinn, *Elizabethans and the Irish*, 70; Alan Haynes, *Robert Cecil, Earl of Salisbury 1563–1612, Servant of Two Sovereigns* (London, 1989), 113–114.

O'Cahan's efforts to engage with the new English order were doomed to failure, not because of any lack of understanding or rationality on his part, but because the English could not permit a powerful Gaelic leader to remain in control of a strategic territory. O'Cahan would die in the Tower of London shortly after sending his last missive to the Privy Council, a petition for justice, on September 30, 1616. Manus O'Cahan, like his brother, saw the advantage in courting the English and, ultimately, in renouncing his brother. A 1610 plea from Donal that Manus "perform a brotherly part to gain yourself a loving brother; and gather both from yourself and from others your best help, that either yourself or some others might come with my wife hither to sue for my liberty" fell on deaf ears, as the younger O'Cahan promptly turned the letter over to Sir Arthur Chichester. The O'Cahan's plea to Manus that he not "let covetous hope of lands debar you" from helping to free him from the Tower suggests that he was well aware of his younger brother's motivations. Manus O'Cahan did receive a grant of land in the Londonderry Plantation, as did Donal Ballagh's wife Honora, but never came close to claiming O'Cahan's Country. Despite the perspective of the pragmatic military man Docwra, who was painfully aware that the cooperation of native leaders like Donal Ballagh O'Cahan had been key to the successful conclusion of the Nine Years' War, English plans for subduing and settling the north of Ireland would not include any significant concessions to native leaders. Although Docwra reasoned that upholding bargains with the native leaders might allow for a more lasting peace, his advice was not followed.[18]

The remainder of the escheated Ulster lands was divided between Scottish and English undertakers, the Church of Ireland, Trinity College, and the Irish Society and London Companies. To plant and subdue territory outside of the Londonderry Plantation lands, the king relied upon individual undertakers and groups of investors. In Counties Antrim, Down, Donegal, and Fermanagh, Scottish planters spearheaded much of the plantation activity, with that of Antrim and Down outside the boundaries of the official Ulster Plantation scheme. Their efforts varied greatly according to the planter's origin and religion. Settlements on the lands of the Catholic earl of Antrim, Randal MacDonnell, built upon the long-established ties with the Scottish Isles, whereas the plantations administered by the Lowland Protestants

18. *Acts of the Privy Council of England,* N.S., XXXV, *1616–1617* (London, 1927), 29–30; Sir Donal O'Cahan to Manus O'Cahan, June 1, 1610, in Russell and Prendergast, eds., *CSPI of the Reign of James I,* III, 504. Rancor continued through the generations, as O'Cahan's son Rory Oge headed a failed conspiracy to overthrow the English in 1615, whereas his other son, Donal Gimhlach, fought and died for the Irish cause in the Rising/Rebellion of the 1640s.

James Hamilton and Hugh Montgomery—Conn McBrien O'Neill's former territory in Counties Down and Antrim—relied upon the importation of extended family groups and the subjugation and attempted displacement of native Irish communities.

Not surprisingly, the Ulster Plantation as a whole was presented as a profitable enterprise for investors and undertakers, but, like so many other ventures, it was to be predicated upon the availability of private rather than public finance, a decision that was recognized as problematic at the time. Sir Arthur Chichester clearly anticipated the same need for crown investment in the venture, as would the leadership of the floundering Virginia colony at Jamestown. Writing in 1609 to Lord Danvers (the Lord President of Munster and formerly Sergeant Major General of the Army under Mountjoy), Chichester expressed his reservations about financing the plantation scheme, noting that he "despairs to see it effectually performed upon private men's undertaking; for such an act must be the work of a commonwealth, and upon the common charge, towards which a subsidy or two were well given. . . . If that be not liked of, let every parish in England contribute towards the planting of a man, two or three, according to their circuit and abilities; the men to be sons or natives of the parish." In seeking civic subsidies for the Ulster Plantation, Chichester might have been reflecting on the failed Roanoke colony and its reliance upon private finance, an understanding gained from his friend and associate Ralph Lane.[19]

Sir Thomas Phillips and the Londonderry Plantation

No aspect of the Ulster Plantation scheme was more widely promoted than the Londonderry Plantation, with propaganda and promises designed to attract the considerable financial power of the City of London. The ideas for the Londonderry Plantation were encapsulated in a treatise reflecting the thinking of numerous individuals, entitled "A Project of Sir Thomas Phillips for the Londoners Plantation in the County of Colrane and the Derry." For an individual central in the planning, implementation, oversight, and, eventually, critique of plantation, little is known about Phillips's background before to his service in Ireland to explain how his ideas developed and how much exposure he might have had to earlier literature on planting colonies in Ireland (such as Thomas Smith's) and elsewhere.[20]

---

19. Davies to Salisbury, Sept. 12, 1607, in Russell and Prendergast, eds., *CSPI of the Reign of James I,* II, 272. See Chapter 1 for a consideration of the friendship between Chichester and Lane.

20. "A Project of Sir Thomas Phillips for the Londoners Plantation in the County of Colrane

Phillips, who was knighted in 1607, was a protégé of Sir Robert Cecil, secretary of state, who sent him to Ireland in 1599; in several letters to his patron, Phillips refers to himself as having been "called out of France," where he had previously spent a decade in service. Like many other military men of his time, Phillips traveled widely, as witness a 1606 reference to his "great industry and continual travail in Spain, Portugal, Italy and Africa." Phillips might have been the son of a prominent member of the Clothworkers' Company or a brother to Francis Phillips, one of the two senior revenue auditors of the English exchequer and a financial officer to the London guilds. Either association could explain Phillips's financial position as well as his initial willingness to involve the London guilds.[21]

Once in Ireland, Phillips fought against rebels in Laois and Munster and in 1601 served under Chichester, then-governor of Carrickfergus. In 1602, Phillips succeeded in capturing Hugh O'Neill's stronghold at Toome, where the Bann flows from Lough Neagh toward the sea. Here, Tyrone had constructed a fort on the western side of the Bann opposite an Elizabethan masonry castle. Phillips was subsequently granted custodianship of the castle and an adjacent thirty acres. The scant traces of this castle, excavated in 1991, revealed the original construction to have been sloppy, with poorly mixed and hastily poured mortar. Of notably better build was a five-sided flanker, interpreted as a later construction that could be physical evidence for Phillips's reedification of Toome Castle, central to maintaining English control over the former O'Neill base. Chichester wrote to Cecil in August 1608 that Phillips had "spent the two years past at Toom, keeping in quietness those parts which lie on the Bann side to the mouth of that river." Chichester further asserted that he knew "no country that better requires looking after, nor a better man for the business than Captain Philips." Phillips had clearly impressed the Lord Deputy, paving the way for their later collaboration in the design of the Londonderry Plantation.[22]

---

and the Derry Sent to Robert Earl of Salisbury, Lord High Treasurer of England," 1611, MS 630, Lambeth Palace Library, London.

21. Phillips to Salisbury, May 10, 1608, in Russell and Prendergast, eds., *CSPI of the Reign of James I*, II, 520; Frank Phillips, "Sir Thomas Phillips of Hammersmith and Limavady," *Irish Genealogist*, VII (1986), 9. Phillips argues for the Clothworkers' connection, whereas Victor Treadwell highlights the connection with Francis Phillips in *Buckingham and Ireland, 1616–1628: A Study in Anglo-Irish Politics* (Dublin, 1998), 243. Terry Clavin suggests that Thomas Phillips was the son and heir of William Phillips, one of the queen's customers of the wool, in his entry on Phillips in *Dictionary of Irish Biography*, http://dib.cambridge.org.

22. As noted by the excavator: "The mortar had been roughly poured (perhaps evidence of the urgency with which the castle was built) with the result that lumps were found adhering to

While Phillips was asserting himself at Toome in the English war against O'Neill's waning forces, English adventurer Bartholomew Gosnold was sailing with thirty-one others to the northeast coast of America to establish a trading post and possible colony. This effort was abandoned after only one month, but it sowed the seeds for Gosnold's next colonial enterprise, the (eventually) successful settlement of Virginia in 1607. It is worth mentioning Gosnold's colonial adventures in light of Phillips's activities in Ulster to again underscore that the planting of Virginia was not carried out on the basis of any well-established Irish model. There is no evidence to suggest Gosnold had ever been to Ireland, although his close association with Edward Maria Wingfield, who fought in Ireland and then served as the Virginia colony's first governor, would have provided him with secondhand information. Given that Wingfield's brother Thomas was the one to lead the English forces in retreat from the Yellow Ford, Gosnold might have reasonably perceived the New World as an easier proposition. By contrast to Gosnold's preoccupations with New World colonization, Thomas Phillips was a soldier whose principal concerns in 1602 were to repel O'Neill's forces. Over the next decade, Phillips transformed himself from a military leader into an outspoken proponent of plantation.[23]

In 1604, Phillips was installed at Coleraine, a former O'Cahan stronghold featuring a thirteenth-century Dominican friary and an English garrison, which Chichester had hopes of developing into a plantation town. Efforts to fortify the locale had been sporadically mooted in the sixteenth century. The earl of Essex informed the Privy Council of his intent "to set upon the building of a town at Coleraine by the Bann and a bridge there over the river" in April 1574. A memorandum by Lord Burghley to Essex, approving of the scheme to build Coleraine and Belfast, yields critical insight into the expected role of towns in a colonial Ulster. Residents of the new towns

---

the face of the wall at various points." See Ruairí Ó Baoill, "Excavations at the Site of Toome Castle, Co. Antrim," *Ulster Journal of Archaeology,* 3d Ser., LVIII (1999), 93; Chichester to Viscount Cranbourne [Cecil], Aug. 28, 1604, in Russell and Prendergast, eds., *CSPI of the Reign of James I,* I, *1603–1606,* 194.

23. For consideration of the Nine Years' War, see Hiram Morgan, *Tyrone's Rebellion: The Outbreak of the Nine Years' War in Tudor Ireland* (Woodbridge, Suffolk, 1993); Morgan, ed., *The Battle of Kinsale* (Bray, 2004); G. A. Hayes-McCoy, *Irish Battles: A Military History of Ireland* (London, 1969); Hayes-McCoy, *Ulster and Other Irish Maps, c.1600* (Dublin, 1964). For Gosnold, see David R. Ransome, "Gosnold, Bartholomew," in *Oxford Dictionary of National Biography,* Oxford University Press, 2004–, accessed May 1, 2013, http://www.oxforddnb.com/view/article/11108?docPos=1; Paul Logue, "Thomas Maria Wingfield, Elizabethan Soldier," paper presented at the Tenth Irish Post-Medieval Archaeology Group Conference, Belfast, 2010.

were to be mostly English, with privileges to sow corn; but their butter and cheese "must come out of England and Wales," presumably to protect English and Welsh commodities in the face of Irish pastoralism. Timber frames for storehouses (100 feet long by 24 feet wide) were to be "made and sent out of England for a house of storage . . . and in these houses must be provided brewing vessels especially cast." Similarly, timber frames for mills were to be provided. Whereas bridges, mills, and houses were ultimately to be built of stone, all masonry work to be attempted in the first year of settlement should concentrate upon the fortifications. Two hundred laborers, of whom fifty were to be skilled, should be provided, along with the use of several ships, including one that Sir Francis Drake "brought out of the Indias," then in the possession of Sir John Hawkins, the English slave trader; an additional four light boats were "to be framed ready in England to carry horses or stores and such like upon the rivers." Such plans were wildly optimistic as well as prohibitively expensive. Three months later, Essex was moved to write to Burghley, "I want [lack] my pioneers, tools for fortification and the storehouses." Although he added a postscript to this letter stating that "the frigates, hoy, mills and tools for the labourers arrived," by June he abandoned his plans to build at Coleraine and at the Blackwater in favor of Belfast, upon learning that the queen had withdrawn her support for his efforts. What became of the materials that had arrived in May, and whether or not Essex put the tools, frigates, and mills to use—and where—is unknown.[24]

Coleraine remained principally a garrison. Captain Christopher Carleill might have also implemented a grander building scheme in 1584, when he found himself assigned there as commander. Carleill was not much impressed with the existing settlement and had little success there, describing it in a letter to Walsingham as the most barren spot in Ireland. The garrison was still in need of investment in 1598, when Ralph Lane suggested to Burghley that a force of nine hundred foot and one hundred horse should be sent to Coleraine in order to keep Scots forces from aiding Hugh O'Neill. Francis Jobson's map of the same year indicates that a garrison was to be established at the Abbey of Coleraine. In 1601, Sir Henry Docwra offered to "make a plantation there (for I have 40 masons and carpenters), which will

24. Earl of Essex to the Privy Council, Apr. 21, 1574, in Mary O'Dowd, ed., *Calendar of State Papers, Ireland, Tudor Period, 1571–1575* (Kew, 2000), 561; "Memorandum by Burghley on the Plat of Walter Devereaux, Earl of Essex," ibid., 743–744; Essex to Lord Burghley, May 8, 1575, ibid., 804; Elizabeth to Essex, May 22, 1575, ibid., 819; Essex to Privy Council, June 1, 1575, ibid., 831; "Instructions Given by Walter Devereaux, Earl of Essex to Mr. Ashton Dispatched towards Queen Elizabeth and the Privy Council," June 1, 1575, ibid., 831–832.

help to end the war" while Captain Humphrey Willis petitioned Cecil for two hundred foot and a posting at Coleraine in order to subdue the "proud traitor" Donal Ballagh O'Cahan. Some force obviously existed there as of September of that year, as Arthur Chichester mentioned using the troops at Coleraine in his plans for an attack on O'Neill's stronghold of Dungannon. Whatever forces were there must have been quite small, as Docwra continued to report his intention to fortify it. In November 1602, the forces recorded for Coleraine, under the command of Captain John Sydney, numbered one hundred foot.[25]

In pressing for Thomas Phillips to be granted an estate at Coleraine, Chichester argued that he "deems the place better put into Captain Phillips' possession than left to the use of priests and friars," and, furthermore, he "thinks it better bestowed upon Captain Phillips, unto whom it is well known, than on a Scotchman, who is said to be a suitor for it, as he will hinder the unlawful excursions of our neighboring islanders." Chichester's distrust of the Highlander Randal MacDonnell is palpable and can be attributed as much to the MacDonnells' mercurial allegiances as to Randal's beheading of Chichester's brother John in 1597. Throughout his deputyship, Chichester continually expressed reservations about permitting the MacDonnells to retain rights to north Antrim. Thomas Phillips also came into conflict with MacDonnell, complaining to Cecil in May 1605 that MacDonnell wanted to renege on an agreement to lease Phillips land at Portrush, on the north coast. Phillips might well have viewed Portrush as an ideal locale for developing a fishing industry, later claiming that "there was long since at Port Rush a fishing used by the Burtons (Bretons) in France, who came every season thither for dogfish and rays, which being well handled are a very great commodity in Spain." One year after this conflict, MacDonnell alleged that Phillips and James Hamilton had illegally claimed his fishing rights on the Bann and that Phillips was conspiring to have him accused of fomenting riots. The dispute over the fishing rights was still unresolved three years later, when MacDonnell again complained to Cecil.[26]

---

25. Rachel Lloyd, *Elizabethan Adventurer: A Life of Captain Christopher Carleill* (London, 1974), 96; Sir Ralph Lane to Sir Robert Cecil, Dec. 23, 1598, in Hans C. Hamilton, Ernest G. Atkinson, and Robert Pentland Mahaffy, eds., *Calendar of the State Papers, Relating to Ireland, of the Reigns of Henry VIII., Edward VI., Mary, and Elizabeth . . .* , 11 vols. (London, 1860–1912), VII, *1598–1599,* 421; Docwra to the Privy Council, Sept. 2, 1601, ibid., XI, 46; Captain Humfry Willis to Secretary Cecil, Sept. 2, 1601, ibid., 48; Chichester to Cecil, Sept. 8, 1601, ibid., 63–64; Docwra to the Privy Council, Jan. 2, 1601/2, ibid., 261–263; "List of the Queen's Army on 20 November 1602," ibid., 525.

26. Chichester to Cecil, June 8, 1604, in Russell and Prendergast, eds., *CSPI of the Reign*

By all accounts, Phillips threw himself into the development of Coleraine with enthusiasm, claiming, in the immediate aftermath of the Flight of the Earls, that "he bought the abbey of Coleraine, and employed all he had in the world on it" and that he had "bestowed all he could get in building, and has made himself a poor man." Phillips converted portions of the Dominican friary, founded in 1244, into a defended residence. The conversion of religious buildings into English garrisons or defended residences is a pattern found throughout post-Reformation Ireland. Notable Ulster examples include the conversion of the Carmelite friary at Rathmullan, Co. Donegal (the embarkation point for the Flight of the Earls), into a residence for Andrew Knox, the Anglican Bishop of Raphoe, and Sir Hugh Montgomery's conversion of the abbey at Newtownards, Co. Down, into his principal dwelling by 1611: "Sir Hugh Montgomery, Kt., hath repaired part of the Abbey of Newtowne for his own dwelling and made a good town of a hundred houses or thereabouts, all peopled with Scots." Within the Londonderry Plantation, Phillips's brother-in-law Sir Edward Doddington converted the Dungiven priory into his manor. Such repurposing of religious structures carried symbolic weight.[27]

Archaeological investigations within Coleraine have yielded traces of the friary (if not specific evidence for Phillips's conversions) and of the late medieval town ditch, which was likely strengthened by Phillips. Finds of fine drinking glass fragments and early-seventeenth-century North Devon pottery were interpreted as domestic rubbish dumped by the Phillips household. By 1609, Phillips claimed to have nearly completed a fort (generally taken to be the fortification of the friary perimeter), to have "induced many English and Scotch to settle," and to have established a "fair market" and a well-attended church. Subsequently, Phillips would also claim to have constructed thirty thatched cottages in the settlement. Whatever the true extent of his developments, in 1610, Phillips was compelled to surrender his lands and rights at Coleraine to the Irish Society. He then moved to Limavady, taking over and reedifying Donal Ballagh O'Cahan's chief castle by the River Roe and acquiring control over 19,400 acres.[28]

---

of James I, I, 178; Phillips to Salisbury, May 19, 1605, ibid., 276; Randall McDonnell to Salisbury, July 16, 1606, ibid., I, 518; McDonnell to Salisbury, Aug. 19, 1608, ibid., III, 21; [Thomas Phillips,] "The Londoners' Plantation," ibid., IV, 225.

27. Phillips to Salisbury, Sept. 22, 1607, ibid., II, 280–281; Gilbert Camblin, *The Town in Ulster: An Account of the Origin and Building of the Towns of the Province and the Development of Their Rural Setting* . . . (Belfast, 1951), 29–30.

28. N. F. Brannon, "Excavations in New Row, Coleraine," in G. Egan, ed., "Post-Medieval

Phillips has been presented as a financially imprudent individual who capitalized upon the king's interests in Ulster to extract himself from his debts, incurred in large part through his efforts to garrison and develop Coleraine. A closer reading of the documents as well as of the archaeology associated with Phillips's developments at Limavady suggests, instead, that although Phillips experienced financial difficulties, they were the result of the seriousness with which he viewed his role as a servitor and planter. To what extent Phillips was responsible for the Londonderry Plantation plan is unclear from the documentary record. What is clear is that Phillips's first-hand knowledge was critical in convincing the companies that the venture might be profitable. His treatise for the development of Ulster and the involvement of the London Companies, although occasionally straining credibility, comes across as a far more grounded document than many other contemporary treatises on plantation and colonization. Rather than promise vast mineral riches, for example, Phillips focuses upon some of the more prosaic yet highly desirable commodities of Ulster, particularly timber, fish, and hides. Phillips was writing from knowledge rather than from speculation; and although a desire to recoup his debts might have been a factor in his enthusiasm for the Londoners' involvement, his commitment to the project is underscored by his own activities as a planter and, ultimately, by his fierce condemnation of the Londoners for not meeting the conditions of the Londonderry Plantation scheme.[29]

Phillips's 1611 treatise summarized all the arguments he marshaled to convince the crown and Council of the need to involve the Londoners in the Ulster Plantation:

Besides the great benefit and profit that the undertakers shall reap by this plantation, it will be a general good for the commonwealth, for by this means London may be not only furnished with all kinds of provisions for the sustenance of man, but also with all sorts of timber, as joists, clap-

Britain and Ireland in 1984," *Post-Medieval Archaeology,* XIX (1985), 168; Brannon, "Where History and Archaeology Unite: Coleraine, Co. Londonderry," in Ann Hamlin and Chris Lynn, eds., *Pieces of the Past: Archaeological Excavations by the Department of the Environment for Northern Ireland, 1970–1986* (Belfast, 1988), 78–79; "Sir Thomas Phillipps's Petition," April 1609, in Russell and Prendergast, eds., *CSPI of the Reign of James I,* III, 202; Phillips to Salisbury, Jul. 12, 1609, ibid., 248; Sir Thomas Phillips, *Londonderry and the London Companies, 1609–1629: Being a Survey and Other Documents Submitted to King Charles I* (Belfast, 1928), 26.

29. For assertions of Phillips's imprudent financial abilities, see Curl, *Londonderry Plantation,* 28–31.

boards, wainscots, barrel boards, hogshead boards, oaken planks for shipping, and other uses. These kinds of commodities I hope in time may be
afforded here cheaper than the boards and timber which the Dutchmen
bring hither.

Phillips's arguments for the wealth that could be gained from developing
Irish timber would prove partially accurate, but he was not immune to hyperbole:

> Since my coming to London I had conference with one Benedict Webb,
> a clothier, who was employed by your Lordship in France, concerning
> clothing, who has very good skill in making oils; he assured me that there
> was 10*l.* to be made of one acres sowing (all charges being deducted). He
> desired me to be an humble suitor to you for license of it for us both, that
> none should make it in the north of Ireland but by our means.

Nothing came of this particular mechanism for profiteering. On his own
lands, Phillips focused upon exploiting ready raw commodities such as timber and fish.[30]

The masterstroke that ensured the implementation of the Londonderry
Plantation scheme was a demonstration of the proposed lands' advantages
to a deputation of Londoners in 1609, an event Phillips spearheaded under
orders from Chichester and the Privy Council. Instructions were sent ahead
that Chichester "select discreet persons to conduct, and accompany them,
who shall be able to control whatever discouraging reports may be made
to them out of ignorance or malice." Furthermore, "the conductors must
take care to lead them by the best ways, and to lodge them in their travel,
where they may, if possible, receive English entertainment in Englishmen's houses." The Londoners were shepherded by Phillips, who was well
equipped to show off only Ulster's attractive side. The finale was a boat trip
down the Lower Bann to its mouth near Coleraine, providing the deputation with a view of the fertile lands, dense forests, and the abundant riverine
life available to them. Encounters with locals were studiously avoided, as
were visits to uncharted upland areas still held by the Irish. As Chichester
reported on September 18, the company representatives "like so well of the
scites *(sic),* the lands adjoining the rivers, and the commodities they think
to raise by their purse and good husbandry, that they assure him the City
of London will really undertake the plantation upon the report they are to

---

30. "Project of Sir Thomas Phillips," 108; Brewer and Bullen, eds., *Carew MSS*, VI, 151–152.

Plate 13. Thomas Raven, division of lands in the Londonderry Plantation, 1622.
With acknowledgment to the Deputy Keeper of the Records at the Public
Record Office of Northern Ireland

make." As a follow-up to this successful mission, Chichester arranged for
Ulster products such as beef, eels, herring, salmon, staves, and hides to be
sent to the London Companies, to further whet their appetites.[31]

The company agents later enthusiastically reported to the City on
Londonderry's economic resources:

> In the woods of Glankankayn and Killatrough are great store of goodly
> oaks, fit for all manner of building, ash also, with elm of great bigness. The
> country in every place is plentiful of stone, apt for any uses; clay and sand
> in divers places thereof for making brick and tile; limestone is there also in
> great abundance. . . . Of timber for shipping or for any other building, the
> woods of Glankankayn and Killatrough [situated in the Bann valley] af-
> ford great plenty, as also good store of pipe, hogshead, and barrel staves,
> clapboard and hoops.

31. Lords of the Council to Chichester, Aug. 3, 1609, in Russell and Prendergast, eds., *CSPI
of the Reign of James I,* III, 266; "Instructions for the Survey of the Derry Plantation," October 1609, ibid., 316; Chichester to Salisbury, Sept. 18, 1609, ibid., 286; Davies to Chichester,
Sept. 20, 1609, ibid., 288; Curl, *The Honourable the Irish Society,* 41.

In addition, the riverine and maritime commodities of the Lower Bann valley exhibited "great store of seals. . . . Sea fowl are found in great abundance. . . . In the rivers of Loughfoyle and Bann, besides salmon and eels, there is great plenty of trout, flounders, and other small fish, and the said rivers by computation yield 120 tons of salmon yearly, and sometimes more." Phillips had pulled off a hard sell. By insulating the company agents from the unsettled realities of social life in Ulster, he created, in effect, ambassadors for his own scheme.[32]

When plans were finalized for the Londonderry Plantation, the Irish Society (made up of representatives of the Great Twelve City of London Livery Companies) accepted responsibility for the development of Londonderry and Coleraine. At Coleraine, east of the River Bann and two miles from the sea, settlement was founded around Phillips's base and the Dominican friary. In exchange for surrendering his holdings there to the Irish Society, Phillips was granted O'Cahan's Limavady lands in April 1611, as referenced in a communication from the Privy Council to Lord Deputy Sir Arthur Chichester:

> As Sir Thomas Phillipps, has, for the convenience of the Londoners, quitted some portions of land which he possessed in this division, and is now returning, having received a recompence from them by an allotment elsewhere, with which they (the Lords) doubt not but he is satisfied, they (the Londoners) have assigned unto him Lymavaddy, with 3,000 acres, Irish measure, adjoining, as also 500 acres next adjoining to the castle of Toome, in respect of the service he may do by commanding still in those parts as he did before, until their plantation be settled.

O'Cahan's seat at Limavady (from the Irish *Leim an Mhadaidh,* or Leap of the Dog) consisted of a late medieval tower house situated in a defensive position atop a rocky promontory above the River Roe. Limavady was the principal castle of the O'Cahan, who also held seats on a crannog in Enagh Lough, outside of Derry, at Dungiven on the River Roe, and, formerly, at Coleraine. Local tradition holds that the O'Cahan maintained another castle at Killane, north of the present town of Limavady, although nothing remains at the site and there are no clear documentary references to it as an O'Cahan seat.[33]

---

32. Instructions for the Survey of the Derry Plantation, October 1609, in Russell and Prendergast, eds., *CSPI of the Reign of James I,* III, 317.

33. Lords of the Council to Chichester, Apr. 14, 1611, ibid., IV, 28–29.

Phillips might have taken especial delight in obtaining O'Cahan's castle and lands at Limavady, given his role in arresting O'Cahan in 1608. There certainly was little love lost between the men. One of the allegations against O'Cahan was that he had incited his brother, Shane Carragh O'Cahan, to rebellion and urged him to capture Phillips. For his part, Phillips had no sympathy for O'Cahan's professed support for the crown, having written candidly to Cecil in March 1602, "It is reported that O'Cane wants to come in to her Majesty. So would they all if they would be received. They only do it to save their goods; and to receive them would be to nurse a new war, for they are now all ready to starve." Certainly enmity toward Phillips fueled the ill-fated conspiracy led in part by Rory Oge O'Cahan in 1614–1615, hatched in an English planter's alehouse with the aim of beheading Phillips, freeing the prisoners in the Tower, and restoring the O'Cahan lands.[34]

When Sir Robert Jacob visited the O'Cahan castle at Limavady in 1609 during a trip of the assizes, he described it as "O'Cane's principal house," an "ill-favoured, ruinous castle, but good land round about it." An earlier (1605) description of the castle similarly referred to it as "O'Cahane's chief house" but made no reference to its condition, suggesting it was in reasonably good order, as O'Cahan was still occupying it. This description also notes the establishment of "a market weekly and one fair to be held yearly" in recognition of the "convenience of the place," although it is far from clear whether the market ever materialized. Few of the markets intended for the Ulster Plantation scheme seem to have existed in any form beyond paper. Whatever the condition of the castle and its designated market, Sir Thomas Phillips wasted little time developing his new lands according to the spirit of plantation. By 1611, when Sir George Carew conducted a survey of Ulster Plantation developments, Phillips "hath toward the building of the castle of Lemavady, and other buildings, felled and squared in the woods good store of timber; and hath raised store of stone out of the ditch, adjoining the castle, being a very hard Rock, whereby he intends to make some good work for the defence of the country." In addition to his work on the castle and its environs, Phillips had begun construction of a new plantation town, Newtown Limavady, a few miles from the castle.[35]

The most informative documentary source for Phillips's developments

34. Phillips to Cecil, Mar. 11, 1602, in Mahaffy, ed., *CSPI 1601–3,* 325–326; Raymond Gillespie, *Conspiracy: Ulster Plots and Plotters in 1615* (Belfast, 1987).

35. Sir Robert Jacob to Salisbury, Apr. 15, 1609, in Russell and Prendergast, eds., *CSPI of the Reign of James I,* III, 194; Lord Deputy and Council to the Lords, ibid., I, 321; Lambeth MS 630 (Carew MSS), ff. 47–47v.

can be found in Phillips's own survey of the Londonderry Plantation, conducted in 1622 and illustrated with a series of maps by the cartographer
Thomas Raven. Raven was a professional English mapmaker, with connections to the City of London, who saw opportunity in the Ulster Plantation.
The carving out of new property boundaries and the tracking of progress
relied upon effective cartography. Raven's map of Limavady provides remarkable insight into the character of the built landscape, but it would be
foolish to accept this depiction at face value. Although he was clearly skilled,
Raven was in Phillips's employ, and Phillips had a vested interest in presenting his activities in a favorable light. The map suggests that Phillips had, by
that time, reedified the castle, built a slate-roofed manor house with ornate
projecting leaded window, and developed the surrounding land. The latter
included formal Renaissance gardens, a fish pond, ancillary structures including a possible brewhouse, and several vernacular structures probably intended to house workers, animals, and produce. As evidenced by this map,
the Roe Valley castle appears to have begun its life as a rectangular tower
house, later augmented with two adjoining circular towers. Although the
veracity of Raven's depiction has been generally accepted, no documentary
evidence speaks so directly to work Phillips carried out, with the exception
of Carew's 1611 comments above. A 1626 reference suggests that the castle
might not actually have been remodeled. Writing on behalf of Phillips's plea
for a pension, Lord Falkland assured the Privy Council that, if they paid
him, Phillips "will fortify his castle, and this will be no small comfort to the
other plantations thereabout." Phillips did receive his pension, but there is
no further mention of whether the castle was fortified. The castle no longer
stands, and the site has not been fully excavated; limited testing unearthed
the traces of a robbed-out wall of likely medieval date, leaving Phillips's
work still to be identified.[36]

Today, the site of Phillips's plantation base lies within the boundaries of

36. For discussion of Thomas Raven, see J. H. Andrews, *Plantation Acres: An Historical
Study of the Irish Land Surveyor and His Maps* (Belfast, 1985), 55–56; Bernhard Klein, *Maps and
the Writing of Space in Early Modern England and Ireland* (Basingstoke, 2001), 127–128; and
Raymond Gillepsie, "Thomas Raven and the Mapping of the Claneboy Estates," *Journal of the
Bangor Historical Society*, II (1981), 6–9. Phillips "added a circular fortified tower" to the castle,
"which was a crenellated tower-house to which were attached sundry structures capped by Irish
crenellations" (Curl, *Londonderry Plantation*, 432); Lambeth MS 630 (Carew MSS), ff. 47–47v.;
Lord Falkland to the English Privy Council, Mar. 15, 1626, in Robert Mahaffy, ed., *Calendar
of the State Papers, Relating to Ireland, of the Reign of Charles I, 1625–[1660]* (London, 1900–1903),
I, *1625–1632*, 105–106; Audrey Horning, "Preliminary Report on Excavations in the Roe Valley
Country Park," unpublished report, September 2009.

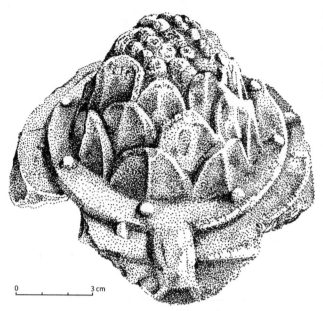

Figure 7.
Dungiven plaster-
work. Drawn for the
author by Elizabeth
Mulqueeny, Queen's
University, Belfast

0   3 cm

the Roe Valley Country Park, a public amenity that consists of a narrow band of woodland straddling the River Roe for a three-mile length, just outside of the present town of Limavady. The castle site itself is recognizable as a promontory defended on the landward side by a still-evident ditch and on the river side by a circa-one-hundred-foot drop. Occasional tree falls and landscaping activities have unearthed material culture from the castle, including decorative plasterwork. An 1835 description of the castle noted the periodic recovery of fragments of ornamental ceiling from the ruins of the building. Although the whereabouts of the nineteenth-century finds are unknown, the plasterwork more recently recovered from the Limavady castle is similar to materials excavated at Dungiven, where another O'Cahan tower house had been adapted by the English servitor and planter Sir Edward Doddington and his wife in the early seventeenth century. Analysis of the Dungiven plasterwork, attributed to Doddington, suggests parallels with late-sixteenth-century examples in Wales and England.[37]

It is possible that the plasterwork at both Limavady and Dungiven relates

37. Angélique Day and Patrick McWilliams, eds., *Ordnance Survey Memoirs of Ireland*, IX, *Parishes of Co. Londonderry II, 1833–5, Roe Valley Central* (Belfast, 1991), 57; A. S. Kennedy Abraham, "Fragments of Decorative Plasterwork from Dungiven Priory, Co. Londonderry," unpublished undergraduate archaeology project, Queen's University, Belfast, 1986.

to the final years of the O'Cahan occupancy, when O'Cahan himself was negotiating his position within the emerging New English–led hierarchy. Remodeling his castle interior in line with current fashions in England might have been a material means of proclaiming his status and cultural awareness. More likely, the exigencies of war and O'Cahan's struggle against paying rent to Tyrone in the period between the 1603 Treaty of Mellifont and his 1608 arrest by Thomas Phillips made investing in expensive interior appointments a lesser priority. By contrast, soldiers and adventurers like Phillips and Doddington were keen to prove their credentials as men of standing, materially marked by their building works. Little early plasterwork survives in Ireland, with important exceptions being the late-sixteenth-century heraldic plasterwork at Ormond Castle at Carrick-on-Suir, which reflects up-to-date continental styles, and the molded plasterwork in the chapel at Bunratty Castle, Co. Clare, dating to approximately 1620.[38]

Beyond symbolizing his status, Phillips's Roe Valley stronghold also exemplified his identity as an early modern entrepreneur. His fish pond was no mere decorative flourish to accompany his formal gardens. Instead, it was intended to preserve one of Ulster's principal commodities: salmon. Phillips had rights to the fish in the Roe, and an extant rock-cut weir below the castle site has been attributed to Phillips's fishing activities. Fish caught from the Roe were placed in the pond, to be removed when needed for the table or the market. Phillips also seems to have engaged in manufacturing activity, to judge from a small structure with a sizable chimney depicted on Raven's map, which might have served as a brewhouse. Documentary evidence supports the practice of brewing on Phillips's proportion. In 1616, a vessel either owned or chartered by Phillips was captured en route from Dublin to Londonderry by Sorley MacDonnell. Among the commodities on board were malt and beer. The malt is suggestive of production, whereas the beer may indicate that the quantities being produced were not sufficient or were limited to ale, or perhaps the local brew was not to everyone's taste. Some of Phillips's products might have supplied the timber-framed inn he constructed within Newtown Limavady, built to provide hospitality to English travelers.[39]

38. Jane Fenlon, "The Decorative Plasterwork at Ormond Castle—a Unique Survival," *Architectural History,* XLI (1998), 67–81; Hanneke Ronnes, "Continental Traces at Carrick-on-Suir and Contemporary Irish Castles," in Thomas Herron and Michael Potterton, eds., *Ireland in the Renaissance* (Dublin, 2007), 255–273; Desmond Guinness, "Plasterwork in Ireland," *The Arts in Ireland,* I, no. 2 (Winter 1972), 39–44.

39. Lords Justices to Winwood, in Russell and Prendergast, eds., *CSPI of the Reign of James I,*

Control over the production, distribution, and consumption of alcohol formed a key element of plantation policy and a lucrative enterprise for entrepreneurs like Phillips. Indeed, Phillips himself had included brewhouses in Coleraine and Londonderry in his 1609 "Estimates of Profit of the Derry Plantation." He also attained a license for distilling aqua vitae "on the 20th of April, 1608, for the next seven years, within the county of Coleraine, otherwise called O'Cahan's country, and within the territory called the Rowte, in Co. Antrim"—a license from which the present-day Bushmills Distillery claims descent. Exactly what was produced in Phillips's distillery, assuming it was constructed, is unknown. Certainly Irish usquebaugh, redolent with spices, was a strong preference of English as well as Irish drinkers. Six years before Phillips received his license, planter Moses Hill of Islandmagee was accused of conspiring with Carrickfergus merchants to disguise the clear aqua vitae shipped into the port: "They have coloured the same yellowish like the Irish usquebaff . . . then sold it to the Irish" at a profit.[40]

It is quite possible that distillation took place alongside brewing in the Roe Valley. Phillips was keen on gaining a monopoly over the production of alcoholic beverages, as he worked to ensure that "no beverage maker . . . dwell but in towns or villages under some British gentleman" and "no alehouses . . . be allowed in remote places." Surviving port books offer further evidence that alcoholic beverages were critical commodities in the Ulster Plantation. During the year 1614–1615, 1,253 gallons of aqua vitae were brought into Carrickfergus, along with 148 hogsheads of wine, 18 hogsheads of beer, and 21 hundredweight of hops. The other major imports consisted of coal (142 tons), building materials for Sir Arthur Chichester's manor house of Joymount, salt (353 barrels), and sugar (1,369 pounds). The hops imply local production, although the significant quantities of imported, finished products suggest the limited nature of alcoholic beverage production within Ulster. Although it is not yet clear whether the structure depicted on Raven's plan of Limavady was a brewhouse, it was designed for a manufacturing process of some kind. Its placement close to Phillips's is not un-

V, 133; T. W. Moody, "Sir Thomas Phillips of Limavady, Servitor," *Irish Historical Studies*, I (1938–1939), 261; for discussion of Phillips's involvement in alcohol production and distribution, as well as a consideration of the cultural role of alcohol consumption in the Ulster Plantation, see Audrey Horning, "'The Root of All Vice and Bestiality': Exploring the Cultural Role of the Alehouse in the Ulster Plantation," in James Lyttleton and Colin Rynne, eds., *Plantation Ireland: Settlement and Material Culture, c. 1550–c. 1700* (Dublin, 2009), 113–131.

40. M. C. Griffith, ed., *Irish Patent Rolls of James I* (Dublin, 1966), 131, 477–478; State Paper Office, State Papers Ireland, Elizabeth I to George III, SP 63/212/61, National Archives, Kew; McGurk, *Sir John Docwra*, 81.

usual: the juxtaposition of elite residences and entrepreneurial manufacturing activities were evident at Jamestown. The most notable example is the placement of the home of John Harvey, governor in the 1630s, in the center of a zone of manufacturing activity, including brewing, distillation, metalworking, pottery production, and possibly tanning. Similarly, excavations at Ferryland, the Avalon colony settlement in Newfoundland, have revealed a combined brewhouse and bakery dating to the 1620s and situated adjacent to a domestic building of the same period, referred to as the "parlour."[41]

Phillips's manor house was not just close to the probable brewhouse—it was also near the castle itself. That Phillips felt the need to construct a manor house in addition to reedifying the castle raises some questions about the extent of his work on the tower house. An early-nineteenth-century description of the castle, long since demolished, portrayed it as a simple square keep with outerworks, suggesting that Thomas Raven's elaborate castle, with its round tower and appurtenances, might have been more aspirational than actual.[42]

On Phillips's death in 1636, the property passed to his son Dudley, but with the proviso that Phillips's second wife, Alice (née Usher), have the use of the plate in his house at Limavady for her lifetime, with all other household goods to be sold to pay his debts. Dudley evidently remained in residence, as he held the castle against Irish rebels in the 1640s, whereas Alice Usher Phillips likely returned to her family near Dublin, where her father (Sir William Usher, clerk of the Irish court) still lived. Dudley's son George, a figure known primarily for his role as a defender in the Siege of Derry in 1688–1689, is named in 1659 as provost of Newtown Limavady, several miles from the castle. In 1662, George Phillips possessed a home in the town, according to the town records, although the 1663 Hearth Money Roll suggests he was still living near or in the castle, as he was credited with four hearths at Limavady (not Newtown Limavady) and his father with six. By 1664,

41. "Orders Conceived by Sir Thomas Phillips, Expressing What in His Judgment Was Fit to Be Done for the Present Reformation and Safety of That Poor Kingdom," June 3, 1623, in Russell and Prendergast, eds., *CSPI of the Reign of James I,* V, 411–413; Robin Sweetnam, "Early 17th-Century Ships' Masters and Merchants," *Carrickfergus and District Historical Journal,* II (1986), 15; Audrey Jane Horning, "'A Verie Fit Place to Erect a Great Cittie': Comparative Contextual Analysis of Archaeological Jamestown" (Ph.D. diss., University of Pennsylvania, 1995), 122–187; Barry Gaulton and James A. Tuck, "The Archaeology of Ferryland, Newfoundland until 1696," *Avalon Chronicles,* VIII (2003), 193, 197–198.

42. The Ordnance Survey Memoirs note, "From the foundations, which can still be traced, it appears to have been merely a large square keep with a ballium (vallum) and outerworks"; see Day and McWilliams, *Ordnance Survey Memoirs,* IX, 92.

he had moved to the model plantation town first established by his grandfather. Although Sir Thomas Phillips never profited from plantation to the extent he had hoped, his grandson prospered in Newtown Limavady and witnessed the completion of plantation's original aims when the Williamite War delivered up Protestant hegemony to Ireland.[43]

Analysis of the O'Cahan's and Phillips's seats indicates well-preserved deposits predating the landscape's eighteenth-century transformation into a deer park. Beyond the castle site, some of Phillips's landscape manipulations can still be discerned in the form of terraces associated with the formal garden and a shallow, water-filled depression that marks the location of the spring that fed the fish pond. Despite the damage caused by the demolition of two nineteenth-century structures and subsequent filling of the fish pond in the 1970s, recent testing unearthed intact deposits containing a mixture of Irish and English pottery of late-sixteenth- or early-seventeenth-century date. The juxtaposition of these materials speaks to the meeting of O'Cahan's Gaelic world and Phillips's plantation world.[44]

Perhaps even more impressive than Phillips's transformation of the

43. Moody, "Sir Thomas Phillips," *Irish Historical Studies,* I (1939), 270–271; E. M. F-G. Boyle, ed., *Records of the Town of Limavady: 1609 to 1808* (1912; Limavady, 1989). The town records stated it was "Ordered that from henceforth forever the Dwelling house of George Phillips, Esq., situate and being within this Corporation of Newtown, with the yard, gardens, orchards, and outhouses thereunto belonging, shall be secured, freed, privileged, and exempted of and from the power, authority, and jurisdiction of the Corporation aforesaid" (5). George Phillips appears to have been resident in Newtown Limavady in 1664, when local tenants were ordered to provide forty loads of gravel apiece to fill in the *sheough,* or ditch, between Phillips's garden and his stable (15). The castle and manor house might have been abandoned following the death of Dudley Phillips in 1672, if not before. George's son William sold the Roe Valley lands to Speaker of the Irish Parliament William Connolly, of County Meath, in 1697, ending the tenure of the Phillips family on the former seat of the O'Cahan lordship. Connolly transformed the lands around the castle into a deer park.

44. This juxtaposition was a central theme of the archaeological project, which aimed to engage the local public in the discovery process. Despite the length of Phillips's occupation of the site and the evident extent of his building works, the location is known locally only as an O'Cahan castle and stronghold. Phillips does appear on interpretive signage in the park, but his significance is overshadowed by the memory of the O'Cahan occupation. In discussing the history of the site with local residents, park staff, and the media, it became clear that, when Phillips is remembered, he is routinely cast as a villain who intentionally swindled O'Cahan out of his lands. That Phillips only received the Limavady lands as compensation for surrendering Coleraine was not well known. The visibility of the archaeological excavations thus provided an opportunity to recast O'Cahan's and Phillips's stories in terms of community understanding. See discussion in Audrey Horning, "*Leim an Mhadaigh:* Exploring Unwanted Histories of the Atlantic World," in Peter E. Pope and Shannon Lewis-Simpson, eds., *Exploring Atlantic Transitions: Archaeologies of Transience and Permanence in New Found Lands,* forthcoming.

O'Cahan stronghold was his establishment of Newtown Limavady, one mile from the castle near a river crossing along the road to Derry. This town was in many ways the embodiment of plantation ideology, with its cruciform plan, central market square, timber-framed "English" houses, custom-built inn, and gristmill. Here Phillips clearly sought to create a model for what he expected the London Companies to build on their lands. He had wasted no time in developing his model settlement, as George Carew attested in 1611: "Sir Thomas Phillips, Knight, hath erected a water mill at Lemavady, unto which he drew water a mile, in a sluice or pond, 12 foot broad and 5 foot deep; he hath put in good forwardness an Inn builded English fashion, for the relief of passengers passing that way, containing in length 46 foot and in breadth 17 foot, two stories high." Two years later, the plantation town boasted a sufficient populace to petition for and receive a royal charter. In 1622, Phillips and Raven were able to record eighteen dwellings in the town, all built in the "English manner," with timber frames and masonry chimneys, and carefully aligned on two cross streets with a market cross in the center. In addition, Raven depicts a flagpole and a set of stocks at the foot of the cross, intended to symbolize a lawful, well-governed society. Phillips's decision to construct his new town several miles away from the existing settlement of Limavady suggests that he viewed it as a symbol of a new order. Content as Phillips was to adapt the O'Cahan castle locale as his own home, Newtown Limavady as a plantation settlement was to be wholly new, rather than built upon existing Gaelic foundations, and thus emblematic of English civility.[45]

Although tradition holds that the present town of Limavady developed from Phillips's model settlement, there are no extant early-seventeenth-century remains, nor is the contemporary town plan easily reconcilable with Raven's. As was the case in other plantation towns (for example, Comber, Co. Down), it seems likely that the town moved from its original location adjacent to the River Roe and up onto higher ground. Insofar as the town records make no mention of any resiting or rebuilding, this posited move must have occurred before 1659, from which date the town records survive. It is possible that damage in the course of the 1641 Rising / Rebellion precipitated a move from what was already an infelicitous location because of flooding. To date, no archaeological traces of Phillips's town have been unearthed within the boundaries of the later town or in the undeveloped land

45. Brewer and Bullen, eds., *Carew MSS,* VI, 572; George Hatchell, ed., *Calendar of Patent Rolls of James I* (Dublin, 1848), 255.

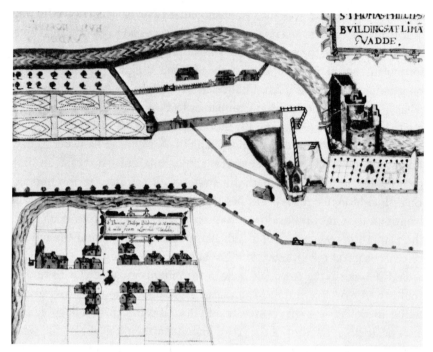

Plate 14. Thomas Raven, Sir Thomas Phillips's settlement at Limavady, 1622. The top shows Phillips's redevelopment of the O'Cahan castle; the bottom of the map depicts Phillips's model town of Newtown Limavady. With acknowledgment to the Deputy Keeper of the Records at the Public Record Office of Northern Ireland

closer to the river. After the 1622 Raven plan, the next extant map of the town was not produced until 1698. This map clearly shows the town in its present location.[46]

For as much as Newtown Limavady was designed as a quintessential plantation town, the fact that Phillips, unlike the Londoners, was permitted to retain Irish tenants suggests that the population of the town was more diverse than implied by the architecture depicted on Raven's map. In reluctantly agreeing to surrender his lands at Coleraine, Phillips had successfully requested the right to retain Irish tenants, as acknowledged in a 1611 communiqué from the lords of the Council to Chichester: "As the lands he parted with to the Londoners were for the most part inhabited by natives,

46. E. A. Currie, "Landscape Development in North-West and South-East Derry, 1700–1840," in Gerard O'Brien, ed., *Derry and Londonderry: History and Society; Interdisciplinary Essays on the History of an Irish County* (Dublin, 1999), 340–341; Boyle, ed., *Records of the Town of Limavady.*

they (the Lords) think that his request is reasonable to be permitted to have the natives likewise on these lands, as other servitors have." Here was Phillips's license to retain the O'Cahan tenants and create a ready workforce for his own endeavors.[47]

Although documentary references to Newtown Limavady are scant before 1659, they are nonetheless illuminating in terms of the town's population. The presence of Irish servants within the "English" households of Newtown Limavady is indicated by Anthony Mahue's April 24, 1615, statement in relation to a failed plot to overturn plantation: "This present day Honora ny Gilligan, wife to James McBrian, came to this examinate's house in Newtown Lymavaddy, and there desired to have some conference in secret with him; whereupon he called a maidservant of his who well speaks and understands the Irish, and willed her to tell him what the said Honora said." That Honora hoped to speak to Mahue in Irish suggests that some English learned the tongue. Mahue's maidservant was most likely Irish and in this instance attained some power over her employer through his reliance on her linguistic abilities. He also trusted that she would accurately recount the words of Honora ny Gilligan.[48]

More signs of Irish living on Phillips's lands can be found in the evidence given against Shane Carragh in the aftermath of Donal Ballagh O'Cahan's arrest. Shane had reputedly plundered the premises of Irish merchant Patrick Roe O'Donnelly, resident of Limavady (the settlement around the castle), and stolen mantles and aqua vitae, which he hid in the home of John Ross. The recent archaeological finds from the castle vicinity also highlight the presence of the Irish, with Irish hand-built cooking pot fragments mixed in with the wheel-thrown, gravel-tempered pottery from North Devon and English pipestem fragments. In effect, the O'Cahan tenants traded one landlord for another. As such, interaction between the Irish and the English residents would have been routine, though punctuated by episodes of linguistic and cultural incomprehension.[49]

To scholars of the plantation, Phillips is best known for his extreme dissatisfaction with the London Companies' achievements (or lack thereof). Despite being the principal proponent for their involvement, Phillips found

47. Lords of the Council to Chichester, Apr. 14, 1611, in Russell and Prendergast, eds., *CSPI of the Reign of James I,* IV, *1611–1624,* 28–29.

48. "Examination of Anthony Mahue, Taken before Sir Thomas Phillips," Apr. 24, 1615, ibid., V, 48.

49. Boyle, ed., *Records of the Town of Limavady,* x. For the 1615 plot, see Gillespie, *Conspiracy,* 19–24.

himself in dispute with them nearly from the start of the plantation, alleging that they had wantonly cut down the forests and failed to import enough British settlers, to build adequate defenses, or, most critically, to expel the Irish, as specified in the articles of plantation. Worse yet, as he reported in 1632, nine Catholic Mass houses had been constructed on company lands. Some of his dislike seems to have stemmed from a power struggle: Phillips had believed himself to have governance over affairs within the London-derry Plantation, whereas the City's agents preferred to maintain control. In their answer to the charge that Phillips should be retained in his governancy, they responded, "For Sir Thomas his superintendency we hope according to the Article to see the country governed and none there to have that power but such as we shall see fit and they to join in Commission with our Agents by us appointed, yet we deny not Sir Thomas Phillips to have the care of the Martial Affairs and Government of his Soldiers, but for the Civil Govern-ment we hope not to need his help." Their obvious hostility toward Phillips further solidified the servitor's opposition to the agents of the City.[50]

However personally he might have taken the companies' actions, Phillips was not the only plantation designer unhappy with the progress of the Londonderry enterprise. Lord Deputy Chichester complained to the king about the Londoners' lack of progress, in particular their failure to take up the patents on their land or to expel the Irish. The king's response, penned in December 1612, was to order a commission to look into the alleged fail-ings of the City. Chichester further pressed his case in January 1613, stating that it his was "his duty" to inform the king

> that the undertakers of that Province (Ulster) goe slowly on the works of the plantation, laboring rather for the most part, to make profit of the Lands, then to erect strong buildings for their Subjects or Bawnes and Court Lodges for their Goods and Cattle so as they lye open to the Will of their ill affected Neighbors who undoubtedly would cut many of their Throats and thrust the rest clean out of the Country. . . . Some gentle-men have begun their Houses of Lime and Stone, but few are finished,

50. Phillips to Secretary Coke, Feb. 1, 1632, in Mahaffy, ed., *CSPI of the Reign of Charles I*, I, 643. For discussions of Phillips and his vendetta against the London Companies, see Curl, *Londonderry Plantation*, 74–81, 86–88; Moody, *Londonderry Plantation, 1609–41*, 194–204, 238–258, 369–374; Moody, "Sir Thomas Phillips," *Irish Historical Studies*, I (1938–1939), 264–269; Canny, *Making Ireland British*, 264–265. For quotation, see "The Points in the Lord Deputy's Letter of the 29th of April 1612 Which Concern the Londoners . . . ," in Phillips, *Londonderry and the London Companies*, 37.

in the mean they lye in weak thatched houses and slenderlie prepared for defence, if they were attempted. For they dwell not in townrids together as they were appointed, but lie scattered up and downe, upon their portions, where every Man affects best for his ease and profit.

Chichester's concerns about profiteering, the lack of defenses, and the failure to remove the Irish from company lands were serious. Although a 1612–1613 commission generally found in favor of the Londoners, later surveys underscored the accuracy of his charges.[51]

The most damning survey was, perhaps unsurprisingly, that undertaken by Thomas Phillips in 1622, which was intended to quantify the companies' failings while highlighting his successes. According to Phillips, "The whole number of British men inhabiting and now found resident in the city of Londonderry, the town of Colraine, the fort of Culmore, and upon the whole 12 proportions planted by the Londoners, doth contain 979, Whereof armed 749. A third part of the 979 British are not serviceable men." The British settlers were well outnumbered by the Irish, according to Phillips, who noted that there "cannot be in the whole county less than 4,000 men." His continued criticisms of the Londonderry Plantation culminated in the Star Chamber lawsuit of 1631–1635, in which he accused the Irish Society of breaking its contract by not adhering to the conditions set forth by the crown. These conditions chiefly stressed the need to plant the escheated lands with English and Scottish settlers to the exclusion of the Irish. As the native inhabitants had a much greater desire to remain on their lands than English or Scottish settlers, who were difficult to attract, they provided surer income for the companies as tenants. When the case went to trial in 1635, the City was uniformly convicted of breach of contract, forced to surrender its patent, and assessed a fine of £70,000. The City's charter was officially revoked in 1638, with the companies' titles attached. Resolution came via the Long Parliament in 1641. In August of that year, the House of Commons formally reinstated the Londonderry Plantation lands to the City and the Twelve Companies. In November, Charles I finally went along with Parliament's decision, but it was a bit late. Rebellion had broken out in October, sweeping through Ulster and taking most of the slim gains of the plantation with it.[52]

51. Chichester to the Lord Privy Seal, Jan. 4, 1613, in Edwards, ed., "Letter-Book of Sir Arthur Chichester," *Analecta Hibernica,* no. 8 (1938), 74–75.

52. Survey of the Londoners' Plantation, in Russell and Prendergast, eds., *CSPI of the Reign*

Archaeology and the London Company Settlements

Although the archaeological investigation of Sir Thomas Phillips's plantation settlement at Limavady was limited, the results can be compared to evidence unearthed at a number of London Company settlements that allows for an assessment of Phillips's claims about the conduct and progress of plantation. Most readily comparable is the evidence from Dungiven, another O'Cahan stronghold situated on the River Roe, nine miles from Limavady. Dungiven consisted of a late medieval tower house appended to an Augustinian priory first established in the twelfth century and associated with the O'Cahans from at least the thirteenth. O'Cahan's seat at Dungiven, like that of Limavady, wound up in the hands of an English servitor, Sir Edward Doddington. Most famous for designing the Londonderry walls, Doddington was resident at Dungiven from 1609 until his death in 1618. In 1609, he was recorded as having a ward of fourteen men stationed at Dungiven, "whereby it is possible that he may clear those parts of such unprofitable members of the commonwealth," meaning the Irish. Doddington would soon be compelled to surrender Dungiven to the Irish Society as part of the Londonderry Plantation scheme, despite the fact that he claimed to have "bestowed the greatest part of his estate" on the castle. Unlike Phillips, who had to quit his lands in Coleraine, Doddington succeeded in regaining his base when he was retained as agent by the Skinners' Company, which had been granted an estate that incorporated the stronghold at Dungiven.[53]

According to the 1611 Carew survey, Doddington had spent £300 of his own money on the "building of the castle and the bawn," supplemented by £200 "from the King." By all accounts, Doddington rapidly set about spending that money, redeveloping the Dungiven tower house to include a manor house and bawn complex, establishing two villages that each boasted twelve houses (as recorded in 1622), and constructing a second bawn at Crossalt (Brackfield), which today is one of the most complete and best preserved examples of a plantation bawn in Northern Ireland. Even Phillips could find little fault with Doddington's work as a servitor when he recorded the condition of the Skinners' proportion. Given the parallels in their careers and their individual acquisition of O'Cahan strongholds, we may imagine the re-

---

of James I, V, 377–378; Curl, *Londonderry Plantation*, 79. In Curl's estimation, "Phillips's survey was so thorough and so damning that he gradually acquired the ear of Government" (80).

53. Jacob to Salisbury, Apr. 15, 1609, in Russell and Prendergast, eds., *CSPI of the Reign of James I*, III, 194; Lords of the Council to Chichester, Apr. 30, 1611, ibid., IV, 34–35.

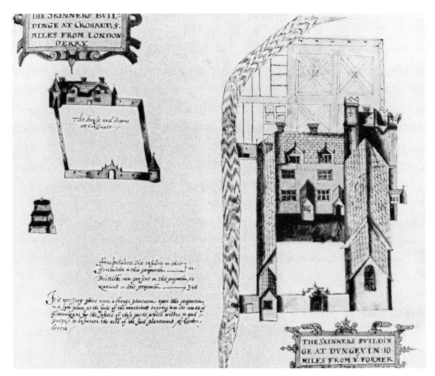

Plate 15. Thomas Raven, Dungiven and the Skinners' lands, 1622. With acknowledgment to the Deputy Keeper of the Records at the Public Record Office of Northern Ireland

lationship between Phillips and Doddington. Considering the time, effort, and money both men spent to transform their respective castles into fashionable (albeit defensive) symbols of their success, it is likely that each man kept a close eye on the other's accomplishments—aided by the fact that their castles were only nine miles apart. Doddington served as a burgess for Newtown Limavady, ensuring his familiarity with Phillips's rather more successful efforts at townbuilding than Doddington's work at Dungiven and Crossalt. The two men were also related by marriage, each having wed a daughter of Sir George Paulett, Dorothy and Elizabeth. Both sisters died young: a memorial in Saint Patrick's Church, Coleraine, commemorates the death of Elizabeth Doddington in 1610, whereas Dorothy Phillips died in 1612. Doddington employed his late wife's memorial to immortalize his own accomplishments, embellishing her plaque with the claim that Doddington was the first to build in the English style in what was then County Coleraine *(primus qui ibi edificabat more Anglicano)*. One wonders what Phillips made of Doddington's claim, given his own developments at Coleraine while Doddington was still holding Dungiven as a garrison.[54]

Excavations at Dungiven reveal where Doddington's funds went. Archaeological investigations in the location of his manor house and the O'Cahan tower house suggest that little was spared in fitting out the building according to the latest fashion, with attention paid to architectural hardware, the fitting of an ornate, molded plasterwork ceiling to the refurbished tower house, and the decoration of the hearths in the manor house with polychrome Dutch tiles. In actuality, the most notable aspect is the abysmal quality of the manor house construction. Even as Doddington invested in his interior appointments and designed his house along recognizably "English" lines, his builders cut corners by employing only clay to mortar the stonework together. Worse yet, one wall of a structure interpreted as a scullery had no masonry at all. Instead, fine, white plaster was directly applied to the clay subsoil through which the structure had been cut. The mustermaster general of the Ulster Plantation, Nicholas Pynnar, was apparently fooled when he visited Dungiven in 1619 as part of his duty of surveying the progress of plantation. Pynnar described the structure as "a strong castle" with "plenty of arms."[55]

Despite its veneer of safety and civility, Doddington's castle rested on shaky foundations, serving as an apt metaphor for the Skinners' Company's entire plantation project. The Skinners' proportion was both the largest and least desirable of all of the Londonderry Plantation grants. Landlocked and interspersed with the lands granted to Manus O'Cahan, Honora O'Cahan, and the church, the Skinners' proportion simply did not appeal to the British settlers who were supposed to subdue and transform its mountains, bogs, and natives. However much Doddington endeavored to meet the conditions of plantation (or at least appeared to do so), he could not meet his brother-in-law Thomas Phillips's expectations for Irish-free London Company lands. That Phillips was not subject to the same requirements he him-

54. "State of the Ulster Plantation in 1611," September 1611, ibid., IV, 122; Curl, *Londonderry Plantation*, 52, 292.

55. Nick Brannon, "Archaeological Excavations at Dungiven Priory and Bawn," *Benbradagh*, XV (1985), 17; N. F. Brannon and B. S. Blades, "Dungiven Bawn Re-edified," *Ulster Journal of Archaeology*, 3d Ser., XLIII (1980), 91–96, esp. 95; "Captain Nicholas Pynnar's Survey of the Works and Plantations Performed by the City of London in the City and County of Londonderry," Mar. 28, 1619, in Russell and Prendergast, eds., *CSPI of the Reign of James I*, V, 384–385; Francis Steer et al., *Dictionary of Land Surveyors and Local Cartographers of Great Britain and Ireland, 1530–1850*, ed. Peter Eden (London, 1997), 419.

self imposed upon the companies must have been galling. Sir Edward Doddington died in 1618, leaving his second wife and widow, Anne Beresford Doddington, holding the castle at Dungiven. The following year, Nicholas Pynnar reported that there were 27 British families resident on the whole of the proportion. By the time Phillips conducted his survey in 1622, only 12 British men remained on the Skinners' lands, in contrast to 348 Irish.[56]

To date, archaeological evidence for the original Dungiven village has not been located to allow for any investigation of the material reflections of the intercultural relations of their Irish and British occupants. It is noteworthy that Raven did not even depict the twelve reported Dungiven houses on his 1622 plan. The three dwellings he does show for Crossalt / Brackfield appear Irish rather than English in character, being single story and constructed of stone or mud with thatched roofs, with one recognizably subrectangular in form. Excavations carried out inside Brackfield bawn unearthed limited evidence for the manor house but only a handful of English materials, including a North Devon sgraffito sherd and North Devon roofing tile fragments. The recovery of a sherd of Ulster coarse pottery from a pit feature within the bawn was considered to be residual medieval material but is equally likely to be a physical indicator of the demographic realities on the Skinners' proportion. The inability to attract British settlers is evident in the accusation leveled against Doddington's widow that she had "brought in no English, but was a great fosterer of Irish Papists." Certainly Doddington's widow (who became the Lady Cooke following her marriage to Sir Francis Cooke) must have enjoyed reasonably cordial relations with her Irish neighbors. When fighting broke out in 1641, she and the company turned the castle at Dungiven over to Manus O'Cahan, entrusting him to hold the English garrison. O'Cahan quickly switched sides and took the castle for the rebel forces. The trust (mis)placed in O'Cahan speaks volumes of the close relations between Irish and English over the thirty years of relative peace that had followed the formal transfer of lands to the Skinners' Company.[57]

Although the Dungiven and Crossalt villages have yet to be pinpointed, other plantation villages have been investigated. The first concentrated ar-

56. "Captain Nicholas Pynnar's Survey," in Russell and Prendergast, eds., *CSPI of the Reign of James I*, V, 384–385.

57. N. F. Brannon, "Excavations at Brackfield Bawn, County Londonderry," *Ulster Journal of Archaeology*, 3d Ser., LIII (1990), 13–14; Sir Ralph Whitfield and Sir Thomas Fotherley to the Privy Council, May 25, 1641, in Mahaffy, ed., *CSPI of the Reign of Charles I*, II, *1633–1647*, 290–291; Brannon and Blades, "Dungiven Bawn Re-edified," *Ulster Journal of Archaeology*, 3d Ser., XLIII (1980), 91–96; Curl, *Londonderry Plantation*, 291.

chaeological effort to sample an entire plantation settlement was carried out at Salterstown, the abandoned settlement of the Salters' Company, close to the shore of Lough Neagh. As Raven depicted it, Salterstown was a sizable settlement boasting ten timber-framed houses and another under construction, along with three smaller cottages and a subrectangular vernacular Irish-style dwelling. These buildings were aligned along a wide street, at the top of which stood a square masonry bawn with corner flankers and, as recorded by both Pynnar and Raven, a timber-framed manor house within. Today, traces of a later two-and-a-half-story masonry castle survive at the site, with only the name of Salterstown Road hinting at the former presence of the plantation town. Both local tradition and the documentary record suggest that Salterstown was destroyed in 1641 and subsequently abandoned, yet excavation revealed that the village was reoccupied when the Salters regained title to their lands in 1657. This second effort at planting Salterstown was no more successful than the first, with the village abandoned again following the Williamite Wars. Major archaeological finds include a rubbish-filled pit, a stone-lined well, and a variety of postholes and areas of burned clay interpreted as earthfast structures with open firehood hearths; such open hearths were a vernacular tradition among settlers from northern England and Scotland.[58]

The physical remains at Salterstown speak directly to the influence of both Irish and British material traditions. Shoes recovered from the well display both Irish thong lacing and English thread stitching, whereas thirty-three sherds of Ulster coarse pottery / everted-rim ware were recovered from sealed seventeenth-century contexts, including the rubbish pit and well, alongside North Devon and London wares. Dendrochronological dating of timbers associated with a platform for that well yielded a date of 1663, indicating that the Irish tradition of producing and using hand-built pottery, often presumed to be of a medieval date, continued well beyond the first few years of plantation. As was true of the other London Companies, the Salters' Company relied upon Irish tenants for rents, and in the early years of the plantation, they devised a means of justifying the retention of such tenants. Instructions to agent Baptist Jones in 1615 specified that "if Irish will go to Church they may continue on [our] land." The Ironmongers' Company also considered any natives who professed to adhere to Protestantism to be eligible for tenancy, possibly counting them as English or Scottish on com-

58. Orloff G. Miller, "Archaeological Investigations at Salterstown, County Londonderry, Northern Ireland" (Ph.D. diss., University of Pennsylvania, 1991).

pany accounts. Although claiming conversion seems an easy, if disingenuous, means to maintain residency, such a decision could have deadly consequences, as related in a report by the Ironmongers' agent George Canning:

> There are yet divers out in rebellion in the woodes, and some tymes light uppon passengers and robb them and sometymes light into the houses and doe manie villanyes; the last weeke they toke an Irishman as he was keeping cattell in the woodes uppon the Mercers' proportion, and hanged him with a withe in a tree, and 'tis thought for no other cause but that . . . being an Irishman, had conformed himself and gone to our church.

Canning's report is a reminder of the challenges facing ordinary Irish tenants as they negotiated the new order. Professing Protestantism might secure tenancy, but it was hardly an easy choice, given the potential consequences of turning one's back on the Catholic faith.[59]

Like Salterstown, the Mercers' Company's village of Movanagher, situated next to the River Bann (north of the present-day town of Kilrea), did not survive the seventeenth century. As the premier of the Twelve Companies, the Mercers' Company was deemed to be integral to the proposed Londonderry Plantation, however disinterested they were in supporting the scheme. Their first response was outright refusal to participate: "That in all humility they return thanks to His Majesty in the gracious remembrance of them in offer of the same precept, but forasmuch as they are for the most part men that live by merchandize and therefore are inexperienced in managing a business of that nature and withal want means and ability for the accomplishment thereof this Company are not willing to have a hand or intermeddle in the same." The company had been similarly reluctant to involve itself in the Virginia venture, pledging £200 in April 1609 but declining to provide any further investment in December 1610, when the Virginia Council again appealed to the companies for investments. Despite their reluctance, the Mercers were compelled to sign on to the Londonderry Plantation scheme in accordance with the majority agreement among the London Companies to participate. When a request for money came, the Mercers again protested, first to the lord mayor and then to the Privy Council. Their pleas for financial leniency fell on deaf ears. Eventually, the company would see its rates lowered slightly.[60]

---

59. Ibid., 179, 448–449, 737; Hill, *An Historical Account of the Plantation in Ulster,* 443; T. W. Moody transcripts, Salters' Company Records, Irish Letter Book, Public Record Office of Northern Ireland (hereafter cited as PRONI), T.853.

60. Audrey Horning, "'Dwelling Houses in the Old Irish Barbarous Manner': Archaeologi-

In January 1613, the Mercers' Company was given the choice of accepting a share of Ulster land (and administering its planting) for the money they had contributed or forfeiting any further involvement beyond allowing the Irish Society to oversee the dispersal of lands. The company agreed to look after its land grant, in hopes of stemming off future requests for moneys. In association with the Innholders, Cooks, Embroiderers, and Masons, the Mercers drew Lot 8 in December 1613, when lands were officially allocated. Even after agreeing to oversee their allocation, the company was tapped for two more contributions. Despite their unwillingness, the company shouldered its new burden; and, unlike most of the companies who farmed their lands out to individual undertakers (as the Skinners did with Doddington), the Mercers endeavored to retain direct management of their estates. A London-based committee was formed to deal with the Irish estate, with weekly meetings, while the company's agent in Ireland undertook daily administration. Initial works were begun under the aegis of the Irish Society, then transferred to the company.[61]

The Mercers' Company lot consisted of 21,600 acres in two parcels incorporating forty-eight townlands—land that was originally described as consisting of only around 3,000 acres. The first parcel lay along the western banks of the River Bann, and the other included large stretches of the forest of Glenconkeyne, running up to the Sperrin Mountains. The western lands of the proportion offered virgin timber, promising the materials required not only for building settlements but also for the fish weirs, for casks to store and ship fish and eels, for boats and rafts to transport such goods downriver to Coleraine, and for exportable lumber. In the middle of the Mercers' two separate yet economically promising tracts lay lands still held by the native Irish McCowells, glebe lands, and land assigned to the Ironmongers' Company. To the north lay lands granted to Manus O'Cahan.[62]

Under the auspices of the Irish Society, the Mercers' primary settlement

cal Evidence for Gaelic Architecture in an Ulster Plantation Village," in Patrick Duffy, David Edwards, and Elizabeth FitzPatrick, eds., *Gaelic Ireland, 1250–1650: Land, Lordship, and Settlement* (Dublin, 2001), 375–396; Audrey Horning, "On the Banks of the Bann: The Riverine Economy of an Ulster Plantation Village," *Historical Archaeology*, XLI (2007), 94–114; Acts of Court, 1595–1629, f. 97v, Mercers' Company Archive, London; T. H. O'Brien, "The London Livery Companies and the Virginia Company," *VMHB*, LXVIII (1960), 141, 146.

61. See Moody, *Londonderry Plantation, 1609–41,* 86–90; Curl, *Londonderry Plantation,* 122–152; Ian Doolittle, *The Mercers' Company, 1579–1959,* ed. Ann Saunders (London, 1994); Horning, "'Dwelling Houses,'" in Duffy, Edwards, and FitzPatrick, eds., *Gaelic Ireland,* 375–396; Horning, "On the Banks of the Bann," *Historical Archaeology,* XLI (2007), 94–114.

62. Moody, *Londonderry Plantation, 1609–41,* 86–90; Curl, *Londonderry Plantation,* 122–152.

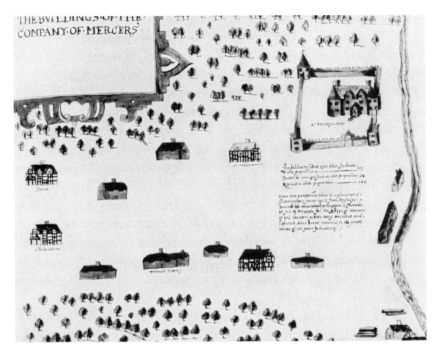

Plate 16. Thomas Raven, Movanagher, 1622. With acknowledgment to the Deputy Keeper of the Records at the Public Record Office of Northern Ireland

was established in the townland of Movanagher, strategically placed to exploit salmon and eel fisheries near a medieval ford on the Bann. The Privy Council spelled out the importance of these resources in establishing the rights and privileges of the City in Ulster: "The salmon and eel fishing of the river of the Ban and Loughfoyle, and all other kinds of fishing . . . in the Ban to Loughfoyle, shall be in perpetuity to the city." The locale was clearly chosen for economic rather than defensive reasons. Movanagher was situated at one side of the entire proportion and could barely defend itself, let alone come to the aid of the western reaches. The economic potential of the Bannside commodities did not counter the site's abysmal defensive qualities. The precarious life of the village that sprouted up outside the bawn's still-surviving masonry walls ended abruptly in 1641, when the village was reportedly destroyed by rebels.[63]

63. "Articles Agreed . . . ," Jan. 28, 1609, in Brewer and Bullen, eds., *Carew MSS,* VI, 37; Curl, *Londonderry Plantation,* 124. Curl further extrapolated on the precarious position of Movanagher by a direct, if startlingly uncritical, reference to relations between the English and Native people in North America: "The parallel of forest clearings in America, where settlers constructed timber-built houses and stockades in woodlands full of hostile Red Indians is not

In 1610, as their Virginia counterparts subsisted on bartered Indian corn and feverishly experimented with glass, iron, and pitch and tar production, the Irish Society embarked upon an ambitious building campaign for their principal settlement at Coleraine, requiring the timber and clay resources at Movanagher. Sawmills and brick kilns were thrown up alongside the Bann, and work was begun on the Mercers' masonry bawn. Dwellings were most likely constructed in tandem with the manufacturing activities, providing housing for the artisans and laborers. Just south of Movanagher, the Irish Society established a fishery at Portna. Eels and salmon would prove to be lucrative commodities for the Londoners. According to the hyperbolic report of Bishop Bramhall, more than sixty-two tons of salmon were caught in a single day near Coleraine in 1635. Regardless of the accuracy of the bishop's claim, sufficient quantities of salmon were available to underpin a significant export market. Salmon were being imported overseas at least as early as 1638. By the eighteenth century, the principal market for Ulster salmon would be North America.[64]

The Mercer's Company itself did not officially take possession until 1618, although the company established its standing committee to direct the development of the entire proportion in February 1614. As with the other company proportions, the Mercers' land was divided into freeholds. Five of these, plus the demesne of Claraletrim, or Claragh, incorporating Movanagher were assigned the same day in October 1618. These freeholds were granted to five individuals, described as "of Mavannahor," which suggests that a village of sorts existed outside of the bawn itself. The deeds granted freehold land to Charles Williams, Thomas Hudson, Thomas Church, Richard Vernon, and Richard Thornton, all resident at Movanagher. Williams received land at Moyeltra, Hudson received land at Tawnyringoy (Tamnyrankin), Church was granted Lanvore (Landmore), Vernon, as company agent, received Claraletrim (Claragh), and Thornton was granted Drummuck (Culnady). Additionally, Coleraine resident William Perry received a freehold at Slaghtneiul. Each deed specified that the holder construct "one sufficient substantiall house of timber, stone or brick of sixe or fouer rooms fitt and convenient for habitation."[65]

---

fanciful." Curl's words could easily have been written in the seventeenth century. See also Angélique Day, *Ordnance Survey Memoirs of Ireland*, XXVII, *Parishes of County Londonderry VIII, 1830, 1833–7, 1839: East Londonderry* (Belfast, 1994), 112.

64. N. C. Mitchell, "The Lower Bann Fisheries," *Ulster Folklife*, XI (1965), 1, 6, 25; Moody, *Londonderry Plantation, 1609–41*, 44.

65. 1618 Deed, Irish Society to William Perry, Mercers' Company Archive.

Nicholas Pynnar rather critically described the Mercers' settlement in 1619:

> This is not set to any man as yet, but is held by one Vernon, agent for the company. Upon this proportion the castle which was formerly begun, is now thoroughly finished, being not inferior to any that is built, for it is a good strong work, and well built, and a very large bawne of *120* feet square, with four flankers, all of good stone and lime. Not far from the bawne there are six houses of cagework, some covered with shingles and some thatched, and inhabitted by such poor men as they could find in the country, and these pay such dear rates for the land that they are forced to take Irish tenants under them to pay the rent. There are divers other houses of slight building, but they are far off, and dwell dispersedly in the wood, where they are forced of meer necessity to relieve such wood kearn as go up and down the country; and as he is informed by divers in the country, there are *46* town lands of this proportion that are set to the Irish of the sept of Clandonells, which are the wickedest men in all the country.

Pynnar's comments make it clear that even as the Mercers were endeavoring to meet expectations in terms of the building program, they were overly reliant upon Irish tenants who were willing to pay high rents to remain on their lands. By contrast, Pynnar's disparaging comments about the quality of the few settlers who could be found to populate the proportion highlights the challenge all of the companies faced in attracting British settlers of sufficient wealth and caliber. That Pynnar was also concerned about the dominance of Clan Donnell further emphasizes the demographic realities of early plantation settlements: Ulster was still very much a Gaelic Irish land.[66]

The castle, or manor house, was situated on the eastern wall of the bawn and was apparently standing when the Irish Society turned the manor lands over to Richard Vernon, agent for the Mercers' Company. He maintained control of the castle, bawn, and Claragh demesne until 1621. Although he is credited with completing the construction of the Movanagher settlement, as well as starting settlements at Carnroe, Kilrea, and Dunglady, he was hardly the best manager that the company might have chosen. Vernon neglected to collect rents, choosing instead to pocket company moneys that were intended to advance the plantation. Whether he did this as a favor to friends or out of fear of retribution by Irish tenants is not clear. Vernon was accused

---

66. "Captain Nicholas Pynnar's Survey," in Russell and Prendergast, eds., *CSPI of the Reign of James I*, V, 383.

Plate 17. Remains of Movanagher bawn wall and flanker (below tree).
Photograph by the author

by freeholder Thomas Church of having "let three townlands under value to some of his friends to be resigned again to his own use" and of making the castle "a taphouse to sell aqua vitae." Vernon's gristmill, sited along the river, was also so poorly built that it ruined grain brought for processing. Church complained to the Mercers' Court of Assistants that Vernon "hath bestowed 120 upon the mill which he might have had built by tenants for 30 and yet this mars the grain in grinding." Vernon was also to provide the company with an accounting of all "Fyer wood barrel staves or pipe staves boards or other things as he hath sold off the ground." It was alleged that he had conspired with the Irish Society agents John Rowley and Tristram Beresford, who were accused of illegally exporting tens of thousands of pipe staves to Spain. As income dropped and complaints rose, Vernon was dismissed from his position as company agent. His staunchest opponent, freeholder Thomas Church, was appointed in his place.[67]

67. The Ordnance Survey Memoirs for Kilrea Parish report an alternative but unconvincing history for Movanagher Bawn, stating, "It was originally built by the O'Cathans, who kept possession of it until they were driven out by the McQuillans." The site of Movanagher was certainly within the O'Cahans' traditional territory, but there is no archaeological evidence to support the attribution of the bawn itself to the clan. Similar claims were made for Brackfield Bawn, suggesting that the O'Cahans loomed larger in nineteenth-century memory than did the

Church was a friend of Sir Thomas Phillips, who was carrying out his survey of the plantation in the same year that Church advanced his career. Consulted by the company, Phillips reported that Vernon had embezzled, to the detriment not only of the company's expected income but the defense of the proportion, as moneys designated for arms "went astray." A variety of weapons and equipment were quickly dispatched and stored in the castle, which was not tenanted by Church, who had instead chosen to remain resident on his freehold north of Kilrea. By the time the Phillips-Hadsor-Raven survey was completed in 1622, the castle at Movanagher was occupied by Valentine Hartopp, who was also the first farmer on the Merchant Taylors' proportion and previously recorded as resident at their principal settlement at Macosquin in 1619. According to the survey, the Mercers' proportion was inhabited by 3 freeholders, 52 British men, and 145 native Irish. Another settlement was also mooted: "Upon this proportion there is a place called Greaneagham, four miles from Dongladye, towards the mountains, whereon a plantation is fit to be made for the safety of that part of the country, where many murthers and robberies have been committed to the great terror of the poor inhabitants." The 1622 survey echoed the concerns Pynnar raised in 1619 regarding the settlement's indefensibility and high ratio of Irish to British.[68]

Unlike Phillips's model town of Limavady, no formal street plan existed at Movanagher, according to the Raven survey. Instead, a scattering of ten dwellings is shown among the trees to the west of the bawn, accompanied by warehouses and a mill by the riverside. Five inhabitants are named on the 1622 map. In addition to Valentine Hartopp, a Mr. Madder, "Minister," apparently occupied a two-story, timber-framed house close to the southwestern flanker of the bawn. Thomas Bromley occupied an oval-shaped, one-story structure, with an addition, near the woods on the southern edge of a cleared "village" space. Charles Williams was associated with another two-story, timber-framed structure on the western margin of the settled area; this was paralleled to the north by another timber-framed building occupied by one Dixon, likely Richard Dixon, recorded as a tenant in 1621.

In the wake of the outcome of Phillips's Star Chamber suit against the

---

early-seventeenth-century London Company planters. See Angélique Day and Patrick McWilliams, eds., *Ordnance Survey Memoirs of Ireland*, XXVII, *Parishes of Co. Londonderry VIII, 1830, 1833–7, 1839, East Londonderry* (Belfast, 1994), 113; Mercers' Acts of Court, 1595–1629; Moody, *Londonderry Plantation, 1609–41*, 143.

68. "Captain Nicholas Pynnar's Survey," in Russell and Prendergast, eds., *CSPI of the Reign of James I*, V, 243; Phillips, *Londonderry and the London Companies*, 158.

London Companies—announced in February 1635 and convicting them of breach of contract—the Mercers attempted to recoup some of their investment. In an exceptionally shortsighted decision, they ordered Thomas Church to sell off "the Armes, weapons, drume, cullours, leading, staffe and materialls that are there remayning and belonging to the Company and their Associates." This foolhardy action, coupled with the continued population imbalance on the Mercers' proportion and the surrounding forested landscape, left the tiny settlement very vulnerable. As a result, it did not survive the 1641 Irish Rising / Rebellion. According to one deposition, following a disastrous defeat for the English at the Ironmongers' settlement at Garvagh on December 13, 1641, Church "raised 2 foot companies of 100 men" after he had been "constrained to leave his Castle to the guard of James McDonnell who then was not in accion of Rebellion and so boating his Men women and children with some luggage and all his ammunition over the Band water marched to Coleraine to safety within the walls of Coleraine." Leaving Movanagher in the hands of James MacDonnell was a disastrous decision for the company. MacDonnell soon joined a mutinous regiment of Irish and Highland Scots, formerly under the command of Archibald Stewart, which killed the British soldiers and settlers near the fisheries of Portna, whom they were meant to protect. The castle was reportedly destroyed in April 1642.[69]

Anecdotal evidence for the destruction of the Movanagher bawn is recorded in the Ordnance Survey Memoirs from the 1830s. According to the story, the bawn was attacked by a rebel with the improbable name of Fairy, who torched the buildings and killed all of Church's men, while Church himself fled to Tamlaght. Fairy then allegedly threw all of the dead into the well inside the bawn. The memoirs also note the nineteenth-century discovery of human bones in the well, then covered with a cowhouse. By contrast to this vivid account, the extant Mercers' Company records contain only a single reference, dated 1645, to the Movanagher castle's being demolished. On October, 10, 1645, "Captaine Thomas Church being shortly going over to Ireland now acquainted this Court that he is laboring to get a Custodian of the lands of Sir Mackdonell and James Mackdonell with whom he left the custody of the Companies Castle there sithence demolished." Although the company pondered its reedification, the subsequent disruptions

69. Mercers' Acts of Court, 1631–1637; Trinity College Dublin Online (hereafter cited as TCD) 1641 Depositions Project, MS 839, ff. 096r–097v, deposition of Charles Anthony, June 12, 1642, online transcript December 2009, http://1641.eneclann.ie, accessed Jul. 15, 2010; ibid., MS 838, ff. 070v–071r, examination of Donnoghy O Cahan, Mar. 8, 1653; Curl, *Londonderry Plantation*, 91, 357.

of the English Civil War and the revocation of the company's charter under Cromwell put paid to any restoration ideas.[70]

Lands were finally conveyed back to the Mercers' Company in 1657–1658 by Cromwell's Parliament. At that stage, the company abandoned the notion of direct management and farmed their proportion out to an undertaker, Gervase Rose, who was awarded a forty-one-year lease. Documentary sources suggest that the Movanagher village settlement was not reoccupied by English following the events of 1641. Poll tax information for 1659 indicates only a taxable population of seven Irish persons living within the townland of Movanagher. Even before the Rising / Rebellion, Movanagher had begun to falter. Quite possibly the lack of a church at Movanagher encouraged the growth of Kilrea, where the church was located. A further draw for Kilrea was the presence of a market; first established at Movanagher, the market shifted to Kilrea in the 1630s.[71]

At present, the site of Movanagher exists as a working farm, with the remains of the masonry bawn enclosing a farmyard. Archaeological exploration in 1999 aimed to identify the traces of the Mercers' haphazard village in the fields to the west and south of the bawn. Although heavily plow-damaged, the soils did yield small concentrations of early-seventeenth-century materials. The probable location of the Reverend Madder's timber-framed dwelling can be intuited from the discovery of a concentration of brick, window glass, and one piece of window lead from plowed soils near the southeastern corner of the bawn. Ceramics from this location include fragments of English tin-enameled earthenware, Donyatt sgrafitto manufactured in Somerset, and Frechen stoneware from the Rhineland. Two musketballs were also recovered from this locale. One of these had been flattened, indicating that it had been fired and hit a solid object. The other had been cut in half to render it more deadly. No structural traces of the dwelling remained, as typically timber-framed houses were constructed atop timber, brick, or stone sills placed on a leveled ground surface. A surviving stone sill from a 1611 timber-framed building constructed in Coleraine was found only a few inches below the present street level, suggesting that traces of any timber sills at Movanagher would have been readily plowed away. The only evidence for Madder's seemingly substantial timber-framed house is the concentration of domestic and architectural artifacts unearthed in the test

70. Day and McWilliams, eds., *Ordnance Survey Memoirs,* XXVII, 112; Mercers' Acts of Court, 1641–1645.

71. Mercers' Acts of Court, 1631–1637, 1641–1645; Séamus Pender, *A Census of Ireland, circa 1659, with Supplementary Material from the Poll Money Ordinances (1660–1661)* (Cork, 1939), 133.

units and trench from the plowed layers. Similarly, experiments on plowed seventeenth-century domestic sites associated with the first capital of Maryland, Saint Mary's City, have demonstrated that up to 80 percent of the artifact assemblages related to these sites are found in the plowed layers.[72]

Like most other company villages, the architecture employed at Movanagher was not solely derived from English traditions, despite the efforts of planners. Of the ten domestic structures rendered on the 1622 map, only four are large, timber-framed dwellings boasting the standard central chimney-lobby entry plan common in England in the early seventeenth century. The lobby entry plan had evolved during the sixteenth century; pragmatically, it permitted the heating of two rooms through the use of a central stack, with the use of the stack itself (as opposed to a hood over an open heath) permitting the insertion of upper floors. The lobby entry house provided additional privacy for the occupants through the insertion of a small vestibule that controlled both visual and physical access to the hall and parlor. The division of the house and the control over access reflects a broader process of closure and the rise of individualism within English society.[73]

A lobby entry house like this was excavated within the Vintners' Company bawn at Bellaghy. The structure rested upon a stone foundation, and its walls incorporated brickwork. The two hearths served by the central H-shaped chimney were lined with pitched cobbles, and one room, likely the kitchen, was floored with cobbles. The form is also common elsewhere in the British colonial world: early-seventeenth-century examples have been excavated at Jamestown and at nearby Rich Neck Plantation on the James River. Planter houses in the Newfoundland colony, on the other hand, more commonly employed gable-end chimneys, reflective of the strong influence of the West Country.[74]

72. Brannon, "Excavations in New Row, Coleraine," in Egan ed., "Post-Medieval Britain and Ireland in 1984," *Post-Medieval Archaeology*, XIX (1985); Robert W. Keeler, "The Homelot on the Seventeenth-Century Chesapeake Tidewater Frontier" (Ph.D. diss., University of Oregon, 1978); Julia A. King and Henry M. Miller, "The View from the Midden: An Analysis of Midden Distribution and Composition at the van Sweringen Site, St. Mary's City, Maryland," *Historical Archaeology*, XXI (1987), 37–59.

73. Anthony Quiney, "The Lobby-Entry House: Its Origins and Distribution," *Architectural History*, XXVII (1984), 456–466; for consideration of closure and architecture, see Matthew Johnson, *Housing Culture: Traditional Architecture in an English Landscape* (Washington, D.C., 1993).

74. Nick Brannon, "The Bawn at 'Vintner's Towne,'" in Emily Murray and Paul Logue, eds., *Battles, Boats, and Bones: Archaeological Discoveries in Northern Ireland, 1987–2008* (Belfast, 2010), 97–102. Jamestown examples include Structure 24 (discussed in Chapter 4), Structure 44 (built by Secretary Richard Kemp in 1638–9), Structure 112 (home to Governor John Harvey), Struc-

Of the other Movanagher houses on Raven's map, three appear to be stone- or earthen-walled with a lobby-entry plan; another, subrectangular with an addition; and two are small and subrectangular to semicircular in shape. These last three clearly reflect Irish vernacular traditions. In an excavation unit situated in the approximate position of one of these small houses, a series of circular soil stains were uncovered, eventually revealing a pattern of postholes interspersed with stakeholes that defined the outlines of a subrectangular structure measuring 4.25 by 6.1 meters and featuring a central hearth separating two rooms. Evidence for the open hearth consisted of an ashy layer defined by a series of rocks and one large, toppled boulder that might have served as a fireback or a support for a smoke flap. One-half of the house appeared to have had a dirt floor and might have housed animals as well as humans. The subsoil sloped on this side, possibly indicative of sweeping, and a thin occupation layer characterized by an organic loam survived.[75]

The building incorporated earthfast posts designed to carry a roof plate or trusses, whereas the driven posts interspersed between the carrying timbers suggest that the walls were covered with wattle woven around the posts and stakes and most likely plastered with a clay and stone daub. The remains of a cobbled yard and a fenced entry were uncovered on the southeastern side of the structure, and a further series of postholes—possibly a fenceline—continued westward from the building into an unexcavated area. Although sparse and highly fragmented, artifacts recovered from the posthole fills, the pit, the occupation layer, and atop the cobbled surface all support an early-seventeenth-century date for the building. The ceramic sherds are

---

ture 158 (kitchen for Structure 112), Structure 198, and the individual houses in the Structure 115 row. See Audrey J. Horning and Andrew C. Edwards, *Archaeology in New Towne, 1993–1995* (Williamsburg, Va., 2000); Horning, "'A Verie Fitt Place to Erect a Great Cittie'"; Cary Carson et al., *Evaluation of Previous Archaeology* (Williamsburg, Va., 2006). The Rich Neck discovery was reported on by Leslie McFaden, "Rich Neck Plantation: An Example of Permanent Architecture in the Seventeenth Century," paper presented at the Annual Conference of the Council for Northeast Historical Archaeology, Williamsburg, Va., 1994; and by David A. Brown, "Domestic Masonry Architecture in 17th-Century Virginia," *Northeast Historical Archaeology,* XXVII (1998), 85–120. Sources for Newfoundland houses include Peter E. Pope, *Fish into Wine: The Newfoundland Plantation in the Seventeenth Century* (Chapel Hill, N.C., 2004), 327–331; Stephen Mills, "Seventeenth-Century Life in Renews, Newfoundland: Archaeological Analysis of an English West Country Planter's House" (MA thesis, Memorial University of Newfoundland, 2002); Douglas Nixon, "A Seventeenth-Century House at Ferryland, Newfoundland" (MA thesis, Memorial University of Newfoundland, 1999); Gaulton and Tuck, "Archaeology of Ferryland," *Avalon Chronicles,* VIII (2003), 189–224.

75. Horning, "'Dwelling Houses,'" in Duffy, Edwards, and FitzPatrick, eds., *Gaelic Ireland,* 375–396.

dominated by a range of English ware types, produced in the London and Hampshire-Surrey region and the West Country. These include green-glazed Border ware, North Devon gravel-tempered and plain coarse earthenware, Donyatt-type sgraffito, and two sherds of white, tin-glazed earthenware, one of which is a fragment of rim from a scalloped plate or possibly from the handle of a porringer. Plain, white, tin-glazed earthenwares were produced in the London region, at Lambeth and Southwark, from the late sixteenth through seventeenth centuries. Similarly fluted rimsherds have been recovered at a range of Chesapeake sites, including Jamestown, Martin's Hundred, and Matthews Manor. The Border ware sherds are likely from drinking vessels or bowls, two of the many utilitarian forms produced by the English potters in the Surrey-Hampshire regions throughout much of the seventeenth century. Border ware products were common in London and, like the London "delft," have been widely found on seventeenth-century sites throughout the English colonial world. A complete green-glazed Border ware drinking jug was recovered from a ditch feature associated with one of the James Fort bulwarks in 1996, and numerous finds of Border ware have been reported from sites associated with the early Plymouth colony in Massachusetts and the Ferryland settlement in Newfoundland.[76]

Both gravel-tempered and plain varieties of coarse earthenware produced in the potteries of North Devon are also common finds on colonial sites, generally representing milk pans and storage vessels (as is the case at Movanagher), or, less commonly, ridged roof tiles and bake ovens. The 1620s bakehouse excavated at Ferryland in Newfoundland contained two North Devon bread ovens, and another North Devon oven was unearthed at Jamestown in the 1930s. The Donyatt-type pottery sherd recovered from Movanagher, with its red body, yellowish slip, and characteristic sgraffito (scratched or incised) decoration is likely derived from a serving vessel.

76. Ian Betts, Kieron Tyler, and Roy Stephenson, *London's Delftware Industry: The Tin-Glazed Pottery Industries of Southwark and Lambeth* (London 2008); Ivor Noël Hume and Audrey Noël Hume, *The Archaeology of Martin's Hundred: Part II, Artifact Catalogue* (Philadelphia, 2001), 334; Ivor Noël Hume, *Early English Delftware from London and Virginia,* Colonial Williamsburg Occasional Papers in Archaeology, II (Williamsburg, Va., 1977); J. Pearce, *Border Ware* (London, 1992); William M. Kelso, Nicholas M. Luccketti, and B. Straube, *Jamestown Rediscovery III* (Richmond, Va., 1997), 53–54; Mary C. Beaudry, Karin J. Goldstein, and Craig Chartier, "Archaeology of the Plymouth Colony in Massachusetts," *Avalon Chronicles,* VIII (2003), 159; Blair Temple, "Somerset and Dorset Ceramics at Seventeenth-Century Ferryland, Newfoundland" (MA thesis, Memorial University, Newfoundland, 2004), table 6.3, 97; Peter Edward Pope, "Ceramics from Seventeenth Century Ferryland, Newfoundland (CgAf-2, Locus B)" (MA thesis, Memorial University, Newfoundland, 1986), 140, refers to "southern white bodied wares," which also appear to correspond to Border ware products.

This type of ware was produced in south Somerset in southwest England throughout the seventeenth century. Although less common on Chesapeake sites than North Devon products, Donyatt-type wares have been recovered from Jamestown and other sites along the James River, including Martin's Hundred and Jordan's Journey, and also from Saint Mary's City, Maryland. Accompanying the English wares in and around the structure were sherds of the same Ulster coarse pottery that were recovered from deposits at Limavady, Brackfield, and Salterstown. Here, again, is evidence that, alongside the more familiar products of the English marketplace, unfamiliar, locally produced wares were swiftly absorbed into the material repertoire of incoming settlers.[77]

The significance of an Irish house form in an English plantation village cannot be overstated insofar as architecture was a means of not only projecting "civilization" but effecting it, as well. In the new Ulster settlements, building leases generally stipulated that houses be constructed "after the English manner" (having, at the very least, a timber-frame structure with a stone or brick chimney). Freeholds granted by the Irish Society to Englishmen resident at Movanagher in 1618 were even more specific: they stipulated that the grantees must build "one sufficient and substantiall house of timber stone or brick containing six or four roomes at the least fitt for and convenyient for habitacion." Leases and regulations are one thing; labor requirements and pragmatism, another. The Movanagher house speaks eloquently to the reliance upon indigenous labor and knowledge in the Londonderry Plantation, the one locale where Irish input was officially prohibited.[78]

Although expediency might have dictated the incorporation of Irish architectural forms by incoming English and Scottish planters, the forms' otherness did not go unremarked. Some commentators even compared Irish building forms with those of New World Natives. In the 1630s, chronicler Thomas Morton noted, "The Natives of New England are accustomed to build them houses, much like the wild Irish, they gather Poles in the woodes

77. Gaulton and Tuck, "Archaeology of Ferryland," *Avalon Chronicles,* VIII (2003), 198; John L. Cotter, *Archeological Excavations at Jamestown Colonial National Historic Park and Jamestown National Historic Site, Virginia,* Archaeological Research Ser., no. 4 (Washington, D.C., 1958), 74; Richard Coleman-Smith, "Excavations in the Donyatt Potteries: Site 13," *Post-Medieval Archaeology,* XXXVI (2002), 118–172; Coleman-Smith, R. Taft Kiser, and Michael J. Hughes, "Donyatt-Type Pottery in 17th- and 18th-Century Virginia and Maryland," ibid., XXXIX (2005), 294–310.

78. P. S. Robinson, "Some Late Survivals of Box-Framed 'Plantation Houses' in Coleraine, County Londonderry," *Ulster Journal of Archaeology,* 3d Ser., XLVI (1983), 129; October 1618 grant to Charles Williams "of Mavannahor," original in Mercers' Company Archive, London.

and put the great end of them in the ground, placinge them in forme of a circle or circumference, and bendinge the topps of them in forme of an Arch." Later in the century, Virginian Robert Beverley drew a direct comparison when commenting upon Virginia Indian dwellings: "Their Chimney, as among the true Born *Irish,* is a little hole in the top of the House, to let out the Smoak." Associations between the housing of the Irish and of Native American people were also made in Ireland, as in the 1672 complaint of Sir William Petty. In his "Political Anatomy of Ireland," Petty estimated that, of 200,000 houses in Ireland in the 1670s, some 160,000 were "wretched nasty cabbins, without chimney, window, or doorshut, and worse than those of the savage Americans." Both Morgan and Beverley helped their readers to envision the Native house forms by referring to the presumably more familiar Irish-style dwellings. Petty, on the other hand, was overtly criticizing Irish domestic architecture, its quality even below that of the supposedly uncivilized New World Native. All three commentators took for granted the efficacy of their ready equation of Irish with Native American, reflecting the broader process of colonial othering associated with English, and later British Atlantic, expansion.[79]

The presence of the Irish-style dwelling associated with Irish and English utilitarian ceramics in an English settlement encapsulates the contradictions of plantation. Far from settling a colonial wilderness, those few planters who made their way to the London Company lands found themselves thrust into a populated Gaelic world where their survival depended upon accommodation and adaptation—processes that are materially echoed in the finds from Phillips's base in the Roe Valley as well as in the later assemblages from Salterstown and can be predicted to be present in other company settlements. Little archaeological excavation has taken place in the Drapers' town at Moneymore, but the documentary record hints at the closeness of relations between natives and newcomers in that settlement as well. Although the early surveys of Moneymore seemed to indicate that the building program was going tolerably well, it appears that the Drapers' choice of an agent, Robert Russell, was as ill-advised, as had been the Mercers' choice of Richard Vernon. In December 1618, a deputation of disgruntled Moneymore tenants journeyed all the way to Drapers' Hall in London to present

79. Thomas Morton, *New English Canaan; or, New Canaan* . . . (Amsterdam, 1637), 24; Robert Beverley, *The History and Present State of Virginia: A New Edition with an Introduction by Susan Scott Parrish* (Chapel Hill, N.C., 2013), 137; William Petty, "The Political Anatomy of Ireland" (1672; rpt. London, 1691), rpt. in *A Collection of Tracts and Treatises Illustrative of the Natural History, Antiquities, and the Political and Social State of Ireland,* II (Dublin, 1861), 77.

allegations against Russell, accusing him of having "built a great and very large and unnecessary brewhouse both to the hindrance and great disturbance of the whole towne." To ensure the profitability of his brewing venture, Russell had diverted the town's innovative piped water supply to service his brewhouse, forbade occupants from producing any ale themselves, and converted five dwellings into alehouses, frequented by a mixed clientele of British and Irish.[80]

The proximity and intimacy of relations between the drinkers in the Moneymore pubs, whatever their cultural identity, gives much pause for thought in considering how alcohol might have lubricated communication. The sharing of alcoholic beverages was a key element in both Irish and English notions of hospitality, albeit governed by different rules, customs, and expectations that could easily be violated. The unintentional delivery of an insult may be the explanation for the violence that erupted on the Mercers' proportion in 1615. As recorded by the Ironmongers' agent George Canning, four Englishmen who were settled on the Mercers' lands (including two leatherworkers, John Browne and John Williams) were assaulted and stabbed to death by nine Irish raiders, or woodkerne. The murders do not seem to have been premeditated acts of resistance, as the attack occurred after John Browne, his wife, and three of their Irish neighbors spent several hours imbibing "beer, wine, and aqua vitae" together with the nine woodkerne in Browne's home. The drunken brawl that ensued might have been sparked by an inappropriate comment or perhaps by a demand for payment on the part of Mrs. Browne, who had turned her home into an unlicensed alehouse. Mrs. Browne's Irish guests viewed the proffering of drink as a gesture of hospitality and would readily take umbrage at its reduction to an economic exchange. Whatever the impetus, such shared consumption of alcohol, be it in the Browne house or in Agent Russell's alehouses, provided the space for exchanges of cultural knowledge, which only become problematic when there is a misunderstanding. Certainly, the widespread practice of intercultural imbibing was a perennial cause for concern to individuals like Sir Thomas Phillips, who recommended in 1623 that no alehouses be allowed "in remote places." As Russell's Moneymore enterprises demonstrated, however, even those alehouses situated within towns could not be effectively regulated in terms of intercultural mingling.[81]

80. Drapers' Company Records, PRONI, D3632/A105.

81. Sir Thomas Phillips, "Reformation of Abuses in the Ulster Plantation," June 3, 1623, in Russell and Prendergast, eds., *CSPI of the Reign of James I*, V, 411–413; Canny, *Making Ireland British*, 435; George Canning, letter, Jan. 15, 1616, MS 17,278, Guildhall Library, London;

Elsewhere in the British colonial world, indigenous people's alcohol consumption would be highly regulated. Plymouth colony officials expressly forbade New England Native peoples from drinking alcohol. Even in zones where indigenous people posed less of a daily threat, as in the Newfoundland colony, alcohol consumption was still a cause for concern. Fishermen benefited from a degree of disposable income and ready access to a range of alcoholic beverages, the latter an integral element of the fishing trade. The result was a level of alcohol consumption excessive enough to merit comment from contemporaries. As would be the case in Ireland, the lucrative nature of the alcohol trade outweighed concerns about the dangers of an inebriated workforce. Newfoundland planter and merchant David Kirke profited from his control over the licensing of alehouses as well as his involvement in the alcohol-for-fish trade. Although excessive drinking by his workforce could lead to disorder and thereby threaten his profits, the widespread desire for imported wine, brandy, and spirit distillates ensured a reliable market. Kirke capitalized on this market even as he, too, was the subject of complaints over his alcohol-related profiteering, much like the Drapers' agent Robert Russell.[82]

Russell clearly illustrated Francis Bacon's lament that "the bane of a plantation is, when the undertakers or planters make such haste to a little mechanical present profit, as disturbeth the whole frame and nobleness of the work for times to come." Firing Russell did not solve the Drapers' difficulties. The company then let the proportion out to absentee farmer and former servitor Sir Thomas Roper, himself no stranger to the profits generated by alehouses, as he held the patent for registering all alehouses in Ireland. Roper had already engaged in unprofitable entrepreneurial activities on his grants in Kerry, including textile and pipe stave manufacturing and commercial fishing; the acquisition of the patent offset Roper's losses. Roper was clearly influenced by the activities of George Villiers (then Viscount Villiers and soon to be the duke of Buckingham), with whom he shared a

Horning, "'Root of All Vice and Bestiality,'" in Lyttleton and Rynne, eds., *Plantation Ireland,* 113–131; Curl, *The Honourable the Irish Society,* 127; Miller, "Salterstown," 166–168. For consideration of intercultural discourse and the ways in which signs and meanings can be misunderstood, see Homi K. Bhabha, *The Location of Culture* (London, 1994).

82. See Yasuhide Kawashima, *Puritan Justice and the Indian: White Man's Law in Massachusetts, 1630–1763* (Middletown, Conn., 1986), 205–224; for a discussion of the desire for alcohol among the Newfoundland fishermen, see Peter Pope, "Historical Archaeology and the Demand for Alcohol in 17th Century Newfoundland," *Acadiensis,* XIX (1989), 72–90; Pope, *Fish into Wine,* 384–395.

family relationship. Villiers had long profited from holding the patent for licensing English drinking establishments. Roper would ultimately advance to the Irish peerage in the 1630s, aided by his association with Buckingham, but his tenancy of the Drapers' lands was short-lived. The company repossessed its lands in 1622, as the castle (poorly built by one George Birkett, rather ironically accused by Russell of being a drunkard) had continued to collapse during Roper's tenure. Birkett was indeed a poor builder: only a portion of the Moneymore bawn wall remains standing, heavily repaired and resting directly upon unstable sands.[83]

The complexity of the interactions between the Irish and the English and Scots planters is discernible outside of the London Company lands, as well. The masonry castle constructed by Scots planter Sir John Hume in 1613 at Tully in Fermanagh reflects Lowland Scottish architectural style in its T-shaped plan and use of projecting turrets. But the masons' construction techniques derived from Irish, not Scottish, architecture, including use of wickerwork barrel vaulting. The Tully Irish masons also took a novel approach to the construction of the turrets. Rather than rely upon cut stone, they employed cones built of rubble, then smoothed the surface of the cones over with mortar to give the superficial appearance of a cut stone turret. Charged with building an unfamiliar architectural form, the Irish workforce simply employed more familiar methods to create a reasonable facsimile of a Scottish corbelled turret. The decision to roof the castle with thatch rather than slate, in another concession to local materials and expertise, proved a fatal error. The castle was destroyed in a fire set by rebels on Christmas Day, 1641.[84]

Clearly, the failure to meet all of the precepts of plantation was not lim-

83. "The Speech Used by Sir Francis Bacon, Lord Keeper of the Great Seal of England, to Sir William Jones . . ." (1617), in James Spedding, ed., *The Letters and the Life of Francis Bacon: Including All His Occasional Works* . . . , VI (London, 1872), 206. Thomas Roper's cousin Rebecca Roper was married to Sir William Villiers, elder brother of Buckingham. See "Commissioners in Ireland to the Marquis of Buckingham, Lord Admiral," Jul. 5, 1622, in Russell and Prendergast, eds., *CSPI of the Reign of James I*, V, 361; king to Viscount Falkland (grant to Thomas Roper for registering licenses for alehouse), Aug. 24, 1622, ibid., 390; Treadwell, *Buckingham and Ireland*, 53; Drapers' Company Estate Archive, D363, PRONI; Moody, *Londonderry Plantation, 1609–41*, 306.

84. Donnelly, "Archaeology of the Ulster Plantation," in Horning et al., eds., *Post-Medieval Archaeology of Ireland*, 41; Brannon, "Archives and Archaeology," in Egan and Michael, eds., *Old and New Worlds*, 102; J. D. Johnston, "Settlement and Architecture in County Fermanagh, 1610–41," *Ulster Journal of Archaeology*, 3d Ser., XLIII (1980), 79–89; Jope, "Scottish Influences," ibid., XIV (1951), 31–47; D. M. Waterman, "Tully Castle, Co. Fermanagh," ibid., XXII (1959), 123–126.

ited to the London Company settlements. Hume did at least build his castle, but other undertakers who accepted grants in the Ulster Plantation did not follow through in developing their lands. One such recalcitrant planter was Sir Maurice Berkeley of Somerset, father of the future Virginia governor William Berkeley (in office 1641–1652, 1660–1677). Sir Maurice, who would also invest in the Virginia Company, had acquired two thousand acres in the vicinity of Lifford, Co. Donegal, but as of 1611 was reported as never having visited his lands nor sent an agent in his stead; "nothing done." He sold the lands to Sir Ralph Bingley sometime before Pynnar's survey in 1618–1619, having planted a grand total of seven British men on the lands while renting to at least five families of the O'Gallagher clan.[85]

Others began developing their lands but often ran out of money or interest before completing the required buildings, or they cut corners. Hearkening back to Doddington's shoddily built manor house at Dungiven, Sir Anthony Cope's builders at Castleraw, Co. Armagh, neglected to employ mortar. Sir Josias Bodley reported the disastrous results in his 1613 survey: "Sir Anthony Cope hath built a fair house of hewn stone with clay, of great charge, which being brought to perfection a great part of it fell suddenly down, so that the whole must be demolished to the ground and newly raised with lime, which is not yet taken in hand by his agent." Although Cope possessed sufficient resources to rebuild his castle before 1622 (this time employing lime mortar!), many lesser planters did not. Indeed, in Chichester's estimation, most English planters were simply not of sufficient means or dedication to follow through with the project of plantation: "Those from England are, for the most part, plain country gentlemen, who may promise much, but give small assurance or hope of performing what appertains to a work of such moment. If they have money, they keep it close, for hitherto they have disbursed but little; and if he may judge by the outward appearance, the least trouble or alteration of the times here will scare most of them away." Chichester's observations reflect the reality that few in England were inspired to gamble their money in Ireland. The rebelliousness of the Irish population was hardly a secret; and, few expected to discover untold mineral riches in a land that was now well surveyed and explored, unlike the New World.[86]

---

85. "State of the Ulster Plantation in 1611," in Russell and Prendergast, eds., *CSPI of the Reign of James I,* IV, 122–23; Hill, *An Historical Account of the Plantation in Ulster,* 514, 520.

86. N. F. Brannon, "Two Fortified Houses at Castleraw, County Armagh," *Ulster Journal of Archaeology,* 3d Ser., XLVI (1983), 165–166; Sir Josias Bodley, "Survey of the Undertakers and Servitors Planted in Ulster between Feb. 2, 1612, and April 25, 1613," in John Harley and

The most successful plantation settlements in Ulster were those spear-headed, not by the London Companies or by individual English under-takers, but by the Lowland Scots Hugh Montgomery and James Hamilton on the former Clandeboye O'Neill lands. In 1605, Hamilton and Mont-gomery each received a one-third share of the Upper Clandeboye estate granted to Sir Thomas Smith in the 1570s. Hamilton's land grant extended along the southern shore of Belfast Lough from Holywood to Bangor and Groomsport, whereas Montgomery received the lands around the settle-ments of Comber, Newtownards, and Greyabbey. Hamilton soon acquired much of the remaining share, originally allocated to Conn McBrian O'Neill, as well as the estate formerly owned by Hugo White at Killyleagh. Here Hamilton established perhaps the most functional and well-populated new settlement of the plantation era. The success of the Scottish plantation in East Ulster was founded upon the importation of families, rather than single males, who were willing to invest their time and effort in developing sustain-able small farms and villages. An apt colonial comparator is the colony of Bermuda, where a demographically stable and gender-balanced community was established in the 1610s. Lured by the promise of landownership on an island blessed with many natural resources, the Somers Island Company had little difficulty attracting settlers. Although the Clandeboye O'Neill terri-tory lacked equivalent sunshine and commodities, its proximity to Scotland, familiar environment, and fixity of tenure attracted settlers from all levels of society. Population increase and the widespread reordering of estates in Scotland, leading to displacement at worst and rent increase at best, ensured a steady stream of willing Lowland Scots migrants.[87]

In the late seventeenth century, William Montgomery, grandson of Sir Hugh Montgomery, set out the history of the Ards Plantation. His version was predicated upon an assumption that the Nine Years' War had left this

---

Francis Bickley, eds., *Report on the Manuscripts of the Late Reginald Rawdon Hastings, Esq., of the Manor House, Ashby de la Zouche*, IV, Historical Manuscripts Commission Report no. 78 (Lon-don, 1947), 174; Chichester to earl of Northampton, quoted in Hill, *An Historical Account of the Plantation in Ulster*, 446.

87. Gilbert Camblin, *The Town in Ulster: An Account of the Origin and Building of the Towns of the Province and the Development of Their Rural Setting* . . . (Belfast, 1951), 35–36; Raymond Gillespie, *Colonial Ulster: The Settlement of East Ulster, 1600–1641* (Cork, 1985), 36–39; Gillespie, "Thomas Raven and the Mapping of the Claneboy Estates," *Bangor Historical Society Journal,* I (1981), 6–9; Robinson, *Plantation of Ulster,* 53; Michael J. Jarvis, *In the Eye of All Trade: Ber-muda, Bermudians, and the Maritime Atlantic World, 1680–1783* (Chapel Hill, N.C., 2010), 24–36; Virginia Bernhard, "Bermuda and Virginia in the Seventeenth Century: A Comparative View," *Journal of Social History,* XIX (1985), 57–70.

part of Ulster devastated and depopulated, and relied upon a direct equation with the settlement of the New World:

> Therefore let us now pause a while, and we shall wonder how this plantation advanced itself (especially in and about the towns of Donaghadee and Newton), considering that in the spring time, Ao. 1606, those parishes were now more wasted than America (when the Spaniards landed there), but were not at all incumbered with great woods to be felled and grubbed, to the discouragement or hindrance of the inhabitants, for in all those three parishes aforesaid, 30 cabins could not be found, nor any stone walls, but ruined roofless churches, and a few vaults at Gray Abbey, and a stump of an old castle in Newton, in each of which some Gentlemen sheltered themselves at their first coming over.

Montgomery overstated his case and the industriousness of his family. In reality, the Hamilton and Montgomery settlements succeeded, first, because they were able to bring over sufficient settlers, and second, because they were able to make use of existing infrastructure. The Clandeboye lands were neither depopulated nor devoid of buildings, fields, or managed woodland. Many of the landscape characteristics attributed to the industriousness of the Scottish settlers derived from medieval Irish field systems and transport corridors. The planters fitted themselves into an existing cultural landscape, one that significantly shaped the character of this unofficial plantation. In this regard, the Scottish settlements of East Ulster diverged markedly from the Bermuda colony. Bermuda was singular among British colonies in the Atlantic world for its lack of an indigenous population. Only there could the principle of res nullius be honestly and effectively employed in the planting of a colony.[88]

Some sense of the Gaelic landscape can be derived from Thomas Raven's extensive 1625 survey of the estate lands held by James Hamilton, first Viscount Claneboye. Following his employ with Sir Thomas Phillips and an

88. John Dennis James O'Keeffe, "The Archaeology of the Later Historical Cultural Landscape in Northern Ireland: Developing Historic Landscape Investigation for the Management of the Archaeological Resource; A Case Study of the Ards, County Down" (Ph.D. thesis, University of Ulster, 2008). William Montgomery compiled his records between 1695–1706. His writings were edited by George Hill in the nineteenth century and published as *The Montgomery Manuscripts (1603–1706)* (Belfast, 1869). The quotation can be found on page 58 of the edited volume. See Neil Kennedy, "William Crashaw's Bridge: Bermuda and the Origins of the English Atlantic 1609–1624," in Nancy Rhoden, ed., *English Atlantics Revisited: Essays Honouring Professor Ian K. Steele* (Montreal, 2007), 107–135, for an expansion of the argument that the lack of a Native population on Bermuda ensured its early stability.

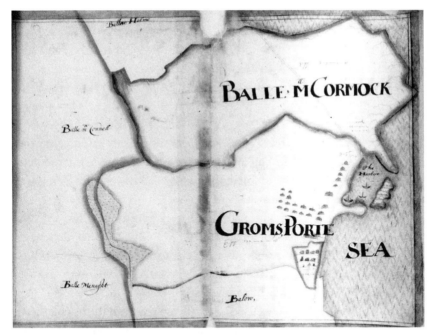

Plate 18. Detail from Thomas Raven's map of Groomsport, depicting Irish houses in the settlement. Courtesy of North Down Borough Council through the North Down Museum

unsuccessful attempt to create an official crown position for himself, Raven turned his hand to surveying the estates of servitors. In addition to detailing the lands, tenants, and economic resources to aid estate management, Raven's survey for Hamilton was also used as evidence in a continuing dispute between Hamilton and Hugh Montgomery over the exact boundaries of their individual grants.[89]

Raven produced a total of seventy-five hand-colored maps, covering the Clandeboye lands of North Down, incorporating Bangor, Holywood, Comber, Groomsport, and Killyleagh, and all of Hamilton's lands around those settlements, including Ralph Lane's former seat at Ringhaddy. Emphasis was placed on the lands' economic potential, as exemplified by

89. Andrews, *Plantation Acres,* 55–56. The boundary dispute between Hamilton and Montgomery was clearly fueled by personal enmity and complicated by each man's separate dealings with Con O'Neill in relation to territory outside of their original grants. Further complicating the dispute was a claim from Sir William Smith, heir to Sir Thomas Smith, who had failed to plant his Ards Colony in the 1570s. See M. Perceval-Maxwell, *The Scottish Migration to Ulster in the Reign of James I* (London, 1973), 234–241.

Raven's frequent depiction of trees, coney burrows (rabbit warrens), and open pasture lands. The imprint of the Scottish settlers is evident in the meticulously outlined towns and in the carefully detailed castle and deer park at Killyleagh. Notably Irish habitations appear, as well, as in the cluster of three low, subrectangular Irish dwellings near Derryboy and in the houses depicted within the seaside settlement of Groomsport. Groomsport itself has fourteenth-century origins, and although the regularly-spaced Irish-style houses evident on Raven's plan are most likely seventeenth century, they reflect the continuing influence of Irish traditions in this medieval port. Surrounding lands were still in the hands of an Irish landowner, Owen Omulcreve, at the time of Raven's survey.[90]

Similarly, the medieval center at Bangor was transformed into a plantation town, albeit one that still incorporated twelve Irish-style houses, as recorded by Raven. Urbanization was a key element in the transformation of East Ulster, with extant towns such as Newry and Carrickfergus expanded and smaller medieval settlements like Bangor subject to development. Bangor had a population of around 226 when Raven recorded the town in 1625. Just five years later, the figure had increased to 987. Regardless of the evidence for continued Irish occupation of the Hamilton and Montgomery lands, the Scottish lords were far more successful in attracting British tenants than were any of their counterparts in the official Ulster Plantation. Muster rolls from the 1630s indicate that the number of adult British men in Counties Antrim and Down numbered 5,600, versus only 6,500 for all of the formal Ulster Plantation (Counties Armagh, Cavan, Fermanagh, Londonderry, Tyrone, and Donegal). The families who traveled to the Hamilton and Montgomery lands, unlike those who journeyed to the New World, already possessed a sound understanding of the land to which they were relocating. Sharing the same climate, they did not need to adapt their knowledge of agriculture to unfamiliar surroundings. Aiding greatly in Hamilton's and Montgomery's colonial ventures was the relative ease of travel to and from Scottish ports such as Stranraer, which facilitated the movement of people, livestock, and building supplies. Taking as little as three hours, the sea journey between County Down and Scotland, although dangerous, is not comparable to a transatlantic voyage. Landlords as well as tenants regularly traveled between the two lands. Migration was fluid and not unidirectional. If the political situation became problematic, one could always return to Scotland. The expansion of trade between Scotland and Ulster facilitated such

90. O'Keeffe, "Archaeology of the Later Historical Cultural Landscape," 329–331.

Plate 19. Excavation of merchant's house, Dunluce, County Antrim, 2009.
Photograph courtesy of Colin Breen, University of Ulster

movement; by way of example, Scottish vessels constituted 80 percent of
the volume of traffic in the port of Londonderry during the second decade
of the seventeenth century.[91]

Archaeological examination of Randal MacDonnell's stronghold at Dunluce has shown that the Highlander also recognized the symbolic value of
townbuilding. As he positioned himself as an ideal British planter in a bid to
retain his lands and influence, MacDonnell followed up-to-date notions of
civic development. He transformed his castle into a gentleman's seat through
the construction of a grand hall featuring projecting mullioned windows; he
also augmented the landscape with a sizable formal garden and established a
village aligned along a formal street plan. Excavation of one house in the village revealed it to be a sizable stone dwelling, likely inhabited by a Scottish
merchant and situated along a wide, cobbled street. Despite MacDonnell's
best efforts, the Dunluce settlement was not to last, as sea access was virtu-
ally impossible. Although a failure as a mercantile center, the Dunluce village and the apparent expense of its architecture and streetscape conveyed its

91. Gillespie, *Colonial Ulster*, 171; Perceval-Maxwell, *Scottish Migration to Ulster*, 59, 294–295.

builder's message: that he was well aware of contemporary British ideas of civility, commerce, and control even as he relied upon Catholic Highlanders to people his ideal plantation landscape.[92]

Indeed, it is becoming increasingly clear that MacDonnell was well aware of the symbolic, as well as pragmatic, importance of townbuilding in the establishment and maintenance of plantation settlements. Townbuilding was viewed as the principal means of organizing and administering colonial zones throughout the British Atlantic world, and the social, political, and military value of townbuilding in the Ulster Plantation had been stressed by Davies, Chichester, and Bacon as plans were laid to reorganize Ulster in the wake of the Flight of the Earls.[93]

Townbuilding as Colonial Strategy

In the words of Edmund Spenser, "Nothing doth sooner cause civility in any countrie then many market townes . . . nothing doth more stay and strengthen the country then such corporate townes . . . Nothing doth more enrich any country or realme then many townes." Towns pro-

92. Jane Ohlmeyer notes MacDonnell's simultaneous promotion of "progressive economic and agrarian policies"; see Ohlmeyer, *Civil War and Restoration in the Three Stuart Kingdoms: The Career of Randal MacDonnell, Marquis of Antrim, 1609–1683* (Dublin, 2001), 24–25; Colin Breen, "The Other Plantation: Settlement on the Antrim Estates," paper presented at the Tenth Annual Irish Post-Medieval Archaeology Group Conference, Belfast, February 2010; Terence Reeves-Smyth, "Community to Privacy: Late Tudor and Jacobean Manorial Architecture in Ireland, 1560–1640," in Horning et al., eds., *Post-Medieval Archaeology of Ireland*, 301–302.

93. Angélique Day and Patrick McWilliams, eds., *Ordnance Survey Memoirs of Ireland*, XXIV, *Parishes of County Antrim IX, 1830–2, 1835, 1838–9, North Antrim Coast and Rathlin* (Belfast, 1994); TCD, 1641 Depositions Project, MS 838, examination of Donnell Magee, Mar. 15, 1653, online transcript December 2009, http://1641.eneclann.ie, accessed Jul. 15, 2010. That the earls of Antrim settled considerable numbers of Roman Catholic Scots in addition to Protestant lowlanders on their Ulster lands is suggested by nineteenth-century sources. The Ordnance Survey Memoirs for the parish of Culfeightrin highlight the prevalence of Scottish surnames and enumerate 430 Protestants, 5,012 Roman Catholics, and only 30 Presbyterians. Even accounting for a significant amount of eighteenth-century Presbyterian emigration to North America, the clear majority of the parish inhabitants were Catholic, of Scottish origin, reflecting the plantation activities of MacDonnell and their continuing links with the Scottish Isles. By way of example, MacDonnell had granted lands encompassing the site of Goodland to Donal and Alexander Magee of Islay. The brothers, like their lord, were probably Catholic, yet they, too, appear to have held conflicting loyalties to crown and to religion. Donal Magee's post-1641 deposition notes that he rushed to "save some British acquaintance of his" ahead of the Irish advance—an advance in which some of his own tenants might well have participated. Despite this documentary evidence, and the existence of sites like Goodland (however poorly understood), there is little public awareness of those Highlanders who made their way to the north of Ireland in both the sixteenth and seventeenth centuries, given the strength of dichotomous understandings of plantation and of its relationship to religious identities.

vided an administrative center and cultural reference point for settlers, as well as facilitated economic activity. Towns would likewise be fundamental to the settlement and management of the Virginia colony, even where they were doomed to minimal success in the face of the demands of the tobacco economy.[94]

As argued by Francis Bacon, towns in Ireland would be "a means to secure the country against future perils." Interestingly, Bacon highlighted the advantages of establishing towns thus:

> And if any man think it will draw people too far off from the grounds they are to labour, it is to be understood, that the number of the towns be increased accordingly and likewise the situation of them be as in the centre in respect of the portions assigned to them: for in the champion countries of England, where the habitation useth to be in towns, and not dispersed, it is no new thing to go two miles off to plough part of their grounds; and two miles compass will take up a good deal of country.

Bacon's notion of imposing an open field system on Ulster so as to enhance the viability and security of its towns was an intriguing notion, founded upon his own critique of English settlement. This serves as a reminder that there was no accepted model for optimum civic administration even within England. What Bacon was proposing was implementing a form of urban development in Ulster that could affect practice within England. Colonial influences can be multidirectional. But his vision for an open field system in Ulster was not put into practice. It would have required a very different set of communal relations and social obligations that were unlikely ever to exist in a new society without ancestral ties to place or person. The incentive for planters and settlers was the acquisition of individual land grants, to be developed individually rather than corporately. Even the London Company plantations, ostensibly corporate efforts, relied upon a system of granting lands, with only minimal oversight of the grantees' activities. A similar problem pertained to the Chesapeake, where efforts to compel Virginia settlers to reside in Jamestown rather than establish dispersed tobacco plantations up and down the many rivers of eastern Virginia failed, despite recognition of the need for urban development.[95]

94. Edmund Spenser, *A View of the State of Ireland,* ed. Andrew Hadfield and Willy Maley (Oxford, 1997), 156–157.

95. Francis Bacon, "Certain Considerations Touching the Plantation in Ireland" (1608), in Maxwell, *Irish History from Contemporary Sources,* 269–273. For considerations of the urban ideal and the Chesapeake reality, see Carville V. Earle, *The Evolution of a Tidewater Settlement System:*

The activities of Munster planter Richard Boyle are a prime example of individual control over the planning and settlement of seventeenth-century Irish towns. Boyle, who became the earl of Cork in 1620, owned one-third of the plantation land in Munster along with George Courtney, enabling the pair to essentially chart the destiny of that portion of Ireland. Boyle, in particular, recognized the virtue of towns in promoting the region's economic development and in retaining a measure of political and administrative control. He concentrated upon restoring the established settlements in Munster as well as creating four new towns, reportedly investing £14,000. The new town of Bandon was designed with a gridiron street plan and protected by walls Boyle described as "stronger, thicker, and higher" than the walls of Londonderry. Excavation confirms the substantial nature of the 2.4 meter-wide walls, which surrounded the town by 1627. Yet seventeenth-century Munster was built upon existing foundations, upon the already flourishing network of towns and trade relations with the south of England and more

All Hallow's Parish, Maryland, 1650–1783, University of Chicago Department of Geography Research Paper no. 170 (Chicago, 1975); Earle, "The First English Towns of North America," *Geographical Review,* LXVII (1977), 34–50; Earle and Ronald Hoffman, "The Urban South: The First Two Centuries," in Blaine A. Brownell and David R. Goldfield, eds., *The City in Southern History: The Growth of Urban Civilization in the South* (Port Washington, N.Y., 1977); Kevin P. Kelly, "'In Dispers'd Country Plantations': Settlement Patterns in Seventeenth-Century Surry County, Virginia," in Thad W. Tate and David L. Ammerman, eds., *The Chesapeake in the Seventeenth Century: Essays on Anglo-American Society* (Chapel Hill, N.C., 1979), 183–205; Kathleen Bragdon, Edward Chappell, and William Graham, "A Scant Urbanity: Jamestown in the 17th Century," in Theodore R. Reinhart and Dennis J. Pogue, eds., *The Archaeology of 17th-Century Virginia* (Richmond, Va., 1993); Lois Green Carr, *Adaptation and Settlement in the Colonial Chesapeake,* St. Mary's City Research Ser., no. 6 (St. Mary's City, Md., 1987); Carr, "'The Metropolis of Maryland': A Comment on Town Development along the Tobacco Coast," *Maryland Historical Magazine,* LXIX (1974), 124–145; Horning, "'A Verie Fit Place to Erect a Great Cittie'"; Horning, "Urbanism in the Colonial South: The Development of Seventeenth-Century Jamestown," in Amy L. Young, ed., *Archaeology of Southern Urban Landscapes* (Tuscaloosa, Ala., 2000), 52–68; Audrey Horning, "English Towns on the Periphery: Seventeenth-Century Town Development in Ulster and the Chesapeake," in Adrian Green and Roger Leech, eds., *Cities in the World, 1500–2000: Papers Given at the Conference of the Society for Post-Medieval Archaeology, April 2002* (Leeds, 2006); Sylvia Doughty Fries, *The Urban Idea in Colonial America* (Philadelphia, 1977); Ronald E. Grim, "The Absence of Towns in Seventeenth-Century Virginia: The Emergence of Service Centers in York County" (Ph.D. diss., University of Maryland, 1977); Henry M. Miller, "Baroque Cities in the Wilderness: Archaeology and Urban Development in the Colonial Chesapeake," *Historical Archaeology,* XXII (1988), 57–73; John W. Reps, *Tidewater Towns: City Planning in Colonial Virginia and Maryland* (Williamsburg, Va., 1972). A recent re-evaluation of this scholarship on urban ideologies in the Chesapeake can be found in Paul Philip Musselwhite, "Towns in Mind: Urban Plans, Political Culture, and Empire in the Colonial Chesapeake, 1607–1722" (Ph.D. diss., College of William and Mary, 2011), 29–32, 35–47.

distant continental ports. The far more rural Ulster Plantation was quite a different matter.[96]

Medieval settlements in Ulster included the ports of Carrickfergus and Newry, the ecclesiastical settlements of Downpatrick and Armagh, and scattered market towns such as Cavan, Omagh, and Dungannon. In addition to expanding these settlements, plans for the Ulster Plantation included the founding of twenty-five incorporated towns, accompanied by a host of villages. In Antrim and Down, as noted above, the former ecclesiastical centers such as Newtownards and Bangor were developed, whereas elsewhere in the plantation—as with Newtown Limavady—towns were entirely new constructions. Each plantation town was to include a church, a market, and a jail and was intended to impose a peculiarly English stamp onto the landscape. Although slow to develop, towns including Coleraine, Londonderry, Belfast, and Newtown Limavady were reasonably diverse and functional by the 1630s, only to have their growth curtailed by the Rising/Rebellion of 1641 and subsequent warfare of the 1640s. It would not be until the end of the seventeenth century that a truly functional network of towns would emerge in Ulster. The overly optimistic nature of the urbanization plans was evident early on, with only fourteen of Ulster's required twenty-five towns established by 1613, forcing planners to reduce the number to sixteen. Ulster was not hampered by the same economic forces that prevented the growth of towns in Virginia and Maryland; there, the reliance upon dispersed tobacco plantations along the navigable rivers stymied efforts to expand central places like Jamestown and Saint Mary's City. Instead, Ulster Plantation again suffered from the inability of planters, particularly the London Companies, to attract sufficient numbers of British settlers. In the case of Cavan, plantation officials were content to allow the Gaelic urban elite to carry out the expansion of the existing market town, further evidence of pragmatism over dogmatism in implementing plantation.[97]

96. Michael MacCarthy-Morrogh, *The Munster Plantation: English Migration to Southern Ireland, 1583–1641* (New York, 1986), 253; Horning, "English Towns on the Periphery," in Green and Leech, eds., *Cities in the World,* 65; R. A. Butlin, "Irish Towns in the Sixteenth and Seventeenth Centuries," in Butlin, ed., *The Development of the Irish Town* (London, 1977), 61–100, esp. 82; Maurice Hurley, "Archaeological Testing at the Town Walls (Gully Townland), Bandon, Co. Cork," unpublished report submitted to Dúchas, Dublin, 2000; Denis Power, "The Archaeology of the Munster Plantation," in Horning et al., eds., *Post-Medieval Archaeology of Ireland,* 23–36.

97. Horning, "English Towns on the Periphery," in Green and Leech, eds., *Cities in the World;* Horning, "Urbanism in the Colonial South," in Young, ed., *Archaeology of Southern Urban Landscapes;* Musselwhite, "Towns in Mind"; Jonathan Cherry, "Colonial Appropriation of Gaelic Urban Space: Creating the First Ulster Plantation Town," *Irish Geography,* XL (2007), 125.

As a plantation town under the control of the Irish Society, Coleraine was designed as an entrepôt. Here, the raw commodities of the Bann Valley that had so appealed to the Londoners—timber, salmon, eels—were to be shipped to England in exchange for finished items, much as the Chesapeake sent its raw tobacco leaves to Bristol and London. Coleraine was duly designated as the only place where ships entering the Bann could be unloaded, but, as with so much of the plantation infrastructure, Coleraine's performance was less than ideal. The port was hampered by a dangerous harbor and the challenge of moving goods on the River Bann. Even in the 1670s, the transportation of timber down the Bann to Coleraine involved two portages overland to avoid two sets of falls, whereas large ships could not use the harbor. Further restricting Ulster's ports was their better proximity to Scotland—where few markets for Ulster commodities existed—than to England.[98]

In 1613, Coleraine consisted of 63 houses (out of an intended 116) described by English observers as "pretty fine houses for there, but many of them slight and weak for that bleak place, and the reparations of manye of them have been and are verie chargeable to the citie." The earliest houses were erected in linear "blocks" of prefabricated timber framework, on stone sills, with brick chimneys and slate roofs. Excavations in 1984 found well-preserved traces of an early-seventeenth-century sill beneath an extant stone house dating to 1674, indicating that the early houses were constructed on sills placed directly on the ground's surface. Although timber was a major Ulster resource and a principal commodity of the Coleraine port, house construction in any material other than brick or stone in Coleraine was prohibited from 1615, reflecting concerns over fire. Judging from the manner in which building regulations were flouted throughout the plantation—as exemplified by Irish-style houses in company villages like Movanagher, Moneymore, and Crossalt/Brackfield—it is likely that timber structures continued to be built in Coleraine. Certainly Sir Thomas Phillips was displeased with the quality and quantity of dwellings in the town, reporting in 1622 that Coleraine required an additional 200 houses plus a strengthening of the earthen defenses first erected in 1611. The eastern wall was "continually falling down and out of repair," in part because of its earthen construction. Phillips had good cause to complain about the state of the ramparts: archaeological examination of a segment of the defenses found that the

---

98. Kenneth Nicholls, "Woodland Cover in Pre-modern Ireland," in Duffy, Edwards, and FitzPatrick, eds., *Gaelic Ireland,* 199–200.

earthen walls had been allowed to significantly erode not long after construction.[99]

Early urban growth in Coleraine was brought to a halt by the events of 1641, which turned the town into a center for settlers fleeing from the outlying, isolated company villages. These refugees reportedly crowded together in temporary dwellings thrown up in the parish churchyard. According to tradition, those who died of conflict or disease were buried in mass graves, although this is archaeologically unsubstantiated. The disarray caused by the Rising / Rebellion was soon exacerbated by the onset of the War of the Three Kingdoms, when Coleraine and other plantation settlements languished without investment. A 1654 commentary notes that many of Coleraine's buildings were badly damaged or demolished. Not until the Restoration would the Irish Society again turn its attention to its Irish estates. Redevelopment in Coleraine was slow, but, in 1679, a new quay was constructed to facilitate shipping. The reversal of crown restrictions on diversification, coupled with the residency of artisans and merchants, revived the stricken settlement toward the end of the seventeenth century, providing the impetus for the development of a viable and diversified commercial network that included the small towns of Ulster as well as corporate centers like Coleraine and Londonderry.[100]

The development of the walled city of Londonderry followed a similar trajectory to that of Coleraine. Long an Augustinian ecclesiastical hub, the locale was also an O'Donnell stronghold centered on a late medieval tower house, which the O'Dohertys had constructed for their overlord. Derry had also supported a short-lived English garrison in the 1560s and was naturally a tactical location in the English struggle against O'Neill toward the end of the Nine Years' War. In 1600, Sir Henry Docwra established a fortified settlement and, like Phillips at Coleraine, strove to establish a viable English town, for which a charter was granted in 1604. Docwra subsequently sold his lands to Thomas Phillips's father-in-law, Sir George Paulett, in 1606. What advances Paulett made are unclear, as the new governor of Derry was killed in the 1608 O'Doherty rebellion. His widow, Dorothy Paulett, was

99. Smithes and Springham Report, Ellis Papers, D683, PRONI, Mic 9B/12B; Brannon, "Excavations in New Row, Coleraine," in Egan, ed., "Post-Medieval Britain and Ireland in 1984," *Post-Medieval Archaeology*, XIX (1985); Philip Robinson and Nick Brannon, "A Seventeenth-Century House in New Row, Coleraine," *Ulster Journal of Archaeology*, 3d Ser., XL (1982), 174; Curl, *The Honorable the Irish Society*, 129; Survey of the Londoners' Plantation, in Russell and Prendergast, eds., *CSPI of the Reign of James I*, V, 372; Brannon, "Where History and Archaeology Unite," in Hamlin and Lynn, eds., *Pieces of the Past*, 78.

100. Bardon, *History of Ulster*, 138; Curl, *Londonderry Plantation*, 91, 98.

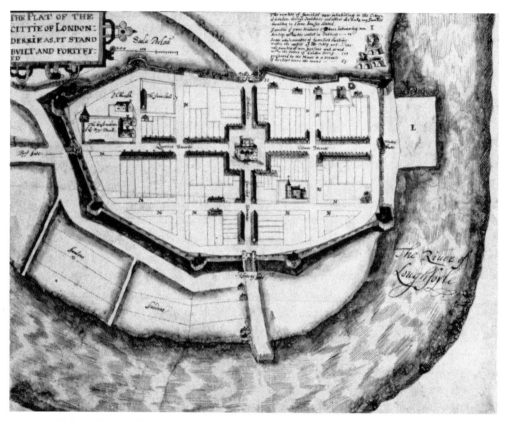

Plate 20. Thomas Raven, Londonderry, 1622. With acknowledgment to the Deputy
Keeper of the Records at the Public Record Office of Northern Ireland

compelled to sell the lands to the Irish Society just as her son-in-law surrendered his holdings at Coleraine.[101]

Under the Irish Society, the new town of Londonderry rapidly absorbed more than three times the initial allocated funding—the result of
poor planning and repeated instances of graft. Nonetheless, by 1622, Sir
Thomas Phillips was able to report that 109 families were resident within
slate-roofed, stone dwellings. Two adjoining masonry structures, which
may be the remains of a pair of the "lyme and stone" houses, were uncovered during rescue excavations in 1980. The structures measured 8.8 by 5.5
meters and boasted 60-centimeter-thick stone walls with flagstone floors
and stone-built corner ovens. The structures' substantial nature suggests at

101. Paul Logue, "Archaeology of Post-Medieval Derry and Londonderry," in Horning et al.,
eds., *Post-Medieval Archaeology of Ireland*, 134–137; Moody, "Sir Thomas Phillips," *Irish Historical Studies*, I (1939), 270.

least the partial success of the Irish Society's efforts, although evidently not enough to pacify Sir Thomas Phillips, who concluded, "The city is well fortified, but wants 300 houses more to be built, and British sent over to guard the town, for as it is now, [it is] a mere bait for an Enemy." Several portions of Londonderry's defenses show themselves to have been sizable constructions, incorporating a ditch measuring up to ten meters wide and two to three meters in depth and making use of earthen ramparts over seven meters in height upon an existing slope. Nonetheless, the walled city was very vulnerable. The hills around the city provided cover and a vantage point for any would-be attackers, whereas the walls themselves were not sufficiently thick to withstand any prolonged shelling.[102]

By 1630, there were approximately 500 able-bodied men living in the city, many of whom were merchants. Londonderry rapidly outstripped Coleraine as an entrepôt, with an average customs income of £937 per annum over the years 1634 to 1639, compared to £215.17 s. for the Coleraine settlement. Yet Londonderry was not immune to the effects of the Rising/Rebellion and the Commonwealth period, enduring a prolonged siege by Royalist forces in 1649. The city slowly recovered and is recorded as having a population of 586 in 1659. With the Restoration came the return of London investment, but just as the companies began to recover from the devastating Great Fire of London in 1666, fire swept through Londonderry in 1668, taking with it much of the fabric of the plantation town. Although rebuilding efforts were successful, with a population approaching 2,000 by 1688, Londonderry then became the stage for one of the principal events in the Williamite Wars: the 1688–1689 Siege of Derry, which saw the town's Protestant population barricade themselves against the Catholic forces of James II.[103]

By the middle of the seventeenth century, new towns like Londonderry and Coleraine, as well as the refurbished medieval settlements at Carrickfergus and Newry, were eclipsed by Belfast, a small medieval settlement that was regenerated at the hands of Lord Deputy Chichester. Belfast (Bel Feirste) was previously the location of a Clandeboye O'Neill castle, defending a ford

---

102. Survey of the Londoners' Plantation, Aug. 10–Oct. 10, 1622, in Russell and Prendergast, eds., *CSPI of the Reign of James I,* V, 367; Brian Lacy, "Two Seventeenth-Century Houses at Linenhall Street, Londonderry," *Ulster Folklife,* XXVII (1981), 57–62; Logue, "Archaeology of Post-Medieval Derry and Londonderry," in Horning et al., eds., *Post-Medieval Archaeology of Ireland,* 139–141.

103. Avril Thomas, "Londonderry and Coleraine: Walled Towns or Epitome?" in O'Brien, ed., *Derry and Londonderry,* 259–278; Logue, "Archaeology of Post-Medieval Derry and Londonderry," in Horning et al., eds., *Post-Medieval Archaeology of Ireland;* Curl, *Londonderry Plantation,* 97; Curl, *The Honourable the Irish Society,* 157.

and point of land between the Rivers Farset and Blackstaff. This castle was the scene of Essex's capture of Brian MacPhelim O'Neill in 1574 and briefly the focus of Essex's colonial ambitions as he informed the Privy Council in May 1574 that he had "begun to entrench a large town here at Belfast." Essex further resolved in June 1575 to abandon plans to build at Coleraine and on the Blackwater in order to concentrate on Belfast: "Therefore I resolve not to build but in one place namely at Belfast and that of little charge. A small town there will keep the passage, relieve Knockfergus with wood, and horsemen being laid there shall command the plains of Clandeboye and with footmen may keep the passage open between that and the Newry and keep those of Killulto, Kilwarlin and the Dufferin in obedience and may be victualled all places by sea without danger of Scot or pirate." Essex recognized the strategic value of Belfast's position, which would aid its growth in later centuries. How much he achieved remains uncertain, as he died in September 1576.[104]

More than thirty years after Essex had targeted Belfast for development, Sir Arthur Chichester began the process that would see Belfast emerge as the key urban settlement in postmedieval Ulster. Chichester funded the construction of a brick manor house at Belfast to serve as his seat, partially incorporating the ruins of the medieval Clandeboye O'Neill castle that had been in the possession of Ralph Lane in 1598, and drafted plans for an ideal plantation town. Like Limavady, Belfast was granted the right to hold a market in 1605, although this should not be taken to mean that either settlement was capable of fulfilling the function of a market at that time. Like Phillips and Newtown Limavady, Chichester found in Belfast his opportunity to construct a model settlement. Chichester, of course, was far better placed both politically and financially to pursue that goal than was Phillips, and he swiftly began construction of a grand residence, as noted by Carew in 1611: "We came to Bealfast where we found many masons, bricklayers, and other laborers aworke who had taken downe the ruynes of the decayed Castle there . . . and had likewise layde the foundation of a bricke house 50 foote longe. . . . The house to be made 20 foote wyde, and two Storys and a halfe high. . . . This work is in so good forwardnes that it is lyke to be finished by the mydle of the next Somer." By choosing to build his manor house out of brick—a material that, although common in parts of eastern England,

104. Earl of Essex to the Privy Council, May 13, 1574, in O'Dowd, ed., *CSPI Tudor Period*, 577; "Instruction Given by Walter Devereux, Earl of Essex to Mr. Ashton Dispatched towards Queen Elizabeth and the Privy Council," June 1, 1575, ibid., 831.

was very unusual for Ireland—Chichester was making a statement about his own identity as an English gentleman. Just as Phillips and Doddington augmented their O'Cahan castles with formal gardens and costly interior appointments to mark their social standing, Chichester also designed his Belfast and Carrickfergus residences with attention to the latest architectural and landscape fashions.[105]

Like Limavady, Coleraine, and Londonderry, Belfast received its town charter in 1613. These charters were designed more to encourage and codify the intended urban network of seventeenth-century Ulster and are not indicative of any particular level of achievement by that year. Townbuilding was a slow process. Bit by bit, a town grew up around Chichester's castle alongside the River Farset, capitalizing upon its outlet to the River Lagan. As noted in the Carew survey, "The towne of Bealfast is plotted out in a good forme, wherein are many famelyes of English, Scotch, and some Manksmen already inhabitinge, of which some are artificers who have buylte good tymber houses with chimneys after the fashion of the English palle, and one Inn with very good Lodginge which is a great comforte to the travellers in those partes." Designed for commerce and not defense, Belfast, unlike Londonderry and Coleraine, was not originally walled, although Chichester encircled his castle with a brick-built bawn twelve feet in height and defended by four half-bulwarks. In response to the 1641 Rising / Rebellion, a rampart enclosing an eighty-six-acre area was ordered to be constructed in 1642, with work commencing that year. Excavations in 1990 unearthed a segment of the three-meter-wide ditch accompanying these defenses, long since buried under late-eighteenth-century developments, indicating that a considerable investment had been made to protect the growing commercial town.[106]

Seventeenth-century manufactures included ironworking, brewing, and hideworking, based on tanning pits discovered in the center of town, highlighting the centrality of this lucrative—if odorous—economic activity. Tanning was similarly an important economic activity in Coleraine and on Phillips's lands at Limavady, as attested to by a May 25, 1618, "grant and

---

105. George Benn, *A History of the Town of Belfast* (1877; rpt. Belfast, 2008), 86; PRONI, Ref T/811/3.

106. Benn, *History of the Town of Belfast,* 86; Raymond Gillespie and Stephen A. Royle, *Irish Historic Towns Atlas No. 12: Belfast Part 1, to 1840* (Dublin, 2003), 2; N. F. Brannon, "Antrim: Belfast, Donegall Street," in Michael Ponsford, "Post-Medieval Britain and Ireland in 1990," *Post-Medieval Archaeology,* XXV (1991), 126–127; Ruairí Ó Baoill, "Archaeology of Post-Medieval Carrickfergus and Belfast," in Horning et al., eds., *Post-Medieval Archaeology of Ireland,* 91–116.

license from the King to Richard Fitz-Symons, Merchant, during his life, for the erection of one Tan-House, and for tanning of hides and leather at Gortneyhanemagh, the Town where the Castle of Lymavadie stands, in the Barony of Keenaught, and County of Londonderry; and also a grant to one Michael Taffe, Merchant, during his life, for the erection of a Tan house to tan hides and leather at the Newtoune of Lymevadie, in the same Barony and County." Leatherworking activity reflected the continuing centrality of pastoralism in Ireland. Cattle raising, long central to Gaelic subsistence, continued to be of significant economic value in plantation-period Ireland. Like timber and fish, good grazing land represented one of the attractive commodities of Ireland. In addition to the Irish breeds, settlers also brought their own livestock to Ireland. Sizeable herds were transported from Scotland to support the Scottish plantation settlements, reflecting the continued reliance upon herding within Scotland in this period. A comparative lack of enclosure in midcentury Ulster (by comparison to Munster) suggests that the English planters also adapted to land use practices associated with pastoralism.[107]

Capitalizing upon the mid-seventeenth-century relaxation of draconian economic policies that sought to keep Ireland as a dependent periphery, Belfast began exporting beef, tallow, hides, butter, and corn to Britain, Europe, and the American colonies and importing cloth, spirits, spices, and tobacco with a fleet of twenty-nine ships in the 1650s. By 1660, Belfast boasted five streets, five lanes, and 150 houses. By 1666, a sugar refinery signaled a critical shift from producing and exporting raw goods to Britain to processing the raw exports of other British colonies. Belfast's ultimate success as a commercial center was predicated upon the residency of merchants as well as viable industries, an important factor separating the colonial towns and cities of Ulster from their counterparts in the Chesapeake. There, the dispersed tobacco plantation system, with its riverine transportation network, continually frustrated attempts throughout the seventeenth century to restrict trade to central places.[108]

107. N. F. Brannon, "In Search of Old Belfast," in Hamlin and Lynn, eds., *Pieces of the Past,* 79–81; Ó Baoill, "Carrickfergus and Belfast," in Horning et al., eds., *Post-Medieval Archaeology of Ireland;* Boyle, ed., *Records of the Town of Limavady,* 2. See Perceval-Maxwell, *Scottish Migration,* 30–31, 129–135, for discussion of Scottish herding practices and the importation of livestock; for consideration of the comparative lack of enclosure in mid-seventeenth-century Ulster, see Canny, *Making Ireland British,* 350; and Philip Robinson, "The Spread of Hedged Enclosure in Ulster," *Ulster Folklife,* XXIII (1977), 57–69.

108. Robert M. Young, *The Town Book of the Corporation of Belfast, 1613–1816* (1892; rpt. Belfast, 2008), xi; George Benn, *A History of the Town of Belfast . . .* (1877; rpt. Belfast, 2008); Peter

Belfast continued to develop its manufacturing sector, establishing its own tin-glazed ceramics, or delftware pottery, in the late seventeenth century and eventually joining mainland British cities as a major industrial center in the nineteenth. The industrial expansion of later centuries destroyed much of the physical evidence for medieval and plantation-era Belfast. Above-ground traces of Belfast's medieval and plantation townscape exist only in surviving fragments of Chichester's street plan. Chichester oriented his town along the River Farset, now culverted beneath High Street. Chichester's grand manor house, incorporating portions of the medieval O'Neill castle, was destroyed by fire in 1708. More than fifty excavations have taken place in the city since 1983, but no trace of the Clandeboye O'Neill settlement has been unearthed. Evidence for the seventeenth century is also scant, although later seventeenth-century midden deposits, possibly from the gardens to the rear of the castle, were uncovered in a small excavation in 1983. Any traces of the castle itself are presumed to have been destroyed during the 1965–1966 construction of a department store, which took place without any archaeological oversight. Inevitably, contemporary political concerns affect understandings of Belfast's history, with a general perception that Belfast is solely an artifact of the postmedieval period. Another reason for myopia regarding Belfast may be the legacy of a considerable movement of Scots into Belfast in the latter half of the seventeenth century, creating a community that emphasized commerce, industry, and the Presbyterian faith.[109]

Francis, *Irish Delftware: An Illustrated History* (London, 2000); Francis, *A Pottery by the Lagan: Irish Creamware from the Downshire China Manufactory, Belfast, 1787–c. 1806* (Belfast, 2001); Ó Baoill, "Carrickfergus and Belfast," in Horning et al., eds., *Post-Medieval Archaeology of Ireland*. For the frustrated development of towns in the Chesapeake, see Horning, "English Towns on the Periphery," in Green and Leech, eds., *Cities in the World;* Earle, *Evolution of a Tidewater Settlement System;* Earle, "The First English Towns of North America," *Geographical Review,* LXVII (1977), 34–50; Kelly, "'In Dispers'd Country Plantations,'" in Tate and Ammerman, eds., *Chesapeake in the Seventeenth Century;* Carr, *Adaptation and Settlement in the Colonial Chesapeake;* Grim, "Absence of Towns"; Musselwhite, "Towns in Mind."

109. Brannon, "In Search of Old Belfast," in Hamlin and Lynn, eds., *Pieces of the Past,* 80–81; Ruairí Ó Baoill, *Hidden History below Our Feet: The Archaeological Story of Belfast* (Belfast, 2011). Despite the considerable documentary and significant, if limited, archaeological evidence relating to Belfast's plantation roots, popular understandings of the city de-emphasize its medieval origins and early-seventeenth-century development in favor of its eighteenth- and nineteenth-century industrial development as well as its turbulent twentieth-century history. Furthermore, the success of Belfast's industry supports contemporary understandings of the city as "British" rather than "Irish." One obvious reason for prioritizing the later history of the settlement is the simple fact that so little survives from Belfast's early history. Philip MacDonald argues that the lack of interest in Belfast's early history is also "in part a result of the fusion of the intellectual legacy of the Elizabethan colonial myth, which portrayed Ulster as a wilderness ripe for plan-

Efforts at creating an urban network in the north of Ireland must also be understood in the context of urban development throughout Ireland. The province of Ulster is notable for its lack of medieval towns compared with the rest of Ireland. As such, new ideas about towns and civic life could be applied (at least on paper) to settlements such as Belfast, Londonderry, Coleraine, and Limavady. By contrast, seventeenth-century development in the well-established medieval urban centers such as Cork, Galway, Limerick, Waterford, Kilkenny, and, of course, Dublin was both constrained and facilitated by existent physical and social structures. In Ulster, where such colonial efforts were carefully planned and monitored, even the most highly regulated plantations were unrealistic in their expectations and haphazard in the implementation. Not surprisingly, then, plantation efforts outside of the province of Ulster were highly variable and inevitably dependent upon the cooperation and even collusion of Native and Old English elites. Although the Gaelic elite of Ulster found their fortunes and influence significantly reduced following the Flight of the Earls, such was not the case throughout the rest of Ireland.

Beyond Ulster

In Munster, the uneven development associated with the implementation of plantation in the 1580s had effectively ended in 1598. Seventeenth-century efforts to rebuild moved slowly and were never as carefully planned or monitored as in Ulster. Official plantation lands were noncontiguous insofar as they derived from the former holdings of the earl of Desmond. Thus, any pretense to the cultural segregation and removal of Irish, as proposed for the Ulster Plantation, was pointless from the start. Undertakers who had fled Ireland following the destruction of 1598 were understandably slow to return and reclaim their lands. Many tracts were sold to new adventurers, including the extensive estate of Walter Raleigh. Raleigh's lands were purchased by Richard Boyle, then clerk of the Munster Court.[110]

The key port of Cork, through the first half of the seventeenth century, remained firmly in the hands of the Old English elite, who frustrated many of the New English incomers' entrepreneurial desires. The elite's hostility toward Boyle contributed to his decision to focus his developments on the

---

tation by denying the significance of any pre-existing settlement or culture, with late Victorian ideological concepts of progress and modernity" (MacDonald, "Medieval Belfast Considered," *Ulster Journal of Archaeology,* 3d Ser., LXV [2006], 29). See also John O'Keeffe, "What Lies Beneath? Medieval Components in Belfast's Urban Development," ibid., 20.

110. MacCarthy-Morrogh, *Munster Plantation,* 141–142.

smaller settlement of Youghal. Youghal, which welcomed the New English, expanded rapidly in the first half of the seventeenth century. Particularly beneficial was the Privy Council's decision, encouraged by Boyle, for Youghal to position itself as one of eight intended staple towns, with control over the woollen export trade. For a brief period, Youghal enjoyed a monopoly over the Munster wool trade.[111]

Although townbuilding was an important element of policy and activity in early-seventeenth-century Munster, the countryside itself was not entirely transformed as desired by plantation theorists. The availability of strongly built, late medieval tower houses on lands granted to incoming New English planters discouraged the construction of wholly new structures. Many Munster planter residences thus represent adaptations to buildings formally constructed by the Gaelic and Old English elite, akin to the English reedification of O'Cahan tower houses at Limavady and Dungiven.

Unlike Ulster, early-seventeenth-century Munster was also still considerably influenced by the Old English and Gaelic elite. Although some of the New English contented themselves with occupying Irish strongholds in the Munster Plantation, it is significant to note that some Old English and Gaelic elite chose to invest in building completely new manor houses reflecting the latest of English and continental fashions. Such efforts were a means of projecting and symbolizing permanence and rootedness. When Edmund and Margaret FitzGerald Supple commissioned the construction of their new home, Ightermurragh Castle, on the eve of rebellion in 1641, they were making a statement about their place in society and their four-hundred-year-old claim to the County Cork lands upon which their new castle was erected. Similarly, the Gaelic elite of West Cork, including the O'Sullivans and O'Driscolls, employed architecture as a means of negotiating their position within the new political order. The old tower house form was replaced with manor houses that retained some defensive features, such as machicolations and corner bartizans, but also nondefensive features, such as large windows, soaring gables, and massive chimney stacks. An example is the early-seventeenth-century house built by Owen O'Sullivan, lord of

111. For Boyle and the development of Youghal, see discussions in Victor Treadwell, "Richard Hadsor and 'Advertisements for Ireland' 1622/3," *Irish Historical Studies*, XXX (1996–1997), 314–315; and MacCarthy-Morrogh, *Munster Plantation*, 242–244. The term "staple" refers to a port through which all wool exports were to pass, with control in the hands of merchants known as "staplers." The decision to limit staples to eight (two for each province of Ireland) chartered staple ports was designed to reduce the amount of trade to the Continent in favor of supplying the English market. Not coincidentally, this move would reduce the power of the Old English merchant oligarchies, but it also was subject to corruption on the part of the New English.

Beara, at Reenadissert on the outskirts of Bantry. O'Sullivan's new house was two stories high and built to a T-plan, featuring mullioned and transomed windows, end chimneys, and five-pointed gables. To the southwest of Bantry, the MacCarthy Muclaghs built a similar two-story fortified house at Gerahameen, whereas the O'Driscolls symbolized their centuries of control over the port of Baltimore by constructing another two-story dwelling with mullioned and transomed windows and projecting chimney stacks.[112]

Features such as the large windows, chimney stacks, and lack of defensive elements also characterized elite architecture in England during the same period and have been broadly linked to an increasing emphasis upon privacy as well as the transition from relations of reciprocity to those dependent upon monetary exchange. Consumption—or being seen to be able to consume—increasingly became a critical means of distinguishing elite status. The incorporation of large windows not only brightened the interiors of homes; more important, it signaled to the wider world that the occupier had the financial means to pay for large and expensive panes of glass. The proliferation of chimney stacks likewise heralded the occupants' financial wherewithal, while also signaling the division of space within the home. Instead of a large, open hall that facilitated communal activities, now the home could be divided into individually heated spaces particular to function or family member. That the Gaelic and Old English elite employed this new architectural grammar should be seen as another example of the manipulation of material culture to mediate social and cultural relations.[113]

The Ulster and Munster Plantations represent the most formalized efforts at imposing English control through the importation of settlers and the restructuring of landholdings. Elsewhere, plantation efforts relied upon the earlier practice of surrender and regrant as a means of ensuring the loyalty of Irish landholders while opening up some new lands for occupation by a new planter elite. Under this system, Irish landholders, both Gaelic and Old English, were compelled to surrender their lands to the crown in ex-

112. Denis Power, "The Archaeology of the Munster Plantation," in Horning et al., eds., *Post-Medieval Archaeology of Ireland,* 23–36; Tadhg O'Keeffe and Sinéad Quirke, "A House at the Birth of Modernity: Ightermurragh Castle in Context," in Lyttleton and Rynne, eds., *Plantation Ireland,* 86–112; Colin Breen, *An Archaeology of Southwest Ireland, 1570–1670* (Dublin, 2007), 131–132; Denis Power, ed., *Archaeological Inventory of County Cork,* I, *West Cork* (Dublin, 1992).

113. See discussion in Terence Reeves-Smyth, "Community to Privacy: Late Tudor and Jacobean Manorial Architecture in Ireland, 1560–1640," in Horning et al., eds., *Post-Medieval Archaeology of Ireland,* 289–326; Maurice Craig, *The Architecture of Ireland from the Earliest Times to 1880* (Dublin, 1978); Johnson, *Housing Culture;* Johnson, "Meanings of Polite Architecture in Sixteenth-Century England," *Historical Archaeology,* XXVI (1992), 45–56.

change for formal, legal title to approximately 75 percent of what they had previously owned. The remaining lands were then made available to loyal servitors and planters. Just as Donal Ballagh O'Cahan saw advantage in accepting an English title and surrendered his lands in exchange for a formal regrant, so, too, did many native landholders in the Irish Midlands. Like their counterparts in Munster, the Gaelic elite of the Midlands employed new architectural styles to proclaim their social standing within the plantation order. Notable examples include Ballymooney Castle, Co. Offaly, built by Donell Carroll around 1622. Now in ruins, Ballymooney featured two towers and an extensive accommodation block, which incorporated fashionable, transomed windows. The inclusion of such windows at Ballymooney proclaimed the O'Carroll wealth and also distinguished the well-lit house from its late medieval counterparts.[114]

While the Offaly Gaelic elite were busy incorporating new English architectural fashions, some of their New English counterparts were selectively incorporating the old Gaelic forms. The new, five-story, fortified dwelling of English planter Sir James Harbert dominated the skyline in Ballycowan Townland near Tullamore but rested upon the vaulted foundation of what is clearly an earlier castle on the site, associated either with the O'Molloys or the O'Melaghlins. The extensive wicker centering on the barrel-vaulted cellars indicate Irish craftsmanship, whereas Harbert marked his proprietorship with an armorial plaque dated 1626 and bearing the family motto: "By god of might, I hold my right." Harbert's adage pithily encapsulated the role of an unwelcome planter in a long-occupied land.[115]

Another significant difference between the Ulster Plantation as designed and the less formal plantation systems operating elsewhere in early-seventeenth-century Ireland is the role of religion. Although the entrepreneurial activities of the Catholic Randal MacDonnell are anomalous for Ulster—where the encouragement of Protestantism was a foundation of plantation strategy—elsewhere, some prominent new settlers espoused the Roman Catholic faith. In fact, of the thirty-five seignories, or plantation estates, of Munster, eight were in the hands of English Catholics by 1641. Ireland was attractive to English Catholics for a number of reasons, most

114. James Lyttleton, "Acculturation in the Irish Midland Plantations of the Seventeenth Century," in Audrey Horning and Nick Brannon, eds., *Ireland and Britain in the Atlantic World* (Dublin 2009), 37.

115. Caimin O'Brien and P. David Sweetman, *Archaeological Inventory of County Offaly* (Dublin, 1997), 155–156; Terence Reeves-Smyth, "Community to Privacy: Late-Tudor and Jacobean Manorial Architecture in Ireland," in Horning et al., eds., *Post-Medieval Archaeology of Ireland*, 300.

notably because the harsh antirecusancy laws of England had no equivalent in early-seventeenth-century Ireland. Coupled with the availability of lands and widespread Catholicism, Ireland appealed to English Catholics who possessed the financial wherewithal and political connections necessary to make the move. The best known of these New English Catholic planters are the Calvert family, who combined their Irish plantation developments with intensive interests in the New World. Sir George Calvert, the first Lord Baltimore, was a founder of the 1621 English colony at Ferryland in New-foundland, whereas his sons Cecil and Leonard Calvert directed the estab-lishment of a Catholic colony in Maryland, settled in 1634. In north Wex-ford, Lord Baltimore concentrated his efforts on developing a new town at Clohamon and exploiting the local timber resources. Following a now well-established pattern, Baltimore occupied an existing castle while he had a new manor house built. The Calvert's temporary home was Ferns Castle, a thirteenth-century Anglo-Norman fortress that had been held by the Gaelic Kavanaghs since the 1360s. Baltimore's new home was constructed by 1626, but it, too, made use of the existing fabric of a late medieval bawn.[116]

The reality that plantation-era Ireland attracted significant numbers of English Catholics challenges common perceptions about the ethnic and reli-gious roots of early modern and modern conflict in Ireland. The compli-cated interplay of religion and identity in Ireland stands as another stark contrast to the English experience in the New World. Commentators might have drawn unfavorable parallels between the supposedly savage indigenous people of both lands, but Catholic planters in Ireland recognized and en-joyed commonalities with the Irish population in terms of religion, broader European identity, use of Latin, and familiarity with legal structures, land-scapes, and elements of the agricultural economy. No such commonali-ties could be found with the far more unfamiliar worlds of the New World Native societies. Simple equations based upon Protestant English versus Catholic Irish cannot be drawn, nor is it any easier to determine which as-pects of identity—religion or ethnicity—guided the actions of individuals. The Calverts were driven by their religious allegiances, but few would claim

---

116. David Edwards, "A Haven of Popery: English Catholic Migration to Ireland in the Age of Plantations," in Alan Ford and John McCafferty, eds., *The Origins of Sectarianism in Early Modern Ireland* (Cambridge, 2005), 95–126; James Lyttleton, "The Lords Baltimore in Ireland," in Pope and Lewis-Simpson, eds., *Exploring Atlantic Transitions;* Michael Moore, ed., *Archaeo-logical Inventory of Co. Wexford* (Dublin, 1996). On other Irish planters in Maryland, see Ronald Hoffman, *Princes of Ireland, Planters of Maryland: A Carroll Saga, 1500–1782* (Chapel Hill, N.C., 2000).

that their New World ventures were not English colonies. Religion also compounded the challenges facing the Old English elite, who were expected to uphold English customs and law in Ireland but found themselves increasingly marginalized by their Catholicism and the religious rhetoric of plantation ideology. The inherent tension between religion and culture was at the core of the midcentury upheavals, which ushered in a far starker process of population displacement and replacement than ever before.

The End of Plantation: The Conflicts of the 1640s

By 1640, the new plantation settlements of Ulster were functioning reasonably well, if not up to Sir Thomas Phillips's original expectations. In contrast to the violence and upheaval that had characterized the first decade of the seventeenth century, the thirty years since the formal establishment of the Ulster Plantation in 1611 were a period of relative peace, as both natives and newcomers accommodated themselves to one another, to the changed landscape, and to the structures imposed by new forms of governance. As implied by the archaeological record and documented in the surveys, relationships between the majority Irish and the minority newcomers were intimate insofar as the demographic and political realities encouraged and required mutual dependency. The Lady Cooke acclimated herself to the reality that the Skinners' Company lands appealed only to Irish tenants. Sir Thomas Phillips might have been more successful at encouraging English tenants to settle Newtown Limavady but pragmatically recognized that the town would also be founded upon the labor of his Irish tenants. By 1659, Newtown Limavady possessed a population of 116 persons eligible to be taxed, out of a total population likely approaching 300. Of those taxable individuals, 46 were identified as Irish and 70 as English or Scottish. Although the town thus had a majority of planters, the numbers of Irish resident there were not inconsequential. Elsewhere—as particularly illustrated by the Calverts' plantation efforts in north Wexford—some of the New English shared religious ideologies with the Old English and Gaels, even where they aimed to supplant local landowners and reshape economic practices. Throughout Ireland, the Old English and Gaelic elites situated themselves within the new political structures, some adopting new architectural fashions as a means of communicating their engagement with the new order. It is significant that the period from the 1610s (which saw the launch of the Ulster Plantation) to the 1640s (when Ireland became embroiled in the wider War of the Three Kingdoms) was characterized by a remarkable lack of violent conflict. That the Irish and the incoming planters were able to at least tolerate one another is evident from both the archaeological and documentary records, which divulge proximity and intimacy.[117]

During this thirty-year period, there were occasional outbreaks of hostility, some related to basic criminal activity (robberies and murders) and others politically motivated. A handful of ill-planned conspiracies were discovered and thwarted, including the 1615 Ulster plot that threatened the life of Sir Thomas Phillips and another in 1625 that linked a feared Spanish invasion with the Maguires' efforts to reclaim their ancestral lands in Counties Fermanagh and Cavan. Although these small-scale plots never came to fruition, their combined effect was a general feeling of unease amongst the planter class. In spite of the considerable degree of discourse, dependency, and accommodation, such disquiet was not misplaced. The events of 1641 would effectively end the experiment of plantation as conceived in the sixteenth century and implemented during the first half of the seventeenth.[118]

The Rising / Rebellion of October 1641, which saw a group of Ulster Irish elites launch an insurrection in a bid to protect their property rights and religious freedom, was the result of the disenchantment of Gaelic and Old English elites with English policies under Lord Deputy Wentworth during the 1630s. Often described as a demonstration of resistance to a colonial power, the armed constitutional protests of 1641 were, in fact, intended to achieve reforms that would restore and guarantee the role of the Catholic elite in the governance of Ireland as a kingdom. In other words, the uprising was not intended to overthrow or eliminate English rule—only to reform it. The action itself began at a dinner party, testament to the closeness of daily relations between native and planter elites. On October 22, 1641, Irish chief and member of Parliament Sir Phelim O'Neill invited himself to a meal with his English neighbor and friend Sir Toby Caulfield at Charlemont Fort in County Armagh. Neatly echoing the events in Belfast Castle seventy-three years before, Phelim O'Neill and his men pulled out their knives and took control of Charlemont.[119]

117. Population figures from Pender, *A Census of Ireland, circa 1659*, 129.

118. Gillespie *Conspiracy;* Moody, *Londonderry Plantation, 1609–41*, 228–229; S. J. Connolly, *Contested Island: Ireland, 1460–1630* (New York, 2007), 377–379.

119. For sources on the causes and outbreak of the 1641 Rising / Rebellion, see M. Perceval-Maxwell, *The Outbreak of the Irish Rebellion of 1641* (Montreal, 1994); Brian Mac Cuarta, ed., *Ulster 1641: Aspects of the Rising* (Belfast, 1997); Jane H. Ohlmeyer, *Ireland: From Independence to Occupation, 1641–1660* (Cambridge, 1995); Toby Barnard, *The Kingdom of Ireland, 1641–1760* (Basingstoke, Hampshire, 2004); Micheál Ó Siochrú, ed., *Kingdoms in Crisis: Ireland in the 1640s* (Dublin, 2001); S. J. Connolly, *Divided Kingdom: Ireland, 1630–1800* (Oxford, 2008) 4–118; Canny, *Making Ireland British*, 461–550; Canny, "What Really Happened in Ireland in 1641?"

Although the conspirators' aims were for constitutional reform, not rebellion, their actions triggered widespread revolt. Whatever control Phelim O'Neill and his conspirators initially had soon evaporated. In Ulster, the same Irish and British neighbors who had peaceably shared food, drink, and labor raised arms against each other, yielding to the underlying anxieties inherent to the plantation system. Half-remembered slights fed the combatants' anger, and their violence spoke to long-standing fears. One such fear was of Spain: Hugh Montgomery, Scottish undertaker of the Ards, was convinced that the Spanish would soon be drawn into the fray. Writing just a few days after the fateful dinner party at Charlemont, Montgomery asserted that the violence had "undoubtedly been fostered by the people who were raising troops for the King of Spain." His alarm highlights the lasting power of Tudor-era preoccupations. Spain in 1641 was dealing with its own internal conflicts, following the outbreak of both the Portuguese and Catalan rebellions. A return to Ireland was not in the cards.[120]

The other fear was confessional. The rhetoric contained within an avalanche of partisan pamphlets, which number more than 250 for the period October 1641–June 1642, framed the conflict as one of religion rather than of constitutional reform. Incendiary descriptions of "bloodthirsty papists" attacking and murdering Protestant planters triggered retaliatory violence. The alliance between Parliament and the Scots sparked further anxiety among the Catholic elite throughout Ireland. The Old English from the Pale, who were increasingly cut off from the corridors of power as Puritan influence rose in England, soon joined forces with the rebels. Following a series of coordinated attacks, the rebels set up their own Confederate government in Kilkenny in June 1642, proclaiming their loyalty to the king but placing them in conflict with the Dublin-based Parliament. The internal Irish struggle expanded into one front in the wider War of the Three Kingdoms, subsumed within the constitutional crises that were sweeping Europe. Religion, more than ethnicity, revealed itself to be a significant element, as underscored by the participation of English and Scottish Catholics in the Confederacy, fighting against the Protestant forces of the crown. For their part, Protestants in Ireland divided their allegiances between the Parliamentarian and Royalist forces, whereas Confederate Catholics ultimately

in Ohlmeyer, *From Independence to Occupation*, 24–42; Pádraig Lenihan, *Confederate Catholics at War, 1641–1649* (Cork, 2001). See also Toby C. Barnard, "1641: A Bibliographical Essay," in Mac Cuarta, ed., *Ulster 1641*, 173–186.

120. Viscount Montgomery to Secretary Vane, Oct. 24, 1641, in Mahaffy, ed., *CSPI of the Reign of Charles I*, II, 341.

forged an alliance with Charles I. All sides relied in part upon Gaelic Irish conscripts to fight their battles.[121]

The 1646 publication of John Temple's *Irish Rebellion* further recast the haphazard and limited nature of the original actions led by O'Neill and his conspirators as outright Catholic-versus-Protestant warfare. According to Temple, upwards of 300,000 Protestant settlers were massacred by Irish forces, a number ten times in excess of the total number of planters who made their way to Ireland in the first half of the seventeenth century. In all, perhaps 30,000 Protestants settled in Ireland as a result of the plantation schemes, a very small achievement considering that the overall population of the country at midcentury was somewhere between 1.3 and 1.5 million. Although plantation spawned radical changes in landholding and settlement, in 1641 Catholics still owned 59 percent of profitable land in Ireland. Even the lands encompassed by the Ulster Plantation, with its pretensions to cultural replacement, were populated by an Irish majority. Following the warfare of midcentury and the ensuing redistribution of land, Catholic landownership dropped to 22 percent by 1688.[122]

Depositions taken from victims and witnesses in 1642 and in the early 1650s underscore the ferocity of the conflict. Although we cannot assume the veracity of the accounts—particularly those taken down a decade after the events—they nonetheless remain a valuable source of insight into the successes and failures of plantation. Nearly four thousand depositions and witness statements survive, some of which report monetary losses in the form of damage to crops and buildings and thievery, and others that stray well into the realms of hearsay. One such deposition is that of Margaret Bromley of County Armagh; after claiming losses to the value of £327, reporting the murder of her husband and twenty-three named neighbors, and identifying her Catholic attackers, she asserted that rebels had drowned hundreds of Protestants at Portadown and at Scarva in separate incidences that, by August 1642, had become legend. Such reports from Armagh, where the worst of the 1641 violence erupted, suggested that many thousands of settlers had been killed. More recent research posits, instead, a figure some-

121. Edwards, "A Haven of Popery," in Ford and McCafferty, eds., *Origins of Sectarianism in Early Modern Ireland,* 125–126; Connolly, *Divided Kingdom,* 100–101.

122. For a discussion of John Temple, see T. C. Barnard, "Crisis of Identity among Irish Protestants, 1641–1685," *Past and Present,* no. 127 (May 1990), 50–72; and Canny, *Making Ireland British,* 461–464. For population figures, see Barnard, *Kingdom of Ireland,* 13, 29, 61; for discussion of the events of 1641 and their significance, see the essays in Mac Cuarta, ed., *Ulster 1641.*

where between 600 and 1,300, out of a total planter population within the county of around 5,000. Bromley further stated,

> It was a Comon report amongst the Rebells that the preists and fryers were the cawse of their killing and putting to death the English and Scottish protestants: And the Rebells alsoe usually sayd that the protestants were worse then doggs, and were noe Christians but those that were Christened at Masse were Christians and *that* the protestants shold be Chistened over againe at Masse before they cold be Christians, And the Rebells alsoe said that they knew that if they themselves shold dy the next morning their sowles sholde goe to god and they were very gladd of the Revenge which they had taken of the English.

Her fear of reprisal and willingness to believe in a papal conspiracy remains palpable centuries later.[123]

Given the historical emphasis upon the breakdown of society and the escalation of violence, it is difficult to gain any sense of how communities and families in Ireland coped during the long decade of warfare. Certainly some Ulster Plantation settlements, like the undefended Mercers' village of Movanagher, seem to have been abandoned. Urban settlements including Coleraine absorbed refugees from outlying locales, although, again, it is difficult to separate reality from hearsay. In 1642, James Redfern reported that "he hath beene credibly told by some of the English in the towne of Coleraine that since the Rebellion began there dyed there of Robbed and stripped people of protestantes that thither hadd fledd for succour the number of seven thowsand or therabouts: besides those of the towne that hadd anciently dwelt there and that the mortalitie there was such and soe great That seven hundreth or eight hundreth more dyed on 2 dayes there." No archaeological evidence for any corresponding mass graves has ever been encountered to support a death rate of that magnitude. Although unsubstantiated, Redfern's report nonetheless relays the extent of people's fears

---

123. Jane Ohlmeyer, "Anatomy of Plantation: The 1641 Depositions," *History Ireland,* XVII, no. 6 (November/December 2009), 56. See also Barbara Fennell, "'Dodgy Dossiers?' Hearsay and the 1641 Depositions," ibid., XIX, no. 3 (May/June 2011), 26–29, and extended discussions in Canny, *Making Ireland British,* 468–469; William J. Smyth, *Map-Making, Landscapes, and Memory: A Geography of Colonial and Early Modern Ireland, c.1530–1750* (Notre Dame, Ind., 2006), 113–119; Hilary Simms, "Violence in County Armagh, 1641," in Mac Cuarta, ed., *Ulster 1641,* 123–138; TCD, 1641 Depositions Project, MS 836, ff. 040r–041v, deposition of Margret Bromley, Aug. 22, 1642, online transcript January 1970, http://1641.tcd.ie/deposition.php?depID=83604or021, accessed Feb. 27, 2012.

as expressed in their willingness to believe in even the most exaggerated reports of atrocity.[124]

Retribution for the attacks of 1641 and 1642 was swift and brutal, albeit far less well recorded. Repeated raids by Parliamentarian forces displaced significant numbers of Ulster Irish, with refugees in the tens of thousands relocating to the provinces of Leinster and Connacht in the wake of attacks during 1644 and 1645. By 1647, much of Ulster and Connacht were declared waste, whereas the provinces of Leinster and Munster fared better. Many of the forces that arrived in Ulster were Scottish covenanters, drawing Ireland more deeply into the wider conflict but helping the Scottish plantation communities of Counties Antrim and Down retain their grip on their settlements. Such raids frequently targeted noncombatants. In July 1642, Scottish forces under the leadership of Robert Monroe were responsible for the deaths of forty Irishmen and more than five hundred Irishwomen and children who were attempting to leave Ulster through the mountains south of Newry. Warfare affected all of Ireland and continued throughout the 1640s with no clear winner and with each side riven by internal disagreement over aims and strategies. The situation was drastically altered with the arrival of twelve thousand troops under Oliver Cromwell in August 1649. Within nine months, Cromwell's troops seized twenty-five Confederate strongholds in the provinces of Leinster and Munster. The troops' brutality in the east coast ports of Drogheda and Wexford, where Cromwell's men routed the garrisons and, notoriously, targeted and killed civilians, rapidly gave rise to a Catholic counternarrative of English savagery.[125]

The victory of Cromwell's forces in 1652 ushered in a period of extensive reprisal against Irish Confederates, with lands confiscated from rebels and granted to a new wave of Protestant settlers. The idea of confiscation and

124. TCD, 1641 Depositions Project, MS 839, ff. 100r–101v, deposition of John and James Redferne, Nov. 7, 1642, online transcript January 1970, http://1641.tcd.ie/deposition .php?depID=839100r068, accessed May 24, 2013.

125. See Kenneth Nicholls, "The Other Massacre: English Killings of Irish, 1641–3," in David Edwards, Pádraig Lenihan, and Clodagh Tait, eds., *Age of Atrocity: Violence and Political Conflict in Early Modern Ireland* (Dublin, 2007), 176–191, esp. 190, for a critique of historiography that ignores the violence directed toward the Irish; see also Pádraig Lenihan, *Confederate Catholics at War, 1641–1649* (Cork, 2001), 89; Smyth, *Map-Making,* 118–119; Raymond Gillespie, "The Irish Economy at War," in Ohlmeyer, ed., *From Independence to Occupation,* 172; Thomas Fitzpatrick, *The Bloody Bridge and Other Papers Relating to the Insurrection of 1641 (Sir Phelim O'Neill's Rebellion)* (Dublin, 1903), xiii; John Morrill, "The Drogheda Massacre in Cromwellian Context," in Edwards, Lenihan, and Tait, eds., *Age of Atrocity,* 245; Mícheál Ó Siochrú, *God's Executioner: Oliver Cromwell and the Conquest of Ireland* (London, 2008).

redistribution was not new, having formed the basis for earlier plantation schemes, with a more extreme version having been mooted immediately following the Rising / Rebellion. Approved by Parliament in June 1642, this new plantation scheme was again based upon private finance and was termed the Additional Sea Adventure. The aim was to capture 2,500,000 acres of land from Catholic hands and provide it as security to the Protestant adventurers as a return for their investment. This scheme was more overtly religious in tone than the earlier efforts, reflecting the impact of the propaganda war that accompanied the conflict in Ireland. One member of this new group of adventurers was the merchant Maurice Thompson, who pledged £1,075 to the venture (which managed to secure more than £43,000) and was promised 16,218 acres in the Ulster counties of Antrim and Armagh. The merchant would also lend considerable sums of money to support Parliamentarian forces in Ireland.[126]

Maurice Thompson had already succeeded against the odds as a Virginia planter, taking up a grant at Blunt Point near Newport News in 1621 and proving himself adept at as an entrepreneur. Most notably, Thompson (with William Tucker and Thomas Stone) had secured a lucrative monopoly over the export of tobacco under the governorship of John Harvey in the 1630s. By then, Thompson had begun trafficking in human lives, taking up a grant of land in Saint Kitts to facilitate his growing involvement in the African slave trade. Thompson also served as an agent for the Providence Island Company and had interests in the Canadian fur trade.[127]

The Additional Sea Adventure raised a militia, which fought for six months in Ireland before running out of funding. Although its martial success was temporary, the Additional Sea Adventure is notable more for the way that it drew together a group of radical Protestant merchants who would influence British overseas policies and practices. Ireland was a rather

126. On December 30, 1645, the Committee of Both Houses for Irish Affairs promised to repay Thompson five thousand pounds plus 8 percent per annum on any outstanding amount for funds he had loaned to outfit the forces of Colonel William Jephson. See Mahaffy, ed., *CSPI of the Reign of Charles I*, II, 424.

127. For discussion of Maurice Thomson's extensive colonial activities, see Robert Brenner, *Merchants and Revolution: Commercial Change, Political Conflict, and London's Overseas Traders, 1550–1653* (Cambridge, 1993); for discussion of the Virginia tobacco monopoly, see 131. For a biography of Thompson and his brother George in relation to their Virginia activities, see Martha W. McCartney, *Virginia Immigrants and Adventurers, 1607–1635: A Biographical Dictionary* (Baltimore, 2007), 689–690. For Providence Island specifically, see Karen Ordahl Kupperman, *Providence Island, 1630–1641: The Other Puritan Colony* (Cambridge, 1993); Brenner, *Merchants and Revolution*, 400–410, 617.

small field of endeavor compared to the expansion of British interests into the Caribbean and the stabilization and growth of colonial societies in the Chesapeake, New England, and Canada.[128]

The Cromwellian land settlement of the 1650s, drawing upon the ideology promoted by the Additional Sea Adventurers, represented a more radical reordering of Irish landholding than the plantations had ever attempted, let alone achieved. Lands were confiscated and divided up between the 1642 adventurers, loyal Protestant planters, and soldiers. Rebels were subjected to a range of punishment, including transportation to the Caribbean, execution, or transplantation within Ireland to poorer lands in Connacht. Although implementation of the Cromwellian land settlement was haphazard and partially reversed during the Restoration, the power once held by the Gaelic and Old English elites was eroded. Protestant hegemony was assured in the aftermath of the Williamite Wars, which saw the accession of William of Orange to the English throne.

Conclusion

Archaeological and historical investigation into the Ulster Plantation and adjacent, nonofficial plantation settlements in the north of Ireland complicates historical memories of the conquest and replacement of the Ulster Irish population. Although the number of investigated plantation-period sites remains small, and some excavations inconclusive, the evidence nonetheless points not only to close relations between incomers and natives but also to the ways in which Gaelic leaders like Donal Ballagh O'Cahan worked the new system to their advantage. The conclusion from this reevaluation of the Ulster Plantation, from its genesis in 1609 to its destruction in the mid-seventeenth century, is that the process was incomplete and characterized as much by relative continuity in Gaelic lifeways and settlement patterns as it was by the efforts of the crown and the Irish Parliament to reenvision and reformulate Ulster land and society.

Stark portrayals of early-seventeenth-century Ireland as a land and people subjected to aggressive colonial control also ignores the complicating factor of religion. The Ulster Plantation was conceived of as an explicitly Protestant settlement, but elsewhere, "Ireland swarms with English recusants, for the laws have no power to deal with them." Even on the lands of the

---

128. Karl S. Bottigheimer, *English Money and Irish Land: The "Adventurers" in the Cromwellian Settlement of Ireland* (Oxford, 1971); Keith Lindley, "Irish Adventurers and Godly Militants in the 1640s," *Irish Historical Studies,* XXIX (1994–1995), 1–12; Canny, *Making Ireland British,* 553; Brenner, *Merchants and Revolution,* 400–459.

Munster Plantation, originally specified for Protestant settlers, a number of planters converted to Catholicism, including two sons of Edmund Spenser. Maryland's founders, the Lords Baltimore, stand as the most well-known English Catholic dynasty in Ireland. Although the lowest population of English Catholics was found in Ulster, they were not by any means absent. Scottish Catholics were present on the lands of the MacDonnells and also under the Hamiltons in County Tyrone. English Catholics were also present on Ulster Plantation grants in both Counties Monaghan and Cavan. Only after the 1640s did a coherent Irish Protestant identity begin to emerge, forged in the fires of the Rising/Rebellion, fanned by lurid propaganda, and given legitimacy in the subsequent land confiscations and resettlements.[129]

Further illustrating Ireland's differing colonial mold to that of the New World is the reality that, outside of the Londonderry Plantation, the Gaelic and Old English elites were not excluded from the ranks of the new political leadership. The legal framework for the Ulster Plantation was also crafted under the aegis of the Irish government in Dublin rather than under direct crown control, as was the case for Virginia after the Virginia Company's royal charter was revoked. Ireland, after all, was formally a kingdom on a level with Scotland and England. James was indeed king of Ireland as he was of Scotland and England, but the kingdoms were not treated equally. Similarities can be drawn in terms of the power wielded by the governor in Virginia and that wielded by the Lord Deputy of Ireland, both of whom were selected by the crown. Nevertheless, an important distinction remains: Ireland was never formally administered as a colony in the way that the New World would be. That distinction would have been intimately understood by the numerous individuals who were involved in both Ulster and the new Virginia colony and whose stories are told in more detail in the next chapter.[130]

The Ulster Plantation, although marking a significant change in the governance of Ireland, was not a process of cultural extermination. On paper, the emphasis on removing the native population and starting anew according to a watered-down version of res nullius would suggest that the Ulster

129. Edwards, "A Haven of Popery: English Catholic Migration to Ireland in the Age of Plantations," in Ford and McCafferty, eds., *Origins of Sectarianism in Early Modern Ireland*, 113, 117–119; Raymond Gillespie, ed., *Seventeenth-Century Ireland: Making Ireland Modern* (Dublin, 2006), 16. See also the discussion in Barnard, "Crisis of Identity among Irish Protestants," *Past and Present*, no. 127 (May 1990), 39–83.

130. Raymond Gillespie, "The Problems of Plantations: Material Culture and Social Change in Early Modern Ireland," in Lyttleton and Rynne, eds., *Plantation Ireland*, 59.

Plantation was an exemplar of colonial theory and practice. In reality, and notwithstanding the relative success of the Scottish settlements in counties Antrim and Down, the Ulster Plantation is not a colonial model. It was no more effective in eliminating native communities than were the Munster and Midlands Plantations, and only partially successful in undermining Gaelic and Old English power. Population figures at midcentury reflect the dominance of Irish over British in Ulster as well as the whole of the island. It is to the latter half of the seventeenth century that one must go in order to see the roots of contemporary sectarianism firmly established through increased numbers of Protestant settlers, a hardening of attitudes toward Catholicism as well as Protestant Nonconformism and the consequent loss of power by the Old English elite. These changes were less the result of plantation than of the conflicts of midcentury and the changing shape of governance both within Ireland and in relation to London. Forasmuch as some individuals at the time might have framed their considerations of New World colonialism in terms of the Irish experience, the future could not be predicted. As will be considered in detail in the next chapter, the Irish and New World ventures were linked, not as model and mirror, but as competitive, contemporary ventures.

CHAPTER FOUR

⧼ Creating Colonial Virginia

Introduction

Nine months before the September 1607 Flight of the Earls provided individuals like Sir Arthur Chichester, Sir John Davies, and Sir
Thomas Phillips with the opportunity to compile their varying designs for
the plantation of Ulster, three small ships set sail from London charged with
renewing England's claim to the New World. This colonial project was the
brainchild of a group that most notably included the chronicler Richard
Hakluyt, military men like Sir Thomas Gates, Edward Maria Wingfield, and
Sir George Somers, and the adventurer Bartholomew Gosnold. Reflecting
earlier models, their project was to be privately financed through the creation of a joint-stock company. The Virginia Company of London received
its charter in April 1606, as did the Western Merchants' Virginia Company
of Plymouth, in which George Popham, nephew of the Munster Plantation
designer Sir John Popham, was a leading figure. Both Virginia Companies
were determined to exploit the New World's natural resources while aiding
in the containment of Spain, and both sent out settlers and supplies in 1607.

Popham's efforts to establish a colony at Sagadahoc, Maine, were short-
lived, whereas the second venture just barely maintained its grasp on the
New World by establishing a fortification on a small island near the Chesapeake Bay. Careful examination of colonial development in the seventeenth
century reveals greater commonalities and manifold interlinkages between
the establishment and development of colonial societies in Virginia and in
Ireland than was the case in the sixteenth century. Yet the Virginia colony
and the Ulster Plantation paralleled one another in their early years—not as
successful ventures, but in the often disastrous decisions made by planters
and planners and the continual failures of settlers to adhere to regulation or
intention. Returning to the military model of the first Roanoke venture—an
approach that contrasted with that taken by the Scottish settlers of the Ards
and that intended for the Ulster Plantation—proved a costly error for the
Virginia colony. By 1650, the societies that emerged from the efforts to plant

Ireland and Virginia continued to proclaim their British roots and character even as each was shaped by its interactions with the indigenous cultures.

Regardless of the significant differences between the planting of colonies in Ireland and Virginia, scholars have routinely noted that numerous individuals involved in the early-seventeenth-century settlement of Virginia had also spent time in the Irish wars, as was the case with Wingfield, Gates, Thomas Dale, Lord De la Warr, Thomas West, and William Newce. Newce's Irish experience was cited by the Virginia Company of London when they granted him the title of marshal in 1621: "And forasmuch as Captaine Newce hath given so large a testimony of his experience and skill in Marshall discipline wherein he hath bene exercised and imployed a long tyme, upon many services in Ireland . . . the Company are pleased to grant him the said place of Marshall." Newce had fought in Ireland during the Nine Years' War and had established himself as a planter in Munster in the early seventeenth century. In 1611, he was recorded as a captain at Kinsale with charge over fifty horsemen while Sir Thomas Phillips still commanded fifty footmen at Coleraine. Newce had also served as lieutenant to Sir Oliver Lambert and was granted a life pension of 10s. by James I in 1614.[1]

Like Phillips, Newce was not satisfied with merely being a military man. By 1600, he had taken on the lease for some of Walter Raleigh's Munster lands and had begun work on Bandonbridge, a Munster Plantation town that would later be developed by the seventeenth-century planter and entrepreneur Richard Boyle. Newce subsequently established his eponymous settlement, Newcestown, in West Cork before opting for one final adventure in the Virginia Plantation. Newce and his wife, along with his brother Thomas (also a captain in Ireland) and Thomas's wife, arrived in Virginia in 1620, where Newce, "out of a generous disposicion and desire to advance the generall Plantacon in Virginia . . . freely offered unto the Company to transport at his owne coste and charges 1000 persons into Virginia" in exchange for the title of general and a patent for lands. Described by Virginia governor Sir George Yeardley as a gentleman of "much worth and suffitienty," Newce received the title of marshal and a patent to 1,500 acres of land, with fifty tenants, in the vicinity of present-day Newport News. Newce's last adventure proved fatal. Both he and his brother died within two years of their arrival in the colony, Thomas having "died very poor," according to George

1. Susan Myra Kingsbury, ed., *The Records of the Virginia Company of London: The Court Book, from the Manuscript in the Library of Congress* (Washington, D.C., 1935), I, 446–447; C. W. Russell and John P. Prendergast, eds., *Calendar of the State Papers, Relating to Ireland, of the Reign of James I*, 5 vols. (London, 1872–1880), IV, *1611–1614*, 475; ibid., V, *1615–1625*, 12.

Sandys. The fate of William's wife is unknown, whereas Mrs. Thomas Newce petitioned the Virginia Company for aid for herself and a young son in August 1623. Neither woman appears in the 1624/25 muster of the colony, strongly suggesting that they, too, had succumbed to the many hazards of early colonial Virginia.[2]

Other Virginia settlers were closely related to Ulster planters, such as the James River planter Stanley Flowerdew, who established his home atop a Weyanoke Indian settlement while his brother Thomas adapted an Irish ráth for his fortified residence in County Fermanagh. Irish Catholics were also implicated in one of early Jamestown's spy stories: this was a 1610 report by one Francis Maguel (probably Magnel or possibly Maguire) about the English developments in Virginia, translated into Spanish and delivered to Madrid by the exiled Franciscan archbishop of Tuam, Flaithrí Ó Maolchonaire (Florence Conry). Conry, an associate and supporter of the exiled Hugh O'Neill, founded the College of Saint Anthony at the Franciscan house at Louvain, where the Gaelic historian Mícheál Ó Cléirigh compiled the Irish manuscripts that would form the core of the *Annals of the Four Masters*. In addition to presenting Magnel's narrative to the Spanish, Conry also offered writings by Philip O'Sullivan Beare and by himself, including a treatise entitled "Statement of the Severities Practiced by England against the Irish Catholics." Both Conry and O'Sullivan Beare saw the future of a Catholic Ireland as dependent upon the strength of ties to Spain. Exactly what Magnel believed is more difficult to ascertain. His unreliable relation seems to have had little to no impact upon the Spanish. Indeed, Magnel's report was more likely to upset than inform the Spanish, as it considerably overstated the achievements of the English and implicitly criticized the Spanish. Magnel's account is replete with tales of the pearls, silver, gold, and diamonds mined by the English, their successes in the boatbuilding industry, and their cordial relations with the Natives of the region. According to Magnel, the "emperor of Virginia" routinely sent envoys to the West Indies, who returned with stories of how Native people there were treated "very badly and as slaves, and the English tell them that those people are Spaniards, who are very cruel and evil disposed." Whatever Magnel's motiva-

2. See discussion in Michael MacCarthy-Morrogh, *The Munster Plantation: English Migration to Southern Ireland, 1583–1641* (Oxford, 1986), 213; Sir George Yeardley to Sir Edwin Sandys, 1619, in Kingsbury, ed., *Records of the Virginia Company of London*, I, 446–447, III, 123; George Sandys to John Ferrar, Apr. 8, 1623, in W. Noël Sainsbury, ed., *Calendar of State Papers*, Colonial Series, I, *1574–1660* (London, 1860), 42–43; Kingsbury, ed., *Records of the Virginia Company of London*, IV, 270–271.

tions, it is unlikely that he saw himself engaged in a black and white cultural struggle against the English or that he perceived himself and his countrymen as sharing any commonalities with the Powhatan peoples.[3]

Magnel was hardly the last Irish Catholic to experience life in the Virginia colony. Francis Wyatt, governor during the 1620s, reported that the Council of Virginia were ejecting a planter, Simon Tutchin, described as being "Dangerous to this Colony" on account of his Catholicism, which had previously seen him "Banished owt of Irelande." Mostly, though, Virginia Company treasurer Sir Edwin Sandys took a pragmatic approach to religion when it came to peopling the Jamestown colony. As he argued, colonists "from every source" were required to ensure the Virginia colony's demographic success, just as Irish tenants would prove a necessity for the London Company settlements of Ulster, despite regulations. Early Jamestown leaders could not afford to be too selective about the settlers' religious beliefs. The presence of Catholic religious items in James Fort–period deposits, including a crucifix and a range of rosary beads, materially attests to Roman Catholic practices in early colonial Virginia. Catholicism did not disappear overnight following the English Reformation; it is not surprising to encounter traces in the Atlantic world.[4]

3. Alexander Brown, ed., *The Genesis of the United States* . . . , 2 vols. (Boston 1890), I, 392–399, 418, II, 940; Stephen M. Donovan, "Conry (or Conroy), Florence," in Charles G. Herbermann et al., *The Catholic Encyclopedia: An International Work of Reference on the Constitution, Doctrine, Discipline, and History of the Catholic Church*, IV (New York, 1908), 261–262, http://www.newadvent.org/cathen/04261c.htm, accessed Jul. 15, 2009. The Annals themselves were compiled and translated by Cú Choigcríche Ó Cléirigh, Fearfasa Ó Maolchonaire, and Peregrinus Ó Duibhgeannain in the 1630s from their base in Donegal; see "Report of What Francisco Maguel, an Irishman, Learned in the State of Virginia during the Eight Months That He Was There, July 1, 1610," in Edward Wright Haile, ed., *Jamestown Narratives: Eyewitness Accounts of the Virginia Colony; The First Decade, 1607–1617* (Champlain, Va., 1998), 447–453. According to Haile, Magnel "was serving his country" because the "Protestant Orange arrived in Ulster in 1607," and therefore "the Irish and the Powhatan were undergoing simultaneous invasion from the same vanguard." In reality, the association of Ulster's Protestants with the House of Orange by definition postdates the Williamite Wars of the late seventeenth century and has nothing to do with the history of the Ulster Plantation or the spy story of Magnel. Haile (447) also expresses doubt about the standing of Conry, describing him as an "Irishman who calls himself the archbishop of an Irish town near Galway." In fact, "Tuam" refers not just to the town of Tuam but to the diocese of Tuam. The title of archbishop of Tuam was first established in 1152, and Florence Conry, or Flaithrí Ó Maolchonaire, was formally consecrated in 1609.

4. Sir Francis Wyatt, Governor, and Council in Virginia, "A Letter to the Earl of Southampton and the Company of Virginia January 10, 1624/5," in Kingsbury, ed., *Records of the Virginia Company of London*, IV, 509; Theodore K. Rabb, *Jacobean Gentleman: Sir Edwin Sandys, 1561–1629* (Princeton, N.J., 1998), 322, 330, 346–347; Kevin Butterfield, "Puritans and Religious Strife in the Early Chesapeake," *VMHB*, CIX (2001), 5–36; William M. Kelso, *Jamestown: The Buried*

Ireland also figured in the Virginia colony's speculative efforts. In 1620, Munster planter Daniel Gookin, an associate of William Newce, convinced the Virginia Company of the efficacy of his plan to import cattle and servants from Ireland to the colony. The subsequent arrival of Gookin's ship gave the Council "great hope (if the Irish Plantacone [prosper]) that frome Ireland greate multitudes of People wil be like to come hither." The ports of Munster were a convenient entrepôt for the provisioning of English ships bound for the New World. Facilitated by these transport links, Irish laborers were sent to the Virginia colony throughout the seventeenth century, although it is often difficult to trace their presence in the documentary record. The shared residences of indentured servants of British, Irish, European, and West and Central African ancestry yield a mixture of artifacts not readily attributable to any one ethnic identity. Rather, their shared material culture likely retained multivalent meanings that ensured the maintenance of cultural boundaries while also facilitating daily discourse.[5]

Of particular note in considering connections between Ireland and Virginia are the roles played by former Irish Lord Deputies Chichester and St. John, along with former Munster Lord President Sir George Carew, in the revocation of the Virginia Company's charter and the reorganization of Virginia as a royal colony in 1624. Illustrating the often convoluted relationship between colonial ventures in Ireland and Virginia is the fact that, at the same time Chichester, Carew, and Grandison were examining the Virginia Company's failings during the treasurership of Sir Edwin Sandys, Sandys himself was appointed as a special commissioner to examine the Irish plantations' failings. Although this commission was never called to duty, sending Sandys to Ireland for an extended period of time would have sidelined him from involvement in both the Virginia and Bermuda colonial enterprises. The enquiries were themselves entwined in the political rivalry between factions associated with the duke of Buckingham, George Villiers, and the earl of Southampton, Lionel Cranfield.[6]

Truth (Charlottesville, Va., 2006), 187; Diarmaid MacCulloch, "New Spotlights on the English Reformation," *Journal of Ecclesiastical History*, XLV (1994), 321; Sarah Tarlow, "Reformation and Transformation: What Happened to Catholic Things in a Protestant World?" in David Gaimster and Roberta Gilchrist, eds., *The Archaeology of Reformation, 1480–1580* (Leeds, 2003), 108–121.

5. Council in Virginia, letter to Virginia Company of London, January 1621/2, in Kingsbury, ed., *Records of the Virginia Company of London*, III, 587; "Newport News," *William and Mary College Quarterly*, 1st Ser., IX (1901), 233–237.

6. "Special Commissioners for Ireland: Warrant for the Payment of Allowances," Jan. 14, 1624, in Russell and Prendergast, eds., *CSPI of the Reign of James I*, V, 456. Sandys, who was disinclined to accept this role, was spared service when the idea for another commission was effec-

The year 1622 proved significant in the fortunes and legacies of each colonial project as determined by the commissioners. In Virginia, Powhatan attacks against the dispersed English settlements, which resulted in the deaths of some 347 colonists, precipitated Captain Nathaniel Butler's scathing report on the colony, entitled *The Unmasked Face of Virginia*. Butler's report contributed to the dissolution of the Virginia Company and the reconfiguration of Virginia as a royal colony as proposed by Chichester, Carew, and Grandison. In the same year, the crown sent out investigators to report on the process of plantation in order to determine why Ireland continued to be a major financial drain. Sir Thomas Phillips and Richard Hadsor, accompanied by the cartographer Thomas Raven, reported from Ulster upon the London Companies' innumerable failings in managing their lands. This report, in particular, provided the basis for the lengthy Star Chamber proceedings against the companies, with the unintended, if predictable, consequence of further taxing their expenditure in Ireland. Meanwhile, reports from 1622 Virginia reached the fledgling Plymouth colony and strengthened its leaders' resolve to begin construction on a fort designed to guard against the Narragansetts and Wampanoags.[7]

Although the year 1622 was thus a turning point for the Virginia colony and the Londonderry Plantation, the problems reported by Butler and by Phillips and Hadsor differed significantly in scale, particularly in terms of the loss of human lives. The London Companies in Ulster were clearly guilty of defying regulations to construct model towns and adequate fortifications and to expel the Irish from their plantation grants; but the Virginia Company was deemed culpable for the deaths of approximately 4,800 settlers. This figure equates to roughly 80 percent of all those who immigrated to the colony between 1607 and 1624. It is far harder to calculate the relative death rates of indigenous Chesapeake and Ulster inhabitants. The balance of documentary evidence suggests that the negative demographic impact of British expansion was far greater for Native peoples of the Chesapeake than it was for Ulster's Irish, notwithstanding the very real hardships that many Irish had been facing since Henry VIII began asserting greater control over Ireland in the 1530s. Simplistic comparisons between early-seventeenth-century British settlements in Virginia and Ireland run the risk of obfus-

tively shelved. See discussion in Victor Treadwell, *Buckingham and Ireland, 1616–1628: A Study in Anglo-Irish Politics* (Dublin, 1998).

7. William Bradford, *Of Plymouth Plantation: 1620–1647*, ed. Samuel Eliot Morison (New York, 1952), 111.

cating and denigrating the many lives lost as a result of the 1607 landing on Jamestown Island.[8]

Ireland did not serve as a model for early Virginia; rather, individuals like Arthur Chichester often spoke in one breath of the two ventures, and many adventurers, including Chichester, perceived the two projects as competing with one another. The unanticipated demand that the London Companies support the Ulster Plantation scheme drew attention and, by extension, investment away from Virginia just when the New World colony needed it most. As discussed above, although the Mercers' Company ventured £200 toward the Virginia Plantation in 1609, they refused to contribute in 1611, even when the lord mayor of London requested it. In fact, fifty-five of the fifty-six companies named in Virginia's second charter of 1609 also became, willingly or not, involved in the Ulster Plantation. When they originally opted to invest in the Virginia Company following its 1606 establishment, the companies had no foreknowledge that the king would soon compel them to invest in Ireland. Furthermore, before the chartering of the Virginia Company and the establishment of the Ulster Plantation scheme, many individual investors were already heavily involved in existent joint-stock companies, such as the Muscovy Company and the Levant Company. More than one hundred members of the Virginia Company were also members of the East India Company, with the Virginia Company treasurer Thomas Smythe also serving as the first governor of the East India Company. In 1610, some of these same people would also sign on to invest in the Newfoundland Company.[9]

The East India Company also had interests in Ireland, exploiting the for-

8. Karen Ordahl Kupperman, "Apathy and Death in Early Jamestown," *Journal of American History,* LXVI (1979), 24–40. See Colin Breen, "Famine and Displacement in Plantation-Period Munster," in James Lyttleton and Colin Rynne, eds., *Plantation Ireland: Settlement and Material Culture, c. 1550–c. 1700* (Dublin, 2009), 132–139, for a consideration of the extent of starvation and disease in Munster during the Nine Years' War.

9. Ian Doolittle, *The Mercers' Company, 1579–1959,* ed. Ann Saunders (London, 1994), 60–61; T. W. Moody, *The Londonderry Plantation, 1609–41: The City of London and the Plantation in Ulster* (Belfast, 1939), 97–98; Edward P. Cheyney, "Some English Conditions surrounding the Settlement of Virginia," *American Historical Review,* XII (1907), 514; Basil Morgan, "Smythe [Smith], Sir Thomas (c. 1558–1625)," *Oxford Dictionary of National Biography,* Oxford University Press, 2004–, accessed Jul. 27, 2009, http://doi:10.1093/ref:odnb/25908; Gillian T. Cell, "The Newfoundland Company: A Study of Subscribers to a Colonizing Venture," *WMQ,* 3d Ser., XXII (1965), 611–625. Cell notes the considerable overlap between individual investors in the Newfoundland, Virginia, and Somers Island Companies but does not address the involvement of some of the same individuals in Ireland beyond acknowledging William Freeman's role in overseeing the Haberdashers' interests in the Londonderry Plantation.

ests and iron resources of Dundaniel, Co. Cork, to supply their considerable shipbuilding needs. According to a petition of 1613, the East India Company had invested £7,000 at Dundaniel, constructing a dock "where they have lately built two ships of 400 and 500 tons apiece; and have built offices, houses, smith's forges, and other storehouses . . . and have likewise at Dundaniel erected an iron-work with divers dwellings for English people to the number of 300 at least." Apart from Sir Thomas Smythe's 1613 request to Lord Deputy Chichester for ordnance to protect Dundaniel from the "wylde Irish," the company's settlement in Co. Cork must be understood as less of a colonial venture in and of itself and much more of an adjunct to the company's colonial interests in more distant lands.[10]

That the London Companies had eschewed Ireland as a target for investment before James I's command may indicate that investing in the unknown New World seemed a better proposition than investing in war-torn Ireland, a land that had nearly ruined adventurers like Sir Thomas Smith. Certainly, interest in Ireland following the submission of Tyrone was decidedly lackluster in comparison to the New World with its promise of untold mineral resources, notwithstanding the testimony of those like Chichester whose New World experiences had been far from positive. No doubt the destruction of the Munster Plantation in 1598 was fresh in the mind of George Popham, as he led the London Company's 1607 effort to plant in Maine, given that his uncle John had been an architect of that first Munster Plantation. Despite this enthusiasm for the unknown over the known, it would not take long before the myriad problems of early Jamestown became a disincentive, exacerbating hardship in the struggling colony. The rapid and successful establishment of a colony on Bermuda, initially under the aegis of the Virginia Company and in 1615 under the Somers Island Company, further siphoned funds away from Jamestown.[11]

10. "Petition of the Merchants Trading to the East Indies and of William Burrell," June 30, 1613, in Russell and Prendergast, eds., *CSPI of the Reign of James I*, IV, 369. For discussion of the East India Company involvement, see Paddy O'Sullivan, "The English East India Company at Dundaniel," *Bandon Historical Journal*, IV (1988), 3–14; Nicholas Canny, *Making Ireland British: 1580–1650* (Oxford, 2001), 313; and for consideration of the archaeological traces of the Dundaniel Ironworks, see Colin Rynne, "The Origins and Technical Development of the Blast Furnace in Ireland, c. 1596–c. 1740," in Conleth Manning, ed., *From Ringforts to Fortified Houses: Studies on Castles and Other Monuments in Honour of David Sweetman* (Bray, 2007), 389; Denis Power, *Archaeological Inventory of County Cork,* I, *West Cork* (Dublin, 1992).

11. James Stevens Curl, *The Londonderry Plantation, 1609–1914: The History, Architecture, and Planning of the Estates of the City of London and Its Livery Companies in Ulster* (Chichester, 1986), 30; Neil Kennedy, "William Crashaw's Bridge: Bermuda and the Origins of the English Atlan-

For those who remained focused on the development of Ireland, the Virginia colony was viewed as a dumping ground for the unwanted. When faced with a thriving community of pirates on Ireland's west coast, servitor Sir Richard Moryson argued to the Privy Council that, as "active men and good mariners," the pirates could be sent to "the intended plantation of Virginia . . . [where] good use might be made of them for the present there." As noted in the previous chapter, Chichester mooted the idea of banishing the Ulster lords O'Cahan and O'Donnell to the New World. Although Moryson's suggested action was not taken, a number of Wexford natives were evidently sent to Virginia in the second decade of the seventeenth century. The threat of being sent to the colony was a means of controlling the remaining "men of the escheated countries of Wexford, who have lately vexed their Lordships with clamours against the distribution of the land there," according to Sir Oliver St. John. In a letter to the lords dated December 8, 1620, St. John advocated "if any more of them trouble the King or their Lordships[,] to send them after their countrymen." Meanwhile, Ireland was also viewed as a source of labor for the Virginia colony, with the company looking favorably upon the 1622 proposition of "certen gentlemen of Ireland" who offered to "trans-port out of Ireland 20 or 30 able youthes of 16: or 17 yeares of age to Virginia to be Apprentices for 6 or 7 yeares in the Companies service." Transplantation to Virginia was later viewed as an appropriate means of disposing of unwanted natives following the upheavals of the 1640s and 1650s. Some survivors of Cromwell's attack on Drogheda in September 1649 were reportedly sent across the Atlantic, and Irish surnames are common on lists of headrights for Virginia in the 1650s. Bristol merchant Richard Netherway apparently sent one hundred Irish natives to be sold as indentured servants in Virginia. Yet Ireland was bound to the New World colonies by far more than these specific population movements. Reliance on funding from the City of London tied together the fortunes of the Virginia colony and the Ulster Plantation, as the king's promotion of the Ulster Plantation scheme brought the two ventures into direct competition.[12]

The requirement that the London Companies invest in the Londonderry Plantation had an immediate and deleterious effect upon the finances for the

tic, 1609–1624," in Nancy L. Rhoden, ed., *English Atlantics Revisited: Essays Honouring Professor Ian K. Steele* (Montreal, 2007), 113–114.

12. Richard Morsyon to Salisbury, Aug. 22, 1609, in Russell and Prendergast, eds., *CSPI of the Reign of James I*, III, *1606–1608*, 277–278; Sir Oliver St. John to the Lords, Dec. 8, 1620, ibid., V, 306; Brown, ed., *Genesis of the United States*, I, 609.

Virginia adventure. To begin with, the amount of money that the companies had pledged to the Virginia Company in 1609 was already considerably smaller than what the king demanded for the Londonderry Plantation in the following year. Little wonder, then, that none of the companies involved in Ulster were named in the March 1612 charter granted to Virginia. As a prominent freeman of both the Skinners' Company and the Haberdashers' Company, Thomas Smythe would have witnessed the wrangling over investment firsthand. Propagandists for each venture began to draw comparisons between the two lands when outlining the wealth to be gained from their respective colonial projects. In 1610, the Council of Virginia contrasted the rich timber resources of Virginia with the limited forests available in Ireland, arguing, "Neither the scattered Forrests of England, nor the diminished Groves of Ireland, will supply the defect of our Navy." Other individuals attempted to balance their commitments to both ventures. Sir Thomas Ridgeway, the first earl of Londonderry, developed a two-thousand-acre County Tyrone plantation grant while simultaneously investing in the Virginia Company. Ironmonger William Canning was a director of the Virginia Company who also patented lands in Ulster, where his brother George, also a director of the Virginia Company, served as the agent on the Ironmongers' proportion. Given George Canning's desultory reports about the progress of plantation and the constant danger posed by rebellious woodkerne—as referenced in the previous chapter—perhaps both brothers hoped that their investments in Virginia might be more successful.[13]

Efforts to develop commodities in each land were also occasionally linked. The Irish Cattle Bill of 1621, never approved, was designed to prevent the importation of Irish cattle into England and Wales, an endeavor supported by Sir Edwin Sandys. Daniel Gookin and Thomas Woode thereby schemed to employ Virginia as a convenient trading partner for cattle raised

---

13. As noted by Ulster historian T. W. Moody, the sum of money ventured by the companies to the Virginia Company in 1609 was "considerably smaller than the amounts demanded from the same companies by the precept of 9 January 1610 for the Irish plantation." As a result, "none of the companies appeared as incorporators in the third charter, granted to the Virginia Company in March 1612." See Moody, *Londonderry Plantation, 1609–41*, 97–98; Council of Virginia, *A True Declaration of the Estate of the Colonie in Virginia with a Confutation of Such Scandalous Reports as Have Tended to the Disgrace of So Worthy an Enterprise* (1610), in Peter Force, ed., *Tracts and Other Papers, Relating Principally to the Origin, Settlement, and Progress of the Colonies in North America, from the Discovery of the Country to the Year 1776* (1836–1846; rpt. Bowie, Md., 1999), III, 4; "Proceedings of the Servitors and Natives in Planting," September 1611, in Russell and Prendergast, eds., *CSPI of the Reign of James I*, IV, 130; "Patents Already Enrolled in Ireland," 1612, ibid., 317; Brown, ed., *Genesis of the United States*, II, 842, 983.

by planters in Ireland. In considering Woode's petition to import cattle into the colony, the company specified that the livestock should be "fayr and lardge Cattle and of our English breed." Exactly what type of cattle were exported to Virginia from Ireland is difficult to ascertain. Although assemblages of cattle bones have been recovered from early colonial sites in the Chesapeake, identifying whether any of the represented species are Irish or English breeds requires comparative assemblages of cattle of known origin. Unfortunately, faunal remains on late medieval and postmedieval archaeological sites in both Ireland and England are not routinely collected or analyzed. Meanwhile, the planting of tobacco in Ireland and England was to be prohibited in order to protect Chesapeake growers: "The same course likewise should be held for Ireland by verie effectuall letters written to the Lord Deputy to prohibite the plantinge of Tobacco there." Fortunately for the Chesapeake growers, tobacco did not flourish in the Irish climate.[14]

Competition for investment ensured that economic speculation was the hallmark of plantation in Ireland and Virginia. Although tobacco would become central in the Chesapeake economy, individual entrepreneurs in both lands engaged in a wide range of manufacturing effects and agricultural innovations in the search for profitable commodities. The glassmaking and ironmaking industries of Ireland, discussed below, were paralleled by similar manufacturing efforts in Virginia, where they left behind a rich archaeological record at Jamestown. Archaeological assemblages from the site of James Fort reveal that, even during the colony's most stressful period, the years 1607–1611, colonists were engaged to some extent in speculative manufacturing and prospecting, as indicated by the presence of distilling dishes, crucibles, copper scrap, glass cullet and slag, and semiprecious stones sourced from the wider region. Artisans remained a core part of Jamestown's fluctuating population throughout the seventeenth century, with the material traces of their activities discernible in the archaeological deposits associated with the town that eventually grew up outside the fort.[15]

14. Efforts to conduct DNA testing on cattle remains from the Nansemond site, discussed later in this chapter and associated with the Munster planter Daniel Gookin, have been inconclusive as to breed or cline. Joanne Bowen, personal communication, Jul. 20, 2009; Richard Thomas, "Bones of Contention: Why Later Post-Medieval Faunal Assemblages in Britain Matter," in Audrey Horning and Marilyn Palmer, eds., *Crossing Paths or Sharing Tracks? Future Directions in the Archaeological Study of Post-1550 Britain and Ireland* (Woodbridge, Suffolk, 2009), 133–148; Court Minutes, Feb. 12, 1623, in Kingsbury, ed., *Records of the Virginia Company of London,* II, 265.

15. Kelso, *Jamestown,* 180–182; Karen Bellinger Wehner, "Crafting Lives, Crafting Society in Seventeenth-Century Jamestown, Virginia" (Ph.D. diss., New York University, 2006).

Alongside analogous efforts at developing commodities, planners in both Virginia and Ireland encouraged the development of towns. The establishment of a civil society was seen as dependent upon functioning towns that would provide economic, political, and social stability. Archaeological data from the Jamestown townsite revealed three distinct peaks of development, with a flurry of activity in and around the 1620s and 1630s, another in the 1660s, and a third in the 1680s. Archaeological materials associated with the three peak periods occurred in distinct areas of the townsite, with limited overlap and therefore little continuity in the development and occupation of individual structures. Such sporadic activity indicates individual speculation rather than a carefully implemented and centrally approved development plan. Pre-1650 activity principally related to manufacturing efforts, whereas the later peaks corresponded with speculative building initiatives sanctioned by the colonial government.[16]

At first glance, these continually unsuccessful efforts at developing Jamestown and the construction of substantial brick buildings in a land of earthfast buildings appear to reflect colonial leaders' insatiable need to symbolize authority. When considered more contextually, however, the attempted development of Jamestown mirrors contemporary speculative development efforts occurring within England and Ireland, even if Jamestown shared the same fate as Randal MacDonnell's doomed mercantile center on the steep cliffs of Dunluce, Co. Antrim. Both Dunluce and Jamestown were as much about projecting an image of urbanity and civility as they were about performing core mercantile functions. The attempted establishment of British colonial societies in both Virginia and Ireland was predicated not just upon negotiating relations with native peoples and overcoming the environmental challenges of new lands but also upon awareness of patterns and politics within Britain itself. Although the pattern of exploration and nascent commodification of new lands and their resources was set during the sixteenth century, it is the seventeenth century that witnessed the maturation of the patterns of economic growth that allowed for the maintenance and expansion of colonial societies in what has become known as the British Atlantic world.

16. Marley R. Brown III, "National Park Service Archaeological Assessment of Jamestown, Virginia: Research Plan, 1992–1994," *Jamestown Archaeological Assessment Newsletter*, I, no. 1 (Fall 1993), 1–5; Audrey Jane Horning, "'A Verie Fit Place to Erect a Great Cittie': Comparative Contextual Analysis of Archaeological Jamestown" (Ph.D. diss., University of Pennsylvania, 1995); Brown and Horning, *Jamestown Island: A Comprehensive Analysis of the Jamestown Archaeological Assessment, 1992–1996* (Williamsburg, Va., 2006); Horning and Andrew C. Edwards, *Archaeology in New Towne, 1993–1995* (Williamsburg, Va., 2000).

The manner in which the English related to the Natives of the Chesapeake region differed substantially from their convoluted engagements with Ireland's Old English, Gaelic, and Scottish peoples—yet, the extent to which English activities were constrained and at times controlled by Native understandings is only just beginning to be recognized. It would not be until close to the end of the seventeenth century that the territory of the Virginia colony would expand beyond the boundaries of the Powhatan world of Tsenacommacah, evidence of the way in which English geographic understandings were unconsciously structured by the Native world. Even by the close of the seventeenth century, Native peoples throughout the Chesapeake region still retained significant roles as traders and cultural brokers. The society that eventually emerged from the 1607 establishment of the Jamestown outpost was heavily shaped by Native influences, even if those influences were seldom acknowledged—and, after 1622, rarely sought.[17]

Background: The Virginia Adventure

The Virginia Company of London's colonial venture began in December 1606, when three ships, the *Susan Constant,* the *Godspeed,* and the *Discovery,* were dispatched from London and began their journey across the Atlantic, landing at Cape Henry in April at the entrance to the Chesapeake Bay. A two-week reconnaissance trip up the James River as far as the fall line (near present-day Richmond) in the territory of the Appomattucks made it clear to the English that the land was densely populated, complicating their search for a suitable location to build a colonial outpost. They eventually settled upon the low-lying and currently uninhabited peninsula of land that would become known as Jamestown Island. Despite its inherent environmental drawbacks, the Virginia Company settlement fared better than that planted by the Plymouth Company at Sagadahoc on the Kennebec River in Maine, which had been beset by difficulties. The Plymouth Company had first sent out the *Richard,* captained by Henry Challons, in August 1606 to

---

17. April Lee Hatfield, "Spanish Colonization Literature, Powhatan Geographies, and English Perceptions of Tsenacommacah / Virginia," *Journal of Southern History,* LXIX (2003), 249. Of particular note is the research being conducted by Maryland archaeologists Julia A. King and Dennis C. Curry into the material and documentary sources relating to post-1660 Native life in the Maryland region and the emergence of Powhatan-descendant Native scholars in Virginia in connection with the Werowocomoco project. See King and Curry, "'Forced to Fall to Making of Bows and Arrows': The Material Conditions of Indian Life in the Chesapeake, 1660–1710," paper presented at the Omohundro Institute of Early American History and Culture conference "The Early Chesapeake: Reflections and Projections," St. Mary's City, Md., Nov. 20, 2009.

select an appropriate site for the Maine settlement. On board were two Abenaki Indians who had been captured and brought back to England in 1605. Their return was designed to facilitate relations between the English and the Native peoples of the region. However, the *Richard* was captured by the Spanish off the Florida coast and never made it to New England. The company was forced to organize another reconnaissance venture, which eventually returned to England and recommended the Kennebec River locale. The settlers themselves did not go out until May 1607, sailing in two ships under the command of George Popham and Raleigh Gilbert. The Maine colony survived for little more than a year after the settlers landed there in August 1607, succumbing to the usual litany of ills: supply shortage, harsh weather conditions, an unfamiliar environment, political instability (George Popham died in 1608, leaving Gilbert in charge), a lack of readily exploitable commodities, and, notably, deteriorating relations with the Natives. Half of the colonists were sent back to England in December because of the lack of food. Despite these difficulties, the site has yielded traces of a sizable, timber-framed storehouse as well as a timber-framed dwelling interpreted as the home of Raleigh Gilbert. Both structures suggest a considerable investment in the colony and the expectation of longevity, but they nonetheless were abandoned when Gilbert received news that, upon the death of his brother, Sir John, he had come into a sizable inheritance, including Compton Castle in Devon. The appeal of the New World swiftly faded. The Maine colony was abandoned in September 1608, while the Virginia colony struggled on.[18]

The Virginia Company of London defined three primary goals for the settlement of Virginia—conversion, transplantation, and wealth creation—in a 1610 pamphlet: "*First,* to preach and baptize into *Christian Religion* . . . to recover out of the armes of the Divell" the Native inhabitants; "*Secondly,* to provide and build up for the publike *Honour* and *Safety* of our *gratious King* and his *Estates* . . . by transplanting the rancknesse and multitude of increase in our people"; and, thirdly, "the appearance and assurance of *Pri-*

---

18. Alfred A. Cave, "Why Was the Sagadahoc Colony Abandoned? An Evaluation of the Evidence," *New England Quarterly,* LXVIII (1995), 625–640; Jeffrey Phipps Brain, *Fort St. George: Archaeological Investigation of the 1607–1608 Popham Colony on the Kennebec River in Maine* (Augusta, Maine, 2007); Brain, *The Popham Colony: An Historical and Archaeological Brief* (Salem, Mass., 2001); Myron Beckenstein, "Maine's Lost Colony: Archaeologists Uncover an Early American Settlement That History Forgot," *Smithsonian,* XXXIV, no. 11 (February 2004), 18–19; Tom Gidwitz, "The Little Colony That Couldn't," *Archaeology,* LIX, no.2 (March/April 2006), 30–35; Richard L. Pfhlederer, "Before New England: The Popham Colony," *History Today,* LV, no. 1 (January 2005), 11–17.

vate commodity to the *particular undertakers,* by recovering and possessing to themselves a fruitfull land, whence they may furnish and provide this King-dome, with all such necessities and defects under which we labour, and are now enforced to buy, and receive at the curtesie of other Princes, under the burthen of great Customs." Not all goals were equal in practice. The aim of producing marketable commodities emerged as a more crucial focus for the colony than either conversion or population absorption, although the latter was an inevitable consequence of both the colony's labor requirements and its appalling mortality rates.[19]

The importance of religious conversion to the Virginia colonial adventure remains a topic of some debate. Although ostensibly central to the colonial mission, converting the Powhatans to Christianity was never at the forefront of initial English diplomatic efforts, which focused much more upon cul-tivating trade relations and extracting knowledge about natural commodi-ties. Yet the political advantages of religious conversion were not entirely overlooked. The 1609 instructions from the Virginia Company to Thomas Gates, then-governor of the colony, specified that, if Powhatan leaders were instructed in English habits and religion, "their people will easily obey you and become in time Civill and Christian." As a means of enforcing conver-sion, Gates was permitted to kidnap native children and "in case of neces-sity, or conveniency, we pronounce it not crueltie nor breache of Charity to deale more sharply with them." Certainly the colonial leaders' military background colored any efforts at voluntary religious conversion, as ac-knowledged in the 1612 admonition of Virginia Company member Robert Johnson: "In steed of Iron and steele you must have patience and humanitie to manage their crooked nature to your form of civilitie." Although prag-matism outweighed evangelism, one should not underestimate the signifi-cance of religion to the Virginia project. In contrast to attitudes toward the Irish, the Natives of the New World were arguably viewed as better subjects for conversion to Protestantism. New World peoples could be for-given for having never been exposed to Christianity, whereas the Catholic Irish had chosen to eschew the "proper" path. As such, the Native people of the Chesapeake were considered more worthy of missionizing activity than were the Irish, and it was naively assumed that, when confronted with European civility and Christianity, Native people would willingly convert. All pretense of treating Virginia Natives as subjects worthy of civilizing was dropped in the aftermath of the March 1622 Powhatan attacks, as best

19. Brown, ed., *Genesis of the United States,* I, 339–340.

exemplified by Edward Waterhouse's condemnation of English efforts to convert "the Savages to Civilitie and Religion." Waterhouse urged his fellow colonists to violence, stating, "Our hands which before were tied with gentlenesse and faire usage, are now set at liberty by the treacherous violence of the Savages, not untying the Knot, but cutting it." Poet Christopher Brooke was even more adamant; he considered the Virginia Natives to be "the very dregs, garbage, and spawne of Earth."[20]

The brutal death, during the 1622 attacks, of George Thorpe, who was responsible for the management of lands at Henrico that had been set aside for an Indian college, could be read as a Native rejection of his conversion plan. As related by Virginia settler Anthony Chester, "The result of Mr. Thorpe's efforts was that the King [Opechancanough] and his subjects began to show much inclination to embrace the Christian religion, from which the English expected much good, but it was not long before they found out that the savages were false and great hypocrites, for in the general massacre mentioned heretofore even Mr. Thorpe was not spared though he could have saved his life by flight." The Powhatans employed their new knowledge of Christianity against the English, timing their attacks during a period they knew was of religious importance: Lent. Clashing religious ideologies played a significant role in the disintegration of diplomatic relations between the English and the Powhatan, yet these were only a contributing factor to the broader process of destabilizing Native society. Although most English colonists were likely sincere in their beliefs, the Jamestown colony's activities were not primarily guided by religious motivations; as in Ireland, however, religion provided a ready justification for military actions against Native people.[21]

The Virginia Company's second stated goal concerned transplanting excess people. Colonization was perceived as a solution for the rising unemployment and population growth that, although relatively low, was viewed as uncontrolled. Estimates place the growth of the English population at

20. Kingsbury, ed., *Records of the Virginia Company of London*, III, 15, 19; Robert Johnson, *The New Life of Virginiea* (1612), in Force, ed., *Tracts and Other Papers*, I, 18–19; Edward Waterhouse, "A Declaration of the State of the Colony and . . . a Relation of the Barbarous Massacre," in Kingsbury, ed., *Records of the Virginia Company*, III 551–553, 556; Christ[opher] Brooke, *A Poem on the Late Massacre in Virginia, with Particular Mention of Those Men of Note That Suffered in That Disaster* (London, 1622), discussed in Stanley Johnson, "John Donne and the Virginia Company," *ELH: A Journal of English Literary History*, XIV (1947), 127–138.

21. "Two Tragical Events," *William and Mary College Quarterly*, 1st Ser., IX, no. 4 (April 1901), 213–214. For consideration of the deliberate timing of the attacks, see Frederic W. Gleach, *Powhatan's World and Colonial Virginia: A Conflict of Cultures* (Lincoln, Neb., 1997), 157.

annual rates of seven per one thousand in the latter half of the sixteenth century and five per one thousand for the first half of the seventeenth century. Increasing urbanization and migration from country to town created an impression of population growth and instability, with colonial settlements perceived as an ideal means of relieving the strain on England's emergent towns and cities. The year 1576 saw the publication of Humphrey Gilbert's discourse encouraging New World settlement as a means of relieving poverty. Gilbert's theme was further developed and elaborated by Sir George Peckham, who in the 1580s provided finance for Gilbert's colonization schemes. In Peckham's vision, new settlements would provide idle men with employment in mines and women and children with employment in processing valuable agricultural commodities such as cotton and hemp. Settlements were widely conceived of as a solution for social problems and for the sloth that so exercised sixteenth-century intellectuals. In the younger Richard Hakluyt's estimation, a successful Norumbega (New England) colony would "keep the mariner from idleness," rescue "great numbers that for trifles may otherwise be devoured by the gallows," and absorb "the fry of the wandering beggars of England." Peckham also optimistically viewed settlement in the New World as a means for England's Catholics (such as himself) to avoid harsh financial penalties in Protestant England.[22]

The "excess population" rationale for New World colonization was also used in encouraging the settlement of the Ulster Plantation, although, for obvious reasons, the Ulster Plantation was never viewed as a haven for recusants. A 1609 promotional statement declared that, if the commodities of the north of Ireland were steadfastly developed by transplanted Londoners, then "it might ease the city of an insupportable burthen of persons, which it might conveniently spare, all parts of the city being so surcharged that one tradesman is scarce able to live by another; and it would also be a means to

22. P. Griffiths et al., "Population and Disease, Estrangement and Belonging: 1540–1700," in Peter Clark, ed., *The Cambridge Urban History of Britain,* II (Cambridge, 2000), 196; E. A. Wrigley and R. S. Schofield, *The Population History of England, 1541–1871: A Reconstruction* (Cambridge, Mass., 1981); Humphrey Gilbert, "A Discourse of a Discoverie for a New Passage to Cataia," Apr. 12, 1576, in David Beers Quinn, ed., *The Voyages and Colonising Enterprises of Sir Humphrey Gilbert,* Works Issued by the Hakluyt Society, 2d Ser., LXXXIII (London, 1940), I, 129–164. For discussion of Peckham's vision, see Philip Alexander Bruce, *Economic History of Virginia in the Seventeenth Century: An Inquiry into the Material Condition of the People, Based upon Original and Contemporaneous Records,* I (London, 1907), 59. See extended discussion of the debate over widespread idleness in Shannon Miller, *Invested with Meaning: The Raleigh Circle in the New World* (Philadelphia, 1998), 26–49; Richard Hakluyt, *A Discourse concerning Western Planting* (1584), in Louis B. Wright and Elaine Fowler, eds., *English Colonization of North America* (London, 1968), 26.

free and preserve the city from infection." Despite such enthusiasm, Ulster was never a principal outlet for England's excess population. By contrast, the policy of reducing England's surplus population by sending them to the New World had been so effective by the end of the seventeenth century that an outcry was raised concerning the draining of workers needed in England's burgeoning industrial centers. Even as early as 1667, the House of Commons held a debate over the remarkable rate at which the Virginia colony was consuming settlers, with one member asserting, "The English at their first arrival lose a third part at least."[23]

It was the third goal of colonization—developing commodities—that would take precedence in the activities of the Virginia Company and their successors in the royal colony, as acerbically described by John Smith: "We did admire how it was possible such wise men could torment themselves and us with such strange absurdities and impossibilities, making Religion their colour, when all their aime was nothing but present profit, as most plainly appeared, by sending so many Refiners, Gold-smiths, Jewellers, Lapidaries, Stone-cutters, Tabacco-pipe-makers, Imbroderers, Perfumers, Silke-men, with all their appurtenances." The centrality of the search for commodities in the early Virginia colony is particularly illuminated by archaeological research. The material evidence for ongoing speculative manufacturing and development in the Virginia colony complicates historical arguments about the overwhelming dominance of tobacco in the Virginia economy and, by extension, the Virginia economic mindset. This constant striving to develop marketable commodities must also be understood as key to the urban ideal that underpinned colonial ideologies. Yes, profits were required to satisfy those who risked investing in the colony. But, for the colony to survive and meet its other aims, towns built around manufacturing and craft activity were needed to support what was intended to become an improved, settled agricultural landscape founded upon tillage: the very epitome of a civil English society.[24]

23. "Motives and Reasons to Induce the City of London to Undertake Plantation in the North of Ireland," May 28, 1609, in Russell and Prendergast, eds., *CSPI of the Reign of James I,* III, 207–208; Russell R. Menard, "British Migration to the Chesapeake Colonies in the Seventeenth Century," in Lois Green Carr, Philip D. Morgan, and Jean B. Russo, eds., *Colonial Chesapeake Society* (Chapel Hill, N.C., 1988), 113; Carl Bridenbaugh, *Jamestown, 1544–1699* (New York 1980), 44.

24. "Advertisements; or, The Path-Way to Experience to Erect a Plantation," in Philip L. Barbour, ed., *The Complete Works of Captain John Smith (1580–1631)* (Chapel Hill, N.C., 1986), III, 272.

Company Period Jamestown (1607–1624)

Understandings of life in the early James Fort has been revolution-ized through archaeological research that has uncovered nearly the entire perimeter of the fort, as evidenced by the soil stains associated with its tim-ber palisade. Much of the fort's interior has been excavated, exposing ten structures and a range of associated features. Several phases in the construc-tion of Jamestown's defenses have been revealed, from the initial triangular-plan timber palisade of 1607 to the creation of a five-sided perimeter by an eastern extension believed to have been constructed in 1608. Ditches approximately 1.83 meters wide and 1.2 meters deep accompany the bul-warks, with demilunes on the river side completing the considerable out-works. The change in authority that occurred with the arrival of Sir Thomas Dale in 1611 can be discerned in the abandonment and filling of ramshackle pit houses and their replacement with rows of timber houses. The remark-able assemblage of more than 750,000 excavated objects constitutes an un-equalled corpus of data referencing the relations of the English with their Powhatan neighbors, their expectations of the new land, their efforts, and their failures—failures underscored by the discovery of twenty-nine human burials believed to date from 1607 alone, some of them buried together in a single grave. Osteoarchaeological analysis indicates that all four individuals in one multiple interment were European males. On the basis of their posi-tion within the fort and the lack of many European objects in the fill, they likely date from the early years of the colony, testimony both to the high death rate and the challenge of expediently coping with the remains of the deceased.[25]

The struggles of the colonists in the first few years at Jamestown are well known. Disease, unrest, spoiled provisions, fire, and simple unfamiliarity with the local environment devastated the small colony. Widespread fam-ine in the winter of 1609–1610 killed many and infamously drove one colo-nist to murder his wife, whereupon he chopped her body into "pieces and salted her for his foode." Archaeological evidence attests to the inexpert

25. Archaeological investigation of the James Fort site was begun in 1994 by the Jamestown Rediscovery archaeological project initiated by the Association for the Preservation of Vir-ginia Antiquities (APVA); see Kelso, *Jamestown;* Kelso and Beverly Straube, eds., "2000–2006 Interim Report on the APVA Excavations at Jamestown, Virginia," unpublished report by the Association for the Preservation of Virginia Antiquities, Williamsburg, Va., 2008. For example, Jamestown archaeologists have interpreted two double interments as "an indicator of the stress-ful times at Jamestown" (ibid., 32–36).

postmortem butchery of one young woman, presumably to provide a meal for the starving. Overall mortality rates suggest that 80 percent of colonists sent to Jamestown between 1607 and 1616 died, although the number of people that actually perished during the winter of 1609 is unclear. Those who did not succumb to starvation reportedly subsisted upon "horses and other beastes . . . vermine as doggs Catts Ratts and myce. . . . Serpents and snakes and . . . wylde and unknowne Rootes," according to the colonist George Percy. Percy's account is supported by the presence of butchered horse bones in association with the remains of snakes, turtles, cats, and dogs in James Fort assemblages dated to the early years of the colony. The colonists' inability to muster sufficient effort to feed themselves on available wildlife resources during the Starving Time must be understood as resultant of a complex interplay of psychological and nutritional factors. Whatever the relative balance of nutritional deficiencies and psychological trauma experienced by the settlers, the result seems to have been widespread apathy, as expressed by Ralph Hamor when he accused settlers of preferring to "starve in idlenesse" rather than "feast in labour."[26]

The extreme stress experienced by the fort occupants is also evident in many remarkable early deposits, such as the fill of a well believed to have been dug in 1609 under the direction of Captain John Smith and replaced in 1611. A wide range of expensive and functional items were retrieved from the well. Still-usable weaponry had been dumped into it, including sword blades and hilts, bandolier fragments, musket shot, and even cannonballs. The deliberate dumping of such costly and important items is highly unusual, an extreme response to stress. By contrast, archaeological sampling of the extensive ditches surrounding the walled Ulster towns of Carrickfergus, Londonderry, and Coleraine has not unearthed a single piece of armor or

26. George Percy, "A Trewe Relacyon: Virginia from 1609 to 1612," *Tyler's Quarterly Historical and Genealogical Magazine,* III (1922), 260–282; Martin H. Quitt, "Trade and Acculturation at Jamestown, 1607–1609: The Limits of Understanding," *WMQ,* 3d Ser, LII (1995), 227–258; Kelso, *Jamestown,* 92–93; Kupperman, "Apathy and Death," *JAH,* LXVI (1979), 24–40; Joseph Stromberg, "Starving Settlers in Jamestown Colony Resorted to Cannibalism," *Smithsonian .com,* http://www.smithsonianmag.com/history-archaeology/Starving-Settlers-in-Jamestown -Colony-Resorted-to-Eating-A-Child-205472161.html, accessed May 21, 2013; Ralph Hamor, *A True Discourse of the Present State of Virginia* (1615; rpt. Richmond, Va., 1957), 26. For disagreement over mortality, see the heated exchange between Thomas M. Camfield, "A Can or Two of Worms: Virginia Bernhard and the Historiography of Early Virginia, 1607–1610," *Journal of Southern History,* LX (1994), 649–662, and Virginia Bernhard, "A Response: The Forest and the Trees; Thomas Camfield and the History of Early Virginia," ibid., LX (1994), 663–670.

Figure 8. Reconstruction drawing of James Fort, based on archaeological evidence. Courtesy, Jamie May, Preservation Virginia, Jamestown Rediscovery Project, Jamestown, Va.

usable weapon. No weaponry was found in the excavations at the O'Neill stronghold of Toome Castle, captured by Sir Thomas Phillips in 1602. None is represented in the metalwork assemblage from the excavation of Doddington's bawn and castle at Dungiven, either. At Jamestown, armor and armaments were not the only expensive goods dumped unceremoniously into a well. Items intended for economic exchange and barter, including coins, jettons, and tokens, were also discarded, alongside still-functional ceramic vessels and a wide variety of personal items including a coral teething stick intended to soothe an infant—one unlikely to have survived the horrors of the Starving Time. The contents of this well are invaluable for understanding the material lives of the early colony and, in popular discourse, have been termed riches. Yet those who poured their worldly goods into that well certainly must not have conceived of the items as riches. Many, perhaps most, of the artifacts now greeted with fascination were the property of dead people, their deposition into wells and pits possibly an act of cleansing by the living. Regardless of their original provenance and the identity of the individuals who cast those weapons, coins, tokens, jettons and pots into the well, we must acknowledge the emotional intensity of this action.[27]

Other early James Fort features are similarly notable for the density of their artifacts, which may tell a similar story of emotional stress while also underscoring the military character of the colonial effort. One feature, which might have started its life as some type of subterranean storage structure based upon its flat-bottomed profile and rectilinear shape, was filled with armor fragments, sword and scabbard pieces, bullet molds, firearms parts, and bandolier cylinders. Amid the weaponry were tobacco pipe fragments, two coins, a leather worker's tool, and one small (1 cm) gold scallop shell ornament lost from a piece of jewelry or rosary possibly associated with Saint James. Furthermore, there were 900 sherds of Native-made pottery and items likely intended for trade, such as copper alloy bells, copper off-cuts, and glass beads. Butchered animal bones included cattle, pigs, deer, dog or wolf, dolphin, and bobcat. The bobcat and dog/wolf remains re-late to animal species that would have ordinarily been considered taboo for consumption. Another possible subterranean storage pit dating to the early years of the fort's occupation yielded a similar assemblage. This feature contained personal objects associated with an individual of status, includ-ing a silver thread button, gilt clothing spangles, cloth seals from Augs-burg fustian, a brass book clasp, an ivory chess piece, a Chinese porcelain wine cup, and a façon de Venise glass. The accoutrements of a gentleman, these valuable objects were discarded into a hole in the ground, along with another array of serviceable weaponry and objects relating to the trade with

27. "Artifacts continue to pour out of what is likely James Fort's first well, built under the di-rection of Captain John Smith in early 1609. Sword blades and hilts, coins, tokens, and jettons, cannonballs, pottery from England, France, Germany and China are among the riches found by the Jamestown Rediscovery team over the past few weeks" (http://www.historicjamestowne .org/the_dig/dig_2009_07_17.php, accessed Jul. 17, 2009; and see this site for further discus-sion of the finds from this early well). Human responses to traumatic events vary enormously but often leave a material signature worthy of interpretation. For a useful discussion of the in-terpretive value and material signatures of traumatic events, see Shannon Lee Dawdy, "The Ta-phonomy of Disaster and the (Re)Formation of New Orleans," *American Anthropologist,* CVIII (2006), 722. For Ulster comparators, see Nick Brannon, "Finds List, Dungiven," unpublished report to the Northern Ireland Environment Agency, 2009. Weaponry that has been recov-ered from Irish sites generally comes from battlefields; see Paul Logue and James O'Neill, "The Battlefield Archaeology of the Yellow Ford," in Audrey Horning and Nick Brannon, eds., *Ire-land and Britain in the Atlantic World* (Dublin, 2009), 7–30; Damian Shiels, "Fort and Field: The Potential for Battlefield Archaeology in Kinsale," in Hiram Morgan, ed., *The Battle of Kin-sale* (Bray, 2004), 337–350.

the Powhatans. Whether all these objects were shoveled into the pits under orders from Governor De la Warr to clean up the fort, or discarded because they were associated with the diseased or dead, or thrown away by individuals in the grip of hysteria and despair is unknowable. Each of these explanations is rooted in the colony's instability and underscores a loss of concern for the future and the importance (or lack thereof) of personal property.[28]

Two nearly complete apothecary jars were found in the aforementioned well, and drug containers are common in all of these early features. Their presence suggests efforts to treat the sick or wounded as well as experimentation with native curative plants. Beyond the demonstrable need for medicine, the potential for New World plants and herbs to produce exportable remedies formed an initial impetus for settlement, with potentially marketable herbs recognized as early as 1607. That year, a report to the king carried by Sir Christopher Newport noted the existence of "apothecary-drugs of diverse sorts, some known to be of good estimation, some strange, of whose vertue the savages report wonders." Two apothecaries, Thomas Feld and John Harford, were then sent along in the first supply to Jamestown in 1608. Macrobotanical samples taken from a 1620s refuse pit adjacent to a structure used for brewing and distillation contained wax myrtle seeds and gallium, or sweet woodruff, seeds—plants that the English recognized as valuable for their medicinal qualities. The pharmaceutical use of wax myrtle was first recognized by Dr. Lawrence Bohun, who arrived at Jamestown in 1610; as William Strachey noted, the wax myrtle "grow in great plenty round about a standing pond of fresh water in the midst of the island, the pill, or rind, whereof is of great force against inveterate dysenterical fluxes, of which Doctor Bohoune made open experiment in many of our men laboring with such diseases, and thereof wisheth all such physicians as shall go thither to make

28. The archaeological designations for the two pits under discussion are Pit 5 and Pit 8. See Kelso and Straube, "2000–2006 Interim Report," 19; Susan Trevarthen Andrews, "Faunal Analysis of James Fort: Structure 166, Pit 5, Pit 8, Pit 9, Pit 10, and Pit 11," report submitted by the Colonial Williamsburg Foundation to William Kelso and Beverly Straube, Jamestown Rediscovery, Williamsburg, Va., 2008, 42; Joanne Bowen and Susan Trevarthen Andrews, "The Starving Time at Jamestown: Faunal Analysis of Pit 1, Pit 3, the Bulwark Ditch, Ditch 6, Ditch 7, and Midden 1," report submitted by the Colonial Williamsburg Foundation to Jamestown Rediscovery, Williamsburg, Va., 2000; for apothecary wares, see Kelso, *Jamestown,* 177. As explained by Jamestown curator Beverly Straube, the fustian was a "linen-cotton weave used in doublets as a fashionable substitute for silk velvet." Another Jamestown pit, Pit 11, yielded four of the same type of cloth seal overlapping one another. Their closed position and proximity suggest that they were still attached to the cloth when thrown away. See Kelso and Straube, "2000–2006 Interim report," 20, for discussion of the contents of Pit 8.

use thereof." Strachey provides a vivid testimony of the struggle to combat the dysentery and other ailments rife in James Fort.[29]

Related to the distillation of medicines was the brewing of beer and ale as a significant component of the diet and an alternative to the brackish water that sickened so many colonists. As early as 1609, broadsides advertised for brewers to settle in Virginia, a sentiment echoed in the *True and Sincere Declaration of the Purpose and Ends of the Plantation Begun in Virginia*. Evidence for brewing and distilling in the early years of the colony includes an earthfast house with a prepared clay floor and three hearths. Associated artifacts include fragments of an alembic and a cucurbit, employed in distillation as well as mineral refining. Although a crucial dietary element, alcohol must also have provided psychological comfort for distressed colonists, be it through communal consumption ritual or attempts to temporarily escape the harsh realities of their existence.[30]

In general, the Ulster planters fared far better than their counterparts at Jamestown, but frequent complaints about drunkenness in the Ulster Plantation settlements signified heightened stress levels among the settlers. In 1612, the Irish Society decreed that drinking establishments in Coleraine were to be limited to three taverns and no more than ten alehouses—certainly sufficient for the tiny population of an incomplete town—as "much 'disorder' was committed by drunken workmen who spent their 'time and substance' in the 'great number of taverns and alehouses.'" Evidence of such behavior can be found in the complaint of the Salters' Company agent Baptist Jones, wherein he relates that, upon returning to Salterstown from a short trip to Dublin in 1614, he found his workmen all drunk and fighting with one another, with work on the Salters' bawn at a standstill. In his estimation, the company's "Master Carpenter is a lazy workman," whereas the "carpenters who came over with me [are] not so good as I expected." Jones also complained about the Salterstown clerk William Smith: "A pot of ale at any time will make him neglect his trust." Such chaotic scenes were repeated on the other company proportions, as small groups of laborers were faced with the often insurmountable, day-to-day challenge of implement-

29. William Brewster to Salisbury, in Alexander Brown, *The First Republic in America: An Account of the Origin of This Nation, Written from the Records Then (1624) Concealed by This Council, Rather Than from the Histories Then Licensed by the Crown* (Boston, 1898), 37; Stephen A. Mrozowski, "Colonization and the Commodification of Nature," *International Journal of Historical Archaeology*, III (1999), 153–165; William Strachey, "The History of Travel into Virginia Britannia: The First Book of the First Decade," in Haile, ed., *Jamestown Narratives*, 687.

30. Kelso and Straube, "2000–2006 Interim Report," 42–43; Kelso, *Jamestown*, 103–105.

Plate 21. Apothecary wares from James Fort. Courtesy, Preservation Virginia, Jamestown Rediscovery Project, Jamestown, Va.

ing the idealized plans for plantation on lands long (and still) occupied by the Irish.[31]

Notwithstanding the challenges facing those charged with constructing, maintaining, and defending plantation settlements, the hardship, stress, and cultural alienation experienced by the English at Jamestown have no ready parallel in Ireland. For the London Companies' many failings in their Ulster efforts, those settlers whom they did manage to entice to their struggling bawns and villages did not face extremes of cultural displacement and deprivation, even if they complained about the lack of supplies or even occasionally feared for their lives. Although the Irish landscape might have been wilder than the one to which English settlers were accustomed, the climate was similar, the foodstuffs were familiar, even if the cuisine was not, and

31. Audrey Horning, "'The Root of All Vice and Bestiality': Exploring the Cultural Role of the Alehouse in the Ulster Plantation," in Lyttleton and Rynne, eds., *Plantation Ireland,* 113–131; James Stevens Curl, *The Honourable The Irish Society and the Plantation of Ulster, 1608–2000* (Chichester, 2000), 127; Orloff Garrik Miller, "Archaeological Investigations at Salterstown, County Londonderry, Northern Ireland" (Ph.D. diss., University of Pennsylvania, 1991), 166–168; Sir Thomas Phillips, "Reformation of Abuses in the Ulster Plantation," June 3, 1623, in Russell and Prendergast, eds., *CSPI of the Reign of James I,* V, 411–413. Quotes from Baptist Jones can be found in the T. W. Moody transcripts of the Salter's Company Records, Irish Letter Book, Public Record Office of Northern Ireland (hereafter cited as PRONI), T.853.

their level of knowledge about their indigenous neighbors was far greater than was the case for the English in Jamestown. The common use of Latin and the presence of individuals fluent in both Irish and English facilitated communication at the elite level. For the nongentry Irish, the arrival and landlord activities of English planters like Thomas Phillips might have been unwelcome but could be accommodated within Gaelic models of socio-political hierarchy. By contrast, the cultural distance between Powhatan and English understandings of social, political, and religious roles and struc-tures was far greater than that between the Irish of O'Cahan's country and the British who arrived as part of the Londonderry Plantation. Further-more, the regular and well-established communication links between Ire-land would have rapidly disseminated awareness of any prolonged outbreaks of disease and starvation. Such news would have precipitated remedial mea-sures, as was the case in 1600 when the Privy Council received reports of rampant dysentery and typhus in Henry Docwra's military encampment at Derry. Docwra was instructed to build a hospital while a number of English soldiers were sent home to Chester to recover. From a comparative perspec-tive, the nadir of the Jamestown effort and Lord De la Warr's arrival in 1610 that signaled an improvement in the colony's fortunes predated any serious settlement of the Ulster Plantation. Arthur Chichester's comments in March 1610 underscore the chronology: "It is hoped the plantation of Ireland may shortly be settled. The Lord Delaware is preparing to depart for the planta-tion of Virginia." When De la Warr arrived to clean up the chaos of James Fort, plans for Ulster were still being debated.[32]

No Ulster planter or overseer encountered anything like the scenes of death and disarray that confronted De la Warr at James Fort. There is no archaeological evidence for extensive clearance deposits comparable to the filled wells and pits of early James Fort on any Ulster Plantation site. Evi-dence for prolonged nutritional stress and starvation in the Ulster Planta-tion is similarly lacking. The only evidence for slaughter of animals not typi-cally considered edible comes from Carrickfergus, where 20 percent of dog bones recovered from medieval and early postmedieval deposits exhibited signs of butchery. Of those exhibiting cut marks, however, only 2 percent date to the sixteenth and seventeenth centuries. Dog butchering in Carrick-

---

32. John McGurk, *Sir Henry Docwra 1564–1631: Derry's Second Founder* (Dublin, 2006), 79–81; Sir William Trumbull et al., *Report on the Manuscripts of the Marquess of Downshire: Preserved at Easthampstead Park, Berkshire,* II, *Papers of William Trumbull the Elder, 1605–1610,* Historical Manuscripts Commission Report no. 75 (London, 1936), 258; David Beers Quinn, *The Elizabe-thans and the Irish* (Ithaca, N.Y., 1966), 121.

Plate 22. Native pottery from James Fort. Courtesy of Beverly Straube, Preservation Virginia, Jamestown Rediscovery Project, Jamestown, Va.

fergus relates to the trade in dog hides rather than human consumption of a taboo food. In sharp contrast to James Fort deposits, Ulster Plantation sites of the first decades of the seventeenth century are characterized by a general dearth of associated material culture. Did settlers to the New World take more personal items, such as the finery, coinage, gaming pieces, and display items found in the trash of James Fort, than their counterparts took to Ireland? Even sites like Dungiven have not yielded many elite personal objects beyond easily lost clothing fittings such as aglets and pins. Assuming that Doddington, of equivalent social status to the Jamestown leadership, did possess some of the same items, they were not discarded at Dungiven or left behind when he died. Similarly, excavations at Phillips's stronghold at Limavady yielded only pottery, pipestems, and architectural material from the plantation period. Again, the most logical explanation for the lack of comparability between deposits associated with the early Ulster Plantation and with early Jamestown would be the extreme hardships, mortality rate, and overall stress that characterized the first few years of James Fort's existence, coupled with the reality that the English elite who journeyed to Ireland were much better able to return to England when necessary. Even Sir

Thomas Phillips, one of the most dedicated Ulster planters, spent considerable time in England. That he died in his home in Hammersmith and not in his manor house at Limavady speaks to Ulster planters' readier ability to maintain a safety net in England.[33]

One similarity between assemblages from both lands can be found in the incorporation of indigenous material culture. Phillips, Doddington, and other Ulster planters relied upon the labor of Irish tenants, visible in Irish architectural forms and material culture of plantation settlements. Materials from James Fort reveal the extent of English reliance on the Native inhabitants of the region. The Native ceramics found in early James Fort deposits underscore the settlers' dependence on foodstuffs acquired from the Powhatans. As noted above, nine hundred sherds of shell-tempered pottery were unearthed from one of the early pits; a further one thousand–plus sherds were recovered from a second pit feature. Evidence not only for the trade in foodstuffs but also for the employment of Native cooking techniques in the English fort appeared in another feature, a 2.43 by 2.75–meter-wide rectangular hole in the ground associated with six postholes, interpreted as a subterranean dwelling. This corresponds to one early report that, when the first supply of ships arrived in 1608, they "found the colony consisting of no more than forty persons—of those, ten only able men, the rest at point of death—all utterly destitute of houses, not one as yet built, so that they lodged in cabins and holes within the ground." In the base of this structure, in an occupation layer, researchers found a crushed Native cooking pot in association with a turtle carapace and the traces of a hearth. The juxtaposition of the finds suggests the application of Native cooking techniques within the fort, which could only have been learned through direct and prolonged contact. Alternatively, the pot and other elements of Native material culture, including a fragment of a woven mat, may signify the residence of Powhatans within the fort, perhaps as Wahunsenacawh's strategy to control cultural relations. The manufacture of a round-bottomed, basket-impressed clay pot recovered from one of the early pits has been attributed to the James Fort clay pipe maker Robert Cotton, suggesting not only that the English were

33. Eileen M. Murphy, "An Overview of Livestock Husbandry and Economic Practices in the Urban Environments of Post-Medieval Ireland," in Audrey Horning et al., eds., *The Post-Medieval Archaeology of Ireland, 1550–1580* (Dublin, 2007), 384–385; Ruairí Ó Baoill, "The Urban Archaeology of Belfast: A Review of the Evidence," *Ulster Journal of Archaeology,* 3d Ser., LXV (2006), 11; finds list, Dungiven priory excavations, on file at Monuments and Buildings Record, Belfast; Audrey Horning, "Preliminary Report on Excavations in the Roe Valley Country Park," unpublished report, September 2009.

able to accommodate Native pots and associated practices but that at least one Englishman was prepared to reproduce the form himself.[34]

Faunal materials from all features associated with James Fort dated to the period 1607–1610 reveal that wild species accounted for 42.4 percent of the fish and meat consumed by fort inhabitants during that period. A wide range of mammals were either hunted by the English or acquired from the Powhatans, including large species such as bear and white-tail deer and smaller animals such as gray fox, raccoon, bobcat, opossum, gray and fox squirrels, and beaver. That these species were also fur-bearing increased their value. A concomitant reliance upon aquatic species suggests that the colonists also internalized at least some Native knowledge about habits and seasonality of fish. The recovery from early fort deposits of more than two hundred objects associated with fishing indicates that availability of equipment was not a problem. The use and maintenance of these tools might have been more of an issue, as documentary accounts highlight the many failures of the English in fishing, exacerbated by unfamiliarity with techniques, lack of salt or other means of adequate preservation, and the seasonality of many species, including sturgeon. That sturgeon did not appear in the James River in the spring of 1610, as in previous years, must have been a source of considerable frustration for the settlers.[35]

Botanical remains provide another important window into subsistence in the early fort. The lowest levels in another well, believed to have been constructed around 1611, yielded both wild and cultivated Virginia plants.

34. Kelso and Straube, "2000–2006 Interim Report," 17–21 (the pits discussed are, respectively, Pit 5 and Pit 8); Ancient Planters of Virginia, "A Brief Declaration," in Haile, ed., *Jamestown Narratives,* 894. There is some ambiguity about the character of the floor deposit. The 2008 report by Kelso and Straube describes the artifacts as having derived from the occupation layer, whereas Kelso, *Jamestown,* 94, suggests they were sealed by it and represent an "accidental time capsule." Similarly, Beverly A. Straube, *The Archaearium: Rediscovering Jamestown, 1607–1609* (Richmond, Va., 2007), 51, describes the assemblage as having "been abandoned suddenly, perhaps with the collapse of the earth and sapling roof." Even if the objects do not relate to an undisturbed "snapshot in time," their association is suggestive of the application of Native cooking methods within the fort. Kelso has further suggested that this pot and the associated activity implied by the assemblage points to the presence of a female Indian cook (95), a compelling suggestion that nonetheless cannot be assumed. Although Indian women were likely present in James Fort, it does not necessarily follow that they performed domestic tasks for the English. Cooking inside the cellar of a pit dwelling would have been an alien activity for a Powhatan woman and presumably an unpleasant activity for anyone—including the handful of Englishwomen who arrived as part of the Second and Third Supplies in 1608 and 1609. Furthermore, the colonists might well have been willing to adapt their own cooking practices to those of Native Virginians.

35. Andrews, "Faunal Analysis," 58–59; Daniel Schmidt, "Subsistence Fishing at Jamestown, 1607–24," *Post-Medieval Archaeology,* XL (2006), 80–95.

Native cultigens came in the form of maize kernels and pumpkin and squash seeds. The majority of botanical materials from this feature were wild berries and nuts. The influence of Native Virginians on cuisine in the fort is clear: not only had the settlers attempted to rely on the Powhatans to supply much of their food, but they also obtained knowledge of Native foodways as they explored the country in their search for commodities. Despite growing hostility, Gabriel Archer noted that, in the summer of 1609, an unspecified number of settlers "were dispersed in the Savages townes, living upon their almes," increasing their knowledge of Native subsistence strategies. Virginia colonists would come to adapt many Algonquian horticultural practices as the colony strengthened, such as slash-and-burn clearance techniques and planting in and around tree stumps.[36]

Fort assemblages also attest to the exchange of nonfood items. Analysis of 179 hafted bifaces found in the fort between 1994 and 1998 suggests that the presence of undamaged small, triangular projectile points made of jasper, dark chert, and orthoquartzite reflects gift giving. All three cryptocrystalline materials are readily fractured. Had they been fired into the fort and hit any kind of solid object, it is likely that there would be a recognizable pattern of breakage. That they are whole and made of nonlocal stone supports the likelihood that their presence is related to social, rather than martial, practices. Orthoquartzite occurs in northeastern North Carolina, whereas the dark chert originated in the Appalachian Mountains and may indicate either direct contact with Siouan-speaking groups or trade via peoples within the Powhatan sphere of influence. Jasper can be found in cobble form in the outer Coastal Plain, in what was then the territory of the Nansemonds, Accomacks, and, before their annihilation, the Chesapeacks. Taken together, the lithic evidence not only reflects regional Native identities but underlines intergroup relationships and Native efforts to weave the English into those existing webs.[37]

Throughout the winter of 1609–1610, some settlers continued to live in Powhatan towns, whereas a second group of colonists located at Point Comfort escaped most of the hardships endured by those at James Fort, report-

36. Steven Archer, "Jamestown 1611 Well Archaeobotanical Analysis Report," submitted by the Colonial Williamsburg Foundation to Jamestown Rediscovery, Williamsburg, Va., 2006. Kelso and Straube report the presence of "blueberries, wild cherry, blackberries, and various nuts such as walnut, hickory, beech, and acorn" ("2000–2006 Interim Report," 68).

37. Dennis B. Blanton, Veronica Deitrick, and Kara Bartels, "Brief and True Report of Projectile Points from Jamestown Rediscovery as of December 1998," *Journal of the Jamestown Rediscovery Center,* I (2001), http://apva.org/rediscovery/page.php?page_id=221.

edly by subsisting on crabs and oysters. In June 1610, those few remaining Jamestown settlers greeted a recently arrived vessel captained by Sir Thomas Gates. Appalled by the condition of the people and the fort, Gates gathered up the survivors and turned his ship around, only to meet three more ships arriving under the leadership of Governor De La Warr. All four ships returned to Jamestown Island, salvaging the colony for England while no doubt seriously disappointing many of those on board who dreamed of a return home. When Sir Thomas Dale arrived the following year, the fortunes of the tiny colonial settlement began to turn for the better as Gates and Dale, De La Warr's second-in-command, instituted martial law over the remaining settlers. The archaeological record from Jamestown materially demonstrates the company's reassertion of authority and order under Dale and Gates, as buildings were demolished and replaced to tidy up and reorganize the fort.[38]

Two timber rows of houses, built atop stone foundations derived from ballast and river cobbles, may be part of the fort's redesign. The structures were orientated along the west wall of the fort palisade and measured 6 meters in width, with overall lengths of 28 meters and 19.5 meters, respectively. The presence of Bermuda limestone in the foundations indicates that the rows could not have been built before 1610, when the first ships arrived in Jamestown from Bermuda. Furthermore, one of the buildings was partially constructed over nineteen human burials presumed to date to 1607. If the row was built as part of Dale's reorganization of the fort in 1611, either these burials were unmarked and forgotten after only a few years—perhaps again indicative of extreme stress—or their presence was of secondary concern to the inhabitants focused upon rejuvenating their residences. Alternatively, the burials may indicate that the rows were built well after 1611 but before the fort fell out of use in the 1620s.[39]

Regardless of the exact construction date of the rows, they bear resemblance to the houses being built in Coleraine and Londonderry. The larger structure incorporated three chimneys and a total of six hearths, interpreted as a row of three spacious lobby entry houses. A stronger possibility is that the structure was originally divided into six individual units measuring 6.09

38. Kelso, *Jamestown*, 103.

39. The structures under discussion include Structure 172 and 175. Kelso and Straube, "2000–2006 Interim Report," give dimensions of 92 by 20 feet for Structure 172, whereas Kelso, *Jamestown*, 106–107, states that structure 172 measured 90 by 18 feet and that Structure 175 measured 66 by 18 feet. The dimensions from the technical report, converted into metric for consistency, are used in this discussion.

by 4.5 meters, or, in imperial, 20 by 15 feet, similar to urban houses in Coleraine that were reported in 1611 to have individual dimensions of 18 by 12 feet. These were constructed of timber and built in rows on continuous timber or stone sills. The 1611 Carew survey noted that a frame was nearly ready to raise for a row of twelve tenements "18 foote wyde and 12 foote toward the streete 2 stories high with dormers and two brick chimneys to every tenement." Although only a trace of one of these structures has been identified in Coleraine, the footprint of a row of tenements with shared chimney stacks would be very similar to that of the largest early Jamestown row. Rows of small, adjoining houses were characteristic of urban buildings in England in this period, particularly in the burgeoning city of London. Such structures had the advantage of making maximum use of small plots and being reasonably cheap and easy to construct. John Stow, in his 1603 survey of London, recorded the conversion of a derelict Shoreditch almshouse into lucrative, speculative housing: "The houses, for a small portion of money, were solde . . . to *Russell* a Draper, who new builded them, and let them out for rent enough, taking also large Fines of the Tenantes, neare as much as the houses cost him purchase, and building: for hee made his bargaines so hardly with all men, that both Carpenter, Brickelayer, and Playsterer, were by that Worke undone. And yet in honour of his name, it is now called *Russels* Row." Whether this Draper by the name of Russell is associated with the similarly avaricious Draper's agent Robert Russell, who endeavored to convert Moneymore into the brewing and imbibing capital of the Londonderry Plantation, is unfortunately uncertain. Either way, population pressure in London ensured a tidy profit from the construction of cheap, closely packed rows of small houses. Population pressure was far less of a constraint in early Coleraine and Jamestown. In fact, the 1613 Smithes and Springham survey of the Londonderry Plantation found that some of Coleraine's smaller dwellings had already been amalgamated to form more commodious houses. The Jamestown dwellings, like those in Coleraine, might also have started life as rows of six small houses and been subsequently enlarged.[40]

Within four years of the arrival of Dale and Gates, the colony had begun

40. Kelso and Straube, "2000–20006 Interim Report," 50; Willie Graham et al., "Adaptation and Innovation: Archaeological and Architectural Perspectives on the Seventeenth-Century Chesapeake," *WMQ*, 3d Ser., LXIV (2007), 451–522; John Rowley, report on the Plantation in Ireland, Oct. 20, 1610, Drapers' Company Records, PRONI; P. S. Robinson, "Some Late Survivals of Box-Framed 'Plantation' Houses in Coleraine, County Londonderry," *Ulster Journal of Archaeology*, 3d Ser., XLVI (1983), 129; Carew Survey of Ulster, 1611, PRONI, MIC 217/2; John Stow, *A Survey of London* (1603; rpt. Oxford, 1908), I, 69–91.

producing its own food supply and trading with the Dutch. The growing strength of the colony, combined with the marriage of John Rolfe and Wahunsenacawh's daughter Pocahontas, temporarily eased the tensions between the English and the Powhatan tribes that had been punctuated by a series of Powhatan strikes on the English following George Percy's 1610 attack on the Paspaheghs. Perhaps most important, from the perspective of the London-based Virginia Company members, tobacco emerged as a profitable commodity that could be produced in the marshy tidewater landscape. Around 1612, John Rolfe first experimented with the crop that promised to reverse the company's fortunes. His accomplishment rested on the cultivation of the West Indian *Nicotiana tabacum* strain rather than the native Virginian *Nicotiana rustica*. The colonists were quick to recognize the potential value of Rolfe's agricultural innovation. In 1615, Ralph Hamor exhorted new arrivals to cultivate the "valuable commoditie of Tobacco . . . which every man may plant, and with the least part of his labour, tend and care will returne him both cloathes and other necessaries." George Yeardley, who became deputy governor of the colony in 1616, encouraged marketing of Virginia tobacco. In fact, so much of it was planted that the following year, Samuel Argall found "the market-place, and streets, and all other spare places planted with Tobacco." The Virginia Company had seemingly found its long-sought economic savior in the drug, yet they did not halt continued efforts to develop other marketable commodities. The company even encouraged settlers to diversify their crops, instructing colony officials in 1621 not to allow artisans "to forsake ther former occupacions for planting Tobacco or such uselesse comodyties." Carpenters, smiths, tanners, tailors, and shoemakers supplied everyday necessities and repair work to alleviate dependence upon imports, yet many were attracted by opportunities that did not exist in England to attain land and property. In response, Virginia planners sought ways of encouraging English tradesmen to settle in Jamestown and ply their crafts. A town was not a town without artisans. A colony without a viable town was unlikely to fulfill its aims of establishing a civil society.[41]

Reflecting the need for support crafts as well as profitable manufactures,

41. Mark Nicholls, "George Percy's 'Trewe Relacyon': A Primary Source for the Jamestown Settlement," *VMHB,* CXIII (2005), 214, 245, 248; George Percy, "A True Relation of the Proceedings and Occurrents of Moment Which Have Hap'ned in Virginia from the Time Sir Thomas Gates Was Shipwrack'd upon the Bermudes . . . ," in Haile, ed., *Jamestown Narratives,* 509–510; Hamor, *True Discourse;* Kingsbury, ed., *Records of the Virginia Company of London,* I, 424. The 1610 attack on the Paspaheghs claimed the lives of the wife and children of the Paspahegh werowance Wowinchopunk.

early economic enterprises at Jamestown were in equal measure aspirational and pragmatic. To encourage settlement and, more important, investments, the Virginia Company kept a steady stream of favorable reports flowing from Virginia back to London. Reverend Alexander Whitaker's 1613 account, entitled *Good News from Virginia,* was typical of company propaganda, as Whitaker extolled Virginia as "a place beautified by God with all the ornaments of nature, and enriched with his earthly treasures." Attempts by Jamestown's early settlers to locate those marketable treasures and to create commodities for export by experimenting with various crops and industries are well known. Some of the most intensive efforts concentrated upon glassmaking, silk production, the search for precious metals and gems, extraction of pitch and tar, potash manufacturing, wine production, and lumbering, as well as attempts to cultivate other West Indian crops such as sugar cane and indigo. Throughout the Virginia Company period, broadsides advertising for craftspersons to come to Virginia were widely circulated. One of these optimistically offered respondents "houses to live in, vegetable-gardens and orchards, and also food and clothing all at the expense of the company of that island." Even then, it was a hard sell.[42]

The company's 1619 instructions to Governor Yeardley further specified the incentives to be offered to those tradesmen who performed their crafts rather than taking up land and cultivating tobacco. They would receive four acres, upon which a dwelling would be constructed, for only the price of the annual four-pence quitrent. Even this not sufficient: the instructions given to the governor and Council in 1621 lamented the colony's failure to produce "those staple Comodities wch are necessarie for the subsisting and Encrease of the Plantation." Not only were colonists failing in their duty to provide marketable treasures other than tobacco; they still could not manage to feed and clothe themselves.[43]

Artisans were similarly of importance to the new settlements in the Ulster

42. A far cry from the pragmatic reality, Jamestown has been celebrated as "the place where many American industries were born in the New World," where innovative craftspeople "never dreamed that the seeds of [their] incessant labors . . . would some day flower into a great industrial and agricultural nation"; see J. Paul Hudson, *A Pictorial Booklet on Early Jamestown Commodities and Industries* (Williamsburg, Va., 1957), iii–iv; Brown, ed., *Genesis of the United States,* I, 248–249, 353, 469; Alexander Whitaker, *Good News from Virginia . . .* , in Haile, ed., *Narratives,* 697–714. For discussion of early manufacturing at Jamestown, see especially Wehner, *Crafting Lives, Crafting Society;* and also Kelso, *Jamestown;* Bridenbaugh, *Jamestown, 1544–1699;* Mrozowski, "Colonization and the Commodification of Nature," *International Journal of Historical Archaeology,* III (1999), 153–165; Horning, "'A Verie Fit Place to Erect a Great Cittie,'" chap. 4.

43. Kingsbury, ed., *Records of the Virginia Company of London,* III, 102–103, 471.

Plantation. In 1610, the Irish Society endeavored to spur the development of its lands through the importation of more than one hundred tradesmen, chiefly to fashion the dwellings and necessary fortifications. Similarly, undertakers of means tried to settle their plantation lands with artisans. In County Tyrone, the plantation settlements of Augher, Benburb, Clogher, and Dungannon relied upon a mixed, proto-urban population of artisans alongside merchants. In contrast to Company-era Virginia's continual search for marketable goods, the Ulster Plantation focused more upon the exploitation of tried-and-true commodities. Unlike the New World, Ireland gave entrepreneurs no expectations of discovering untold riches. Ireland's value lay in its strategic location, and its wealth came in the form of cattle and related dairy products, fish and eels, and the development of iron and timber. Artisans were critical to plantation settlements in developing these resources and providing day-to-day necessities, but less so for the speculative development of undiscovered commodities.[44]

At Jamestown, on the other hand, archaeological expressions of the pursuit of diverse industries have been uncovered. Amethysts, garnets, and quartz recovered from inland Virginia attest to the adventurers' hopes of discovering profitable gemstones. Similarly, the presence of pearl beads alongside Native-made mussel shell beads in the fill of an early fort ditch has been associated with the Council of Virginia's 1610 request for "Pearle drillers" to be sent to the colony. Although many of the thousands of strips of copper unearthed from features within James Fort were intended for trade with the Powhatans, copper was also necessary for processing into brass for export. Echoing the finds from Joachim Gans's furnace at Roanoke are crucibles, alembics and cucurbits, and distilling dishes (scorifiers) and dippers recovered from fort period deposits, representing the necessary implements for mineral assaying and processing. Several triangular and beaker-type crucibles have been unearthed, including one containing copper residue. Early Jamestown settler John Martin likely spearheaded these efforts to develop metallurgy, given his association with the Society of Mineral and Battery Works. Other copper objects recovered from early Jamestown contexts include eighty-one Irish pennies, providing a tangible material link between the lands. But rather than representing pocket change acquired in Ireland, it is likely that the coins—reviled at the time for their low value—were destined, instead, either for the Indian trade or for use in manufacturing.[45]

---

44. Canny, *Making Ireland British,* 239.
45. Kelso, *Jamestown,* 181; Carter C. Hudgins, Marcos Martinón-Torres, and Thilo Rehren,

Evidence for other early attempts at manufacturing include waste products from the 1609 "trial of glass," including more than seven thousand fragments of cullet, traces of slag, and crucibles exhibiting glass residue. Glass was similarly viewed as an important industrial commodity in Ireland. Efforts to produce glass on the Salters' Proportion in the Londonderry Plantation are confirmed by the recovery of moils (waste glass left on the blowpipe during production) and green and gray glass tubing associated with production, along with glass products including window panes and tableware. Salterstown was the locale of a glasshouse operated by William Robson between 1614 and 1618. Robson was a member of the Salters' Company who directed the expansion of glass production in England in the early seventeenth century, including a glasshouse at Blackfriars, which was operational by 1601. Glassmaking was undertaken elsewhere in Ireland during the same period, with the establishment of an English-run glassworks at Drumfennig, near the Cork-Waterford border, documented for the 1580s. Upstanding remains of an early-seventeenth-century glasshouse still survive at Shinrone, Co. Offaly, associated with the Henseys, a glassworking family of French Huguenot descent. This manufactory produced both window glass and vessel glass, employing forest glass technology. Forest glass requires considerable quantities of wood ash, making it heavily reliant upon timber resources; as a consequence, it was a technology that had ceased to be used within England but was deemed appropriate for colonial regions such as Ireland and Virginia. Archaeomagnetic dating of fired clay associated with the Shinrone furnace indicated its use in the first half of the seventeenth century. It is likely that the furnace ended operation by 1640 in response to recent legislation preventing the manufacture and export of Irish glass.[46]

"From the Mines to the Colonies: Archaeological Evidence for the Exchange and Metallurgical Usage of English Copper in Early Seventeenth-Century Ireland and Virginia," in Horning and Brannon, eds., *Ireland and Britain in the Atlantic World*, 157–180; Kelso and Straube, "2000–2006 Interim Report," 24. Coins: Robert Heslip, personal communication, Jan. 25, 2010; Beverly Straube, personal communication, Jan. 26, 2010. Martin's experiments can be understood both in the context of the Roanoke efforts as well as the earlier copper processing efforts of Sir Thomas Smith and Sir Humphrey Gilbert.

46. Miller, *Salterstown*, 483–490; see also Nick Brannon, "A 1614–1618 Londoners' Glasshouse at Salterstown, Co. Derry?" *Archaeology Ireland*, XII, no. 2 (Summer 1998), 23; Nessa Roche, "The Manufacture and Use of Glass in Post-Medieval Ireland," in Horning et al., eds., *Post-Medieval Archaeology of Ireland*, 405; M. S. Dudley Westropp, *Irish Glass: An Account of Glassmaking in Ireland from the XVIth Century to the Present Day*, rev. ed. (1920; Dublin, 1978), 20–24; Sarah Paynter, Caimin O'Brien, and Jean Farrelly, *The 17th-Century Glasshouse at Shinrone, Co. Offaly, Ireland*, English Heritage Centre for Archaeology Report, no. 39 (Portsmouth, 2005), 1–2; Jean Farrelly, "Lost and Found: One Glasshouse," in Joe Fenwick, ed., *Lost and Found: Dis-*

The development of commodities in both Ireland and Virginia was crucial to providing a financial return for investors. In 1621, George Sandys was appointed treasurer of the colony in Virginia and received an official mandate to encourage manufacturing. Instructions to the governor and Council specified to Sandys's "spetiall and extreordinarie care the execution of all o[u]r orders Charters and instructions tending to the setting upp, Encrease and maytaininge of the said Staple Comodities." That Sandys, as official enforcer, did not have an easy time of encouraging manufactures is patently clear in a letter written by him in March 1622 / 3 wherein he describes some of the difficulties encountered in a renewed effort at glassmaking. The excavated remains of this 1620s glassmaking complex included a working furnace, a fritting furnace joined to an annealing furnace, as well as a pot kiln, cullet pile, clay pit, and well. This second attempt to develop a glassworks at Jamestown relied upon importing a number of skilled Italian glassmakers, who were to "sett upp a Glasse furnace and make all manner of Beade and Glasse" under one Captain William Norton, who paid for their passage. On arrival in Virginia, Norton succeeded in directing the construction of a glass furnace, but the glassmakers were apparently none too impressed with life at Jamestown. Noting the "ill successe of the glasse workes" and the discontent of the workers, George Sandys, who was forced to take over when Captain Norton died, described the challenge of leading the glassmaking venture:

> They built up the furnace, wch after one forthnight that the fire was put in, flew in peeces: yet the wife of one of the Italians (whom I have now sent home, havinge receaved many wounds from her husband at severall times, and murder not otherwise to bee prevented, for a more damned crew hell never vomited) reveald in her passion that Vincentio crackt it wth a crow of iron: yet dare wee not punish theise desperat fellowes, least the whole dessigne through their stubbornesse should perish.

As unhappy as these Italian craftsmen were in Virginia, they also must have been cognizant of how much was riding on their success. In the end, everyone was disappointed.[47]

---

covering Ireland's Past (Bray, 2003) 265–272; J. Farrelly and C. O'Brien, "Glasshouse, Shinrone, 17th-Century Glasshouse," in Isabel Bennett, ed., *Excavations 1999: Summary Accounts of Archaeological Excavations in Ireland* (Bray, 2001).

47. Kingsbury, ed., *Records of the Virginia Company of London*, I, 493, III, 468–482; J. C. Harrington, *Glassmaking at Jamestown: America's First Industry* (Richmond, Va., 1952); George Sandys, "Letter to Mr. Farrer by the Hopewel," March 1622/3, in Kingsbury, ed., *Records*, IV, 23–24.

The 1620 Virginia Company records highlight attempts to develop com-modities at Jamestown by importing other European craftsmen. In Novem-ber of that year, a Gabriell Wisher was contracted "to procure out of Swead-land, and Poland men skillfull in makinge Pitch, and Tarr, Pottashes, and Sopeashes, Dressers of Hemp and Flax, Clapbord and Pipestaves and for makinge Salt Peter and Powder," and in 1621, a contract was "made with frenchmen procured from Languedock and sent to Virginia for planting of Vynes." Although demonstrating the broad knowledge and trade connec-tions of its prominent members in casting their net widely both for possible manufactures and available artisans to be employed in Jamestown, neither of these efforts was to prove any more successful than the exploding Italian glassworks.[48]

Sir Edwin Sandys, who preceded his brother as treasurer of the Virginia Company, had himself forcefully led many of the efforts to develop com-modities. His first year in office, Sandys sent 150 people to Virginia to set up three ironworks. One of these was established at Falling Creek, now within Chesterfield County. The Falling Creek Ironworks began operation in 1620. In 1621, the Mercers' Company sent John Berkeley to serve as ironmaster, along with twenty skilled workers to operate both the furnace and forge.[49]

Ironworking was also a focus for other colonial ventures. Newfoundland investor Sir Percival Willoughby, son-in-law of the Tudor entrepreneur Sir Francis Willoughby, sought iron ore to complement the abundant forest re-sources on the northerly island. Willoughby had already speculated heavily in mining and manufacturing in Nottinghamshire, to pay off family debts that had been incurred, in part, through financing abortive efforts at both iron and textile manufacturing in the first Munster Plantation. He was to be disappointed in his hopes for Newfoundland as a center of iron manufactur-ing. Although iron ore is indeed present there—most notably at Bell Island just north of St. John's—it would not be successfully mined until the close of the nineteenth century. The Newfoundland Company simply did not pos-sess the financial wherewithal to support the large-scale exploitation of iron and to bear the subsequent costs of transporting such a heavy commodity back across the Atlantic.[50]

48. Kingsbury, ed., *Records of the Virginia Company of London*, I, 423, 466.

49. Charles E. Hatch Jr. and Thurlow Gates Gregory, "The First American Blast Furnace, 1619–1622: The Birth of a Mighty Industry on Falling Creek in Virginia," *VMHB*, LXX (1962), 261–296.

50. For Wollaton Hall, see Mark Girouard, "Solomon's Temple in Nottinghamshire," in Girouard, *Town and Country* (New Haven, Conn., 1992), 187–196. On Willoughby and his

The history of Virginia's Falling Creek Ironworks was also short-lived, as twenty-seven individuals were recorded as having been killed by Indians at the furnace in 1622, including ironmaster John Berkeley. Reportedly, the industrial structures were also destroyed. Sporadic examination of the site revealed considerable surviving traces of iron manufacturing activity, which could allow for more direct comparisons with the ironworking industry of seventeenth-century Cork, where ironmasters employed up-to-date technological methods in exploiting Ireland's timber and mineral resources. Systematic archaeological survey at Falling Creek in the 1990s revealed extensive charcoal and slag deposits, whereas earlier antiquarian reports suggest the presence of buried structural remains. Whether this evidence corresponds to the 1620s or, more likely, to later efforts at restarting the industry has yet to be determined. Although the Falling Creek operation of the 1620s was far from a success, entrepreneurs continued to envision a future for iron manufacturing in the colony. As in Ireland, the vast timber resources of Virginia allowed for the establishment of the iron furnace and fueled entrepreneurial dreams, shared by Sir Thomas Phillips. In 1632, Phillips put forth a plan to construct an ironworks near Slieve Gallion, although the plan never came to fruition. Iron manufacturing in both regions ultimately failed. In Ireland, the industry was hampered by a get-rich-quick mentality that ensured the destruction of the resources needed to support the long-term manufacturing. A similar mindset in Virginia ensured the replacement of iron manufacturing by tobacco production.[51]

---

activities, see Cell, "Newfoundland Company," *WMQ*, 3d Ser., XXII (1965), 620–621, 625; MacCarthy-Morrogh, *Munster Plantation*, 231–232; M. Harvey, "The Economic Condition of Newfoundland," *Journal of the Canadian Bankers' Association*, III (1896), 148–149; R. S. Smith, "Willoughby, Sir Francis (1546/7–1596)," in *Oxford Dictionary of National Biography*, Oxford University Press, 2004–, accessed Aug. 25, 2011, doi:10.1093/ref:odnb/49827. Another branch of the Willoughby family would become more intensively involved in the seventeenth-century plantations in Ireland, including another Sir Francis Willoughby who acquired a grant of two thousand acres in County Tyrone in 1612. See State Paper Office, State Papers Ireland, Elizabeth I to George III, SP 63/232/33, National Archives, Kew.

51. Hatch and Gregory, "First American Blast Furnace," *VMHB*, LXX (1962); Colin Rynne, "The Social Archaeology of Plantation-Period Ironworks in Ireland: Immigrant Industrial Communities and Technology Transfer, c. 1560–1640," in Lyttleton and Rynne, eds., *Plantation Ireland*, 248–264; E. Randolph Turner III and Antony F. Opperman, "Searching for Virginia Company Period Sites: An Assessment of Surviving Archaeological Manifestations of Powhatan-English Interactions, AD 1607–1624," MS, Virginia Department of Historic Resources, Richmond, Va., 2004; Lyle E. Browning, "Falling Creek Ironworks: Past, Geophysics, and Future," *Quarterly Bulletin of the Archaeological Society of Virginia*, LX (2005), 43–55; Moody, *Londonderry Plantation, 1609–41*, 344. As noted by Rynne, a "colonial mindset" in Ireland, "in-

By contrast to industries like glassmaking and ironworking, which relied upon the knowledge of skilled craftspeople, timber was the most widespread and readily exploitable commodity, requiring minimal processing before being shipped back to England—although shipping timber from Virginia was far less cost effective than shipping it from Ireland. The Virginia Company contrasted the abundance of timber in Virginia with the "diminishing" stocks of Ireland in order to direct investment away from Ireland. Archaeological evidence underscores the significance of timber exploitation in the Virginia colony. A rectangular saw pit was unearthed underlying the bulwark ditch on the west point of the triangular James Fort, indicating that it was in use during the earliest period of the settlement and might have provided materials for export as well as in the construction of fort defenses and buildings. Woodworking tools are identifiable in Jamestown assemblages from the entirety of the seventeenth century and can be associated with the work of particular trades (carpenters, coopers, joiners, turners, shipwrights, and wheelwrights) through recognition of specialist tools.[52]

Although many craftsmen were no doubt principally employed in constructing and maintaining the fabric of the fort and subsequent town, others worked in more specialized commercial ventures. Virginia's abundant forest resources rendered the colony a seemingly ideal locale for shipbuilding, and early in the Company period, a number of vessels were constructed, as well as facilities for repairing other ships. Thomas Woode, in his bid to import cattle from Ireland to Virginia, promised to build the necessary ships. George Sandys led efforts to encourage shipbuilding in Virginia, arranging for the importation of twenty-five shipbuilders in 1621 and providing them with twelve hundred forest acres to use as raw material. This venture was to be sited near the then-operational Falling Creek Ironworks, where it could make use of an extant sawmill, the timber being exploited by the furnace, and the ironworks' products. Eight of the newcomers succumbed to disease, resulting in the failure of this venture.[53]

Unsuccessful or not, shipwrights were clearly active in Company period Jamestown. For example, two cases involving shipwrights were heard in the

spired by a short-term and ultimately short-sighted strategy of economic gain," precipitated the destruction of forests that impeded the industry ("Plantation-Period Ironworks," 262).

52. Kelso, *Jamestown*, 180; Kelso and Straube, "2000–2006 Interim Report," 8. Wehner, "Crafting Lives, Crafting Society," 237–238, provides a helpful list of seventeenth-century toolkits associated with each specialty.

53. Bruce, *Economic History*, II, 428–429; Wehner, "Crafting Lives, Crafting Society," 164–165 (I am grateful to Karen Wehner for sharing this research).

Virginia court on the same day in 1622. In the first case, Captain William Eppes was taken to court for his failure to pay for the construction of "a smalle Shallop"; in the second case, shipwright Brian Caught contracted to build an eighteen-foot shallop for John Utie, even though Utie still owed him payment of "sixscore pownd waight of Tobacco for A boate formerly builte." Colonists also acquired and utilized Native canoes. The example recovered in the 1960s from Powhatan Creek, just a few miles from Jamestown Island, exhibited tool marks from iron implements, indicating a colonial date for the reworking of this vessel. Whether this was a canoe acquired and modified by the English or produced and repaired by Powhatans employing metal tools—or, indeed, made by an English artisan following Powhatan practice, just as pipemaker Robert Cotton replicated a Native pot—is impossible to know. What is certain is that the advantages of the Native canoe for navigating the often shallow and marshy waters of the tidewater region did not go unnoticed by colonists. In 1629, Jamestown gunsmith and churchwarden John Jackson complained that one Edward Wigg had stolen his canoe. For Jackson and most other Virginians, a vessel of some variety was essential for travel within the colony. The colonial reliance upon the waterways for communication and in structuring understandings of place echoed that of Native society.[54]

A related industry that depended upon Virginia's ample woodland was the production of pitch and tar. Like timber, pitch and tar were main commodities imported into England from Poland and Russia by the Muscovy Company. As such, the development of the industry in Virginia had the potential to erode the Muscovy Company's profits—welcome news to those in the Virginia Company who were not engaged in the trade from the east, but a source of potential conflict for individuals like Thomas Smythe, who was extensively involved with both companies. In 1608, German and Polish workmen were sent to the colony to develop the pitch and tar industry, as well as glassmaking and soap ash production. Some archaeological evidence for the production of pitch and tar at Jamestown was encountered in 1941, on the edge of the appropriately named Pitch and Tar Swamp. Although

54. H. R. McIlwaine, ed., *Minutes of the Council and General Court of Colonial Virginia: 1622–1632, 1670–1676* (Richmond, Va., 1924), 34, 99; Ben C. McCary, "An Indian Dugout Canoe, Reworked by Early Settlers, Found in Powhatan Creek, James City County, Virginia," *Quart. Bull. Arch. Soc. Virg.,* XIX (1964), 14–19; Martha McCartney, *Documentary History of Jamestown Island,* III, *Biographies of Owners and Residents* (Williamsburg, Va., 2000), 186. See April Lee Hatfield, *Atlantic Virginia: Intercolonial Relations in the Seventeenth Century* (Philadelphia, 2004), 56–59, for the centrality of the rivers to the development and function of the Virginia colony.

the excavation was terminated before completion, a progress report on the 1941 excavations describes the feature as a rectangular pit containing deposits of pitch.[55]

The emphasis upon production of commodities and the raising of livestock within the colony during the Company period was designed not only to create more exportable goods but to cultivate a degree of self-reliance. The continued struggle for Virginia to support its own subsistence requirements would contrast markedly with the situation in Ulster, particularly the Scottish plantations in the Ards Peninsula. There, the importation of entire families with their livestock and farming implements aided the replication of a reasonably sustainable society and agricultural economy. In both Ireland and the New World, a fundamental tension existed between the bid for colonial self-sufficiency and the crown's desire to maintain control through economic dependency. The political value of maintaining an unequal economic relationship between Britain and Ireland was overt in the policies of Irish Lord Deputy Sir Thomas Wentworth, the earl of Strafford (in office 1632–1639), who in 1633 advised the treasurer thus:

> I am of Opinion, that all Wisdom advises to keep this Kingdom as much subordinate and dependent upon England as is possible, and holding them from the Manufacture of Wool (which unless otherwise directed, I shall by all Means discourage) and then inforcing them to fetch their Clothing from thence, and to take their Salt from the King (being that which preserves and gives Value to all their native staple Commodities) how can they depart from us without Nakedness and Beggary?

Such concerns informed the aforementioned legislation that halted the manufacture of glass in Ireland and precipitated the abandonment of industries such as that at Shinrone.[56]

Meanwhile, in the New World context, the Virginia Company was growing frustrated over the lack of compliance to orders to increase production. This is patently clear from the threats incorporated in a 1622 book of instructions to the governor and Council: "And if you shall finde any person, either through negligence or wilfulnesse, to omit the planting of Vines, and

---

55. Bruce, *Economic History*, I, 49. This potentially very early manufacturing feature was in all probability destroyed when the former Jamestown Visitor Center was constructed in the 1950s. This Visitor Center was itself demolished to make way for a new complex as part of the 2007 anniversary commemoration. See J. C. Harrington, *Progress Report on the 1941 Excavations in the Grounds of the Association for the Preservation of Virginia Antiquities* (Williamsburg, Va., 1942), 11.

56. William Knowler, ed., *The Earl of Strafforde's Letters and Dispatches* (London, 1739), I, 193.

Mulbery trees, in orderly and husbandly manner, as by the Booke is pre-
scribed, or the providing of convenient roomes for the breeding of Wormes;
we desire they may by severe censures and punishment be compelled thereunto." The continued failure of manufacturing in Virginia during the Company period served as a final rationale for the revocation of the company's
charter in 1624, as noted in a sharp indictment contained within Sir Francis
Wyatt's commission to the governorship: "And that if industry were used
it would produce divers good and staple comodities though in the sixteene
yeares government past it had yealded fewe or none, And that this neglecte
they conceaved must fall on the governors and companie here whoe had
power to direct the plantacions." The Virginia Company had indeed failed
to produce the massive profits hoped for by their investors, but it was not
through lack of trying. As evidenced in the finds from the James Fort, even
in the settlement's earliest, bleakest years, colonists were engaged in metallurgical experimentation, geological prospecting, botanical recording, viniculture, glassmaking, and the production of trade goods alongside the necessary (if more prosaic) efforts at providing food and maintaining shelter.
No matter how hard the English tried, however, Virginia was not a land
of milk and honey. No gold and silver mines worked by Natives existed
to underpin British colonial endeavors as they had done for the Spanish in
Mesoamerica and South America.[57]

From Private Venture to Royal Colony

The issue of governance in the new Virginia colony was not as
straightforward as it had been in Ireland after Tyrone's submission in 1603,
when the existing structures of the Dublin-based English government were
extended and more effectively implemented throughout Ireland. In 1618,
under a newly ratified charter, the Virginia Company accorded the settlers
a representative government, and martial law was abandoned in favor of an
English-style judicial system. The company also began to permit individual
ownership of land as a means of encouraging settlement, with profits going
to the landowner rather than to the company or the colony as a whole.
Known as the headright system, this was a grant of fifty acres of land in
the new colony to any immigrant who paid his or her passage and lived in
Virginia for at least three years. Entrepreneurs who paid for another person's passage also received fifty acres for each indentured servant that they

57. Kingsbury, ed., *Records of the Virginia Company of London*, III, 663; Minnie G. Cook, "Sir
Thomas Wyatt, Governor: Documents, 1624–1626," *WMQ*, 2d Ser., VIII (1928), 159.

funded, a significant incentive that provided not only land but labor to work it. Reforms also allowed for the granting of particular plantations, such as Martin's Hundred, to groups of investors, while relative economic and political stability in the colony led to the expansion of settlement along the navigable rivers of the Virginia tidewater. The English policy of situating their settlements both on existing Native settlements and along the margins of the Powhatan world precipitated a carefully planned, if ultimately unsuccessful, strategy of resistance culminating in the coordinated attacks of March 1622.[58]

One of these particular plantations that was attacked in 1622 brought Ireland and Virginia together through the involvement of Munster planter Daniel Gookin and his sons Daniel Jr. and John. In 1604, Gookin Sr., along with his brother Vincent, left their lands in Kent and took up property in Munster, as the plantation was being reestablished following the end of the Nine Years' War. There, both prospered through their involvement in developing and marketing traditional Gaelic commodities including cattle and fish. It was the potential for expanding the cattle trade that brought Virginia to Daniel Gookin's attention, and in 1621, he was granted 1,600 acres, provided that he transported cattle and settlers to the colony. Gookin acted swiftly, sending the *Flying Harte* to Virginia "well furnished wth all sortes of provisione, as well as wth Cattle, as wee could wishe all men would follow theire example, hee hath also brought wth him aboute 50 more uppon that Adventure besides some 30 other Passengers." Gookin also attained an agreement from the Virginia Company to allow him a free market if he successfully established a plantation peopled by Irish. Gookin was energetic and convinced of his New World venture's success, readily selling his property at Carrigaline, Co. Cork, to the entrepreneurial Munster planter Richard Boyle to finance his new venture. Gookin settled at Newport News, near lands granted to the other Munster planters William and Thomas Newce, and established a plantation named Marie's Mount in honor of his wife. Daniel Jr. later developed a grant situated near the confluence of the James and Nansemond Rivers.[59]

---

58. As expressed by Peter Wilson Coldham, "The way was open for private landlords to enrich themselves without the necessity of passing on any benefit to their hired labourers." See Coldham, *Emigrants in Chains: A Social History of Forced Emigrants to the Americas of Felons, Destitute Children, Political and Religious Non-conformists, Vagabonds, Beggars and Other Undesirables, 1607–1776* (Surrey, 1992), 43.

59. Kingsbury, ed., *Records of the Virginia Company of London*, III, 587. As described by John Smith, "The 22. of November arrived Master Gookin out of Ireland, with fifty men of his owne, and thirty Passengers, exceedingly well furnished with all sorts of provision and cattle, and

Gookin picked the wrong year to move to Virginia. Although Marie's Mount withstood the events of March 22, 1622, within a few years, the population had dwindled from the original fifty men to only eighteen men and two women, as indicated by the 1624/5 muster. Only eight of these individuals are listed as having arrived in the *Flying Harte* alongside Gookin, whereas a further three arrived in the *Providence*, sent by Gookin in 1623. The twenty individuals evidently shared a total of four houses and fifteen head of neat cattle, with foodstuffs dominated by dried fish. Although Gookin might have indeed arrived "well furnished wth all sortes of provisione," those provisions had not been replaced. Gookin's intended Irish plantation in Virginia was clearly not prospering as the Council had hoped. His sons remained convinced that they could prosper in the New World, but Gookin Sr. himself soon gave up on Virginia. He returned to Munster seeking the comfort of his previous life, even taking up the lease of the lands at Carrigaline that he had formerly owned. Gookin was unable to financially recover from his Virginia investment before he died in 1632/3, with the excessive debts forcing him to relinquish the lease of his former lands back to Richard Boyle. An inventory of Gookin's estate recorded in April 1633 gives material testimony to the financial impact of Gookin's Virginia adventure. Although he had a range of household furnishings, tablewares, and a handful of books, his only possession of significant monetary value was an ironic echo of Virginia: two thousand pounds of (improperly cured) tobacco, valued at twenty-five pounds, set against recorded debts of nearly seventy pounds.[60]

Daniel Gookin's financial position at his death contrasts markedly with that of his brother Vincent and, as such, exemplifies the very different risk factors involved in planting in Ireland versus planting in Virginia. Like Daniel, Vincent established himself as a planter in Munster in 1604. Rather than become distracted by the promise of the New World, Vincent Gookin

planted himselfe at Nuports-newes." See "The Government of Sir Francis Wyat," in Barbour, ed., *Complete Works*, II, 286–287. For discussion of the Gookin family, see Frederick William Gookin, *Daniel Gookin, 1612–1687, Assistant and Major General of the Massachusetts Bay Colony: His Life and Letters and Some Account of His Ancestry* (Chicago, 1912); and Luke Pecoraro, "'Of Chusinge and Takinge Some Place of Advantage, and There to Make Some Pallysadoes': Atlantic Connections at the Nansemond Fort, Virginia" (MA thesis, Boston University, 2010). I am very grateful to Luke for sharing his research.

60. Gookin, *Daniel Gookin*, lists twelve as arriving in the *Providence*. The Council had expressed that "we doe conceave great hope (if the Irish Plantacone prosper) that from Ireland greate multitudes of People wilbe like to come hither" (Kingsbury, ed., *Records of the Virginia Company of London*, III, 587). Gookin's inventory is printed in *Daniel Gookin*, 54–55.

concentrated his efforts on traditional Irish commodities—cattle and fish—becoming a very wealthy man, albeit one who never felt at home in Ireland. Gookin held strong views on the perceived inferiority of his Irish neighbors and on the manner in which he felt English control should be imposed. Content to profit by employing Irish economic strategies, Vincent nonetheless castigated other planters for intermingling with the Irish through "marriage and gossopry or the like" in order to secure local status. Unlike them, Gookin had "and ever will stand at a distance with the Irish, and will not so much as suffer my children learn their language." Gookin's comments, written around the time of his brother's death, puts integrationist strategies into sharp relief, as they suggest that at least some planters adopted traditional Gaelic practices such as gossiprid. His comments about language imply that it was unusual for a planter not to learn at least some Irish. Gookin's stance and palpable bitterness might well have been influenced by his brother's failed struggle to regain his standing in Munster and traumatic experiences with the Powhatans in Virginia. Vincent equated the habits of the Irish with those of New World Natives, asserting that the Irish "live in their houses more beastly than barbarians or Indians." Such parallels were also drawn by individuals with no experience regarding New World Natives, but Vincent would have been familiar with his brother's firsthand accounts. Although no direct written evidence survives of Daniel Gookin's perspective, his actions speak clearly to disenchantment with the New World, even as his sons endeavored to continue their father's project. Their activities in the 1630s and 1640s provide valuable perspective on English-Native relations in that period, several decades after the colony was established. Before focusing on those insights, we must examine how activity in Virginia shifted in the wake of 1622 and the subsequent revocation of the company charter. Cultural relations between the colonists and the indigenous peoples of the Chesapeake region were irretrievably changed by the events of 1622.[61]

The Powhatan victory was short-lived, being that English revenge was swift. As recounted in an anonymous chronicle first published in 1707:

When the occurrence of this massacre became known in the mother country, the English were ordered to take revenge by destroying with fire and

61. Andrew Hadfield, "Gookin, Sir Vincent (d. 1638)," in *Oxford Dictionary of National Biography,* Oxford University Press, 2004–, accessed Apr. 15, 2010, doi:10.1093/ref:odnb/11007. Gookin was forthright in his negative opinion of Ireland (Gockins to Wentworth, in Mahaffy, ed., *CSPI of the Reign of Charles I,* III, *1647–1660,* 181–186, esp. 184–185); and see T. C. Barnard, "Crises of Identity among Irish Protestants, 1641–1685," *Past and Present,* no. 127 (May 1990), 70.

sword everything of the Indians; consequently they set out for Pamun-key, destroyed both the houses and crops of the Indians, took Opechan-kenough prisoner and shot him on the very place where his house stood before it was burned down. On this spot the English then built a new town. By these means the Indians became very much subdued and lived in constant dread of the English.

The chronicler overstated the submission of the Chesapeake Natives and conflated events of the 1620s with those of the 1640s (Opechancanough was shot to death in 1646 while imprisoned in Jamestown), but the account highlights the role townbuilding played as colonial policy. Although towns were emblematic of English civil society, the Chesapeake reality was that the Native landscape was characterized by well-developed towns, whereas the colonial English landscape was one of dispersed, poorly defended settlements. Forcibly taking a Native town and destroying its buildings and crops in order to plant a new English town was deliberately symbolic, even if not practical from the perspective of urban development. As previously discussed, English expansion beyond the confines of Jamestown and its immediate locale had long been predicated upon acquiring and developing Native lands, as exemplified by the archaeological evidence from Jordan's Journey and Flowerdew Hundred, where English habitations were juxtaposed with, and in places imposed upon, Native dwellings. In post-1622 Virginia, colonists became more likely to destroy and replace Native structures than to acquire and adapt as they once had.[62]

Alongside revenge, defense and rebuilding were central to recovery and the reorganization of Virginia into a royal colony. Outlying settlements were to be rebuilt and fortified. Answering to suggestions made by Lord Arthur Chichester, the Privy Council directed that "some convenient number of houses [be] . . . built together of Brick and enclosed with a Brick wall" at both Henrico and Charles City, although there is no physical or documentary evidence to suggest this ever occurred. In fact, no mention of a settlement at Charles City even appears in the 1624 / 5 muster. In addition to concern over the state of the colony's nucleated settlements, official attention also focused upon the colonists' failure to adequately secure their settlements by realizing Dale's original plans for fortification. Those fortifications that were constructed made use of both timber and earthen defenses, as indi-

62. *Voyage of Anthony Chester to Virginia, Made in the Year 1620: Narrated by a Distinguished Passenger, Who Participated in This Expedition* . . . (Leyden, 1707), transcript at http://etext.lib .virginia.edu/etcbin/jamestown-browsemod?id=J1022.

cated by instructions for the reedification of Henrico and Charles City: "In most places and particularlie about Henrico and Charles citie the Sods are very good to fortifie with all—especiallie if they be cut in the sedgie ground which is so full of roots that it binds the earth close and keeps it from falling in pieces." Governor Francis Wyatt reiterated the importance of fortifications in a 1623 letter: "We know of no other course, then to secure the forrest by running a pallizade from Marttin's hundered to Kiskyack." This palisade across the James-York Peninsula was finally constructed by 1634, according to a report by Governor John Harvey to the Privy Council: ". . . secured a great part of the Country from the incursion of the natives with a strong pallisado which I caused to be built between two creeks, whereby they have a safe range for their cattle near as big as Kent." Harvey was not exaggerating. In 1994, archaeologists recorded a 17.67-meter-long segment of this palisade line in Williamsburg. Unusually for the Chesapeake, traces of it still survive above ground in the form of a slight berm. Below-ground evidence revealed that the ditch and berm feature with its timber pales was an impressive 2.7 meters in width and was placed on the landscape in a straight line, rather than following natural topographic features that would have enhanced its defensive function. Clearly, the palisade's tactical value lay, not in its defensive capabilities, but in its symbolic and psychological role. The palisade delineated English territory, symbolized the permanence of the colonial hold, and made manifest the new separation between settler and Native, in a rejection of the earlier interdependencies. Furthermore, the imposition of a recognizably straight line across the landscape obscured the shapes and contours of the Native landscape, which had been so influential in directing and constraining English settlement. That said, the palisade only reordered cultural space on the James-York Peninsula. Outlying English settlements were still situated within Native territories.[63]

Post-Company Development at Jamestown

By the time the company lost its charter following the events of 1622, Jamestown had evolved out of the confines of the palisaded wooden

63. Brown, *First Republic in America,* 500, 545; Brown, ed., *Genesis of the United States,* I, 545; Records of the Colonial Office, CO 1/3 ff 21–23, 1/8 f74, National Archives, Kew; Martha McCartney, *Land Ownership Patterns and Early Development in Middle Plantation: Report of Archival Research* (Williamsburg, Va., 2000), 2; John Metz et al., *"Upon the Palisado" and Other Stories of Place from Bruton Heights* (Williamsburg, Va., 1998); Philip Levy, "'The Foundacion of All Other Great Works': The Strange Career of the Middle Plantation Palisade," in Dennis B. Blanton and Julia A. King, eds., *Indian and European Contact in Context: The Mid-Atlantic Region* (Tallahassee, Fla., 2004), 265–288.

fort. Lands outside of the fort were formally opened to settlement in 1618, and sometime between 1621 and 1623, town lots were laid out by the Cambridge-educated surveyor William Claiborne. A census taken in 1624 recorded 125 persons within the town, which was composed of twenty-two houses, three storehouses, and the church, with a total of nine boats owned by residents. Of those 125 Jamestown inhabitants, 35 were women, including 6 African servants; 17 were boys under the age of eighteen, and 8 were girls under the age of eighteen. Resident on the island, but outside of the townsite, were a further 29 men, 14 women, 5 boys, and 3 girls. By way of comparison, in 1622, Sir Thomas Phillips and Richard Hadsor reported that there were 110 able-bodied, armed British men resident in the city of Londonderry and 100 in Coleraine. Phillips and Hadsor did not record the numbers of women and children in the two Ulster Plantation towns, but the ratio of men to women is likely to have been more balanced than that of Virginia, with its early emphasis upon a male military model. Although the British population of Coleraine and Londonderry was still vastly outnumbered by the Irish in the surrounding countryside, both settlements, located only thirty miles apart, boasted far larger male populations than that of Jamestown, the only functioning English town in the entire Virginia colony in 1624. The Chesapeake was a land of nucleated settlement, but those settlements were Native, not English.[64]

Even as it became more and more evident that the plantation economy limited expansion of towns, efforts continued to develop Jamestown as a means of economic diversification and relief of dependency. Early royal governors were given explicit instructions to develop commodities other than tobacco, and a number of individuals invested heavily in nascent manufactures in and around Jamestown's New Towne, which were designed not only to create more export products but also to address the growing need for commodities within the colony. Hampered by the lack of a fully functioning, diversified urban settlement, Virginians struggled to make do in the early colony. Seventeenth-century household inventories indicate a lack of material possessions and a preponderance of enumerated objects that were broken and worn out. This low standard of living is generally attributed to high mortality, unfavorable economic conditions, and reliance upon British trade for essential items. But a lack of sufficient trades in the Chesapeake

64. 1624/5 Muster database, http://www.virtualjamestown.org/Muster/muster24.html; Edward M. Riley and Charles E. Hatch Jr., *James Towne: In the Words of Contemporaries* (Washington, D.C., 1955), 21–22; Sir Thomas Phillips, *Londonderry and the London Companies, 1609–1629: Being a Survey and Other Documents Submitted to King Charles I* (Belfast, 1928), 52, 53.

does not presuppose a lack of necessity. Although tobacco producers did not require the same devices necessary for wheat cultivation, a variety of manufactures were still required, including the basic tools used in tobacco cultivation, pottery, and building materials. Coopers to produce tobacco hogsheads were in demand and were often able to obtain large tracts of land following foreshortened periods of indenture. Carpenter, joiner, and cooper Gerrard Hawthorne was indentured to Virginian Thomas Vause for a period of only three years rather than the customary seven. Hawthorne's transportation was paid for, and he had to right to refuse to perform services for colonists other than Vause. At the end of his indenture, he received his tools, bedding, furniture, and fifty acres of land.[65]

Such favorable terms emphasize the high demand for artisans in the early colony. Some were attracted: a total of 222 artisans associated with Jamestown between 1607 and 1700 have been identified, representing fifty-two individual trades. At least 111 remained in Jamestown practicing their craft for at least one year, whereas 21 remained in residence for a sustained period. Brickmakers, potters, carpenters, sawyers, smiths, feathermakers, tanners, leatherworkers, tailors, brewers, distillers, ironworkers, bakers, shoemakers, and numerous other craftspersons made their way to Jamestown, many patenting lands in the colonial center. The story of one such artisan, the aforementioned gunsmith John Jackson, whose canoe had been stolen in 1629, illuminates the advantages of being an artisan in demand in early Jamestown. Jackson and his family resided on a waterfront property adjoining a ⅜-acre lot held by merchant Richard Stephens. In January 1625, their household at Jamestown consisted of John Jackson and his wife (unnamed), their nine-year-old son, John, the orphaned ten-year-old Gercian Buck, and a grown son or kinsman named Ephraim Jackson. Livestock included three cows, three goats, and four pigs. The archaeological traces of the Jackson home, excavated along with an associated refuse pit and well, provide an opportunity to evaluate the material life of an early artisan household.[66]

65. James Horn has suggested, "Lacking towns and industry and with a relatively small and dispersed population, the Chesapeake did not require the range of specialist trades and crafts to be found in the Vale of Berkeley and elsewhere in England"—but it must be remembered that the Chesapeake, like Ulster, was never intended to be without towns. See Horn, "Adapting to a New World: A Comparative Study of Local Society in England and Maryland, 1650–1700," in Carr, Morgan, and Russo, eds., *Colonial Chesapeake Society,* 147. See also Carr, "Diversification in the Colonial Chesapeake: Somerset County, Maryland, in Comparative Perspective," ibid., 354. See Bruce, *Economic History,* II, 420–421, for examples of Virginia-based artisans, and for Hawthorne, see 404.

66. Wehner, "Crafting Lives, Crafting Society," 127. Jackson's holdings are referenced by

The Jackson residence was, by early Virginia standards, a comfortable dwelling. When fully uncovered by archaeologists in 1999, the structure was found to measure 4.87 meters by 7.31 meters and exhibited a two-room hall-and-parlor floor plan. Architectural materials suggest that the building was of wattle and daub supported on a low brick foundation. Although the Jackson home was not large, it did incorporate brick at a time when the overwhelming majority of Jamestown and Chesapeake planter houses were constructed entirely of earthfast timbers and daubed walls. The use of brick implies a financial and psychological investment. Jackson's home also served as his workplace. Artifacts and soil chemistry suggest that the north bay, or hall, accommodated smithing activity. Of all raw materials associated with gunsmithing, such as lead-casting waste, gunflints, and worked flint, 92 percent were recorded around the hearth and storage area inside the hall and in the spread of hearth ash and refuse to the north of the hall, suggesting that Jackson melted lead and cast shot in the home. Although the melting of lead shot did not require specialist skills, Jackson likely augmented his smithing income with this simple task. Most striking is a clear difference be-

---

Stephens, who patented a ⅜-acre waterfront lot in 1623 that was bounded on the east by Ralph Hamor's 1.5 acres and on the west by John Jackson's property. See Virginia Land Office Patent Books, 1619–1660, I, 1, microfilm on file, John D. Rockefeller Jr. Library, Williamsburg, Va.; Nell Marion Nugent, *Cavaliers and Pioneers: Abstracts of Virginia Land Patents and Grants, 1623–1800*, I (Richmond, Va., 1934), 2; McCartney, *Land Ownership Patterns*, 295–296; Irene W. D. Hecht, "The Virginia Muster of 1624/5 as a Source for Demographic History," *WMQ*, 3d Ser., XXX (1973), 65–92; Martha McCartney, "An Early Census Reprised," *Quart. Bull. Arch. Soc. Virg.*, LIV (1999), 178–196; Virginia M. Meyer and John Frederick Dorman, eds., *Adventurers of Purse and Person: Virginia 1607–1624/5* (Richmond, Va., 1987). For a full account of the reinterpretation and re-excavation of this structure, see Audrey Horning and Karen B. Wehner, *Archaeological Investigations at Jamestown's Structure 24* (Williamsburg, Va., 2002). This case study also underscores the potential for examining individual households within Irish plantation settlements, an approach that has yet to be fully explored, notwithstanding the documentary aids to the identification of such households. The Jackson dwelling is known by its archaeological designation as Structure 24. The building, an ephemeral brick foundation, was apparently the first structure uncovered in the government-sponsored archaeological initiative of the 1930s. Unfortunately, the structure was never recorded in plan, artifacts were only casually retained, and only one photograph was taken. The only notes extant from the excavation of Structure 24, which commenced on December 1, 1934, were written in August 1936 by an anonymous author and state simply: "Only excavation here was by 'pot-holes.' A small foundation was exposed, but one photograph is only record. Even the exact location is now uncertain—since it has been backfilled" (Lot B–98, map form, August 1936, Colonial National Historic Park archives). In the 1950s, evidence for the structure was reviewed, and it was then associated with two newly uncovered features, Well 20 and Refuse Pit 5. According to John Cotter, Structure 24 "was an early 17th century feature of considerable significance" (Cotter, *Archaeological Excavations at Jamestown, Virginia*, National Park Service Archaeological Research Ser., no. 4 [Washington, D.C., 1958], 62).

tween the north and south ends of the house as marked by soil pH, calcium, and magnesium, underscoring the fact that the inhabitants used each bay in very different ways. Utility earthenwares were concentrated in the north bay near the hearth, whereas heightened soil potassium and phosphate levels on the outside rear of the north bay reflects the dumping of wood ash, food wastes, and other hearth refuse. Fragments of case bottle glass and decorative ceramics were clustered in the northeast corner of the house near a series of small, interior postholes, possibly associated with shelving or a cupboard. A spread of fragmentary dining wares and glass vessels were unearthed outside the house on the south side, possibly debris swept from the house following a domestic accident. Not surprisingly, tobacco pipe fragments were also concentrated near the hearth, attesting to time spent relaxing or mixing a smoke with a routine task such as casting lead shot. Despite serving as a workshop as well as a home, Jackson's residence seems to have been comfortably furnished on the interior. Fragments of plaster hint that at least some of the interior walls were finished. Findings of window glass suggest that at least one window boasted glass panes, which would have been diamond-shaped and fitted into lead quarrels. Brass curtain rings suggest that at least one window was trimmed with curtains, whereas copper furniture tacks and a brass key provide clues as to the movable furnishings.[67]

Other smithing items found in the house include a portion of an iron file; five musket fragments; raw materials for repairs, including copper alloy sheets; a copper finial; rolled brass and iron; and considerable amounts of lead shot, sprue, and gunflints. Smithing materials recovered from the associated well include a file, a crucible, scrap brass, lead shot, three pieces of flint, and two tinker's dams, suggesting that Jackson also engaged in more general smithing, such as minor repairs to cookware. Tools from two nearby refuse pits, probably filled when the property was abandoned, included a claw hammer, two files, a clamp, and a chisel. A spread of coal and slag in the soils northeast of the dwelling may pinpoint the former location of Jackson's forge. Forty-eight pieces of flint (including two nodules and a variety of flakes) were also found in the pits, suggestive of gunflint manufacture. Lead shot was recovered from the pits, as was another tinker's dam and a quantity of lead scrap, whereas an andiron and an iron wagon-tire might have been brought to Jackson for repairs he never completed. The presence of gunflints in the assemblages from the well, refuse pit, and house indicate that at least a portion of the guns Jackson repaired (and potentially pro-

67. Horning and Wehner, *Structure 24.*

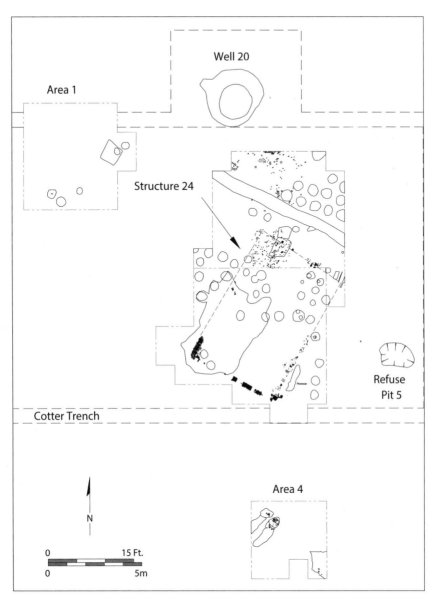

Figure 9. Location of 1998–1999 excavations at Structure 24. Courtesy of
the Colonial Williamsburg Foundation, Williamsburg, Va.

duced) employed flint in their firing mechanism. Although matchlocks were frequently employed in the early years of the colony, snaphances incorporating flintlocks became common in Virginia in the second quarter of the seventeenth century.[68]

Materials found at the Jackson house and its associated well and refuse pits also reflect the ways in which this colonial outpost was connected to the widening Atlantic and Asian commercial trade. Imported ceramics included a Dutch earthenware candlestick base, Spanish costrels and olive jars, Italian and Portuguese tablewares, Chinese porcelain, Rhenish Wanfried slipware, and Rhenish stoneware, alongside English earthenwares, locally produced earthenwares, and just four shell-tempered Native pottery sherds. Unlike the early fort wells, the Jackson well was not filled with abandoned, yet still functional, personal goods. Although two nearly whole, lead-glazed earthenware pitchers were discovered in the well, their presence suggests a clumsy water drawer rather than the desperate or cathartic clearance of a dead person's property. A total of 649 individual artifacts were excavated from the well, of which 242, or nearly 37 percent, were ceramic sherds. Of those, locally produced wares, including the two water pitchers, numbered 154, accounting for an overwhelming 63 percent of the ceramic assemblage. Similarities between these Jamestown earthenware vessels and those produced at Martin's Hundred by a potter identified as Thomas Ward link the two settlements. Accounting for the dominant presence of Ward's wares in the Jackson home is that fact that Ward served as an apprentice under the Martin's Hundred brickmaker John Jackson—a relative of Jamestown's John Jackson.[69]

The Jamestown Jacksons provided welcome shelter to the Martin's Hundred Jacksons in the wake of the 1622 attacks, when four indentured servants

68. Beverly A. Straube, "'Unfit for Any Moderne Service'? Arms and Armour from James Fort," *Post-Medieval Archaeology*, XL (2006), 54; Ivor Noël Hume, *A Guide to Artifacts of Colonial America* (New York, 1969), 213–214.

69. Field notes for Feb. 14, 1956, record, "After protracted heavy rains which flooded the well to the five foot level, a whole Spanish earthenware bottle with handles on opposite of neck, floated to the surface and was fished out by A. B. Moore." The well apparently remained in its flooded, half-excavated state for five more months, until July, when it was recognized that "much artifact material missed when the mud [which] was cleared in the first operations was recovered, including several pieces of shoe leather." Conditions were no better on the second attempt, described as "excavation of muck in Well 20." For the identification of Thomas Ward, see Martha W. McCartney, "The Martin's Hundred Potter: English North America's Earliest Known Master of His Trade," *Journal of Early Southern Decorative Arts*, XXI, no. 2 (Winter 1995), 139–150; and Beverly A. Straube, "The Colonial Potters of Tidewater Virginia," ibid., 1–40.

in the household at Martin's Hundred were killed. The Jacksons' hospitality extended beyond kinship, as Richard Frethorne, an apprentice or servant under Martin's Hundred leader William Harwood, wrote to his parents in England in 1623 and noted that the Jacksons, whom he viewed as surrogate parents, had constructed a "Cabbin" for Frethorne and his fellow servants to stay in during their visits to Jamestown; the alternative would have been to huddle overnight in their vessel. By 1624, the Jackson household had re-established itself at Martin's Hundred, with the muster of 1624 enumerating Jackson, his wife, Ann, a twenty-week-old child, and two servants, including the forty-seven-year-old potter Thomas Ward and thirty-five-year-old John Stephens. Another (unnamed) female child had died during the year. In contrast to the difficulties experienced by the Martin's Hundred family, Jamestown's John Jackson managed to establish himself quickly in Virginia society, serving as a churchwarden, an administrator for the estates of deceased neighbors, and, most notably, an assemblyman in 1632 and 1633. Jackson's ability to rise in Jamestown society was likely because of, rather than in spite of, his occupation as a gunsmith and his willingness to extend his craft activities into more general smithing. Although the lure of profit from tobacco led many craftsmen to abandon their trades—despite legislation to the contrary—and to take up small holdings outside of the fledgling town, artisans like Jackson who opted to ply their trades profited from being in demand.[70]

In Ireland, the centrality of townbuilding to the overall plantation project was similarly dependent upon the presence of artisans. Beyond the entrepreneurial activities of individuals such as Richard Boyle, who imported ironworkers and glassworkers, even the smallest plantation settlements needed artisans for basic supplies and repairs. Those employed by the Irish Society in the early years of the Ulster Plantation often faced an uphill battle, as the agents were often slow to pay their laborers, who were also expected to acquire and care for their own tools. Smiths in the Londonderry Plantation were not treated with the same respect that Jamestown's John Jackson enjoyed. Although dependent upon the work of smiths, the Irish Society insisted that "smiths be not trusted with iron and steel with above £10 at a time and that at such rates as the City be no losers and the same to be paid in money or work." In Moneymore, agent Robert Russell added the local

70. Horning and Wehner, *Structure 24;* Cary Carson et al., *Evaluation of Previous Archaeology* (Williamsburg, Va., 2006), 45–47; McCartney, *Documentary History of Jamestown Island,* III, 185–186; Kingsbury, ed., *Records of the Virginia Company of London,* IV, 58–60.

smithy to his extensive property portfolio, funded by the profits from his brewhouse and multiple drinking establishments. Insofar as Russell paid workmen and artisans in ale rather than in cash, it is easy to see how the smith might have been compelled to sell his shop. Even though the Irish plantations depended upon the labor of craftsmen just as much as their counterparts in Virginia, they did not go to any of the same lengths to attract or to retain artisans. Whereas planters lured craftsmen to the Chesapeake with promises of land and housing, their counterparts in Ireland knew that they could always turn to the Irish to provide labor if sufficient numbers of English or Scottish artisans were not available or were not deemed suitable.[71]

As was true of those who settled in the Chesapeake, many of the British artisans who relocated to Ulster Plantation settlements did hope to acquire land in addition to pursuing their crafts. The depositions taken in the wake of the 1641 Rising / Rebellion indicate that most artisans also engaged in some agricultural pursuits. Examination of Newtownbutler, Co. Fermanagh, reveals that the majority of craftspeople whose accounts were recorded in the depositions (including smiths, tanners, innkeepers, weavers, butchers, and shoemakers) also kept cattle. The importance of cattle to provide a supplemental income stream reflects both the influence of Irish practice and the traditional willingness of artisans to diversify their economic activities. In late medieval English towns such as York, artisans commonly kept livestock for extra revenue. Despite the efforts by Ulster's craftspeople, the opportunities seized and exploited by John Jackson simply were not available. Blacksmith Robert Barton testified that he was "robbed of and lost" his home and shop in Newtownbutler on October 25, 1641, when Irish forces under Rory Maguire attacked the town. Barton provided a value of £35 for his household goods, with a further £7 lost in smithing tools and raw materials. His material wealth places him at the lower end of the scale for tradesmen in England in the mid-seventeenth century, albeit in line with midcentury probate values in the Maryland colony. Although we have no corresponding probate data on Jackson, the archaeological record at his residence and documentary references suggest that Jackson's economic and social status was considerably higher than Barton's. In short, the society that developed in seventeenth-century Ulster adhered much more to a traditional model of class hierarchy than was the case in early Virginia. For Jackson, the demand

71. T. W. Moody and J. G. Simms, *The Bishopric of Derry and the Irish Society of London,* I, *1602–1670* (Dublin, 1968), 89.

Plate 23. Martin's Hundred 1630s homelot. Courtesy of
the Colonial Williamsburg Foundation

for his craft services combined with the colony's demographic instability
provided him with freedom from the social norms that constrained Ulster's
artisans.[72]

The experience of the Jackson family also stands out in comparison with
rural settlements along the James, further indicating that those artisans who
did choose to live in Jamestown profited both from their own rarity and
from their proximity to the town's amenities, however limited those might
have been. Archaeological evidence from a Martin's Hundred rural homelot of the second quarter of the century provides a sharp contrast to the
finds from the Jackson property at Jamestown. One of a series of outlying
homes built following the 1622 destruction of Wolstenholmetowne, the site
encompassed the postholes of a 4.87 by 7.31–meter earthfast, clay-walled
dwelling, matching the dimensions of the Jackson house. The Martin's Hundred house also possessed a lean-to addition, measuring 3.04 by 2.1 meters,
flanked by three refuse pits and a small yard enclosed by a paling fence.
No structural traces for ancillary outbuildings survived, although it is quite

72. Canny, *Making Ireland British,* 348–349; Heather Swanson, *Medieval Artisans: An Urban
Class in Late Medieval England* (Oxford, 1989), 6. Probate values employing measures suggested
by Horn, "Adapting to a New World," in Carr, Morgan, and Russo, eds., *Colonial Chesapeake
Society,* 133–175.

likely that rudimentary animal shelters and grain stores once existed on the site. Artifacts were scarce—mainly residing in the plow zone—and there was no window glass associated with the structure. The ceramics assemblage was dominated by coarse earthenwares, at 61 percent. By contrast, the ceramics assemblage from the Jackson home was comprised of only 26 percent coarse earthenwares. The remaining ceramics at the Martin's Hundred site, 22 percent tin-enameled wares and 17 percent stonewares, were represented by utilitarian storage forms rather than the more elite serving or dining vessels used at the Jackson home. Evidence for tobacco smoking was common to both sites. A total of sixty-six imported pipe bowls and pipestems and twenty-nine locally made pipestems were recovered at the Martin's Hundred lot, readily explained by the overwhelming reliance upon tobacco monocrop culture, even if the tobacco had been shipped across the Atlantic for processing and returned ready to smoke. The inhabitants of this house surely realized that their pipes bore a strong resemblance to those employed by local Native people, although they might not have appreciated—or, indeed, cared—that the design of their pipes was modeled upon those used by the Indians of the Albemarle Sound, copied by the Roanoke adventurers, and transformed by English craftsmen. By the 1620s, the Native practice of tobacco smoking had been first mimicked and then wholly transformed into an English activity with attendant new social meanings.[73]

Notwithstanding the Native derivation of the tobacco pipes that are ubiquitous on colonial Chesapeake sites, it is significant that excavations at these two sites of the 1620s did not unearth many recognizably Native items, unlike the early James Fort assemblages. The only Native-made objects were the scant four sherds of Native pottery from one of the refuse pits near the Jackson house and a single sherd of shell-tempered late Woodland pottery found in the plow zone at the Martin's Hundred homelot. This reflects the major changes in relations between the English and the Powhatan peoples after the 1622 attacks. No longer would Indians be such routine visitors to English homes. Planters separated themselves from the daily intercourse with Native people that had characterized the first fifteen years of colonial settlement. Colonists were no longer as dependent upon the Powhatans for subsistence and were intensely wary of reestablishing the cultural prox-

73. Andrew C. Edwards, *Archaeology of a Seventeenth-Century Houselot at Martin's Hundred, Virginia* (Williamsburg, Va., 2004); Edwards, "Inequality in Early Virginia: A Case Study from Martin's Hundred" (MA thesis, College of William and Mary, 1994); Dane T. Magoon, "Chesapeake Pipes and Uncritical Assumptions: A View from Northeastern North Carolina," *North Carolina Archaeology*, XLVIII (1999), 107–126.

imity that had provided cover to the Powhatan raiders. Both colonists and Native peoples began to avoid encounters. Documentary records provide scant hint of Powhatans in Jamestown beyond formal visitations such as the delivery of messages or, after 1646, tribute. No Native people are listed as members of Jamestown households on the 1624/5 muster. Sporadic laws as well as physical barriers restricted Native movement within the colony and, particularly, in the vicinity of the James River, as John Smith observed in 1629: "Upon this River they seldome see any Salvages." In that same year, the Assembly passed legislation that would allow for planned attacks on Native communities three times per year. Jamestown archaeological assemblages dating after the first quarter of the seventeenth century similarly reveal little material that can be easily attributed to Virginia Indians, although the material impact of the fur trade will have left little physical trace in terms of English consumption of furs. Native influences on colonial society were still significant, but their material traces became far more subtle.[74]

Similar to the rarity of Native goods at Martin's Hundred and post-1622 Jamestown, only five sherds of Native-made Roanoke simple-stamped pottery were found at a site on Neck of Land, just outside Jamestown, occupied by indentured servants of the Reverend Richard Buck and his family from c. 1630 to 1650. Excavation of a pre-1650 dwelling in Kicoughtan Parish, later to become the port of Hampton, uncovered a wide variety of European ceramics but not a single sherd of Native pottery. The same was true for a pre-1650 domestic site along College Creek, within the bounds of the present City of Williamsburg. In Jamestown itself, post-1622 assemblages from the townsite beyond the fort are notable for the almost complete absence of recognizably Native-made materials. Although the lack of excavated seventeenth-century sites in Ireland hampers comparisons, Irish-made Ulster coarse pottery has been found in planter assemblages from the second half of the seventeenth century, implying continuity in both material practice and cultural discourse; this is exemplified by the finds of Ulster coarse pottery and shoes made following Irish techniques from the settlement at

74. "The True Travels, Adventures, and Observations of Captaine John Smith . . . ," in Barbour, ed., *Complete Works,* III, 215–218; William Waller Hening, ed., *The Statutes at Large; Being a Collection of All the Laws of Virginia, from the First Session of the Legislature in the Year 1619,* 13 vols. (New York, 1809–1823), I, 141. The fur trade does leave a recognizable material signature in terms of the production of furs. Kill-off patterns, in particular, have been used as indicators of the impact of the fur trade on Native hunting practices. See Heather A. Lapham, "'Their Complement of Deer-Skins and Furs': Changing Patterns of White-Tailed Deer Exploitation in the Seventeenth-Century Southern Chesapeake and Virginia Hinterlands," in Blanton and King, eds., *Indian and European Contact in Context,* 172–192.

Salterstown. Given the comparative absence of Indian-made materials on the James River sites, the artifacts suggest very different attitudes to cultural relations in Ireland and Virginia. Similar strategies of avoidance were not practicable in Ireland, as Vincent Gookin overtly acknowledged in his complaint that his English neighbors adapted Irish practices in order to protect their plantation holdings.[75]

Back in Virginia, the new policy of avoidance went hand in hand with redoubled efforts to encourage self-sufficiency and to diversify manufacturing. Although John Jackson appears to have set himself up as an individual tradesman, other craft activity was associated with entrepreneurs, arguably none more active than Sir John Harvey. Harvey, who served as governor from 1630 to 1635 and again from 1637 to 1639, was one of the chief proponents of townbuilding and manufacturing at Jamestown, pushing through one of a series of acts designating Jamestown as sole port of entry for the colony. This act, passed in 1631 / 32, specified that

> every shipp ariuinge in this colony from England, or any other parts, shall, with the first winde and weather, sayle upp to the porte of James Citty and not to unlade any goods or breake any bulke before she shall cast anchor there, uppon payne that the captayne and mayster of the sayd shipp shall forfeite the sayd goods or the value thereof, and shall have and suffer one mounthes imprisonment.

Requiring all ships to break bulk at Jamestown was not only designed to account for the amount and variety of goods entering in the colony; it was also intended to concentrate stores and warehouses at the port, forcing colonists to journey to Jamestown to purchase goods as well as attend to legal matters.[76]

Enforcing the port act proved difficult, in part because of opposition from officials in England who feared disruptions in trade and who acted to

---

75. Seth William Mallios and Garrett Fesler, "Archaeological Excavations at 44JC568: The Reverend Richard Buck Site," unpublished archaeological report, Association for the Preservation of Virginia Antiquities, Richmond, Va., 1999, 50. The singular recovery of a nearly complete Colonoware pot of Afro-Caribbean origin from this site is a reminder of the complexity of cultural relations in the Virginia colony reflective of its broader Atlantic context and connections. For other comparative sites, see Andrew C. Edwards and Marley R. Brown, *Hampton University Archaeological Project: A Report on the Findings* (Williamsburg, Va., 1989); Edwards, *Archaeology at Port Anne: A Report on Site CL7, an Early 17th Century Colonial Site* (Williamsburg, Va., 1987). For the presence of Ulster coarse pottery on the Salters' Company settlement, see Miller, *Salterstown*, 438–471.

76. Riley and Hatch, *James Towne*, 23.

suspend the law in 1638, on the grounds that Jamestown did not have sufficient storage facilities. Irritated, Governor Harvey and the Privy Council refused to comply, asserting that Jamestown did indeed have more than adequate facilities as well as a growing population. According to Harvey, "there was not one foote of ground for half a mile together by the Rivers syde in James Towne but was taken up and undertaken to be built before yor Lords' order arrived commanding that until stores were built all men should be p'mitted to Land theire goods in such places as should be for theire owne conveniencye." Patents for a number of riverside lots issued to prominent merchants, including George Menefie, Richard Stephens, and John Chew, support Harvey's claim. After the revocation of the port act was made known, Harvey observed, "Wee found the undertakers generally disheartened by this Order." It was far easier for ship captains to patent land in the colony and avoid breaking bulk in the struggling port of Jamestown, where they would have to engage with middlemen.[77]

Comparison of the early plats for Jamestown with the site's archaeological base map reveals that, although John Harvey was correct regarding the land being bought up along the waterfront, there is no evidence for the extensive construction of warehouses and dwellings in response to Jamestown's designation as sole port of entry. Instead, there is evidence only for sporadic craft activity and clear traces of only two warehouses. One of these structures was probably built by the Kecoughtan planter-merchant William Parry in the late 1630s. Built into the riverbank and employing a brick foundation to support a long frame structure above, possibly of double pile construction, Parry's warehouse would have been impressive. Parry himself owned a lot measuring six by four poles (30.1 by 20.1 meters) in Jamestown, suggesting that he used his warehouse just for times when Jamestown was the only port of entry. Parry's property was bounded by that of another merchant, William Barker, who was involved in the fur trade with a range of Native peoples. However, no archaeological evidence has been found to indicate whether Barker developed his Jamestown lot. The second excavated warehouse appears to have combined residential with storage facilities. Built of brick and set back from the waterfront in the west end of town, this building measured 14 by 9.1 meters and might have been constructed as early as the late 1620s, continuing in use until it burned down in the 1640s. At that time, the property was owned by John White, a business associate

77. Bruce, *Economic History,* II, 533; "Virginia under Governor Harvey," *VMHB,* III (1895–1896), 30.

of the Jamestown merchant George Menefie, who owned lands in the east of New Towne. Menefie had begun his career at Jamestown as the official merchant for the corporation of James City while also operating a forge in New Towne. He later became engaged in the African slave trade.[78]

Two other waterfront structures, possibly warehouses, were unearthed in 1935 and 1955 respectively. All that remained of these features were two single lines of brick parallel to the riverfront, near John Jackson's property. These may date to the 1640s, when two Dutch brothers, Derrick and Arent Corstenstam, owned the same tract, but there is not enough evidence to prove this theory. No doubt other warehouse structures eroded into the James River, as the first excavated warehouse was partially exposed through such river erosion, and others might have gone undiscovered by virtue of their not being constructed in brick. The more ephemeral traces of wooden buildings, consisting of soil stains, were not always recognized during the early archaeological projects at Jamestown. Nevertheless, archaeological evidence—or rather the lack thereof—confirms John Harvey's worst fears. Regardless of crown disapproval, keeping Jamestown as sole port of entry was an insurmountable task. Increased settlement on the York River encouraged direct shipping on that waterway, across the peninsula from Jamestown. In addition, Jamestown's position as an entrepôt continued to be weakened by legislation permitting ships owned by colonists to sail directly to any port within the colony.[79]

Recognizing, like Virginia Company officials before him, that Jamestown and the colony could never become even marginally self-sufficient without the presence of numerous tradesmen and artisans, Governor Harvey empha-

---

78. The first warehouse in question, Structure 26, was excavated in 1935 and found to measure 16.15 by 4.87 meters. Anecdotal evidence for a second set of foundations below the water's edge, in the general vicinity where the building was later excavated, was recorded in 1927, possibly relating to a second bay for this warehouse and making it a double pile building similar to warehouses constructed in contemporary London. Unfortunately, artifacts from the site were not securely recorded in terms of context. Those associated in some way with the dwelling date generically to the entirety of the seventeenth century. William Parry patented his New Towne lot in 1638. Parry owned tracts of land on the Nansemond River and at Kecoughtan (Elizabeth City, later Hampton), likely his principal residence. See Cotter, *Archaeological Excavations,* 63–66; Carson et al., *Evaluation of Previous Archaeology,* 48–49; McCartney, *Documentary History of Jamestown Island,* III, 265. The second warehouse, Structure 163, was excavated by the Jamestown Rediscovery project. See Nicholas Luccketti and Beverly Straube, "1998 Interim Report on the APVA Excavations at Jamestown, Virginia" (Richmond, Va., 1999); Wehner, "Crafting Lives, Crafting Society," 455.

79. Carson et al., *Evaluation of Previous Archaeology,* 50–51; Cotter, *Archaeological Investigations,* 150; McCartney, *Documentary History of Jamestown Island,* III, 90.

sized to the Privy Council in 1631 Jamestown's need for shipwrights, smiths, carpenters, tanners, and other skilled workers, especially brickmakers and bricklayers. Harvey was aware that concentrating manufactures in the town would force colonists to patronize the settlement. By extension, building up Jamestown would enhance Harvey's own prestige as governor and make his job far more manageable. In 1633, to forestall artisans from turning away from their trades in order to plant tobacco, Harvey forbade brickmakers, carpenters, joiners, sawyers, and turners from agricultural pursuits. As an incentive, anyone who proposed to build sawmills would receive property at Jamestown. Harvey attempted to revive the moribund shipbuilding industry, reporting in 1632 that the industry was back on its feet with the establishment of a new sawmill. The 1635 experience of David DeVries, forced to sail a leaking ship from Jamestown to New Netherlands for repairs, points out the shallowness of Harvey's claim. Although boats were constructed throughout the colony to facilitate travel and communication, no facility dedicated to large-scale shipbuilding emerged despite continual efforts.[80]

Governor Harvey had also attempted to rebuild the ironworks begun by the Virginia Company at Falling Creek. In 1630, Harvey sent word to England of his intent to restart the industry, which had been devastated in 1622. Harvey included ore samples with his correspondence and apparently piqued the interest of London Company member Sir John Zouche, who, with his son John, relocated to Virginia from the family seat at Codnor Castle in Derbyshire. The Zouches invested heavily in reviving the ironworks, but it was unsuccessful. Yet ample precedent existed in Ireland for the establishment of iron smelting as a potentially lucrative colonial enterprise. The ironworking industry encouraged by Raleigh on his Munster lands has already been mentioned, whereas the abundant forest resources of Ulster spurred the development of ironworking as one of the more intensive industries attempted in the plantation. The practice of employing only English and continental European laborers on plantation ironworks, rather than local workers, might have led to the destruction of eleven furnaces by Irish rebels in the turmoil of 1641. The most significant challenge for ironmaking in Ireland was the finite nature of available woodland. By contrast, Virginia forests offered the vast quantities of timber required to fuel an iron industry. Iron manufacturing remained of interest to Virginia's colonial develop-

80. Hening, *Statutes at Large*, I, 208; David Peterson deVries, *Voyages from Holland to America, A.D. 1632 to 1644,* trans. Henry C. Murphy (New York, 1853), 108; Bruce, *Economic History,* II, 431–438.

ers throughout the century; for example, in 1658, the General Assembly attempted to prohibit the exportation of iron in an effort to see the materials employed in building projects within the colony. Such regulation served the interests of colonial planners, but not those seeking profits on exports. The 1658 law was repealed a year later, reenacted in 1662, repealed again in 1671, and reenacted in 1680. Not surprisingly, the enactment and reenactments of the law also correspond to two major building efforts in the colony: the Town Acts of 1662 and 1680.[81]

More generally, spatial analysis of artifact distributions suggests that the placement of craft activities at Jamestown was determined by the property holdings of speculators, dispersed haphazardly across the townsite. Examination of the spatial distribution of 9/64-inch tobacco pipestem bores, with a date range of 1580–1620, and 8/64-inch pipestem bores, with a date range of 1620 to 1650, revealed three discrete zones of pre-1650 development, all corresponding to manufacturing activities. The most intense concentration of early pipestems was located in the northwest portion of New Towne, corresponding to a number of industrial features including brick, tile, lime, and pottery kilns with associated borrow pits, a brewery and apothecary, bloomery furnace and ironworking area, possible ice storage pit, two dwellings, two wells, and a number of boundary ditches. Smaller concentrations of 8/64-inch pipestems and 9/64-inch bores were located on the far eastern portion of New Towne, close to Orchard Run, clustering around a brick and tile kiln, an associated pit, and a possible dwelling. The third concentration was noted along the Jamestown shoreline, in the vicinity of the aforementioned warehouse of William Parry, and a pottery kiln.[82]

The apparent independent nature of development at Jamestown is significant in that a properly planned new town should be expected to regulate the placement of odorous activities. Manufacturing activities within towns

81. The Zouches were also connected to the Ormond earldom in Ireland, insofar as Gearóid Óg Fitzgerald, son of the eighth earl of Kildare, married Elizabeth Zouche in 1503. Fitzgerald would become Lord Deputy of Ireland in 1513. See Diarmaid Ó Catháin, "Some Reflexes of Latin Learning and of the Renaissance in Ireland, c. 1450–c. 1600," in Jason Harris and Keith Sidwell, eds., *Making Ireland Roman: Irish Neo-Latin Writers and the Republic of Letters* (Cork, 2009), 27; Bruce, *Economic History*, II, 451–454; Eileen McCracken, "Charcoal-Burning Ironworks in Seventeenth and Eighteenth Century Ireland," *Ulster Journal of Archaeology*, 3d Ser., XX (1957), 125; Rynne, "Plantation-Period Ironworks," in Lyttleton and Rynne, eds., *Plantation Ireland*, 248–264; Martha W. McCartney, *Virginia Immigrants and Adventurers, 1607–1635: A Biographical Dictionary* (Baltimore, 2007), 777–778.

82. The brick and tile kiln is Structure 127, the pit is Feature 76, and the dwelling is Structure 126. On the shoreline, the buildings include the Structure 26 warehouse and the Structure 27 pottery kiln.

and villages are best situated on the outskirts of settlement, where the sights, sounds, and smells of manufacturing are least intrusive and where the incendiary nature of most industries present the least threat to the fabric of the town. Officials in English towns often tried to regulate the location of industries. As early as the fourteenth century, it became common for trades to be limited to certain streets within a town, accounting for the prevalence of street names such as Butcher Row or Fish Street. Archaeological evidence from Chester indicates that the late medieval tanyards there were placed outside of the town walls, whereas potters in the Hampshire town of Andover were ordered to move their kilns to the riverside in 1668 "and sufficiently tile them" because it was recognized "by sad experience" that the kilns had nearly burned the town down.[83]

Because efforts to create manufacturing in Jamestown were spearheaded by individuals, who were encouraged by official acts and proclamations, the industries were located on the entrepreneurs' properties rather than determined by a centrally managed plan. Any effort to regulate these nascent New World industries would have been counterproductive, given the great desire for industry coupled with the low rate of success. Although early colonial entrepreneurs also were—perhaps contrarily—often those most heavily involved in the tobacco trade, the major efforts to create manufacturing at Jamestown and in Virginia were carried out by these individuals, such as Governor John Harvey, long after tobacco had already emerged as Virginia's chief export product. Similarly, the implementation of town plans was often haphazard in the new towns of the Ulster Plantation. Archaeological evidence for tanning within Chichester's developing town at Belfast suggests that zoning of crafts was not a priority. In Coleraine in 1622, despite the 1615 banning of timber in favor of more fireproof stone and brick construction, the town boasted only eighteen stone houses alongside fifty-two timber dwellings. Even the guardhouses for Coleraine were constructed out of timber, compromising their defensive utility. In both lands, expediency took precedence over intention. The difference lay in the degree of oversight and the relative value of adhering to the plans. The economic value of Virginia as a periphery to Britain's core, providing raw materials like unprocessed tobacco, far outweighed the significance of establishing urban settlements

83. Mick Aston and James Bond, *The Landscape of Towns* (1976; Gloucester, 1987), 98; Peter Carrington, *Book of Chester* (London, 1994), 82; E. L. Jones and M. E. Falkus, "Urban Improvement and the English Economy in the Seventeenth and Eighteenth Centuries," in Peter Borsay, ed., *The Eighteenth-Century Town: A Reader in English Urban History, 1688–1820* (London, 1990), 123.

along recognized English models. By contrast, the many complaints about the failings of the Irish plantations, especially Ulster, reflected the significance placed upon urban settlements as a means of defense against the Irish as well as a locus for converting the Irish to English notions of civility. Sir Thomas Phillips's case against the London Companies emphasized the lack of successful urbanization on the individual proportions, contrasted against the town he built at Newtown Limavady, which he attempted to employ as a model of good practice.[84]

Illustrating the same reliance upon individual entrepreneurship as Phillips, two of the areas within Jamestown exhibiting archaeological evidence of early craft development are associated with Governor Harvey's actions. The property surrounding the brick and tile kiln and associated features in the eastern end of town near Orchard Run lay within a six-and-a-half-acre parcel of waterfront land Harvey patented in 1624. There, Harvey seems to have headed a brick and tile production center while he was governor. Harvey's presence in the manufacturing zone in the northwest portion of New Towne can be inferred through referencing properties on the north, west, and east, as Harvey's property—including a dwelling and orchard—was described in 1640 as adjoining the land "lately belonging to Sir George Yeardly." Yeardley owned a seven-and-a-quarter-acre parcel abutting on Back River, directly to the north of the manufacturing zone. The Glasshouse Point property, where George Sandys's attempts at making glass had so spectacularly failed in 1624, was also under Harvey's control as another speculative venture.[85]

One of the most obvious manufacturing features situated on Harvey's property was a rectangular, brick-footed frame structure; this measured 6.55 by 6.18 meters in the interior, with a tiled roof and a square-tiled ceramic floor thirty to sixty centimeters below grade, and three circular boiler furnaces clearly indicating a manufacturing, rather than domestic, function. The structure bears a close resemblance to a brewhouse depicted on Ralph Treswell's 1612 survey of a Clothworkers' Company property in London, which incorporated two very similar circular boiler ovens. The presence of

84. N. F. Brannon, "In Search of Old Belfast," in Ann Hamlin and Chris Lynn, eds., *Pieces of the Past: Archaeological Excavations by the Department of Environment for Northern Ireland, 1970–1986* (Belfast, 1988), 79–81; Ruairí Ó Baoill, "Archaeology of Post-Medieval Carrickfergus and Belfast," in Horning et al., eds., *Post-Medieval Archaeology of Ireland,* 91–116; Ó Baoill, "Urban Archaeology of Belfast," *Ulster Journal of Archaeology,* 3d Ser., LXV (2006), 8–19; Audrey Horning, "English Towns on the Periphery: Seventeenth-Century Town Development in Ulster and the Chesapeake," in Adrian Green and Roger Leech, eds., *Cities in the World, 1500–2000: Papers Given at the Conference of the Society for Post-Medieval Archaeology, April 2002* (Leeds, 2006).

85. McIlwaine, *Minutes,* 496–497; McCartney, *Land Ownership Patterns,* 109–110.

scrap copper, a portion of a copper kettle, lead pipe, and fragments of a lead cistern, coupled with mortar analysis indicating low temperature activity, further points to the use of the Jamestown building as a brewhouse. It also likely served as an apothecary, based on the recovery of sixty-nine fragments of apothecary jars. As noted above, the two activities were closely linked. The presence of an alembic and a large quantity of drug pots and jars recovered from the manufacturing structure, a nearby trash-filled clay borrow pit, and the cellar of an associated dwelling points towards the distilling of herbal remedies, an activity begun in the earliest years of the colony.[86]

In addition to the production of medicinal remedies, brewing remained one of the colony's essential operations. Although significant to the English diet in Ireland as well, the consumption of beer had taken on an element of necessity in Jamestown's unhealthy environment. The dangers of drinking Jamestown's notoriously brackish water continued to be a matter of concern. In 1623–1624, the Assembly recommended that all coming to the colony bring malt and brewing supplies in order to avoid having to consume Jamestown water, at least until seasoning (acclimation to the local disease environment) had occurred. Unfortunately, not all brewers were good at their trade. According to George Sandys, the "stinking beer" produced by a brewer named Dupper had "been the death of 200 persons." Regardless of the quality of the products, by 1625, there were two brewhouses in operation in the colony, and they had begun to make use of persimmons and Indian corn in addition to imported malt. Captain John Smith, in summarizing colonists' observations in 1629, again noted the presence of two brewhouses. As was the case in the Ulster Plantation, legislation was passed in 1620 to restrict production in Virginia to common brewers. The act was designed "for the represeinge of the odious . . . sinne of Drunkenesse," but it also assured that alcoholic beverages remained marketable commodities, as indicated by the statement that "noe person . . . shall at any tyme . . . brewe anie beere or ale, and sell the same againe in his or her house . . . unlesse it bee in Townes where there is noe Common Brewer." Whereas Jamestown managed to centralize some of the colony's brewing activities, in Ulster, corrup-

---

86. Cotter, *Archaeological Excavations,* 102–109; Horning and Edwards, *Archaeology in New Towne,* 129–138; Wehner, "Crafting Lives, Crafting Society," 414–417; Carson et al., *Evaluation of Previous Archaeology,* 88–91; John Schofield, *The London Surveys of Ralph Treswell* (London, 1987), 118–120. Instructions from the Virginia Company to Sir Francis Wyatt in 1621, for example, recommended "employing yo'r Apothecaries in distilling of hott waters out of yo'r Lees of beere and searching after mineral dyes, gummes, druggs and the like things," indicating that apothecaries were expected to engage in brewing (Kingsbury, ed., *Records of the Virginia Company of London,* III, 476).

tion was a prime determinant for the location and operation of brewhouses in the early years of the Londonderry Plantation. In addition to the activities of the Drapers' agent Robert Russell—who diverted his town's water supply to his own extensive brewing operation—the Irish Society's agent John Rowley, charged with overseeing the City's development at Coleraine, diverted production from Coleraine's official brewhouse to an unsanctioned establishment on his own holdings at Castle Roe. In Virginia, the establishment of common breweries not only aimed to control the sin of drunkenness but, more important, to encourage manufacturing and manufacturing centers in the colony by limiting individual production.[87]

Traces of other manufacturing efforts were situated near the brewery and apothecary, including a cluster of one circular and two rectangular kilns atop a pit filled with debris from metalworking. The pit contents indicated small-scale iron tool repair work, whereas the kilns saw use in the production of pottery as well as oyster-shell lime, bricks, and tile—all essential for constructing urban dwellings and businesses. In the midst of all of this noisy and smoky activity, Governor Harvey lived in a relatively modest brick-and-frame house where he enterained visiting dignitaries, given his 1632 complaint that there was "no other house but his for hospitality in James Island." Artifacts recovered from the excavation of this dwelling hint at Harvey's involvement in other manufacturing activities, as they included tenter-frame parts used in textile production as well as three crucible fragments, a piece of slag, and lead and copper scrap.[88]

Like Sir Thomas Phillips, Harvey was a determined, if unlikable, man whose dogged efforts to impose control over the colony's development earned him many enemies. By 1635, Harvey had fallen victim to the ill winds of political posturing, accused of being too supportive of Lord Baltimore's Roman Catholic colony of Maryland. He was also deemed monarchical in his leadership, violent in temperament, and too lenient on Indians. This last accusation stemmed from Harvey's role in implementing a 1632 statute to

87. George Sandys to Ferrar, Apr. 8, 1623, in Sainsbury, ed., *CSP*, I, 43; Bruce, *Economic History*, II, 211–212; House of Lords, "'An Act [Bill] for the Repressing of the Odious . . . Sinne of Drunkenesse . . . ,'" Feb. 14, 1620/1, in Kingsbury, ed., *Records of the Virginia Company of London*, III, 427–428. Agent Rowley also was accused of having "committed great havoc in the woods" by profiting from the timber trade in direct contravention of the rights of the Irish Society. See the king to Sir Arthur Chichester, Dec. 23, 1612, in Russell and Prendergast, eds., *CSPI of the Reign of James I*, IV, 311. See also Moody, *Londonderry Plantation, 1609–41*, 145–146; T. H. Mullin, *Coleraine in By-gone Centuries* (Coleraine, 1976), 61.

88. Governor Harvey to the Virginia Commissioners, May 27, 1632, in Sainsbury, ed., *CSP*, I, 151.

halt the regular raids on Powhatan villages and the indiscriminate killing of Native people that had been permitted since 1622. Now, action against Natives could only be taken if provoked. Considering the profits many colonists made in their raids upon Powhatan storehouses and crops, any action taken to limit such activities would be unpopular. Harvey was also instrumental in brokering a September 1632 peace treaty with the Pamunkey and Chickahominy, a mutual agreement to cease warfare. This was equally unpopular with many English, and Harvey was impeached and returned to England to plead his case. Reinstated in 1637, he lasted in office until December 1638, when he was replaced by Francis Wyatt, who finally arrived in the colony for his second term as governor in April 1640. Forced to sell all of his property to the government to pay off his debts, Harvey had returned to England by late 1641 and died by 1650. The archaeologically documented failure of the craft activities in the enclave zone following the governor's fall in fortune highlights the extent to which development in Jamestown and the colony was linked to individuals; it also highlights the difficulties in creating alternative commodities to tobacco.[89]

Harvey's struggle to develop Jamestown as the political and commercial center of the colony is also linked to the importance of the town in colonial ideology. Like the designers of the Ulster Plantation, he envisioned towns as key to the establishment of civic society and, critically, to the maintenance of royal power. Harvey's principal opponents in Virginia were the members of the elite mercantile class. Virginia's merchants and their London associates were, of course, opposed to any strengthening of royal, and by extension gubernatorial, control over their profitable activities. The mercantile focus upon the profits to be derived from Virginia's tobacco monocrop economy and its attendant scattered settlement pattern challenged the development of the civitas as an instrument of security and stability. In their struggle to develop and promote towns as the sociopolitical bedrock of their respective colonial societies, Sir John Harvey and Sir Thomas Phillips were kindred spirits.[90]

89. For consideration of relations with Powhatans under Harvey, see discussion in Gleach, *Powhatan's World,* 168–169. Sources on Harvey's time in office include "Virginia under Governor Harvey," *VMHB,* III (1895–1896), 21–34; "Declaration of Sir John Harvey," ibid., I (1893–1894), 425–430; "Virginia in 1635: The Deposing of Governor Harvey," ibid., VIII (1900–1901), 299–306; "Virginia in 1635: The Deposing of Governor Harvey (Continued)," ibid., 398–407; J. Mills Thornton III, "The Thrusting out of Governor Harvey: A Seventeenth-Century Rebellion," ibid., LXXVI (1968), 11–26.

90. Thornton, "Thrusting out of Governor Harvey," *VMHB,* LXXVI (1968), 11–26. For a useful consideration of Harvey's understanding of towns, see Paul Philip Musselwhite, "Towns

Any town aiming to fulfill Harvey's and Phillips's civic goals would also require a market. Phillips's Newtown Limavady included a designated market zone, but Harvey did not manage to establish one at Jamestown, nor did his successor, Francis Wyatt. When Wyatt's gubernatorial replacement, Sir William Berkeley, son of Virginia Company investor and recalcitrant Fermanagh planter Sir Maurice Berkeley, arrived in 1642, he was carrying instructions to create a market. It would take seven years. To be held every Wednesday and Saturday, Jamestown's market encompassed a large zone between Orchard Run and Sandy Bay, between the James and Back Rivers. Thirteen years after its establishment, it had apparently failed to establish itself as an integral function of the town: the act that had created it was repealed in 1664. A decision was then made to establish one market in each county, situated along an accessible waterway. Even this attempt failed to attract merchants, as two years later, another act labeled any one person who established a market, "whether the merchants shall willingly come for the sale," a public benefactor. In the Irish plantations also, markets often failed, even though Ireland possessed a superior communication network and a large number of towns. Although some markets thrived in the Ulster Plantation, such as those at Belfast and Londonderry, smaller ones did not always survive, as with the replacement of the Movanagher market with one at Kilrea. The intended, if not necessarily actual, presence of markets in the smaller company settlements is underscored by the depiction of market crosses on many of Thomas Raven's 1622 maps, including Newtown Limavady. How successful these efforts were in reality is open to question.[91]

Sir William Berkeley, whose tenure as governor stretched from 1642 until 1677 (with a hiatus during the Commonwealth), was aware of the challenges facing the creation and maintenance of towns and markets in Ireland. Berkeley acknowledged the failings of plantation in Ireland—possibly thinking of his own father's failed investment but more likely referencing the 1641 Rising/Rebellion—in discussing a Virginia land grant policy that promised title to anyone maintaining and defending a settlement for a period of five years:

> This wee did because every plantation being almost equally a frontier, if it were deserted would give easy approaches to the enemy, and no man will lay out his money and labour on that which he had not some hopes

91. Hening, ed., *Statutes at Large,* I, 362, 397; Bruce, *Economic History,* I, 391.

to injoy . . . if I mistake not there were divers notable men in England outed of their lands in Ireland, because in times of warre they kept not sufficient strength to defend them.

Later in the seventeenth century, close family members of his were involved in efforts to transform Ireland following the Cromwellian reconquest. His nephew Charles was created Baron Fitzhardinge of Berehaven Kerry and named baron of Rathdowne, Co. Wicklow, in 1663, a title that passed to his father, the governor's brother Charles, in 1665. Another brother, Sir John Berkeley, served as Lord Deputy of Ireland from 1670–1672.[92]

By the time that Sir William Berkeley took office as the Virginia governor, tobacco had clearly established itself as the colony's chief export and preoccupation. But, like Harvey before him, Governor Berkeley's primary economic aim was to identify additional agricultural commodities. Berkeley encouraged planters to experiment with other luxuries, such as silk production and viniculture, as well as more prosaic crops. A description published in 1649 hints at the extent of Berkeley's agricultural experimentation: "The Governour *Sir William,* caused half a bushel of Rice (which he had procured) to be sowen, and it prospered gallantly, and he had fifteen bushels of it, excellent good Rice, so that all these fifteen bushels will be sowen again this yeer. . . . The Governour in his new Orchard hath 15 hundred fruittrees, besides his Apricocks, Peaches, Mellicotons, Quinces, Wardens [winter pears], and such like fruits." Berkeley invested heavily in his botanic experimentations, intended in part to diversify the agricultural economy but also to signal his cosmopolitan identity as a man of science.[93]

Despite the stabilization of Virginia's economy and the spread of settlement, as in Ireland the 1640s were a period of instability and violence, marked by the Powhatans' final effort to stay the expansion of English settlements through an attack in April 1644. Between four hundred and five hundred colonists perished in the attack, which was focused upon English settlements on the periphery of the Virginia colony. Contemporary commentators attributed the timing of the assault to Native awareness of warfare within England: "Their great King was by some English Informed, that all was under the Sword in *England,* in their Native Countrey, and such

92. [Sir William Berkeley], "Petition to the Council for Foreign Plantations" (1662), in Warren M. Billings, ed., *The Papers of Sir William Berkeley, 1605–1677* (Richmond, Va., 2007), 171.

93. "A Perfect Description of Virginia . . ." (1649), in Peter Force, ed., *Tracts and Other Papers, Relating Principally to the Origin, Settlement, and Progress of the Colonies in North America from the Discovery of the Country to the Year 1776,* II (1844; rpt., Bowie, Md., 1999), 14.

divisions in our Land; That now was his time or never, to roote out all the *English.*" The attack was further timed to coincide with Maundy Thursday, during the holiest week in the Christian calendar and echoing the intentional Lenten timing of the 1622 violence.[94]

One of the outlying settlements attacked in 1644 was the Nansemond River holding of Daniel Gookin Jr. Whereas his father had given up on Virginia and returned to Munster, Daniel Jr. and his brother John were evidently determined to make something of the Virginia grants that were their inheritance. Daniel Gookin Jr. took up the patent for the Nansemond River lands, in today's Suffolk County, using headrights granted to his father. As commander of the militia for Upper / Lower Norfolk (appointed 1641), Gookin might have overseen construction of an extensive enclosure that incorporated a four-sided, asymmetrical timber palisade 70.1 meters in length, defended by corner bastions, and protecting two dwellings and outbuildings within the circumference. This fortification was most likely constructed during the 1640s to replace an earlier palisade. The physical similarities between the Nansemond Fort and an Irish bawn are inescapable. Although both forms derive from more general Renaissance fortification styles, the decision to construct a bawnlike defense at the confluence of the James and Nansemond Rivers—when most Chesapeake settlements did not rely upon formal defensive enclosures (despite official encouragement)—is clearly suggestive of Gookin's own agency and Munster experience. The Nansemond defenses, which relied on two round bastions providing cover for marksmen employing small arms, were designed to repel attacks by Native warriors rather than to defend against other Europeans through the use of heavy ordnance. The plan echoes that employed at the Cork castle of Carrigaline, where Gookin spent part of his childhood. There is little specific information as to Gookin's relations with the Powhatans beyond a report given by his brother John to the court at Jamestown about "certayne Outrages and Robberyes committed by the Indians belonging to the Nanzemond," for which Daniel, as commander, was authorized to approach the Nansemond chief, for return of the stolen items and to apprehend the culprits.[95]

94. Robert Beverley states that "near Five Hundred Christians" were killed, whereas the General Assembly recorded "near four hundred" killed. See Beverley, *The History and Present State of Virginia: A New Edition with an Introduction by Susan Scott Parrish* (Chapel Hill, N.C., 2013), 46; Gleach, *Powhatan's World*, 174–176, esp. 175; J. Franklin Jameson, ed., *The Wonder-Working Providence, 1628–1651* (New York, 1910), 265–267.

95. Meyer and Dorman, eds., *Adventurers of Purse and Person*, 100–101; Martha W. McCartney, *Virginia Immigrants and Adventurers, 1607–1635: A Biographical Dictionary* (Baltimore, 2007),

Gookin's later life provides clues to the manner in which he might have dealt with the Nansemond Indians. A committed Puritan, Daniel Jr. left the Virginia colony before the attacks of 1644, first settling in Maryland in 1643 and then in the Massachusetts colony by 1644; his brother John died in Virginia at age thirty in 1643. Gookin Jr. lived out his days in Massachusetts, earning fame for his missionary work among the "Praying Indians" alongside the Reverend John Eliot (transcriber of the Bible into Algonquian and founder of the Praying Town at Natick) and for serving as major general of the Massachusetts Bay colony. He continued to maintain trade relations with the Chesapeake region and retained his Virginia lands. In Massachusetts, Gookin concentrated his efforts on converting and containing Massachusetts's Natives, applying lessons first learned at Marie's Mount and then on the Nansemond River. While Gookin balanced religious conversion with military might, his first cousin Vincent Gookin Jr. was engaged in a prolonged war of words over the issue of the transplantation of Irish natives to Connaught in retribution for the 1641 Rising/Rebellion. In sharp contrast to his father, who espoused a deep-seated hatred for the Irish, Vincent Jr. opposed efforts to divide communities of Irish from settlers. He was of the opinion that the transplantation of the native Irish was more likely to create a unity in opposition, whereas returning to the pre-Rebellion model of co-habitation would ensure stability.[96]

332–333; Pecoraro, "'Of Chusinge and Takinge Some Place of Advantage,'" 24; Gookin, *Daniel Gookin*, 60. Nicholas M. Luccketti reports on the site in "Nansemond Pallizado and Virginia Palisade Fortifications," in Eric Klingelhofer, ed., *First Forts: Essays on the Archaeology of Protocolonial Fortifications* (Leiden, 2010), 85–104. Charles T. Hodges explores the defensive capabilities of early Chesapeake fortifications in "Private Fortifications in 17th-Century Virginia: A Study of Six Representative Works," in Theodore R. Reinhart and Dennis J. Pogue, eds., *The Archaeology of 17th-Century Virginia,* Archaeological Society of Virginia Special Publication no. 30 (Richmond, Va., 1993), with a focus on the Nansemond (Harbor View) Fort on 199–202 and 209–211; and in Hodges, "Forts of the Chieftains: A Study of Vernacular, Classical, and Renaissance Influence on Defensible Town and Villa Plans in 17th-Century Virginia" (MA thesis, College of William and Mary, 2003).

96. Gookin, *Daniel Gookin,* 58; Barnard, "Crises of Identity," *Past and Present,* no. 127 (May 1990), 62; Alden T. Vaughan, "'Expulsion of the Salvages': English Policy and the Virginia Massacre of 1622," *WMQ,* 3d Ser., XXXV (1978), 85; Pecoraro, "'Of Chusinge and Takinge Some Place of Advantage,'" 25. The Nansemond territory was home to a sizable community of Puritans, many of whom had been brought to the colony by brothers Richard and Philip Bennett. These Virginia Puritans found themselves unwelcome in Royalist Virginia during the 1640s and 1650s, and many relocated to Maryland to take advantage of the Maryland colony's policy of religious toleration, codified in 1648. For further discussion, see Kevin Butterfield, "Puritans and Religious Strife in the Early Chesapeake," *VMHB,* CIX (2001), 5–36. Gookin settled on Pequot lands, served as Superintendent of the Praying Indians, and eventually produced two

Both the Gookin cousins were characterized by their enemies as traitors to Britain, with Vincent Jr. caricatured as a "teagish person" and Daniel Jr. criticized for being too lenient on the New England Natives. Although the extent of their personal relationship is unclear, they shared philosophies in ensuring control over, respectively, the Irish and the Indians. Vincent Gookin Jr.'s arguments against transplantation in favor of cohabitation were founded upon a belief that familiarity and immersion within modes of English civil society would succeed in converting the Irish to Protestant Christianity and accommodation to English-style political rule. His cousin Daniel advocated the same policy for New England's Natives, suggesting that English and Indians should "cohabit together, without which neither religion nor civility can prosper." Daniel Jr. expressly cast his arguments in comparison with the situation in Ireland, suggesting that, if the strategy of cohabitation "had been effectually taken with the Irish, their enmity and rebellion against the English had been long since cured or prevented, and they better instructed in the Protestant religion." There is a remarkable similarity between the writings of both junior Gookin cousins, owing to their Irish upbringing and, more than likely, personal discourse as adults.[97]

Like New England's Native people, Virginia Indians found themselves subjected to conversion and containment during the latter part of the seventeenth century. In the aftermath of 1644, the colonial government authorized a number of raids and forbade trade with the Powhatans. Sporadic violence continued over the next two years, particularly targeting the Chickahominies, Pamunkeys, and groups south of the James River, including the Nansemonds. The capture and subsequent murder of the now-elderly Opechancanough ended the conflict. A new Powhatan leader, Necotowance, reluctantly signed a treaty with Berkeley on October 5, 1646, ceding territory and establishing terms for yearly tribute, a practice still symbolically followed by the Pamunkeys and the Mattaponis today. After 1646, the Powhatan chiefdom ceased to exist as a political entity, with no further mention of

works often labeled proto-ethnographies; see Gookin, "Historical Collections of the Indians in New England" (Boston, 1792); and "An Historical Account of the Doings and Sufferings of the Christian Indians in New England . . ." (Cambridge, Mass., 1677).

97. See especially the comparisons made by Patricia Coughlan, "Counter-Currents in Colonial Discourse: The Political Thought of Vincent and Daniel Gookin," in Jane H. Ohlmeyer, ed., *Political Thought in Seventeenth-Century Ireland: Kingdom or Colony* (Cambridge, 2000), 56–82. For in-depth consideration of Vincent Gookin Jr.'s perspective on transplantation and civil society, see Barnard, "Crises of Identity," *Past and Present,* no. 127 (May 1990). For quotes from Daniel Gookin Jr., see his "Historical Collections of the Indians in New England," 179, 222.

Necotowance in the documentary record. However, the disintegration of the chiefdom should not be seen as the diminution of Native identity nor of the power and organization of individual polities, most of which had been forced to become part of the paramount chiefdom. Factionalism among the Powhatan-related groups was common even at the height of Wahunsena-cawh's power in 1607. Despite the waning of the chiefdom, the colonial government viewed the subdued Powhatans as an integral part of the colony itself, insofar as they could be employed as a buffer against the incursions of other Native groups.[98]

Cultural Relations

Although the violent resolution of the 1644 conflict severely damaged Powhatan infrastructure and ability to resist English encroachment, in no way did it end Native presence and influences in Virginia. Whatever the realities of early colonial relations, the archaeological record from later seventeenth-century sites continues to demonstrate that, far from being wiped out by disease or absorbed through acculturation, Native people in the post-1644 Chesapeake maintained their presence and cultural identities. As hinted at by the dearth of Native ceramics in post-1622 English assemblages, the hardening of attitudes encouraged separation of residences. More subtle material influence continued, as indicated by the English absorption of Powhatan crops and spatial geography, but daily interactions were constrained by conflict and its memory.[99]

Although Indians, English, and Africans engaged in material, linguistic and conceptual exchanges, as exemplified by archaeological assemblages mixing together Native materials, European imports, and Afro-Caribbean ceramics, this should not be read as evidence for loss of identity. Artifacts are complicated, and objects carry a multiplicity of often contradictory meanings for both the users and observers. New forms of behavior and material culture can simultaneously challenge and reify ethnic and cultural boundaries, as exemplified by one of the Chesapeake's most iconic artifacts: the

98. Gleach, *Powhatan's World*, 174–176, 184–192; Helen C. Rountree, "The Powhatans and the English: A Case of Multiple Conflicting Agendas," in Rountree, ed., *Powhatan Foreign Relations, 1500–1722* (Charlottesville, Va., 1993), 192–197; Martha W. McCartney, "Cockacoeske, Queen of Pamunkey: Diplomat and Suzeraine," in Peter H. Wood, Gregory A. Waselkov, and M. Thomas Hatley, eds., *Powhatan's Mantle: Indians in the Colonial Southeast* (Lincoln, Neb., 1989), 173–195.

99. See, for example, L. Daniel Mouer, "Chesapeake Creoles: The Creation of Folk Culture in Colonial Virginia," in Reinhart and Pogue, eds., *Archaeology of 17th Century Virginia*, 105–166.

Plate 24. Colonoware tobacco pipe from Rich Neck Plantation. Photograph by the author, courtesy of Kelly Ladd-Kostro, Colonial Williamsburg Foundation

Colonoware tobacco pipe. Made of local terra-cotta clay and often incised with a five-pointed star motif, these pipes are ubiquitous on seventeenth-century Chesapeake sites and were smoked by individuals from a cross section of the Chesapeake's multiethnic population. The object was common, and its shared use linked together individuals in a routine practice. At the same time, the act of smoking and particularly the symbolism of the star could hold very different meanings dependent upon religious and cosmological beliefs and practices. Such an object, on one level, was a piece of material culture connected to a communal practice; yet disparate understandings of the motif as well as the significance of the act of smoking itself strengthened cultural boundaries as much as the familiarity of the pipe and the practice transcended them.[100]

In short, material influences travel in multiple directions but do not necessarily presage a change in identity. English people did not become Native through incorporation of maize, and Native people did not become English through incorporation of English materials, practices, or livestock. An apt illustration of this simple point can be found in the excavated evidence

100. See Kathryn Sikes, "Stars as Social Space? Contextualizing 17th-Century Chesapeake Star-Motif Pipes," *Post-Medieval Archaeology*, XLII (2008), 94. In presenting evidence for the disparate understandings of stars and the night sky held by the Europeans, Africans, and Indians who smoked tobacco through these pipes, Sikes suggests that the multivalency in the perceived meanings of the star "enabled communication" in social situations, "facilitating dialogues of both collaboration and dissent across ethnic boundaries."

from the Buck Farm site, located along the Chickahominy River. In the late 1960s, this late Woodland palisaded site was unearthed, which also exhibited evidence for colonial-era use. Buck Farm is notable for the presence of up to eleven animal interments, all presumed to be ritual. Such burials, generally of dogs, have also been found at Native sites throughout eastern North America and at three other sites in the Chickahominy River region. These animal burials are associated with sites linked to communal activities, including locales with evidence for feasting and for ossuaries containing human remains. At the Buck Farm site, reanalysis of the faunal materials revealed that three of the animal burials were of pigs rather than dogs as originally interpreted. These pig burials postdate the destruction of the palisade at the site but hint at the continuing significance of the locale for a Native community. Pigs were introduced by Europeans but substituted for dogs in the ceremonial activity at the Buck Farm site. In other words, Native people (probably the Chickahominies) incorporated new livestock into their cultural repertoire. The keeping of pigs, then, does not connote acculturation—only cultural dynamism.[101]

In another example, the Posey site in Charles County, Maryland, appears to have been occupied by Mattawoman Indians from the precontact period through the end of the seventeenth century. Adoption of European materials was selective, as reflected in the artifact assemblage. Although a single iron knife was incorporated, the lithic assemblage implies continuity in the use of stone-cutting implements. As also seen at the seventeenth-century Cape Creek site on Hatteras Island, European copper objects were refashioned into projectile points and ornaments, according to a traditional material grammar. Faunal remains were almost entirely from wild species, with the exception of a single pig, represented only by five tooth fragments, which might indicate an unknown, but nondietary, use. Comparisons of the faunal assemblage from Posey with three precontact Maryland Algonquian sites revealed few differences, suggesting continuity of foodways. Although some European ceramics were present at the Posey site, these items were in-

101. State designation is 44CC37. For discussion of the Buck Farm animal burials, see Jennifer Fitzgerald, "Late Woodland Dog Ceremonialism on the Chickahominy and Beyond," *Journal of Middle Atlantic Archaeology*, XXV (2009), 105–110; and Christopher Shephard, "A Late Woodland Protohistoric Compound on the Chickahominy River: Multiscalar Investigations of the Buck Farm Site," ibid., 111–117. Radiocarbon dating was equivocal. One burial was tested, yielding a calibrated date of 110+−40 BP (Beta 249895), with a two-sigma calibrated range of AD 1670–1960.

corporated into and used as part of a Native culinary and storage repertoire alongside the Native-made Potomac Creek and Yaocomico vessels whose broken remains accounted for 85 percent of the total ceramic assemblage.[102]

Evidence from the Camden site in Caroline County, Virginia, a portion of a Native Nanzatico or Portobago settlement occupied between 1650 and 1700, similarly underscores the selective nature of the incorporation of new practices and objects. The single structure excavated at the site outwardly followed the design of the colonial "Virginia house," but the inside of the home featured an open fire in the center of the floor. Furthermore, the material culture associated with the site was dominated by recognizably Native materials. For example, 93 percent of the ceramics were of local, Native-made Potomac Creek ware, suggesting at the very least a continuity in culinary practices. European glass was present on the site but, in one case, had been fashioned into a projectile point.[103]

Such dominance of Native material culture at the Posey and Camden sites, when locally made and European style wares were available, must be seen as significant and reflective of a conscious choice on the part of the Nanzaticos at Camden and the Mattawomans at Posey. Like the Croatans at Cape Creek, the Mattawomans might have been operating as traders, insofar as they were situated on the periphery of the Maryland settlement. By contrast, the Camden inhabitants, closer to English settlement, might have been more concerned about presenting the outward illusion of conformity. The adoption of an English-style house does not mean that the Indian inhabitants conceived of or used the space in the same ways as an English settler, just as the use of the Gaelic house by the Movanagher planters does not presume the adoption of Gaelic understandings of dwelling spaces.[104]

102. Julia King and Dennis Curry, "'Forced to Fall to Making of Bows and Arrows': The Material Conditions of Indian Life in the Chesapeake, 1660–1710," 17, paper presented at the Omohundro Institute of Early American History and Culture conference "The Early Chesapeake: Reflecting Back, Projecting Forward," St. Mary's City, Maryland, Nov. 20, 2009. Laura J. Galke, "Perspectives on the Use of European Material Culture at Two Mid- to Late 17th-Century Native American Sites in the Chesapeake," *North American Archaeologist*, XXV (2004), 104, states 79 percent.

103. Mary Ellen N. Hodges and E. Randolph Turner III, "Historic Contact at Camden NHL," *CRM*, XVIII (1995), 25–28, describe the site as Nanzatico, whereas King and Curry attribute it to the Portobagos in "'Forced to Fall to Making of Bows and Arrows,'" 11, 17, 23; Howard MacCord, "Camden: A Postcontact Indian Site in Caroline County," *Quart. Bull. Arch. Soc. Virg.*, XXIV (1969), 1–55; Galke, "Perspectives on the Use of European Material Culture," *North American Archaeologist*, XXV (2004), 103. Galke gives 89 percent (104).

104. As argued by Galke, "Perspectives on the Use of European Material Culture," *North American Archaeologist*, XXV (2004), 91–113.

While in Ireland, English and Scots planters readily adapted Irish forms of housing; in the Chesapeake, the dominant colonial form of housing relied upon earthfast timber construction attributed to a minority medieval tradition. The seventeenth-century earthfast "Virginia house," as it has become known, is characterized by the use of hole-set timber posts, with the timber superstructure covered either in wattle and daub or riven wooden clapboards, and chimneys, more often than not, expediently built of timber and earth. The form is clearly rooted in medieval English architectural traditions but was uncommon in early-seventeenth-century England. Given the readiness of English planters in Ireland to adapt unfamiliar dwellings, Powhatan influence on colonial Virginian architecture should not be discounted. Powhatan techniques also relied upon earthfast construction, albeit to secure frameworks of bent saplings rather than load-bearing posts, and presented another in a range of possible construction choices for English settlers. Although the inhabitants of James Fort elected to build some timber houses employing the standard, ground-laid, timber sills of early-seventeenth-century England—such as the row of adjoining buildings referenced earlier—they also constructed earthfast buildings. Several of these referenced a localized Lincolnshire earthfast tradition known as "mud and stud." Perhaps they elected to build earthfast houses not just because such buildings were expedient and vaguely familiar to some but because they might have been led to that choice by the presence of Native examples. In other elements of daily life, such as foodways, the English in Virginia showed themselves willing to selectively adapt new practices. If the earthfast Virginia house was as ubiquitous as the archaeological record implies, then it was being occupied by individuals from varying cultural backgrounds, including the Natives at Camden and the increasing numbers of indentured and, later, enslaved Africans. What was gained by sharing this form? Like the Chesapeake tobacco pipe, perhaps the Virginia house allowed for a point of convergence between the disparate groups who formed Virginia society. Its earthfast construction and clay daub walling echoed Indian, English, Scottish, Irish, and a range of African traditions, perhaps providing a physical link to remembered pasts while signifying a connection—be it willing or not—with the present.[105]

105. Cary Carson et al., "Impermanent Architecture in the Southern American Colonies," *Winterthur Portfolio*, XVI (1981), 135–196; Graham et al., "Adaptation and Innovation," *WMQ*, 3d Ser., LXIV (2007), 451–522. Although the seeming lack of investment in permanent (read: masonry) architecture may reflect the volatility of the tobacco economy and the stress of high mortality rates, the archaeological identification of an increasing number of brick-built dwell-

Conclusion

By 1650, colonial settlements in the Chesapeake had achieved a level of stability that would not be matched in Ireland until the close of the seventeenth century. The continual arrival of new British settlers alongside an increasing stream of African and African-Caribbean laborers augmented the growing numbers of whites born in the colonies. Although the colonies were far from immune to the disruptions of the War of the Three Kingdoms, neither Virginia nor Maryland served as a battleground in that conflict. Still too dependent upon England for trade, defense, and immigrants, colonial elites steered a careful course. Even a committed Royalist like William Berkeley was unwilling to risk warfare, permitting Virginia to surrender peaceably to Commonwealth forces in March 1652. Political institutions established in Virginia during the 1620s continued to operate, in sharp contrast to the complete disintegration of the delicate balance once struck between the Irish, Old English, and New English elites that allowed plantation society to function during the first three decades of the seventeenth century. The firm establishment of colonies in the American northeast had provided further stability through the development of intercolonial trade and, less tangibly but no less important, by normalizing awareness of the British New World colonies in the Old World. Although the Algonquian-speaking inhabitants of the region continued to outnumber colonists in both Virginia and Maryland, there was no chance that the incomers could be forced out. Powhatan resistance had been quashed by 1646. The English remained dependent upon trade with other Native groups—especially the fur trade

---

ings and a refinement of notions of permanence have considerably complicated this economic interpretation. See, for example, David A. Brown, "Domestic Masonry Architecture in 17th-Century Virginia," *Northeast Historical Archaeology,* XXVII (1998), 85–120. The most recent article on earthfast building in the Chesapeake, published in 2007 by architectural historians Willie Graham and Carl Lounsbury, historians Carter Hudgins and James Whittenburg, and archaeologist Fraser Neiman, focused entirely upon the meaning of and English precursors for earthfast architecture in the Chesapeake. The authors discount any potential Native influence on Chesapeake society and its architecture in the seventeenth century in one short sentence: "During this period English and African settlement encompassed the entire coastal plain, displacing the region's native peoples." In reality, the Coastal Plain was not emptied of its Native inhabitants, making it counterfactual to presume that all material impact was unidirectional (Graham et al., "Adaptation and Innovation," 4). For consideration of the use of mud and stud buildings at Jamestown, see J. Eric Deetz, "'For When Our Houses Were Builded of Willow, Then We Had Oaken Men': Early Architecture at James Fort," paper presented at the Society for Historical Archaeology Conference, January 2002. It should also be noted that some English commentators directly compared Irish house forms with those of the New World; given English willingness to inhabit Irish houses in Ireland, we should not assume any aversion to adapting Powhatan dwellings in Virginia on the basis of form.

brokered by groups along the Potomac—but such trade was increasingly on colonial terms, as many Native groups shifted their own residences to avoid encroaching colonial settlements.[106]

That English settlement in the Chesapeake could surpass plantation Ireland in terms of social and political stability by midcentury would have been inconceivable to anyone suffering through the Starving Time. As vividly attested by the extensive clearance deposits of early James Fort—where expensive and meaningful personal belongings were tipped away into the brackish depths of hand-dug wells—the first colonists had lost faith in their own survival and, by extension, that of the colonizing mission itself. The reliance upon the Powhatans' largesse, materially marked by the Native-made ceramics that dominate the early deposits, increased anxiety but also impressed upon the survivors the need to accommodate themselves to Native people and practices. The familiarity that characterized these early relations eventually helped to provide cover for the attacks of 1622, when Powhatan frustration at the expansion of English settlement associated with the introduction of the headright system boiled over into warfare. After 1622, relations changed drastically. Efforts at diplomacy, conversion, and accommodation were replaced by antagonism, punishment, and avoidance, reflected in the archaeological record by a precipitous drop in the presence of Native-made goods in colonial assemblages and redoubled efforts by leaders like John Harvey to impose the development of towns as emblems of civil English society.

From the very beginning of English expansion, the experiences of Ulster and the Chesapeake were dissimilar, each the product of unique demographic, environmental, economic, political, and religious conditions and concerns. Ulster was not a model for early Jamestown, which itself did not even capitalize upon the lessons of Roanoke. The societies that developed in Ulster and the Chesapeake, and indeed other colonial zones, were products of the locally situated cultural entanglements between natives and newcomers. As graphically illustrated by the archaeological record from James Fort—and, more subtly, by those of Camden and Posey, as well as the ubiquitous adoption of the Virginia house from 1607 onward—the relationship

---

106. For consideration of the position of Virginia and Maryland during the period of the War of the Three Kingdoms, see Carla Gardina Pestana, *The English Atlantic in an Age of Revolution, 1640–1661* (Cambridge, Mass., 2004). As noted by Pestana, there were some small-scale outbreaks of violence attributable to Parliamentarian versus Royalist feeling in the Chesapeake, most notably Ingle's "Rebellion" in Maryland during the period 1645–1646. See ibid., 116, for a description of Berkeley's surrender to Parliamentarian forces.

between the Powhatan peoples and the English was paramount but never wholly predictable in its outcome, ever dependent upon individual actions, perceptions, decisions, and (more often than not) miscommunications. Despite displacement, disease, violence, subjugation, and ongoing prejudice, Native peoples in the wider Chesapeake region endeavored to maintain individual and community identities throughout the seventeenth century, and some into the present. Yet injecting their stories and contributions back into the narrative of early colonial Virginia is a task as challenging as that of acknowledging the material influence of Gaelic society on plantation-era Ireland.[107]

107. Consider the comments of Chief Stephen R. Adkins in his Senate testimony arguing for federal recognition for the Chickahominies: "I often say this country is here today because of the kindness and hospitality of my forebears who helped the English Colonists at Jamestown gain a foothold in a strange and new environment. But what do you know or what does mainstream America know about what happened in those years between the 17th century and today. The fact that we were so prominent in early history and then so callously denied our Indian heritage is the story that most don't want to remember or recognize." See Thomasina Jordan, Indian Tribes of Virginia Federal Recognition Act: Hearing on S. 480, *Before the Committee on Indian Affairs,* 109th Cong. 101–103 (2006) (statement of Stephen R. Adkins, Chief, Chickahominy Indian Tribe).

Convergence and Divergence
Ireland and America

Fynes Moryson was both correct and incorrect in situating Ireland in the Virginian Sea. He knew that his readership would be familiar, and perhaps even directly involved, in New World expansion. As the quintessential traveler, known for his chronicles of Turkey, Bohemia, Poland, and Germany, Moryson might have longed to cross the Virginian Sea himself. Had he done so, he surely would have revised his understanding of the links between the two lands. The relationship between English (and, later, British) expansion into Ireland and across the Atlantic in the sixteenth and seventeenth centuries was not one of model and mirror, despite the significant connections between individuals engaged in both ventures.

Ireland during the sixteenth century was not an unknown land to the English but rather a focus for religious, political, and economic reform. In 1599, Francis Bacon clearly distinguished English activities in Ireland from those of the New World when he described the Irish conflict as "no ambitious war against foreigners, but a recovery of subjects," even as he was concerned to elevate the Irish from "more than Indian barbarism." At the same time, the fact that the attempted implementation of such reforms in the Kingdom of Ireland was informed by colonial philosophies derived from the Renaissance fascination with the Roman Empire does validate the use of colonialism as a theoretical framework for understanding the character of relations between people on the ground. However, this does not mean that Ireland was itself a colony or that it was necessarily a field for colonial experimentation to aid in Atlantic expansion. Furthermore, as addressed in Chapters 1 and 2, the Roanoke efforts were less influenced by, and more formative for, the Irish endeavors of protagonists such as Ralph Lane, Thomas Hariot, John White, and Walter Raleigh. The principal period of each of those individuals' involvement in Ireland postdated the failed Roanoke colonies of the 1580s. Lane, in particular, expressed little desire to return to the New

World, finding that Ireland's familiar terrain, coupled with his understanding of Scots and Irish military tactics, was a better field upon which he could demonstrate his talents and loyalty to Queen Elizabeth.[1]

Hariot's writings and White's illustrations clearly influenced later English efforts in the New World, as considered in Chapters 2 and 4, and informed the Jamestown colonists' expectations as well as provided a context for comparisons drawn by the English in Ireland. As an example, the commander of English forces during the Nine Years' War, Lord Mountjoy, caged his plans for Irish plantation in terms that referenced New World Natives: "Because the Irish and English-Irish were obstinate in Popish superstition, great care was thought fit to be taken that these new colonies should consist of such men as were unlike to fall to the barbarous customs of the Irish, or the Popish superstition of Irish and English-Irish, so as no less cautions were to be observed for uniting them and keeping them from mixing with each other than if these new colonies were to be led to inhabit among the barbarous Indians." Mountjoy's proscription against cultural intermingling in Ireland would be undone by the realities of plantation. Decades later, political writer Vincent Gookin Jr. would unsuccessfully argue in favor of cohabitation as a means of ensuring peace in Ireland.[2]

Aside from the lasting power of such tropes of barbarism, there is little that knits the experience of the Native peoples of North America to the experience of the native Irish in the sixteenth and early seventeenth centuries. Even in the context of plantation, designed to redraw political boundaries and redistribute landholdings, many Irish maintained control of their lands. Those who found themselves displaced or discriminated against as a result of plantation employed the structures of English regulation to plead their cases, a response that would not be widely employed by Chesapeake Native people until the latter half of the seventeenth century. Most notable are the complaints lodged by Irish from Leitrim and other planted counties in the Midlands with the 1622 Commission, citing abuses of plantation regula-

1. Francis Bacon to earl of Essex, March 1599, in James Spedding, ed., *The Letters and the Life of Francis Bacon: Including All His Occasional Works* . . . , II (London, 1862), 129–133.

2. C. Litton Falkiner, *Illustrations of Irish History and Topography, Mainly of the Seventeenth Century* (London, 1904), 298. David Beers Quinn suggested that Mountjoy might have based his comments about the New World on information obtained from Ralph Lane; see Quinn, *The Elizabethans and the Irish* (Ithaca, N.Y., 1966), 119. For the writings of Vincent Gookin Jr., see T. C. Barnard, "Crises of Identity among Irish Protestants, 1641–1685," *Past and Present*, no. 127 (May 1990), 50–72; and Patricia Coughlan, "Counter-Currents in Colonial Discourse: The Political Thought of Vincent and Daniel Gookin," in Jane H. Ohlmeyer, ed., *Political Thought in Seventeenth-Century Ireland: Kingdom or Colony* (Cambridge, 2000), 56–82.

tion but not calling for the abolition of plantation itself. These "hordes of aggrieved and impoverished natives from the recently planted counties" demanded more accurate measurement of lands (implying an understanding of the commodification and ownership of land), protested extortionate rents, and bemoaned the quality of land they had been assigned. They argued their cases to the Old English lawyer Richard Hadsor (who spoke Irish) and used the plantation instructions as the basis for their complaints. Although few were successful in gaining redress, their knowledge of and ability to participate in the investigations contrast strongly with the Powhatans' experience when a similar commission examined the failings of the Virginia Company. No Indians were invited to the table. Such was the cultural distance that, even if an invitation had been extended, the parties would likely have been at cross-purposes.[3]

Concluding that Ireland was not a testing ground for American colonialism does not denigrate the value of comparative analysis. Instead, it actually promotes comparison, particularly in an effort to question insular national histories. Ideas of America lie at the root of assumptions about Irish coloniality. Attendant upon the testing-ground theory is an assumption of the inevitability of America's colonization and the emergence of the American nation. The expansion of the British into Ireland thus appears as just a dress rehearsal for the real thing—the founding of the United States of America. At the same time, there remain important similarities between British expansion in both lands—similarities that need to be recognized to further the study of history in both places. Insights garnered from archaeology in combination with more traditional documentary research brings us closer to understanding the impact of colonialism and plantation on unnamed individuals.

Comparative Archaeologies of British Expansion

A premise throughout this study has been the central importance and interpretative value of the physical traces from the past, with a focus upon the complementarities as well as the often meaningful disjuncture between the source materials. Understanding of the Native experience in the New World has long employed and interrogated material sources. If we were to leave understandings of Gaelic society entirely to the examination of documentary sources, our understandings would be limited, in-

3. Brian Mac Cuarta, "The Plantation of Leitrim, 1620–41," *Irish Historical Studies,* XXXII (2000–2001), 311.

deed, given the culturally specific roles of Gaelic literature and the intrinsic biases of English accounts. However, physical evidence should not be seen as merely a substitute for documentary sources when they are deemed to be nonexistent or problematic, nor as some unbiased or democratic device capable of elucidating subaltern experiences. All sources are subject to misinterpretation; all interpreters select their own emphases and means of translation. Historical archaeology unearths and untangles disparate forms of data, allowing for a more informed consideration of lives lived fully, if never recorded in documents.

Material sources also illuminate the experiences of the planters and colonizers in both lands, sometimes in ways obscured by the documentary record. It is the archaeological record that reveals the shakiness of Edward Doddington's reimagining of the O'Cahan castle at Dungiven, with its ornate plasterwork concealing the lack of mortar in the castle walls. The presence of Irish pottery and architecture within Ulster Plantation villages such as Movanagher and Salterstown exemplify the proximity of those cultural contacts between natives and newcomers that so incensed Sir Thomas Phillips, even when he, himself, as revealed through the archaeological and documentary records from Limavady, was clearly dependent upon Irish as well as English tenants. Moving west across the Atlantic, it is the archaeological evidence from later seventeenth-century sites like Camden that reveal distinctly Native activities occurring behind the façade of an apparently English house, whereas it is the critical and intimate role played by Native people in early Jamestown that stands as the most significant revelation of the early-twenty-first-century excavations at James Fort.

At a more interpretative level, the contested interplay of sources is often the most revealing. A visitor to Doddington's manor house at Dungiven might have been distracted by the brightly glazed fireplace tiles and molded plaster ceiling, temporarily fooled by the lack of mortar and stone hidden behind the plasterwork. At the same time, Doddington's precarious position as a planter would have been obvious in the lack of development on his land; in the Irish tongue spoken by his servants; in the way the fifteenth-century marble effigy of O'Cahan warrior Cooey na Gall, lying in state in the adjacent chapel, anchored the O'Cahans to Doddington's manor house; and, most notably, in the copious written surveys tracking the progress, or lack thereof, of the Londonderry Plantation. Knowing what was hidden underneath Doddington's plasterwork does not necessarily alter the broader-scale understanding of the plantation process, but it does expose the manner in which an individual manipulated his position and self-presentation—

perhaps even to the point of believing his position was more stable than it really was. What all these sources most strongly reveal is the ambiguity and uncertainty that lies at the heart of colonial experiences, often written out of history altogether.

Where next, then, for comparative analyses of Ireland and America? This study, with its particular focus on Ulster and the Chesapeake / Albemarle region, has interrogated just a portion of the convoluted relations between the two lands, which, in turn, must be understood within a wider European, Atlantic, and ultimately global historical framework. From an archaeological perspective, the work has barely begun. Movement away from a focus on fortification styles and presumed similarities in Irish and Indian warfare tactics would certainly be a good place to start. In both lands, increased attention to the European experiences of so many English servitors and settlers, which contributed to the ways in which they understood and constructed their physical worlds, is long overdue. Any similarities between the defenses built in Ireland and North America must take that broader context into account. Too much time spent focusing on identifying the similarities and dissimilarities between the physical manifestations of colony and plantation detracts from both macroscale examinations of processes of change and microscale investigations of local context and lived experience. Rather than foregrounding the hunt for parallels, archaeological research on early modern British expansion might benefit, instead, from an evaluation of practices and approaches in both lands. As noted in earlier chapters, North American historical archaeology places great weight upon environmental materials that permit close analyses of diet and of landscape change, such as those that have addressed the impact of the Jamestown colony's establishment. Such materials on Irish post-medieval sites are rarely analyzed, despite good preservation.

At the same time, Irish archaeology has long focused upon landscape approaches that allow for large-scale considerations of how individuals and groups understand and interact with the physical environment. The reconstruction of patterns of Gaelic land use, linked to clan territories, holds great promise for considered evaluations of the actual impact of plantation. Given the survival of the townland system and the increasing recognition of the maintenance of preexisting boundaries, it is becoming clear that planters accommodated themselves to an existing cultural landscape that would prove to be remarkably persistent. By contrast, the persistence of the Powhatan cultural landscape is only now being considered. In Virginia, the Highway Marker project has begun to make visible this newly recognized landscape.

Driven by the concerns of the contemporary Virginia Indian community, this project has erected a number of new signs targeting sites of Native significance.

In both lands, artifacts and buildings are the mainstay of most archaeological research. The extensively researched collection from Jamestown, encompassing a wide range of objects reflecting the nascent global trade of the early modern world, provides an understanding of the movement of material goods in that period. Given the unique context of the early Jamestown deposits, attributable to the extreme stress the settlers experienced in the first few years, it is unlikely that any Irish site of the period will yield the same volume or variety, as noted in Chapter 4. At the same time, the collection puts the material lives of early modern English adventurers into context, informing speculation about what is missing from the Ulster assemblages associated with servitors such as Doddington, Phillips, and Chichester, or what might have graced the mantel of Walter Raleigh's temporary Irish home at Myrtle Grove.

Considerable work remains to be done in both lands to gain a better appreciation of local material lives. In the Chesapeake, finds of Native-made ceramics and smoking pipes can no longer be written off as prehistoric, particularly given their dominance in the Jamestown assemblages. Similarly, the lack of understanding of Gaelic Irish material culture, and in particular the production of hand-built Ulster coarse pottery—not to mention the poorly understood establishment of a vernacular thrown earthenware tradition in the latter part of the seventeenth century—deserves consideration. Is it possible to refine the chronology of Ulster coarse pottery so as to evaluate its significance in plantation-period sites such as Sir Thomas Phillips's stronghold at Limavady? There is no shortage of archaeological research questions, both small and large. Scholars in both lands need to be open to unexpected possibilities—such as the influence of Native technology on Virginia colonial architecture or the multiple readings of ubiquitous objects such as the tobacco pipe—and to be skeptical of simplistic parallels and comparators.

Individual and Communal Responses to British Expansion

Other insights emerge from a comparative consideration of British expansion that highlight the ways in which individuals as well as communities responded to and engaged with colonial processes. For example, factionalism can be seen as a key element for understanding the events that took place in such disparate locales as Rathlin and Roanoke or Werowocomoco and Londonderry. In sixteenth-century Ulster, there was no unified Gaelic opposition to English aggression even at the height of the Nine Years' War. The propensity of the MacDonnells of north Antrim to switch allegiances from the Irish to the English and back again must be understood as part of a factional strategy to regain the Lordship of the Isles. The 1575 massacre of Sorley Boy's settlements on Rathlin Island, under orders from the earl of Essex, was just one occurrence in a confusing sequence of events that saw the English first ally with the Irish forces of Shane O'Neill against the Scottish MacDonnells and then applaud the MacDonnells' murderer of Shane O'Neill in 1567.

Factionalism likewise characterized the relationship between many New World Native groups. The beheading of the Roanoke chief Wingina by Ralph Lane's Irish servant Edward Nugent did not provoke a unified response from the Algonquian societies of the region, with groups like the Croatans engaging with the English and perhaps even absorbing the members of the Lost Colony following John White's departure. Factionalism was an even stronger deterrent to Native unity within as well as on the boundaries of the Powhatan chiefdom. To take the example of the Chickahominies, their ability to withstand incorporation into the Powhatan chiefdom was a more significant motivating factor in their early-seventeenth-century history than was any opposition to the English. What unity did underpin Powhatan opposition to the English, most notably under the leadership of Opechancanough, evaporated following his death in 1646. The English in both lands were similarly not immune to the perils of factionalism. Governor John Harvey was brought down by his rivals in the Virginia government, whereas Phillips's vendetta against the London Companies only succeeded in further weakening the ability of the City of London to invest in their Irish estates. The companies themselves might have seen some poetic justice in Phillips's bankruptcy. In Northern Ireland today, it is the London Companies who are remembered, not Phillips. The eighteenth- and nineteenth-century company-financed improvements to the built fabric of Londonderry villages are a particularly noticeable legacy. In terms of the contemporary economy, the Irish Society still retains rights to fisheries on the River Bann. The seventeenth century is never far away from the twenty-first century in Northern Ireland.[4]

Although factionalism characterized politics in both lands, pragmatism

4. Buck Woodard and Danielle Moretti-Langholtz, "'They Will Not Admitt of Any Weroance from Him to Governe over Them': The Chickahominy in Context; A Reassessment of Political Configurations," *Journal of Middle Atlantic Archaeology*, XXV (2009), 85–96.

might have been more of a motivating factor in determining intercultural discourse for the lower orders of society. The lot of an indentured servant in Virginia was likely less enviable than that of a laborer in the Ulster Plantation, but they shared similar challenges. A letter written by a carpenter employed by the Ironmongers' Company on their Londonderry Plantation lands highlights necessary accommodation to Irish practices but echoes the well-known pleas of Martin's Hundred servant Richard Frethorne, who complained of his "most miserable and pittiful Case both for want of meat and want of cloathes." The Ironmongers' carpenter wrote,

> And seeing I have transported myself and my family into this rude kingdom to doe the Cittie service. . . . I think your Worshipful Company indulge me of more than ordinary favor. For coming over hither from a civll place where is all plenty our entertainment was hunger for a dyett and our Lodging upon Rushes in dity cabbings where we lay pyled up on upon another and having often occasion to make jorneyes to the woods for Timber for the Cities work, I eyther had the skey for a Canopy or if I found any covers by chance it was an Irish Cabin where wee had kearne and cowes for our companions, our dyett be scradocks and Irish butter our drink water and our beds upon Rushes at such tymes of the yeare as wee especially myselfe had cause to wishe for a hott drink and warm lodgingh in respect of my age and my manner of living in the place from whence I came, I am hardened and resolved to stay if I doe you service.

This letter, likely engineered by partisans, was intended to encourage the company to pay greater attention to its Ulster lands, which it never wanted in the first place. Similarly, Richard Frethorne's letters, however genuinely phrased, served as useful propaganda in the effort to discredit the Virginia Company.[5]

5. Richard Frethorne, "Letter to Mr. Bateman," Mar. 5, 1622/3, in Susan Myra Kingsbury, ed., *Records of the Virginia Company of London,* IV (Washington, 1935), 41. Emily Rose described Frethorne as "America's most pathetic settler" in "The Politics of Pathos: Richard Frethorne's Letters Home," in Robert Appelbaum and John Wood Sweet, eds., *Envisioning an English Empire: Jamestown and the Making of a North Atlantic World* (Philadelphia, 2005), 92, 104. Rose suggests that Frethorne, despite the tone of his correspondence, was "better off than many of his fellow servants in Virginia," given his literacy, family background, and connections to London politicos. A contrasting view is given by Sandra L. Dahlberg, "'Doe Not Forget Me': Richard Frethorne, Indentured Servitude, and the English Poor Law of 1601," *Early American Literature,* XLVII (2012), 1–30. Dahlberg presents a compelling case for Frethorne's having been involuntarily indentured by his parish as a mechanism for alleviating poverty. Ironmongers' carpenter's letter in the Ironmongers' Company Papers, D382, Public Record Office of Northern Ireland.

Bearing in mind that both accounts served political purposes, each still provides insight into the perspectives of nonelite participants in both ventures. The most valuable insight from the Ironmongers' account is the forthright acknowledgement of the reliance upon and familiarity with the Irish population on the proportion. Manus McCowy Ballah O'Cahan retained possession of a freehold that divided lands assigned to the Ironmongers, which themselves were occupied by the O'Cahans and O'Mullans and their respective tenants. Such mutual accommodation between native Irish and English and Scots settlers is similarly implied by the evidence for intercultural sharing of drink in the Ulster Plantation's proliferating alehouses. Presumably, the Irish language vied with English in Robert Russell's Moneymore taphouses, just as it would have in Coleraine's three sanctioned taverns and nearly a dozen alehouses. Although Sir Thomas Phillips might have reserved his model inn at Newtown Limavady for the benefit of British travelers, it is more than likely that the establishment was staffed by Irish, in the same way that Newtown Limavady resident Anthony Mahue employed an Irishwoman as his maidservant. Proximity, of course, can breed conflict as well as accommodation, as underscored by the murders that took place in Mrs. Browne's illicit alehouse on the Mercers' lands in 1614.[6]

War and plantation undeniably changed the Gaelic world of late medieval Ireland. However, that change was not necessarily forced upon an unwilling and subjugated population. Rather, Gaelic and Old English elites were often willing participants in the new order, seeking ways in which to enhance their own social and political positions. Donal Ballagh O'Cahan's effort to employ English law to gain independence from his O'Neill overlord is only one example of an adaptationist strategy employed by an elite actor, regardless of the outcome. Other Gaelic elites were more successful. A prime example can be found in the experience of the leader of the Ulster rebels in 1641, Sir Phelim O'Neill, whose father and grandfather died fighting for the English during the revolt of Sir Cahir O'Doherty in 1608. Sir Phelim O'Neill had benefited from the loyalty of his family, inheriting and retaining five thousand acres in County Tyrone when others of his clan were dispossessed.

---

6. In 1612, the Irish Society decreed that Coleraine would be limited to no more than three taverns and ten alehouses. Given both the difficulty of regulating such establishments and their potential for profit, it is likely that the number was higher. See Audrey Horning, "'The Root of All Vice and Bestiality': Exploring the Cultural Role of the Alehouse in the Ulster Plantation," in James Lyttleton and Colin Rynne, eds., *Plantation Ireland: Settlement and Material Culture, c. 1550–c. 1700* (Dublin, 2009), 128; James Stevens Curl, *The Honourable the Irish Society and the Plantation of Ulster, 1608–2000* (Chichester, 2000), 127.

In addition to his considerable landholdings, O'Neill was politically and socially well established, representing Dungannon in the House of Commons. No wonder his neighbor Lord Caulfield had no qualms about allowing O'Neill and his retinue into his home at Charlemont on the River Blackwater on the evening of October 22, 1641, only to find his home and garrison seized by his neighbor's men. O'Neill's decision to rebel was not guided by any straightforward sense of ethnic pride but rather by his heavy debt and concern over his own position in the face of the emergence of a Puritan Parliament. The structures of inequality founded on essentialized ethnic and religious differences that defined Ireland in the eighteenth and nineteenth centuries were not as firmly in place when Phelim O'Neill resorted to violence to maintain his social position. The foundations of division might have been laid during the plantation period, but more often than not—like Doddington's manor house at Dungiven—those foundations lacked the mortar that would have rendered them impermeable to machinations such as O'Neill's. Furthermore, it is historical memory that imposes unassailable and dichotomous ethnic identities on individuals—be they Gaels, Old English, or Planters—who might have first conceived of themselves as loyal to the Kingdom of Ireland and its head of state than as colonial overlords or dupes of a colonial regime.[7]

Gaelic literary traditions likewise accommodated the changing order, as bards composed praise poetry for the established Gaelic lords that nonetheless signaled loyalty to the crown. Similarly, examination of the material lives of the Irish throughout the seventeenth century reflects the ways in which the elite sought new material items and means of self-presentation, even in parts of Ireland that did not undergo plantation. The thirst for luxury items is reflected in the Gaelic tract *Pairlement Chloinne Tomáis,* likely composed within the surviving MacCarthy lordship in Munster, a satire that aimed its barbs at the Gaelic elites' new hunger for luxury goods, including tobacco and imported textiles. Participation in the nascent capitalistic economy knitted together Gaels and planters but did not determine the ways in which individuals incorporated new ideas and objects into their daily lives. Just as the Nanzaticos' (or Portobagos) use of an English-style house at Camden does not imply a loss of a Native identity, just as Movanagher planters' use of an Irish-style house does not presume the loss of English-

7. S. J. Connolly, *Divided Kingdom: Ireland, 1630–1800* (Oxford, 2008), 41–42. As aptly phrased by Barnard, "Seventeenth-century self-perceptions should not be dismissed too readily as self-deceptions"; see "Crises of Identity," *Past and Present,* no. 127 (May 1990), 43.

ness—so, too, the incorporation of luxury goods and the sharing of architectural grammars by Gaelic as well as British elites cannot be understood in a simplistic framework of acculturation. Material culture assisted individuals in negotiating their place in society and in their relationships with others, as also demonstrated by the English incorporation of Gaelic notions of hospitality, a practice that contributed to Lord Caulfield's fateful welcome to Sir Phelim O'Neill in 1641. The intersection of such practices can conveniently mask difference as they facilitate discourse.[8]

Material accommodation and negotiation occurred at all levels of society. Although there are few archaeological studies focusing upon seventeenth-century nonelite life, the ones that have taken place shed light upon the interplay of ideas and objects circulating in early modern Ireland. A useful instance comes from the excavation of two adjacent mid- to late-seventeenth-century structures in Linford Townland, above the east Antrim coast. One of these was built of sod, similar to the late medieval examples associated with Gaelic architectural tradition considered in Chapter 1; the other was constructed of stone. Artifacts recovered from the sod house included locally made, lead-glazed coarse earthenwares, clay tobacco pipe stems with bore diameters indicating an early- to mid-seventeenth-century date, and fragments of a Rhenish stoneware jug, all in association with sherds of Ulster coarse pottery. Artifacts recovered from the stone house and an associated pit include a 1691 William and Mary coin, wine bottle glass dated after 1650, and imported Staffordshire slipware of very late-seventeenth- or early-eighteenth-century date, suggesting it may have been occupied slightly later than the sod structure. But rather than reflect a simple transition from Gaelic- to English-style housing, the presence of the two different building forms underscores the range of housing available to individuals within a particular socioeconomic stratum. Despite the efforts of plantation theorists and planners earlier in the century, many Ulster planters occupied Irish-style dwellings rather than constructed houses in the recommended English timber frame form. The Linford assemblage suggests a year-round occupation, with subsistence based upon agriculture and cattle- or sheep-raising, whereas the mix of native and imported ceramics and architectural styles reflects a pattern of material blending—evidence that speaks to sig-

8. Michelle O Riordan, "The Native Ulster *Mentalité* as Revealed in Gaelic Sources, 1600–1650," in Brian Mac Cuarta, ed., *Ulster 1641: Aspects of the Rising* (Belfast, 1997), 90–91. See discussion of *Pairlement Chloinne Tomáis* in Raymond Gillespie, "The Problems of Plantations: Material Culture and Social Change in Early Modern Ireland," in Lyttleton and Rynne, eds., *Plantation Ireland*, 56–57.

nificant discourse among all participants in a process that, whether colonial or not, was certainly rife with ambiguity.[9]

Another significant avenue for comparative analysis lies in the rise and role of entrepreneurialism and its archaeological signatures in the early modern Atlantic. Understandings of the activities of Jamestown's John Harvey or William Berkeley, of the earl of Cork Richard Boyle or the earl of Antrim Randal MacDonnell, must place them into that broader economic and cultural context. Harvey's experimentation with manufacturing at Jamestown is not evidence for frontier adaptation or nascent American exceptionalism. Instead, it echoes his peers' practices in England as well as in Ireland and is indicative of his belief in the role of towns as key elements in the development of a stable colonial society. The similarity of efforts to establish ironworking and glassmaking in the Irish plantations and in Virginia is a reminder of the widespread awareness and interconnectedness of contemporary commercial ventures, just as the emphasis upon the building of towns in both lands is linked to concerns over political and social control as much as economic advancement. The outcomes of those efforts were very different. By 1659, Ireland enjoyed a network of ninety-five small towns, defined by the presence of between 120 and 500 taxable individuals as determined through the poll tax returns. Undermining the colonial rationale for the original establishment of these towns is the reality that the towns were home to a mixed population. Even after the warfare of midcentury, Ulster plantation towns still accommodated significant numbers of Irish. Belfast had a population of 589 taxable persons, of whom 223 were Irish. Even the walled city of Derry had a taxable Irish population of 480 out of a total of 1,072. In the Chesapeake, the only network of towns consisted of those remaining Native nucleated settlements that had not been destroyed or converted by the English. In the aftermath of 1622, these settlements were culturally exclusive.[10]

As an early modern entrepreneur, Virginia's Governor Harvey was not exceptional. Notwithstanding his failure to lessen the stranglehold of to-

9. The structures were uncovered during the investigation of an area of extensive prehistoric and Bronze Age activity, and as such were not the primary focus of the research. See Brian Williams and Dermot Moore, "Excavations in Linford Townland," unpublished report, Belfast, 2002.

10. For consideration of Ireland's towns as recorded in the 1659 "Census," or poll tax, see Raymond Gillespie, "Small Towns in Early Modern Ireland," in Peter Clark, ed., *Small Towns in Early Modern Europe* (Cambridge, 1995). For population figures, see Séamus Pender, *A Census of Ireland, circa 1659, with Supplementary Material from the Poll Money Ordinances (1660–1661)* (Cork, 1939), 8, 124.

bacco through diversification, later governors picked up where Harvey had left off. Most notable was William Berkeley, whose primary economic aim was to identify additional agricultural commodities. Berkeley encouraged planters to experiment with other luxuries, such as silk production and viniculture, as well as more prosaic crops. In 1663, he noted in a personal letter that he had "sent home another Tunn of Potashes" and planned that "the next year we shall make a visible entrance into those stable commodities as flax and hemp."[11] Excavations carried out at Berkeley's Green Spring Plantation in 1928 and 1929 uncovered evidence of brick kilns and a glass furnace containing a brick inscribed with the date of 1666, whereas investigations in the 1950s pinpointed a seventeenth-century pottery kiln. Like Harvey, Berkeley invested personally in efforts to develop manufactures. Also like Harvey, Berkeley was concerned about the development and diversification of Jamestown, even making an effort to develop one of Ireland's staple commodities: linen. Berkeley's plans included the establishment of two flaxhouses, which were to employ children sent from each of Virginia's counties.[12]

In addition to their efforts at economic development and diversification, Harvey and Berkeley in Virginia, Boyle in Ireland, and their counterparts in England shared in the elite culture that also attracted the Gaelic hierarchy of the period. One incarnation of this culture can be seen in the development of the landscape garden, itself a manifestation of the desire to commodify and control nature intrinsic to colonial expansion. Many years before Berkeley sought to transform his Green Spring Plantation into both a productive and pleasurable landscape, Richard Boyle had established a three-acre garden and orchard at his estate of Lismore, which even boasted a bowling green and a planned "wilderness," along with schemes for a water mill and summerhouse. Much of this garden was built and designed by 1626 and served an additional, defensive function by being enclosed by a stone wall and guarded by turrets. No less ambitious, albeit on a far smaller scale, were Sir Thomas Phillips's alteration of the O'Cahan landscape in the Roe Valley.

11. Berkeley to Lord Egerton, April 18, 1663, MSS 2395 f. 365, microfilm on file at John D. Rockefeller Jr. Library, Williamsburg, Va.; Berkeley, "Discourse and View of Virginia," in Peter Force, ed., *Tracts and Other Papers, Relating Principally to the Origin, Settlement, and Progress of the Colonies in North America from the Discovery of the Country to the Year 1776,* II (1844; rpt. Bowie, Md., 1999), 14.

12. Berkeley to Egerton, Apr. 18, 1663, microfilm; Berkeley, "Discourse and View of Virginia," in Force, ed., *Tracts and Other Papers,* 14; William Waller Hening, ed., *The Statutes at Large; Being a Collection of All the Laws of Virginia, from the First Session of the Legislature, in the Year 1619,* I (New York, 1823), 336.

There, Phillips set out formal gardens, as pictorially recorded by Thomas Raven in 1622, that incorporated orchards as well as terraces, walkways, and geometrical ornamental plantings. Gaelic and Old English elites similarly shared in these new passions, as did the Scottish Randal MacDonnell, who established the formal gardens at Dunluce Castle, Co. Antrim.[13]

Boyle, Berkeley, and England-based entrepreneurs operated in terms of a complementary logic, albeit in dissimilar lands. The transformations of the seventeenth century clearly contributed to the emergence of an economic system inspired by capitalism and rooted in the commodification of lands and people. However, even as colonial spaces such as Virginia and Ireland grew ever closer to one another in terms of social and economic structure and entanglement with Britain, these large-scale societal transformations do not easily translate into a wholesale erasure of difference, as perhaps most notably underscored by the continuing presence of Powhatan-descendant communities in the heartland of what was colonial Virginia. Focus on the micro-scale—such as that which can be aided by the archaeological lens or revealed through the rare personal letters of a disgruntled carpenter or in-dentured servant—reminds us that, although the broad structures of early modern colonialism and capitalism imposed severe constraints and muted difference, individuals nonetheless retained the capacity to construct their daily lives and negotiate their identities and relationships in meaningful ways worthy of scholarly consideration.

Conclusion: Ireland in the Atlantic World

The context for the histories considered in the preceding chapters lies in the emerging British Atlantic world of the early modern period, itself understandable only in terms all of the other polities engaged in Atlantic endeavors and the role of the more geographically, if not culturally or eco-nomically, distant lands of Asia. However, the more we seek to appreciate global connections and influences in such a broadly contextualized under-standing of the early modern world, the more danger there is in obscur-ing and misrepresenting local nuance. Comparative histories by their very nature almost inevitably privilege the view from one direction. In the case of Ireland in the Atlantic, that view has long elided the history of natives by prioritizing the English experience or has accepted stereotypes about

13. Michael MacCarthy-Morrogh, *The Munster Plantation: English Migration to Southern Ire-land, 1583–1641* (Oxford, 1986), 185–186; Terence Reeves-Smyth, *Irish Gardens and Gardening be-fore Cromwell* (Cork, 1999), 124.

natives in one land while finding complexity in another. This study of Ireland in Moryson's "Virginian Sea" has accorded nuance to considerations of native and settler life both in Gaelic Ireland and in the wider Albemarle and Chesapeake regions. Despite the divergent experiences of life from 1550 to 1650, understandings of the connections between Ireland and America more broadly will continue to be complicated by more recent histories and by the very real economic and political ties between the two lands that combine to obscure the earlier histories examined in this study. The historical and cultural connections oft proclaimed for Ireland and North America are more the product of the eighteenth- and nineteenth-century Irish emigration that contributed to the emergence of a distinctive Irish-American identity than they are divergent experiences and legacies of early modern colonialism. This later relationship must be decoupled from that of the period 1550–1650. To return to the contemporary value of this study, reflected upon in the preface, distinguishing the early modern history of colonial expansion from the later history of Ireland and Irish emigration weakens the long-assumed direct link between plantation and the Troubles of the late twentieth century. As such, the greatest relevance of comparative study of Ireland and America from 1550 to 1650 may not be what it tells of the past, but what it means in the present—and where it may lead in the future.[14]

14. For a more global approach to the Atlantic world, see Peter A. Coclanis, "Atlantic World or Atlantic/World?" *William and Mary Quarterly*, 3d Ser., LXIII (2006), 725–742. When it comes to Atlantic histories, the view is often from the American coastline. Similarly, Christopher Grasso and Karin Wulf, "Nothing Says 'Democracy' Like a Visit from the Queen: Reflections on Empire and Nation in Early American Histories," *Journal of American History*, CXV (2008), 773, note that, "though the goal was to reach across and around the ocean, recent, sustained attention paid to the Atlantic comes mostly from early Americanists." The potential of historical research to contribute meaningfully to overcoming contemporary conflict is discussed in Audrey Horning, "Exerting Influence? Responsibility and the Public Role of Archaeology in Divided Societies," *Archaeological Dialogues*, XX (2013), 19–29.

Index

Page numbers in italics refer to illustrations.